The Hardball Times Baseball Annual 2008

Featuring contributions by THT's staff writers:

Richard Barbieri • Sal Baxamusa • John Beamer

Brian Borawski • John Brattain • Matthew Carruth • Derek Carty

Chris Constancio • David Gassko • Chris Jaffe

Dave Studenmund • Steve Treder • Tuck • John Walsh

With additional contributions by guest writers:

Bill James • John Dewan • Tom Tango

Will Leitch • Mitchel Lichtman • Vince Gennaro

David Vincent • David Cameron • Brian Gunn

Bill Ferris • Jonathan Helfgott • Jon Daly • Greg Rybarczyk

Produced by Dave Studenmund

Edited by Bryan Tsao, Carolina Bolado and Joe Distelheim

ACTA SPORTS

The Hardball Times Baseball Annual 2008

New articles daily at www.hardballtimes.com

Edited by Bryan Tsao, Carolina Bolado, and Joe Distelheim
Stats developed by Dave Studenmund and Bryan Donovan
Cover design by Tom Wright
Typesetting by Dave Studenmund

Published by: ACTA Sports
                 5559 W. Howard Street
                 Skokie, IL 60077
                 1-800-397-2282
                 info@actasports.com
                 www.actasports.com

ISBN: 978-0-87946-341-0
ISSN: 1940-4484
Printed in the United States of America by Versa Press.
Year: 12 11 10 09 08 07 06
Printing: 10 9 8 7 6 5 4 3 2 1

What's Inside

What's Inside (cont.)

Welcome to Our Book

The *Hardball Times Baseball Annual 2008* is an outgrowth of an Internet website, called the *Hardball Times*, natch (www.hardballtimes.com). THT is sort of a gathering place for people who like to write about baseball. We're not really a discussion board or a blog—more of an online magazine featuring well-written and edited, in-depth articles every day. We're a bunch of passionate amateurs, though several THT writers have been scooped up by major league teams and major media outlets, and one of our writers just signed a book deal.

So we wouldn't be here, talking to you out of a book, if it weren't for the Internet. And the Internet has yielded some other important contributors to this *Annual*.

The first section of the *Annual* is an overview of the 2007 season, organized by division. THT's writers have done their best to discuss the dynamics and wonders of the baseball season that was.

The second section is called 2007 Commentary, and it includes a number of contributors from THT and other websites. For instance, we make use of those unique WPA statistics that are available during the season on *Fangraphs* (www.fangraphs.com). An instance in which the Internet actually influenced a player is chronicled by its main protagonist, David Cameron of *U.S.S. Mariner* (www.ussmariner.com). Jonathan Helfgott, who traveled extensively for a year to explore baseball's international scene, has a contribution. And Bill Ferris, who follows the Tigers on his blog (www.detroittigersweblog.com) has added a "General Manager in a Box" analysis of the Tigers' Dave Dombrowski.

David Vincent, the "Sultan of Swat Stats" and author of *Home Run: The Definitive History of Baseball's Ultimate Weapon*, offers his perspective on the many home run milestones we witnessed this year. Chris Constancio, who manages the wonderful minor league site called *First Inning* (www.firstinning.com) contributes a piece on the minors' top prospects. And Derek Carty, whom we recruited to cover fantasy baseball for THT because he was doing such a fine job with his own blog, has a fantasy-oriented chapter.

You may notice something new in this year's *Annual*: Toons! They're the creation of Tuck, a graphic artist who offered to help us expand beyond the written word. Tuck's toons are featured every week on our site, and you'll find several scattered throughout the *Annual*.

Our History section includes pieces from folks we've come to know through the *Baseball Think Factory* (www.baseballthinkfactory.org), including a guest piece by Jon Daly, covering the career of manager Billy Southworth.

Speaking of history, one of the most important baseball events of the year involved the Internet: *Retrosheet* (www.retrosheet.org) published their full play-by-play event files of virtually every game from 1957 to the present. This is a gold mine for baseball statisticians, and several of our writers took full advantage of this wonderful resource.

For instance, guest author Tom Tango used the data to examine the best catching talents of the past 50 years, and to ask, yet again, whether Derek Jeter is really a good fielder or not. As always, his methodology is ironclad. Other contributors to our Analytic section include Mitchel Lichtman, who has written the definitive before-and-after statistical review of the season. Mitchel co-authored *The Book*, with Tom Tango and Andy Dolphin. Tom and Mitchel also co-host one of the best blogs and discussion boards for baseball statisticians, *The Book Blog* (www.insidethebook.com).

Another exciting event on the Internet this year was Major League Baseball's decision to make their Pitch f/x data available to the general public. This is very exciting information, and many bloggers are making tremendous use of it. To learn more, read John Walsh's article "The Origin of the Platoon." Then, read Greg Rybarczyk's "Of Home Runs and Free Agents" immediately after it. Greg runs the site *Hit Tracker* (www.hittrackeronline.com) and has develped a system to track the particulars of every major league home run. Greg combines his cutting-edge analysis with the Pitch f/x data in a way never seen before.

There's so much good baseball on the Internet that even old friend Bill James, who set the standard for the *Annual* with his *Baseball Abstracts*, has decided to join the fun. His guest piece here is just a hint of what his new website, *Bill James Online*, will hold.

So many people to thank—so little room. John Dewan has helped us in so many ways, it is impossible to thank him enough. Steve Moyer and Damon Lichtenwalner of Baseball Info Solutions, who provide our stats, are always on call and responsive to our frantic requests. Charles Fiore of ACTA Sports is a tremendous writer's resource, and Steve Treder performed yeoman work at the last minute to dig up all those "stat facts" you'll find in our stats section. Finally, a big thanks to the secret behind THT's success, our editors: Bryan Tsao, Carolina Bolado and Joe Distelheim. And thank you for coming along for the ride.

Happy Baseball,
Dave Studenmund

The *Hardball Times Annual 2008* is dedicated to the memories of...

Betsy Studenmund, who taught me intellectual honesty and curiosity,

Russ Studenmund, who taught me the value of hard work and attention to detail, and

Jeff Newhall, who taught me to do everything possible with joy and humor.

All three passed away this past year. All three now lie in Cooperstown, NY, overlooking Otsego Lake. I hope you discover their influence throughout this book.

- Dave Studenmund

The 2007 Season

Ten Things I Learned This Year

by Dave Studenmund

For sheer highs and lows, milestones and millstones, heroics and devilry, the 2007 baseball season ranks among the best ever. This past year featured the breaking of baseball's most cherished record, a great season from its best player on the cusp of deciding whether to take the money or run, the most-lopsided regular season game and World Series of all time, and season-ending winning and losing streaks that rank among the best, and worst, ever.

With so much going on, baseball proved once again to be the sport you can't pin down and that always teaches you something new. Some of the year's insights that top my list are...

We don't have to feel bad for Red Sox fans any longer.

In 2004, most of us joined in the jubilation of Red Sox Nation, feeling that an unjust and tragic baseball curse had been revoked at last. This year, with their second World Championship in four years, the Sox have joined the Yankees in that part of our moral landscape we reserve for over-privileged, overpaid and over-hyped baseball teams. In the world of baseball, that's a backhanded compliment.

This was the Red Sox's year from start to finish. Boston managed to grab headlines and the biggest free agent prize of the offseason when the Sox bid $51,111,111.11 just to be able to negotiate with Daisuke Matsuzaka of Japan. The Sox approached the negotiation with agent Scott Boras skillfully, eventually signing the pitcher to a six-year, $52 million deal. In the current free agent market, that is quite a good deal, and it made the $51 million bid a little less nonsensical.

Signing Matsuzaka allowed the Red Sox to return Jonathan Papelbon to the bullpen, where he was once again unhittable. Add a fantastic season from Josh Beckett, who managed to remain injury-free all year long, a find in Japanese import Hideki Okajima, depth (Curt Schilling, Tim Wakefield, Javier Lopez) and youth (Jon Lester, Clay Buchholz) and you have one of the best pitching staffs in recent memory.

The Sox started strong, going 36-16 and leading by 10.5 games by the end of May. The rest of the AL East, most notably the Yankees, couldn't make up the difference and the Sox reestablished their dominance in the postseason, running into severe competition from only the Cleveland Indians.

With such a dominant season, and the semi-breakup of the Yankees after the season, this could be the beginning of a dynastic run by the Sox. No, we don't have to feel bad for Red Sox fans any longer. They should be feeling bad for us.

There's a difference between a milestone and a record.

Most of us happen to have 10 fingers on our hands and 10 toes on our feet. As a result of this seemingly random assignment of digits, we count in tens, and we put special emphasis on numbers that end in a couple of zeroes, like one hundred, one million and one googol. We call them milestones.

However accidental the setting of the standard, a number of players achieved historic career milestones this year.

- Tom Glavine won his 300th game
- Craig Biggio smacked his 3,000th hit
- Sammy Sosa hit his 600th home run
- Trevor Hoffman recorded his 500th save—the first player to do so
- Alex Rodriguez, Frank Thomas and Jim Thome hit their 500th career home runs—A-Rod was the youngest player to hit 500
- Pedro Martinez recorded his 3,000th career strikeout

We even saw a rare seasonal milestone in 2007, when Jimmy Rollins and Curtis Granderson both hit 20-20-20-20, those being a minimum number of doubles, triples, home runs and stolen bases in one season. Only two other players had hit those milestones before—and Rollins and Granderson did it in the same year.

A number of records also were broken in 2007. For instance, Hoffman's 500th save was both a milestone and a record at the time, but his career saves total at season end, 524, is the current record—not really a milestone. It doesn't have a couple of zeroes at the end of it. Still, records are cool, too.

Bobby Jenks, the White Sox closer, tied a record by retiring 41 batters in a row over 13 appearances, briefly resuscitating the profile of Jim Barr, who set the record in 1972.

On Sept. 27, Ryan Howard set a record for strike-outs in a season, breaking Adam Dunn's previous high and finishing with 199 strikeouts. The next day, teammate Rollins broke Willie Wilson's single-season record for most at bats in a season, finishing with 716.

Perhaps the second-most impressive career record set in 2007 was Bobby Cox's 132nd ejection from a game, breaking the legendary John McGraw's record. Among the many facts culled from the colorful history of Cox's ejections is the fact that he's been thrown out of games with the Phillies most often—13 times—and the Braves have won only one of those games.

Perhaps the biggest disap-pointment of the season was the record that wasn't broken. Biggio came within two painful fastballs to the body of tying Hughie Jennings' career record for being hit by a pitch (287). He seemed to lose his "touch" this year, getting hit by pitches only three times, after totaling as many as 34 HBPs in previous years. Biggio retired at the end of the season, meaning that Jennings' record will stand for the foreseeable future.

Biggio's pursuit of the record even became the subject of a satirical piece from *The Onion*, headlined: "Craig Biggio Blames Media Pressure For Stalling At 285 Hit-By-Pitches."

With over 50 games remaining, Biggio has ample time to break the record, though there are several tangible factors that can be blamed for his recent stall. Most significant is the simple fact that the closer he gets to the immortal mark, pitchers around the league have been throwing to, instead of at, Biggio.

> **Streaky records**
> - Greg Maddux became first pitcher to win at least 10 games in 20 straight seasons.
> - Albert Pujols became first player to hit 30 HR and 100 RBI in first seven seasons.
> - Ichiro had 200 hits for the seventh straight year; Wee Willie Keeler holds the record at eight.
> - Moises Alou had the longest hitting streak for batters over the age of 40: 30 games.
> - Placido Polanco has played second base a record 182 straight games without an error.

"No one wants to be the guy who throws that record 288th bean-ball," New York Mets pitcher Tom Glavine said. *"From this point on, when Craig comes up to bat, he is only going to get pitches he can hit. Still, I am sure some pitcher will make a mistake, and serve up a wild pitch on a silver platter. When that happens, Craig will definitely know to lay into it."*

It didn't happen. But another player did survive intense media scrutiny to break a hallowed career mark.

A very few numbers are both milestones and records.

The most important career record of all was set by the bay in San Francisco, where Barry Bonds hit his 756th home run on Aug. 7, breaking Hank Aaron's record of 755—a number that had come to represent both a record and a milestone, just as Babe Ruth's 714 stood as a hallowed number before Aaron broke it.

Before the season even began, a favorite pastime of baseball pundits was guessing which date Bonds would break the record, with most estimates in August or September. Bonds seemed to make all the guesswork irrelevant, however, when he blasted eight home runs in April. It seemed that the record might fall before the All-Star break. But his bat cooled as the weather warmed, and the accompanying media circus seemed to last forever.

Or as Stephen Colbert said on *The Colbert Report*: "The media continue to wait for Barry Bonds to break the home run record, continuing baseball's proud tradi-tion of waiting for something to happen."

Bonds tied the record in San Diego on Aug. 4, then came home to San Francisco to break it. The San Francisco fans cheered, but the rest of the nation was torn between loathing and confusion. No one represented the attitude of those fans more than commissioner Bud Selig, who personally witnessed the 755th home run, stood when it was hit, didn't applaud, and released a curt press release after the event. He didn't attend the 756th, sending a repre-sentative instead.

The issue, of course, was Bonds' alleged use of performance-enhancing drugs, particularly steroids. "Alleged" is the legal term, though very few people actually would use it in normal conversation. That Bonds took steroids is almost a certainty. And Bonds' self-centeredness has fanned the flames of loathing further.

The ultimate testament of how fans feel about Bonds was conducted by fashion designer Marc Ecko, who bought the 756th home run ball and ran a poll on the Internet to determine what should be done with it. More than 10 million people voted:

- 47% voted to brand the ball with an asterisk and donate it to the Hall of Fame
- 34% voted to bestow it to the Hall of Fame without an asterisk
- 19% voted to launch it into space forever, banishing it from our earthly realm

Lost in the brouhaha was the fact that Bonds, who turned 44 in July, had the greatest season of anyone over the age of 42, as measured in Win Shares. He accrued 27 Win Shares in 2007, blasting the previous record, 44-year-old Jack Quinn's 18 in 1928.

The era is dead. Long live the era ... not.

There is more than just antipathy towards Bonds at work here. There is anger over something we've lost. When Babe Ruth set the original record-that-is-also-a-milestone, it came to represent a Golden Age of baseball, when play was pure and players heroic. When Aaron set a new mark, he represented the best of baseball's Grand Experiment—integration of the national pastime—as well as personal courage in the face of life-threatening hostility. At the time, many rued the end of an era (as people always do), but over time most came to appreciate the institutional and personal courage Aaron's mark symbolized.

Bonds' new mark represents a great athletic achievement, but much less, too. It represents a new era in baseball, one in which the millions and millions of dollars thrown at players has goaded them into looking for every competitive edge, including illegal ones. Underneath our rage is a sorrow that the reality we now face isn't going to disappear in the face of more stringent drug testing or legal proceedings.

New undetectable drugs will be invented; new pharmaceutical ways will be found to gain an edge. And some players will try them, no matter what penalties are at risk, putting those who don't try them at a competitive disadvantage (and potentially costing them millions). This is baseball now, an ethical quagmire. We wish we could banish it to the moon, but we can't. And so we mourn, and we boo, and we seethe.

More than any other sport, baseball once served as a refuge from sordid affairs like politics and capitalism. But it is no longer the game of purity, heroes and innocence. It is now a professional game, with no illusions. This isn't Barry Bonds' fault, but he is the icon of our loss.

It was also the year of the A-Rod

In a weird parallel, another great ballplayer, the one most likely to break Bonds' new home run mark, had his best year ever in New York. Yankees third baseman Rodriguez set career highs in runs scored (143), runs batted in (156), on-base percentage (.422) and slugging percentage (.645). He led the league in home runs (54, including his 500th career homer) and will almost certainly be voted the league MVP when the award is announced after this book goes to press. Yet, in a way, A-Rod continued to be almost as controversial a presence as Bonds.

In the 1990s, Craig Biggio ranked:
- 1st with 147 hit by pitch
- 2nd with 1,515 games played
- 2nd with 1,042 runs scored
- 2nd with 362 doubles
- 3rd with 1,728 hits
- 8th with 319 stolen bases
- 12th with 730 walks

A-Rod doesn't have Bonds' egomaniacal personality, but he does seem to be lacking something ("fire in the belly?") that sportswriters like to see. Combine that with the intense New York media atmosphere, the largest contract in baseball history (which almost bankrupted the Texas Rangers), some questionable behavior on the field (such as slapping a ball out of Bronson Arroyo's hand in a playoff game in 2004) and a lack of production in the postseason, and you've got a combustible situation.

A-Rod's laidback manner didn't jibe well with aggressive New Yorkers, and constant comparisons to Derek Jeter didn't help either. And his contract, which paid $252 million over 10 years—by far the largest contract in baseball history—added suspense to the proceedings because it contained a clause that allowed A-Rod to opt out at the end of the 2007 season.

Imagine. The guy has the largest contract ever, and he plays for the Yankees. And he might opt out? Yes he might, and he did. At the end of the season, A-Rod decided to walk away from a guaranteed $81 million over the next three years, in the hope of finding a better deal, or perhaps just a more welcoming atmosphere, somewhere else.

Incredibly, agent Boras announced Rodriguez's decision during the fourth game of the World Series. This was during the Red Sox's clinching world championship victory, and the news was covered by Fox television as the Rockies were scrambling to stay in the ballgame and the Series. A satiric *Onion* headline said it best: "Slow Month In Baseball Saved By A-Rod."

The unusually slow month, the only interesting point of which was a seemingly unending array of baseball games—some of which even went past their usual nine-inning limit—was very nearly a complete disappointment for the league. Now, however, the clutch statement by Rodriguez has inspired fan interest once again and has many fans and members of the baseball media calling Rodriguez "a contemporary Mr. October."

It was a sad, pathetic attempt by Boras to upstage baseball's main event, and a true insight into how classless he is. And it isn't going to help A-Rod establish a new image. He isn't Barry Bonds, but he remains an enigma, someone who is not likely to restore baseball to its fans' good graces.

Teams can set records and milestones too.

There was a significant milestone attributed to a team this year. On July 15, the Phillies lost to the Cardinals, 10-2. It was the 10,000th loss in Philly history, making them the losingest franchise in not only major league history, but in the history of professional sports everywhere.

This year's Phillies turned out to be winners, however, when they overcame a seven-game deficit in the NL East with 17 games to play. The Phillies went 13-4 in those final contests, the Mets went 5-12, and the Phillies finished in first place on the final day of the season. By some measures, it was the greatest come-from-behind streak in baseball history.

But the greatest season-ending streak was Colorado's. Sporting a 76-72 record on Sept. 15, the Rockies won 13 of their last 14 regularly scheduled games to tie San Diego for the National League Wild Card slot. They beat the Padres in a classic tiebreaking game, qualifying for the postseason, and then swept series from both the Phillies and Diamondbacks to qualify for the World Series. Their 21 wins in 22 games was the greatest streak ever heading into the World Series.

Never a franchise encumbered with great expectations, the often-overlooked Colorado squad captured the hearts of many baseball fans with their wildly improbable run. In a year characterized by a lack of heart from its major protagonists, the Rockies displayed heart a-plenty for all of baseball. In a small way, they may have saved baseball from itself—at least for now.

The guard is changing.

Last year, one of our 10 lessons was "youth has been served." This year, we recognize that something a little more substantial is going on: The popular face of baseball is changing from the old—all those players who reached milestones this year—to the young. This generational changeover could not have come at a better time for the game.

Over the past 30 years, the average age of baseball players has been rising fairly steadily, as medical advances and new training techniques (cough) have enabled players to stay in the game longer. Obviously, the lure of free agent money has provided the motivation to do so.

But in the past two years, the average age of baseball players has trended downward to an extent not seen since the early 1960s, when expansion and the full fruits of integration produced a stellar group of young players. As Bill James points out in this year's *Bill James Handbook*, the 1964 class of youngsters included Pete Rose, Carl Yastrzemski, Gaylord Perry, Tony Oliva, Dick Allen, Lou Brock, Ron Santo, Willie Stargell and many, many other notable talents under the age of 25.

It will be interesting to see who among today's youngsters eventually will rank in the same class of baseball greats as Rose, Yaz and Allen. Felix Hernandez, David Wright, Grady Sizemore, Ryan Howard, Scott Kazmir, Hanley Ramirez, Fausto Carmona, Ryan Braun, Prince Fielder and Jose Reyes, to name a few, all could be there when their careers are over.

> **Single Digits**
>
> Jon Rauch led the Nationals with eight wins and Matt Chico had the most losses among Nats hurlers: nine. This was the first time in major league history that a team didn't have a pitcher break double digits in either wins or losses.

> **Positive Buc Facts**
> - The Pirates hit 45 home runs in August; highest monthly total in club history
> - 322 doubles for season also a team record
> - Also set club records in fielding percentage, most errorless games and fewest errors in a season

Most importantly, these players are providing a breath of fresh air and personality at a time when baseball sorely needs it. Let's hope they fulfill every expectation we have of them, and that they can establish a new, more vibrant and ethical era in baseball.

Even individual game records were set.

The Rockies and San Diego solved their differences in a classic tiebreaking game, but history was also made in an Aug. 22 game, when the Rangers beat the Orioles, 30-3. It was the most lopsided game and the most runs scored in a game since they started counting foul balls as strikes. A memorable game in so many ways...

- The Orioles actually led, 3-0 after three innings. Their win probability at that point was 82%.

- Yes, the Rangers scored 30 runs in the last six innings. In fact, they scored 30 runs in just four separate innings.

- Wes Littleton earned a save for the Rangers, illustrating how ridiculous saves are.

- Texas' team batting average rose five points, from .253 to .258.

- Baltimore's ERA sank from seventh in the league (4.39) to 11th (4.60).

- The player with the longest last name in major league history, Jarrod Saltalamacchia, tied for the most RBIs on the team, seven.

- The bottom three Rangers hitters were 13 for 19, with four homers and 16 RBIs.

- One of them, David Murphy, swung at 14 pitches and missed only once.

- Baltimore pitchers threw 120 more pitches than Ranger hurlers.

The clincher: it was only the first game of a doubleheader. The Rangers won the second game as well, 9-7.

The Internet is bringing us closer to the game.

How great is the Internet? It has not only brought you *The Hardball Times*, but a wealth of other pretty cool baseball stuff, too. For instance, many baseball players now

> **How to turn around a season**
> The Cubs went 21-10 (.677) in their last 31 games decided by one run after starting the season just 2-12 (.143) in those contests through May 27. Overall, Chicago went 23-22 (.511) in one-run games in 2007.

have their own blogs, in which they talk directly to fans (sometimes immediately after games are over), without any media or publicity middlemen.

It's now easier for fans to hear an insider's perspective. Schilling (who had the most entertaining and widely read blog this year) told us how you file for free agency: "So this huge thing, free agency, was accomplished by doing the following: Place a phone call to the MLBPA, tell them you want to become a free agent, hang up."

> **How to turn around a career**
> Carlos Pena had a big year, with 46 home runs for the Devil Rays, after hitting just one with Boston in 2006. That's the second-biggest increase in baseball history, behind Mark McGwire (3 in 1986 to 49 in 1987).

No bureaucratic forms to fill out? Who knew? Other players, such as Granderson and Todd Jones, posted frequently on their blogs and MySpace pages. This is a positive development for major league baseball, bringing the game and its personalities closer to its fans.

The Internet even changed a pitcher's pitching strategy. Dave Cameron, of *U.S.S. Mariner* (www.ussmariner.com) posted an "open letter" to Felix Hernandez's pitching coach and, well, you can read all about what happened in David's review of the Seattle season, "The Year of the Improbable."

Baseball statistics took a giant leap forward when Sean Forman added new features to his site, www.baseball-reference.com, at a hair-raising pace. As I write these words, you can now look up detailed game logs, performance breakouts, minor league records and a gajillion other statistics from baseball's past. *Baseball Reference* has become the ultimate baseball resource.

This development was triggered by *Retrosheet's* release of play-by-play data for nearly every game since 1957 early in the year, a stunning accomplishment for the nonprofit site (www.retrosheet.org). As they say, "God bless Retrosheet."

Fangraphs (www.fangraphs.com) started posting live Win Probability graphs of all major league games on its site. Tracking games is perhaps the best use of Win Probability Added, as discussed in my *Annual* article, "The Story Stat." Having live WP graphs adds to your enjoyment and understanding of what's happening during a game.

But probably the biggest statistical breakthrough was MLB.com's rollout of its Pitch f/x system across most major league ballparks. Pitch f/x is an addition to MLB.com's popular Gameday application, in which you can track a live ballgame on a pitch-by-pitch basis over the Internet.

The Pitch f/x system uses video cameras to measure the speed, trajectory and spin of each pitch at 30 frames a second. The results are posted on the Gameday application, and saved in XML format, for any baseball fan with the requisite technical skills to download.

This has led to a wealth of new information on the Web, such as John Walsh's article in this *Annual* about platoon advantages. Other major contributors to the Pitch f/x dissection have been THT's Josh Kalk, Joe Sheehan of *BaseballAnalysts.com*, Mike Fast's *Fastball* blog (http://fastballs.wordpress.com), Dan Fox of *Baseball Prospectus* (www.baseballprospectus.com) and Professor Alan Nathan's Pitch f/x resource page (http://webusers.npl.uiuc.edu/~a-nathan/pob/pitchtracker.html).

Thanks to these analysts, we now have a much deeper feel for how well umpires follow the prescribed strike zone, the pitching performance of some high-profile pitchers like Pedro Martinez and Schilling, and when pitchers throw certain types of pitches and what happens when they do. The subjects are seemingly endless, and writers and bloggers are stepping up to the challenge.

Still, baseball has its real-life tragedies and heroes.

Baseball is still just a game played by a bunch of grown boys. But every once in a while, something happens in the baseball world that suddenly gives you real-life perspective.

One such instance was the death of minor league first base coach Mike Coolbaugh, when he was struck in the head by a line drive. Such a needless death; you're likely to see more coaches wearing batting helmets in the future.

In St. Louis, pitcher Josh Hancock died in an automobile accident while driving under the influence of alcohol. St. Louis was the scene of many dramatic incidents during the year, and Cardinals fan Brian Gunn has contributed a review of the Cardinals' highs and lows to the *Annual*.

Not all human interest stories in baseball were tragic, however. Some were inspiring. Zach Greinke overcame horrible bouts of depression and social anxiety, which caused him to walk away from baseball a year ago, to perform admirably for Kansas City this year.

And Cincinnati's Josh Hamilton, unwanted a year ago, picked up in the Rule 5 draft by the Cubs and subsequently sold to the Reds, had a breakout season (batting .292/.368/.554 in 337 plate appearances). Hamilton overcame his own demons and an addiction to crack to become a model of courage and redemption for baseball fans everywhere. As he observed in *ESPN The Magazine*:

A father will tell me about his son while I'm signing autographs. A mother will wait outside the players' parking lot to tell me about her daughter. They know where I've been. They look to me because I'm proof that hope is never lost.

In spite of everything, baseball still has its heroes. Baseball still gives hope.

American League East Review

by John Brattain

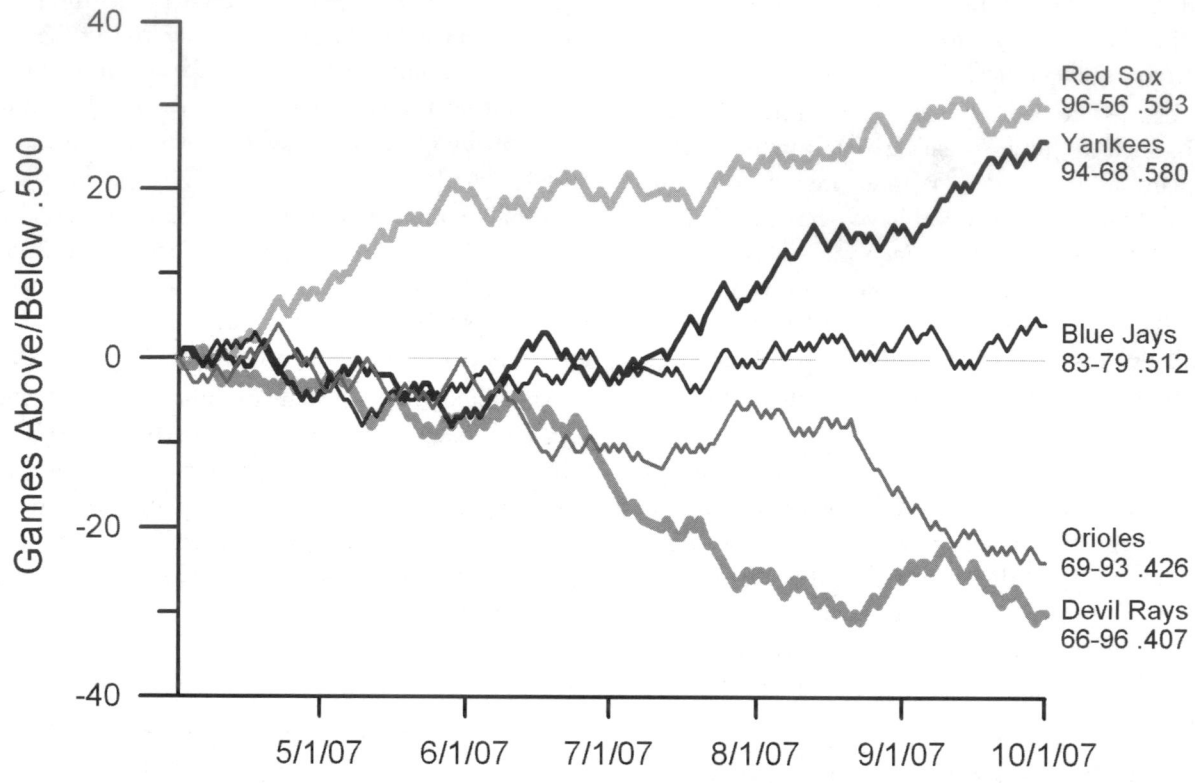

After finishing third for the first time since 1997, the Boston Red Sox prepared for 2007 by reloading in a big way, winning the bidding for Japanese sensation Daisuke Matsuzaka and adding southpaw Hideki Okajima from the Land of the Rising Sun for the relief corps.

Boston also unveiled a new keystone combination, signing troubled shortstop Julio Lugo and debuting highly touted prospect Dustin Pedroia. Replacing Trot Nixon in right field was the highly talented and equally fragile J.D. Drew.

The defending AL East champion New York Yankees were their usually busy selves in the off-season. They addressed their starting pitching by inviting former Yankees hero Andy Pettitte to return, re-upped Mike Mussina for two years, and, to counter the Red Sox' Matsuzaka signing, paid a smaller posting fee and smaller, five-year contract to Kei Igawa.

Other transactions brought more pitching, but the biggest of those moves proved to involve one of the Yankees' own—a spring training invitation to highly touted right hander Philip Hughes. As the season went on, the Yankees would stretch across the age spectrum, signing Roger Clemens and promoting the exciting Joba

Chamberlain and Ian Kennedy, both of whom started the year in Single-A and finished it in the Bronx.

There was less activity among the position players; other than trading away Gary Sheffield, the only other change of note was to shore up the infield defense by inking Doug Mientkiewicz.

Among the other American League East teams, Toronto added some veteran starters to their stable of fine young pitchers and, with a solid bullpen featuring flame-throwing lefty B.J. Ryan, felt they had enough pitching to compete.

The Baltimore Orioles retooled their bullpen, signing free agents Chad Bradford, Jamie Walker and Scott Williamson. They were equally busy with their starters, bringing in veterans Steve Trachsel and Jaret Wright and, in what turned out to be an offseason masterstroke, claiming Jeremy Guthrie off waivers from the Cleveland Indians.

What the Tampa Bay Devil Rays lacked in activity, they made up for in quality. Probably the biggest coup was inviting failed prospect Carlos Pena to spring training; he wound up with a season that was MVP-worthy most years. In 148 games, Pena narrowly missed the 100/100/100 club (runs/RBIs/walks) by one run,

14

batted .282/.411/.627, thumped 46 home runs and posted an OPS+ of 167.

They did likewise with 36-year-old reliever Al Reyes, who over his first 28 games had 15 saves with a 1.95 ERA and struck out 33 in 27.2 innings. He would pick up only 10 more saves over his last 32 games with a 7.59 ERA, largely due to a nasty case of gopher-itis (10 home runs in his final 32 innings). The Devil Rays also dipped into the Japanese talent pool, emerging with third baseman Akinori Iwamura, who provided a slightly better than league average bat (.285/.359/.411) and even led his team in three-base hits with 10.

Tampa Bay didn't have a big effect on the division, but with a talent pool of promising youngsters will be a force to be reckoned with in the near future. That pool includes B.J. Upton, who enjoyed a 20/20 season (24 home runs, 22 steals) and hit .300/.386/.508, Delmon Young (.288, 13 home runs, 93 RBIs and a cannon in right field), speedster Carl Crawford (.315/.355/.466, 10 home runs, 50 steals), 23-year-old future Cy Young contending lefty Scott Kazmir (13-9, 132 ERA+, a league leading 239 strikeouts in 206.2 innings) and 25-year-old James Shields (12-8, 120 ERA+, 184 strikeouts in 215 innings with a tiny walk rate of 1.51 per nine innings).

The season's first two weeks saw the Blue Jays reach their high point of 2007: an 8-5 mark had them in first place after winning the opener of a three-game set with the Red Sox. Boston then won the next two to take the division lead it would never relinquish. After leaving Toronto, the Red Sox came home for their first series against their main rival, the Yankees, and swept with tennis-like scores of 7-6, 7-5 and 7-6. The Yankees were 8-9 and had lost Chien-Ming Wang, Mussina and, to the surprise of absolutely no one, Carl Pavano, to injury.

Injuries hurt both the Yanks and Blue Jays. New York found itself pressing the likes of Chase Wright, Darrell Rasner, Matt DeSalvo, Tyler Clippard and young phenom Hughes (who would soon join the wounded) into starting service during the season's early months. By the end of May, the Yanks were eight games under .500 at 21-29, their offense sputtering because of slow starts by Bobby Abreu, Hideki Matsui and Johnny Damon and written off for dead.

The Blue Jays lost B. J. Ryan, their closer, to Tommy John surgery. Left-handed starter Gustavo Chacin went down in late April, along with Victor Zambrano in May. Left fielder and leadoff hitter Reed Johnson barely made it out of the gate before being lost for

three months. Third baseman Troy Glaus was in and out of the lineup, setup man Brandon League was out, catcher Gregg Zaun was lost with a damaged thumb in late April, and snake-bitten ace Roy Halladay was felled with appendicitis. The injuries to the pitching staff did give some of the Jays' young arms a chance, and they acquitted themselves quite well. Toronto ended up with the second-best pitching staff in the AL in 2007.

The Yankees' record through the end of May could have been far worse save for the mashing of Alex Rodriguez (.292/.386/.641; 19 home runs), Derek Jeter (.343/.431/.461) and Jorge Posada (.357/.414/.560). Regardless, the Red Sox finished the month 20 games over .500 with a 10-game cushion over second place Baltimore, which got surprising contributions from its starting rotation.

It was an odd game at the end of the month that seemed to trigger the Yankees' resurgence. They were in Toronto for a three-game set and had dropped the first two. In the getaway game, the Yankees chased rookie Jesse Litsch in the first inning with five runs. In the seventh, however, Matt Stairs brought the Jays even with a two-run homer.

The score remained knotted at five when the Yankees had a wild ninth. With two out, a Rodriguez single drove home Melky Cabrera, putting men on first and second. Posada hit a high pop fly to third base and utility man Howie Clark was lining up to gather in the third out. With the runners going on contact, Rodriguez was coming into third when he distracted Clark by yelling "HA!" or "MINE" (depending on whom you asked) and Clark let the ball drop, thinking shortstop John McDonald was calling it. Hideki Matsui scored, Jason Giambi drove in Rodriguez and Posada with a single and the game was 9-5, and over.

It was the beginning of a 14-3 run by the Bronx Bombers that vaulted them into second place in the East. More importantly, they gained 3.5 games in the wild card standings. The Yankees were getting hot right on time to welcome back a baseball legend: Roger Clemens was signed to a $28 million pro-rated contract in early May.

Just when the Yankees looked to be back in it, they fell right out again, dropping seven of eight and falling three games below .500 and eight back in the wild card hunt. The Clemens arrival did little to stem the tide; he was just 1-2, 4.86 ERA after three starts.

The Orioles went into free fall in June, going 8-18, including a nine-game losing streak, and skipper Sam Perlozzo was replaced by Dave Trembly. The Blue Jays had befallen a similar streak in the previous month—a hole from which they had been unable to extract themselves despite impressive pitching in both the rotation and the bullpen. The month ended with only the Red Sox above .500, enjoying a 10.5 game cushion and seemingly poised to cruise to an easy AL East title.

Of course, when it's Red Sox-Yankees, things are never easy. Despite the lead, the Red Sox scuffled in June, finishing the month 13-14, and their lackadaisical play continued into July, while the Yankees came back to life. Robbie Cano started to heat up, as did Matsui and Abreu, while the rotation started to regain order. The Yankees won 19 of 28 July contests, while the Red Sox were 15-12. New York was now just three games out in the wild card race and only seven games behind Boston with 56 games left—six of those contests head-to-head. The Pinstripes also had three game sets upcoming at Cleveland and against Seattle—the teams ahead of them in the wild card standings.

Despite the impending key schedule, the Bronx Bombers were uncharacteristically quiet at the trade deadline (save for trading reliever Scott Proctor to the Dodgers in exchange for third baseman Wilson Betemit) while the Red Sox pulled a coup—landing Texas Rangers closer and 2003 Cy Young Award winner Eric Gagne.

As things turned out, it was anything but a coup. Gagne was hit hard and saw his ERA balloon from 2.16 to 3.81 after the trade.

However, the Yankees would make two moves within the following week, one of which would soon set baseball abuzz. On Aug. 4, the Yankees reinstated Hughes from the 60-day DL. Three days later, they brought up a pitcher from their Triple-A Scranton Wilkes-Barre affiliate who had opened 2007 in the Florida State League: Joba Chamberlain.

On Aug. 3, behind a strong start by Tribe ace C.C. Sabathia, Cleveland finally overtook Detroit atop the AL Central, relegating the Tigers to the wild card lead. The following day, the Yankees' bats (including Rodriguez's 500th career home run) routed the Royals 16-8 to pull within 1.5 games of the wild card lead. The following day they finished the sweep and were a half game behind the Tigers.

Six games later, the Yankees were tied with the Mariners with the Tigers one game back. Ten games later, the Yankees were thumped 16-0 in the finale of a series in Detroit, leaving them eight back in the East and two in the wild card standings. Making things worse, Mussina couldn't seem to get anyone out anymore, having given

up 19 earned runs over his last three starts for a 17.69 ERA.

The Yankees were now coming into the biggest games of the season: a nine-game home stand that opened with three against Boston and closed with three against the Mariners. The Red Sox had survived a Yankees charge earlier in the month that closed the gap to four games by winning 10 of 15 while the Yankees lost eight of 15. What was the worst thing that could happen? A Yankees sweep? All three games had marquee pitching matchups: game one was Pettitte vs. Matsuzaka; game two featured Clemens vs. Josh Beckett and the final head-to-head would be Wang vs. Curt Schilling.

Other than Matsuzaka's 6.1 inning, five earned runs outing in the opener, the starters lived up to their billing. However the Yankees prevailed in all three games, putting them five back in the East and back atop the wild card standings to stay. The question remained whether the Yankees could overtake Boston for the division. Meanwhile the Blue Jays briefly entered into the mix by winning seven of ten after going 4-3 on a West Coast swing and sweeping slumping Seattle. That gave the Mariners their second nine-game losing streak; they would go on to lose 15 of 17, taking them out of the playoff picture.

On Sept. 1, Red Sox rookie Clay Buchholz stunned the baseball world by tossing a no-hitter in a 10-0 romp over the Orioles in Fenway Park. It was just his second major league start.

On Sept. 3, the Jays were just 5.5 games back and the proud owners of the best pitching in the major leagues since the All-Star break. However, Toronto lost two of three in Boston in early September and followed that up with seven more losses over their next 10. Despite sweeping Boston at home and splitting a four-game set against the Yankees, it was too little too late.

It looked like the three-game series from Sept. 14-16 would be the final chance for the Yankees to catch the Red Sox. The series started with the Yankees 5.5 games back. The Red Sox needed to win only one of the three to put themselves in the driver's seat in the AL East. Being swept again would bring the Yankees to within two with 13 to play and New York would finish its schedule against Baltimore, Toronto and Tampa Bay.

In the first game, the Red Sox roughed up Pettitte early, while Matsuzaka didn't get out of the sixth although he had given up just two runs. The Yankees broke through against the usually reliable Okajima and Jonathan Papelbon, sending 10 men to the plate and putting a six spot on the board. They won the opener and the lead was down to 4.5.

Game two saw Beckett come through in big fashion for his 19th win, giving up just three hits and one run over seven innings while Wang gave up five runs and didn't get out of the sixth. In the closer, the Yankees whittled the lead back down to 4.5 games as Clemens tormented his old team, besting Schilling after Jeter touched off a three-run shot. The Red Sox made it close, getting a run in the eighth and one in the ninth—loading the bases with two out for David Ortiz. Mariano Rivera got him to pop out to short.

The Yankees swept Baltimore and the Jays swept Boston, cutting the lead to 1.5 games. The Yankees then took two of three off Toronto while the Red Sox did likewise with Tampa Bay and the lead was still 1.5 games on Sept. 23. Three days later, the Yankees routed the Devil Rays 12-4, getting Wang his 19th win and clinching the AL wild card. The Red Sox closed out the season with four games against the Minnesota Twins. They split their first two and Boston's win in the second game—behind a superb eight innings of work by Matsuzaka—clinched at least a tie for the division. The following day, knuckleballer Tim Wakefield pitched a solid seven innings for win No. 17 and the Red Sox finally and indisputably broke the Yankees' stranglehold on the AL East.

Different Paths

When the Red Sox won it all in 2004, their season got off to an uninspiring start; they were only 10 games above .500 on August 9th. But a fantastic run in the rest of August and into September set them on their way to their first Series title in a zillion years. This year was different. The Sox were already 10 games over .500 on May 4th and 20 games over on May 28th, but the result was the same: a World Series title in Beantown. There's more than one way to break a curse.

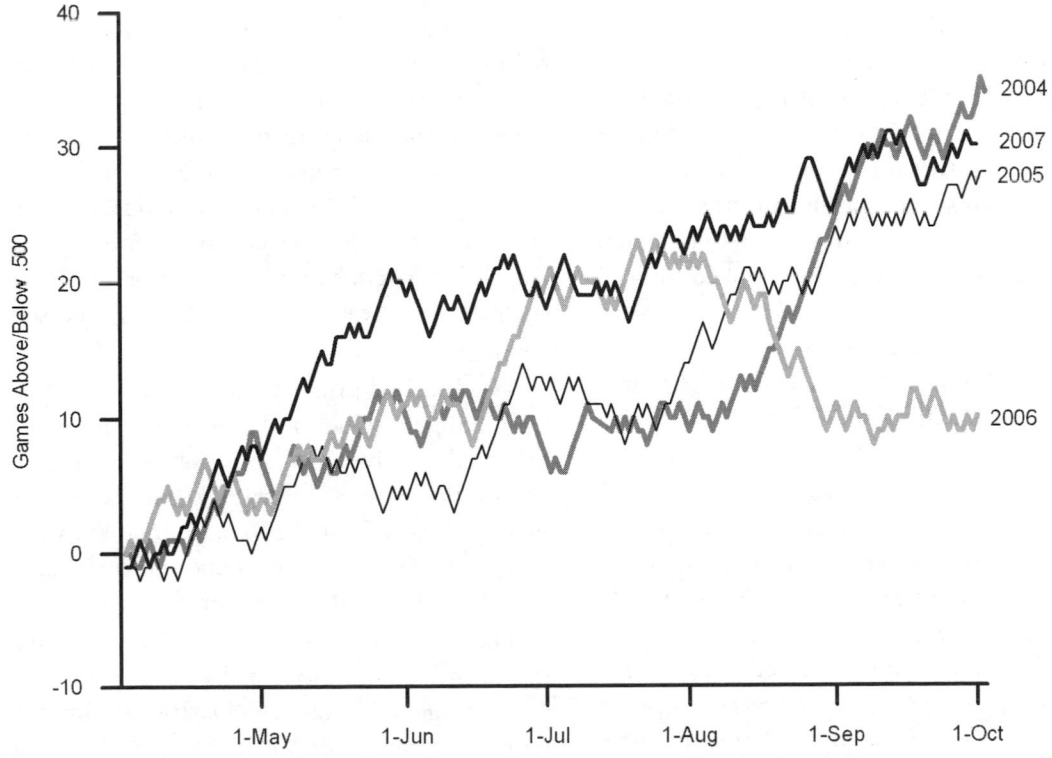

American League Central Review

by Brian Borawski

In 2006, the teams in the American League Central catapulted their division from one of the worst in baseball to one of the best. The Detroit Tigers came from nowhere to become the first AL Central team to ever win the wild card, and the Minnesota Twins mounted an amazing late-season stretch run to capture the division on the final day. The defending world champion Chicago White Sox won 90 games but finished in third place while the Cleveland Indians, who were picked by many to win the division, fell flat in the first half and never recovered. With four solid teams, the race to win the American League Central in 2007 was pretty wide open, and any of the four top teams looked like they had a chance to walk away with the title.

The Tigers didn't waste much time shoring up their 2007 lineup. Just two weeks removed from their World Series loss to the St. Louis Cardinals, the Tigers traded three pitching prospects for New York Yankees slugger Gary Sheffield. The Tigers extended Sheffield's current contract by two years and also got him to agree to serve as the team's primary designated hitter. A potent Tigers lineup got better, and many thought that if the Tigers could replicate their pitching success in 2007, they'd be the favorites to walk away with the Central.

The White Sox, on the other hand, seemed to be going in reverse. With six quality starting pitchers, it was expected that they'd deal one to make room for Brandon McCarthy. Instead, they traded both Freddy Garcia and McCarthy, receiving Gavin Floyd and Gio Gonzalez from the Phillies for Garcia and John Danks and two other prospects from Texas for McCarthy. This left the fifth spot in the rotation up for grabs, and surprisingly, it was the rookie, Danks, who secured the spot.

The Indians' primary concern in the offseason was their bullpen, which lacked a bona fide closer. They appeared to solve that problem by signing former closers Joe Borowski and Keith Foulke. Borowski, despite saving 36 games for the Marlins in 2006, was slated to be the team's setup man while the oft-injured Foulke would be used as the team's primary closer.

The Minnesota Twins, as usual, didn't make a major splash in the offseason, while the Kansas City Royals and new general manager Dayton Moore made a big move by signing Gil Meche to a controversial, above-market five-year $55 million contract. The Twins lost phenom rookie Francisco Liriano to a shoulder injury and Brad Radke to retirement. Nonetheless, the Twins' track record of sustained success meant nobody was counting them out.

The Indians were then dealt two blows before the season even started: Foulke's unexpected retirement and Cliff Lee's abdominal strain. Foulke's exit pushed Borowski into the closer's role, while Rafael Betancourt became his setup man. Cleveland replaced Lee with Fausto Carmona, who had made a failed attempt to close for the Indians in 2006.

The season kicked off and it was the Tigers, Twins and Indians who jockeyed for position at the top of the standings. The Twins were the first team to reach 10 wins on April 20, but the Tigers and White Sox were right behind them with nine and eight wins respectively. By the end of April, the Indians took first place after winning seven of their last eight games. The Tigers and Twins were 1.5 games back while the White Sox were 2.5 games back, despite being in danger of falling below .500.

The beginning of May was the Tigers' time to shine. They won their last two games in April and extended that to an eight-game winning streak before finally losing their first game of the month. They then rattled off three more wins and on May 12, the Tigers had pushed themselves to a 1.5 game lead. The Twins were going in the other direction—3-8 in May at that point—and had fallen all the way to fourth place with the Indians and White Sox sandwiched between the other two teams.

The Tigers were riding two hot bats during their winning streak. The re-emergence of Magglio Ordonez as an elite hitter was a huge boost to the Tigers. Through his first 13 games, Ordonez hit just .216 with one home run and six RBIs. Then in his next 15 games, he failed to get a hit in just one game and he boosted his batting average to .349 with four home runs and 20 RBIs.

The other big hitter for the Tigers was perennial slugger Gary Sheffield. The right hander got off to a rough start in April, hitting just .200/.369/.306 during the month. He was showing his typical patience at the plate with more runs (22) than hits (17) because of his 19 walks. In May, he turned that all around, finishing the month at .321/.385/.642 with 10 home runs, 22 RBIs and 24 runs.

The Indians then went 13-6 from May 12 through the end of the month. They turned a 1.5 game deficit to the Tigers into a 3.5 game lead, turning the American League Central into a two-team race because of the declines of the Twins and the White Sox. The primary

reason behind the Indians' success was C.C. Sabathia's transformation into an elite pitcher and the surprisingly good performance of fill-in starter Fausto Carmona.

Sabathia had always been considered an excellent starter, but in his six previous seasons he had never garnered a vote for the Cy Young Award. And despite very good seasons in 2005 and 2006, he had been absent from the All-Star Game both years. 2007 appeared to be Sabathia's season though, because by the end of May, he was an impressive 8-1 with 75 strikeouts and just 14 walks in 81 innings.

While Sabathia's elevation to a Cy Young contender wasn't all that surprising, the fact that Fausto Carmona, a pitcher who wasn't even expected to be in the rotation, was right there with him was a surprise. At the end of May, Carmona was 6-1, and while his strikeout and walk rates weren't as spectacular as Sabathia's, Carmona was able to get the job done because he kept the ball down and held batters to a league-leading 64.3% ground ball percentage.

By the end of June, the Tigers had picked up a couple of games on the Indians and they stood 1.5 games back while the Twins held on at 5.5 games back. The month was more notable for the complete collapse of the White Sox though. They finished June with a 12-18 record; it was their offense that was pretty much downright horrible. Their first-half OPS was a paltry .696, and they'd finish the season with the fewest number of runs scored in the American League.

The Tigers won their final five games heading into the All-Star break, and they supplanted the Indians at the top of the division with a slim, one-game lead. Gary Sheffield and Magglio Ordonez remained red hot, but it was center fielder Curtis Granderson who was on his way to a historic season. He already had 15 triples to go along with 62 runs and an .884 OPS. He also had nine stolen bases without a single time getting caught, and he hadn't grounded into a single double play.

The Tigers then won six of their next nine games after the break and on July 23, they led the division by two games. At that point, the Tigers' collapse began. They finished July losing seven of nine and went 11-18 in August. It had seemed like a lock that the team, between the Indians and Tigers, that didn't win the division would nab the wild card, but by the end of August both the New York Yankees and the Seattle Mariners had inserted themselves into the mix with solid second halves. The Indians, on the other hand, struggled in July but got it together in August and finished the month

17-11, turning the Tigers' one-game lead into a 5.5 game Indians lead, a 6.5 game turnaround in one month.

The Tigers put together a fine September, but the deficit was just too great and on September 23, the Indians wrapped up the division with a win over the Oakland Athletics. They finished the season with an eight-game lead through a nice mix of quality hitting and rock-solid pitching. Victor Martinez provided the lineup with a great hitting option at catcher, and he led the team with 25 home runs, while Grady Sizemore played in all of the Indians' games for the second straight season and led off in 151 of the Indians' 162 games. Even Travis Hafner, who had an off year with just 24 home runs, drove in 100 runs and walked 102 times.

Sabathia and Carmona continued their spectacular seasons, each finishing with 19 wins. Carmona was second in the league with a 3.06 ERA, while Sabathia was fifth at 3.21. Paul Byrd provided a nice third option in the rotation, and he walked fewer batters per nine innings (1.31) than any pitcher in the American League. Joe Borowski struggled at times as the team's closer, and he became the first pitcher ever to save 45 games while having an ERA north of 5.00. The stars in the pen were Betancourt and Rafael Perez. Betancourt was virtually unhittable as the team's setup man, while Perez provided the Indians with a top-notch left-handed option coming out of the pen.

The Tigers' second-half collapse can be partly attributed to injuries and partly to a set of players who had career years in 2006 but who couldn't follow up in 2007. Gary Sheffield missed substantial time in September because of a shoulder injury and even when he was in there, he wasn't the same hitter. The Tigers' rotation turned into a revolving door that included more than one player from the Tigers' minor league affiliates. Magglio Ordonez and Placido Polanco had career years, but that couldn't offset mediocre seasons from Brandon Inge, Ivan Rodriguez, Craig Monroe and Marcus Thames.

The highlight of their season was a no-hitter by sophomore Justin Verlander, who was the Tigers' one reliable starter. He finished with 18 wins while no other Tiger finished with more than 11. Jeremy Bonderman, who was 10-1 at one point in the season, dropped eight of his final

nine decisions and his ERA ballooned to 5.01. He was eventually shut down in September with a sore elbow. The Tigers' bullpen was also subpar—what was a major strength in 2006 (3.55 ERA) was mediocre in 2007 with an ERA of just 4.40.

The Twins finished with a sub-.500 record for the first time since 2000, and while Justin Morneau followed up his 2006 MVP season with another solid campaign that included 31 homers and 111 RBIs, injuries to Joe Mauer and a mediocre infield resulted in a Twins offense that finished just 12th in the American League in runs scored. Torii Hunter was the only other standout at the plate with 28 home runs and 107 RBIs. The team's 4.18 ERA, fourth-best in the league, couldn't make up for the lack of offense. Johan Santana was his old self, and while he was probably the best pitcher in the league, he finished with a career-high 13 losses. Carlos Silva, Scott Baker and Matt Garza also had fine seasons from the mound, but they couldn't overcome the lack of offense.

The White Sox and Royals slugged it out for last place for most of the season, with the Royals losing six of their last eight games to help the White Sox finish in fourth place. The highlight of the White Sox's season was Jim Thome belting his 500th career homer; they were out of the race in the second half. The Royals actually got out of the cellar a few times, but when the season ended, that's where they ended up. Gil Meche actually had a very good season with a 3.67 ERA, and Brian Bannister had a respectable second half with a 7-4 record.

The division had its share of league leaders. Magglio Ordonez became the first Tiger since 1961 to bring home the batting title with his .363 average. Ordonez also belted a league-leading 54 doubles and Curtis Granderson became just the third player to have 20 homers, doubles, triples and stolen bases. C.C. Sabathia led the league with 241 innings pitched, and Joe Borowski had a league-leading 45 saves.

In the end, the Indians finally got their due. They had suffered a near-spectacular finish in 2005 and an early collapse in 2006, but in 2007 they held off all comers and won the division for the first time since 2001.

American League West Review

by Sal Baxamusa

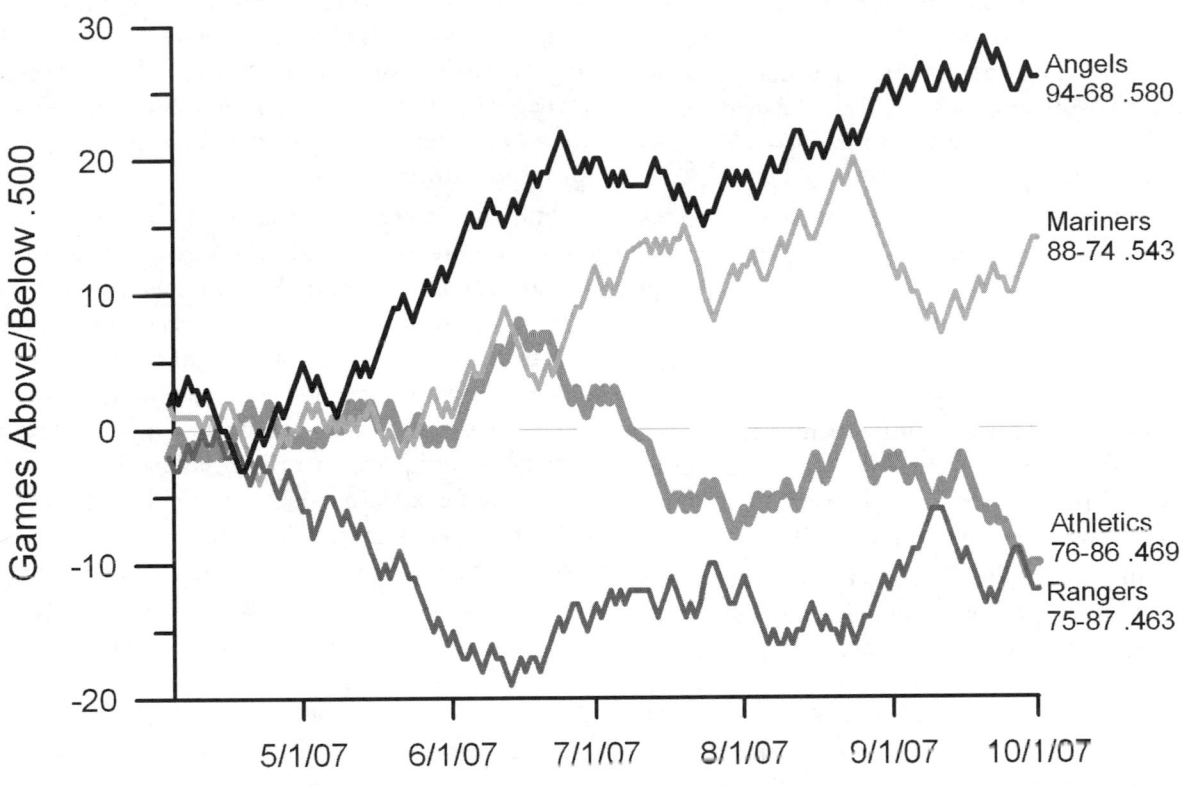

For years, AL West fans would tell you that the best baseball happened after most of the country went to sleep. I told anyone who would listen that the 10 p.m. EST games would not disappoint. I hope 2007 wasn't the year that they tuned in, because unlike every year since 2001, there was no down-to-the-wire race for the division title.

The performance of Seattle, Oakland and Texas suggests that all three teams were of similar quality, as all three finished with identical Pythagorean records (79-83). It was a remarkable display of mediocrity. Seattle gave it their best shot, but their run fell short in late August. Superb pitching kept Oakland around the peripheries in the early going, but they were done in by poor performance and injuries. Texas got off to a brutal start and had an unsuccessful late charge at third place.

The Angels scuttled Seattle's playoff dreams with a three-game sweep in Safeco in late August, dropping the Mariners five games back and allowing the Halos to waltz to their third division title in four years. Despite the departure of longtime pitching coach Bud Black, Angels hurlers were once again impressive. Their top three starters combined for 3.76 runs allowed per nine

innings and over seven strikeouts per nine innings. For most teams, that's an ace; John Lackey, Kelvim Escobar and Jered Weaver did it over 61 starts. The back end of the rotation was a mess—Bartolo Colon (elbow) was injured and Ervin Santana (8.38 road ERA) was ineffective—but the Angels had the depth to plug holes with the non-terrible Joe Saunders (4.38 FIP) and Dustin Moseley (4.16 FIP). They had their usual strikeout bullpen (8.1 strikeouts per nine innings), and though Francisco Rodriguez and Scot Shields had down years, they combined with Justin Speier to form a fearsome end-game troika.

None of that was surprising, but who expected the Angels to score the fourth-most runs in the American League? Preseason analyses of the Angels' offense started "Outside of Vladimir Guerrero..." This year, outside of Vlad, Angels hitters ranged from acceptable to excellent. Among regulars (and not counting the predictably-ditched-in-midseason Shea Hillenbrand) everybody save Orlando Cabrera and Gary Matthews, Jr. had an above-average GPA.

Casey Kotchman, written off as a bust at age 23, and Mike Napoli looked like Mark Grace and Mickey

Tettleton. Chone Figgins' .409 BABIP—the product of a 26.4% line drive rate and his speed—fueled a career year. Garret Anderson reversed a three-year decline to net a .279 GPA.

And Vlad? Per usual, he hacked at everything and succeeded wildly. He saw only 150 called strikes all year. He struck out looking once. Once! All he does is swing, which doesn't work for most batters. But it does for him, and like most years, he was a force. His .326 GPA was sixth in the AL.

Outside of Vlad, the Angels didn't rely much on power (123 home runs, ranked 12th) or patience (507 walks, ninth in the AL). Instead they rode the strength of their batting average. Despite ranking just 10th in the American League in walk rate, they had the third-best on-base percentage in the league. They hit singles (over 1,100, second-most), struck out infrequently (fewer than 900 times, third fewest) and ran the bases aggressively. They were the opposite of the cartoon version of *Money-ball* ("good offense = walks and homers").

More than other teams, the Angels relied on batting average, which is not without disadvantage since batting average—more so than power and patience—is prone to fluctuation. In 2006, the Angels' batting average was league average, and the offense struggled. In 2007, they walked at the same rate and hit for less power, but an extra 10 points on their batting average led to lots more runs.

The Angels weren't the only AL West team with a surprising offense. Seattle drew the fewest walks in the league; Safeco kills the right-handed power of hitters like Adrian Beltre and Jose Guillen; Jose Vidro was the Mariners' primary designated hitter. Yet Seattle managed to score nearly 800 runs by out-Angeling the Angels, hitting for a higher average (tied for second highest) and striking out even less frequently (second fewest).

Not only did the offense exceed expectations, the Mariners won more games than their underlying performance would normally suggest. Based on their team OBP/SLG and ERA, we might have guessed the Mariners would win 76 games; in reality they won 88.

Part of that difference—3.6 wins—was attributable to the bullpen. Ace closer J.J. Putz was spectacular. Opposing hitters were fortunate to reach base at all against Putz (league-leading 0.70 WHIP) and, once there, were fortunate to score (league-leading 94% LOB%). Only the Indians' Rafael Betancourt had more Pitching Runs Created among relievers.

The rest of the 12-game gap was due to the timely performance of hitters and starting pitchers. Repeatable? Maybe, although probably not. These numbers indicate that a good deal of their success will not persist, and I submit that winning 88 games was not a Great Leap Forward. Management, however, was pleased and capped the year by announcing that both general manager Bill Bavasi and manager John McLaren—who took over after Mike Hargrove resigned unexpectedly—would return in 2008.

Still, there were major positives in the Pacific Northwest. The first was Ichiro, who signed a five-year, $90 million extension in the midst of another fantastic season (20 WSAB, third in the AL). The second was production from a core of young players (infielders Jose Lopez, Yuniesky Betancourt and Beltre and outfield prospects Adam Jones and Wladimir Balentien) who will provide average-to-star performance in the coming years. The last is that Felix Hernandez—only 21 in 2007—posted his second consecutive 30-start groundball-inducing strikeout-heavy year. King Felix had the poise to one-hit Boston and the maturity to call for a trainer in his next start when his elbow barked. His continued health is critical to this franchise.

Health dominated Oakland's year, as they lost over 1,200 player-days to the disabled list, and 54 players rotated through the 25-man roster. A litter of regulars (Eric Chavez, Bobby Crosby, Dan Johnson, Travis Buck, Mike Piazza, Milton Bradley, Mark Kotsay and Bobby Kielty), two-fifths of the rotation (Esteban Loaiza and Rich Harden), and the top relievers (Huston Street, Kiko Calero and Justin Duchscherer) each missed a month to four months.

Oakland's notion of a second-half run was torpedoed by a nine-game losing streak around the All-Star break. General manager Billy Beane had already curiously designated Milton Bradley for assignment, and the losses marked the beginning of the end. Jason Kendall was traded, Kielty was released and Loaiza was claimed off waivers by the Dodgers. Duchscherer, Kotsay, Chavez, Buck, Crosby, Harden and Calero were shut down rather than rehabilitated.

Could the A's have contended at full health? It's a moot point. The team was banking on full seasons from players with known chronic conditions (Chavez, Kotsay) or histories of nagging injury (Bradley, Harden). Beane may have taken that risk consciously—it's not an awful idea for a mid-market team—but nevertheless got burned. As players went down, Beane was nothing if not creative as he scrambled to find free or cheap talent.

Players with no trade value (Kendall and Bradley) were flipped for useful relievers (Jerry Blevins and Andrew Brown) and a backup catcher (Rob Bowen). Hole at the hot corner? Acquire Jack Hannahan (.280 GPA) for peanuts. Out of credible center fielders? Ryan Langerhans for cash. Done with him? Flip him for Chris Snelling. Claim Jeff Davanon and Kevin Thompson on waivers. Hey, look, Dee Brown! Solutions from within? How about 174 transactions for the Triple-A team? The pace was dizzying, and the moves kept the A's from being awful.

The best of these acquisitions was Jack Cust, who is the designated hitter on the Sabermetric Parody All-Stars. Acquired a few days after Piazza hit the disabled list, Cust (.319 GPA) was second only to David Ortiz among DHs. He was a caricature of the take-and-rake approach: striking out in a third of his plate appearances (a maddening 44% were called punchouts), walking up a storm (highest walk percentage in the league) and hitting the ball hard (an unsustainable .437/.861 AVG/SLG when making contact).

There were other good performances: Nick Swisher (.294 GPA) and Mark Ellis (.884 RZR, tops among second basemen in the AL) were productive in the field while Joe Blanton (3.59 FIP, 230 innings) and Dan Haren (3.82 FIP, 222.7 innings) impressed on the mound. But on the whole, the season was a disappointment for a team that had seen the ALCS in the year prior.

And then there was Texas. Nobody ever notices the Rangers, although they were notable early on for being awful—through the end of June they owned the league's worst mark, 33-47. But even that bit of notoriety escaped them, and Texas finished strong, relatively speaking, missing third place by a single game.

Before the season, the Rangers upgraded their offense by acquiring Frank Catalanotto and Kenny Lofton and promoting Gerald Laird to starting catcher. Pundits guffawed, claiming that the Rangers needed to focus on pitching. Conventional wisdom is that they are a team of sluggers backed by little pitching. Such wisdom gives too much credit to their hitters, too little to their pitchers and none to their ballpark. The Ballpark in Arlington is a hitter's park, and the team's park-adjusted numbers showed that they had slightly above-average pitching and slightly below-average hitting in 2006. The offseason plan to upgrade the offense on the margins while bringing back the core of a not-terrible pitching staff was a good one.

The pitchers kind of held up their end of the bargain, coming in a few ticks below league average (98 ERA+).

This is remarkable considering that their rotation turned into a disaster in which nobody tossed more than 175 innings and the ERA leader checked in at 4.87. If not for a stellar relief corps—third-best ERA and by far the most innings pitched—the pitching might have been calamitous rather than mediocre. Reliever Joaquin Benoit created almost as many pitching runs (55) as "ace" Kevin Millwood (59). Seattle was the only other AL team that came close to having a reliever (Putz, 81) create as many runs as their best starter (Hernandez, 87).

The offense, however, did not improve. Shortstop Michael Young had superficially good numbers—.315 AVG, 201 hits, 94 RBIs—but saw his power evaporate (9 HR) and his GPA drop to .256. His 2004 was probably the career year of a good infielder, not the breakout of a superstar shortstop. His value is now tied to his relative ironman status, and it's hard to imagine his five-year, $80-million extension as a net positive in anything but a public relations sense.

But Young was not the problem, nor were Ian Kinsler, Marlon Byrd and the traded-at-midseason Mark Teixeira and Kenny Lofton. Hank Blalock also hit very well when he wasn't missing time with rib and shoulder problems, although he was limited to designated hitter by year's end.

Other hitters, however, offset those positive contributions. Frank Catalanotto was a below-average corner outfielder when he wasn't disabled. Nelson Cruz bested only Jay Gibbons and Reed Johnson in GPA among corner outfielders. Sammy Sosa cranked his 600th homer, but he was the worst regular DH in the league (.245 GPA).

The offense wasn't bad; it was just average. Coupled with average pitching, the Rangers churned out another unremarkable season.

General manager Jon Daniels did his best to salvage the year with some shrewd midseason trades. The itinerant Kenny Lofton was spun for catching prospect Max Ramirez. Eric Gagne looked awful but managed a good enough ERA to be shipped to Boston for pitcher Kason Gabbard, outfielder David Murphy and pseudo-prospect Engel Beltre. And when superstar first baseman Mark Teixeira declined an eight-year, $140 million extension, he was traded to the Braves. The booty included four of the top five Braves prospects: catcher Jarrod Saltalamacchia, toolsy infielder Elvis Andrus, flamethrowing Neftali Perez and lefty Matt Harrison.

None of the three traded players were likely to help this or the next relevant Rangers team, while the return included a good mix of high-upside and low-risk prospects. Daniels did a very good job of building for the future when the present looked bleak.

The Angels had a successful season. The other teams should measure success by what they learned. An early poor performance caused Texas to take a long-term view. If Oakland ("but for the injuries") and Seattle ("we won almost 90 games") conclude they are at the cusp of contention, they could make franchise-crippling mistakes. It's possible that the Angels will fall back—their underlying statistics weren't that impressive—but a poor bet considering their youth and payroll advantages. If that happens, the division buzzword will be parity. If not, the buzzword will be mediocrity.

Not This Time

From 2004-2006, the Athletics had puttered around in the first half of the year only to surge in the second half and battle for the division title. For a while, it looked like the pattern might repeat itself this year, as the A's were in the same position at the end of May as they had been in previous years. But injuries and disappointing performances sunk them in the second half, and they finished with their worst record of the past nine years.

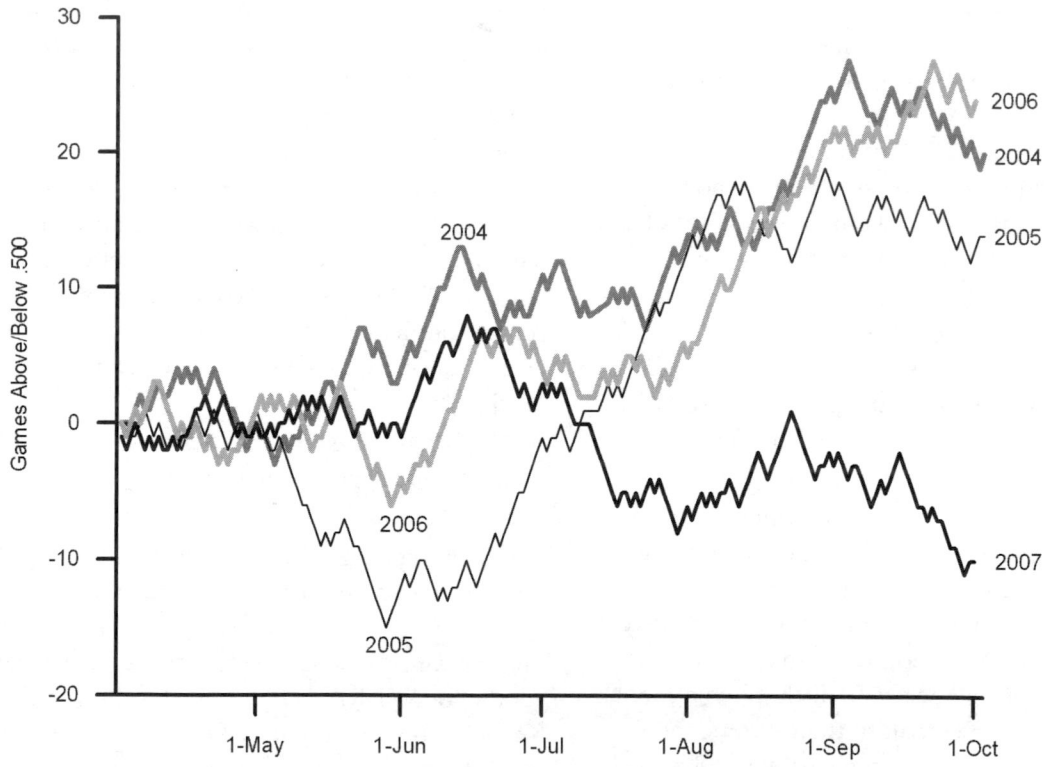

National League East Review

by John Walsh

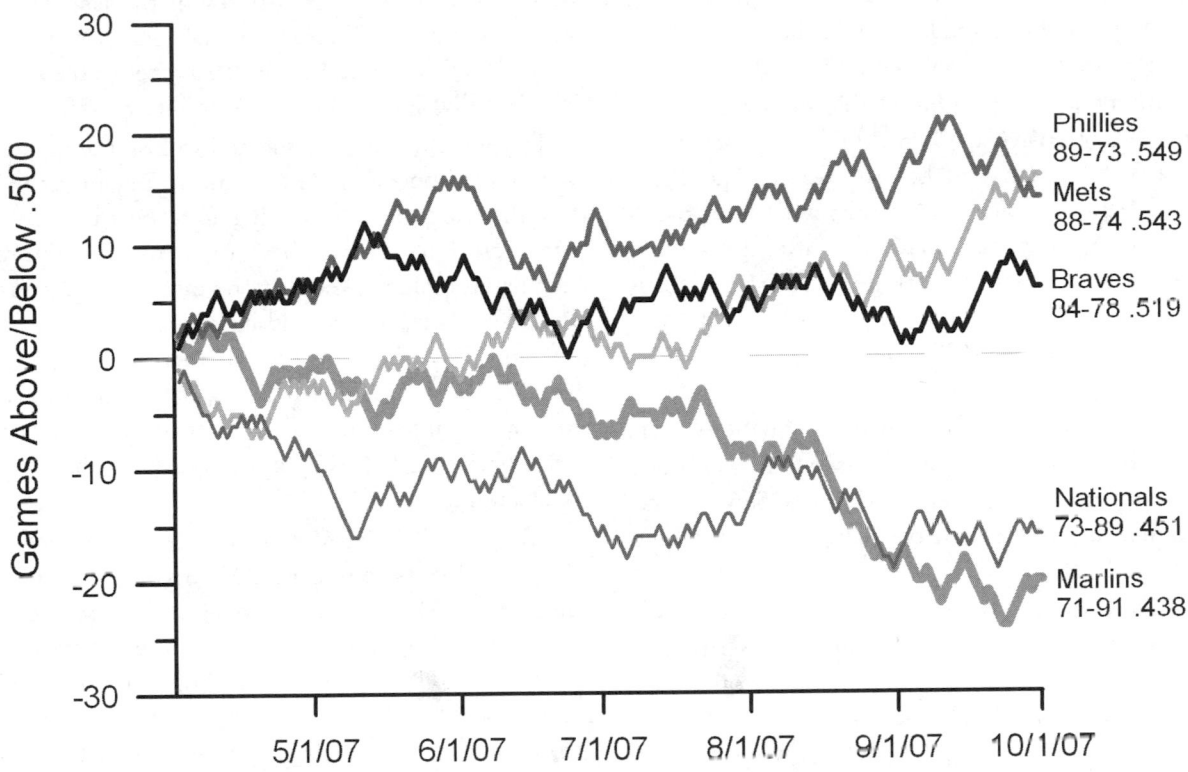

As the 2007 season opened, it was generally agreed that the National League East was up for grabs. Yes, the New York Mets, who had coasted to a largely uncontested divisional crown in 2006, were back with much of their lineup intact. But the Philadelphia Phillies, who had finished 12 games behind the Mets in 2006, took some comfort in knowing that, measured by run differential, the real distance between the rivals was closer to five games. The same can be said of the Atlanta Braves, who posted a 79-83 record last year despite outscoring their opponents by more than 40 runs.

The Mets, who came so close to reaching the World Series last year, were returning most of their 2006 team. Their two outfield corners (their two non-Carlos Beltran outfielders) and their second baseman would be different in 2007, but these were not key players. The pitching presented a question mark, since Pedro Martinez would miss nearly the whole season, and Steve Trachsel, who made 30 starts in '06, had moved on via free agency. The bullpen was in flux as well, and it wasn't clear if the Mets could match their excellent bullpen results of 2006.

Like the Mets, the Phillies had the core of their everyday players back for 2007. The infield trio of Ryan Howard, Chase Utley and Jimmy Rollins was back, although, unfortunately, so was third baseman Abraham Nunez. In the outfield Shane Victorino replaced Bobby Abreu and Carlos Ruiz took over behind the plate. As with the Mets, there was more uncertainty about the pitching staff. The Phils added starters Adam Eaton and Freddy Garcia to round out the rotation of Brett Myers, Cole Hamels, Jamie Moyer and Jon Lieber.

The Braves traded one of their better 2006 offensive players, Adam LaRoche, for bullpen help and slotted Kelly Johnson in at second base to replace Marcus Giles. As with their fellow NL East contenders, the Braves had some holes on the pitching side. The top of the rotation, Tim Hudson and John Smoltz, looked very strong, but after those two the cast wasn't inspiring. The bullpen looked like a bright spot, however, with Mike Gonzalez and Rafael Soriano coming over in trades.

While any of these three teams had a chance at winning the division, the same could not be said of the Marlins and Nationals. The Fish were coming off an upbeat season in which they exceeded expectations, but they still were not considered contenders. The Nationals looked like an utterly dismal team after losing Alfonso Soriano to free agency and starting the season with-

25

out their other good hitter, Nick Johnson. People were predicting a historically bad season for the Nats.

That's how things stood at the start of the season. We wouldn't know how it turned out until a Sunday afternoon some six months later, when the Phillies won the division pennant on the last day of the season. Let's have a closer look to see how that happened.

The Phillies, as has been their habit the last few years, were a great offensive club in 2007. They outscored every other NL team and before you go squawking about that bandbox they play in (just what is a "bandbox," anyway?), they still ranked first after accounting for park effects. This run-scoring machine was led by first baseman Howard, who slugged 47 home runs, drove in 136 and hit .268/.392/.584.

No wait, the offensive standout was second baseman Chase Utley, who topped 100 in both runs and RBIs and cranked 48 doubles, despite missing a month due to a broken hand. His gorgeous .332/.410/.566 line was accompanied by nine stolen bases in 10 attempts and only seven GIDP.

What am I saying? Wasn't Jimmy Rollins, who just might win the MVP award, the key to this offense? Thirty home runs, more than 200 hits, the fourth 20-20-20-20 (doubles, triples, home runs and stolen bases) player in the history of the game. All this while playing, by most accounts, solid defense at a premium position.

Add in fine seasons by Pat Burrell and Aaron Rowand and some excellent contributions from fill-ins Jason Werth and Tadahito Iguchi, and you have a very, very good offensive team.

The pitching was, well, not as good. Hamels (183.1 innings, 3.39 ERA) emerged as the undisputed staff ace, particularly when Myers was moved to the bullpen early in the season. The surprise of the rotation was 22-year-old rookie righthander Kyle Kendrick, who started 20 games and went 10-4 with a 3.87 ERA. He may not have the peripherals to keep that up (3.8 strikeouts per game, 1.25 home runs per game), but he managed to do it this season.

Beyond these two, however, things started falling off quickly. Kyle Lohse did what he usually does: pitch a fair number of innings of average (or below) quality ball. Moyer slipped to a 5-plus ERA, perhaps starting to feel all those 44 years of his. Lieber and Garcia started a dozen, mostly ineffectual, games each before succumbing to injury.

Worst of all was Eaton, who was handed the ball 30 times and responded with a frightening 6.29 ERA in 161.2 innings. Unlike Kendrick, the Eaton Rifle **does**

have the peripherals to back up his, ahem, performance: 1.3 strikeout to walk ratio and 1.59 home runs per game.

Despite the pitching woes, the Phillies won when they had to, including 13 times in the last 17 games, when the pitching more than held its own, posting a 3.44 ERA. That stretch included a three-game sweep of the then division-leading Mets at Shea Stadium.

In contrast, the Mets seemed to lose the games that were most important. They went 6-12 against the Phillies, the team they absolutely had to beat in the stretch run. You don't have to be a math whiz to figure out that had the Mets taken just one more game against the Philadelphians, they would have ended up tied for the division. But why were they in this position, anyway? The Mets won 97 games in 2006, cruised to the division title by 12 games and had most of the key parts of that team back in 2007. Why did they drop nine games in the standings?

Well, in 2006 the Mets scored 103 runs more than their opponents, while in 2007 that run differential dropped to 54. That 50-run dropoff can be laid at the door of the bullpen. After pacing the league in 2006 with a 3.25 ERA, the Mets' bullpen was eighth in reliever ERA (3.99). The difference in runs prevented works out to 53, which is almost exactly the dropoff in run differential. The front of the bullpen—Billy Wagner, Aaron Heilman and, for the most part, Pedro Feliciano—was solid, but what sunk the Mets in 2007, simply killed them, was 172 innings of 5.39 ERA relief work from Scott Schoeneweis, Guillermo Mota and Aaron Sele. Yuck.

Turning to the starting rotation, did you realize that this year's version was actually superior to the 2006 model? Me, neither. The improvement was mostly due to a fine year by Ollie Perez, who led the staff in ERA (3.56) and tied for the lead in wins with 15. It's easy to forget that Perez, who was pitching in the Padres rotation before he started shaving, is only 25. The other bright spot for the starting rotation was the long-awaited return of Pedro Martinez (3-1, 2.57 ERA) late in the season. Pedro can get the fastball up to only 88-89 mph now, but he still struck out 32 batters in 28 innings. It will be fun to see if the new Pedro can continue to confound hitters with his bag of tricks in 2008.

When David Wright woke up on the morning of May 1, he may or may not have worried about his stats, but many Mets fans were fretting about his .244/.370/.311 line. Even more worrying were the mere eight home runs that Wright had managed going back to July 1, 2006.

On this day, though, Wright went 3-for-4 with a double and a homer and so kicked off his official campaign for the office of National League MVP. The Mets third baseman, who is still only 24, hit .339/.425/.588 the rest of the way. Even his counting stats over that span, 38 doubles, 30 homers, 101 RBIs, would be good work over a full season.

Jose Reyes, the other budding Mets superstar, lost a bit of his luster in 2007. After a fast start, he was merely average (.263/.336/.385) from mid-May on. Perhaps most disturbing were whispers of Reyes's problems of concentration and, perhaps, dedication while the Mets were struggling to hang on to their division title. But a four-month slump can play with your mind, especially for a youngster like Reyes. I'm betting on a big step forward next season.

The Braves copped the Pythagoras Trophy, awarded to the team with the best run differential in its division. Yes, the Braves' Pythagorean record, estimated from runs scored and allowed, was 88-74, tops in the NL East. In fact they ranked third in the NL in runs scored and third in run prevention, which is not too shabby for a team many considered a disappointment this year.

Perhaps the biggest news in Atlanta in 2007 was the horrible offensive numbers put up by center fielder Andruw Jones in his contract year. Jones got off to a slow start and never broke out of his funk, hitting .222/.311/.413 on the year, the worst performance of his career (discounting 100-odd at-bats as a 19-year-old). Here's a question: If Jones had had his normal year, would the Braves have won the NL East? No, not quite. Jones was worth about 3.5 wins fewer this year than last, while the Braves finished five games behind the Phillies.

On the positive side of the offensive ledger, we have the other Jones. Chipper batted .337, his career best, on his way to an OPS+ of 166, his best mark since his MVP year of 1999. Although he was bothered by minor injuries throughout the season, he did manage 600 plate appearances, his best total in four years. Another plus for the Braves was the fine (.276/.375/.457) year by converted second baseman Kelly Johnson, who was a big upgrade over the departed Marcus Giles.

The starting rotation was quite top-heavy: Sinker-baller Hudson, after a disappointing 2006, bounced back big-time: 224.1 innings, 16-10, 3.33 ERA. Perhaps the most amazing performance by a Brave came from the ageless Smoltz. The 40-year-old starter finished in the top five in the NL in six pitching categories: ERA, walk rate, strikeout rate, strikeouts, strikeout to walk ratio, and ERA+. He also went 14-8 over 205.2 innings. We're getting used to over-40s excelling on the mound, but Smoltz's performance is truly extraordinary.

Chuck James was a serviceable No. 3 starter (11-10, 4.24 ERA), but after that the cupboard was usually pretty bare. The bulk of the remaining starts went to Buddy Carlyle, Kyle Davies (since exiled to Kansas City) and Jo-Jo Reyes.

The Braves bullpen, third best in the NL this year, was unexpectedly led by setup man Peter Moylan, a sidearming righthander, who managed a 1.80 ERA in 90 innings pitched. Soriano, who became the closer after the team released Bob Wickman late in the season, was no slouch either: 72 innings, 3.00 ERA, with 70 strikeouts against only 15 walks. A key feature of the Braves bullpen was that it didn't have any real stinkers: only one Braves reliever (Tyler Yates) pitched more than 20 innings with an ERA over 5: that's fewer than any other NL East team.

Five reasons why the Washington Nationals should be satisfied with their 2007 season: 1) They lost only 89 games. Preseason pundits were predicting at least 100 losses for the Nats and I remember seeing some down-right silly forecasts like 120 losses. 2) The bullpen was very solid, as evidenced by their NL fourth-best 3.81 ERA. Six relievers pitched at least 40 innings with a sub-4 ERA. 3) Shortstop Christian Guzman put up a delightfully uncharacteristic line of .328/.380/.466. He then did his team a favor by getting injured before he could regress back to his normal level of play. 4) Wily Mo Pena was acquired in August from the Red Sox for a player to be named later. The 25-year-old Pena, who never seemed to get untracked in Boston, took over in left field for the Nats and hit .293/.352/.504 over the final six weeks. If Wily Mo is really finally realizing his potential, this is a big boost for the Nats. 5) They finished fourth in the NL East, after three straight seasons in the cellar. In fact, after a terrible start that saw them at 9-25 on May 10, they went 64-64, bettering the Braves and the Marlins.

I'm not going to give you five negatives about the Nats in 2007, but just one: The starting pitching was bad. Granted, they essentially had to build a rotation from scratch after losing the entire 2006 staff to either free agency or injury. While there were, perhaps, a couple of bright spots (Shawn Hill and Jay Bergmann), the rest of the staff ranged from sub-par to horrifying. Only one rotation member (Matt Chico) made more than 21 starts and the bottom of the rotation consisted of 37 starts by five pitchers, all of whom boasted ERAs north of 6.00. Ouch.

In contrast to their neighbors one floor up, the Marlins have to be disappointed in their 2007 campaign. After an uplifting 2006, in which seemingly half the team was in the running for NL Rookie of the Year, the 2007 version took a couple of giant steps back. Last year I wrote about the Marlins' fine quartet of young pitchers: Josh Johnson, Scott Olsen, Ricky Nolasco and Anibal Sanchez. In 2006 as a group these guys went 45-21 with a 3.74 ERA in 592 innings pitched. The same crew, this year, struggled mightily: 13-21, 5.76 ERA in 244 innings. Only Olsen was healthy the whole season and the Marlins probably wish he hadn't been.

On offense, the Marlins were fine. Shortstop Hanley Ramirez continued his march towards superstardom, hitting .332/.386/.562. Miguel Cabrera (.320/.401/.565)

is only 24 years old, which is hard to believe, since he's been among the best hitters in the NL for four years running now. Jeremy Hermida had a breakout sophomore year, hitting .296/.369/.501, after having a disappointing rookie season. Overall, the Marlins got above average production from six of their eight regulars: only catcher Miguel Olivo (OPS+ 73) and center fielder Alfredo Amezaga (OPS+ 81) dragged down the offensive attack.

When all is said and done, the Phillies, Mets and Braves all had quite similar seasons. The Braves got a bit unlucky, perhaps, which dropped them back from the other two. In the end, the Phils out-clubbed their opponents and won the big games when they had to, taking the division crown for the first time in 14 years.

National League Central Review

by John Beamer

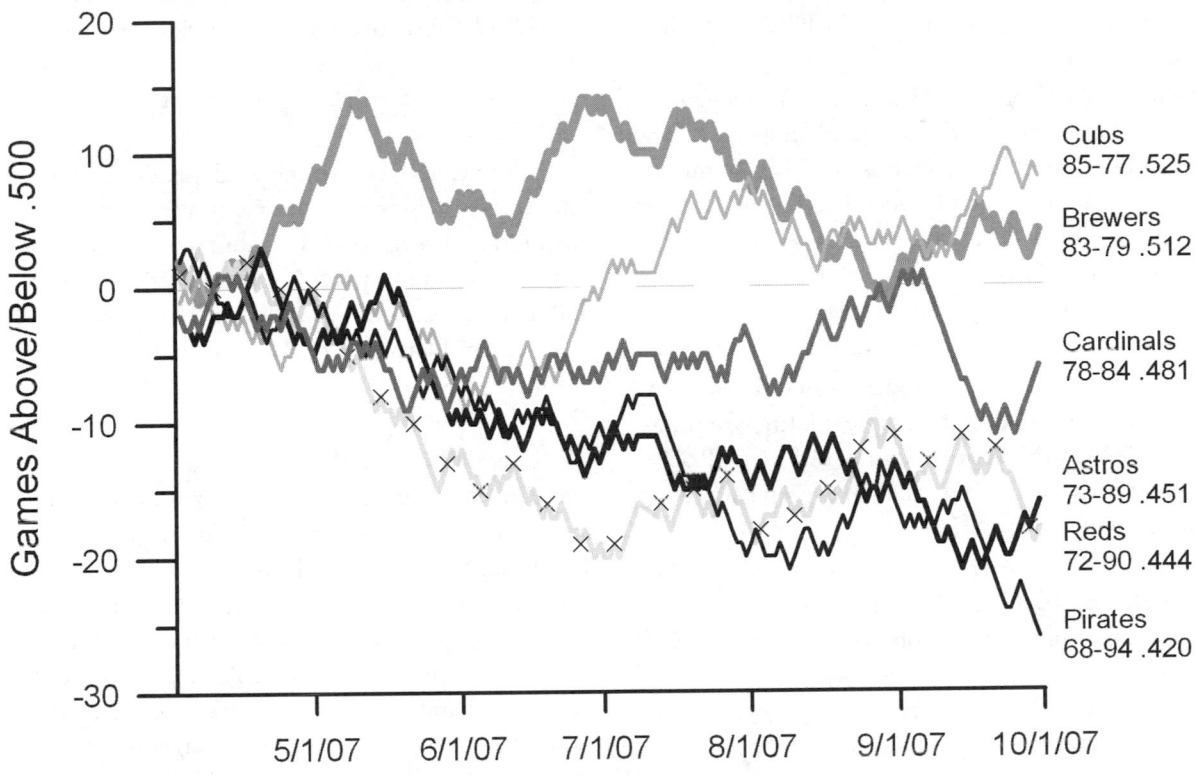

It is surprising that a division that produced the last three National League World Series representatives, the defending World Series champion, and the winningest team in the bigs two out of the last three years should enter 2007 touted as the weakest in the game. But such is baseball. In response, NL Central teams splurged close to $500 million on free agents. Would it be enough to shake off the moniker of "worst division in baseball"?

No. As new Cubs manager Lou Piniella quipped in the heat of the battle, "The only way to gain ground in our division is by getting rained out." That was generous. Totting up the numbers, the NL Central was a collective 54 games below .500. The next worst was the AL Central, two games below. The impotence of the NL Central cannot be overstated.

The tone was set in the season-opening series as the Mets routed the Cardinals in a reprise of last year's NLCS. To make matters worse, the Cards' Chris Carpenter lasted only six innings before succumbing to an injury that required Tommy John surgery. He won't retake the mound until 2009.

Off the field, things weren't much better for St. Louis. Tony La Russa was found dozing at the wheel of his car after drinking heavily. Worse still, a month later, reliever Josh Hancock was killed in a car crash while inebriated. At the end of April, the Cards were a sorry 10-15 with only 16 home runs—just two more than Albert Pujols himself had in April last year.

The Brewers took the early lead, opening April 16-9 and losing only one series at home, to the Chicago Cubs. The Brewers' record was built on pitching—the staff ERA for the month was a miserly 3.81 even though ace Ben Sheets pitched woefully. In two consecutive games, he was ripped for 13 runs in 11 innings as the Brew Crew lost four of his first five starts. It was immaterial by mid-May—the Brewers had stretched their record to a major league best 25-12, with Prince Fielder hitting a battery of home runs, setting a new franchise record with 13 in the month of May.

Of the remaining contenders, Cincinnati started with the most pomp and after a dozen games had even opened up a small lead, reprising the team's strong start of 2006. However, three weeks in the Reds slipped below .500 and would remain there for the rest of the season. Save some power from lefties Josh Hamilton, Adam Dunn and Ken Griffey Jr., there were few bright spots for Cincinnati in 2007.

Houston also stood at the summit for a day but swiftly plummeted to 22-31 through May, a sequence that included seven- and nine-game losing streaks. The Astros were always going to struggle after losing Roger Clemens and Andy Pettitte. Sure enough they did. Their rotation clocked a disappointing 5.25 ERA excluding Roy Oswalt.

Bullpen woes also plagued Houston. Brad Lidge blew his first save opportunity, then imploded spectacularly against St. Louis, giving up five runs in 2/3 of an inning. He wouldn't close again until mid-June. The acquisition of Carlos Lee did little to inspire the team, although he partly justified his extortionate salary with a line of .303/.354./.528, taking advantage of the proximity of the Crawford Boxes, where he hit half his home runs.

In Pittsburgh, expectations were suitably low. The Bucs haven't finished within a dime of first for more than a decade and the acquisitions of Adam LaRoche, Shawn Chacon and Tony Armas Jr. weren't about to vault the team into contention.

The problem was that there was no apparent strategy. Take the LaRoche trade, for instance, in which the Pirates gave up a high-potential prospect, Brent Lillibridge, for a lollygagging first bagger coming off a career year in 2006. LaRoche, perhaps predictably, could only muster an ugly .206/.315/.353 by Memorial Day. He'd improve, but not much. Surprisingly the Pirates didn't sink as fast as some expected, keeping within 10 games of the lead until late June.

Meanwhile the Cubs, laden with $300 million of free agent contracts, struggled to live up to their billing and had losing records in both April and May. Disaster was averted only because of the ineptitude of the other teams—incredibly, all posted losing records in May, allowing everyone to stay in touch. On June 1, the Brewers had a 6.5-game lead over Pittsburgh, St. Louis and Chicago, with Cincinnati and Houston both within a further three.

In early June, the fractious Cubs' clubhouse finally reached boiling point. In the first of a three-game set against the Braves, Carlos Zambrano and Michael Barrett had a ruckus after a pitch-calling disagreement that would end the catcher's career at Wrigley. The next day Lou Piniella vented his frustration by starting a kafuffle with umpire Mark Wagner over a call at third. In an incredible display, Piniella punted his cap around the turf and kicked dirt over Wagner's shoes. Piniella was tossed and suspended as the Cubs lost their sixth straight in a 2-12 rut.

It was to be their nadir. From that point, the Cubs turned their season around. The following two weeks they played .600 ball but failed to dent Milwaukee's lead

as the Brewers, inspired by the promotions of rookies Ryan Braun and Yovani Gallardo, went 17-9 in June. Braun had an immediate impact, clubbing a homer in his sixth big league at-bat. Gallardo opened with a 4-1 record. Sheets showed a welcome return to form, posting a 2.17 ERA for June. As July dawned, the Brewers had a 7.5 game lead over the Cubs with the Cardinals a further three back. The remaining teams were fighting for last.

Fittingly, it was around Independence Day when the fireworks started. The Cubs went on a 19-5 tear, inspired by a revived Zambrano, who, after his rumpus with Barrett, ran up a 9-2 record on the back of a 1.41 ERA to the end of July. The offense also sparked to life, led by Derrek Lee, Alfonso Soriano and Aramis Ramirez, who collectively accounted for more than half the team's home runs in the season.

In early July, the Brewers lost three in a row against the Pirates and their lead was down to 4.5. There was worse news in Milwaukee as the pitching started to crumble. First, Sheets tweaked his finger and landed on the DL for six weeks. Gallardo coughed up 11 runs in three innings at Coors Field and then the Cardinals blazed him for seven. Matters weren't helped by Ned Yost's seeming inability to manage his bullpen. He put ill-equipped relievers into high-leverage situations, drawing repeated criticism across the blogosphere.

By July 31, the Brewers were dethroned at the top of the Central after 99 days in the lead. The Cubs, however, suffered their own injury blow a few days later: Soriano ruptured his thigh muscle, which considerably slowed the team's momentum. For a soporific four weeks, the division lead jumped back and forth depending on which team had the most recent loss.

Meanwhile, La Russa was planning his October assault. A 15-11 surge in July was the first hint of a revival and then came the remarkable tale of former pitcher Rick Ankiel, who fleetingly became Pujols reincarnate. In his first game, on Aug. 9 against the Padres, Ankiel slammed a 2-1 curveball from Doug Brocail over the right field wall. A couple of days later he hit two more against the Dodgers. The hot streak continued, climaxing Sept. 6 with a three-hit, two-home run game in a 16-4 blowout against the Bucs. Ankiel had seven RBIs in that game to cap an astonishing month's stretch that saw him thump nine homers for a line of .358/.409/.765.

However, what baseball gives, baseball takes. A day later, Ankiel was at the center of a drug scandal involving HGH. His production suffered, and he batted .220/.250/.330 to the end of the season with only two more homers. His hot streak had coincided with the

Redbirds going 19-10 to vault over .500 and within a game of the lead. As Ankiel went cold, the Cards lost their hopes of a World Series repeat.

While three contenders fought at the top, the division's other teams gave their front offices a cleaning. The Reds fired manager Jerry Narron on July 1 with Cincinnati sporting a league-worst 51 losses. Replacement Pete Mackanin did a credible job, leading the club to a winning record in his short tenure. Over at Mission Control, the Astros dispensed with both manager Phil Garner and general manager Tim Purpura. It seemed a harsh firing, given that owner Drayton McClane's sole objective at the start of the season was to help celebrate Craig Biggio's 3,000th hit—a feat he accomplished on June 28 despite batting an anemic .250/.283/.378.

In September, the Pirates completed the hat trick as they parted ways with GM David Littlefield, who left the franchise in the same position he found it back in 2001—in last place. Littlefield's parting shot was the head-scratching acquisition of Matt Morris at the trade deadline, which saddled the franchise with $13 million of salary. Did the front office believe that 12 games back counted as contending? Morris had an ulcer-inducing 6.71 ERA in the 10 games he started.

The battle for the bottom was intense: by early September; barely a game separated the three. The Bucs triumphed, losing their last 11 of 14 and securing their 15th consecutive losing season. Next year, expect them to join the Phillies as the losingest franchise in sports.

By the first week of September, the division race was shaping up as a humdinger, with the Brewers and Cubs tied for first. The Brewers' charge was led by Rookie of the Year candidate Braun, who had a torrid September. In one three-game stretch, he went 7-for-11, single-handedly winning games against the Pirates and 'Stros. On Sept. 9, Braun jacked two shots into the seats to secure a 10-5 victory over the Reds and the Brewers stood atop the division. The Cubs responded by winning a rescheduled game against the Cardinals behind Ramirez's four-hit, two-homer night. They upped the ante by taking series against Houston, St Louis and Cincinnati. The Brewers matched, winning four in a row, and on Sept. 18 the teams were still level.

Then, however, the Brewers' hopes faded when they lost three of four against the Braves at Turner Field. The first two games were split, but it was in the third game that things went wrong. The Braves came back from 2-0 down to win in extras on a Rickie Weeks fumble. Game four was worse, as the Brew Crew blew a 4-1

seventh-inning lead. That meant the Brewers' record on the road was 32-49 for the season, only one game off the worst in the National League.

The Cubs took advantage and comfortably swept Pittsburgh to build a 3.5 game advantage. It wasn't quite over, though. The Cubs got run over by the Marlins, allowing the Brewers to claw back within two as they beat out the Cardinals. In the middle game, Prince Fielder belted his 49th and 50th home runs, besting the previous franchise record set by Gorman Thomas 26 years ago, and also becoming the youngest man to club 50 round-trippers.

As the Brewers faced the Padres for the season's last four games, they had to win at least three to have a chance of reaching the playoffs. They blew the first, suffering some shoddy glove work from Braun, who committed three errors, running his major league-leading total to 26. The next day, in a lunch game, the Cubs beat the Reds 6-0 behind Soriano's leadoff home run, his 32nd overall and his 11th in the leadoff spot, a big league record. (He'd add one more a couple of days later to extend the record.)

The Brewers had to beat the Padres in a nightcap to stay alive. Chris Capuano was on the mound in place of the injured Sheets. The omens were bad—Capuano had been involved in 22 straight losses after the Brewers won his first seven starts. He was better this night and gave up only three runs, but back-to-back doubles by the Padres in the seventh triggered a 6-3 loss and saw Cubtown celebrating its first division title since 2003.

Despite the power bats of Soriano, Ramirez and Lee, the statistics say that it was the pitching rotation that carried the Cubs to the title. Adjusting for park, Chicago allowed a miserly 4.1 runs per games—the fewest in the majors. Ted Lilly was an unexpected revelation, winning 15 and sporting a 3.83 ERA. Jason Marquis had a respectable ERA of 4.61 yet still was the worst regular starter.

The bullpen was less effective, but unearthed a gem in Carlos Marmol, whose devastating heat/slider combo saw him strike out every other batter. For all the wheezing about the lack of talent in the division, the Cubs aren't a terrible team and on balance are worthy champions in a weak division. After the All-Star break, they had a division-best 44-39 record, the eighth best second-half record in the majors.

None of the other franchises, not even the Brewers, should be especially proud of their achievements. Maybe next year NL Central teams should march out to Amy Diamond's ditty "It can only get better." It can't get worse, can it?

National League West Review

by Steve Treder

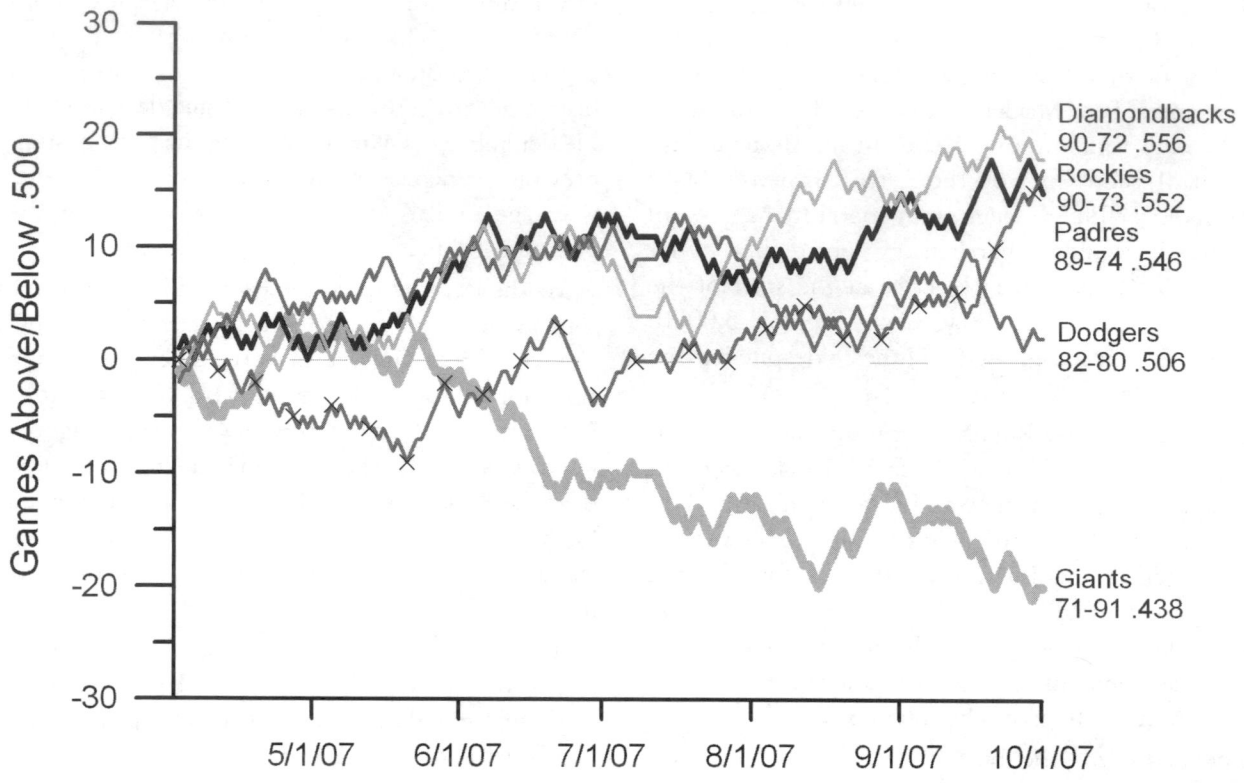

The most competitive, interesting, and highly enter-taining NL West season in many years wasn't resolved in 162 games. Nor was it resolved through nine innings of its 163rd. And when that extra-inning extra game featured a tie-breaking two-run homer in the top of the 13th (clouted by an unheralded journeyman who was not only hitting his eighth home run in 87 at-bats since being acquired by his new team, but was notching his fifth such blast of the dramatic, late-inning, game-changing variety), rapidly answered by a four-line-shots-in-a-row-off-one-of-the-all-time-greatest-closers three-run game-winning rally, finishing with an eyelash-close tag play at home in which the catcher dropped the ball, the runner missed the plate, and the ump blew the call—well, baseball just doesn't get much more fun.

Remember 2005, when this division was the runt of the MLB litter, its first-place team at 82-80? Ancient history. The 2007 NL West division's .520 winning percentage was the very best in the game. The NL West mopped the floor with NL East opponents at a .568 rate and easily handled the NL Central as well, to a .547 tune. (Oddly, the West performed the most poorly among the National League divisions in inter-league play, with a feeble .436.)

This division produced not only the winningest team in the National League, but also both of its tied-for-the-Wild-Card combatants. And, of course, this division produced both of the NLDS winners, in matching three-game sweeps.

This was the division that housed the redoubtable Barry Bonds, persevering through the acrid storm of steroid-controversy negativity with yet another amazing performance, surpassing Hank Aaron's four-decades-old career home run record with room to spare. This was also the division that featured the high-profile Los Angeles Dodgers, widely predicted to strongly contend, but falling apart down the stretch while exhibiting a weird form of dissension. And this was the division that featured the ne'er-do-well Colorado Rockies, widely predicted to finish last (though not by me! I knew my Giants would be up to that task), picking up steam after a stumbling start, roaring past the wire as the hottest team in baseball, and riding that tremendous momentum all the way to the World Series.

This division's champion was the Arizona Diamond-backs, putting together its first winning season since 2003 while making liberal use of smoke and mirrors: the Dbacks joined the 1932 Pirates, 1984 Mets, and 1997 Giants as just the fourth team in history to post a .550-plus winning percentage despite a below-.500 Pythagorean record. The Snakes became the very first team in history to post the best record in its league while being outscored.

Arizona won despite presenting one of the weakest offenses in the game. Many of their highly regarded young talents were disappointing with the bat: 24-year-old shortstop Stephen Drew, in his first full season, hit far less than expected, and 24-year-old right fielder Carlos Quentin hit so badly that he wound up back in the minors; his replacement, 20-year-old rookie Justin Upton, hit no better. Twenty-five-year-old sophomore first baseman Conor Jackson didn't hit badly, but neither did he step forward into his anticipated stardom, while 23-year-old rookie center fielder Chris B. Young delivered power, speed and defense, but also a dreadful .295 OBP, which was all the more problematic because manager Bob Melvin insisted on batting Young leadoff most of the year.

But the Diamondbacks' organizational depth paid dividends: When 27-year-old young veteran third baseman Chad Tracy was sidelined by injuries, 23-year-old rookie Mark Reynolds came straight up from Double-A and filled in splendidly. And both of the "oldest" regulars in the Arizona lineup contributed fine all-around seasons: 31-year-old left fielder Eric Byrnes (26 Win Shares) and 29-year-old second baseman Orlando Hudson (20 Win Shares).

But mostly the key to the Diamondbacks' success was excellent pitching. Ace Brandon Webb was predictably brilliant. And while Arizona's 47-29 performance in one-run and two-run decisions was probably mostly a function of good luck, having a great bullpen sure didn't hurt. The Dbacks got exceptional results from their no-name relief staff, especially closer Jose Valverde and middle-inning man Juan Cruz, who combined for 165 strikeouts and 91 hits allowed in 125 innings.

The Rockies presented a structure similar to Arizona's: a generally young ball club, with most of its talent produced by the minor league system, and with an extraordinarily good bullpen. But unlike the Diamondbacks, Colorado featured some serious offensive thump. The extravagant numbers at the core of the Rockies' lineup weren't just a mile-high park effect: 27-year-old left fielder Matt Holliday emerged in 2007 as a first-order star (his 30 Win Shares tied with Miguel Cabrera for third in the National League), and his supporting cast of veteran first baseman Todd Helton (not what he once was, but still a robust run-producer), right fielder Brad Hawpe, third baseman Garrett Atkins (who came on like gangbusters after a very slow start) and rookie

shortstop Troy Tulowitzki all contributed genuinely fine years with the bat.

On the pitching side, southpaw Jeff Francis, at age 26, quietly developed into a premium starter. The rest of the Rockies' rotation was something of a patchwork, but it held together pretty well, enjoying the support of the remarkable relief corps. In midseason, 24-year-old setup man Manuel Corpas and veteran closer Brian Fuentes swapped roles, and over the second half they combined for a 1.53 ERA and a sub-1.00 WHIP. Behind them, journeymen Jeremy Affeldt, LaTroy Hawkins and Jorge Julio were outstanding. Even 37-year-old Matt Herges, designated for assignment in April, was raised from the dead in July and made a solid contribution in the second half.

But Colorado's most impressive aspect was their fielding. The Rockies committed just 68 errors, by far the fewest in baseball, and their second-in-the-league DER of .701 was exceptional given that the ultra-spacious Coors Field is the most hit-fertile environment in the major leagues.

The Rockies' team-wide improvement over the course of the season was extraordinary. In April, putting up a record of 10-16, Colorado scored 4.1 runs per game while allowing 5.0. They steadily improved in both categories, until in their 20-8 September (including a 13-1 sprint to the finish to force the wild card playoff) the Rox were scoring 6.2 while surrendering just 4.4.

For the San Diego Padres, losers of that memorable 163rd game, 2007 will be remembered as a season of frustration. They were in first place for 43 days throughout the year, and up to the very end the Padres held the inside track on the wild card. But they provided the opening for Colorado by being swept in a late-September series with the Rockies in San Diego, including a nightmarish final game in which the Padres lost both center fielder Mike Cameron (22 Win Shares) and left fielder Milton Bradley (.313/.414/.590 in 42 games) to injuries. Bradley, incidentally, that day set the major league record for times tearing-ACL-while-being restrained-by-own-manager-from-attacking-umpire-who-instigated-rhubarb, with one.

Still the Friars could have clinched the wild card on the season's final weekend by winning either one of two games against the Brewers, who'd already been eliminated. But San Diego lost both, including the Saturday contest in which their august closer Trevor Hoffman (the all-time career saves leader, who'd passed the 500 mark in June) blew the save by surrendering a two-out ninth-inning pinch-hit triple to, of all people, Tony Gwynn, Jr.

In distinct contrast to the young, largely home-grown Diamondbacks and Rockies, the 2007 Padres featured uber-veterans in key roles (along with the 39-year-old Hoffman were 36-year-old right fielder Brian Giles and 41-year-old starter Greg Maddux), and their only organizationally developed talents of significance were ace Jake Peavy (who was phenomenal, leading the league in wins, strikeouts, WHIP, ERA, and ERA+) and power-hitting shortstop Khalil Greene.

The fruits of general manager Kevin Towers' wheeling and dealing were abundant. First baseman Adrian Gonzalez (leading the team with 27 Win Shares) and starting pitcher Chris R. Young (just as dominant as Peavy in the first half) were both plucked from Texas in a steal of a January 2006 trade. In a surprising November '06 deal, Towers sent standout rookie second baseman Josh Barfield to the Indians in exchange for unproven prospect third baseman Kevin Kouzmanoff; while Barfield flopped in Cleveland, Kouzmanoff had a fine year in San Diego.

Heath Bell, nearly unhittable as Hoffman's set-up man, had been pilfered from the Mets. Bradley, who hit a ton in his as-per-usual brief stretches of good health, had been scavenged from Oakland in late June '07. And at the end of July, Towers relieved Arizona of the services of utility outfielder Scott Hairston, who proceeded to make stunning late-game home runs his specialty, including the Oct. 1 bomb that came oh-so-close to winning the wild card berth.

If the Padres' season was frustrating, then 2007 for the Dodgers was agonizing. This deeply talented ball club spent most of the first half leading the division, in the top spot for 68 days. Then they encountered a sudden, horrible 6-18 slump in late July/early August—a 24-game span in which they were shut out four times and scored one or two runs nine times—and the Dodgers dropped all the way to fourth. They then pulled themselves together and were back in the thick of the race in mid-September, only to drop 11 of their last 14 games.

Worse, perhaps, was the manner in which the team appeared to handle its disappointments: Those final sour two weeks featured almost daily quotes in the media from Dodgers veterans Luis Gonzalez, Jeff Kent and Derek Lowe that seemed desperate to lay blame for the collapse exclusively at the feet of its youngest performers, in particular 22-year-old outfielder Matt Kemp and 23-year-old first baseman James Loney.

This palpable disintegration was odd not only to the degree that such public finger-pointing by experienced players is appallingly impolitic. It was also strange in that it was plain that the Dodgers' problems were utterly unattributable to failings on the part of their youngsters, especially not Kemp and Loney, each of whom batted a gaudy .382 in September, with Loney tossing in nine home runs and 32 RBIs for good measure. Meanwhile Gonzalez and Kent, both 39 and dogged by injuries, were struggling (Gonzalez hit .240 with four homers after July 25, and Kent drove in just one run after September 12), and the 34-year-old Lowe put up a 5.94 ERA over his final six starts.

There was, in fact, an array of highly impressive young talent in Los Angeles. Twenty-four-year-old sophomore Russell Martin led the team with 24 Win Shares, emerging as one of the game's premier catchers. Chad Billingsley, 22, was strong in a long relief role in the first half and terrific as a rotation starter the rest of the way, while 23-year-old Jonathan Broxton was lights-out all year long as a setup reliever. A couple of veteran pitchers were outstanding as well: ace starter Brad Penny had a career-best season, while Takashi Saito was as wickedly effective as any closer in baseball.

In San Francisco, big-contract signee Barry Zito disappointed with a mediocre 11-13, 4.53 performance (though he distinctly improved in the second half), and the home run heroics of that other Barry couldn't prevent the team from sliding into the basement for the first time since 1996. The Giants' graybearded lineup mounted virtually no offense at all outside of their 42-year-old cleanup hitter, who whacked 28 homers in 340 at-bats, led the league in walks and intentional walks, and whose 170 OPS+ would have led the league had he not fallen 25 plate appearances short of qualifying.

Other than Bonds' record chase, the only excitement in San Francisco was over its Mutt-and-Jeff pair of hard-throwing young right-handers. In his second full big-league season, 22-year-old Matt Cain, 6-foot-3 and 235 pounds, was among the league's better starters, though he went 7-16 as the Giants scored fewer than five runs in 28 of his 32 starts. And 23-year-old 5-foot-11, 160-pound Tim Lincecum, in only his second year of pro ball, was promoted to the majors in May with a grand total of 13 minor league games under his belt—in which he'd surrendered 26 hits in 63 innings, with 104 strikeouts and an ERA of an even 1.00. Lincecum was inconsistent in his first tour in The Show, but he fanned 150 big leaguers in 146 innings. And in his best outings—such as July 1 against the Diamondbacks, in which he expended just 97 pitches while striking out 12 and walking none in seven shutout innings—the raw rookie's lightning two-seam fastball and hard, sharp curve simply awed all observers.

The Postseason Sweeps

by Matthew Carruth

When the calendar turned to October (the one and only!) we officially began the postseason. Or not.

NL Wild Card playoff: San Diego Padres at Colorado Rockies

Technically, the one-game playoff for the NL Wild Card between the San Diego Padres and the Colorado Rockies counted as a regular season game, but let's not be technical. This game had more riding it than most postseason games, and what a game it was, pitting perennial NL Cy Young contender Jake Peavy against Josh Fogg (?!) in the cozy confines of Coors Field.

Striking first and often, the Rockies piled up a 3-0 lead after two innings. But humidor or not, this is still Coors Field, and anything short of a double-digit lead that early in the game, especially when you are relying on Josh Fogg, does not feel safe. The Padres drove that point home in the third when a single, walk and another single loaded the bases to start the inning. One batter later, Adrian Gonzalez launched a monster shot into the right field seats for a 4-3 Padres lead. The Padres would tack on another run to make it 5-3, but the score didn't stay that way long; in the bottom half, Todd Helton mashed a no-doubter himself to right to cut the lead in half.

Amazingly, no more scoring would take place for two whole innings, until the bottom of the fifth, when a leadoff double from hero of the game Troy Tulowitzki was followed by a line drive single from Matt Holliday that knotted the game again at 5-5. In the sixth, Seth Smith (remember that name), pinch-hitting for the pitcher, tripled with one out and scored on a Kazuo Matsui sac fly. Tulowitzki would follow that up with another triple, but Holliday stranded him, striking out. Still the Rockies had a 6-5 lead.

During the top of the eighth, it looked like a leadoff Geoff Blum single was going to waste after a popup and a strikeout, but Brian Giles delivered a two-out double that Holliday misplayed and we were tied again at six. While Colorado closer Manny Corpas came in for the ninth and shut down the Pads 1-2-3, Padres manager Bud Black stuck with Heath Bell rather than go to his closer, Trevor Hoffman, in the bottom of the ninth. Bell responded with another easy inning, finishing his night after 2.2 innings while allowing just two baserunners and striking out five.

San Diego threatened in the 10th, getting two runners on with two outs, but Matt Herges coaxed a Brian Giles ground out to end the frame. Of note was the pinch-running appearance of Mike Cameron, who by all accounts before the game was physically unable to swing a bat or even field. Nonetheless, Cameron remained in the game as the center fielder. Both teams got runners on in the 11th, but San Diego was foiled by a Khalil Greene double play and Colorado by a Brad Hawpe strikeout.

In the 13th, Jorge Julio entered the game for the Rockies, much to the dismay of diehard fans who would have preferred the team use anyone, including a Padre. Julio started the inning with a five-pitch walk and after ball one to Scott Hairston finally threw a strike. Unfortunately for him, it was a strike only because any batted ball is counted as a strike—Hairston put his bat on the ball and around 425 feet later it was 8-6 Padres.

Julio would allow another single before getting yanked for Ramon Ortiz, the 10th Colorado pitcher of the night, bringing new meaning to the phrase "everyone is available." Ortiz would retire the next three Padres, but it was now 8-6 Padres heading to what looked to be the final home inning. That meant that Black, having withheld Hoffman all game, now had the chance to hand the ball to the all-time saves leader with three outs to get and a two run cushion.

Those who were not paying close attention to the game, and this includes the announcers and pretty much every paid analyst in the mainstream media, would later conclude that Hoffman choked in the situation. But those who were paying attention might have noted that Hoffman was anything but fresh. Getting loose for the bottom of the 13th marked the **fourth** time Hoffman had warmed up that night. People do not make enough of the fact that relief pitchers will throw around 20 pitches in the pen to loosen up. Hoffman hadn't yet thrown an official pitch and his pitch count was already well north of 50. As far as Hoffman's arm was concerned, he was on his fourth inning.

It really should not have been a big surprise when the Rockies led off going double-double-triple to quickly tie the game and put the winning run on third with zero outs. Hoffman gave Helton a free pass, but Jamey Carroll took the first pitch he saw to right field and plated Holliday with a sac fly for a 9-8 Rockies win and a rousing kickoff to postseason baseball. Unfortunately, it also turned out to be the peak of the drama.

NLDS: Colorado Rockies at Philadelphia Phillies

Jeff Francis and Cole Hamels faced off in a match-up of young aces in a postseason where youth would become a major story throughout. While neither pitched poorly, Francis endured longer. Although he surrendered consecutive solo homers to Pat Burrell and Aaron Rowand in the fifth, he otherwise shut down the Philly offense. For their part, the Rockies put up three runs in the second and never relinquished the lead, tacking on another with Holliday's solo home run in the eighth and finishing the game with a 4-2 victory.

Game 2 featured a letdown, with the pitching match-up going from Francis-Hamels to Franklin Morales against Kyle Kendrick, prompting a gigantic "who?" from probably 95% of non-local viewers. Neither starter would make it even four innings. Tulowitzki and Holliday welcomed Kendrick to the postseason with back-to-back home runs in the first and Jimmy Rollins reciprocated to Morales in the bottom half. Rollins would add a triple in the second, giving the Phillies a 3-2 lead until the fourth.

Then, with Garrett Atkins on second after a lead-off double and two outs, Kendrick intentionally walked eight-hole hitter Yorvit Torrealba. Colorado manger Clint Hurdle responded by pinch-hitting Smith again. He got on board with a slow infield hit, which signaled the end of the day for Kendrick, who was replaced by Kyle Lohse. Lohse managed to throw a very successful first three pitches to Matsui, if you define successful as not getting hit out of the park. Unfortunately, the fourth pitch was not quite as successful and Matsui made it 6-3 Rockies.

Colorado put the game away for good in the sixth; a pair of walks and Matsui's triple led to four more runs and a 10-3 lead. With a 10-5 victory, the Rockies had a 2-0 series lead heading back to Colorado.

With their season down to one road game, things did not look good for Phillies fans. Heading out to Coors Field for a pair, the Phillies tabbed Jamie Moyer, a fly ball pitcher, to oppose rookie Ubaldo Jimenez. It turned out that Moyer was not a problem at all, tossing six innings and allowing just a lone run on yet another Matsui triple. Jimenez was equally good, going 6.1 innings and allowing just a solo home run to Shane Victorino in the seventh.

In the bottom of the eighth, though, after the first two Rockies hitters went down, three straight singles from Atkins, Hawpe and the pinch-hitting Jeff Baker gave the Rockies a 2-1 lead and put them just three outs from the win. Sure enough, Corpas came in, struck out Ryan Howard looking and retired Rowand and Victorino on harmless ground balls, locking up the series sweep for torrid Colorado. The Rockies had now won 17 of their last 18 games.

NLDS: Chicago Cubs at Arizona Diamondbacks

Brandon Webb and Carlos Zambrano dueled for six innings, after which we had a 1-1 game. Zambrano came out, having struck out eight, allowed one walk and given up four hits, including a solo homer to Stephen Drew. Webb lasted one more inning, also allowing four hits and walking three with nine strikeouts.

Neither starter threw 90 pitches, with the managers limiting pitch counts for possible Game 4 starts, but it was Zambrano's early exit that provided lots of fodder for the Chicago second-guessers. Carlos Marmol relieved Zambrano and Mark Reynolds said hello with a leadoff home run that put the Diamondbacks up 2-1. They would add another and Brandon Lyon and Jose Valverde shut the Cubs down with little trouble to wrap up a 3-1 Arizona win.

When Doug Davis and Ted Lilly squared off in Game 2, the Cubs got the first runs. Matt Murton led off the second with a single and scored a moment later on a Geovany Soto home run. Davis would go on to strike out the side in the inning but the Cubs had a 2-0 lead. The Cubs got to savor that lead for approximately 10 minutes—Chris Young's two-out, two-on homer in the bottom half flipped the 2-0 lead to a 3-2 deficit.

An Eric Byrnes triple added a fourth run in the inning and Drew's triple in the fourth made it 6-2. Arizona stretched it out to 8-2 after five. The Cubs added back a pair, but that would be it. Another Lyon-Valverde appearance in the eighth and ninth kept anything further from brewing in Arizona's 8-4 win.

With Arizona up 2-0, the series shifted to Chicago where Rich Hill took the mound opposite Livan Hernandez as the Diamondbacks attempted to finish the sweep. Arizona took no time getting to work. Young's leadoff homer was followed by a double from Drew, who scored on Justin Upton's single a few batters later. Each team scored a run in the fourth, but a Byrnes homer in the sixth made it 4-1 Arizona and time was running thin for Chicago with Lyon and Valverde waiting.

Sure enough, Arizona took that lead to the eighth, and Lyon took over, allowing only a harmless two-out single. Another bases-empty homer from Drew took it out of the realm of a save, but Valverde came in nonetheless and did his thing, freezing Jason Kendall and Darryl Ward on called strike threes before inducing a fly out from Alfonso Soriano to finish the game with a 5-1 victory and a 3-0 series sweep.

ALDS: Los Angeles (Anaheim) Angels at Boston Red Sox

The story of the opener was clearly Josh Beckett, who is quickly garnering a reputation as a big-game pitcher. Beckett faced just 31 hitters while tossing a complete game, four-hit shutout. Kevin Youkilis and David Ortiz homered, but the Sox needed just one while Beckett shut down the Angels' offense. First game to Boston, 4-0.

Game 2, pitting Kelvim Escobar against Daisuke Matsuzaka, was much more of a contest. Boston struck in the first with a pair of runs off walks and singles, but the Angels answered with some small ball of their own for a first run and then back-to-back doubles for another two to take a 3-2 lead.

Things settled down for a while after that. While neither pitcher was dominating—Matsuzaka allowing 10 baserunners in 4.2 innings and Escobar nine in five—they were able to keep the runs off the board until Boston tied it in the fifth on a leadoff double, walks to David Ortiz and Manny Ramirez and a Mike Lowell sac fly.

The relief corps for the Angels didn't have much luck keeping runners off base, typified by Scot Shields walking three in his two innings. Boston's, on the other hand, had a clean three innings until turning the ball over to Jonathan Papelbon in the eighth. He issued a pair of walks in his inning and a third, but allowed no runs.

In the bottom of the ninth, Boston's Julio Lugo led off with a single and Dustin Pedroia's ground out moved him to second. That's when Angels manager Mike Scioscia brought in Francisco Rodriguez. Rodriguez got Youkilis to strike out swinging and then intentionally gave Ortiz his fourth walk of the game. Didn't work. Ramirez got a 1-0 fastball over the inner half and sent it into orbit. That ended the game in a dramatic 6-3 win.

Heading back to Anaheim facing elimination, the Angels turned to Jered Weaver, whose 2007 campaign was much more indicative of his talent level than his sensational but fluky 2006, against Curt Schilling for

the Sox. The pitchers got out of jams until the fourth, when Ortiz and Ramirez led off with back-to-back homers. That was all Schilling needed over his seven shutout innings, setting it up for Hideki Okajima and Papelbon to close the series.

Bullpen heroics weren't needed: The Boston offense went to work in the top of the eighth with two walks, two singles and three doubles, which added up to seven runs, a 9-0 lead and a giant nail in the Angels 2007 season. Okajima came in anyway for the eighth and Eric Gagne was able to hold on to the nine-run lead in the ninth, and the Red Sox joined the Rockies and Diamondbacks with first-round sweeps.

ALDS: New York Yankees at Cleveland Indians

My name is Johnny and I'll be leading off this series with a home run.

Johnny Damon probably didn't say that, but he could have. He sent the Yanks to a quick 1-0 lead, but nearly as quickly as the lead came, it vanished. After Chien-Ming Wang got two outs in the bottom of the first by inducing a Asdrubal Cabrera double play, the next five Indians went walk, single, single, walk and single, scoring three runs. In fact, of the seven hitters who came to the plate in the first, only Cabrera failed to reach base—the third out came on the basepaths.

Cabrera made up for that with a leadoff homer in the third, matched by his Yankees counterpart at second base, Robinson Cano in the fourth. The Yanks added a run in the fifth, bringing it to a 4-3 game, but a Victor Martinez two-run homer and a double-single walk-double string later added another three runs and the Yanks trailed 9-3. The Indians didn't let up and finished the game out 12-3.

Game 2 was a bit more like what we figured we would see given the strength at the top of each team's rotation. Andy Pettitte matched up with Fausto Carmona and both were brilliant. Carmona's only run allowed in his nine innings pitched was on Melky Cabrera's homer in the third. Pettitte went 6.1 scoreless before yielding to Joba Chamberlain, who couldn't find any sense of control and wasn't helped by a invasion of bugs that swarmed around. He walked two and uncorked a pair of wild pitches, which tied the game at one apiece.

Much was made later about the bugs, but Carmona pitched through the same swirling insects with little effect. Mariano Rivera came into the game in the ninth for the Yankees and pitched a scoreless pair and Carmona gave way to Rafael Perez, who did the same. Luis Vizcaino took over for Rivera in the 11th and quickly allowed a pair of runners on via a walk and single. Casey Blake bunted them over, opening a base for Vizcaino to take the bat out of Grady Sizemore's hands and put it into those of Cabrera, who popped up.

With two out and the bases loaded, Travis Hafner stepped up and after watching a ball and swinging through a couple strikes, lined one into the right field gap for a game-winning single. Cleveland had won 2-1, pushing the Yankees to the edge.

The story of game three was the prospect of Roger Clemens making possibly his last start (again) in New York (again). The Indians chipped away at Clemens, plating a run in each of the first three innings and driving him from the game in the third. But the Yankees weren't out just yet, struggling back before a Damon three-run homer in the fifth gave them a 5-3 lead. Trot Nixon's error with the bases loaded in the sixth allowed Cano to clear the bases with a single and run the lead to 8-3. The Indians would get a run back in the eighth, off Chamberlain again, but never threatened the outcome of the game and we finally had a series go to a fourth game.

Game 4 highlighted the familiar debate about pitchers on short rest. The Yankees, facing elimination, turned back to Game 1 starter Wang while the Indians avoided rushing C.C. Sabathia back and went with Paul Byrd. One wonders how long it took Joe Torre to regret his decision: Sizemore made it 1-0 Cleveland three pitches into the game and Jhonny Peralta made it 2-0 four batters later with an RBI single. Ten minutes later the Indians were threatening again with the bases loaded and nobody out in the second, and Wang was done, replaced by would-have-been starter Mike Mussina. A run-scoring double play and Cabrera's single later made it 4-0.

The Yankees answered with a run in the bottom half with a bases-loaded, two-out single by Derek Jeter (to cries of "here come the Yankees" from a broadcast booth desperate for the big market of New York to stay), but Byrd kept further runs from scoring by getting Bobby Abreu to fly out.

Byrd continued to work around the baserunners he was allowing (10 over five innings), and in the fourth, the Indians struck again with a double, a pair of walks and a two-RBI single from Martinez, making it 6-1. The Yankees would get home runs from Cano, Alex Rodriguez and Abreu, but they were unable to get any runners on beforehand. Thanks in part to Jeter's .353

October OPS and Wang's ineffectiveness, the Yankees were headed home without a championship for a seventh straight postseason. (There go the Yankees, Joe. So long).

ALCS: Cleveland Indians at Boston Red Sox

Since Cleveland saved Sabathia for a potential Game 5, both rotations started at the top with Beckett and Sabathia. Cleveland led off with a Hafner home run, interrupting Beckett's striking out the side. The Red Sox answered with three straight singles to even the score at one.

Boston added four more in the third thanks to a bases-loaded walk to Ramirez after Sabathia had him 0-2 and an ensuing ground-rule double from Lowell. Two innings later came more Boston fireworks: Ortiz and Lowell walked around a Manny single to load the bases and two would score on Bobby Kielty's single. Boston added a third run later on Jason Varitek's double and after five it was 8-1, Sabathia was gone, Beckett was cruising and the game was all but over. Each team got two more runs, but Cleveland never threatened crooked numbers and Boston took game one in a 10-3 rout.

Game 2 saw Carmona and Schilling both knocked out in the fifth inning, Carmona getting touched for four runs, Schilling for five. Both pitchers allowed an alarmingly high nine baserunners; Schilling all by hits (solo home runs by Peralta and Sizemore), Carmona split between four hits and five walks. Ramirez and Lowell homered for the Sox following Carmona's departure.

After a seesaw six innings which saw the lead change four times, the game was even at six all and finally some stability ensued. Cleveland's Jensen Lewis, Rafael Betancourt and Tom Mastny combined for 5.2 one-hit, no-run, no-walk innings in relief and Okajima, Mike Timlin and Papelbon were right in stride with 4.2 two-hit, shutout innings of their own for Boston.

All that brought us to the 11th inning and with Papelbon done after two frames, in came Gagne, who had been terrible for Boston since coming over from Texas at the trade deadline. Red Sox fans could have saved themselves some horror by changing the channel. Gagne recorded the first out, but then allowed the next two runners on before handing off to Javier Lopez, who yielded two more singles, a walk and a wild pitch before he get yanked for Jon Lester, who gave up a double and finally a three-run shot to Franklin Gutierrez before Casey Blake bookended the inning with his second strikeout. Ten hitters came to the plate and none were left stranded, Cleveland putting a big seven on the scoreboard and waltzing back home with a series even at 1-1 after a 13-6 win.

Matsuzaka, perhaps used to the shorter season and six-man rotations common in Japan, had shown signs of fatigue toward the end of the season and had some fans worrying about his durability come October. These fears had not been eased with his first postseason start, so it was with trepidation that Boston fans approached Game 3.

Matsuzaka was matched with Jake Westbrook, exactly the sort of pitcher—a strike-thrower who pounded the lower half of the strike zone—who on paper posed the biggest threat to shutting down Boston's offense. That's exactly what Westbrook did, recording 14 groundball outs and getting three key double plays. Westbrook would hold Boston scoreless until the seventh, when a Varitek home run with J.D. Drew aboard netted the Red Sox their only two runs all night. The momentum of the game was really decided in the second, when Westbrook escaped a bases-loaded, nobody out jam and Kenny Lofton delivered a two-out, two-run home run. In the span of five minutes, Boston had gone from anticipating at least a couple of runs to getting none and yielding a pair.

The Indians would knock Matsuzaka out in the fifth with two more runs, this time off the more mundane combination of walks, singles and RBI ground outs. The Indians' pen retired seven straight batters and Cleveland pulled ahead in the series with a 4-2 victory.

Although they were down only 2-1, Game 4 looked like a must win for the Red Sox, who wanted no part of facing elimination and having to work through Sabathia, Carmona and Westbrook again to come back. But in a battle of put-it-in-play pitchers, Byrd finished with the victory over Tim Wakefield. Neither pitcher faced a big threat until Blake led off the fifth with a home run. Three singles and a hit batsman later, the Indians had added another two runs and had a pair on base when Peralta welcomed Manny Delcarmen to the game with a three-run homer, making it 6-0. Lofton added a seventh run, singling, stealing a base and then scoring on Blake's second hit of the inning.

Right on the heels of that big inning, Byrd faced the meat of Boston's lineup in the top of the sixth and didn't make it through, giving up consecutive leadoff home runs to Youkilis and Ortiz before giving way to Lewis. Ramirez promptly made it three in a row, standing and watching the ball leave the park and drawing the ire

of many. Lewis shut down the inning, however, and while Lester did a fine job of giving the Boston offense a chance to come back with three scoreless innings, the Red Sox couldn't do anything more against Lewis and Betancourt.

Just like that, it was a 7-3 Cleveland victory and the Indians held a 3-1 series lead with two of the best pitchers in 2007 ready to close it out.

Nothing could keep Beckett from taking over Game 5. He pitched his third consecutive postseason gem with eight strong innings, allowing just six baserunners while striking out 11 Cleveland hitters. The lone run he surrendered was in the first on a Sizemore double and Cabrera's single. After that he was golden, allowing just four of the next 28 batters to reach base.

Boston got early offense from a Youkilis home run and a bizarre "single" in the third from Ramirez that scored Ortiz from first. Yes, you read that right. Ramirez launched a long line drive that appeared to hit off the very corner top of the wall and bounce back into play. With two outs, Ortiz was hustling and scored quite easily, but Ramirez, loafing down the line and then protesting the lack of a home run call, never got past first.

The scored stayed 2-1 until the seventh, when Pedroia doubled, Youkilis tripled and Ortiz knocked Youkilis in with a sac fly to make it 4-1 and reach the Cleveland bullpen, which this time did not prove to be a rock. Perez loaded the bases in the eighth and Mastny, relieving him, tossed a wild pitch and walked a pair, which ran the score up to 7-1. Papelbon finished the game out at that score and ensured that Cleveland would have to win in Boston.

Game 6 was certainly about redemption. Redemption for Schilling who went seven strong innings this time, allowing just two runs, and for Drew, who had been a bust in year one of his five year mega-contract.

First, Drew. In the bottom of the first, the Sox loaded the bases with nobody out, but Ramirez struck out and Lowell flied out too short to warrant a sac fly. With two outs, it fell on Drew, who worked the count to 3-1 and then utterly destroyed a Carmona fastball, whacking it into center field for a series-changing grand slam.

Baseball is a more static game than, say, soccer or basketball, so talk about momentum isn't usually apt, but right at that moment, many Cleveland fans must have had a distinct sinking feeling that they were going to have to face a road Game 7 with the pressure on. For a second, Cleveland put some of that feeling away with a Martinez home run in the second and then singles from Nixon and Blake to lead off the third, but nothing further would come of that and in the bottom half of the third Boston would send 11 men to the plate. Key hits from Lugo and Youkilis among others pushed across six runs and put the game away with a 10-1 lead. Aaron Laffey did a wonderful job in relief for Cleveland with 4.2 scoreless innings, but it was of no consequence as Boston cruised to a 12-3 victory and set up a deciding game seven.

In a rematch reminiscent of Game 3 through its first two-thirds, Westbrook and Matsuzaka battled it out for the pennant. Matsuzaka kept retiring the Indians in order and the Red Sox kept getting just enough ground balls through the infield defense to score runs (three in the first three innings), in between not getting them through the defense and causing double plays (three in total). The Indians, down 3-0 entering the fourth, got on the board with doubles from Hafner and Ryan Garko, and then in the fifth Lofton singled off the Green Monster in left and was called out trying to stretch it into a double. Replays made it pretty clear that Lofton was actually safe, but that wouldn't stop Fox announcers Joe Buck and Tim McCarver from complimenting Ramirez for the rest of the game on his "assist."

Umpire Brian Gorman's call proved costly for the Tribe: Gutierrez and Blake followed up with singles of their own, which would have scored Lofton. Sizemore got one of them home with a sac fly, but what could have been a 3-3 game was still a 3-2 Boston lead.

Things stayed that way until the seventh, when Lofton reached second on Lugo's fielding error and Gutierrez singled over the third base bag, with the ball caroming into the middle of left field. Lofton would have scored easily on the play, but third base coach Joel Skinner stopped him and the tying run was held on third with one out. Blake promptly hit into a double play.

Blake didn't help matters in the bottom half, booting a grounder that put Jacoby Ellsbury on base. Two batters later, Pedroia made it 5-2 Red Sox with a home run over the Monster. Cleveland wasn't ready to die just yet, getting the first two batters on in the eighth, but Boston manager Terry Francona summoned Papelbon, who got a Hafner strike out, Martinez ground out and Garko fly out. It was still 5-2 and the Tribe had just three outs left.

The challenge grew larger. Pedroia added three RBIs on a bases-clearing double in the bottom half and the Red Sox tacked on another six runs. Papelbon stayed on the mound to record the final three outs and Boston had won 11-2 and overcome a 3-1 series deficit,

ensuring that for the next 50-plus years the broadcasters will mention 2004 and 2007 in every Boston playoff series where the Red Sox trail.

NLCS: Colorado Rockies at Arizona Diamondbacks

With the NL West division rivals coming off sweeps and extra days of rest, we got to see the rotations reset again for the NLCS. Game 1 featured Francis against Webb, who got a couple of strikeouts in the first before Francis gave up the first run on Drew's single and Eric Byrnes' double. Webb couldn't maintain his momentum, though, and gave that run right back. He was fortunate in fact, not to do worse—the first three Rockies reached base in the second, but Colorado scored only one run, which came when Tulowitzki hit into a double play. Colorado went right back at it in the next inning, getting singles from Willy Taveras, Matsui, Holliday and Hawpe, scoring three runs and making it 4-1.

After that, both pitchers cruised. Francis defused Arizona threats, twice inducing double plays, until the seventh, when the Rockies gave him another run. Torrealba, on board via a walk from reliever Juan Cruz, scored on Conor Jackson's error.

The Diamondbacks got the first two hitters on in the bottom half, but Francis coaxed yet another double play. Still, Arizona wasn't finished, getting a bunt single that brought in Herges to replace Francis. After walking Young, Herges was replaced himself by Jeremy Affeldt, who got Drew to fly out with the bases loaded to end the inning. Though Corpas allowed some well-struck balls in the ninth, Arizona went down in order and Game 1 belonged to Colorado, 5-1, to keep its remarkable winning streak intact.

Game 2 matched Jimenez with Davis. They combined to throw 10 innings (five apiece), allow 10 hits (five apiece), two earned runs (one apiece), eight walks (four apiece) and 11 strikeouts (5.5 a pie ... no, I'm kidding. Six for Jimenez, five for Davis).

In other words, there was a lot of sloppy pitching extricated by bouts of missing enough bats to keep runs off the board.

For example, in the second inning, 11 batters came to the plate with Colorado scoring on an error, a pair of strikeouts and consecutive singles before another strikeout. Arizona failed to score after a leadoff double, which was followed by two strikeouts, a walk and finally, the sixth out of the inning—on, of course, a strikeout.

Arizona did level the game in the next inning, this time capitalizing on a leadoff double (from Doug Davis, no less!) followed by Young's RBI single, but Colorado recaptured the lead in the fifth when Taveras scored on a Helton sac fly. The respective relief corps settled both teams down as Cruz, Tony Pena and Lyon combined for four one-hit, no-walk innings for Arizona and Herges, LaTroy Hawkins and Brian Fuentes went three shutout innings for the Rockies. Corpas came in for the bottom of the ninth with a one-run lead. After hitting Young with one out and giving up a single to Drew, he blew the save when Young scored on Byrnes' ground out. Neither team got a runner in the 10th, but the 11th saw the Rockies grab another run on the back of three Valverde walks and the bottom half saw no more drama. The Rockies held on for a 3-2 victory and 2-0 series lead.

The Diamondbacks started Game 3 off with singles from Young and Drew, but Byrnes lined back to Colorado starter Fogg for a double play to kill the potential rally. Then, in the bottom half, after Arizona's Hernandez retired the first two Rockies, Holliday homered, making it 1-0 Colorado and that was the game in a nutshell. Arizona hit into double plays in each of the first three innings and didn't send more than four men to the plate in any inning. Reynolds would tie the game in the fourth with a solo home run, but Torrealba untied it in the sixth with a two-out, three-run blast, making it 4-1, which is where the score stayed.

Game 4 saw power-hitting Micah Owings start for Arizona, facing a 3-0 series deficit against Franklin Morales. Both teams had two-out opportunities early with runners on, but failed to cash in until the third, when Arizona's Jackson singled in Owings for the first run. But the series ended, for all intents and purposes, an inning later when after walks to Hawpe and Tulowitzki, Owings had the pitcher's spot due up in the order with two outs after making a spectacular play on a Torrealba ground ball that left him a bit shaken up.

Clint Hurdle elected to pinch-hit Smith, ending Morales' night after just four innings. Smith was quickly down but Owings couldn't put him away. He lofted a Texas League double to left field that scored a pair and made it 2-1 Colorado. Jackson then misplayed a ground ball and the flood gates opened wide. Matsui's single and then a mammoth Holliday home run made it 6-1. Arizona managed only one baserunner (on an error) over the next three innings until getting close in the eight with Chris Snyder's two-out, three-run home run. That made it made it 6-4, and Upton's triple brought the

tying run to the plate, but Corpas came in and struck out Tony Clark swinging.

Arizona would try again in the ninth, Young doubling with one out, but Drew popped out and Byrnes made the final out, grounding to short. Colorado had completed another sweep, was 7-0 in the playoffs, had won 21 of its last 22 games and was headed to the Rockies' first World Series.

World Series: Colorado Rockies at Boston Red Sox

Game 1

The Rockies hadn't lost in seemingly forever and the Red Sox had just climbed back from a 3-1 series deficit, besting two Cy Young contenders in the process. With the Rockies' eight-day layoff, it was a tossup as to which team had the most momentum going into the series.

Twenty minutes into Game 1, we had an answer: It was Boston.

Pedroia ripped a leadoff home run. The Sox would get two more in the inning on pairs of singles and doubles and quickly had a 3-0 lead. Doubles by Atkins and Tulowitzki got Colorado back into it at 3-1, but Beckett escaped further damage and from there would be the Beckett we'd come to expect in the 2007 postseason, finishing with seven innings, six hits, a walk and nine strikeouts. Meanwhile, the Red Sox offense had 12 more hits, six of them doubles, and scored another 10 times to make game one a 13-1 rout and send the Rockies to their first loss in nearly a month.

Game 2

A hit-by-pitch, single, error and RBI ground out allowed the Rockies to post a quick 1-0 lead against Schilling in Game 2 and Jimenez navigated his way through trouble for the first three innings before a walk, single and sac fly evened the game in the fourth and a walk, single and double gave the Sox a 2-1 lead and drove Jimenez from the game. Things stayed that way the rest of the way, with a noted highlight coming in the eighth when, with two outs, Holliday singled. With Helton coming up, in came Papelbon, relieving a fantastic effort from Okajima (2.1 innings, no runners, four strikeouts). Papelbon promptly picked off Holliday. The Rockies went 1-2-3 with a pair of swinging strikeouts in the ninth and the Red Sox had held serve at home, up 2-0 in the series.

Game 3

Home proved to be no more welcoming than the road for Colorado, especially when Boston batted around in the third and threw up a 6-0 lead that included a bases-loaded single from Matsuzaka and a pair of doubles from Ellsbury, the second of which knocked starter Fogg out of the game. The Rockies would get a pair back in the sixth, but Timlin came in with two on and one out and retired the threat.

After Herges came in and struck out the Boston side, Timlin surrendered consecutive singles, causing Francona to summon Okajima to face Holliday. Holliday launched the first pitch way out to center field and suddenly it was just a one-run game, but after allowing next batter Helton to single, Okajima retired the next three hitters to end the seventh.

Ousted Colorado closer Fuentes came in for the eighth inning and it was there that Boston put the game away. After Varitek grounded out, Lugo drew a walk, Coco Crisp singled and Ellsbury topped off the game of his life with his third double. Pedroia did similarly right after him, making it three runs in the inning and a 9-5 lead. Boston added a meaningless insurance run in the ninth to make it 10-5, and there it ended with Boston now up 3-0 in the series.

Game 4

The starters for this elimination game, Lester and Aaron Cook, both had faced serious medical problems, Lester with lymphoma and Cook with blood clots, which made the overused term life-or-death, when applied to sporting events, a little more trite than usual.

The scoring began early as Ellsbury secured his spot as soon-to-be most-overhyped young player of the offseason with a leadoff double and scored on Ortiz' single. The Rockies got a leadoff double from Helton in the second and a one-out double in the third from Matsui, but made nothing of either opportunity while Cook retired the next 10 batters through the fourth.

The Sox broke Cook's streak with another leadoff double, this time from Lowell, and cashed in on Varitek's single, making it 2-0. For five consecutive innings, from the second through the sixth, the Rockies got at

least one runner on base. But after six innings, it was still 2-0 Boston. If you needed a summary of the series, that would be an apt one.

The seventh began with Lowell's leadoff homer and the end of Cook's night afterward. It also saw Hawpe bypass Colorado's knocking-in-runners problem by homering himself. Fuentes made an appearance in the eighth and got to face Kielty, pinch-hitting for Timlin. Kielty quickly homered to push the lead back to three at 4-1. Fuentes and Corpas worked around a single and walk to keep the score there.

With six outs remaining in Colorado's season, things got closer. Francona brought in Okajima, who got Holliday to ground out before Helton singled and Atkins finally got a hit with a runner on, this one going over the wall for a two-run home run that made it 4-3.

Francona wasted no time going early to ninth-inning man Papelbon, in a move reminiscent of Torre using Rivera for extended saves in the 1996-2000 era. Papelbon responded by retiring Ryan Spilborghs and Hawpe to end the eighth. The Sox went down in order in the top half of the ninth and we were three outs from the end of the 2007 season with Colorado's 8-9-1 hitters due up.

Papelbon wasted no pitches, going all gas and getting Torrealba to ground out on an 0-2 pitch and Carroll to line out on an 0-2 pitch. Not even Smith, postseason pinch-hitter extraordinaire, could do anything against Papelbon, working the count to 2-2 before swinging through a high fastball for strike three.

With that, another Boston championship was in the books. This one was filled with some of the stars of 2004, and a few new ones who should be sticking around a lot longer than Johnny Damon, Dave Roberts and Pedro Martinez. With a solid core of young talent, nearly unlimited monetary resources that they're not afraid to use, and Rodriguez' seemingly sure departure from New York, the Red Sox head into the 2007 offseason as perhaps the closest bet to a sure thing to return to the postseason in 2008.

2007 Commentary

The Story Stat

by Dave Studenmund

I know what you're thinking: We don't really need another baseball statistic, do we? Aren't there enough esoteric baseball stats, with their funny little acronyms and names, that just repeat what we already know?

Well, yes, I know how you feel. But every once in a while, a statistical concept so different comes along that it deserves to be added to our daily jargon.

Imagine a statistic that captures the drama of a game, play by play. Imagine a stat that allows us to quantify the current status of a game, and the importance of a situation. Imagine a statistic that assesses the true impact of a play's outcome, based on what we know of the game at that moment.

In short, imagine a single statistic that tells the stories, as opposed to the facts, of each baseball game. If you can imagine that, well, you're pretty imaginative. And you're probably imagining something very similar to WPA: Win Probability Added.

WPA assigns a percentage (anything between 0% and 100%) to the probability that one team will beat the other at any point in a game. It accounts for the score, inning, number of outs and base situation, and assumes the teams are evenly matched.

Now, we know that many teams aren't evenly matched, but using an average "background" gives full credit to the teams and players who make the plays as they're made. And, besides, why not assume everyone is even at the beginning of a game? Seems to me that's the best way to let the story of a game unfold.

Thanks to the baseball site called *Fangraphs* (www.fangraphs.com), we now have the WPA for every play of the year, as well as live WPA game graphs, play logs and player totals. Believe me when I tell you that this is a stat you want to know.

Let's take a real live example from the most important game of the 2007 regular season: the tiebreaker between Colorado and San Diego on Oct. 1. It was just the 12th tiebreaker in major league history, and only Bobby Thomson's "Shot Heard 'Round the World" in 1951 can compare for sheer tie-breaking game drama.

Here is how the 13th inning of the Colorado/San Diego game played out, from a WPA perspective:

- At the top of the 13th, the score was 6-6 and both teams had a 50% chance of winning.
- Brian Giles led off the inning with a walk, and the Padres' win probability (or WP) rose to 58%.
- Scott Hairston smashed a dramatic home run, putting San Diego ahead, 8-6, and giving the Padres a 92% WP. That homer was worth 0.34 in Win Probability Added, the difference in Win Probability as a result of the play.
- Chase Headley singled to center, increasing the Pads' WP to 93%.
- The next three batters made outs, and the Padres held a 90% probability of winning going into the bottom of the inning.

The Rockies had other thoughts, however, when they came to bat in the bottom of the 13th.

- Kaz Matsui led off with a double, and the Rockies' WP, which had been 10%, jumped to 20%.
- Troy Tulowitzki doubled to center, scoring Matsui and making the score 8-7. Down by only one run, with a runner on second and nobody out, the Rockies' WP was 45%. Tulowitzki's blast had a WPA of 0.25.
- Matt Holliday tripled to right, scoring Tulowitzki. Tie score, man on third, nobody out, and the Rockies' WP was 94%. Holliday's triple was worth a WPA of 0.49, the single biggest play of the game. At this point, a Rockies win was extremely likely.
- Todd Helton was intentionally walked, which raised Colorado's WP a minuscule amount.
- Jamey Carroll hit a sacrifice fly, Holliday scored, and the Rockies won 9-8. End of game—WP of 100%.

In one inning, we saw a rise of 40%, followed by a swing of 90% in the other direction. That is pure baseball drama. By the way, here's how the bottom of the ninth of the Giants' fabled comeback against the Dodgers in 1951 played out:

- The Giants were losing, 4-1, at the beginning of the bottom of the ninth. Their WP was 4%.
- Alvin Dark singled to first, WP rose to 9%.
- Don Mueller singled to right and Dark went to third. The Giants' WP was 19%, a 10% increase.
- Monte Irvin fouled out, and New York's WP dropped to 11%.
- Whitey Lockman doubled, scoring Dark and sending Mueller to third. With one out and runners on second and third, trailing by two runs, the Giants' WP was 29%.
- Bobby Thomson smashed a home run to left field, a play worth 0.71 WPA.

Perhaps this gives you a little perspective. As big as Matt Holliday's triple was for the Rockies, Thomson's home run was much bigger.

You may be wondering how Holliday's triple compares to the biggest hits of 2007. From a pennant-winning perspective, there was none bigger. But from a game perspective, each of the following blows were struck with two out in the bottom of the ninth, making them worth an amazing 0.90 WPA:

- On April 15, Marco Scutaro hit a three-run home run with two out in the ninth to lead Oakland over the Yankees, 5-4.
- Stephen Drew hit a two-run homer to put the Diamondbacks up over the Padres, 3-2, in an early April 25 game.
- Aramis Ramirez homered on June 29 to lead the Cubs to victory over the Brewers, 6-5, when the Cubs were in the midst of winning 11 of 13.
- Also on June 29 (a big day for dramatic home runs), the Rockies lost to the Astros when Mark Loretta hit a two-run homer to cap a 9-8 victory for Houston.
- What goes around comes around: In a key Sept. 18 game, Todd Helton hit a two-run homer to lead the Rockies to a 9-8 win over the Dodgers.
- B.J. Upton hit a two-run homer for the Devil Rays on Sept. 8, capping a win over the Blue Jays, 5-4.

The biggest defensive play of the year occurred on June 23, in an interleague game between the Nationals and the Indians. Victor Martinez had hit a three-run homer off Chad Cordero in the top of the ninth to put the Indians up 4-3 (0.52 WPA on the play), but the Nationals had fought back and loaded the bases with one out against Joe Borowski. At that stage, the Indians' win probability was down to 46%.

But Felipe Lopez bounced into a force out at home, and catcher Kelly Shoppach managed to nab Nook Logan off third base on the same play—end of game. With a turnaround of 54% on one play, the Indians managed to pull out the win.

Those were some of the most dramatic moments of the 2007 baseball season. Let's see what other stories we can pull out of Fangraphs' WPA statistics.

The Rockies' Streak

There was no bigger story in baseball this year than the Rockies' phenomenal streak at the end of the year. They won 15 of their final 16 regular season games, including that tiebreaking cliffhanger against the Padres, to grab the wild card slot on the last play of the season.

Here is the WPA record of that remarkable streak. I've broken down the WPA contributed by Colorado's batters, starting pitchers and relievers:

Date	Opp	Score	Batting	Starters	Bullpen
9/16	FLA	13-0	0.33	0.16	0.00
9/18	LAN	3-1	0.00	0.32	0.18
9/18	LAN	9-8	0.99	-0.13	-0.36
9/19	LAN	6-5	0.50	-0.03	0.03
9/20	LAN	9-4	0.36	0.13	0.01
9/21	SD	2-1	-0.61	0.29	0.82
9/22	SD	6-2	0.21	-0.15	0.44
9/23	SD	7-3	0.30	0.19	0.01
9/25	LAN	9-7	0.64	-0.50	0.36
9/26	LAN	2-0	-0.14	0.41	0.23
9/27	LAN	10-4	0.39	-0.06	0.17
9/28	ARI	2-4	-0.44	-0.13	0.07
9/29	ARI	11-1	0.36	0.14	0.00
9/30	ARI	4-3	0.09	0.29	0.12
10/01	SD	9-8	0.54	-0.37	0.33
Totals			3.52	0.57	2.41

You may be able to spot the logic in these numbers. In most blowouts, such as that 13-0 pasting of the Marlins, the Rockies' largest WPA totals were contributed by their batters and starters. Relievers don't really get a chance to contribute when the game is already decided by the sixth or seventh inning. In low-scoring affairs, the team was led by its pitchers; in games that went down to the wire, credit (or blame) was taken by the bullpen.

The 9-8 win over the Dodgers in the second game of a doubleheader on Sept. 18 was a particular doozy. Starter Mark Redman gave up a 3-0 lead in the first inning, but the Rockies' batters fought back and led, 5-4, in the fifth. However, the Rockies' bullpen couldn't hold onto the lead, and the Dodgers were winning 8-5 in the eighth. Colorado's batters battled back, closing the gap to 8-7 in the bottom of the eighth and winning in the ninth on that two-out home run by Helton. The Rockies' batters refused to quit, and won the equivalent of two games in one!

The batters were the biggest contributors to the Rockies' streak, with 3.52 WPA points. Individual leaders were Holliday (1.9 WPA), Helton (1.2 WPA) and Brad Hawpe (1.0 WPA).

But the surprise contributor to the Rockies' streak was their bullpen, which contributed 2.41 WPA to the 16 games. Before Sept. 16, Rockies relievers were rocky indeed, actually contributing a negative WPA (-2.22) to the team. Their resurgence, led by Matt Herges (0.70), Brian Fuentes (0.61) and Manny Corpas (0.44), was the true story behind the story.

The Mets' Un-streak

While the Rockies were putting together their historic run, the National League East was the scene of another historic run of games: The Mets lost 12 of their final 17 games, losing their hold on first place in the NL East to the Phillies. Here is a WPA scorecard of those 17 games:

Date	Opp	Score	Batting	Starters	Bullpen
9/14	PHI	2-3	-0.64	0.24	-0.10
9/15	PHI	3-5	-0.17	0.24	-0.57
9/16	PHI	6-10	0.19	-0.30	-0.39
9/17	WAS	4-12	0.04	-0.37	-0.17
9/18	WAS	8-9	0.10	-0.62	0.02
9/19	WAS	8-4	0.42	-0.24	0.32
9/20	FLA	7-8	0.44	-0.25	-0.68
9/21	FLA	9-6	0.49	-0.09	0.09
9/22	FLA	7-2	0.23	0.26	0.01

Date	Opp	Score	Batting	Starters	Bullpen
9/23	FLA	7-6	0.52	-0.06	0.04
9/24	WAS	4-13	-0.16	-0.27	-0.07
9/25	WAS	9-10	-0.11	-0.34	-0.05
9/26	WAS	6-9	-0.14	-0.14	-0.22
9/27	STL	0-3	-0.48	-0.04	0.03
9/28	FLA	4-7	-0.12	-0.44	0.06
9/29	FLA	13-0	0.36	0.14	0.00
9/30	FLA	1-8	-0.10	-0.41	0.00
Totals			0.87	-2.69	-1.68

During the Mets' run of ignominy, their batters were slightly above average, but their pitching and defense, particularly their starting pitching, was horrendous. Like Colorado's resurgent bullpen, this trend was a surprise; up to Sept. 14, the Mets' starters had compiled a WPA of 4.38 and the bullpen's WPA was 3.12. Their pitching collapse in the final 17 games of the season was a shock to most baseball observers.

The biggest culprits were reliever Jorge Sosa (-1.04) and starters Tom Glavine (-0.76), John Maine (-0.54), Mike Pelfrey (-0.50) and Oliver Perez (-0.48).

WPA doesn't account for fielding (it could, but Fangraphs hasn't quite figured out how to make that work) and the Mets' fielders developed holes in their gloves in September.

Before Sept. 14, the Mets' Revised Zone Rating (RZR) was .847, meaning that they successfully handled nearly 85% of all balls that were hit into their fielders' zones. From that point on, however, their RZR was .771. That might not look like a big difference to you, but it's equivalent to the difference between a .253 and .329 batting average.

Let me put it this way: Mets fielders allowed two more hits per game during their September plunge than they had the previous part of the season. That's worth more than a run a game. The positions that took a particular turn for the worse in RZR were:

	Pre 9/14	9/14+	Diff
Second Base	.835	.640	-.195
Shortstop	.886	.756	-.130
Third Base	.699	.605	-.094
Left Field	.920	.750	-.170

Despite the fact that their bats stayed relatively healthy, the Mets' everyday players still deserve part of the blame for the Mets' collapse.

Clutchiness

Bill James has an article in these pages about clutch hitting. We like to call this "clutchiness," Stephen Colbert style, because it's a subject that is difficult to pin down. We're pretty sure it exists, but we're just not sure what "it" is, or how to find it.

A statistical offshoot of WPA is something called Leverage Index. Leverage Index (LI) was invented by Tom M. Tango (who also has a couple of articles in this *Annual*) to estimate the relative importance of a plate appearance. LI uses the WPA framework to determine how critical a plate appearance is by evaluating all possible outcomes of the plate appearance. The greater the potential difference in outcomes, the more critical the situation.

An average plate appearance is 1.0, but critical plate appearances (such as a tie game, two outs in the bottom of the ninth) can be 7.0 or more. We call the most critical plays high-leverage situations, or "clutchy" situations.

There aren't a lot of high-leverage situations. Of the 195,190 plays tracked by Baseball Info Solutions and Fangraphs last year, 118,725 had an LI below 1.0. Only 18,901 (less than 10%) had an LI over 2.0. Only 6,111 (just 3%—slightly more than one a game) had an LI over 3.0.

To determine a player's clutchiness, I (arbitrarily) chose an LI cutoff of 3.0, and listed all batters who made at least 10 plate appearances with an LI of 3.0 or more. I then ranked them by WPA gained for every 10 high-leverage plays. Using this methodology, the 10 clutchiest batters of 2007 were:

Name	Tm	LI	WPA	Plays	WPA/P
Tulowitzki, T	COL	3.77	2.76	23	1.20
Loretta, M	HOU	3.70	2.23	21	1.06
Logan, N	WAS	4.43	0.99	10	0.99
Matsui, K	COL	3.80	1.88	20	0.94
Hatteberg, S	CIN	4.01	1.15	13	0.89
Escobar, Y	ATL	4.02	1.08	13	0.83
Suzuki, K	OAK	3.89	0.91	11	0.83
Flores, J	WAS	4.53	1.39	18	0.77
Drew, S	ARI	3.88	1.54	20	0.77
Michaels, J	CLE	4.16	0.70	10	0.70

Rockie rookie Troy Tulowitzki had a tremendously clutchy year, particularly in the first half of the season. In April and May, he had eight plate appearances with an LI of 3.0 or more, and made a positive contribution in each one. He was walked twice, hit by a pitch, singled twice, doubled twice and tripled. Each contribution came in the ninth or extra inning of a close game.

Although Tulowitzki also made some positive contributions later in the year, such as the very last game of the year, his clutchy performances in the first two months of the season really stand out.

If you're like me, the rest of the list consists of a bunch of "huhs?" Nook Logan? Kaz Matsui? Jesus Flores? What about some of the "well-known" clutchy hitters of our day, perhaps those mentioned in the James article?

David Ortiz? Though he's been a clutch hitter in the past, WPA doesn't rank Ortiz highly in 2007. In 25 plate appearances with an LI of 3.0 or more, his WPA was -0.02. That's negative.

Chipper Jones was better, contributing 0.55 WPA in 25 clutch plate appearances. Albert Pujols contributed 0.17 in 22. Alex Rodriguez, who had some big late-inning home runs early in the year, finished with 1.13 WPA in 18 clutch plays. He ranks 17th among major leaguers with 0.63 WPA per 10 plays.

How about the least clutchy batters? Here they are, using the same methodology, only in reverse:

Name	Tm	LI	WPA	Plays	WPA/P
Gutierrez, F	CLE	4.95	-1.40	12	-1.17
Jacobs, M	FLA	4.07	-1.24	11	-1.13
Spilborghs, R	COL	3.76	-1.30	13	-1.00
Mientkiewicz, D	NYA	3.56	-0.99	10	-0.99
Granderson, C	DET	4.49	-1.38	14	-0.98
Ramirez, M	BOS	4.29	-1.25	13	-0.96
DeJesus, D	KC	4.16	-1.28	14	-0.91
Chavez, E	OAK	4.19	-1.91	21	-0.91
Crosby, B	OAK	4.26	-1.08	12	-0.90
Fick, R	WAS	4.04	-1.11	13	-0.85

The funny thing is that there are probably more "star" names on this list than on the list of clutchiest hitters. One trend is clear: Batters who have a severe platoon disadvantage, such as Curtis Granderson, can be beaten in critical situations. You can read more about this in the introduction to our statistics, "Now You Has Stats."

Some teams managed to deliver more often than other teams in the "clutchy." Here are the top five teams, ranked by batting WPA in situations with LI over 3.0. You may not be surprised to see Colorado at the top of the list…

COL	3.85
NYN	2.78
SEA	1.51
ARI	1.00
FLA	0.70

…but the Mets also performed very well in critical situations. Their major clutchy contributors were Carlos Delgado (0.67 WPA/P), Jose Reyes (0.51), Shawn Green (0.32), Endy Chavez (0.25) and Luis Castillo (0.18).

For the other perspective, here's the list of the five least "clutchy" WPA totals:

PIT	-6.26
KC	-4.77
OAK	-4.70
MIN	-3.99
BOS	-3.82

I won't name specific players here, but it is interesting that the World Champion Red Sox are on the list. As dominant as they were, delivering clutch hits wasn't a hallmark of the 2007 Red Sox team.

Pitching Clutchiness

The interesting thing about critical situations is that pitchers usually win them. Of last year's 6,111 clutchy situations, pitchers managed a positive WPA 3,773 times, or 61% of the time, even though WPA is generally distributed evenly between batting and pitching. Altogether, pitchers compiled a 37.50 WPA total in those high-leverage situations.

Said differently (and just for fun), if pitching and batting were two separate teams, pitching would have a record of 118-44 in critical situations.

The reason is pretty obvious: Teams have an advantage in high-leverage situations because they can bring in a fresh reliever, often creating a platoon advantage (for instance, bringing in a LOOGY—Left-handed One-Out GuY—to face a left handed batter). In fact, new pitchers entered the game in 879 of those 6,111 clutchy situations (that is, new pitchers were brought in to face batters in 14% of high-leverage situations), and they compiled a 13.2 WPA in those single plate appearances.

Who were the best pitchers in critical situations last year? Like the list of clutchiest batters, it will surprise you:

Name	Tm	WPA	Plays	WPA/P
Saarloos, K	CIN	0.97	10	0.97
Dohmann, S	TB	0.88	11	0.80
Marte, D	PIT	1.03	13	0.79
Herges, M	COL	0.86	11	0.78
Romero, J	PHI	1.24	16	0.78
Sele, A	NYN	0.85	11	0.77
Perez, R	CLE	1.21	16	0.75
Putz, J	SEA	3.58	48	0.74
Qualls, C	HOU	2.65	36	0.74
Feliciano, P	NYN	1.00	14	0.71

Kirk Saarloos had a truly awful 2007, with a 1-5 record and a 7.17 ERA. But in 10 high-leverage plays, Saarloos gave up three double plays, two fly outs, two strikeouts, two fielder's choices and a walk. Not a bad record at all. Too bad he stunk the rest of the time.

In limited playing time, Tampa Bay's Scott Dohmann managed to compile a similar clutchy record. Damaso Marte was used as a classic LOOGY last year, to great effect. And we've already mentioned the impact Herges had on the NL West pennant race.

Really, the only "mainstream" relievers on this list are J.J. Putz, who had a fantastic year in Seattle, and Houston's Chad Qualls. Still, I'm guessing you'd like to see the list of least clutchy pitchers:

Name	Tm	WPA	Plays	WPA/P
Aquino, G	MIL	-1.37	10	-1.37
Julio, J	FLA	-1.06	13	-0.82
Majewski, G	CIN	-0.87	11	-0.79
Correia, K	SF	-1.54	23	-0.67
Brown, A	OAK	-0.85	13	-0.65
Hoey, J	BAL	-0.61	10	-0.61

Name	Tm	WPA	Plays	WPA/P
Santos, V	CIN	-0.78	14	-0.56
Ray, C	BAL	-2.11	38	-0.56
Eyre, S	CHN	-0.55	10	-0.55
Ohman, W	CHN	-0.81	15	-0.54

On the surface, Milwaukee's Greg Aquino (who spent April and September with the big club) had a mediocre year: 4.50 ERA in just 14 innings. But in nine of 10 situations when the leverage index was above 3.0, he made a negative contribution to the Brewers' effort. In fact, he had a 0.27 WPA when the LI was below 2.0, and a -1.68 WPA (that's negative) when the Leverage Index rose above 2.0. That's the opposite of clutchy pitching.

And I'm guessing that Orioles fans aren't surprised to see Chris Ray on this list, nor are Cubs fans surprised to see Scott Eyre and Will Ohman.

The Cubs and Orioles had some of the least clutchy pitching of all, as evidenced by their WPA totals in critical situations:

BAL	-3.42
COL	-3.08
TOR	-2.21
CHN	-1.72
MIL	-1.46

Baltimore's Chris Ray may have garnered 16 saves in 20 opportunities, but that doesn't begin to describe the poor season he had; his WPA record does. Colorado's bullpen ranks as the second-least clutchy staff in the majors, although the Rockies' September run more than atoned for their un-clutchiness.

Scads could be written about the Blue Jays, Cubs and Brewers bullpens, too, but I'll leave those to your vivid imagination.

But let's end this discussion on a positive note: the clutchiest pitching staffs of the year:

ARI	6.11
SEA	5.22
LAA	4.99
BOS	3.84
MIN	3.53

Two of the biggest surprises of the year, Arizona and Seattle, can point to their bullpens as major reasons for their success.

The Diamondbacks' Fluky Season

Speaking of Arizona, WPA can help us understand one of the major riddles of the year: How did the Diamondbacks manage to compile a 90-72 record and finish first in the NL West, despite being outscored by 20 runs? In all of baseball history, this feat has been matched only by the 1984 Mets, who also went 90-72 despite giving up 22 more runs than they scored.

On average, a team that is outscored by 20 runs can expect to finish a full season with 79 wins, because it takes about 10 runs to convert a loss to a win and 79 is two fewer than the 81 games an average team would win. Arizona beat this expectation by an astounding 11 games. Can we track down the difference using WPA? Sure we can.

Let's start with the Diamondbacks' bats. Arizona scored 712 runs, 57 fewer than the National League blended average of 769. In general, you would expect 60 runs under average to result in -6.0 WPA. In real life, Diamondbacks bats compiled -1.2 WPA, nearly five games out of the 11-game difference.

How about pitching? Well the Diamondbacks allowed only 732 runs last year, 37 fewer than the blended average of 769. You'd typically expect a pitching staff with that record to compile a WPA of 4.0, but the Diamondbacks pitchers actually had a WPA of 10.2, six more than expected.

So, give the Diamondbacks offense credit for five out of the 11-game difference, and give the pitchers the remaining six-game credit. The credit for Arizona's amazing run was shared almost equally by the offense and the defense.

How did they do it? Primarily by performing better when it mattered most. Here is a table of how much WPA the D-back batters contributed by several degrees of Leverage Index (less than one, between one and two and more than two):

LI	Plays	WPA
0-1	3853	-0.94
1-2	1937	-3.28
>2	525	3.01
Total	**6315**	**-1.21**

To give this table some perspective, remember two things: First, the Arizona batters would be expected to compile a WPA of -6.0. Second, batters tend to perform worse as LI increases. You can see that D-backs batters followed this pattern when their LI exceeded one, but they certainly turned things around when LI reached two or more.

As for their pitching, we've already seen how well Diamondbacks pitchers performed in clutchy situations. But let's break it down a bit more.

Here is a table of how the Diamondbacks starting pitchers performed (as measured by WPA) according to the Leverage Index. As you can see, they matched their performance to the criticality of the situation extremely well:

LI	Plays	WPA
0-1	2450	-0.87
1-2	1565	-0.50
>2	271	4.10
Total	4286	2.73

Now, here's the same table, for the Diamondbacks bullpen:

LI	Plays	WPA
0-1	1318	-0.30
1-2	429	1.37
>2	400	6.41
Total	2147	7.48

Now, that's pitching to the situation. Virtually every Diamondbacks pitcher delivered in high-leverage situation, but particular props go to Jose Valverde (2.52 WPA in 65 critical situations) and Brandon Lyon (1.79 WPA in 53 critical situations). And credit also goes to manager Bob Melvin for calling on the right pitchers in the right situations.

To finish the story, let's post a comprehensive table which displays the average WPA per 1,000 plays for batters, starting pitchers and relievers. For each group, the table includes the major league average and the Diamondbacks' average. As you can see, every group of Diamondbacks players rose to the occasion:

	Batters		Starters		Bullpen	
LI	MLB	ARI	MLB	ARI	MLB	ARI
0-1	-0.11	-0.24	-0.03	-0.36	0.35	-0.23
1-2	0.15	-1.69	-0.38	-0.32	0.63	3.20
>2	-2.52	5.73	-0.73	15.13	4.39	16.02

There are thousands of stories in a baseball season; these have been just a few of them. WPA crosses the divide between what we see on the field and what we see in the statistics. That's why I call it the "story stat," and why you can expect to see it in more and more baseball venues.

Our Appendix lists the WPA stats for every player who played a minimum amount of time, and you can download a spreadsheet with the WPA stats of all major leaguers from http://www.hardballtimes.com/THT2008Annual/. The username is "tht08" and the password is "utley." This is a service to book purchasers only.

The Deadspin Spin on 2007

by Will Leitch

We can find ourselves, sometimes, so far deep inside the game of baseball that we forget it's supposed to be *fun*. Fortunately, there's always enough off-the-field weirdness to remind us that no matter how seriously we take the great game, its participants and those who cover it will always make sure they remind us how silly they can truly be.

Here's a look at a season's worth of goofiness and malfeasance.

April

Adhering to a decades-old policy of making sure its most loyal customers are the ones they value the least, Major League Baseball takes part in a protracted feud with cable providers over their MLB Extra Innings package. After a bunch of rich people yell at each other and make muscle poses, they finally reach an agreement, which they announce triumphantly to fans, expecting them to be joyous that they have been given the opportunity to give Bud Selig 160 bucks. Mostly, they are.

The Toronto Blue Jays pull an advertisement that features designated hitter Frank Thomas smashing his son in the face with a pillow after the Television Bureau of Canada refuses to approve the ad because of its "violence." The Blue Jays call the decision "ridiculous," and then, in protest, set a nine-year-old on fire.

ESPN broadcaster Gary Thorne, for reasons unbeknownst to other humans, claims on a Red Sox-Orioles broadcast that, "The great story we were talking about the other night was that famous red stocking that he wore when they finally won, the blood on his stocking, it was painted. Doug Mirabelli confessed up to it after. It was all for PR." Schilling responded with an angry denial on his blog that didn't include a single ROTFL which, to prove his story, was typed with his feet. Thorne backed off his claim after Schilling offered $1 million to anyone who could prove Schilling painted his sock, an offer that made sure no other players would contradict his story, considering he made the $1 million paid exclusively to charity rather than to the player himself.

May

Cardinals pitcher Josh Hancock is tragically killed in a drunk driving accident, and in response, the St. Louis Cardinals ban alcohol from the clubhouse. (For a while, anyway.) This makes the Cardinals clubhouse the one place in *Busch* Stadium that is not paid for by and devoted exclusively to promoting alcohol consumption.

In order to boost attendance to their then-first-place baseball team (and, of course, help people), the Milwaukee Brewers offer free rectal exams outside Miller Park, offering two free tickets for anyone who is examined. Mercifully, the Brewers do not hold the examinations on bat day.

After a dramatically convenient announcement at Yankee Stadium, Roger Clemens signs a pro-rated, $28 million, one-year contract with the then-struggling Bronx Bombers. He will ultimately make only 18 starts for the team and "hurt" himself when he's trying to muddle through Game 3 of the American League Divisional Series. He will, however, give Andy Pettitte someone to talk to other than random women Derek Jeter has discarded.

A man at Dodger Stadium, after playfully heckling Reds future Hall of Famer Ken Griffey Jr., is shocked by Griffey, who tosses the fan his (presumably used) jock strap on his way out to right field. He actually tossed him a brown paper bag with the jock in it and refused to head to the outfield until he opened it. The fan later says he's now a big booster of Griffey, though he does not reveal whether or not he ever wore the jock.

The front page of the *New York Post* exclaims: "STRAY-ROD!" The night before, a reporter followed Alex Rodriguez back to his hotel in Toronto and took pictures of him entering the lobby with a buxom, mannish blonde who was not Rodriguez's wife. Later, the paper interviews a woman who claims A-Rod likes the "she-male, muscular type," thus finally allowing Jason Giambi to release a sigh of relief and finally come out of the clubhouse shower.

June

In the first in a series of unfortunate incidents, the wife of Devil Rays outfielder Elijah Dukes claims that he sent a photo of a gun to her cellphone and left a voice mail stating, "You dead, dawg. I ain't even bullshitting. Your kids, too." He is immediately traded to the Cincinnati Bengals.

During their yearly exhibition baseball game at Fenway Park, reporters who cover the Red Sox nearly come to fisticuffs with their pasty brethren, who cover the Yankees. Bob Klapisch accidentally hit the Boston Spanish radio broadcaster in the helmet with a pitch, causing him to "charge" the mound. Yankees beat reporter Pete Abraham documented his team's intestinal fortitude: "I will say this about the New York media, we don't back down when the benches clear. We were more riled up than the Yankees were on Friday night. I wish I were kidding, but I'm not. We were a few seconds away from a full-out scrap."

In a recap of Tony La Russa's spring training arrest for driving while intoxicated—or, more accurately, "parking and sleeping" while intoxicated—*The Miami Herald* scoops that several cops, when they realized the man asleep in the car was La Russa, "prepared a dazed-and-confused La Russa for jail by teaching him gang signs." Immediately, La Russa responded by calling for a double switch and bringing in three cops to pitch to three batters in the sixth inning of an 11-2 game.

Sammy Sosa hits his 600th home run to the cheers of a few thousand Rangers fans who, mercifully for him, don't speak English and lack the ability to put together words to form accusatory questions.

July

The Brewers, during a road stand in Pittsburgh, end up staying at the same hotel at a convention of Furries, the grown human beings who attempt to procreate with other human beings who are wearing the costumes of dogs, bears, kittens and other cute animals. Players "reported neighboring rooms generating loud animal noises, barking and other, deep into the night," but broadcaster Bob Uecker is unfazed, posing for pictures with several of the furry fornicators.

Gary Sheffield, displeased by a fortnight of sports coverage that didn't feature him saying something "controversial," claims that all black players "had an issue" with beloved Yankees manager Joe Torre. Fortunately for Sheffield, none of the teams who trade him every other season so he'll be somebody else's problem have had managers as blatantly racist as Torre. The then-Yankees skipper refuses to acknowledge Sheffield's allegations because he was napping in the fourth inning again.

More Elijah Dukes fun: During divorce proceedings, Dukes' wife accuses him of smoking marijuana, having a serious drinking problem and threatening to kill her. No one is fazed by this, but public uproar ensues when she says he used steroids.

August

Showing foresight beyond human comprehension, the U.S. Army Reds Legends Baseball Camp invites Pete Rose to speak to campers and children. Shockingly, it doesn't go well; Rose says that he saw Joe DiMaggio in the shower and that "he saw more of him than Marilyn Monroe ever did." Rose also liberally drops "the F-bomb" and tells the kids that if they finish in second place in anything they do, they're "losers." Rose could not be reached for comment, because no one thought to look for him at one of the several thousand weekly appearances he makes at Las Vegas casinos signing his own merchandise.

Barry Bonds breaks Hank Aaron's home run record, at home, in front of the only fans who don't hate him, and is greeted by a Jumbotron message from Aaron himself, the man whose scorn of Bonds had started all this mess in the first place. Sadly, Bonds was not chased around the bases by Jim Grey; that would have been funny.

After a near-decade chasing down the demons that pushed him out of the game, former Cardinals phenom Rick Ankiel returns to the major leagues and hits three home runs in four games. His story is inspirational and heartwarming, and absolutely nothing could come across that could sully it in any possible way.

During a break between innings of a Mariners-Red Sox game, Mariner Moose, the "beloved" Seattle mascot, runs over Boston outfielder Coco Crisp with his four-wheeler while Crisp swung in the on-deck circle. Crisp is unhurt but now notoriously terrified of the species *Alces alces* and is known to wet himself in fear while watching reruns of "Northern Exposure."

Ray Zerba, assistant general manager of the minor league Jacksonville Suns, is fired by the team after he is caught smoking pot under the bleachers during a game. He is immediately hired by the Pittsburgh Pirates, where he trades Jason Bay for Elijah Dukes' cell phone.

Jose Offerman, out of major league baseball for years and playing for the Long Island Ducks, responds to a hit-by-pitch by attacking pitcher Matt Beech and catcher John Nathans with his bat. (He actually smacked Nathans in the head, giving him a concussion.) Offerman, despite a dozen photographers there to document the incident, later pleads innocent to all charges.

September

Oddly, a fight between Major League Baseball and ESPN breaks out. The rift started because the network released the names on the All-Star roster before it was supposed to, and MLB responds by banning the network from on-site studio remotes from various post-season series. Baseball fans, aghast at being denied John Kruk's incisive commentary and delightful conversational *bon mots*, rebel by storming Bud Selig's office, but Selig, a leader who stands on his principle at all points, refuses to budge.

October

Dane Cook, the logical spokesperson for Major League Baseball, informs us that the month of October only comes around once a year, no matter how much you might believe otherwise. Dope, dude.

During a tense American League Divisional Series Game 3 at Jacobs Field between the Yankees and the Indians, midges—tiny insects once thought to be the far more innocuous-sounding "Canadian Soldiers"— swarm New York rookie pitcher Joba Chamberlain and briefly force him to pitch like Rick Ankiel. The midges ultimately cost the Yankees the game and the series. It also inspires George Steinbrenner to cede control of his team to two men he calls his "sons," but who are actually millions of midges combining to impersonate a human form. The coalition of midges instantly brings a steady hand to the Yankees' franchise.

Tim McCarver, while calling the American League Championship Series points out, with a straight face and with the tone of a man who has discovered cold fusion, that innings in which a batter leads off with a home run more often end in multiple runs than innings in which the leadoff batter walks. He claims that he and statisticians have "studied" the issue. Tim McCarver is very smart in ways that you and I will never be able to understand.

The Boston Red Sox make the World Series, proving once again that, someday, underdogs the likes of the Red Sox always have a chance to win. Crazy game, that baseball.

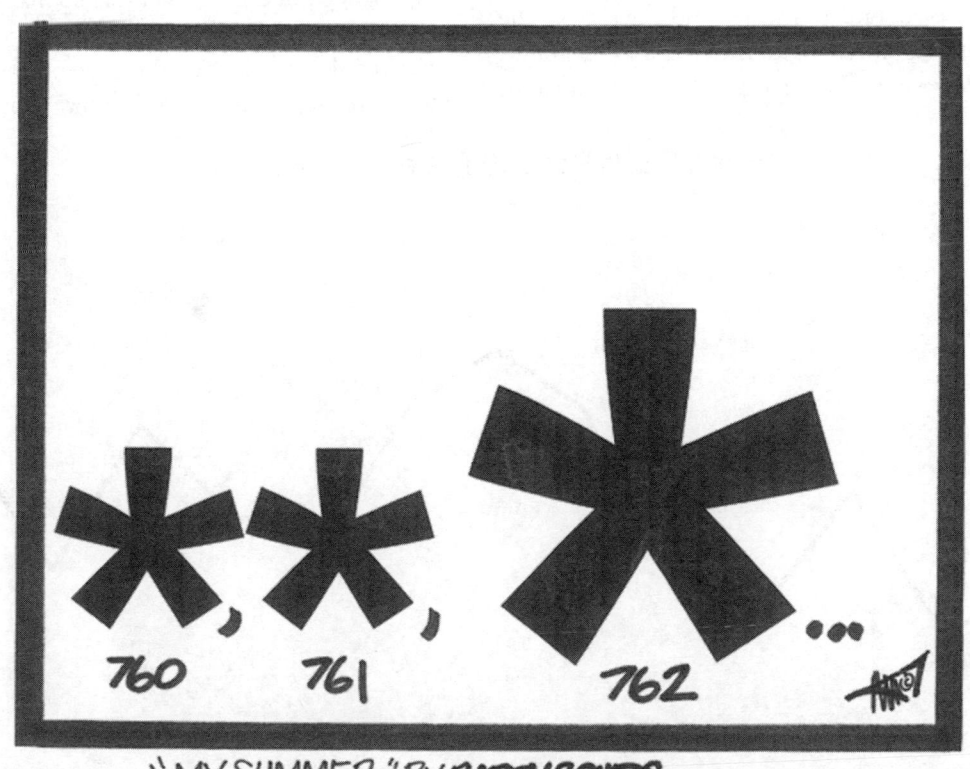

"MY SUMMER," BY BARRY BONDS...

The Year in Home Runs

by David Vincent

Baseball fans witnessed many memorable home run events in 2007, including record-setting performances by teams and individuals. Home runs and home run hitters were hot topics, so let's take a look at the home run events of 2007.

Major league batters slugged 4,957 home runs during the 2007 season, the first time that the yearly total did not top 5,000 since 1997. This 5,000 milestone was first reached in 1998 and has been the norm every season since then, with the most hit in 2000 (5,693). While a yearly total might be instructive, it has no context and thus is hard to interpret.

A better measure of home run hitting is a "home run production rate," defined as how many circuit drives were hit for every 500 plate appearances in the major leagues. Over the course of the 2007 season, all hitters combined hit 13.1 homers for every 500 plate appearances, a rate that was down by 1.3 homers from the previous season but within the range of numbers for the time period 1994-2007, as shown in the graph below. This figure is expanded from *Home Run: The Definitive History of Baseball's Ultimate Weapon.*

The 2007 season rate is the second-lowest on the chart and more in range with the 1994-1998 period than the last few years. Few single-season production

drops have been larger than that of 2007. Since 2000, the home run production rate has hovered around the 14.0 level with a pendulum-like swing back and forth around the line for the last five years.

Batters started the season slowly, perhaps due to the horrid weather conditions in April. The April production rate (11.8) was the lowest of any month in the last eight years, and it clearly dragged down the rate for the season:

Month	PA	HR	HR/500
Apr	28,751	681	11.8
May	33,490	944	14.0
Jun	30,250	765	12.6
Jul	31,503	845	13.4
Aug	32,228	822	12.8
Sep	32,276	900	13.9

Usually, the highest production rate occurs in the hotter months of June through August, but in 2007 the highest rates were in May and Sept.. The latter month's rate might be due to the fact that so many teams were still in the pennant (or Wild Card) race. This probably caused more regulars to play and the September call-ups to spend more time than usual on the bench. Whatever the explana-

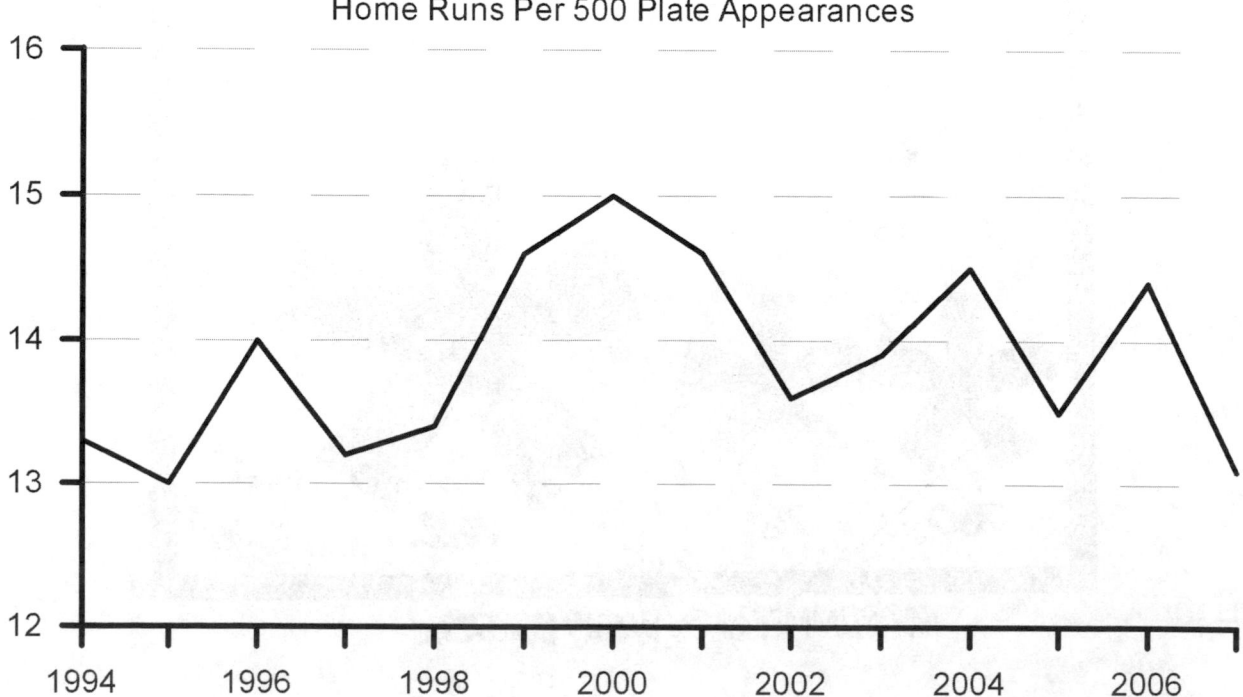

Home Runs Per 500 Plate Appearances

tion, it is clear that the very low rate in April dragged down the rate for the season more than it might have otherwise. Leaving April out produces a rate for the rest of the season of 13.8. This is still down from 2006 but not quite as much, and it is about the same as the 2003 rate.

Alex Rodriguez of the Yankees led the American League with 54 long balls for the season. This is A-Rod's third season with 50-plus homers and eighth with at least 40. His 14 homers in April tied Albert Pujols' record for most in that month. Rodriguez extended his own record for most homers in one season by a right-handed Yankees batter; he had hit 48 in 2005 to break the previous mark of 46 set by Joe DiMaggio in 1937. Rodriguez has hit at least 30 home runs for the 10th consecutive season, which is the third-longest streak of all time and the longest current streak. Barry Bonds hit at least 30 homers for 13 straight seasons (1992-2004) for the longest streak of all time.

After hitting 28 home runs in 2006, Prince Fielder of the Brewers led the National League with 50 in 2007. This is not close to the largest such increase, held by Davey Johnson of the Braves who smacked five in 1972 and 43 the next year and never hit more than 18 in any other season. Fielder, by hitting his 50th homer of the season on Sept. 25, became the youngest player in history to reach the 50 plateau. At 23 years and 139 days old, he beat the previous mark of Willie Mays, who was 24 years and 137 days old when he hit No. 50 on Sept. 20, 1955. Prince's dad, Cecil, slugged 51 home runs in 1990, so the Fielders are the only father/son pair to each hit 50 in one season.

In addition to the two sluggers with 50 homers, three batters had season totals in the 40-49 range (Carlos Pena, Ryan Howard and Adam Dunn) and 21 concluded the season in the 30-39 range. The next table shows the breakout of individual hitter totals for the last few years. The number of hitters in the 40-49 range dropped in 2007, although the other two columns remained about the same. As with other numbers quoted in this article, one season does not make a trend, but it will be interesting to watch home run totals over the course of the next few years to see if a trend does develop.

Year	30-39	40-49	50+
2001	29	8	4
2002	20	6	2
2003	20	10	0
2004	28	9	0
2005	18	8	1
2006	24	9	2
2007	21	3	2

Carlos Pena of the Devil Rays hit 46 home runs in 2007 to improve his personal best of 27 set in 2004. Pena also topped the DRays' team record of 34, set by Jose Canseco in 1999 and tied by Aubrey Huff in 2003. Prince Fielder also set a new single-season record for his team with his 50, beating the Brewers' mark of 45 hit by Richie Sexson in both 2001 and 2003. Julio Franco set a mark of a different sort on May 4. On that day, Franco hit his only circuit clout of the season at the age of 48 years and 254 days to extend his own record as the oldest player to hit a home run. Franco holds four of the top five marks for homers by well-aged sluggers, with only pitcher Jack Quinn of the 1930 Philadelphia Athletics sneaking into the fourth spot.

At the start of the season, much of the baseball world's attention was focused on Barry Bonds and his attempt to set a new career record by topping Hank Aaron's mark of 755 home runs. A lot of the discussion was not about baseball but about chemistry class. I will leave that topic to others and only say that emotionally charged words and phrases used by pundits are not helping anyone understand the history being made.

Bonds tied the record on Aug. 4 in San Diego, hitting the home run off Clay Hensley. The fact that Bonds hit this home run against the Padres is significant because he has hit more homers against the Padres than any other opponent in his career. Three days later at home in San Francisco, Bonds hit his record-breaking 756th home run off Mike Bacsik of the Washington Nationals. In an interesting quirk of history, Bacsik's dad had faced Hank Aaron after The Hammer had hit his 755th home run in 1976. Bonds hit No. 756 to one of the deepest parts of SBC Park into a group of fans and ended the season with 762 career blasts to became the third player to hold the career record in the last 85 years.

On July 18, 1921, Babe Ruth captured the career mark with his 139th home run, passing Roger Connor. Ruth held the mark for almost 53 years until Hank Aaron passed him on April 8, 1974. Now after 33 years, Aaron has stepped aside as Barry Bonds has acquired the mantle of home run king, based on the career total.

Just as raw numbers for a season are not the best way to examine that season, career totals are not the best method of determining who might be the best home run slugger. Using the same home run production rate discussed above, this time applying it to batters with at least 300 career homers through 2007, produces the following list:

Batter	Debut	HR	HR/500
Mark McGwire	1986	583	38.3
Babe Ruth	1914	714	33.7
Ralph Kiner	1946	369	32.5
Barry Bonds	1986	762	31.4
Sammy Sosa	1989	609	30.8
Alex Rodriguez	1994	518	30.7
Juan Gonzalez	1989	434	30.6
Jim Thome	1991	507	30.5
Dave Kingman	1971	442	30.3
Albert Belle	1989	381	29.6

The top two sluggers are probably no surprise. Babe Ruth changed the way the game is played with his batting heroics, and his home run production rate was unchallenged for decades. Only Jimmie Foxx, who debuted in 1925, and Hank Greenberg, who debuted in 1930, came within six of Ruth's rate until the late 1940s. Foxx hit 27.6 homers for each 500 plate appearances, while Greenberg slugged 27.2. Foxx retired with the second-best rate in 1945 but is now 20th, while Greenberg ranks 24th on the all-time list. Mark McGwire, at the top of the list, hit 49 home runs in his rookie season, with a rate of 38.2, which is near his career rate.

Let's look at the production rate for the big boppers after eliminating walks and only counting at bats. The next table shows the top 10 with production rates based on 500 at bats instead of plate appearances.

Batter	Debut	HR	HR/500
Mark McGwire	1986	583	47.5
Babe Ruth	1914	714	42.6
Barry Bonds	1986	762	40.4
Ralph Kiner	1946	369	39.2
Jim Thome	1991	507	37.6
Ted Williams	1939	521	36.5
Alex Rodriguez	1994	518	35.5
Harmon Killebrew	1954	573	35.2
Manny Ramirez	1993	490	35.0
Sammy Sosa	1989	609	34.6

Barry Bonds moves from fourth to third, and Jim Thome jumps from eighth to fifth. Harmon Killebrew breaks into the list from the 12th spot, but the largest jump comes from Ted Williams, who was 14th but moves into the sixth spot in this table. Sluggers who moved up the list walk more than other hitters, while batters such as Sammy Sosa, Juan Gonzalez and Dave Kingman move down the list due to fewer walks in their careers.

One player to watch in the next few years is Ryan Howard of the Phillies. He has slugged 129 home runs in 1,695 plate appearances for a production rate of 38.1 in his short career. These numbers can change radically, but if he produces anywhere near this rate for another nine years, he will be well over the 500 homer milestone and only 36 years old, which is about average for the members of the 500 Home Run Club. Again, however, projecting numbers for Howard after only three seasons is risky. Let's check back with him in a few more years.

Other sluggers achieved career milestones in 2007. Sammy Sosa, who had not played in 2006, hit his 600th home run on June 20. Sosa, playing for the Rangers, hit a solo shot off Jason Marquis of the Cubs to become the fifth player to reach that plateau. It was the first home run Sosa had hit off a Cubs pitcher in his career, after slugging 545 for the North Siders. He ended the 2007 season with 609 career dingers. Three players joined the 500 Home Run Club in 2007. On June 28, Frank Thomas of the Blue Jays became the 21st player in the club when he smacked a three-run shot off Carlos Silva of the Twins in Minnesota. In the ninth inning of that contest, Thomas was ejected for arguing a called third strike. He became the first guy in history to hit that milestone and be ejected from the same game.

Alex Rodriguez became the youngest player to hit 500 homers on Aug. 4, the same day that Bonds hit No. 755 to tie Hank Aaron. A-Rod hit the homer off Kyle Davies of the Royals at Yankee Stadium eight days after his 32nd birthday. He beat the record for youngest to 500 held by Jimmie Foxx by 330 days. The third player to join the club was Jim Thome, who hit his 500th on Sept. 16 off Dustin Moseley of the Angels. Thome's four-bagger came in the bottom of the ninth inning to win the game for the White Sox, the first time a player hit a game-ending homer for No. 500. One player topped the 300 mark in 2007: Todd Helton. The Rockies' first baseman smacked the milestone circuit drive on Sept. 11 off Adam Eaton of the Phillies, the team that the Rockies would sweep a month later in the National League Division Series.

Three times in history before 2007, there have been two sluggers who have hit their 500th career home run in the same season. In 1967, Mickey Mantle and Eddie Mathews reached the milestone, in 1971 it was Harmon Killebrew and Frank Robinson, and in 2003 Sammy Sosa and Rafael Palmeiro joined the club. The three players in 2007 are more than any other season in history.

At the end of 2007, there were six active players with at least 500 career home runs. They are Barry Bonds (762, first all-time), Sammy Sosa (609, fifth), Ken Griffey Jr. (593, sixth), Alex Rodriguez (518, 17th), Frank Thomas (513, 18th) and Jim Thome (507, 22nd). These six represent the greatest number of active players in the 500 home run club ever, topping the previous high of five in 1971 (Hank Aaron, Willie Mays, Frank Robinson, Harmon Killebrew and Ernie Banks).

Four Boston Red Sox batters hit home runs in succession on April 22 at Fenway Park. Manny Ramirez, J.D. Drew, Mike Lowell and Jason Varitek each hit a solo shot off Yankees rookie pitcher Chase Wright, who was sent back to the minors the next day. The BoSox became the fifth team to hit four consecutive dingers, and it was the second time that one pitcher surrendered all four; Paul Foytack had surrendered four to the Indians in 1963.

Other teams to hit four in a row were the 1961 Milwaukee Braves, the 1964 Twins and the 2006 Dodgers. J.D. Drew was also part of the Dodgers' quartet of homers; thus, even though this feat has only been accomplished five times in major league history, one player has participated in two of the five events.

On Sept. 9 in Cincinnati, the first three batters for the Brewers each smacked a four-bagger. Rickie Weeks, J.J. Hardy and Ryan Braun became the first trio to start a game with home runs. Two other teams had their first three hitters slug home runs, but in both cases the clubs had performed the feat at home. Those teams were the 1987 Padres (Marvell Wynne, Tony Gwynn and John Kruk) and the 2003 Braves (Rafael Furcal, Mark DeRosa and Gary Sheffield).

On May 15-17, the Tampa Bay Devil Rays hosted the Texas Rangers in a three-game series at The Ballpark at Disney's Wide World of Sports in Lake Buena Vista, Florida. The park is the spring training venue of the Atlanta Braves, and this DRays series at Disney was used as a marketing tool by the club. Eight homers were slugged in the three games, including one by Sammy Sosa on May 16.

Sosa started the season having hit at least one home run in 42 different ballparks. In April, he homered at Rangers Ballpark in Arlington and Jacobs Field in Cleveland to set a new record for most parks homered in, passing Ken Griffey Jr. and Fred McGriff. Disney became the 45th park for Sosa and is a record that will take a few years to break, as only Gary Sheffield has a shot at it right now. Sheffield has hit home runs in 40 parks in his career but has six current parks to add to his list, as well as the new park that will open in Washington in 2008. Only one of the parks is in the American League (U.S. Cellular Field).

The All-Star Game played in San Francisco on July 10 featured the first inside-the-park home run in the history of the Midsummer Classic. Ichiro Suzuki hit a fly ball off the right-center field wall at SBC Park where the barrier juts out into the playing field. The ball caromed away from Ken Griffey Jr., and Suzuki was able to complete the circuit before the ball was returned to the infield.

Later in the game, Alfonso Soriano homered for the National League as a representative of the Cubs. This was Soriano's third All-Star homer, and each has been hit for a different team; in 2002, he homered as a Yankee and in 2004 he homered as a Ranger. Soriano is the only player to hit an All-Star home run as a representative of three different squads and only the second player to homer for both leagues, matching the feat first performed by Frank Robinson. The fact that other players have not homered for both leagues in the All-Star Game is astounding given the amount of player movement in the last 20 years.

There was a lot of talk during the 2007 season about who might be the next batter to hold the career home run record, with much of the attention focused on Alex Rodriguez. For the seven-year period of 2001 through 2007, A-Rod has hit the most homers (329), an average of 47 per season. Albert Pujols is a distant second with 282 four-baggers. As the 2008 campaign begins, Rodriguez needs to hit 244 home runs to match Bonds' total of 762. If A-Rod averages 40 homers per season (seven fewer than he has been averaging), it will take him a little more than six years to get to 762. In six years, Rodriguez will be 38 years old, which is two years younger than Hank Aaron when he passed Babe Ruth and five years younger than Bonds last August. If Rodriguez stays healthy, it seems inevitable that he will pass Bonds in 2014.

What conclusions can be drawn from 2007? Even though the home run production rate was down in 2007 from 2006, production was still within the range of values for the 1994 through 2006 period. The one-year drop has not created a trend and, although production is down slightly from the peak years of 1999 through 2001, it has not changed in a significant manner. It will be interesting to watch the next few years to see if a real trend does develop.

Thanks to Dave Smith of Retrosheet (www.retrosheet.org) for generating the monthly home run production rate and temperature numbers.

Championship Hangover: The 2007 St. Louis Cardinals

by Brian Gunn

The Cardinals' season began, more or less, just past midnight on March 22 at an empty intersection in Jupiter, Fla., with the manager of the defending world champions behind the wheel of a Ford SUV, passed out drunk. Tony La Russa was idling at a green light, his foot on the brake pedal, when two undercover cops tapped on his window. When he came to, his eyes were glassy, his speech was slurred and he reeked of alcohol. During a roadside sobriety test, he nearly fell over trying to stand on one leg, then flubbed the alphabet.

He was arrested on suspicion of DUI and taken to a holding cell in Palm Beach. The attending officers mockingly prepped him for the ordeal by teaching him gang signs.

When news of the arrest broke the following morning, the response was swift and harsh. ESPN's Keith Law said that La Russa should be given two choices by the Cardinals: either enter rehab or resign as manager. Jose De Jesus Ortiz, a beat writer for the *Houston Chronicle*, opined that La Russa, a noted animal-rights activist, "proved that he puts the threat of running over a dog above the possibility that he could have killed some poor child by his recklessness."

But in Cardinals Country, La Russa was generally excused, if not embraced. Before the team's next spring training game, La Russa received a rousing ovation from the home crowd at Roger Dean Stadium—a dubious reaction to a man charged with a misdemeanor. One fan yelled, "Don't worry about it, Tony!" while Kevin Slaten, a radio jock for the Cards' flagship station, wrote off the incident as mere hoopla: "It's not like the president was assassinated," he said.

This no-big-deal attitude shouldn't have been surprising. After all, La Russa wasn't the first manager to mess with the bottle—Bill James estimates that, of the 25 greatest managers of all time, at least 18 were alcoholics. What's more, drinking has been part of baseball since the game began. Just look out in the bleachers or up on the Jumbotron and you'll see how deeply it's ingrained in the culture. This is especially true in St. Louis, where the Cardinals play in a stadium named after a brewing company, and every year players are introduced to fans in a parade of Anheuser-Busch

Clydesdales. Maybe that's why La Russa got a free pass from the home crowd.

But of course that overlooks the obvious. The real reason La Russa was treated so charitably by Cardinals fans was because just five months earlier he had guided the franchise to its first world championship in 24 years. He was in his honeymoon period. Or, as one Cards season-ticket holder put it, "The guy won us a World Series … You think we're going to be upset with him because he got a DUI?"

In the end, however, Cardinals fans wouldn't be able to shrug off the incident quite so easily. Because, strangely, it never really went away. The same scenario, with the team embroiled in turmoil and scandal, kept rearing its ugly head throughout the 2007 season. Each time Cardinals fans were put to the test, and each time the glow of October '06 faded just a little more.

If a baseball season were a boxing match, the 2007 Cardinals would've been knocked out about 10 seconds into the first round. In their first regular-season series of the year they squared off at home against their NLCS rivals, the New York Mets. The Mets pounded them three straight nights by a combined score of 20-2, serving notice that although the Cards held the championship belt, they weren't going to keep it without a fight.

A few days later, Chris Carpenter, the team's perennial ace, landed on the DL with bone spurs in his elbow. The Cards had to make do with a rotation that was already relying on youngsters like Anthony Reyes and Adam Wainwright, retreads like Kip Wells, and projects like Braden Looper, who hadn't started a single game since his first year in Single-A ball.

The hitters also stumbled out of the gate. Jim Edmonds, suffering from offseason shoulder and toe surgery, as well as persistent headaches from a concussion in '06, was a ghost of his former self. New acquisition Adam Kennedy failed to live up to preseason expectations. Most surprisingly, Albert Pujols started the season in a woeful 1-for-17 rut. It was a full three weeks into the season when he finally crossed the Mendoza line.

By the end of the month, the Cards had dropped 10 of 13 games at home while falling five-and-a-half games behind the *arriviste* Brewers. On April 29, St. Louis sports columnist Bernie Miklasz wrote that "the Cardinals aren't very good … Brace yourselves to deal with the harsh reality, and a hard summer." Miklasz's words proved prophetic, for that very night the Cardinals' season would get a lot worse, a lot sooner than anyone expected.

Josh Hancock could best be described as a "good ol' boy." A chunky Mississippi native, he liked to drink, hated working out, and loved playing baseball for a living. In fact, he was the only player to attend the premiere of a DVD documenting the Cards' unlikely run to their 10th world championship the previous autumn.

But he also suffered from some serious demons. In the early morning hours of a day at the end of April, Hancock, allegedly drunk, edged his car into traffic and got clipped by a tractor-trailer going 40 to 50 mph. He walked away from the accident unhurt, but he showed up late and hungover for a ballgame that began just a few hours later. "We were all a little nervous," closer Jason Isringhausen told the *Post-Dispatch* after Hancock ignored several frantic phone calls. "That's why it's so different here, because of what happened with Darryl." He was referring to his old teammate Darryl Kile, who in 2002, after repeated phone calls to his Chicago hotel room, was found dead at age 33.

Despite these warning signs, Hancock got involved in another car accident just two nights later. He was driving down U.S. 40 in St. Louis—drunk, speeding, texting on his cell phone, not wearing a seat belt—when he plowed into a tow truck that had stopped to assist another motorist. He died on impact.

The Cardinals were devastated. And although one hesitates to cast judgments on the people closest to this tragedy, particularly a Cardinals clubhouse racked with confusion and grief, it's still safe to say that Tony La Russa did not handle the situation well. When reporters asked him for details regarding Hancock's alcohol intake the night of the crash, La Russa snapped, "I'm not into investigative reporting." Later, La Russa held a fungo bat in his hand while warning reporters not to turn Hancock's death into some probing exposé: "The first time I hear insincerity, I'm going to start swinging this fungo."

It was an old La Russa tactic, one that allied him with cutthroats like Billy Martin and Dick Williams: Draw the wagons, feed into paranoia, turn your weak spots into tests of loyalty, us versus them. But as strategy, it failed. If anything it only led to more questions about La Russa's fitness for leadership:

Didn't he himself get arrested for drunk driving in spring training? Did he lack the moral high ground to confront Hancock about his drinking when he had the chance? And why paint the media's questions about Hancock as a witch hunt? Doesn't that just worsen an already-bad situation? Is La Russa the best guy to manage this team? Is he even stable?

These were the conditions under which the Cardinals had to go out and play baseball games—although at that point in the season, baseball felt less like a game and more like something approaching drudgery.

As spring turned to summer, it became clear that the Cardinals were playing not to repeat as division champs, but merely to stave off embarrassment. Since integration, the worst record of any World Series winner through the first two months of the following season is the 17-38 mark put up by the '98 Marlins. They, of course, were victims of a very public fire sale the previous winter and weren't expected to compete. The second worst record, however, belongs to the 2007 Cardinals, who limped along at a 22-29 pace heading into June.

The main culprit was the Cards' starting pitching. Over those first two months, the rotation had a 16-27 record with a 5.33 ERA. Wells was especially wretched, starting off 3-11 with a 6.30 ERA. Improbably, Reyes was even worse: he began the season with an 0-10 record and a 6.40 ERA. To be fair, Reyes inherited more than his share of bad luck—his peripheral numbers weren't terrible, and he had the weakest run support in the league (1.79 runs per nine innings). But he clearly wasn't the same guy who was once touted among the game's top pitching prospects, nor was he the same guy who buzzsawed through 17 straight Tigers hitters en route to a Game 1 victory in the 2006 World Series.

In fact, Reyes became something of a lightning rod among Cardinals fans, who argued incessantly over who was to blame for his troubles. Was it Reyes himself? Or was it the regime under which he suffered? See, La Russa and pitching coach Dave Duncan love groundball pitchers—two-seam specialists like Jeff Suppan and

Woody Williams, pitch-to-contact guys who thrive by passing the buck to the Cardinals' sure-handed infielders. Reyes, unfortunately, is not cut from that cloth. He's a high-risk/high-reward hurler who likes to challenge hitters up in the zone with his four-seam fastball. That's fine, unless you leave too many pitches over the meaty part of the plate (which Reyes did often; opposing hitters had a blistering .203 isolated power average against him on the season), or if you can't wriggle your way out of jams (and indeed, Reyes allowed a .346 slugging percentage with the bases empty, but a monstrous .637 slugging percentage with runners on). This drove Duncan nuts.

So partisans fell into two camps. One side—call them the left-wingers—said that Reyes was merely a victim of his upbringing. The other side—the right-wingers—said he was a victim of his own stubborn inability to adapt. Either way, Reyes sank further down the depth charts as the season wore on. At the end of May he was sent to the minors for reprogramming. (At the time, Duncan said, "He really needs to develop more confidence in a pitch he can get a ground ball with.") Reyes was recalled a month later, and even had some decent stretches here and there. But by the end of September, he was relegated to menial tasks, like pinch running for Pujols when the slugger's calves gave out, or trying to get the last couple outs in a 16-3 game against the Pittsburgh Pirates. In other words, he had been demoted from future savior of the rotation to, in essence, team janitor.

Pujols shook off his early-season cobwebs and rolled into the All-Star break with numbers that would be the envy of just about any other player in the league—a .310 batting average, 16 homers, 53 walks. But of course Pujols is not just any other player. Like Michael Jordan or Tiger Woods, he's an athlete to whom second place is the same as last, who must not only win, but dominate. It was one thing for Alex Rodriguez to knock Albert from his perch as the designated "best player in baseball"—after all, A-Rod is a legend in the making, an Inner Circle Hall of Famer. It was quite another for Prince Fielder, four years Pujols' junior, leading the NL with 29 jacks at the All-Star break, to surpass him as the top vote-getter at first base for the midseason classic.

To make matters worse, Pujols didn't even get to play in the game. With the National Leaguers down a run, the bases loaded and two outs in the bottom of the ninth in San Francisco, manager Tony La Russa passed up Pujols and instead called on Aaron Rowand to pinch hit. Rowand flew out to right to end the game. Asked about La Russa's choice afterwards, Pujols sulked, "If I wasn't expecting to play I wouldn't have come up here."

If Pujols was frustrated by the way the All-Star Game ended, his general manager, Walt Jocketty, was surely more frustrated by the way it began, with Oakland's Danny Haren taking the mound as the starting pitcher. Haren was a critical piece (along with Kiko Calero and hitting prodigy Daric Barton) of a trade Jocketty made two years earlier to land left-hander Mark Mulder. While Haren was 10-3 with a 2.30 ERA at the break, Mulder was languishing on the DL, and Cardinals fans were daydreaming about returning him to Oakland under some kind of lemon law.

The need for a young, cheap Danny Haren-like pitcher became even more acute when, less than a week after the All-Star break, Carpenter was diagnosed with damage to his elbow ligament. He would miss the rest of 2007—and most of 2008—with Tommy John surgery.

Obviously this was not part of Jocketty's plan. In fact, last winter Jocketty voluntarily tore up Carpenter's bargain-basement contract—$7 million for 2007 and $8 million for 2008—and replaced it with a five-year contract just shy of $17 million a year. It was a costly gamble. Joe Sheehan of *Baseball Prospectus* was puzzled why Jocketty "bought Carpenter's age 34-36 seasons at $17 million per without yet knowing what he's going to be at 32 and 33." As it turns out, Carpenter will spend those years on the shelf.

Jocketty made a similar miscalculation with Edmonds, who filed provisionally for free agency last November, awaiting a decision by the team on a $10 million option. Instead, Jocketty renegotiated the entire contract, not only rewarding Edmonds for 2007, but tacking on an additional $8 million for 2008. Most fans were happy to see Edmonds back, but when he slumped in the first half of the season—he missed a month with a pinched nerve in his back and struggled to keep his OBP over .300—people began to question the wisdom of that bonus year. Surprisingly, Edmonds seemed as baffled by the decision as anyone. "I don't know why they did what they did," Edmonds told the *Post-Dispatch* in late June. "You'd have to ask them."

It would be easy to conclude from these moves that Jocketty was operating under the Paul Konerko rule of contract negotiation, which says that loyalty trumps reason if you've just won a world championship. But that wasn't really the case. After all, Jocketty cut ties with some key players in the offseason, including most of his 2006 starting rotation: Jeff Suppan, Jeff Weaver and Jason Marquis. So clearly Jocketty's problem was not excess allegiance to the boys who took him over the top.

No, Jocketty's real problem was replacing them. How the Cardinals would go about doing that—whether they would seek talent from within the system or from without—was the central question in a front-office war that raged behind closed doors throughout the summer. It was a war that turned what had been one of the most stable organizations in the game (with the same owner, GM and manager for the past dozen years) into the Bronx Zoo Midwest.

No one is sure when Jocketty's troubles began, but it was probably sometime in the winter of 2006. The Cards had just won a world championship, they had a brand-new stadium, and they packed the house every night. The franchise was a cash cow. According to Kevin Wheeler of KMOX.com, the Cards raked in somewhere in the neighborhood of $225 to $250 million, and that's before counting local TV and radio revenue, corporate sponsorships, or the team's share of the MLB Extra Innings money. Forbes valued the franchise at $460 million, sixth highest in all of baseball.

Nevertheless, the Cardinals' consortium of owners froze payroll and balked at authorizing any big-ticket signings. This may have been a blessing—most of the free agents the Cards targeted (notably flamethrower Jason Schmidt) turned out to be busts. But the owners' frugality reportedly irked Jocketty.

Jocketty was further irritated when his boss, principal owner Bill DeWitt, promoted Jeff Luhnow to oversee both amateur scouting and player development. Luhnow was not Jocketty's choice for the job. A Wharton Business School grad with a fondness for sabermetric analysis, Luhnow didn't fit in with the chummy, backroom-negotiating style favored by Jocketty's inner circle. The old guard disparagingly referred to him behind his back as "the accountant" and "Harry Potter"—although considering the way he divided the front office, a better nickname may have been "Yoko Luhnow."

See, it wasn't just Luhnow's style that rubbed Jocketty the wrong way. It was what he represented in terms of organizational philosophy. Jocketty was a big game hunter, looking elsewhere to bag established stars like Mark McGwire and Jim Edmonds, whereas Luhnow was all wonkish efficiency, urging the Cards to save money by rebuilding from the ground up. To Jocketty this was a decidedly "lose now" approach.

Things got so bad by the summer of 2007 that half of the front office wasn't talking to the other half. According to a source close to the situation, "Jocketty and his cronies treated Luhnow like some sort of baseball war criminal," with Luhnow terrified of being seen around Busch Stadium for fear it would get back to Jocketty. These reindeer games infuriated DeWitt and team president Mark Lamping. Around midseason, Jocketty intimated to friends that he might quit at the end of the season— that is, if he wasn't fired first.

Despite these tensions, Jocketty never gave up on the team. Quite the opposite. When it became clear that the Cardinals were in danger of sinking into irrelevance, Jocketty put aside whatever gripes he had about his bosses, and played the only card he had left to play: He began tinkering at the margins like a madman.

Jocketty spent the rest of the summer engaging in baseball's version of dumpster diving. When Carpenter went down, Jocketty hauled in Todd Wellemeyer—waived by the Royals, of all teams, with a cover-your-eyes 10.34 ERA—and the Cards immediately inserted him into the starting rotation. When outfielder Preston Wilson was scratched from the season with a torn-up knee, Jocketty called on journeyman Ryan Ludwick to fill his shoes. Adam Kennedy, who barely out-hit the Cardinals' pitchers this season, eventually succumbed to season-ending knee surgery and was replaced by no-name prospect Brendan Ryan.

And so it went. Reyes lost his spot in the rotation and was replaced by slowball specialist Mike Maroth. Wells lost his spot in the rotation and was replaced by Red Sox castoff Joel Piniero. Scott Rolen went down for the season with a bum shoulder and was replaced by Dave Kingman impersonator Russell Branyan. Kelly Stinnett was picked up to sub for injured Yadier Molina for a few weeks. Troy Percival, who actually retired two years earlier, became one of the Cards' go-to relievers after Tyler Johnson strained his biceps.

Some of these gambits didn't work. Maroth, for example, was a calamity of biblical proportions (after a good debut against the Mets in late June, he was 0-5 with a 12.91 ERA). But most of the new guys made for surprisingly useful spackling. Ryan hit better than he ever did in the minors, Ludwick produced league-average numbers for a corner outfielder, and Piniero—who had the very *worst* ERA of any starter in '06—revived memories of his days as a young Mariner, finishing with an ERA a smidge under 4.

The man holding things together was none other than the Cards' embattled manager. One might think La Russa's hair-trigger disposition was a poor fit for a team that needed to relax and play ball. (Quick story: In the middle of the season there was speculation that La Russa might leave the team or retire at the end of the year. La Russa was asked if he had lost his verve for the job, and he replied that no, he had not. How come? Well, because "there are still times," he said, "when you've got a five-run lead, when it's tense and I can't swallow. I've got a headache, and I'm afraid I'm going to throw up. You only feel that stuff because you're anxious about the outcome." Headaches, anxiety, vomiting—to La Russa, these are sure signs of a healthy work environment.)

Anyway, despite La Russa's ulcerous personality, and despite his fumbling approach to public relations, his stubborn refusal to phone it in actually suited the team well. Never one to just sit back and lose, he kept trying something, anything, to goose the team along. Whether throwing Looper into the starting rotation, reshuffling the lineup, bunting in the early innings, starting runners, or—gasp!—batting the pitcher eighth, La Russa never stopped throwing spaghetti against the wall. Some of these strategies made sense (as both SABR's Mark Pankin and THT's own John Beamer showed, there are sound statistical arguments for batting the pitcher eighth) and some clearly did not (for example, Cardinals baserunners were caught stealing 37% of the time, the worst rate in the majors).

La Russa also wrung decent seasons from a few of the younger Cards who were not expected to do well. Chris Duncan, the big galoot with the loopy swing, enemy of MLE mavens everywhere, posted surprisingly solid numbers. (If you want a sense of what he's like in left field, though, imagine Tonto trying to scat.) And Molina bingled his way to a passable .275 batting average while remaining the best defensive catcher in baseball. But La Russa's finest work was with the bench and the bullpen. The Cardinals hit .293 in the pinch, far and away the best mark in the majors, and their foul rag-and-bone shop of a bullpen actually performed superbly: second in the NL in WPA.

Add it up and the Cardinals found themselves in OK shape on Aug. 1. They were only three games under .500—or, "right in the thick of things" if you play in the NL Central—on the strength of a break-even June and a winning July. Of course, their overall run differential was atrocious, 75 under through 103 games, which works out to six Pythagorean wins fewer than their actual total. But that's what makes 2007 one of La Russa's more impressive managerial efforts. The Cardinals were having their worst season of the decade, but they hung in the race by playing over their heads.

On July 28, the Cards scored three runs in the bottom of the ninth to nip the Brewers 7-6. They reeled off two more wins against the Brew Crew, and were flush with optimism heading into August; a six-day road trip would take them to cellar-dwelling Pittsburgh and Washington, the patsies of the National League. If the Cards could take four, maybe five of those games, they'd be right back in the thick of the division race.

Instead the Cards dropped five straight. They lost the easy ones (by scores of 15-1 and 12-1) and the hard ones (four straight in which they held the lead). "That was ugly," said Rolen after the trip had ended. "We played well at home against the Brewers, and then went on the road and soiled the bed." They were eight games under .500, eight games out of first, and fading fast.

And then, in a pattern that was becoming almost routine, the Cards amplified their problems on the field with yet another crisis off it. In their first game back home, utilityman Scott Spiezio—one of the more affable members of the team, a second-generation Cardinal who sported a clownish *crimson imperiale* soul patch—found himself sitting in the dugout, basically freaking out. His heart was racing; he was irritated and anxious, sweating profusely, taking in intravenous fluids. When someone suggested he check into a hospital, Spiezio pulled the IV from his arm and split from the stadium.

The next day Spiezio informed the club that he was suffering from substance abuse, and that his dependency was abetted, in part, by heartache over the death of Josh Hancock. Given that this was the Cards' third drug- and alcohol-related incident of the year (reviving memories of the mid-80s Pirates), the organization immediately checked Spiezio into an outpatient treatment program and granted him an indefinite leave of absence from the team.

His replacement on the roster was a 28-year old outfielder who, before the season began, was not listed among the Cards' Top 30 prospects by *Baseball America*. But even casual baseball fans knew him well. His name: Rick Ankiel.

At the time of his call-up, Ankiel was widely considered a project. Just three years earlier he was a full-time pitcher who shifted to the outfield only because he suffered from incurable performance anxiety on the mound. In the years since, he was plagued by injuries and setbacks, and even though he was finally healthy in 2007, he still needed sandpapering as a hitter. He rarely walked and he struck out in a quarter of his at-bats. But when he did make contact, the results could be ferocious—half his hits went for extra-bases, including a PCL-leading 32 home runs.

In his first game back with the big club, Ankiel broke open a tight game against the Pads by drilling a three-run homer into the right field stands. La Russa, who, even in the best of times lurks in the dugout like a wound-up coil, erupted with joyous glee. Afterwards a misty-eyed La Russa said, "I'm fighting my butt off to keep it together. Short of winning the World Series … it's the happiest I've been in this uniform."

In one sense Ankiel's homer was the culmination of a long journey, but in another he was just getting started. Two days later he cranked a pair of homers against the Dodgers, then later in the game added a sprawling catch at the warning track. The following week in Wrigley, he showed off his prized arm by firing a bullet into third to gun down Ryan Theriot on the basepaths. Rolen received the throw and marveled, "I just saw something that maybe I hadn't seen before." A few innings later Ankiel belted his fourth homer of the year.

By this point Ankiel was a YouTube folk hero, and his rousing exploits seemed to lift the rest of the team. In the weeks after Ankiel arrived, the Cards went 18-9. Their starting pitchers, who practically qualified for FEMA grants earlier in the season, tossed 14 quality starts over 20 games, with a group ERA of 2.75. Ankiel became the poster child for this resurgence.

Of course, it wasn't all good times for the Cards. On Aug. 31, during a game against the Reds, Cards right fielder Juan Encarnacion was standing in the on-deck circle when he took a foul ball in the face. The impact shattered his orbital bone —the technical term is a "blowout fracture"—and brought to mind the eye injuries that ruined the careers of Tony Conigliario and Dickie Thon (not to mention the heart-rending death of Mike Coolbaugh, a minor-league coach who, just a few weeks earlier, was killed by a line drive while standing in the first-base coaches box). A few moments after Encarnacion went down, Ankiel hit a grand slam to cap a come-from-behind Cardinals victory. The twin incidents—Encarnacion's tragedy and Ankiel's triumph—were odd, even somewhat eerie, especially considering Ankiel was the man who replaced Encarnacion as the Cards' everyday right fielder.

By the first week of September, the Cards were officially back in the race, hot on the heels of the Brewers and Cubs. As much as one is tempted to view Ankiel as a quick fix—a Cardinals cortisone shot—the team had actually been playing well for the last couple months. In fact, for a full half season the Cards were the best team in the NL, at least by wins and losses:

NL Standings, June 1 – Sept. 6

ST. LOUIS	49-39	.557
Chicago	49-39	.557
Colorado	47-38	.553
Philadelphia	47-39	.547
Arizona	46-40	.535

Now of course, this chart may speak more to the general mediocrity (er, parity) of the National League c. 2007—presumably you could rig the dates so that virtually *any* NL team would look like a hot property at some point. Nevertheless, in a Cardinals season marred by disappointments, misbehavior, and even death, it was an encouraging stretch.

The high water mark for the team came on Sept. 6, when the Redbirds lambasted the Pirates 16-4 on the strength of two home runs and seven RBIs from Ankiel. At that moment, Ankiel sported a .358/.409/.765 line that looked like something out of young Stan Musial's career. The Cards were over .500 for the first time all year, only a game out of first, about to square off against division-leading Arizona and Chicago. It was a hopeful time.

And then Ankiel turned into a pumpkin. Just hours after Ankiel's big game against Pittsburgh, the New York *Daily News* leaked word that the Cards' right fielder had received shipments of human growth hormone while rehabbing from an injury in 2004. There were plenty of extenuating circumstances to absolve Ankiel—HGH was not on baseball's banned substances list at the time; Ankiel used it under the care of a physician; he used it to aid his pitching, not his hitting; there was no indication that he'd tampered with HGH after '04; and perhaps most importantly, clinical studies suggest that HGH has no performance-enhancing benefits whatsoever.

But the damage was done. Ankiel went from a feel-good story to a feel-sorta-lousy story. The same editorial writers who held him up as the savior of the Cardinals' season (if not the savior of a sports world rocked by the Michael Vick dog-fighting scandal, Barry Bonds' steroid-clouded home run quest, and the game-fixing bombshell surrounding NBA ref Tim Donaghy) now considered Ankiel just another embarrassment. The Unnatural, they called him.

Weirdly, the controversy seemed to affect the Cards' on-field performance. The team had a disastrous series in Arizona, dropping three straight games after a series of bizarre, down-the-rabbit-hole plays (e.g. Aaron Miles about to turn a game-changing double play, then tripping over his own feet and falling flat on his face). Things got worse from there. Rolen—who had been feuding with La Russa for months about the condition of his damaged left shoulder—finally succumbed to season-ending surgery. Chris Duncan aggravated a hernia and was also lost for the year. Same deal with Mulder: out for the year after an abortive comeback attempt.

Thinned by injuries and playing a wicked string of 35 games in 34 days (the longest ever stretch without an off-day to end a season), the Cardinals never got back on track. They ended up losing 14 of 16 games, including nine in a row, a trick that hadn't been turned in St. Louis since the Carter Administration. "They say everything happens for a reason," reliever Brad Thompson told *USA Today*, "But we have no idea why this is happening to us."

No Cardinal sank faster than Ankiel himself. In the two weeks after the HGH story broke, he went .127/.169/.164, with 14 strikeouts and nary a home run. One night at Great American Ballpark, amid chants from the crowd of "H-G-H! H-G-H!", Ankiel dropped two easy fly balls. Cardinals fans began to wonder if the immense self-criticism Ankiel carried with him on the mound was bleeding into his performance at the plate and in the field.

The Cards finally hit rock bottom on Sept. 20, when they were drubbed 18-1, at home, by the lowly Astros.

Their best reliever that night was none other than Miles. Busch Stadium was officially sold out—same as every home game all year—but no one will know the game's actual attendance figures. Why? Because the Cardinals' organization, presumably embarrassed by the tide of no-shows, refused to release them.

The Cardinals managed to end the regular season on an up note: a five-game winning streak, including wins against the Brewers and Mets that torpedoed those teams' playoff hopes. But despite the small potatoes, most people in St. Louis were just thankful the season was over. It was only the second time in eight years the Cards went home without playing in the postseason. Their pitching staff, which led the majors in ERA just two years ago, finished near the bottom of the league. (Although to be fair, most of that ugliness can be laid at the feet of four players: Wells, Reyes, Maroth and Mulder. Combined they went 9-39 with a 6.63 ERA. The rest of the staff: 69-45, 4.11.)

A few days after the season ended, Jocketty was ousted as general manager. The team he guided still owned the most regular-season wins, playoff wins and league titles of any NL team this decade. But clearly that team is now gone.

It's funny: In the fall of 2006 Cardinals fans felt like the luckiest folks on earth. After all, who can forget the improbable, ridiculous events that tilted their way that postseason? There was Yadier Molina's homer to beat the Mets in the NLCS, Curtis Granderson slipping on the outfield grass at a key moment in the World Series, all those Tigers pitchers throwing all those balls into the outfield corners. Luck wore Cardinal red that October, no doubt.

The 2007 Cardinals season was, by contrast, so haunted, so hexed, that St. Louisans couldn't help but wonder if it was karmic payback for the gratuities that befell them a few months earlier.

In the end, 2007 seemed like the black mirror of 2006, with more than a few Cards fans, myself included, reporting the same odd experience. During our darkest days, in the midst of defeat and tragedy, the mind would calm itself by flashing back to a misty October night in Queens, when Wainwright dropped the hammer on a frozen Carlos Beltran to clinch the pennant for the Cards. It was an image we carried in our pockets, like a lucky penny we turned over and over and over…

The Year of the Improbable in Seattle

by David Cameron

For many of us, the understanding of statistical probability is a stabilizing force in our lives. It allows us to avoid blaming an angry deity for every disappointing event, while also keeping us grounded when things go perfectly. Probability is rational, calm and emotionally detached.

In the case of the 2007 Seattle Mariners, however, it was totally useless on many occasions.

The Mariners began the season as prohibitive underdogs, coming off three consecutive last place finishes and having spent the winter loading up on new players with enough serious questions to fill a week's worth of "Jeopardy" episodes. Almost universally pegged for last place, the team seemingly had one legitimate hope: that 21-year-old uberphenom Felix Hernandez would take his King Felix nickname seriously and carry the team every fifth day.

His first two starts of 2007 bore witness to the possibility of the remarkable: an eight inning, 12-strikeout shutout of the A's on Opening Day, followed by a one-hit complete game domination of the Red Sox in Fenway Park in the game that ESPN had decided was Daisuke Matsuzaka's arrival on the national scene. King Felix had stolen the show yet again, and the improbability of a 21-year-old Cy Young contender seemed on the verge of reality.

However, five days later, Felix would walk off the Safeco Field mound after recording just one out against Minnesota, complaining of pain in his elbow and causing the city of Seattle to stop breathing. The diagnosis turned out to be as positive as any arm injury can be, and he returned to the mound a month later. However, post-DL Felix was not pre-DL Felix. He was loathe to throw at max effort and became fairly hittable. A degradation of his top-shelf stuff proved enough of a problem to take him from legitimate ace to struggling youngster.

With his raw ability to overpower no longer present in each start, his inexperience and lack of a pitching plan became more and more obvious. Hernandez had always thrown in a fairly predictable pattern. Through the USS Mariner blog (www.ussmariner.com) that I've maintained with several friends for the past few years, I had been charting his starts since the 2006 season. The trends became overwhelmingly obvious. It didn't take long to see that he began every start the same way, throwing as hard as possible to "establish the fastball." Without fail, the first 10 pitches of each start would be straight cheese, regardless of count, batter or situation. For the opponents, Hernandez' first inning was like a trip to the batting cage, and the results were predictably terrible.

After chronicling these issues for more than a year and watching a lack of a plan sabotage the success of a guy with a golden arm, on June 27 I published "An Open Letter To Rafael Chaves," the Mariners' pitching coach, and the guy Hernandez trusted most in the organization. It was just a chance for me to vent and lay out some of the problems that were keeping Hernandez from pitching to his potential. Considering I'd been raising the issue for over a year, I was resigned to thinking that the post wasn't going to be much beyond personal therapy.

However, through a series of circumstances that involved a dedicated blog reader, a printer and fan access to the bullpens in the Oakland Coliseum, the "open letter" eventually found its way to Chaves. He took the case to Felix, handed him the printout of my personal therapy, and essentially told him that if random fans on the Internet could figure out what pitches he was going to throw, so could opposing hitters.

That was good enough for the young Venezuelan to try something new, and on the afternoon of July 7, he took the hill in Oakland. After a couple of fastballs to start the game, he busted out a third pitch curveball. Pitch five was a slider. Pitch eight was another curve. Establishing the fastball took a back seat to mixing his pitches, and success wasn't far behind—he threw an eight-inning, two-hit shutout in his best start since returning from the disabled list. In the post-game interview, he was quoted as saying "the Internet says I throw too many fastballs, so today, I changed it up."

With players bypassing the media and starting their own blogs, the line that kept fan and player at a distance had been blurring already, and the "open letter" incident continued this trend. The world we live in is certainly changing, and things that were once considered out of the realm of probability, such as a fan influencing the pitch selection of his team's ace, were now becoming quite possible.

Hernandez wasn't the only Mariners pitcher on a roller coaster ride in 2007. For Jeff Weaver, and those who endured the ride with him, the only word that comes close to explaining his '07 season is inexplicable. Signing him as a free agent to be the No. 5 starter, the team hoped Weaver could solidify the back end of what had been an inconsistent rotation in 2006. It was not to be.

Weaver's start to the season was delayed by a snowstorm that wiped out the Mariners' entire four-game series in Cleveland. As it turned out, he undoubtedly would have preferred that the snow not let up until mid-May. Weaver's first six starts as a Mariner were historically awful (22 innings, 50 hits and a 14.32 ERA). He couldn't locate his 88 mph fastball and his slurvy breaking ball wasn't fooling anyone.

Each time he took the hill, it looked like some kind of hitting competition. Yankees, Red Sox, Royals—it didn't matter. He didn't look like a guy who could get outs against a junior college team, much less major league hitters. The Mariners tired of sending him out to get pummeled, and on May 11, they placed him on the disabled list with acute inability to pitch, or, as they called it, "arm problems."

Weaver dropped off the map for the next month, alternating hanging out at home with rehabbing in Arizona, and was mostly an afterthought in Seattle. He was an $8 million experiment gone terribly wrong, and no one was in any hurry to see him in Safeco Field again.

However, as the fill-ins from Tacoma either got injured (Cha Seung Baek) or struggled (Ryan Feierabend), the team found itself in need of a starting pitcher and decided to give Weaver another chance. On June 9, he returned to the mound in San Diego, getting through four innings while giving up only two runs and lowering his season ERA to 12.46. In normal circumstances, a short stint in Petco Park isn't something to celebrate, but Weaver's season was anything but normal.

The outing in San Diego was enough to earn him another start. As the Mariners attempted to keep up with the Angels, they simply wanted innings, and expectations for Weaver's performance weren't particularly high. Mediocrity would have made the organization ecstatic. The M's would get something slightly better than mediocrity.

From his return in San Diego until his Aug. 23 appearance in Texas, Weaver made 14 starts and posted a 3.38 ERA over 90.2 innings. After allowing a 1.208 OPS in his first six starts, he held opposing hitters to a .718 OPS in his next 14. For two and a half months, the guy who made a fan base loathe his every pitch in record time became the team's best starting pitcher. He threw complete game shutouts on June 20 (when he entered the game with a 10.97 ERA, making it one of the most shocking performances of the year) and Aug. 12. The team went 9-5 in those 14 starts.

Aug. 28, however, played midnight to the Cinderella run. It was the first of Weaver's final seven starts, appearances in which he posted an 8.47 ERA and allowed opposing hitters a .997 OPS. The fade down the stretch came as quickly as the season-saving turnaround in mid-June. After re-establishing himself as a major league pitcher from June through August, Weaver's September left all observers with a bitter taste in their mouths.

Weaver made 27 starts for the Mariners. In the 13 of those that covered April 10-May 10 and Aug. 28-Sept. 28, he threw only 56 innings, gave up 101 hits and posted a 10.97 ERA. If those starts were the total of his 2007 performance, it would be one of the worst pitching seasons of all time. However, those two months of historic awfulness bookended two and a half months of getting people out.

From worst pitcher ever to rotation saver and back again, all in the span of six months—Jeff Weaver's 2007 will go down as one of the most improbable pitching years in baseball history.

Not everyone enjoys the unpredictable. Manager Mike Hargrove almost certainly would have preferred the mundane to what the Mariners provided him this year. After being publicly placed on "the hot seat" by team president Chuck Armstrong last winter, heading into the final season of his three-year contract and having the front office declare that anything short of a division title in '07 would be disappointing, his position was on shaky ground.

The mandate was to win. After beginning the season 5-3, the team dropped six consecutive games, the last culminating a sweep at the hands of the Los Angeles Angels. The hot seat had been turned to burning by both fans and local media, and less than a month into the season, the calls for Hargrove to be replaced by bench coach John McLaren (a personal friend of Ichiro's and an understudy of Lou Piniella) grew louder by the day.

However, the team immediately responded, winning seven of its next eight games, saving Hargrove's job and putting the team back in the division race. It was a precursor of things to come: The Mariners would continue their yo-yo act throughout the season. They lost five of six games in mid-May, again causing questions about the manager's job security, but followed that with six wins in seven days. Every time the team's record approached a level where a firing would seem justified, the Mariners rallied.

After a 10-game stretch that saw the team go 9-1 from June 2-June 12, the Mariners stood at 35-26, only three games out of the division lead, and the questions about Hargrove's future seemed to have been put to bed for the remainder of the season. The team overcame adversity to stay in contention into the summer, and talk of a managerial change took a back seat to pondering how to improve the roster and make a legitimate playoff run. The team was on a high, and Hargrove's confidence seemed justified.

The Mariners proceeded to drop six consecutive games to the Cubs, Astros and Pirates, losing 4.5 games in the standings as the Angels surged while the M's collapsed. In just a week's time, the idea of a division title seemed to slip away, and fans fired up the hot seat once again. The up-and down season had taken its toll on Hargrove, and having tired of the daily grind, he called general manager Bill Bavasi and told him he wanted to resign. Bavasi, attending the graduation of his daughter, asked Hargrove to hold off until the team returned to Seattle and they could talk face to face, and the man once known as The Human Rain Delay agreed to keep managing for a few more days.

The flight back to Seattle didn't change his mind, but he agreed to continue managing the team through the All-Star break (and keep all these discussions from everyone, including the players), just to make sure that he wasn't walking away because of temporary frustration. In typical Mariners fashion, the team responded to the six-game losing streak by going on a 10-1 run and rescuing the season. Again.

Hargrove had had enough, however. The winning didn't make him want to stay, and on July 1, with the team at 44-33, he made his resignation official. The team had won seven consecutive games, and Hargrove quitting was the last thing anyone expected. However, he told the media, "the lows were too low and the highs just weren't high enough."

Hargrove had been in baseball for 35 years, but a half season of the maddening 2007 Mariners was enough to make him want to do something else. Even with his team playing its best baseball during his tenure and the Mariners in a good position in both the division and wild card races, Hargrove left the team, and baseball, for a life that didn't involve hot seats, cold streaks or Jeff Weaver.

While Hargrove chose to get off the roller coaster, the rest of the organization and its fans couldn't make a similar choice. For better or worse, we're tied to this team, and we were going to see this crazy season through. Following the manager's departure, the team continued to experience ups and downs, with the ups outnumbering the downs 28-20 in the first 48 games of the McLaren era.

With a win on Aug. 24, the team stood at 73-53, 20 games over .500 and only one game behind the Angels in the AL West race, while holding a three-game lead over the Yankees in the wild card chase. The Mariners were legitimate contenders. They'd survived an injury to their ace, Hernandez, three separate losing streaks of six games or longer, and the resignation of their manager. Only two days away from hosting a series at Safeco Field against the first-place Angels, the city began to ramp up for a real pennant race—the first one Seattle had seen in years. The Mariners were the hot ticket again.

Aug. 25 and 26 brought losses in Texas leading into the pivotal Angels series, but they were just two games, and the team had been playing good baseball for most of the past two months. Certainly, this team that had come so far and bounced back so many times wouldn't fold now. How many times can a team fall apart in one season, anyway?

One more time, apparently. The Angels rolled into Seattle, sweeping the Mariners and pushing the division lead to five games, effectively ending the Mariners' chance of winning the AL West. On the way to Toronto for a three-game series, they had to stop in Cleveland for a one-game makeup of the early season snow series. They lost again. Arriving in Canada on a six-game losing streak, the Mariners lay down again, losing three more to the Jays and pushing the losing streak to nine.

Hernandez ended that streak by winning a game in Yankee Stadium, but his teammates then dropped the next four games, solidifying a two-week stretch that saw the team win exactly one game and essentially secede from playoff contention. From Aug. 25 to Sept. 8, the Mariners punted their 2007 season, going from contender to pretender in a brutal stretch of baseball that saw them lose every way possible. They didn't hit and didn't pitch, and the previously rock-solid bullpen couldn't hold the few leads the Mariners did manage to bring into the late innings.

It took only two weeks to cancel out nearly everything that had been accomplished in the first four months. The fans returned to their cynical ways. They couldn't even call for Hargrove to be fired this time. It was just a bewildering experience: 20 games above .500 headed into the last week of August to completely out of contention at the end of the first week of September.

The Seattle Mariners closed the 2007 season with 88 wins (predictably, they rebounded from their collapse with a strong finish), but the path they took to those wins was anything but ordinary. From the team's ace getting advice from a blogger, Weaver taking pitching inconsistency to a whole new level, Hargrove announcing he was tired of managing during a winning streak, and the team flushing a pennant race down the toilet in record time, this was no ordinary 88-win campaign.

So 2007 was the year Seattle turned probability on its ear. It was quite a ride, but one I'd imagine most participants would rather never take again.

The Top Minor League Prospects

by Chris Constancio

The value of young talent was never as apparent as during the 2007 season.

The small-market Rockies relied on young pitching during their amazing late run to the playoffs and rookie shortstop Troy Tulowitzki was among their most important contributors in the lineup and on the field. The American League champions Red Sox team received big returns from little rookie leadoff hitter Dustin Pedroia. Both Pedroia and Tulowitzki were featured in last year's list of the top 30 prospects.

This year I would like to try something different. Instead of ranking players, which can exaggerate the difference in value of players ranked far apart, I will write about a handful of important prospects at each position. I restricted this list to players who have not yet passed the rookie eligibility threshold (130 major league at bats or 50 innings pitched). This means some notable prospects, such as Justin Upton, have to be excluded.

In addition to summarizing each player's strengths and weaknesses, I am referencing similar performances to help put each player's achievements in context. For each player, I searched for similar performances among players of the same age and at the same level of competition within the past 10 years. Players included demonstrate significantly similar strikeout rates and walk rates as the target player. I also require similar isolated power (slugging minus batting average) for hitters and ground-ball rate for pitchers when possible.

Rather than give a false sense of precision with similarity scores for each of these players, I list five to seven significantly similar performances. These are organized in terms of "best case" and "worst case" career trajectories based on how each player's career turned out. These lists of similar performances are not included for every player; some performances just don't generate a meaningful group of comparison players.

The similar player lists are based only on characteristics of hitting or pitching performance (not fielding). Although I don't recommend basing player projections on a handful of similar performances, I hope these lists will help shape realistic expectations. It is easy to demonstrate an optimistic bias when comparing prospects to good major leaguers, but these similar performances can remind us of a range of potential outcomes

for each prospect. The years in parentheses are the years of comparable performances.

Now, on to the prospects…

Projected Catchers

Bryan Anderson
St. Louis Cardinals | 21
ETA: 2009

Anderson handled an aggressive 2007 promotion to the Double-A Texas League, where he hit for a high average for the second year in a row. He maintained a respectable on-base percentage against older pitchers but he did not hit for power, particularly when playing away from his home park. There are questions about his ability to remain behind the plate, but he still has plenty of time to improve and his left-handed bat will be an asset if he can catch in the major leagues.

Best Case: Edwin Encarnacion (2003) and James Loney (2005)

Median Case: Robert Andino (2005)

Worst Case: Alexis Gomez (2001) and Nathan Haynes (2000)

Jeff Clement
Seattle Mariners | 24
ETA: 2008

The third overall pick from the 2005 draft had a solid season for Triple-A Tacoma this year. His defense has never been a strength, but Clement continued to improve behind the plate. He was a better hitter all-around than in 2006, when he was rushed to the upper minor leagues. Clement walked more often, struck out less often, and hit for more power in 2007. While he probably won't hit for a high average, his well-rounded approach at the plate should make him an above-average offensive catcher in the American League as soon as next year.

Best Case: Chase Utley (2003) and Adam LaRoche (2003)

Median Case: Damon Hollins (1998) and Gerald Laird (2003)

Worst Case: Jason Hart (2001) and Guillermo Quiroz (2005)

Hank Conger

Los Angeles Angels | 20

ETA: 2010

He's a switch-hitting catcher with solid contact skills and power potential. Like most Angels prospects, Conger doesn't demonstrate much patience at the plate; he walked in just 6.6% of plate appearances in 2007. Four of every five baserunners were successful in stealing against Conger, so he has his work cut out for him behind the plate.

Best Case: Robinson Cano (2002) and Brian McCann (2003)

Median Case: Jeff Mathis (2002) and Carlos Gonzalez (2005)

Worst Case: Rudy Guillen (2003)

Geovany Soto

Chicago Cubs | 25

ETA: 2008

Soto experienced a major breakout when he slugged 26 home runs and hit 20% of his batted balls for line drives in the Pacific Coast League. He earned a promotion to the National League and found himself on a playoff roster in October. Do not be surprised if Soto's results are less impressive when he starts for the Cubs in 2008, as he had never had a batting average higher than .272 and never hit more than nine home runs in a year until this past season.

Projected First Basemen

Lars Anderson

Boston Red Sox | 20

ETA: 2010

The Red Sox paid more than $800,000 to sign Anderson, an 18th round pick from the 2006 draft. The left-handed hitter did not disappoint in his full season debut; he showed reasonable power potential and a solid approach at the plate in the South Atlantic League. Anderson walked in 13.5% of his plate appearances there and showed poise against much older players during a late-season promotion to the California League, where he reached base in 23 of 47 plate appearances.

Best Case: Matt Holliday (1999) and David Wright (2002)

Median Case: Ryan Langerhans (1999)

Worst Case: Brent Clevlen (2003) and Jayson Nix (2002)

Daric Barton

Oakland Athletics | 22

ETA: 2008

The former catcher does not project to be more than adequate at first base, but his bat warrants a role in Oakland's starting lineup. Barton is a strong contact hitter with exceptional plate patience that should yield a high batting average and on-base percentage as soon as next season. While he has never hit for much power, he was among the league leaders in lifting balls in the air during his 2007 campaign in the Pacific Coast League and was able to launch 13 of 25 hits for extra-bases for Oakland in September. Don't give up on his power potential just yet.

Bill Rowell

Baltimore Orioles | 19

ETA: 2010

Rowell has been a high-profile prospect since before becoming the first high school hitter taken in the 2006 draft. His raw power is on display in batting practice, but he swings and misses too often to produce much in games. He is young and has time to make adjustments, but some of the comparison players below serve as reminders of how difficult it is to improve on strikeout problems that are apparent at a young age. Rowell currently plays third base, but will likely move to first or a designated hitter role in the major leagues.

Best Case: Chris Duncan (2000) and Felipe Lopez (1999)

Median Case: Franklin Gutierrez (2002) and Brandon Wood (2004)

Worst Case: Edgardo Baez (2005) and Sean Rodriguez (2004)

Joey Votto

Cincinnati Reds | 24

ETA: 2008

Votto regressed to more typical levels of power production after a breakout season in 2006, and it seems unlikely that he will be more than an average first baseman in the short term. Still, his patient approach at the plate and hitting in the friendly confines of Great American Ballpark should result in solid production overall. He hit four home runs in his brief stint with the Reds and should be starting at first base in 2008.

Best Case: Adam LaRoche (2003) and Kelly Johnson (2005)

Median Case: Chris Duncan (2005) and Ryan Langerhans (2004)

Worst Case: Eric Valent (2001) and Justin Huber (2005)

Projected Middle Infielders

I won't distinguish between projected shortstops and second basemen because most major league second basemen start as shortstops in the minor leagues. Often, these changes are difficult to predict because factors other than player talent come into play. Note the transition of Cleveland Indians second baseman Asdrubal Cabrera last year: He was widely regarded as a strong defensive shortstop but earned a starting job as a second baseman due to the team's need.

Matt Antonelli

San Diego Padres | 22

ETA: 2009

Antonelli cruised through advanced Single-A and Double-A leagues in 2007, posting an OBP near .400 at both stops while moving from third base to second base. The 17th overall pick from the 2006 draft could demonstrate above-average on-base skills and 15-20 home run power for the Padres within two years.

Reid Brignac

Tampa Bay Devil Rays | 22

ETA: 2009

Brignac's 2007 campaign, which included a .260 batting average at Double-A Montgomery, was viewed as a disappointment following his breakout season in the California League the previous year. However, he cut down on his strikeouts while walking more often and maintaining above-average power in a much more challenging league for hitters in 2007. What's not to like?

Best Case: Justin Morneau (2002)

Median Case: Brandon Phillips (2002) and Shin-Soo Choo (2004)

Worst Case: Josh Kroeger (2004) and Cody Ross (2003)

Chris Coghlan

Florida Marlins | 22

ETA: 2010

The 36th overall pick from the 2006 draft made contact to all fields while walking more often than he struck out for Single-A Greensboro. The second baseman's overall numbers looked worse when he hit .200 after a promotion to the Florida State League, but he continued to demonstrate above-average contact skills and a solid line drive rate that should serve him well in the upper minor leagues.

Hector Gomez

Colorado Rockies | 20

ETA: Early 2008

Gomez is a toolsy shortstop who earned rave reviews despite making 39 errors at shortstop in 2007. His plate discipline can be most kindly described as a work in progress. Gomez struck out in 21% of plate appearances while posting the third worst walk rate among South Atlantic League players with at least 500 plate appearances last year.

Best Case: Adam Jones (2004) and Brandon Phillips (2000)

Median Case: Jason Pridie (2003) and Luis Montanez (2001)

Worst Case: Robinson Chirinos (2003) and Victor Hall (2000)

Chin-Lung Hu

Los Angeles Dodgers | 24

ETA: 2008

Hu is a slick-fielding shortstop who also played second base in 2007 and earned Futures Game MVP honors during the MLB All-Star break. He could be an above-average major league shortstop if he could complement his good contact skills with a more consistent ability to walk and get on base. Hu does not project to more than 30 extra-base hits a season in the majors and probably will hit in the bottom of the order when he earns a starting role.

Best Case: Cesar Izturis (2002)

Median Case: Nate McLouth (2004) and Tike Redman (2000)

Worst Case: Matt Watson (2003) and Omar Quintanilla (2005)

Jed Lowrie

Boston Red Sox | 23

ETA: 2009

Lowrie rebounded from a disappointing and injury-plagued 2006 season to post the fifth-highest OBP among qualifying players in the Eastern League. He launched a combined 68 extra-base hits across Double-A and Triple-A leagues. Lowrie has remained at shortstop, but his limited range may require a move to another infield position.

Best Case: Marcus Giles (2001) and Kelly Johnson (2005)

Median Case: Jason Conti (1998) Luis Matos (2002)

Worst Case: Jason Hart (2001) and Eric Valent (2000)

Carlos Truinfel

Seattle Mariners | 18

ETA: 2010

Truinfel held his own as the youngest player in the Midwest and California Leagues this year. He was an aggressive hitter and didn't show much power (even at the hitters' haven of High Desert), but he has plenty of time to develop his offensive skills.

Projected Third Basemen

Chase Headley

San Diego Padres | 23

ETA: Late 2008

Headley has always had a mature plate approach that characterizes Padres prospects, but in 2007 he hit the ball harder than ever. He hit well from both sides of the plate and led his Texas League team to a championship while finishing with the league's best on-base and slugging percentages in 2007. He also paced the league with a 24% line drive rate on batted balls. Headley will challenge for a role on the Padres in the spring and could be a surprise Rookie of the Year contender.

Best Case: Curtis Granderson (2003) and Nick Swisher (2003)

Median Case: Adam LaRoche (2003) and Joey Votto (2006)

Worst Case: J.D. Closser (2002) and Laynce Nix (2003)

Evan Longoria

Tampa Bay Devil Rays | 22

ETA: 2008

Longoria has hit well at every level during his brief minor league career. He posted an OBP over .400 while hitting 21 home runs for Double-A Montgomery during the first two-thirds of the 2007 season. He led the Southern League with a 23% line drive rate on batted balls. He did more of the same during Triple-A Durham's stretch drive to the postseason. Longoria strikes out too often to hit for a high average in the majors, but he is otherwise a very complete hitter who can contribute solid defense at third base for the Devil Rays as soon as 2008.

Andy LaRoche

Los Angeles Dodgers | 24

ETA: 2008

LaRoche struggled during an early stint with the Dodgers in 2007, but he proved too good for Triple-A pitchers when he returned to the Pacific Coast League.

LaRoche's power potential might be overstated by his results due to his hitter-friendly home park; 17 of his 28 Triple-A home runs over the past two seasons have come at Las Vegas. LaRoche has demonstrated an elite plate approach that should result in above-average on-base skills at the major league level when he finally earns an everyday job in 2008. When his shoulder is healthy, LaRoche is at least an average major league third baseman. As the comparison players below suggest, LaRoche is a relatively safe bet to become at least an average major league third baseman.

Best Case: Mike Lowell (1997)

Median Case: Edwin Encarnacion (2005) and Aubrey Huff (2000)

Worst Case: Ben Davis (1999) and Carlos Quentin (2005)

Ian Stewart

Colorado Rockies | 22

ETA: 2008

Stewart continued more of the same in 2007, demonstrating sound on-base skills and moderate power production at a higher level of competition than the previous season. Stewart hit only six home runs with a meager slugging average of .377 away from hitter-friendly Colorado Springs, so he may need more time in Triple-A before earning playing time as a corner infielder in the big leagues.

Best Case: Wes Helms (1998) and Mark Teahen (2004)

Median Case: Josh Barfield (2005)

Worst Case: Todd Linden (2003) and Brad Nelson (2005)

Neil Walker

Pittsburgh Pirates | 22

ETA: 2009

Walker nicely handled the transition from behind the plate to third base. Although his offensive production trailed off at the end of the year, he did make some important improvements in plate discipline and posted the best OBP (.362) of his minor league career. The switch-hitting Pittsburgh native may earn a promotion to the National League as soon as 2008.

Best Case: Alex Rios (2003) and Edwin Encarnacion (2004)

Median Case: Wily Aybar (2004) and Bobby Crosby (2002)

Worst Case: Brian N. Anderson (2004) and Scott Thorman (2004)

Angel Villalona

San Francisco Giants | 18

ETA: 2011

The teenager earned a $2.1 million signing bonus in 2006 and held his own with a .344 OBP and .450 SLG in the Arizona Rookie League in 2007. The big-bodied third baseman should start the 2008 season as one of the youngest Single-A players.

Projected corner outfielders

Wladimir Balentien

Seattle Mariners | 23

ETA: 2008

Balentien has always had exceptional raw power, and over the past two years he has developed about as well as a hitter of his type could in the upper minor leagues. He started walking more often in 2006, which allowed him to finish the season with a respectable on-base average in spite of his .230 batting average. Toward the end of the 2006 season, Balentien started cutting down on his strikeouts. This carried into the 2007 season, when he struck out in 19.2% of his plate appearances while walking at a healthy rate and hitting 24 home runs for Triple-A Tacoma.

Best Case: Rickie Weeks (2005)

Median Case: Chris Young (2006)

Worst Case: Michael Coleman (1998) and Michael Restovich (2003)

Carlos Gonzalez

Arizona Diamondbacks | 22

ETA: 2009

Gonzalez is frequently criticized for his inconsistent effort, but he can hit; he posted a 20% line drive rate in the Southern League. His plate discipline is mediocre, but he did substantially improve his walk rate in the second half of the 2007 season.

Best Case: Jeff Francoeur (2005) and Corey Hart (2003)

Median Case: Mike Morse (2004) and Ronny Paulino (2003)

Worst Case: David Kelton (2001) and Josh Kroeger (2004)

Chris Marrero

Washington Nationals | 19

ETA: 2010

Marrero had no trouble with South Atlantic League pitching, and the Nationals rewarded him with a promotion to the advanced Single-A Carolina League in July. The results were less impressive there, but he incrementally improved his walk rate and contact rate throughout the season. Marrero hit 23 home runs across the two levels of competition, and he could emerge as an elite power hitter in the major leagues.

Travis Snider

Toronto Blue Jays | 20

ETA: 2010

Snider roped 58 extra-base hits and finished his first full season with a .377 OBP in 2007. He was prone to slumps that involved a lot of strikeouts, but Snider could emerge as baseball's top hitting prospect if he can demonstrate consistency and improvement in that area next year. Although Snider is big and has limited range in the outfield, he has a strong arm and is athletic enough to break into the major leagues as a corner outfielder.

Best Case: Austin Kearns (1999)

Median Case: Eric Duncan (2004) and Delmon Young (2004)

Worst Case: Jeff Winchester (1999) and Jorge Moreno (2000)

Jose Tabata

New York Yankees | 19

ETA: 2010

Tabata is a rare type of young prospect: a teenager who makes contact at a high rate against more experienced pitchers and prefers to drive the ball to the opposite field. Despite occasional comparisons to sluggers, the 5-foot-11 Tabata doesn't hit the ball particularly hard and for the second year in a row was among the league leaders in groundball rate. There is plenty of time for Tabata to evolve and he may develop more power if he stays healthy, but as of now he looks on track to become a high-average hitter with limited power.

Fernando Martinez

New York Mets | 19

ETA: 2009

Martinez suffered from a hand injury in 2007 and never got much of a chance to show that he could handle his aggressive promotion to the Eastern League. If he returns to the Eastern League next year, he still will be among the league's youngest players. Martinez played center field almost exclusively in 2007, but he is unpolished in the field and probably will need to move to left if the Mets continue to push him toward the big leagues.

Projected Center Fielders

Jay Bruce
Cincinnati Reds | 21
ETA: 2008

Bruce is one of baseball's top all-around prospects. He remained in center field for the 2007 season while his bat forced the Reds into aggressively promoting him all the way from the Florida State League to Triple-A Louisville. Bruce posted an OPS above .900 at every level of competition in 2007. The results looked spectacular, but the young left-handed hitter does strike out at an above-average rate. In 2008, Bruce may struggle to put the ball in play and suffer from a disappointing batting average and on-base-average, much as Alex Gordon did last season. This isn't much of a long-term concern, however, and Bruce should make up for his swings and misses with power to all fields while playing his home games in one of the major leagues' most hitter-friendly parks next year.

Jacoby Ellsbury
Boston Red Sox | 24
ETA: Early 2008

Ellsbury started his 2007 season at Double-A Portland and found himself starting playoff games for the Red Sox by October. Ellsbury's minor league career has been characterized by consistency; he has struck out in only 10 to 12% of his plate appearances at every stop in the minor leagues but has never posted a slugging percentage above .434. The speedy contact hitter seems a sure bet to hit .290 with a .350 OBP in the major leagues, though he probably won't collect more than 10 home runs in a season.

Cameron Maybin
Detroit Tigers | 21
ETA: Late 2008

Maybin is exciting to watch; his raw power and exceptional speed have drawn a lot of attention over the past two years. Unfortunately his speed has been hiding some of the shortcomings in his game: Maybin was relying on his legs to beat out infield hits and boost his batting average. At the same time, he was striking out once every four plate appearances and turning in dreadfully low line drive rates. It remains to be seen whether that approach will work at higher levels of competition. Maybin's major league promotion predictably resulted in many strikeouts and ground outs, so he should return to the minor leagues at the beginning of the 2008 season.

Best Case: Kelly Johnson (2002)

Median Case: Scott Moore (2004) and Elijah Dukes (2004)

Worst Case: Xavier Paul (2005) and Ben Johnson (2001)

Andrew McCutchen
Pittsburgh Pirates | 21
ETA: Late 2008

McCutchen found himself hitting .189 at the end of April, but he bounced back and hit over .300 with six home runs over his final two months at Double-A Altoona. The Pirates probably won't be able to resist calling up McCutchen, a fast runner and patient leadoff type of hitter, at some point in 2008.

Colby Rasmus
St. Louis Cardinals | 21
ETA: 2009

The last five 20-year-olds who slugged at least .525 in 300 or more at-bats at the Double-A level are Brandon Wood, Jack Cust, Milton Bradley, Nick Johnson and Eric Chavez. Now we can add Rasmus to that list. Rasmus is a patient hitter who lifted the ball in the air more often than any other Texas League hitter in 2007. He could take over starting center fielder duties for the Cardinals within the next year.

Jordan Schafer
Atlanta Braves | 21
ETA: 2009

Schafer experienced what was widely viewed as a breakout season when he led the minor leagues with 176 hits in 2007. Unfortunately, he is unlikely to hit for a high batting average at higher levels. He still strikes out too often and, like Maybin, enjoyed great success when hitting ground balls. Schafer did improve his power production and walk rate, so 2007 was certainly a step in the right direction. He is a solid center fielder and has a strong enough arm to play any outfield position for the Braves in a couple of years.

Best Case: Matt Holliday (2001)

Median Case: Chris Duncan (2002) and Rob Bowen (2002)

Worst Case: Chris Aguila (2000) and Brian Gordon (2000)

Pitchers

Nick Adenhart
Los Angeles Angels | RHP | 21
ETA: 2009

Adenhart's recovery from Tommy John surgery out of high school could not have been better; he has thrown 150 innings in each of the past two seasons and succeeded against older competition. Adenhart does not project to rack up a lot of strikeouts in his major league career, but at his best he is a good control pitcher who can keep the ball on the ground.

Best Case: Bronson Arroyo (1998) and Ryan Dempster (1998)

Median Case: Tony Armas (1999) and Kevin Gregg (1999)

Worst Case: Nate Cornejo (2000) and Yorman Bazardo (2005)

Brett Anderson
Arizona Diamondbacks | LHP | 20
ETA: 2009

Anderson is a big finesse lefty with impeccable control. He walked only 22 batters in 120 innings while pitching for two Single-A teams in 2007. He also struck out about a quarter of the batters he faced while getting 57% of batted balls hit on the ground.

Best Case: Dontrelle Willis (2001)

Median Case: James Shields (2001) and Ian Snell (2001)

Worst Case: Tyler Clippard (2004) and Chris Narveson (2001)

Homer Bailey
Cincinnati Reds | RHP | 21
ETA: 2008

Bailey's repertoire, which includes a 95 mph fastball and an above-average curveball, has inspired visions of a frontline starter. Unfortunately, Bailey has failed to improve his mediocre control over the past three years and has walked at least 10% of opposing hitters at nearly every stop of his minor league career. He missed time due to injury in the second half of 2007, but should compete for a role in the starting rotation next year.

Best Case: Matt Cain (2005) and Freddy Garcia (1998)

Median Case: Gil Meche (2000) and Dennys Reyes (1998)

Worst Case: Kyle Davies (2005) and Edwin Jackson (2004)

Clay Buchholz
Boston Red Sox| RHP | 23
ETA: 2008

Buchholz earned national attention when he pitched a no-hitter for the Red Sox in only his second major league start. The 23-year-old struck out more than a third of opposing batters at both Double-A and Triple-A this year, and he could make an immediate impact in the Sox starting rotation in 2008. The last starting pitcher prospect to strike out more than 30% of opposing batters over 100 or more innings at Double-A and Triple-A in one year was Francisco Liriano, who won 12 games with a 2.16 ERA for the Twins in the following season.

Trevor Cahill
Oakland Athletics | RHP | 20
ETA: 2010

Cahill's stuff doesn't get scouts excited, but he struck out 27% of opposing batters while demonstrating strong groundball tendencies in 2007. Cahill got better as the season progressed, and he posted a 0.74 ERA in the final month of the season for Single-A Kane County.

Best Case: Jake Peavy (2000)

Median Case: Jorge Julio (1998) and John Patterson (1997)

Worst Case: Fernando Cabrera (2001) and Kris Honel (2002)

Joba Chamberlain
New York Yankees | RHP | 22
ETA: 2008

Chamberlain rocketed all the way from the Florida State League to the majors in four months. At every level, he demonstrated good control and an exceptional ability to get batters to swing and miss. Chamberlain will make full use of his repertoire as a starter in 2008.

Johnny Cueto
Cincinnati Reds | RHP | 22
ETA: 2008

A fastball/slider power pitcher with great control, Cueto struck out five times as many batters as he walked while climbing the rungs of the minor leagues in 2007. He has only four games of Triple-A experience, but Cueto could start the 2008 season on the Reds pitching staff with a strong spring performance.

Best Case: Dustin McGowan (2003)

Median Case: Zach Duke (2004) and Chin-hui Tsao (2003)

Worst Case: Rich Fischer (2002) and Edinson Volquez (2005)

Wade Davis

Tampa Bay Devil Rays | 22

ETA: Late 2008

A third-round pick from the 2004 draft, Davis improved his control in 2007 and continued to strike out about a quarter of the batters he faced. The Rays could use his impressive fastball/curveball combination in their bullpen in 2008.

Best Case: Adam Wainwright (2003)

Median Case: Anibal Sanchez (2005) and Claudio Vargas (2001)

Worst Case: Brandon Claussen (2001) and Jon Rauch (2000)

Luke Hochevar

Kansas City Royals | RHP | 24

ETA: 2008

The first overall pick from the 2006 draft has not lived up to expectations thus far. While he maintained good control, Hochevar struck out only about 20% of Double-A and Triple-A hitters and his stuff induced a lot of fly balls that left the park. His ceiling is perceived to be as a No. 2 starter in the major leagues, but the list of similar performances below indicates that is not a likely outcome given his record in the minor leagues.

Best Case: Aaron Heilman (2002)

Median Case: Jose Capellan (2004) and Ricky Stone (1998)

Worst Case: Adam Bernero (2000) and Scott Randall (1999)

Eric Hurley

Texas Rangers | 22

ETA: 2008

The Rangers' best pitching prospect continued to show above-average command of his repertoire in 2007, but as he started allowing more batted balls against older hitters in the upper minors, home runs became a problem. Hurley demonstrated strong fly ball tendencies in 2007, and he will need to induce more strikeouts if he is to be more than a back-of-rotation starter in the major leagues.

Best Case: Kevin Millwood (1997) and Ben Sheets (2000)

Median Case: Ryan Dempster (1999) and Joel Pineiro (2000)

Worst Case: Sean Douglass (2001) and Wilton Chavez (2003)

Will Inman

San Diego Padres | RHP | 21

ETA: Early 2008

Inman doesn't overpower anyone, but he has used his exceptional command of his fastball to get ahead of hitters in the minor leagues. Unfortunately, he was pitching around batters more often in the higher minor leagues and saw his walk rate go up. He also allowed 13 home runs in only 81 innings pitched at that level, and his tiny 25% groundball rate at San Antonio suggests that home run total might not be a fluke.

Ian Kennedy

New York Yankees | RHP | 23

ETA: 2008

Like Chamberlain, Kennedy started the season in the Florida State League and worked his way up to the major leagues by September. Kennedy doesn't throw his fastball much harder than 90 mph, but he was able to dominate hitters in the lower minor leagues by commanding four pitches. He was a bit more hittable at the Triple-A and major league level and is prone to home run troubles due to his fly ball tendencies. He still projects as an average major league pitcher and could stabilize the back of the Yankees' rotation in 2008.

Best Case: Ramon Ortiz (1999) and Octavio Dotel (1998)

Median Case: Tim Redding (2001)

Worst Case: Jorge de la Rosa (2004) and Dennis Tankersley (2002)

Clayton Kershaw

Los Angeles Dodgers | LHP | 20

ETA: 2009

Kershaw might be the most popular pitching prospect in baseball. The 19-year-old southpaw led the Midwest League with a 32.4% strikeout rate, but he did struggle with control. He walked at least three batters in four of his five late-season starts with Double-A Jacksonville. His ability to control his remarkable stuff could determine if he makes a mark in Los Angeles or if he stalls in the upper minor leagues like wild left-handed Dodgers pitching prospects Scott Elbert and Greg Miller.

Best Case: Joel Zumaya (2003)

Median Case: Boof Bonser (2001) and Homer Bailey (2005)

Worst Case: Matt Riley (1999) and Justin Jones (2003)

Jake McGee

Tampa Bay Devil Rays | LHP | 21

ETA: 2009

McGee led the Florida State League with 145 strikeouts and a 31% strikeout rate in 117 innings pitched with Vero Beach. While he has the makings of a good curveball and changeup, those pitches are still works in progress. His mid-90s fastball could carry him to the Tampa Bay staff within the next year.

Best Case: Scott Kazmir (2004) and Adam Wainwright (2002)

Median Case: Kyle Davies (2004) and Gio Gonzalez (2005)

Worst Case: Clint Nageotte (2002) and Chuck Tiffany (2005)

Adam Miller

Cleveland Indians | RHP | 23

ETA: 2008

While Miller finished his injury-plagued season with an underwhelming 5-4 record and a 4.82 ERA, his fielding-independent ERA of 3.06 tells a story of a pitcher who continues to baffle hitters when he is healthy enough to step on the mound. Miller does a nice job of pitching to contact and inducing ground balls when he needs to. His fastball can reach the high 90s and his slider is a major league out pitch. He just needs to stay healthy to contribute to the Cleveland staff in 2008.

Best Case: Kevin Millwood (1997) and Adam Wainwright (2004)

Median Case: Ramon Ortiz (1999) and Ted Lilly (1998)

Worst Case: Sergio Mitre (2004) and Jason Hammel (2005)

Franklin Morales

Colorado Rockies | LHP | 22

ETA: 2008

Morales is a power lefty who relies on a mid-90s fastball and above-average curveball to get opposing hitters swinging and missing. Morales started the 2007 season in Double-A Tulsa and finished with a successful run against National League hitters in September and October. His fielding-independent ERA at Tulsa was 4.36 and he has walked more than 11% of opposing batters at every stop in his minor league career, so his control may be an obstacle to continued major league success.

Best Case: C.C. Sabathia (2000)

Median Case: Boof Bonser (2003) and Ubaldo Jimenez (2005)

Worst Case: Brad Baker (2002)

The Business of Baseball Report

by Brian Borawski

Welcome to the third *THT Annual* Business Baseball Year in Review. This installment will be slightly different from the first two, which were almost completely dominated by a single story. In both years, the Montreal Expos' relocation to Washington, D.C. was such a saga that it took on a life of its own. In 2007, though, the city and the team had a stadium deal that was acceptable to the league and all that needed to get done from then on was to build the stadium.

In a way, baseball had almost reached what can be considered a golden age in 2006. Attendance was at an all-time high and as the season came to a close, the owners and the Major League Baseball Players' Association concluded the negotiations for a new collective bargaining agreement that seemed downright peaceful. There were still some black marks, like the ongoing investigation into performance-enhancing drugs by former Senator George Mitchell, but it looked like at this point, nobody wanted to mess things up. It was just interesting to see how, if possible, baseball could top itself in 2007.

Stadium Issues

In 2006, several teams made headway towards the construction of new stadiums. The Minnesota Twins, New York Yankees and New York Mets all agreed with their municipalities to get new stadiums done, and the Oakland Athletics were well on their way towards moving to Fremont, Calif., a suburb of San Francisco. There was one holdout though: the Florida Marlins. In yet another setback, the Marlins were unable to secure a stadium deal in 2006, but if you use the Twins as an example, you don't give up after one try or even 10 tries. With the support of the commissioner's office, the Marlins once again went all out to secure a stadium in 2007.

In early February, the Marlins received some backing from Florida Governor Charlie Crist, who said he approved a plan that would use sales tax money to help pay for a new stadium. The plan had Miami-Dade County pitching in $120 million and the Marlins going in for $210 million. That left a $90 million shortfall though, and the hope was that the state would pitch in with $60 million in sales tax receipts to make up most of the gap.

It didn't last long before things hit a wall, and a plan that could have put a new stadium on a nine-acre plot of land near Miami's Government Center fell through in March when the deal appeared to put the construction of a children's courthouse and a new Miami police training academy in jeopardy. This is around the same time that the Orange Bowl was looked at as a viable site to move the team.

In April, Marlins owner Jeffrey Loria got picky and he began to once again pitch for a downtown Miami stadium. While he didn't completely rule out the Orange Bowl idea, he also made a plea that the downtown option would be better for the fans. By late April though, it seemed like once again, the Marlins were going to fall short of getting their new stadium. With a couple of weeks before the legislature adjourned, the state's Revenue Estimating Conference began questioning how beneficial a new stadium would be to the area.

The saying goes, the more things change, the more they stay the same and for the sixth time in eight years, the Florida Legislature failed to give the Marlins what they wanted as the May deadline came and went. It looked like Miami-Dade County might try to solely provide the funding, but like every other plan, it just seemed to fizzle out.

In August, the Marlins' public relations machine began working and the team announced that, with their lease at Dolphin Stadium running out in 2010 and a two-year construction time, something had to be done as soon as possible. They didn't use the word relocation though because that would almost seem hollow after the Marlins backed out on a deal with San Antonio in 2006. MLB Commissioner Bud Selig even made an appearance in the Miami area to meet with government officials; in the past, Bob DuPuy, the league's chief operating officer, provided most of the face time with respect to the Marlins' stadium issue.

Then near the end of August, the Orange Bowl idea resurfaced. The University of Miami came to an agreement to move its home games to Dolphin Stadium, which left the Orange Bowl site all but ripe for the picking. As this story went to press though, nothing had been resolved. The team was still sticking to the downtown stadium idea, and the state wasn't yet willing to pony up the money to bridge the funding gap.

In the meantime, the stadiums for the Yankees and Mets were progressing nicely. The Athletics closed on the land that would be the site for their new stadium in Fremont in May. Only the Twins hit a roadblock before breaking ground: the city had failed to secure the land. The city was able to procure it through eminent domain, but the landowners were fighting for what they thought were fair prices.

The two sides came in over $17 million apart, but the Twins eventually won out as the panel gave the land to the Twins for $23.8 million. There was one dissenting opinion that stated the land was worth $33.2 million, and while that opened the way for an appeal by the landowners, the two sides eventually settled the case at a price of $28 million. As part of their agreement with the county, the Twins pitched in $15 million. The Twins then broke ground on the stadium site in late August and so far, things are progressing as planned.

Aside from the Marlins, everyone pretty much got what they wanted when it came to prospective stadiums. You could see this area dry up because aside from the Marlins, there isn't a lot of noise with regard to teams pitching for new stadiums, mostly because a lot of the ones out there are younger than 15 years old.

Baseball Teams for Sale

The Braves had been up for sale since January 2006, and since April 2006, it was pretty much a certainty that Liberty Media, a Colorado-based media conglomerate, would end up with the Braves. The hang up was a complicated transaction that would basically allow both parties to defer the tax on the transaction, so not only were Time Warner, the owner of the Braves, and Liberty Media at the negotiating table, but a slew of attorneys and MLB were waiting in the wings to make sure they got an ownership group that would play ball.

Finally, in February 2007, Liberty Media and Time Warner came to an agreement, and the sale was sent to the league's office for approval. Finally, on May 17, 2007, the sale was approved by the owners. Time Warner received approximately 68.5 million shares of its own stock from Liberty Media valued at $1.479 billion and in exchange, Liberty Media received the Atlanta Braves, Leisure Arts, Inc., a group of lifestyle titles and $984 million in cash.

While the league was approving the Braves' sale, Tribune Company, the owner of the Chicago Cubs, was purchased by local real estate developer Sam Zell. The Cubs remained with Tribune throughout the 2007 season, but a sale was imminent because Zell already held a stake in the Chicago White Sox. Shortly after the purchase by Zell, Dallas Mavericks owner Mark Cuban surfaced as a potential buyer. Cuban's name was mentioned when the Pirates sale rumor happened in 2006, so that wasn't much of a surprise.

The only other development that revolved around the Cubs sale occurred in September. Apparently the Tribune Company contemplated separating the assets that surrounded the Cubs and selling them separately to make a little bit more cash. Along with its stake in the Cubs, the Tribune is looking to sell its 25% stake in Comcast Sportsnet as well as Wrigley Field. It was estimated that if sold separately, the assets could net the Tribune Company $1 billion as opposed to the $600 million price tag if everything is sold together.

The only other ownership change that occurred in 2007 was with the aforementioned Pittsburgh Pirates. While the team wasn't sold, a change of control did occur in January 2007. Kevin McClatchy gave up the reins to Robert Nutting. McClatchy kept control of the team's day-to-day operations as its chief executive officer, but all other decisions would be made by Nutting. Both McClatchy and Nutting were owners, and the change didn't alter the fortunes of the Pirates, as they suffered their 15th consecutive losing season.

Cable Versus Satellite

In early January, an interesting rumor surfaced that the league and DirecTV were contemplating an exclusive agreement that would make DirecTV the exclusive vendor of the MLB Extra Innings package, which gives viewers the ability to view any MLB games that aren't subject to a local or national blackout. Whether the news was leaked by design or not, the reaction was immediate, as many cable subscribers accused the league of chasing the almighty dollar at the expense of fans, because cable subscribers would then be blocked from the Extra Innings subscription package.

It wasn't until mid-March that the deal was finalized, and as a concession to potential FCC scrutiny, the league gave the cable companies a short window to match the deal with DirecTV. One of the major issues wasn't the actual Extra Innings package itself; it was a new MLB channel that the league was pushing. As part of the deal with DirecTV, the MLB channel would come on line with the basic cable package, and that was something the cable companies didn't appear to be willing to do.

The March 31 deadline came and went, and it was eventually scrapped by the league. In the end, InDe-mand, a consortium of cable operators, came to an agreement with the league that essentially matched the deal with DirecTV. They got it done just a couple of weeks into the season so the Extra Innings package was made available to cable subscribers in the end.

The Mitchell Investigation Grinds On

The investigation into performance-enhancing drugs led by former Senator George Mitchell continued throughout 2007. Similar to the Jason Grimsley plea agreement in 2006, in April 2007 a former clubhouse employee of the New York Mets, Kirk Radomski, pleaded guilty to distributing anabolic steroids to dozens of current and former baseball players over an 11-year period. As part of his plea agreement, Radomski agreed to cooperate with the Mitchell investigation, but the names of the players were redacted from public court files. In June, the Hearst Company, which owns 12 daily newspapers including the *San Francisco Chronicle,* filed a lawsuit saying that the names of the players that Radomski named in his plea agreement should be made public because when the government released the names to Mitchell, who is a private citizen, the public should have been allowed access. Shortly thereafter, the Associated Press followed the Hearst Company with its own lawsuit. Both the government and the Major League Baseball Players' Association filed papers to keep the names of the players redacted, and in late July, a federal magistrate in Phoenix rejected the Associated Press' request to have the names revealed.

While all of this was going on, Jason Giambi opened up his big mouth and all but admitted to using performance-enhancing drugs, or in his words, "stuff." Rumors began to swirl around Giambi that consisted of everything from the Yankees voiding his contract to an extended suspension. Bud Selig highly recommended that Giambi meet with the Mitchell investigators, and in mid-July, he became the first—and to date only—player to voluntarily cooperate with the investigation. For his troubles, Giambi got off without a suspension, and he was able to play out the rest of the season with the Yankees.

In September, one of the feel-good stories of the season was tarnished. Rick Ankiel, the former Cardinals pitching prospect turned slugger, was found to have received a 12-month supply of human growth hormone during the investigation of online drug supplier Signature Pharmacy. Toronto Blue Jays third baseman Troy Glaus and Los Angeles Angels of Anaheim center fielder Gary Matthews, Jr. were also named.

In mid-October, a rumor began to float around that the investigation was almost complete and that a list of players who used performance-enhancing drugs would be released sometime between the end of the 2007 World Series and the beginning of 2008. According to the rumor, some teams asked to see the list beforehand to review it for accuracy, but they were denied access. Regardless, like last year, this story hadn't been resolved as this report went to press.

Baseball Card Wars

In 2006, baseball announced that they'd be granting licenses to just two baseball card companies: Upper Deck and the mainstay in the baseball card industry, Topps. In March 2007, a group led by former Disney chairman Michael Eisner called Tornante Co. agreed to purchase Topps for $385 million in a deal that would leave management largely intact.

Whether it was just the ability to take out a competitor or just because it was a good deal, Upper Deck then attempted to take over Topps. Upper Deck was offering $10.75 for each share of Topps, whereas the offer made by Eisner's Tornante Co., came in at only $9.75. It seemed like a slam dunk, but the management made life so difficult for Upper Deck that they eventually withdrew their tender offer because Topps management was withholding key information during the due diligence process.

In October 2007, the sale finally went through and Tornante Co. and a second company called Madison Dearborn Partners LLC got Topps for $9.75 a share. The sale was contested by a few board members who thought the sales price was too low considering Upper Deck was willing to pony up $10.75 a share. The sale was approved by a razor-thin margin with just 53.4% voting in favor of the sale, but that was still enough to push things forward.

MLB Goes International

More than any other year, it appeared that MLB and its teams were trying to stretch their reach overseas to places they had never gone before. Even prior to 2007, it appeared that the league was looking more and more at expanding its overseas presence, and in November 2006, MLB opened up an office in China to promote baseball.

In January, two different groups went on international excursions. The first was headed by Yankees president Randy Levine and Yankees general manager Brian Cashman, both of whom traveled to China to both promote the Yankees brand as well as explore the possibility of opening a baseball academy in China.

The other excursion was headed up by New York Mets general manager Omar Minaya. He and a group that included former major league players Dave Winfield, Bob Watson, Dusty Baker, Reggie Smith and Dave Stewart traveled to Ghana to donate baseball equipment and survey land so they could build baseball fields and set up a four-team league. Minaya was impressed with Ghana's performance in the soccer World Cup, and he was hoping to harness some of that athleticism and hopefully turn it into baseball talent.

While not MLB related, a six-team baseball league in Israel was formed with the hope that with some success, the country could field a team in the 2009 World Baseball Classic. The league did have its share of growing pains, and it was plagued by everything from poor playing fields to payment delays and shortages of equipment. Former major league pitcher Ken Holtzman went over to Israel to manage one of the teams, but he eventually left with two weeks before the end of the season and he wouldn't supply an answer as to his abrupt departure.

In June, the Yankees announced that they had received a sponsorship deal from a Chinese company, the first ever by a major league team. The Yiii Group, the largest dairy company in China, got some signage at Yankee Stadium as well as a spot in the Yankees' official game program. This came just two weeks after the Yankees became the first team to sign a player from China.

In August, the Puerto Rican Winter League cancelled its season. A month later, Dr. David Bernier, the Puerto Rican Secretary of Sport, outlined a proposal that would remove Puerto Rico from the First-Year Players Draft because teams were largely ignoring Puerto Rico in favor of other Latin American countries; teams could go elsewhere and not have to deal with the draft. The report was to be analyzed, but nothing has been determined yet.

Finally, in late September, it was announced that the Chinese National Team would be the first national team to play in the Arizona Fall League. Team China played each of the six Arizona Fall League teams, and to prepare for the contests, they competed in 16 Instructional League games. Former manager Jim Lefebvre and pitching coach Bruce Hurst were slated to be in charge of the Chinese team.

Fantasy Stats Case Wins Appeal

In 2006, Major League Baseball Advanced Media (MLBAM) lost its lower court battle with CBC Distribution and Marketing, Inc. At issue was the use of player names and statistics for fantasy baseball, an industry that's estimated to generate more than $1.5 billion in revenue annually. MLBAM was trying to control the use of fantasy statistics; CBC filed a lawsuit contesting whether MLBAM could dictate who could and could not use baseball statistics and player names in fantasy baseball leagues.

In August 2006, United States District Court Judge Mary Ann Medler upheld CBC's argument and ruled that MLBAM could not force businesses to pay for baseball statistics. She claimed that CBC hadn't violated the player's claimed right of publicity and that MLBAM could not stop CBC from offering fantasy baseball leagues using MLB statistics.

In September 2006, both MLBAM and the MLBPA appealed the decision and in October of 2007, in a split 2-1 decision, the 8th U.S. Circuit Court of Appeals panel upheld the ruling of Judge Mary Ann Medler. The one dissenting opinion came from Judge Steven Colloton, and while he didn't disagree with CBC's claim of First Amendment protection, he did take issue with the fact that CBC initially signed a contract with MLBAM to pay fees but then backed out and filed a lawsuit instead.

Attendance and the Almighty Dollar

For the fourth consecutive season, MLB broke its attendance record with 79,502,524 fans compared to 76,042,787 last year. Along with the overall attendance record, MLB broke the average attendance record as well; 32,785 fans made it out to each ballgame on average. This broke the record that had stood since the strike in 1994.

In addition, five of the top 15 largest attendance days ever occurred in 2007, including July 28, when 717,478 fans paid to see a baseball game. That broke the previous record of 640,412 set back on July 3, 1999. That 1999 record was almost broken just a week earlier on July 21 when the now third-largest attendance day occurred. On that day, 639,628 fans paid to see a baseball game.

Eight baseball teams set franchise attendance records in 2007. The Detroit Tigers eclipsed the 3 million mark for the first time in franchise history, and they broke an attendance record that had held since the last time they won the World Series in 1984. The Los Angeles

Dodgers went over the 3.8 million fan mark for the first time; their 3,857,036 total was the fifth highest total in National League history. The Yankees broke the American League attendance record with 4,271,083 fans while the Boston Red Sox, Chicago Cubs, Milwaukee Brewers, New York Mets and St. Louis Cardinals all set franchise records as well. Ten different teams went over the 3 million mark in attendance while 24 went over the 2 million mark.

Minor League Baseball also broke its attendance record with 42,812,812, which was 1.1 million fans more than the record set the previous year. Thirteen of the 15 minor leagues showed an increase in attendance, while the Pacific Coast League, the Midwest League, the South Atlantic League and the Pioneer League all set attendance records in 2007. The two Triple-A leagues, the International League and the Pacific Coast League have combined to set records in seven of the past eight years.

To go along with increases in attendance, money came in the door hand over fist. MLB.com had record traffic in 2007 and its owner, Major League Baseball Advanced Media, continued to be a cash cow for the league. The numbers weren't final when I finished this report, but it was estimated that MLB would earn somewhere between $5.6 billion and $5.8 billion. Bud Selig even said he hoped to one day surpass the National Football League in revenue, which was something that would have been unheard of just five years ago.

Fantasy Baseball: Thinking Ahead

by Derek Carty

When fantasy baseball owners prepare for their draft or auction, the first thing most do is come up with a set of projected numbers for each player. While this is a great first step, it is often the final step for fantasy owners. This is a huge mistake.

It is not enough to simply know that a player is good or bad. It isn't even enough to have a set of projected numbers. You have to know every player's value in relation to every other player. Virtually any player would be worth drafting or auctioning for the right price, and virtually any player could be passed up for the wrong price, regardless of skill level.

For example, Alex Rodriguez figures to be the top-rated fantasy player going into 2008. Even so, if the bidding in a standard fantasy auction goes up to $60, you can be sure I won't be involved. There is little chance he would provide positive value at this price. In my opinion, Carlos Zambrano is generally overvalued. If the bidding stops at $1, though, I'm bidding $2.

That's why this article will be referring to players in terms of being generally overvalued or undervalued. It won't be the case in every league, but this should indicate a player's true value in relation to his market value. We'll be talking a lot more about player valuation at the THT Fantasy Focus blog this offseason, eventually systematically assigning numeric values to every player using many factors. For now, though, this should get your feet wet.

First, let's look at some attributes that fantasy players tend to overrate. First is past success. Past success does not equal future success. We need to look beneath the surface and decide whether a player's past results are repeatable.

I'd also warn against getting too attached to a player because of his name or his star appeal. Maybe a player is exciting to watch or fun to cheer for or has an engaging personality, but these things don't win you fantasy championships. I'm sure you've heard that going with your first instinct is best, but in my experience, the guys who do this wind up at the bottom of the standings.

The last things I'll mention here are a couple of stats. In fantasy baseball, batting average tends to get overrated because it is the only offensive stat (in a traditional 5x5 league) that is a ratio instead of a number. But a guy with a high batting average yet few homers isn't necessarily better than a guy with a lot of homers and a low batting average.

On the flip side, strikeouts are underrated. Not only are they a category unto themselves, but they have a great effect on ERA and WHIP. You could finish in the top half of your league in strikeouts, ERA, and WHIP (and possibly wins) simply by drafting guys who are at the top of the strikeout rate leader board. You'll notice a lot of these guys are also toward the top in ERA and WHIP, but the real problem here is that guys with low strikeout rates get drafted too high (see: Chien-Ming Wang, Barry Zito).

Now let's look at some players.

Likely to be Overvalued

Pitchers

Carlos Zambrano | CHC | SP

Zambrano's 2007 season went from bad to worse. His strikeout rate dropped more than a point from 2006 as he put up a first-half strikeout-to-walk ratio of 1.98. In the second half, his strikeout rate got even worse and his walk rate blew up. Despite this, Zambrano managed a 3.95 ERA that should have been higher; his FIP ERA was 4.55. I expect Zambrano's strikeouts to come back in 2008—at least to some extent—but his problem has always been his high walk rate, and he hasn't shown any signs of improving it. He'll have a chance to improve going into his age-27 season, but so will a number of other guys that aren't being ranked in the top 10 among starting pitchers. Too risky for his hype.

Brad Penny | LAD | SP

Penny was aided by an incredibly low home run per fly ball rate (second in the majors) that allowed him to post a 3.03 ERA despite a 4.38 xFIP. The home run per fly ball rate will surely regress in 2008, causing those who draft Penny early to lose a great deal of value. He posted the worst strikeout rate of his career and his worst walk rate since 2002. What's even worse is that his first half was better than the second. These rates could bounce back a bit, but even if they reach 2006 levels, Penny is simply not the top 20 starter many are billing him as for 2008.

Chien-Ming Wang | NYY | SP

Being a Yankee has resulted in Wang being drastically overvalued. His ground ball tendencies and 94 mph fastball allow many people to look past his poor strikeout-to-walk ratios, but one year this will catch up with him. Wang improved his strikeout rate in 2007, but there is no way a pitcher who strikes out fewer than five batters per nine innings should be ranked in the top 25. This fact alone makes him unattractive. Besides, a low strikeout rate directly increases a pitcher's WHIP and has a large effect on his ERA.

Barry Zito | SF | SP

People just haven't learned their lesson with Zito. He's a fly ball pitcher who hasn't posted a strikeout-to-walk ratio above 2.00 since 2004. In addition, his team has a terrible offense and is casting out its best hitter this offseason. His 4.94 FIP in 2006 barely improved in 2007 (4.79) with the move to the National League. Despite all of this, I'm still seeing him ranked in the top 40 starting pitchers for 2008. Fantasy baseball isn't about picking guys who have rock-star personas attached; it's about making the pick that will provide the most value. Zito is not the right choice if you're trying to get value.

Brian Bannister | KC | SP

While many have criticized the Mets for trading Bannister, he really was playing over his head in 2007. The comparison between his 3.71 ERA and 4.52 FIP explains a lot. He, essentially, was Chien-Ming Wang without the ground balls: a strikeout rate below five and a strikeout-to-walk ratio below two. Not exactly a formula for success. It also doesn't help that he has the Royals offense instead of the Yankees for support. His .264 BABIP was ridiculously low and will surely regress in 2008. While not everyone is buying into the Bannister hype, he is still likely to be overvalued in drafts and auctions. He is not a top 50 or 60 starting pitcher and doesn't figure to provide much value in any one category. Like Wang, he'll get significant negative value in the strikeout category, but unlike Wang, he won't be able to compensate with wins.

Hitters

Reggie Willits | LAA | OF

Willits took everyone by surprise in 2007, bursting onto the scene and posting a .391 OBP and 27 steals in just 136 games. He figures to take a step backward in 2008, though. His .363 BABIP is unsustainable, and his lack of power to make up for a drop there will cause his batting average to plummet. He is great at drawing walks, so he'll be helpful with steals and runs, but a two-category player shouldn't be among the top 50 or 60 outfielders. A guy like Kenny Lofton will help in three categories—assuming he finds some regular playing time—and will be valued far less.

Jorge Posada | NYY | C

Posada's reputation as a power hitting catcher has been maintained in recent years by Yankee Stadium's right field fence, 314 feet at its shortest point. At 36, though, Posada can no longer hit many balls past deeper fences. If he doesn't remain in New York, there is a real chance his home run production will fall off a cliff. A drop in his home run rate and a regression on his ridiculous .389 BABIP would hurt Posada's batting average as well. His RBIs and runs will depend on what team he goes to, but if Posada isn't in the Bronx next year, he looks a good bet to be a bust if drafted as top five catcher.

Howie Kendrick | LAA | 2B

Kendrick came to the majors reputed to be a great contact hitter. While this may be the case, there are reasons for concern. The first is that he has had BABIPs of .329 and .382 in his first two years. The .329 mark could be legit, but the .382 is not. He hasn't supported either mark with line drives. While he is still likely above average in terms of converting balls in play into hits, he doesn't bring much else to fantasy teams. He doesn't have much power or speed, hurting his prospects for home runs, stolen bases and RBIs. He rarely walks, and with a drop in BABIP (and batting average), he won't be able to score many runs. This leaves Kendrick as a guy who will struggle to hit .300 and won't be able to do much else. I don't see Kendrick as a top 10 second baseman, as many do. I'd much prefer a guy like Ryan Theriot, who can help in three categories, can also play shortstop, and isn't even cracking some top 25 lists.

Likely to be Undervalued

Pitchers

Tim Lincecum | SF | SP

As a rookie, Lincecum displayed a fantastic ability to strike out major league batters, but his walk rate was below league average. Despite this, Lincecum posted a FIP of 3.56. With a modest improvement in his control, Lincecum would have the chance to be a top 10 fantasy starter. He already will get you great value with strikeouts, and improved control would better his ERA and WHIP prospects. The only downside to Lincecum is his poor offensive support. Even so, he is a good bet to outperform his market value as a top 30 starter.

Dave Bush | MIL | SP

A favorite sleeper for a lot of owners in 2007, Bush disappointed and was even dropped in a lot of leagues. While he posted a 5.12 ERA, his xFIP was a solid 4.43. His strikeout rate regressed a little from 2006, but his

3.05 strikeout-to-walk ratio was still quite good. Even if he doesn't pitch like he did in 2006, Bush is still better than a lot of the 70 or 80 pitchers ranked ahead of him on many lists. Several owners will be gun-shy, and a lot were never high on him. As such, Bush figures to provide good value in 2008.

Scott Baker | MIN | SP

He's certainly not one of the first guys you would think to mention in a conversation about good pitchers, although he may be if he helps you win a 2008 fantasy championship. He shouldn't be counted on to anchor your staff, but Baker is barely making the top 100 starters on many preliminary rankings; he should be much higher on your list. He has great control and can post a league average strikeout rate, giving him a 3.52 strikeout-to-walk ratio in 2007. He had a 3.94 FIP this year, and I don't see any reason why his actual ERA can't get there in 2008. He'll be a great pick in the later rounds of the draft.

Andrew Sonnanstine | TB | SP

Sonnanstine is a pitcher in the Baker mold (peripherals-wise) but with much less hype. He showed top-notch, if somewhat inconsistent, control in his first crack at the majors and a league-average ability to strike batters out. His 5.85 ERA masked his 4.35 FIP, which is good news for the opportunistic fantasy owner. For a guy who isn't even making top 100 lists, Sonnanstine is capable of putting up some great numbers and giving you excellent value. The downside to Sonnanstine is the appalling defense behind him, which led to a .333 BABIP this year. While he is somewhat risky, I'd be hard-pressed to find a pitcher I'd rather take at the end of my draft or for a couple of bucks at auction.

Hitters

Frank Thomas | TOR | DH

Thomas, despite his age and limitations, is still a very good ballplayer. The past two years he has put up very good contact rates for a power hitter and is capable of posting adequate batting averages. His HitTracker profile shows that he still has a lot of power, and he hits in a pretty good lineup for RBIs. Despite this, I've seen Thomas left off lists of the top 10 fantasy DHs. While using him to fill your utility spot hinders your team's flexibility, I think the excellent value Thomas will provide late in a draft more than makes up for it.

Rafael Furcal | LAD | SS

It's been said that a sore ankle caused Furcal trouble all year. It's also been said that Furcal and his doctors are expecting it to be completely healed by spring training. His opposite-field power disappeared this year, and

he wasn't hitting his pulled homers quite as far as he did in 2006. If the ankle truly was the source of the troubles, Furcal could provide good value to his 2008 owners. A healthy ankle would bring more steals, and an increased home run rate and a slight increase in his BABIP (which seems likely) would allow Furcal to approach .300 again. Furcal is risky, but the reward would be a four-category contributor exceeding his top 15 billing, possibly resulting in a top seven shortstop.

Jack Cust | OAK | OF

One of the feel-good stories of 2007, Cust still doesn't get much respect from fantasy players, probably because he is a "Three True Outcomes"-type player; even Adam Dunn hasn't gotten much respect until this year. Cust's .366 BABIP will drop some, and his batting average will hurt you, but he should still be helpful with homers, RBIs and runs given regular playing time. With other three category guys like Juan Pierre and Nick Swisher cracking some top 30 lists, Cust figures to be a pretty good value in the top 70.

Nick Johnson | WAS | 1B

He didn't play at all in 2007 due to a broken leg and subsequent hip troubles, but he was excellent in 2006. It is difficult to say how these injuries will affect him, but if he can improve even a little on 2006 he would be a fantastic bargain. His power was excellent and showed the potential for improvement, and his incredible walk rate allowed him to score 100 runs while batting cleanup for the Nationals. He has consistently good BABIPs, so it isn't ridiculous to see Johnson as a real four-category threat. The injury concerns and the poor Washington offense have him outside the top 25 on some first base lists, but he has the potential to be much better. Keep in mind, though, that he isn't even guaranteed to be ready for spring training.

When people think about winning a fantasy baseball league, they generally think about picking the right players. While this is certainly the first step, fantasy baseball is actually much more complex.

To win in a competitive league, you need to incorporate not only good player evaluation and valuation, but the ability to create a strategy and think creatively. During the offseason at THT Fantasy Focus (http://www.hardballtimes.com/main/fantasy), we'll be going into much more detail on players, digging deeper into valuation principles, explaining strategies, and discussing many other fantasy topics. If you're serious about winning next year, make it a priority to stop by.

The Growing Game Abroad, The Changing Game at Home

by Jonathan Helfgott

To the avid baseball fan, it comes as no surprise that the quintessentially "American" game of baseball has a vibrant and thriving tradition outside of our country's borders. Fans have been cheering for guys named Ramirez, Martinez and Rodriguez for decades without thinking twice about the origins of their favorite players. The story of Roberto Clemente, the first Latin American player inducted into the Hall of Fame and an internationally recognized humanitarian, warms the hearts of baseball fans and serves as a reminder of the power of sport to give rise not just to icons, but to heroes.

Yet despite the widespread knowledge of the existence of an international aspect to the game of baseball, very few people know anything about the game outside of the United States. Unlike professional soccer, where the game is played on multiple grand stages across Europe and nationalism gives the sport one of its most compelling subtexts, baseball has one stage for all the world's elite talent. At least in this country, that seems to satisfy all but the most hardcore fans.

The World Baseball Classic in 2006 marked the first time baseball's widespread international appeal was brought to the forefront as a compelling narrative. Though concerns persist about how the March tournament affected players' readiness for the upcoming season, the event was a rousing success. Casual fans learned that they actually play baseball in places like Australia and South Africa. Peter Moylan, a pharmaceutical representative from Sydney, got the opportunity to resurrect his career and enjoyed a successful season in the Atlanta Braves' bullpen a year later. The world got to see the Cuban national team face off against the best players from other countries rather than simply dominating teams full of overmatched youngsters in international competition. Above all though, the origins of major league baseball talent were displayed before a large American audience for the first time.

Two full seasons removed from the inaugural WBC, the game has continued its rapid international growth, and players are popping up in minor league farm systems from places that would shock the casual observer. This piece will examine the growth of the international game, what it means for the sport's future, and how it affects the countries where the game's significance stretches far beyond which team will win the "World" Series each year.

Laissez Faire Economics and International Scouting

To understand the world of international baseball scouting, one must first understand the system that brings players from their home countries to chase the dream of playing major league baseball. Amateur ballplayers from the United States, Canada and Puerto Rico all have to go through a draft process that affords them considerable protection under baseball's collective bargaining agreement. The agreement requires that players graduate high school before signing, sets strict rules for the acquisitions of agents, and caps the percentage of a player's signing bonus that an agent can demand for his services.

In contrast, the only restriction on signing international talent is that the player must turn 17 before the end of the season in which he is signed. Without guarantees of equal access or oversight of the actions of trainers and agents, the international scouting game is somewhat of an economic free for all.

The Dominican Republic: International Baseball's Standard-Bearer

While Venezuela and Cuba both placed players at the game's highest level before Ozzie Virgil became the first Dominican to crack a major league roster in 1958, the Dominican Republic (along with Puerto Rico, which has since moved to the Rule 4 draft) is where MLB's international scouting divisions developed the international academy system.

To say that Dominicans are passionate about the game of baseball is a little like saying the Grand Canyon is a decent sized hole in the ground. Fifty fans at a rookie-level Dominican Summer League game make as much noise as a crowd of thousands in the United States—assisted in part by noisemakers, drums, trumpets and the corrugated tin roofs of the fan seating sections.

In the Dominican Republic, the nation's most widely circulated newspaper, the *Listin Diario*, routinely publishes the names of youth league MVPs, occasionally publishing the names of players as young as seven. In August 2006, while I was living in Santo Domingo, the paper ran an article complete with color photo about an 8-year-old named Juan Carlos Custodio who threw a no-hitter in a small private league's semifinal game.

The attention paid to players at such an early age may seem excessive, but the reality is that the road to the major leagues for the average Latin American player begins around the age of seven. For kids in large cities like Santo Domingo, the first step is to find a local trainer who will agree to accept them into a program. For the next nine years, the most committed players drill for hours on end. Some go to school, most do not. The system makes no demands either way.

For all of that training, it is extremely rare for a child in an organized training program to actually play complete games. Kids in the big cities have to play in the middle of streets, and rural areas lack proper fields. Equipment is a luxury, and the elite private training programs are more concerned with drills and developing athleticism than staging games. "The problem with these kids is that they never play baseball," Milwaukee Brewers' Latin American Coordinator Fernando Arango said. "They only practice."

As for the training programs themselves, there is a huge degree of disparity.

Flavio Ortega, the lone trainer in the small town of Monte Criste on the Haitian border, works with anyone who comes by. His field was built by the city and a pack of goats keeps it free of weeds. It is not easy for a trainer in such a remote location to draw scouts, so he spends a lot of time ferrying players to larger facilities in Santiago and Santo Domingo. He is a beloved figure in town, and nearly everyone you meet seems to have trained with him at one point or another.

José Medina, who shares a field with another trainer behind Santo Domingo's *Estadio Olímpico*, has a similar outlook. An independent organization (the *Associación Independiente de Programas de Beísbol*) assigns kids to Medina and he trains them six days a week. Through his membership in the *Associación Independiente*, he agrees to take only 10% of any signing bonuses his players might earn. Medina, whose most successful pupil is Cleveland Indians starting pitcher Fausto Carmona, is unlikely to negotiate more than one or two contracts a year. However, he is quick to point out that the work has other rewards. "The kids know that I won't train them if they don't attend school," he told me one day during a break from training. "And even if they don't sign, at least they are here and not on the streets."

Wealthier, more prestigious trainers called *buscones* (literal translation: seeker) develop relationships with agents in the United States and offer a much larger range of services to attract the best athletes in the country. Their players are housed, fed and given gym memberships. Their lives are closely monitored, every aspect of their training supervised, and the expectation is that their bonuses will be higher when it comes time to sign.

Generally, kids do not sign contracts with prominent *buscones* until around age 12. To find athletes with the potential to sign large bonuses, the *buscones* employ people whose job is to scour the countryside for promising talent. On any given day, it is common to see a dozen such individuals prowling the grounds near programs like the ones run by Ortega and Medina, looking to lure the best athletes away. Because of this, in certain circles the word *buscón* is treated the same as the word *ladrón*, meaning thief.

The *buscones*, who expect to make a significant amount of money from the players they represent, have different priorities than those of low-level trainers like Ortega and Medina. In a system with zero oversight, corruption flourishes. In the best-case scenario, the *buscones* feed their players well, properly represent them, and negotiate fair market value contracts in exchange for a cut no less than 30%. Hector "Eliud" Acevedo, who runs a private training program with his father out of the University of Santo Domingo, was quick to defend the higher fees his program charges its players. "Honestly, I think [a 30% cut] is fair," Acevedo told me. "We invest a lot of money in our players. When they don't sign, we ask nothing from them and we lose our investment. To make a living, we have to take a big cut from the players who sign."

While the ethics of the *buscón* system under the best conditions can be debated, it clearly has major flaws. Major league scouts routinely pay *buscones* to give them exclusive access to players they like. Rumors float through Latin American baseball circles about which *buscones* pump their kids full of steroids or change identification papers to falsify ages, which ones have been shot for stealing clients, and worst of all, which ones force kids to perform sexual favors in return for training and representation.

"It's a mess," said José Escarramán, president of the *Associación Independiente*, who dreams of a day when all private trainers will be forced to follow the same regulations. "We can pass laws, but they do nothing. Dominicans are not used to following rules."

Clearly, the simple act of signing a contract is a huge ordeal for an international player. Once he has navigated this process though, he finds himself facing a whole new set of challenges.

The odds of any player signed to a professional contract making the major leagues are slim. Those odds go down considerably for players signed at the age of 16—an age when it is virtually impossible to tell which promising kid will mature into a man capable of throwing or hitting a 95 mph fastball. The vast majority of them don't make it.

"[The players who get released] come home and do nothing," Escarramán said. "They have no education, no skills, and they come home depressed. Maybe one in 100 of these kids will make the major leagues. I think Major League Baseball needs to help us find a way to deal with the other 99. The first step is increasing the signing age from 16 to 18. At least then kids can graduate from high school before they sign."

Jaime Torres, an agent whose work representing Cuban defectors (including major leaguers José Contreras and Yuniesky Betancourt) brings him to the Dominican Republic often, expressed a similar opinion. "These kids have such huge egos," Torres said. "When they get their first contract, they buy cars and fancy clothes and walk around their home towns saying *'estoy firmado'* [I'm signed]. When they get released, they feel like they have failed and can never go home. You hear stories of kids trying to kill themselves after they get released. It is a bad situation."

Though reforming such a flawed system seems like a daunting task, the last decade has seen a number of positive strides. The *Associación Independiente de Programas de Beísbol* succeeded in passing a law capping the fees of trainers and *buscones* at 10%. At this point, enforcement is nearly impossible. Many trainers have not heard of the law, and scouts and *buscones* alike laugh at the idea that it will ever be applied successfully. Nevertheless, attempts at oversight are a positive step.

The influx of agents like Scott Boras into the Dominican game, while doing little to fix the problems with the *buscón* system, has driven the international market closer to the standards set by the Rule 4 amateur draft.

On the MLB side, teams are beginning to realize the importance of education in their Latin American academies to prepare their players for life in the United States. All teams offer some form of English instruction, though most do not require that their players attend. The New York Yankees hire private educators to teach a four-course program that all players must attend and the Cleveland Indians pay to send their kids to a private school near their academy in Boca Chica on the country's Southern coast.

In the United States, colleges and four-year universities are working to establish connections with local trainers to bring Latin American players over on student visas.

None of these developments provide a definitive solution to the problem, but the system is much better now than it was even 10 years ago. "It usually feels like we are not accomplishing much, but really I am happy," Escarramán told me after informing me that he had secured a spot for a Santo Domingo player at Miami-Dade Community College. For now, small steps will have to do.

Exporting the System: Baseball in Australia

While the Dominican Republic largely established the rules by which the international scouting game is played, the recent history of scouting in Australia is an interesting counterpoint. The sport has existed in Australia for over a century. For decades, cricket players used baseball as a way to stay in shape during the offseason. Operating on a club system sustained by government land grants and the work of small groups of devotees, baseball has survived as a niche sport in an extremely lighthearted and nurturing environment. Only in the past 15 years or so have major league scouts realized Australia's potential as a source of major league talent.

A relatively wealthy country, Australian baseball players do not face the same challenges as Latin American players for whom baseball is their one shot at wealth. However, Australians are subject to the same regulations, or lack thereof, as players in any other country not covered by the rules of the amateur draft. When scouts began discovering Australian talent, they pounced on an opportunity to acquire players who had little concept of their worth. "In the mid-90s, I saw a lot of players who were getting used and abused," Australian player agent Trevor Jarrett explains. "I have a lot of friends who are scouts, but the truth is the scouting profession encourages a lot of dishonesty. It is a scout's job to sign good players for as little as possible. I decided it was time for someone to step in and act on players' behalves."

Jarrett was not the first agent to negotiate a lucrative contract for an Australian baseball player. That title goes to Scott Boras, who represented infielder Glenn Williams in 1993 and negotiated a $1 million contract with the Atlanta Braves. In representing the vast majority of Australian signings in the past decade, however, Jarrett has been instrumental in driving up the price for Australian talent. Jarrett runs an open business, posting his standard contract on his website for all potential clients to examine. He describes his negotiating method succinctly. "When I get an offer, I call every scout I know and tell them about it. If they want my player, they'll beat the offer," he said. "Teams don't like it when I do that, but it works well."

Jarrett's methods are an interesting example of how a little openness can dramatically alter the nature of a process that thrives on secrecy.

Australian baseball itself has hit a bit of a lull after a dramatic rise in the mid-90s. In 1988 a group of entrepreneurs started a professional league that featured several players from the American minor leagues. The league brought baseball to Australia on a level never seen before, and it stayed afloat for 10 seasons before eventually going bankrupt in 1999. Though the league died out, many credit it with the measurable increase in Australians playing affiliated baseball. "The league was huge for Australian interest in baseball," Joe Clarke, author of the book *The History of Australian baseball* told me. "All of the players who are close to the major leagues now, guys like Chris Snelling and Justin Huber, they all grew up watching the Australian Baseball League. If baseball is going to really take off, we need something like that again."

While nothing has been officially confirmed, Major League Baseball appears ready to fund a revival of an Australian professional league to be played during our winter. Rumors abound that the league is set to open as early as the winter of 2008. With international investment, the prospect of a successful Australian professional baseball league and another renaissance for the game down under appear greatly improved.

Europe and South Africa: New Frontiers

While the past few decades of international scouting have been first and foremost an attempt to integrate the entire baseball playing world into the Major League system, the past decade has seen new efforts by MLB to spark and cultivate interest in the game where little existed previously. Nowhere has this been more prevalent than in Europe and Africa—most notably South Africa. In 1995, Major League Baseball opened an office in London. This office is responsible for the game's development in both Europe and Africa, which pretty accurately reflects the relative strength of the game in the western half of the Eastern Hemisphere.

Though the overall European and African presence in affiliated baseball remains small, the number of players who have signed out of the Major League Baseball European Academy has increased every year since the academy's inception in 2005—from three that year to seven in 2006 to nine this past year.

"Holland still is producing the most professional-ready players, [but] the Czechs, Italians and even the Germans are quickly gaining ground," Jason Holoway, manager of game development for MLB's European office explained. "The Dutch have a semi-professional league which is at least of the quality of good university baseball, maybe even the low minors." In European competition, the Dutch league shares its supremacy with the semi-pro Italian league. The two countries have traded championships in the two largest European tournaments every year since 1968.

The Seattle Mariners and Minnesota Twins are currently the teams most actively scouting European talent, and as players like Florida's Rick Vanden Hurk and Seattle's Gregory Halman continue to demonstrate major league tools, European representation in affiliated baseball should increase dramatically.

While Major League Baseball's efforts in Europe are already bearing fruit, South Africa is the real gold mine. "Nowhere in Europe or the rest of Africa has the game spread as quickly as it has in South Africa," Holowaty said. "The elite levels in Holland and Italy are a little better right now, but according to our numbers, there are over 300,000 kids playing baseball in South Africa right now. That is more than all of Europe combined."

The explosion of baseball in South Africa is a result of the combined efforts of Major League Baseball and the South African government, which has long considered sports an integral part of raising the nation's international profile. Major League Baseball and the South African Baseball Union have installed organized baseball in roughly 1,300 of the country's 28,000 schools, primarily in poorer neighborhoods where the children are overwhelmingly black and colored (not a slur, but rather an ethnic identity officially recognized by the South African census).

Like Australia, baseball has long existed in South Africa as a club sport played by a small minority of the nation's citizens. Nick Dempsey, the first South African player to play in the minor leagues, learned about the game from his grandfather, who discovered it while in a

POW camp with Americans in World War II. Roderick Siljeur, South African baseball's youth commissioner, came to the game a different way: "The local cricket club cost 15 rand a year," Siljeur said. "Baseball only cost 2 rand a year, so I grew up playing baseball."

Though baseball has had a presence for decades, the explosion of baseball in South African schools could not exist without the efforts of Major League Baseball. MLB began investing resources into South African baseball in the early '90s through something called the Pitch Hit and Run program. Holowaty estimated that over the past 12 years or so, MLB had spent over $10 million dollars on various development tools in South Africa. The sheer numbers make baseball officials optimistic that many South African players will eventually make their way to the major leagues. "This will eventually be a huge source of talent," Holowaty said. "There is so much athleticism and passion in this country. [South Africa] will not be a huge resource in the next two years, but it will be eventually."

The future of South African baseball is up in the air. As Holowaty acknowledges, "…there are no agents in this country." Major League Baseball is first and foremost a business, and "up to now, the South Africans who have signed have come very cheap."

As of now, though, baseball is unquestionably a positive influence in the lives of many South African children. "Our motto for a long time has been simply, 'Let the Children Play,' Bennett said. "With everything that has happened in this country, just let the children play. We are not concerned with producing millionaire baseball players."

In 2009, the South African Department of Sport will open the first national sports academy, which will house elite athletes in 19 officially targeted sports, including baseball. The academy will house 30 baseball players and provide them with state of the art training facilities as well as a free boarding school education.

In his enthusiasm over the growth of baseball in South Africa, Bennett boasted that Alan Klein, author of the book *Sugarball: The American Dream, the Dominican Game* is on record with a prediction that South Africa will be "the next Dominican Republic." Those familiar with the way scouting has operated in that country might find that an odd thing to be proud of. In any case, the growth of baseball in South Africa— particularly the character of that growth—will be one of the most fascinating developments in the global game in the next few decades.

Back to Latin America: What Will Happen to Cuba?

Baseball is casting a wider net than ever before to draw talent from all over the world and change the face of the game. However, the country with the longest and most storied baseball tradition outside of the United States is the one most likely to profoundly change the game at the major league level in the next few years.

Scouts and analysts have long debated the effect of a potential "opening up" of the Cuban baseball market for years. Long thought to be host to the greatest living ballplayers never to don a major league uniform, the merely modest successes of Cuban league standouts like José Contreras and Liván Hernández has left some doubting the greatness of Cuban baseball.

When discussing Cuban league veterans making immediate transitions to the major leagues, such doubts are warranted. However, if Cuba were to truly open up, if its 16-year-olds were eligible to sign professional contracts and major league teams allowed to open academies on the island, there is little reason to doubt that Cuba's influence will be at least as profound as that of the Dominican Republic.

Cuba has a larger population than the D.R. (over 11 million citizens to the Dominican Republic's 8 million), and while other sports like basketball have begun to captivate the interest of young Dominicans, Cubans play baseball to the virtual exclusion of every other sport. As Cuban baseball historian Peter Bjarkmann points out, "The young athletes [in Cuba] also have enjoyed better nutrition and health care [than young Dominicans], and are far better educated. They all read and write, and some of the Cuban Leaguers work on graduate degrees in sports management in the offseason."

While the immediate impact on baseball of Cuba's hypothetical re-entry into the international economy cannot be entirely known, it is a near certainty that the introduction of an entire nation into the universe of potential major league baseball players will make the talent pool far stronger than it has ever been.

The Future

Baseball has never been exclusively America's game. Only recently has the game's highest level reflected the sport's broad appeal beyond American borders. The World Baseball Classic has spurred the development of a new professional baseball league in Israel, the possible revival of the Australian Baseball League, and increased interest in professional leagues in Europe, Taiwan, Japan and Korea, not to mention MLB's recent flood of investment into developing baseball in China. It is not difficult to imagine a scenario in the near future where fewer than half of the players in the majors will be of American origin, a prospect that would have seemed ludicrous 20 years ago.

As baseball continues into this era of unparalleled expansion, communities in the countries affected by the sport's growth will face the difficult task of protecting the interests of child athletes from a system largely stacked against them. Major League Baseball's role is clear. As with any industry, its goal is to maximize profits and minimize costs, and that will not change anytime soon.

Some have speculated on the possibility of an international draft, which would be a crucial step towards standardizing the process of talent acquisition but which is unlikely to happen anytime soon. Extension of the Major League Baseball Players' Association representation to minor league talent would be an even larger step in the right direction, but it is considerably less practical.

The different social, economic and infrastructural conditions in the nations that will begin to contribute talent to the major leagues opens the door to a wide variety of possibilities for the game moving forward. The greatest hope for those who have seen this process occur unregulated is that these countries will move quickly to protect players' interests, "letting the children play" as much as possible.

GM in a Box: Dave Dombrowski

by Bill Ferris

Record and Background

Age: 51

Previous Organizations:

White Sox: Various positions 1978-1986

Montreal Expos: General manager 1988-1991

Florida Marlins: General manager 1992-2001

Years of service with current organization: Six

Cumulative record: 1,369-1,640 (Montreal: 318-329, Florida: 627-764, Detroit: 424-547)

Did he play professional baseball, and if so, what type of player was he? His playing career ended after high school.

Personnel and Philosophy

Any notable changes from the previous regime?

The Tigers had spent the better part of a decade losing, seeming to shift strategies and focus regularly. When Dombrowski took over in 2002 he had a plan, even if it wasn't entirely apparent at the outset. Detroit still lost a lot early in Dombrowski's tenure while he cleared out bloated contracts like those of Bobby Higginson and Damion Easley, and tried to acquire young talent in exchange for the few Tigers players who still had value.

Before Dombrowski, the Tigers had tried to assemble a core group of young talent, only to trade much of it away to get Juan Gonzalez. Francisco Cordero, Frank Catalanatto, Justin Thompson and Gabe Kapler were among the players sent to the Rangers for one year of Gonzalez and five years of Danny Patterson.

It was an ill-conceived move to bring a right-handed hitter in the last year of his contract in to the biggest left and center fields in the big leagues. The Tigers tried to extend Gonzalez with an obscene $150 million offer, but he declined as the team sniffed the .500 mark. Fans expecting to see the Tigers add a major piece or two instead saw Gonzalez replaced with Roger Cedeno and Hideo Nomo replaced with Chris Holt. It marked the end of the Brad Ausmus-trade-era. Trading Ausmus was a staple of the Randy Smith reign with no less than four trades in a four-year span.

Dombrowski came to the Tigers not as the GM, but as the president and CEO. One of his first moves was to oust then general manager Smith and manager Phil Garner. He then prepared to ride out some lean years as he flipped Mark Redman, Randall Simon and Jeff Weaver for multiple prospects.

For those to be the Tigers' most valuable pieces says quite a bit about the state of the organization. Regardless, Redman netted the Tigers Nate Robertson and Gary Knotts. Weaver was turned into Jeremy Bonderman, Carlos Pena and Franklyn German. Simon was used to obtain Roberto Novoa (who was later part of a deal to get Kyle Farnsworth) and Kody Kirkland.

The plan was to go into 2003 with a young team and young manager and have everyone grow together. By the time that the 2003 season ended, the team had amassed 119 losses. The talent wasn't there and free agents like Rondell White, Jason Johnson, Fernando Vina and Pudge Rodriguez were used to help bridge the gap while Dombrowski worked to build a cadre of young pitching prospects. While the plan needed to be amended, there was no wavering from a commitment to developing young talent, even with the free agent expenditures.

Another difference is that owner Mike Ilitch seemed to have more trust in his new GM than the previous leadership. With that trust came a bigger budget, and that was used to make blockbuster deals with Rodriguez and Magglio Ordonez, and to retain newly acquired talent like Carlos Guillen long term.

Those changes transformed Detroit from a laughingstock to a league leader in short order.

What characterizes his relationship with ownership? What type of people does he hire? Is he more collaborative or authoritative?

Dombrowski has worked under varied guidelines from ownership. For the bulk of his time in Montreal and Florida, he had significant financial constraints except for 1996 and 1997 in Florida, when he could spend like crazy.

With Ilitch and the Tigers, he has earned the trust of his owner, and with that trust came a respectable payroll. Ilitch drew the ire of many fans when he seemed to be pretty frugal during the Smith years and the early part of Dombrowski's tenure. But starting in 2004, Ilitch took the reins off and the payroll has since doubled. While Ilitch stays outside of day-to-day baseball operations, he will get heavily involved with Dombrowski while recruiting big name free agents.

It is this involvement that makes it ambiguous who is driving some of the bigger signings or decisions to pick up expensive options (like Rodriguez's $13 million option for 2008). My impression is that in some cases Ilitch will drive decisions that aren't always a great value proposition, but will improve the team.

As he's moved from team to team, Dombrowski has kept many of his closest advisers. When he left for Florida, he took his assistant GM and his director of scouting with him, in addition to a number of scouts. The same was true in his move to Detroit, where he brought Al Avila and Scott Reid.

Given the loyalty that is shown both ways, it's safe to say that he maintains strong relationships with those who work for him and whom he trusts.

What kinds of managers does he hire? How closely does he work with them?

Rene Lachemann, John Boles, Jim Leyland, John Boles, Luis Pujols, Alan Trammell, Jim Leyland. I can't really find a pattern here except that he likes Jim Leyland. We won't count Pujols, who was a stopgap in the 2002 season and who had Felipe Alou (another Dombrowski blast from the past) as his bench coach. And he inherited Buck Rodgers in Montreal.

I think he likes younger managers, especially with younger teams. He told *The Sporting News* as much when he was looking for his first manager with the Marlins:

"You can hire an older guy and then groom someone on his staff who will be your manager of the future. Or you can hire a young guy, someone who will be patient and be around when the club is ready to contend years down the road."

He went the young route with Boles and Trammell. And he replaced both with a veteran manager in Leyland. And that is another Dombrowski trait: He keeps going back to those he is comfortable with. Leyland and Dombrowski worked together in Chicago before heading their separate ways.

Trammell's hiring probably served a dual purpose in that it was an opportunity to let a young manager grow with a team and it had public relations cachet: The Tigers would have someone in uniform that Detroit fans could root for.

In Detroit, Dombrowski seems to give the managers quite a bit of say in building the roster. Trammell was allowed to bring back an over-the-hill and expensive Higginson while a more productive Marcus Thames was left in the minors. Leyland has been allowed to retain underperforming players such as Neifi Perez, Sean Casey and Jason Grilli. It's usually unclear who ultimately makes these decisions, but the feeling here is that these were the product of the manager and not the GM.

Also of note: When Leyland was with the Marlins, he earned a reputation as someone who would allow his young pitchers to throw a ton of innings. With Detroit, it has been the opposite. Given that both the GM and manager are the same as in Florida, it is hard to say which party had the philosophical change on pitch counts.

Player Development

How does he approach the amateur draft? Does he prefer major league-ready players or "projects?" Tools or performance? High schools or college? Pitchers or hitters?

Dombrowski has developed a reputation for going after the highest ceiling players available and isn't intimidated by signability concerns. This has worked to the Tigers' advantage with the signings of Cameron Maybin (2005), Andrew Miller (2006) and Rick Porcello (2007). The Porcello bonus broke Josh Beckett's record for a high school pitcher. Beckett was also a Dombrowski signing, in Florida.

Of course, this is also a function of an owner's willingness to spend, but Dombrowski makes the business decision to invest money in the draft, where he feels he has a better chance to compete with large market teams for top talent, rather than in the free agent market.

This emphasis on scouting and amateur players is part of what brought his success in Florida and Montreal. The Florida Marlins were born in 1991 and by January 1992 already had 30 scouts (11 of whom came with Dombrowski from the Expos) and a baseball academy in the Dominican Republic. Edgar Renteria and Luis Castillo were signed as teenagers before the Marlins had even played a game.

Dombrowski favors tools, especially in the case of pitchers, among whom he covets hard throwers. He'll draft from either the high school or collegiate ranks, going where the talent is.

He has a reputation for building pitching depth through the draft, but he's had fair success with positional draft picks as well. He has made the following first round selections:

- Charles Johnson (twice)
- Rondell White
- Cliff Floyd
- Mark Kotsay
- Adrian Gonzalez
- Cameron Maybin

While he'll draft position players high, he emphasizes building pitching depth through the draft, where it is at its cheapest. He is a subscriber to the adage that you can never have enough pitching, and desires to stockpile it to help the big club either directly or through a trade.

Does he tend to rush players to the majors or let them marinate?

Dombrowski won't hold a young player back. Jeremy Bonderman was in the rotation before he could drink. Justin Verlander spent one season in the minors before becoming a mainstay. Miller didn't even have that long: He got a September call-up months after the College World Series and went into the rotation with less than a full year of professional ball.

Dombrowksi's propensity for pushing guys through the system manifested itself again last August. After six games at the Double-A level, the 20-year-old Maybin was inserted into the Tigers' starting lineup.

The Marlins typically had young players playing major roles; in 1997, their keystone combo of Renteria and Castillo was a combined 42 years old. And Livan Hernandez was a member of the rotation at 21.

In all these cases except Bonderman, Leyland was the manager, so it's hard to say who was making the call.

Roster Construction

Is he especially fond of certain types of players? Does he like proven players or youngsters? Offensive players or glove men? Power pitchers or finesse guys?

Power arms. Power arms. Power arms. He likes them in the rotation. He likes them in the bullpen. He likes them in the majors. He likes them in the minors.

Aside from that, he tends to favor the same traits that are common throughout baseball. He likes defense up the middle and power at the corners. However, that hasn't always come to fruition.

Save for one outburst from Brandon Inge, the Tigers haven't had a 20-homer third baseman under Dombrowski's tenure. The past two years, the team has had more offense from the shortstop position than first base, but with less defense.

In many cases, though, it seems he prefers regulars who have some way to contribute offensively. Dombrowski has been willing to overlook defensive shortcomings and find a position for players who can hit. The Tigers took a flyer on Chris Shelton, who was available because the Pirates didn't think he had a position. The Tigers taught him first base. They moved Eric Munson around hoping that he could provide a big bat and learn third base.

In center field, the team tried Alex Sanchez, who could at least hit for average, and Craig Monroe, who could at least hit for power, despite neither being able to play in a park as big as Comerica. And with the outfield full going into 2007, the club taught Thames to play first base during spring training.

For the bench players, there seems to be a preference for defense. Neifi Perez and Ramon Santiago have recently found spots on the Tigers bench despite limited offensive skills.

Dombrowski doesn't seem to be scared off by either end of the age spectrum. His teams have had players in their early 20s and others in their late 30s.

While the Tigers have been among the league leaders in strikeouts the past few years, the biggest contributors (Inge, Curtis Granderson, Monroe) were players who came through the Tigers' minor league system. Many players Dombrowski has acquired have been batting average-heavy players like Casey, Placido Polanco, Rodriguez and White. I'm not sure if this is a preference in player type, or an effort to achieve some balance. The latter seems a possibility as Dombrowski acquired Gary Sheffield to lend patience to an aggressive lineup.

Does he allocate resources primarily on impact players or role players? How does he flesh out his bullpen and his bench? Does he often work the waiver wire, sign minor league free agents or make Rule 5 picks?

Dombrowski isn't afraid to commit big years and big dollars to special players. He signed Sheffield in 1997 to a contract extension that was the richest at the time. When other GMs would offer Rodriguez only two years, Dombrowski was willing to go four. And when Ordonez was looking for a big deal after coming off a controversial knee procedure, it was Dombrowski who inked him to a deal that could total more than $100 million.

But Dombrowski tends to save those types of deals for the real difference makers. He'll also fill in with role players and veterans who can be had for manageable one- or two-year deals. These are the Whites, Jason Johnsons, Todd Joneses. And even though he may pay more than market on a per year basis, those deals that don't work out, like Troy Percival and Vina, don't have long-term ramifications.

After years of dealing with small market payrolls, it's clear that Dombrowski prefers to be able to rely on home-grown talent. The long-term signings come when he knows he can't provide talent at a given position. The shorter-term deals are designed to bridge the gap until one of those prospects in A-ball is ready to make the jump.

He will try to take advantage of the Rule 5 draft when he has roster spots available. In 2003, three members of the bullpen (Matt Roney, Wil Ledezma, Chris Spurling) were Rule 5 pickups. The next year, he stashed Shelton on the bench for a full season. In 2005 and 2007, he selected more bullpen arms who ultimately spent the season on the 60-day disabled list.

He'll also sign a cadre of minor league free agents each year to provide depth at the Triple-A level and help fill in for injuries in the bullpen. Players such as Bobby Seay, Chad Durbin and Grilli all had roles on recent Tigers teams. While not top shelf talent, these players all served their roles as fill in starters and LOOGYs quite well.

When will he release players? On whom has he given up? To whom has he given a shot? Does he cut bait early or late?

Dombrowski has been fairly liberal in terms of releasing players while with Detroit. He's had no qualms letting starters go. Contract status or timing haven't seemed to play a large role in the decisions.

- He let Damion Easley go with two years and more than $14 million left on his contract—the most expensive cut in MLB history at the time.
- He released Sanchez outright before the 2005 season because he was failing to get with the program (and a drug test).

- Pena was let go before the 2006 season.
- Dmitri Young was released during a rain delay late in 2006 after a year of struggling on and off the field.
- Monroe was designated for assignment during a pennant race in 2007 while in the middle of a horrendous slump.

In only one of those instances did he give up on a player too early: the Carlos Pena release. Pena was still young, and still in his arbitration years. Given Pena's success in 2007, it looks like a mistake in hindsight. However, Pena struggled with both the Red Sox and Yankees organizations in 2006 and it is far from sure that he would have had the same success had he stayed in Detroit.

Is he active or passive? An optimist or a problem solver? Does he want to win now or wait out the success cycle?

Throughout his career, Dombrowski has tended to be active. He went after Mark Langston early in the season in 1989. He was aggressive in getting Sheffield after the 2006 season. He rapidly built and disassembled the 1997 Marlins team.

At the same time, he is patient. He knew success would be a long time coming for the Marlins when he took over an expansion franchise and tried to stick to the development cycle even when his team was being compared to the more successful Rockies.

He faced the same uphill battle with the Tigers and realized that there wouldn't be a quick fix that would make the team competitive until young talent began to emerge.

In 2006 he was perhaps too proactive after Polanco's shoulder injury. A ground ball went through Omar Infante's legs, and shortly thereafter the Tigers acquired Neifi Perez.

While he's typically acquired the pieces he's needed when his teams have been close, he decided to stand pat during the 2007 trade deadline while the Tigers bullpen struggled with poor performance and injuries to Joel Zumaya and Fernando Rodney. According to Dombrowski, he tried to add a bullpen arm and made what he considered a fair offer. But he wasn't going to mortgage the future because it appears this is the first time that he has a team that has a chance to stay on top for a long time.

Does he favor players acquired via trade, development or free agency?

Dombrowski has shown that he'll use all three avenues to acquire talent, but I feel he prefers to build through the minor leagues. But that can mean a variety of avenues—finding and drafting his own players, trading veterans for multiple prospects from other teams, or dealing his own minor leaguers to find a missing piece.

Of course, it would be disingenuous to claim that Dombrowski's success has been exclusive to building up organizational depth. After all, he did acquire Al Leiter, Kevin Brown, Bobby Bonilla, Moises Alou, Rodriguez and Ordonez on the open market.

Dombrowski prefers to develop pitchers because he believes it is easier to acquire position players via free agency or trade.

Trades and Free Agents

Is he an active trader? Does he tend to move talent or horde it? To whom does he trade and when?

He was much more active earlier in his career while with the Expos and the Marlins. With the Tigers, he has made only three big moves: moving Weaver and acquiring Sheffield and Polanco. A fourth, which later became key to the Tigers' success, was the acquisition of Carlos Guillen for Ramon Santiago and minor leaguer Juan Gonzalez.

I don't think he necessarily hordes talent, but he tries to avoid situations where he has to move players. The 1997 post-World Series situation was different, because he had an edict to cut payroll. In situations where he's had more latitude, he won't move a player until he gets what he wants, and sometimes it has cost him.

With the Marlins, he had a hot commodity in reliever Brian Harvey. Dombrowski contended he was going to hold on to Harvey despite his team not really being in the race. Harvey was injured and Dombrowski got nothing in return.

In 2004, the Tigers were in a position to deal Ugueth Urbina to a contending club. The San Francisco Giants were looking for help, but Dombrowski set the price tag at multiple prospects, including Matt Cain. Early in the 2005 season, Dombrowski was forced to deal Urbina after a fight on the team flight. Things turned out a little better this time: He got Polanco from the Phillies, who were making room for Chase Utley.

With less than top talent, it seems that Dombrowski will just let players go, or in the case of players who have

been good citizens and teammates, will try to find a situation that will be a good fit for them. Mike Maroth going to St. Louis and Monroe going to the Cubs for PTBNLs are recent examples.

Dombrowski will trade at all times of the year, during the season, after the season, before the season. He's made blockbuster trades both in and out of season.

Will he make deals with other teams during the season? How does he approach the trading deadline?

Dombrowski is comfortable making marginal trades as well as blockbusters during the season. The famed Langston for Randy Johnson (and others) came during late May when the team was .500. Langston was the best pitcher available, and the July addition of Zane Smith made the Expos the team to beat before a late-season collapse.

The next year, with the team nine games out in August, he traded Smith, who was going to be a free agent, within the division and netted Moises Alou in return.

He's also played the role of seller during the summer with Detroit, when he shipped out his only valuable commodity, Weaver, in a three-way deal netting Pena, Bonderman, and German.

He's also been willing to add role players to a couple of his World Series teams—Darren Daulton in Florida and Casey with the Tigers—neither time having to surrender much.

With the Tigers, Dombrowski has done a good job of adding to the team without giving up top talent.

Are there teams or general managers with whom he trades frequently?

Dombrowski seems to trade in the National League more than the American League. Since coming to Detroit he has hooked up with the Cubs, Mariners and Braves multiple times. But his two biggest deals have involved Brian Cashman and the Yankees. Those deals were the Weaver trade, then the Sheffield trade following the 2006 season.

Under what circumstances will he sign free agents?

Dombrowski will sign two types of free agents.

The first is the marquee, All-Star, represented by Scott Boras type who will be expensive in terms of years and dollars. These are players who will be cornerstones of the franchise for the next four years and who play positions where there is no help coming from the system.

Dombrowski has done well with Boras' players over the years. The Tigers were carrying three Boras clients in 2007: Kenny Rogers, Rodriguez and Ordonez. Whether it is because Dombrowski doesn't shy away from dealing with Boras or because his owner is willing to pay what it takes to get the players signed, Team Boras has been quite good to Team Dombrowski. I'm sure that fact isn't lost on either of them.

Ordonez and Rodriguez were the big signings that actually happened. How much credit Dombrowski should receive is debatable. The Tigers went into the 2004 offseason with a hefty budget and reports had them making plays for Troy Glaus, J.D. Drew, Adrian Beltre and Carl Pavano. But recruiting players to Detroit proved difficult. It was the same difficulty they faced the year prior when they unsuccessfully tried to woo Miguel Tejada and Rich Aurilia to the Motor City.

Committing $75 million (which could still balloon to $105 million if vesting options kick in) to Ordonez could be considered a lot of things, but prudent wasn't a word floated around at the time. It was a huge overpayment, one that the Tigers had attempted with several other players.

In several cases, Dombrowski was fortunate that Detroit wasn't an attractive destination. Aurilia picking the Mariners over Detroit led to the trade in which the Tigers sent Ramon Santiago and Juan Gonzalez (a different one) to Seattle for Guillen.

It is doubtful that the Tigers could have absorbed Pavano's contract without getting any production.

But even the hefty contracts handed Ordonez and Rodriguez haven't deterred the Tigers from spending heavily in the draft or retaining their home-grown talent.

The second type of free agent Dombrowski will sign is the stop-gap. These are the players he can get on one- or two-year deals because the player is coming off injury or coming to the end of his career. These aren't the difference makers, but the effective major league regulars like White.

Contracts

Does he prefer long-term deals or short? Does he backload his contracts very often? Does he lock up players early in their careers or is he more likely to practice brinksmanship? Does he like to avoid arbitration?

Dombrowski has no problem going with long term contracts for top-shelf talent. He went for four years on Rodriguez when no one else was offering more than two. He gave five years with two option years to Ordonez, who was coming off of knee surgery. However, he also was negotiating from a point of weakness, trying to attract talent to a losing team.

It's worth noting that in both of those cases Dombrowski and his legal counsel, John Westhoff, worked language into the contract protecting the team in case of specific injuries to the areas of greatest risk. In the case of Ordonez, a knee injury resulting in significant lost playing time in the first season would have voided the rest of the deal. In the case of Rodriguez, missing time due to back injury in the first two years would have shortened the contract.

He has proved to be a big fan of the two-year contract for non-marquee talent like White, Vina, Johnson, Rogers, and Jones. While he may overpay per year, he also maintains considerable flexibility and avoids blocking upcoming players.

He also seems to prefer to lock up known commodities. He re-signed Sheffield with the Marlins before he hit the free agent market

With the Tigers, Dombrowski worked out four-year contract extensions with both Guillen and Polanco in the last year of each of their contracts. He also extended Sheffield at the time of the 2006 trade.

And if he can't get an impending free agent inked, he's not afraid to trade him and take what he can get in return, as evidenced by a trade deadline deal shipping out Farnsworth.

With Detroit, he has locked up Bonderman and Inge during their arbitration years, buying out their first years of free agency. But with other players, he'll try to sign them to a two-year deal during arbitration (Maroth, Rodney) providing the club with some cost certainty while not committing a large chunk of resources.

He prefers to work things out with players prior to arbitration. No Tiger has made it to arbitration hearings during his tenure.

Anything unique about his negotiating tactics? Is he vocal? Does he prefer to work behind the scenes or through the media?

It is hard to analyze Dombrowski's negotiating tactics, because you don't hear anything until after the deal is made. He doesn't comment on free agents he's pursuing, and he doesn't comment on a trade until after it happens, or has no possibility of happening. The exception was when the Tigers announced that negotiations with first round pick Verlander were over. It proved a successful move—Verlander's father began to deal directly with the Tigers to get a deal done.

Bonus

What is his strongest point as GM?

Dombrowski's strongest point is his adaptability. In his professional career he's been in circumstances that demanded different approaches. With the Expos, and with the majority of his time with the Marlins, he was working with payrolls that can be described as meager. Then, he focused the bulk of his dollars and energy on amateur scouting, both in and out of the United States.

When he had money to spend with the Marlins, he spent wisely, sinking big dollars into players who would have a big impact. When he needed to cut, he managed to assemble many of the pieces for another World Series team despite trading bulky contracts with little leverage.

With the Tigers, he figured out quickly that there was a lot of dead weight and that the team wouldn't be competing in the near term. He didn't spend on free agents and decided to go with a raw team in 2003. The hope was that some of the pieces of a young team could grow together with their new manager.

Instead, 119 losses happened and some of those young pieces clearly weren't going to be a lot of help. Dombrowski responded by making a series of smaller free agent signings, signing veterans he could get on two-year deals that would give the team an element of competitiveness while the talent in the lower parts of the organization matured.

In short, he knows what he wants to do, and doesn't lose sight of the plan, but he isn't stubborn enough to keep from adjusting and correcting.

What would he be doing if he weren't in baseball?

The Sporting News reported that being a baseball general manager was his plan as far back as high school. His honors thesis was titled "The Man in the Middle. The Role of the General Manager in Baseball." After finishing college as an A student in accounting, he went to work for his favorite childhood team, the Chicago White Sox.

If Dombrowski weren't in baseball, he'd probably be trying to figure out how to get into baseball. That was the plan all along

History

The Months of 2007 in History

Richard Barbieri

On our *Hardball Times* site, each week I tackle an event from the many years of baseball history and give it the full historical perspective.

It is not always necessary to look far back for noteworthy events; each season contains its share. Below are 12 events, one for each month since our *Annual* last arrived at your doorstep. Most were big pieces of news you probably heard. A couple are more obscure.

All have in common that they did not stand alone in baseball history. They all have a place in the historical context of the game.

November 2006: *Mets announce stadium naming rights.*

As we go to press, there is much talk of Alex Rodriguez' new contract. Will it top $300 million?

It might, but it still wouldn't be the richest deal in baseball. That deal is one signed by the New York Mets, and involves money coming *into* the team, to the tune of $400 million. That money will be coming over the next 20 years from Citigroup. In return the Mets' new stadium will be known as "CitiField."

In the 2007 season, 14 teams had stadiums with what might be described as "pure" corporate names. A few others play in stadiums with corporate names, but those refer to either the current or past ownership, so it is not quite the same.

Excluding stadiums named for their ownership, the first modern stadium with a corporate name was Denver's Coors Field when it opened in 1995. This was the start of a trend in the late '90s. The trend is slowing; some teams have "reclaimed" their park names. Among new parks, only the Mets have announced a corporate name for a previously unbranded stadium.

If that holds, exactly half the parks in baseball will bear corporate names, a lower percentage than the NFL or NBA. Of course, a lot can change in a couple of years—ask fans who thought they would be attending games at Enron Field for decades to come— but for now it appears the influence of corporate names has not reached as far into baseball as is sometimes imagined.

December 2006: *Jeff Bagwell retires.*

Some players are doomed to toil in relative obscurity, no matter their accomplishments. Jeff Bagwell is one of those players. He's one of the 10 best first baseman ever.

Despite this, his whole career is a series of *buts*, beyond his control.

He won a Rookie of the Year, *but* it was on a team that lost nearly 100 games. He won an MVP Award, *but* it was for strike-shortened 1994. He appeared on four All-Star teams, *but* was beaten out for starting spots by players like Gregg Jefferies and Fred McGriff.

For much of his career, his team was a regular playoff contender, *but* the Astros lost in the first round four years in a row. The Astros finally made it to the World Series in 2005, *but* by then Bagwell had been reduced by injury to a backup role and hit just .125.

He posted impressive numbers while playing in the cavernous Astrodome, *but* could not accumulate 500 home runs or even 2,500 hits. For Bagwell, it puts a rather unfortunate spin on his nickname as a member of the Killer Bs.

Even in retirement, Bagwell managed to be underrated. After suffering a shoulder injury, Bagwell did not play at all in the 2006 season but was a *de jure* active player. His retirement was anticlimactic, merely making official something that was already widely assumed.

In 2011, Bagwell will be eligible for the Hall of Fame. He should be elected on the first ballot, achieving a career milestone without any *buts*.

January 2007: *Carlos Peña signs with Devil Rays.*

Although a minor move at the time—Peña was brought in to compete with the likes of Ty Wigginton, Greg Norton and Hee-Seop Choi—it turned out brilliantly. Peña made the Rays coming out of spring training and went on to have the season of his career. He hit more home runs than anyone not named Rodriguez, Fielder or Howard.

Peña was given the Comeback Player of the Year Award for his performance, which is nice, but highlights one of my problems with the award. Peña was establishing a new level of performance. It wasn't a "comeback" in the traditional sense; rather, he was finally living up to his potential.

To be fair, the Comeback Player of the Year Award, which has been an official MLB Award since only 2005 (earlier, it was given out by *The Sporting News)* doesn't do that very often. But it does happen. In 1991 Terry Pendleton was voted Comeback Player of the Year. He also won the MVP Award. It was wrong to say Terry was coming back to that quality; in the seven years prior, he had earned one vote for the MVP.

A more typical winner is someone like the 2007 NL Comeback Player, Dmitri Young, who put together a strong bounce-back season for the Nationals. And some players who win when establishing a new level of performance, like Gil Meche in 2003, do so after missing major time due to injury.

It might be a few years before another player has a "comeback" to a new level of play, but when it happens I'm sure there will be an actual comeback going unrewarded.

February 2007: *1956 perfect game footage shown.*

If you watch enough baseball games, you eventually will see the end of Don Larsen's 1956 World Series perfect game. Larsen throws a pitch, it is called strike three, and 5-foot-8 Yogi Berra runs out and leaps into the arms of 6-foot-4 Larsen.

What most people don't know is that, for many years, that was thought to be the only existing footage of the game. Although it was broadcast on TV (with commentary from Vin Scully and Mel Allen), such broadcasts were rarely preserved. The networks taped over them or threw them out, and without VCRs or DVRs, many famous moments have been lost.

Bobby Thomson's "Shot Heard 'Round the World," is just that, only heard, not seen. With the exception of Bill Mazeroski's home run, most of the footage of Game Seven of the 1960 World Series is also lost. Much to the NFL's chagrin, there is no surviving copy of the broadcast of Super Bowl I.

(This phenomenon extends beyond sports; NASA recently admitted it lost the original tapes of the first moon landing.)

The surviving perfect game footage is not actually a copy of the original broadcast, but a kinescope recording. That's the fancy term for recording something by literally setting up a camera in front of a monitor and filming what is being broadcast.

The Larsen game was kinescoped as part of a program to record World Series games to be viewed by military personnel stationed internationally. It was shown publicly for the first time in February at the Yogi Berra Museum in New Jersey.

As the story of the perfect game proves, footage long thought lost to time does sometimes appear. One hopes more will be found, providing the chance to see great moments again.

March 2007: *Angel Berroa sent to minors.*

It is easy to look back on past Rookie of the Year Awards and criticize the choices. The past few years voters have rated Eric Hinske in front of John Lackey, and Ben Grieve in front of Magglio Ordonez *and* Orlando Hernandez.

And that isn't even touching on famous historical misses: Alvin Davis ahead of Kirby Puckett and Roger Clemens, Jim Lefebvre over Joe Morgan, Walt Dropo instead of Whitey Ford.

Ultimately, that's too harsh on the media members who vote on the awards. It is called "Rookie of the Year" Award, not the "Player Who Debuted This Year with the Best Long Term Career Chances" Award.

Many of the biggest busts in Rookie of the Year history are justifiable within the confines of their season. Bob Hamelin won the 1994 award, beating out Manny Ramirez, Rusty Greer and Jim Edmonds, among others. But Hamelin was honestly the best player that season, despite not being half the prospect his competitors were.

This makes Angel Berroa's fall more perplexing. Berroa was 25 when he won his award in 2003, and probably deserved it. The other leading contender was Hideki Matsui, a rookie in name only. Yet Berroa has never reached that level again; 2003 represents his career high in nearly every offensive category.

Berroa's fall from Rookie of the Year to albatross was complete when the Royals acquired the punchless Tony Peña Jr. Pena was slotted in at shortstop, and Berroa was demoted back to Triple-A Omaha, where he spent most of 2007.

Barring a miracle comeback, Berroa will be consigned to the Ben Grieve-Jim Lefebvre dustbin of history.

April 2007: *Indians snowed out.*

Every once in a while, the YES Network will replay the Yankees' 1996 home opener, a game played in a light snow. The players (and fans) don't look especially comfortable, but they managed to get through it in just over three hours.

The Cleveland Indians would have no such luck in 2007, as snow wiped out all four games of their home opening series with the Mariners. With the prospect of more snow to come, their second series was moved to Milwaukee's Miller Park.

Moving to Milwaukee was somewhat appropriate, given that Milwaukee's County Stadium had doubled for Cleveland's "Mistake by the Lake" Municipal Stadium in 1989's movie *Major League.* The Indians went

2-1 in the series, and also won a "home" game played in Seattle in September, giving them a good record in home-away-from-home games.

This sort of thing does happen, but only very occasionally. The last time teams shifted cities entirely was in 2004, when a hurricane forced the Marlins to "host" the Expos at Chicago's U.S. Cellular Field. In September 1991, a piece of concrete fell in Olympic Stadium, necessitating that the Expos play out their schedule on the road. In 1998, a falling beam required the Yankees to play a game at Shea Stadium.

These probably aren't the home games teams have in mind but, like everything else in the world, circumstances upset the best laid, or best scheduled, plans.

May 2007: *Orlando Cepeda caught with drugs.*

It is popular for certain media types to theorize that the performance-enhancing drug scandal will be, if not quite a death blow, then at least a harsh wound to the game of baseball.

These critics are unaware, or choose to be, of facts like baseball's record-setting attendance in the past couple of years. Fans are almost certainly unhappy with the "PED Era," but they are still coming out to the ballparks.

And ultimately, why would they not? The use of PEDs is a mark against baseball, and the players who used it, but it is hardly the only drug-related blow the game has suffered. Orlando Cepeda was arrested this month after police stopped him for speeding. Cepeda—a Hall of Famer—is listed on the Giants' website as a community representative, whose job entails "speaking to 'at-risk' children about the dangers of drugs and alcohol."

He should have spent more time speaking to himself—police recovered marijuana and other drugs when they arrested him. This was not the first run-in with the law for Cepeda, who served 10 months in jail on drug charges in the '70s.

A decade later, baseball had an even bigger drug controversy: Pittsburgh drug trials revealed widespread use of drugs by players. Those who admitted cocaine use included Tim Raines, Paul Molitor, Lee Mazzilli and Keith Hernandez. Molitor is now in the Hall of Fame, while Raines and Mazzilli both served as coaches (and as manager, in Mazzilli's case) and Hernandez is a Mets' broadcaster, proving reputations can be rehabilitated.

It might be some time before fans view huge home run totals as unquestionably clean—should such totals return. But to think that baseball will be crippled by

such a scandal is demonstrating ignorance of both current events and past history.

June 2007: *Carl Pavano undergoes Tommy John surgery.*

After their humiliating defeat in the 2004 ALCS, the Yankees decided to enhance their pitching. To that end, they brought in, among others, Carl Pavano. He signed a four-year contract that will earn him $39.95 million before it ends. Since Pavano is unlikely to appear for the 2008 Yankees, his four-year total is a 5-6 record and a 4.76 ERA in 111.1 innings.

That puts Pavano in some exclusive company: the "All-Bust" starting rotation. Anchoring that rotation is Jaime Navarro. He signed a four-year, $20 million contract with the White Sox in 1997. In the first three years of the deal, Navarro led all AL pitchers in losses, earned runs and wild pitches. The Sox dispatched him to Milwaukee.

Next on the mound is Darren Dreifort. After signing a five-year, $55 million contract with the Dodgers after the 2000 season, Dreifort missed the entire 2002 and 2005 seasons and averaged less than 70 innings in the years he did pitch. For good measure, those years featured a collective 9-15 record with a 4.63 ERA.

Finally the rotation comes around to a pair of Rockies. After the 2000 season, Denver signed Mike Hampton and Denny Neagle. Neagle signed first, earning $51.5 million over five years, followed by Hampton's $121 million over eight years. Hampton was traded to Atlanta after two years (with the Rockies responsible for $49 million of the contract). Neagle lasted just three years, and would later see his contract terminated after he was arrested with a prostitute.

Navarro, Dreifort, Pavano, Hampton, Neagle. A rotation only a long man could love.

July 2007: *Kenny Lofton traded to Indians.*

If you've watched a baseball game the past few months, you've seen two things for sure: that Chevrolet ad with the John Mellencamp song and that DHL ad about trading Kenny Lofton.

It's not a bad ad, all things considered. (It gets a little tiresome after the 350th time, but that's a separate point.) As baseball ads go, it is based on reality. Kenny Lofton is a pretty good player. Nearly a .300 hitter for his career, he has more than 2,400 hits and 1,500 runs, and is the active leader in steals.

Despite all that, Lofton has been traded a lot, especially in the later portion of his career. He was traded just twice from 1988 (when he was drafted by the Astros) through 2001. Since 2002, however, he has been traded four times, including three times at the deadline.

Six trades may not sound like a lot, especially over a career as long as Lofton's. The other way to look at it is that he has been traded for (deep breath) Willie Blair, Eddie Taubensee, Marquis Grissom, David Justice, Felix Diaz, Ryan Meaux, Jose Hernandez, Matt Bruback, Felix Rodriguez and Max Ramirez.

Sadly, several of them are pitchers, so I can't assemble an "All-Traded for Kenny Lofton" team, but there's some pretty good talent on that list. I don't know if Kenny plans to return next year, but if he does, I'll be on the lookout should he once again be dealt.

August 2007: *Joba Chamberlain debuts.*

On Joba Chamberlain's *Baseball Reference* page, the sponsorship states that "if (they) told you half the things (they've) heard about this Joba, you'd probably short circuit." That might be true, so I'll stick to just one incredible fact about him.

Some of you may have seen the ERA+ statistic. It measures a pitcher's ERA relative to the league average and his home ballpark. An ERA+ of 100 is exactly league average. Anything above it is better than average. Pedro Martinez' 2000 season, for example, produced an ERA+ of 285.

This season, in his limited time, Joba Chamberlain posted an ERA+ of 1,156. That is the highest single-season total ever. It is also only the second four-digit ERA+ in baseball history.

Before Yankees fans get too excited, it is worth pointing out that the list is a mixed bag. With a minimum of 20 innings, the list does feature names like Dennis Eckersley (606 in 1990) and Jonathan Papelbon (500 in 2006). But the list also features names like Brian Bruney (503 in 2006, left off Yankees postseason roster in 2007) and Paul Kilgus (625 in 1993, never pitched in the majors again).

Perhaps the worst-case comparable for Joba and the Yankees is Joel Johnston. Until Chamberlain, Johnston was the only player with an ERA+ over 1,000. He did that as a 24-year-old for the Royals in 1991. In 1992, he pitched just 2.1 innings, and his ERA+ was 30. He never pitched in the majors after 1995 and ended his career with a 3-5 record in fewer than 100 innings.

If that's the fate of Joba, Yankee fans may indeed short circuit.

September 2007: *Diamondbacks make playoffs.*

One of the easier, if crueler, articles to write at the end of the season is the wrapup of active players who have never made it into the postseason. The all-time leader in this category is Ernie Banks (2,528) with Luke Appling (2,422) in second place. (Ron Santo is in fifth, giving Chicago players three of top five spots.)

Until the Diamondbacks clinched their playoff spot, the active leader in this category was Jeff Cirillo. He had played 1,617 games in the majors with six teams without seeing postseason action. Cirillo finally got into a playoff game during the NLDS, pinch-hitting during the ninth inning of Game 3.

That's not one of the higher totals all-time—there are 32 players over 1,750—but it is high for the wild card era. Another player who had never tasted the post season was Todd Helton, whose 1,578 regular season games ranked him third on the active list.

Helton needed the dramatics of a one-game playoff to secure his postseason spot, but he finally did so. He struggled in the NLDS, but did scorch a triple in his first playoff at-bat, once he'd waited for a long time.

Some unfortunate souls remain on the list. The new active leader is Damion Easley (1,593) whose career might be over at age 38. If that is so, Jose Vidro (1,333) takes over the top spot, with Tony Batista (1,309) and Randy Winn (1,297) trailing.

October 2007: *Rockies host Padres.*

I cannot do justice to the incredible, 13-inning, nearly five-hour classic the Padres and Rockies played for the National League wild card spot. However, that game was rather the exception when it comes to one-game playoffs. They have an underwhelming history despite their inherent drama.

The average margin of victory in the seven one-game playoffs is four runs. Only three have seen a margin of one or two runs. In addition to this year's close game, the justly famous Yankees-Red Sox 1978 playoff ended with the winning run on third base. The third game is the 1998 Giants-Cubs match-up, which finished with a 5-3 score but only after a furious rally by the Giants.

In one-gamers, great pitching performances are more common than close games. Joe Niekro (1980), Randy Johnson (1995) and Al Leiter (1999) have thrown complete games in one-game playoffs. Leiter's was a shutout, Niekro allowed just one unearned run and Johnson only a ninth inning home run when already up by nine runs.

This year's was the first one-game playoff in almost 10 years. Maybe it will not be so long before another game creates more history.

The Decline and Fall of the MLBPA

by John Brattain

"In my mind, ballplayers were among the most exploited workers in America."
—Marvin Miller

Baseball is a game of cycles. There have been eras on the field where speed and "little ball" were hallmarks of the game. There have been times when power and the long ball reigned supreme. Various pitching eras have come and gone.

The sport's cyclical nature also has extended to the business side of the sport. In professional baseball's earliest period, there was the freest of free agency. Not only did players change teams at the end of seasons, they often sold their services to the highest bidder in midseason. With different leagues both large and small, it wasn't unheard of for a player to wear more than one uniform.

This practice, called "revolving," cost team owners a lot of money, especially for top talent. Eventually, the "powers that were" reached a gentleman's agreement to "reserve" their best players—making them untouchable to competing clubs. Initially a team could reserve five players. Gradually the number increased until finally all players on a given team belonged exclusively to the club that held their rights. This was a part of every contract.

Further, clubs "capped" how much a given player could make in a season.

It didn't take long for the players to realize they were being shafted. In an attempt to counteract the restrictions being placed on them by the clubs in organized baseball, organizations such as The National Brotherhood of Base Ball Players (which gave birth to the Players League) cropped up, later followed by the Players' Protective Association in 1900, the Fraternity of Professional Baseball Players of America in 1912 and the American Baseball Guild in 1946.

All of these events came and went in a relatively short period of time. Their efforts were doomed from the start because not every player was with the program. For every player willing to take a stand, there were 10 others ready to take his place. Team owners simply hired players who wished to play for pay and not make waves.

In the 20th century, players had little leverage until the Federal League of 1914-15. The threat of players jumping to the better-paying new league caused the

American and National Leagues to offer more money. It would be the high water mark for professional baseball players for decades and from that brief perch, they would fall a long way.

The inevitable lawsuits stemming from the demise of the Federal League ultimately led to baseball's antitrust exemption. Simply put, this allowed teams to deny qualified players from working in the major leagues without repercussions. It was a practice called "blackballing" which is quite illegal—unless you are exempt from anti-trust law.

The irony is that a lot of players that were members of The National Brotherhood of Base Ball Players in the 19th century became owners and general managers who exploited the next generation of players in the game.

After the Black Sox Scandal of 1919, organized baseball created the office of commissioner and hired former federal judge Kenesaw Mountain Landis, who was empowered to act "in the best interests of baseball." This "best interests" power was used to bar the eight Black Sox from playing in MLB again. It would be used by future commissioners as a whip to keep players in line.

At this point, the players had no leverage. There was no third league you could sell, or threaten to sell your services to and you were completely at the pleasure of the team holding your contract save for a few blips on the radar.

There was an aborted attempt by Robert Murphy in 1946 to unionize the players in Pittsburgh. Also in 1946, several players jumped their contracts to play in the ill-fated Mexican League.

After that, there were lawsuits by players Danny Gardella (he signed with the Mexican League and, even though no MLB team held his rights, when the league folded he was blacklisted by organized baseball) and George Toolson (a talented Yankees farmhand who felt he could make the big leagues with another team that didn't have Joe Collins, Johnny Mize and Tommy Heinrich to play first base). However, ownership still held the whip hand after settlement of the Gardella case, confirmation of the 1922 decision that baseball was exempt from anti-trust law (Toolson) and congressional indifference.

One has to wonder if the old non-fraternization on-field rules were more about keeping the players from uniting than about competitive integrity.

By the time Marvin Miller came on the scene, the players union was an illegal company union financed by the owners. The executive director of the union was Judge Robert Cannon, a man in so tight with ownership that he once lobbied for the job of commissioner. Amazingly, nobody save Miller found that to be at all unusual.

This is the situation Miller was dealing with: a constituency that was, for the most part, politically conservative—hence anti-union. Also the players had been told by their own executive director (Cannon) that they had it so good that they didn't know what to ask for next and that the commissioner of baseball was neutral, represented both management and player and held a powerful stick: "the best interests of baseball."

With all this in ownership's favor, Miller faced a daunting task of breaking management's iron grip on the game. He realized the most important thing was unity. Other attempts to unionize had failed so badly because nobody got all the players on board. Miller knew he had to unite the entire group from Willie Mays and Hank Aaron all the way down to Bob Uecker and Bobby Wine.

It would take time and it would take education. Miller started by enlightening players on how badly they had actually been exploited, demonstrating ownership's failings and finding positions that 100% of the players could unite behind.

Miller was willing to take the time to let everybody have his say and build a consensus among the players. No matter how long a meeting took, it continued until the players understood the issues at hand and came to a position that had the unconditional support and comprehension of all.

There is an axiom in baseball: "Swing for singles and the home runs will come." Miller understood that small victories were important; they helped the players understand how powerful a consensus among them was and it gave them confidence that unity would better their circumstances.

Instead of calling a strike, (anathema to political conservatives), Miller explained a 1969 job action over pensions as something that was more familiar and palatable to the players: a mass holdout. By 1972, the players sensed their new power and were indignant at their employers' belligerence (capped by St. Louis Cardinals owner Gussie Busch's pronouncement that the players

wouldn't get "another goddamned cent … if they want to strike—let 'em."). They decided to strike and called it that.

Miller took a building-block process to player gains: First, he negotiated a basic agreement, followed by a grievance procedure for player complaints that would be acceptable to ownership (the commissioner would be the final arbitrator in these cases).

Curt Flood's suit against organized baseball, while unsuccessful, was a godsend to the players, since it brought publicity to the unfairness of baseball's power structure. It also gave Miller the leverage he needed to get the most important concession the players ever required—a genuine, neutral arbitrator to hear player grievances. No longer did the commissioner (Bowie Kuhn at the time) have final say.

Miller had contended from the first time he read it that rule 10A (in the standard player contract) that read:

"On or before January 15 … the Club may tender to the Player a contract for the term of that year by mailing the same to the Player. If prior to the March 1 next succeeding said January 15, the Player and the Club have not agreed upon the terms of such contract, then on or before 10 days after said March 1, the Club shall have the right … to renew this contract for the period of one year."

…gave the owner a single option year and not perpetual options on the players' services. The owners contended that since the renewed contract had this clause, it would be in effect the following year, and the year after that, etc. Miller had told the players he thought it meant that once the option was played out, there was no longer a contract between player and club. In other words, it made the player a free agent.

Now Miller had an arbitrator in place who wouldn't automatically side with the owners. Next, he needed somebody to play out his option year and test Miller's theory before a neutral arbitrator. He was emboldened when a contract violation by Oakland A's owner Charlie O. Finley gave Catfish Hunter an opening to terminate the contract, making him a free agent. The question went before arbitration Peter Seitz, who sided with Hunter, and the righthander landed a record-breaking contract with the New York Yankees.

It also gave the players an idea how badly they had been exploited and how much money free agency could be worth.

After some close calls, finally a player played out his option year, filed for free agency and asked the arbitrator to view rule 10A as a one-year option. He was Dodgers ace Andy Messersmith. As a backup (in case the Dodgers met Messersmith's demand for a no-trade clause, which was the sticking point in negotiations), Miller enlisted the help of former Baltimore Orioles 20-game winner Dave McNally. McNally had retired during his option year but the Montreal Expos—to whom he had been traded—still held his rights.

Since arbitrator Seitz had once noted a 1969 court of appeals decision that confirmed that a similar clause in NBA player contracts meant a one-year renewal (in the case of Rick Barry and the San Francisco Warriors), Miller felt he had the right guy to hear the Messersmith/McNally case.

He was right and the players won free agency.

After that decision, owners tried to nullify that decision, first through the courts, then by locking the players out of spring training. Finally a collective bargaining agreement was ratified that allowed for free agency. Ownership tried to roll back the huge financial gains made by the players in 1980-81, 1985 and 1990 but each time the union (now headed by Don Fehr) held firm and players emerged with their free agency and salary arbitration rights intact.

It could rightly be said that the MLBPA was the most successful union in existence.

Then came 1994 and the strike that caused the cancellation of the World Series. The tide turned. On the surface, it appeared to be a Pyrrhic victory at best for the owners. Judge Sonia Sotomayer ruled that ownership had bargained in bad faith and re-instituted the previous work rules until a new collective bargaining agreement was reached, an agreement that gave ownership a few small concessions.

It had literally saved the players' collective hide. Under U.S. labor law at that time, management, after a reasonable period of negotiations, could declare an impasse and impose new work rules. In the 1994-95 off-season, ownership had done just that. The game now had a hard salary cap and new revenue sharing rules, and re-opened for business. Sotomayer's decision overturned management's impasse and with it went the cap and the revenue sharing.

It didn't change one fact, however: Fehr and his No. 2 man, Gene Orza, got their constituents to believe that ownership would crack under pressure, as it had so often in the past. Owners had capitulated regularly because of the differing financial interests of large and small revenue clubs and because of media, political and big market team owners' pressure on the commissioner.

This time, with commissioner Bud Selig also owner of the Milwaukee Brewers, ownership had hung tough and the players had to be bailed out by Sotomayer. Chances are this wouldn't have happened if a Republican were in the White House at the time (Sotomayer was an appointee of President Clinton).

Further, the players weren't adequately briefed on what was at stake. A number of Florida Marlins, for example, complained about the strike itself. They didn't know why they had walked out save for the fact that the MLBPA had told them they were on strike. They had been told little more than "the MLBPA is the most successful labor union on earth and turned indentured servants into multi-millionaires. That's all the explanation you need, son. Now do your part."

After the strike, salaries started to skyrocket: Albert Belle of the Cleveland Indians broke the $10 million per year barrier by signing a five-year $55 million contract with the Chicago White Sox after the 1996 season. Kevin Brown became baseball's first $100 million man, inking a then-staggering seven-year/$105 million deal with the Los Angeles Dodgers after the 1998 season.

Finally, after the 2000 season, both the $20 million per year and $200 million threshold were smashed. Manny Ramirez got an eight-year/$160 million dollar package from the Boston Red Sox and, in the grand-daddy of them all, there was the now-notorious 10-year/$252 million contract that Tom Hicks of the Texas Rangers bestowed upon Seattle Mariners shortstop Alex Rodriguez.

Salary disparity in 1985 was causing some passionate debate among the players, leading to a two-day strike. Now the gulf between the major league minimum and Alex Rodriguez was as vast as the one between the rich man and Lazarus.

The MLBPA celebrated every new salary breakthrough—as well it should since the salary bar had become the raison d'etre of the union. This was in sharp contrast to Miller's simple desires to give the players power over their own careers, keep the market as free as possible and protect the value of the free agent and arbitration rights.

During Fehr's term, one of Miller's ideals had mutated. Miller felt that the best players should set the salary scale—the proverbial "rising tide lifting all boats." Fehr had determined to see just how high the tide could rise regardless of the effect on other boats. While players like Belle, Brown, Ramirez and Rodriguez were setting new salary heights, the clubs had learned that certain talent was replaceable. If a free agent signing/arbitration award set a new market for a certain stripe of player that clearly wasn't worth that amount of money, then clubs simply didn't offer those sorts of players arbitration and didn't tender them contracts.

This caused Marvin Miller's biggest fear—flooded player markets—to become a reality.

The superstars were getting their money, but a lot of veteran players were being squeezed out by promising youngsters or had to accept smaller contracts and minor league deals to try to win a job in spring training. This caused no little grumbling, and several journeymen players complained that the union represented the superstars and they were being largely ignored. Even some of the salaried elite, players such as Mark McGwire, Tony Gwynn and Jeff Bagwell, started wondering what was going on within their ranks.

These players complained about the MLBPA's influence on their careers. Miller had preached freedom while Fehr and Orza stressed taking the most money. McGwire passed on free agency with the Cardinals and signed an extension to prove he didn't need top dollar to play. Gwynn repeatedly butted heads with Orza, who urged him to go to a team that would pay him market value if San Diego wouldn't pay him more. Shawn Green intimated in the *Toronto Star* that he wanted to go somewhere where he could make what the union felt he was worth. He said he didn't want to make the other players angry by "hurting their earnings."

The journeymen felt ignored and the superstars started to feel that they had a new master—the salary bar. There were rumors about severe grumbling among the union executives over the contract extension Ken Griffey Jr. signed with the Cincinnati Reds after his trade from the Mariners. *Sports Illustrated* mentioned how Selig almost cried with relief when he heard what the total package was. The irony was that while it wasn't ground-breaking in annual salary terms, Griffey's total deal was then the largest ever given a player, though far less than what many thought he would fetch on the open market.

The biggest dollars went to the sluggers and to the pitchers who could keep them in check. The era of "Chicks Dig The Long Ball" meant incredible salaries to those who could hit it. As milestones belonging to the game's gods began to fall, crowds packed stadiums, bought cable packages, went online, and bought team merchandise in record amounts.

Eventually suspicion began to fall upon those who made 50-homer seasons seem routine, 60 homers a

"been there and done that" phenomenon and 70 home runs no longer the product of a deluded mind.

Doping had finally caught up with MLB. While the superstars got the headlines, the real damage was being done at the fringes of the sport. Players right on the bubble of the big leagues were faced with a difficult choice: take anabolic steroids or give up the dream. Finally, through congressional pressure brought on by shocking revelations from several high-profile players, drug testing came to baseball.

Debate was fierce and emotions ran high. The most surprising thing that had come out of all of this was the revelation that Fehr and Orza were out of touch with the feelings of their constituency. It reached the zenith of absurdity after a *USA Today* player poll revealed that 79% of players favored independent steroid testing. Forty-four percent said they felt pressure to juice to keep their jobs. Shortly thereafter, Fehr told the U.S. Senate not to consider unsubstantiated newspaper reports as fact. It became clear that Fehr and Orza hadn't touched base with their membership on an issue of critical importance to the players.

While all this was transpiring, Selig had taken a page from Marvin Miller's book on the value of consensus. He increased media revenues (especially through the Internet) and made sure they were shared, and he got the fractious ownership group to share more traditional revenue. Selig increased the value of their product by tinkering with the game itself: three divisions, a wild card, an extra round of playoffs and inter-league play. This gave them more inventory to sell to the networks and advertisers. He helped owners strong-arm communities into building luxurious ballparks and obtained sweetheart leases for their clubs.

All of this helped franchise values skyrocket over a very short period of time.

Selig showed the owners the power of consensus. As Miller had done so brilliantly four decades before, he settled for small gains here and there. With each added revenue stream, Selig gained the other owners' confidence.

Profits hadn't been so healthy since the days of Peter Ueberroth and collusion. Even though 1994-95 was a disaster, he proved to owners that they could stick together—much as the players learned the same lesson during the mass holdout of 1969 and the strike of 1972. They came within an eyelash of implementing the economic system of their dreams. With franchises being merely one part of massive corporate portfolios, they could weather any challenge from the MLBPA.

Since a lot of these corporations were also mass media outlets, they had a degree of control over the press.

Adding to the owners' clout was the lack of institutional memory among the players. Most players involved in the strike of 1994-95 are no longer playing and some who remain in the game are now part of management. Very few remain from the lockout of 1990, still fewer from the collusion era and none from the strike of 1981. They have little knowledge of the history of their union and the fight to achieve the gains they take for granted. In the early 1990s, union stalwart Gene Tenace was stunned to learn how many players didn't know the name Marvin Miller. The modern superstar feels that if he plays well and has a sharp agent, that's all he needs. They are insulated by entourages and some keep themselves above their teammates and union brethren.

Adding to the mix is the influx of talent from around the world, men who have differing values that may not include a union consciousness. There are those who have opinions that stem from pop culture which disdains authority (whether union or management) and have a self-centeredness that precludes putting other's interests above their own. In Miller's time, top players like Joe Torre, Reggie Jackson, Brooks Robinson, Willie Mays, Curt Flood, George Brett, Catfish Hunter, Bob Boone and Tom Seaver gave up much so Alex Rodriguez can potentially become baseball's first $30 million a year player.

Miller stated: "I tried to pound this message home to the players each spring. If one side becomes complacent, the other side becomes bolder. Either you push forward or you're going to be pushed back. In the type of labor-management situation in baseball, attempting to hold your ground, marking time, is an invitation to being shoved backward."

Time has shown that Fehr and Orza are guilty of just that. They became so fixated on the salary bar that they've lost the union. Miller recognized this years ago when he wrote: "(Fehr's) error was not at the bargaining table, but in the clubhouses and elsewhere, in not instilling in the players the determination to fight the good fight … Trying to instill morale in troops after the battle has started is foredoomed. Once negotiations are underway, it is too late."

Judge Sotomayer saved the MLBPA from an ignominious defeat in 1995. Fehr wasn't counting on unity to win the day during the strike. He was counting on the owners to crack. When they didn't, he needed judicial help.

The last two collective bargaining agreements have been negotiated without a stoppage, but not because the MLBPA has "seen the light" and decided to act in the best interests of baseball. It's because they realize there isn't consensus among its constituents. This was revealed during the last strike and through the so-called "steroid era." The union couldn't hang tough over a long strike., realizing that a journeyman ballplayer isn't going to risk his career and money for a principle that allows A-Rod to make $32 million in 2008 rather than $27 million. The stratification of monetary interests, which helped build the power of the union when it was ownership's problem, is now its undoing when it's an issue for the players.

The fixation on the salary bar came at the cost of the MLBPA's power base—player consensus. It benefited only a minority. Among the reasons for so much resistance to drug testing was an unstated one: While there were legitimate privacy issues (which also makes good copy), steroids landed the biggest boys the biggest bucks. So the union leaders didn't consult their membership on the issue since it affected the new master of the union—the salary bar. The rest of the union membership were simply expected to fall into line. It took being cornered by Congress to finally move Fehr and Orza into action.

The biggest piece of evidence that the MLBPA's power has waned is that the last two collective bargaining agreements have been negotiated without a stoppage or even the threat of one. Ownership even got the union to re-open a live collective bargaining agreement twice to strengthen drug testing. It made Miller borderline apoplectic.

During Selig's tenure as commissioner, 21 new parks have been built (plus one massively publicly financed renovation of Ewing Kauffman Stadium), almost all with a large degree of public money. (Even San Francisco paid a sizable subsidy to the Giants). Major League Baseball has become a cash-cow of epic proportions and local and national TV deals are reaching new highs. Despite all this, the last two bargaining agreements have included strong disincentives to overspending on players.

So, the Yankees will have to pay 40% more than any other team to re-sign Alex Rodriguez now that he has opted out of his current contract. Ownership is enjoying record revenues and may pass the NFL in the near future. There appears to be no limit to how high management's profits or equity can climb, but the players' slice of that pie is becoming smaller.

The only reason Selig hasn't gotten a salary cap is that owners don't need one and don't wish to risk the massive revenues MLB enjoys. Unless the MLBPA regroups, a cap is coming. Soon the Yankees and Mets will have new stadiums and their revenues and franchise value will go stratospheric. The luxury tax hasn't slowed the Yankees spending and soon they'll pull even further away from the pack.

There is only one way to slow the Yankee Empire—a hard cap on how much they can devote to payroll.

The three other major professional leagues have salary caps, which increase franchise values. The only thing keeping baseball from having one is the MLBPA and the expiration of the current agreement. If Fehr and Orza continue to attempt to hold their ground, marking time, they're inviting ownership to shove them backward and ram a salary cap down their throat.

Then the fall of Marvin Miller's empire will be complete.

Manager Grinders and Boppers

by Chris Jaffe

I've always had an interest in studying managers. In part, it's sabermetric's wide-open frontier. We've got all this really mathematically solid stuff like WARP and Win Shares and what-not to evaluate players. For managers? Neh. This is one reason one of my favorite books is *Bill James' Guide to Managers,* in which he sinks his teeth into this most forsaken of subjects.

One interesting bit in James' book was a two-page blurb on managerial tendencies. James had then-assistant John Sickels find out how often a manager's teams came in first or last in various categories to get a sense of what aspects a manager stressed or minimized. Obviously the managers' players and their talents came into play, but I think there's more to it than that. I'm going to take James' tendencies information a step further. Instead of counting only times in first or last, I want to account for and quantify every single ranking.

With such a formula, I can find out fun things, like which managers were the biggest fans of "small ball" techniques and which held themselves above those practices. To find the heroes and villains of small ball, I'm focusing on the two classic stats for playing for one run: sacrifice bunts and stolen base attempts.

I'll use Alan Trammell's proclivity to bunt as an example. In his three years as manager, Detroit led the league in sacrifice hits just once, but the Tigers were always near the top in sacrifices.

The simplest way—ranking all teams in a given league from most to least by sacrifice hits—doesn't work for two reasons.

First, there's the issue of opportunity. A team can sacrifice only if it has a runner on base. Thus, if the teams with the best and worst OBP in their league have the same number of sacrifice hits, the offensively challenged squad is more bunterific. You need to account for opportunity.

To do so, I use the following formula: SH/(H+BB+HBP+ROE-HR). ROE stands for Reached on Error, if you're curious. I want to keep the math here fairly basic. I'm not aiming for utter perfection; reasonable effectiveness works. By this formula,

Trammell had the most bunt-happy team in 2003 and was third in the AL the next two years.

That leads to the second snag. Coming in third in a 14-team league is different than third in an eight-team league. Solving this is a bit more vexing. You can't just divide rank by the number of teams in a league and leave it like that. If you did it for an eight-team league, you'd find that the teams had an average score of .5625, but if you do it for a 14-team league it's .5357. There is a reason for this, and if you grab a calculator you can figure it out, but I want to avoid getting caught in the numeric glob. The important point is that league sizes screw up comparisons across eras.

Fortunately, there's a way around this. With Trammell's 2002 season, take his rank in sacrifice hits (first), divide by teams (14), and then divide by the league average (.5357). This way all leagues from all eras will be centered at the same point; which will be 1. Lower scores mean the manager called for bunts or stolen bases more often, and higher means the team avoided small ball strategies. For Trammell's 2002, 1/14/0.5357 = 0.1333. He scores 0.4000 for each of his third place finishes. That averages to 0.3111—the score of a man who really liked to bunt.

With this method, I put every team from 1876-2006 in the database except the 1884 Union Association, which was a major league only for census purposes. Adding managers to the database, I can find out which ones loved/hated the classic small ball approach. I'm going to limit this to guys with at least 10 seasons, because otherwise I'd talk about managers no one ever heard of.

The wrinkle is trying to determine what constitutes a manager's season and what doesn't, because managers are sometimes fired in midseason. For this study, I attribute a team's stats to a manager if he ran the team for over half its games. It ain't perfect, but it works well enough.

Now that the explanations are done, I can get on with the results. Which managers were the most/least likely to sacrifice?

The results are on the following page.

Bunts have been recorded only since 1894, giving me 71 managers since then who've lasted at least a decade. Here are the ones who liked to bunt:

Manager	Bunt Score
Gene Mauch	0.442
Tommy Lasorda	0.479
Billy Southworth	0.519
Roger Craig	0.554
Joe Cronin	0.593

Not too surprising. Mauch was well-known for his fondness in this regard. I have him as the top bunter nine times, at least once with every squad he ran. He was runner-up eight times. Not bad. By my system, Southworth was the first or second most bunt-happy manager in the NL eight straight times.

The surprise is Joe Cronin. People don't think of him as a manager, but he led the Senators and Red Sox to the only pennant either had from 1925-1964. He was a big bunter when he began managing. His squads came in first or second in all but one of his first nine seasons before he cooled his ardor for the tactic. I should note that as a one-run strategy, bunting made less sense in the high-octane 1930s AL when he did it the most.

Next are the men who guarded their outs:

Manager	Bunt Score
Bruce Bochy	1.656
Buck Showalter	1.606
Tom Kelly	1.538
John McGraw	1.443
Jimmy Williams	1.440

With all this "Moneyball" talk these days, you'd think it would be some Beane-affiliated manager atop the list. Nope. In Bochy's last eight years in San Diego, the Padres were last or next-to-last every year except 2005.

John McGraw is a huge surprise. He came out of the 1890s Baltimore Orioles team that emphasized the inside game of playing every little edge. But while he loved to steal bases, he disdained the bunt. Admittedly, McGraw led the league in bunt-rificness twice, 1903 and '04, but he quickly shifted. Beginning in 1909, he was either last or next to last in bunting every year except once in the nearly quarter-century he remained

on the job. As a player, he loved getting on base, and as manager, he jealously guarded his outs. Until the 1990s, he was the most anti-bunting manager in baseball history.

Like sacrifice hits, thefts are a product of opportunity, so I'll base felicity for felony with feet on a formula that roughly accounts for chances: (SB+CS)/(H+BB+HBP+ROE-HR-3B-2B). It ain't perfect, but close enough.

Stolen bases weren't always recorded, but they've been around since the 1880s. That gives me slightly more managers to play with, 73. Here are the men who lived to run:

Manager	SB Likelihood
Whitey Herzog	0.368
Red Schoendienst	0.491
Walter Alston	0.507
Clark Griffith	0.538
Mike Hargrove	0.569

If you're surprised by Herzog's listing, then you weren't alive in the 1980s. His teams were in the top two in willingness to run every full season he managed except 1981 (which wasn't a full season) and 1989, when he was about done. Alston was the most larceny-minded man in the NL in each of his first eight seasons in LA except 1961, when his Dodgers were in second place. Though he and Maury Wills didn't revive the stolen base all by their lonesomes, they played a big role.

Here's the other half.

Manager	SB Likelihood
Bill Terry	1.600
Danny Murtaugh	1.506
Jimmy Williams	1.500
Johnny Oates	1.493
Buck Showalter	1.442

Some repeat names here, with Williams and Showalter. Bill Terry learned at the feet of John McGraw, who showed up on the least likely to bunt list. I get the feeling the Giants weren't into small ball much in the first half of the century.

So far, I've looked at thefts and bunts in isolation, but there's an underlying theme of the manager trying to scrape out one run. I've designed both so that lower scores indicate more small ball propensities. I'm going to add these two scores and see who were the least and most small-ball mangers since 1894, when we have data for both strategies. Since I'm combining data, an average score is 2, not 1.

Here are the most small ball minded managers ever:

Manager	S. Ball Score
Walter Alston	1.13
Paul Richards	1.35
Frank Chance	1.35
Whitey Herzog	1.40
Jack McKeon	1.49
Dick Williams	1.56
Joe Cronin	1.56
Bill Southworth	1.56
Phil Garner	1.56
Mike Hargrove	1.57

Initially Alston wasn't especially prone to play for one run. With the mighty "Boys of Summer" lineup, he'd be in the bottom half in bunts. While the 1955 Dodgers led the league in steals, that was partially a product of their OBP. Things changed with the move to LA. From 1958 to 1966, Alston took advantage of the skills of a new generation of Dodgers, the offense-deflated Dodger Stadium and the enlarged strike zone to become the all-time champion of small ball. The Dodgers were the top base path felons seven times in those years; coming in second the other times. They led the league in bunt frequency half the time, and were always in the top three. Though the departure of Wills in 1967 lessened his extreme offensive grinding, Alston remained a small ball practitioner.

One widely respected current manager who narrowly missed the top 10 (in fact, before 2007 he was 10th) is Tony La Russa. He has changed over the years, becoming less a grinder the longer he's been around. He was the league's most bunt-happy manager in his first two full seasons. In the next quarter century, he's led the league only twice more. Going team by team, his small ball score was a mere 1.311 with the White Sox, thanks to his bunts. In Oakland, with its powerful lineup, he bunted far less; slightly less than league average. That's still more than most managers would bunt with that lineup, though. Instead, he ran more with players like Rickey Henderson, giving him a small ball

score of 1.570 there. In St. Louis, he steals and bunts a little more than most, but not a huge amount more, for a score of 1.761.

Finally, men who lived for the big inning:

Manager	S. Ball Score
Buck Showalter	3.05
Jimmy Williams	2.94
Jimmy McAleer	2.75
Danny Murtaugh	2.74
Ralph Houk	2.71
Johnny Oates	2.68
Bill Terry	2.58
Bruce Bochy	2.56
Miller Huggins	2.51
Bill Virdon	2.38

Buck Showalter has almost always finished near the bottom in both categories. He ran a little more in Arizona, but in 1993 with the Yanks he became one of only four men (along with Bob Lemon in 1977, Don Zimmer in 1979 and Carlos Tosca in 2003) to come in dead last in both categories in a 14-team league.

The most impressive name on the list is Miller Huggins. He never liked to bunt, but with the Cards he frequently had his runners go. With his powerful Yankees lineup in the new live ball era, he cut back on that tremendously. He knew what his talent was and fit his style to match the players' abilities rather than force the situation; just what a good manager is supposed to do.

Looking over the anti-small ball lists, there's one glaring omission: Earl Weaver. He's the game's all-time great proponent of the big inning with his denunciations of such tactics in his book "Weaver on Strategy." Yet not only did he miss the least small ball list, he's not especially close, coming in as the 18th most station-to-station manager with a bunt score of 1.132 and a stolen base mark of 1.108. That's not at all what one would expect given his reputation. What is going on?

Simple: Weaver underwent a managerial metamorphosis. Through 1976 he was actually a moderate small baller, with a combined score of 1.672 (0.862 with steals, and .810 with bunts). The Orioles were one of the four most likely teams to bunt in the AL six times in his first eight years. He finished in the top half in at least one of those two categories each year in that first phase.

Then came his historic shift. From 1977 onward, his squads never again wound up in the top half of either tendency. In his remaining eight seasons, his small ball score was 2.838 (1.333 with steals, and 1.505 with bunts). Figuring small ball scores for single season, here's how Weaver ranked in the AL each year:

Year	Rank	
1968	4	(out of 10)
1969	4	(out of 12)
1970	6	
1971	7	
1972	7	
1973	3	
1974	2	
1975	3	
1976	6	
1977	10	(out of 14)
1978	12	
1979	12	
1980	11	
1981	11	
1982	13	
1985	14	
1986	14	

For a while there, even when his offenses had lots of power and ability, he was no less likely than average to try these tactics. Reading his book is like reading Walt Whitman's final version of *Leaves of Grass*. You get what the old man thinks about what the young man did. That's especially noteworthy because his earlier teams were actually a bit better. That doesn't mean that they were better because they bunted and stole more, but his writing tells you more about the 1985-6 Orioles than the 1969-71 glory run.

I guess here's where I'm supposed to make some brilliant statements about the small ball vs. big inning approaches. Certainly there's a script ready for me to follow. Bazillions of sabermetric researchers smarter than I'll ever be have deduced that small ball is for the birds. Playing for one run, as Weaver once put it, only gets you that run.

However, this study tells you about a manager's proclivities, not abilities. For the latter you'd have to dig deeper. The devil, as they say, is in the details. While I generally support the big inning strategy myself, I can't help but notice the top small ballers are a more impressive cast of characters. All approaches have their place depending on the era, park, players and game situation. But these were the men most extreme in their strategic predilections.

Billy Southworth ... in a Box

by Jon Daly

Editor's Note: in his classic book, The Bill James Guide to Baseball Managers from 1870 to Today, *Bill James used the "Manager in a Box" format he had pioneered in his earlier Abstracts to great effect, encapsulating the careers of many managerial greats. Arguably, the best manager James didn't include was Billy Southworth, who managed the Browns and Braves for 13 seasons. Jon Daly has come to Southworth's rescue.*

Year of birth: 1893
Years managed: 1929, 1940-1951
Managerial record: 1,044-704, .597 (similar to Frank Chance)

Characteristics as a player: He was a left-handed NL outfielder from 1915 to 1929. His career was similar to that of Casey Stengel.

Where does he fall on the managerial tree?: Southworth played for Joe Birmingham, Lee Fohl, Hugo Bezdek, George Gibson, Fred Mitchell, John McGraw, Rogers Hornsby and Bob O'Farrell in the majors, mainly Bezdek, McGraw, and Mitchell. We all know about McGraw. Mitchell was a pitcher who played for Frank Selee and Ned Hanlon. Hugo Bezdek was a college football coach at Penn State and his training methods may have been an influence for Southworth's regimented spring training camps. (McGraw had tough camps, too, but Bezdek's players looked forward to the games because they were easier than the practices.)

Other influences include Branch Rickey. Rickey was an innovator, an early user of such items as batting cages and sliding pits. Perhaps Bob Quinn, an executive at Columbus when Billy played there, was an influence.

Southworth was an influence on Earl Weaver, who second-guessed him as a teenager in the stands of Sportsman's Park. In fact, there were a number of future managers from the St. Louis area who were around for Southworth's teams. Whitey Herzog and Dick Williams are two others. (But Whitey was a Yankees fan, a front-runner.)

Players he managed who later became managers themselves include Del Crandall, Alvin Dark, Jim Elliot, Roy Hartsfield, Tommy Holmes, Lou Klein, Marty Marion, Gene Mauch, Terry Moore, Eddie Stanky and Harry Walker. I'm not sure how much of an influence Southworth was on Dark and Stanky. They did not get along.

What He Brought to a Ball Club

Was he an intense manager or more of an easy-to-get-along-with type?: In the middle. He wasn't a McGravian hardass, except for his first tour in 1929. But his tough training camps and occasional lectures to players weren't always appreciated.

Was he more of an emotional leader or a decision maker?: He was a quiet man and a decision maker. In *Baseball in '41*, Robert Creamer describes Southworth as a "hands-on manager. During a game, making changes that he felt had to be made…"

Was he more of an optimist or more of a problem solver?: A problem solver, as per the Creamer quote.

How He Used His Personnel

Did he like to platoon?: Platooning was a strategy that became popular after the Miracle Braves won the 1914 World Series. Later it fell out of favor as players complained about it and managers appeased them. Along with Stengel, he was instrumental in bringing back platooning as a strategy, although it wasn't called that in those days. (Both were platooned as players.) Newspapers sometimes called it the Southworth Shuffle or the Army game—his players had their own words for it. He used a three-headed platoon at third base with the Braves one year. With the Cardinals, he may have used platooning to counter an inordinate number of lefties that opposing teams would pitch against them in order to keep Stan Musial and Slaughter in check. Ken Heintzelman and Fritz Ostermuller were among those who started often against the Redbirds.

Did he try to solve his problems with proven players or with youngsters who still had something to prove?: He had young teams with the Cardinals, who had a well stocked farm system thanks to Branch Rickey. With Boston, he went with older players, particularly in the lineup. He seemed to work better with youngsters. In a way he was like a football coach who has had success at the college level but failed at the pro level. In his first go-around in 1929 his veteran ex-teammates mutinied. He had his greatest success with a relatively young Cardinals team during the war. And the veteran Braves descended into turmoil after the 1948 pennant winning season, causing Southworth to take a leave of absence late in the 1949 season.

How many players did he make regulars who had not been regulars before, and who were they?: (For hitters I went with first season with 100-plus games. For pitchers, I went with first season with 100-plus innings.) With St. Louis, 21: Charlie Gelbert, Ernie Orsatti, Fred Frankhouse, Bill Hallahan, Creepy Crespi, Johnny Hopp, Ernie White, Howie Krist, Stan Musial, Whitey Kurowski, Walker Cooper, Johnny Beazley, Murry Dickson, Howie Pollet, Harry Walker, Lou Klein, Ray Sanders, Harry Breechen, Emil Verban, Ted Wilks, Red Schoendienst. With Boston, six: Johnny Sain, Warren Spahn, Earl Torgeson, Alvin Dark, Vern Bickford, Sam Jethroe (special case).

Did he prefer to go with good offensive players or did he like the glove men?: Using Win Shares, a balanced team tends to have a ratio of roughly 2.84 hitting win shares to each fielding win share. With the Cardinals, his teams were balanced. With Boston, they tended more towards offense. This may be because he no longer had the gloves of Marty Marion and Terry Moore. It may be a characteristic of teams that platoon. It may have been because they were older.

Did he like an offense based on power, speed or high averages?: Averages. His teams led the league in hits six times and average five times. He did like speed, but more in the sense of taking the extra base rather than stealing. I'm not sure if he was averse to power, but when Branch Rickey traded Johnny Mize, the Cards replaced him with Ray Sanders and Johnny Hopp. Neither was a longball threat, but both could run.

Did he use the entire roster or did he keep people sitting on the bench?: He spread out the playing time with Boston, and most of his players saw action due to platooning.

Did he build his bench around young players who could step into the breach if need be, or around veteran role players who had their own functions within a game?: Veterans. He usually started the youngsters that he had.

Game Managing and Use of Strategies

Did he go for the Big Inning offense, or did he like to use the one-run strategies?: He definitely played small ball. "Southworth's idea was to get a lead …put the pressure on the other team." —Bill James

Did he pinch-hit much, and if so, when?: According to Retrosheet, Southworth's teams pinch-hit 23 times, while their opponents pinch-hit 20 times in World Series games. Usually, this was to pinch-hit for a pitcher, but he occasionally pinch-hit for others in the bottom third of the order. In Game 6 of the 1948 World Series he hit Clint Conatser for Marv Rickert and Phil Masi for Bill Sakeld when lefty Gene Bearden came in. Those appeared to be part of a platoon arrangement.

Was there anything unusual about his lineup selection?: Alvin Dark said that he would sometimes make lineup decisions based on how players looked in batting practice. Nowadays, lineups are up hours before game time. One time, Sibby Sisti was raking in batting practice and Southworth wanted to start him over Dark, but Dark begged to stay in the lineup, so Sisti played third for Bob Elliot.

Did he use the sac bunt often?: Yes, more than any manager since him, 150 times a year or so. In 1943, his Cards sac bunted 172 times; the most by a team ever since 1931. They won 105 games. He had Stan Musial bunt in the third inning of Game 1 of the 1944 World Series. Only Gene Mauch bunted more often relative to the other managers of his time.

Did he like to use the running game?: His teams didn't steal much, but they would take an extra base. The only year that I have caught stealing data for (1951), they were efficient; 80 for 114. That's a success rate of over 70%.

In what circumstances would he issue an intentional walk?: A sportswriter named Joe King wrote that Billy would use an intentional walk to set up a force play.

His teams issued seven intentional walks in the World Series versus 12 issued to them by the opponent. Blix Donnelly walked George McQuinn in Game 2 of 1944 to face Mark Christman. This set up a force, and it allowed Donnelly to avoid a lefty. Three intentional walks were issued to eighth-place hitters to face the pitcher. The other three were to load the bases.

Did he hit and run very often?: Stan Musial said that he did. With the Braves, Eddie Stanky would have his own signal for putting the hit and run on while he was at the plate. Alvin Dark thought that this was a convenient way for him to evade responsibility.

How did he change the game?: According to Robert Creamer in *1941*, Southworth and Leo Durocher are the reasons that managers can only visit their pitcher once an inning before having to remove him. He'd hold long meetings with the pitcher and the catcher and the infield, pushing games past the two-hour mark. He was also one of the first managers averse to criticizing his players in public. This was in reaction to how John McGraw treated him.

Handling the Pitching Staff

Did he like power pitchers or did he prefer to go with people who put the ball in play?: Billy's teams led the league in strikeouts four times. Although they only gave up the fewest walks per game one year, they usually gave up fewer than an average amount of walks.

Did he stay with his starters or go to the bullpen quickly?: Southworth's teams led the league in complete games six times. This was unlike Durocher who was in the vanguard of using relievers.

Did he use a four- or five-man rotation?: He was the first manager in the lively ball era to have three

starters start 37 or more games. He would leverage his starters by matching up his better ones against better teams and his lefties against teams with left-handed power. In 1942, other than Mort Cooper and Lon Warneke, he used his pitchers as swingmen. Max Lanier had 20 starts, seven against runners-up Brooklyn.

Did he use the entire staff, or did he try to get five or six people to do most of the work?: With Boston, at least, he usually had three pitchers pitch over half of the innings.

How long would he stay with a starting pitcher who was struggling?: Sain complained about being pulled. In four World Series, he had three quick hooks and one slow hook, while the opposing managers had one quick hook and two slow hooks. Not sure if this was similar to the regular season usage patterns.

Was there anything unique about his handling of pitchers?: Gerald Hern wrote a poem about this.

First we'll use Spahn
then we'll use Sain
Then an off day
followed by rain
Back will come Spahn
followed by Sain
And followed
we hope
by two days of rain

What was his strongest point as a manager?: Getting his players to play beyond expectations. Platooning put his hitters in situations where they'd be more likely to succeed. He even platooned Musial a bit when he was young. Were the battles of summer and fall won on the spring training fields of Florida? His camps were tougher than Joe McCarthy's. Not sure how he did with pitchers; Mike Gonzales and Johnny Cooney were his pitching coaches.

If there were no professional baseball, what would he probably have done with his life?: South-

Analysis

Signals and Noise

by Mitchel Lichtman

Separating signal from noise is one of the fundamental challenges of a baseball analyst. In recent years, teams, analysts and fans alike have become more sensitive to the problem of noise. For the most part, we now know not to overrate or underrate players based on one season, and that even the best of projections can be confounded by randomness on many different levels, in addition to any flaws in the system itself. Unexpectedly losing a Chris Carpenter can scuttle a team's season; avoiding the injury bug as the Indians did can spur a team to the playoffs.

So how do we determine whether a team like Cleveland's overachievement was due to the manager's influence, chance, the players themselves, their hitting coach, pitching coach, or perhaps some combination thereof? Maybe it was none of the above and the Indians simply had far fewer injuries than the average AL team, such that they were supposed to win 96 games, despite most people's less lofty preseason expectations.

There are a multitude of reasons why a team might under- or overachieve, not the least of which is the aforementioned chance alone. Beyond injuries, there can also be sudden improvements in individual performance brought on by good coaching, or a dramatic decline based on any number of factors.

So when we look back at the 2007 season, how can we pierce the fog, to paraphrase Bill James, and understand why some teams won while others lost?

To address that, we first must arrive at a reasonable expectation for each team going into the season, which is not a trivial task. Who determines what was "expected" of a team? I was listening to a Nats game on XM radio the other day, when one of the announcers stated that Manny Acta (the Nats skipper) should be a candidate for manager of the year because, "Everyone expected the Nats to win only 50 or 60 games, and they are on pace to win around 70."

First of all, who is "everyone?" Surely not anyone with any reasonable baseball prognostication skills. The preseason "Vegas line" for the Nationals was 68.5 wins. Most of the analytical forecasters had them in the mid 60s (OK, Buster Olney projected them with 49 wins). They ended the season with 73 wins.

What about the Indians? They finished the '07 campaign with 96 wins. The preseason Vegas line was 86.5 wins and most of the good forecasters predicted them to win 89 or 90. So, apparently they managed almost 10 more wins than expected. Perhaps their surprising success was the result of Eric Wedge's managing skill, as many have suggested.

The problem with that premise is that it is not difficult for a team, by chance alone, to over (or under) perform its expectation or true talent by eight or 10 games. One standard deviation in wins for a 162-game season is almost seven games, by chance alone. So, around one out of 20 teams per season will exceed its true talent by more than 10 games, with or without any influence by the manager.

With a little analytical gymnastics, we can in fact figure out how many games the Cardinals, Phillies and every other team, were expected to win before the season, how they were supposed to do once we found out their exact personnel and playing time, whether they exceeded or fell short of either or both of those expectations, and from whence that over- or underachievement came.

The Methodology and Results

Let's start with the preseason win/loss projections. I used Baseball Prospectus' playing time projections and depth charts for pitchers and batters, along with my own Superlwts (offense, defense, and baserunning) and pitcher projections in order to come up with a basic runs scored and runs allowed per game for each team.

For example, if the Cubs' non-pitchers, prorated by their estimated playing time, were collectively projected at 10 runs below average per season in offense, defense and baserunning, and their pitchers combined were projected at 20 runs above average, then they would have an average runs scored per game of 4.5 (I use that as the NL average) minus $10/162$ runs, and runs allowed of 4.5 minus $20/162$. From that, I used a simple Pythagorean formula (with a 1.86 exponent) to compute a baseline win percentage. After doing that for all 30 teams, I simulated the entire 2007 season 10,000 times, using each team's win percentage and a log5 formula to determine the outcome of each game. The results are in the following table:

119

Teams	Projected pre-season wins
AL East	
NYA	93
BOS	90
TOR	84
BAL	78
TB	74
AL Central	
CLE	89
MIN	84
DET	79
CHA	77
KC	71
AL West	
OAK	86
LAA	84
TEX	80
SEA	77
NL East	
ATL	85
PHI	85
NYN	84
FLA	79
WAS	69
NL Central	
STL	85
MIL	84
CHN	81
HOU	78
PIT	76
CIN	71
NL West	
SD	89
ARI	84
LAN	82
COL	77
SF	77

While a manager may deserve some credit (good or bad) for the difference between playing time and personnel estimates before the season starts and that which ultimately plays out, I think much of that is within the domain of injuries and the front office.

In any case, as you will see, the difference between the preseason win projections and the win projections based on actual personnel and playing time is in most cases pretty small. That's probably because most major league players are fungible. Even the loss of so-called star players for significant periods of time usually costs a team no more than a couple of games in win expectancy.

Once we have our preseason "blind" win projections in place, step two is to take our player projections and prorate them for the actual playing time of each player on each team, after the season is over. This next table adds our win projections for each team based on actual personnel and playing time, again using preseason player projections only.

	Projected pre-season wins	Projected wins based on actual playing time	Diff
AL East			
NYA	93	95	+2
BOS	90	89	-1
TOR	84	82	-2
BAL	78	75	-3
TB	74	79	+5
AL Central			
CLE	89	91	+2
MIN	84	84	0
DET	79	80	+1
CHA	77	76	-1
KC	71	72	+1
AL West			
OAK	86	82	-4
LAA	84	83	-1
TEX	80	78	-2
SEA	77	81	+4
NL East			
ATL	85	85	0
PHI	85	83	-2
NYN	84	84	0
FLA	79	78	-1
WAS	69	74	+5
NL Central			
STL	85	83	-2
MIL	84	82	-2

Keep in mind that these win projections are based on estimates of player personnel and playing time. When the smoke clears and the season is over (or even begins) all kinds of things can and will wreak havoc on these estimates. Players, especially pitchers, will get injured and miss substantial playing time—in some cases, an entire season. Managers and GMs will make roster moves and playing time decisions that may not correspond to our initial estimates.

	Projected pre-season wins	Projected wins based on actual playing time	Diff
CHN	81	79	-2
HOU	78	76	-2
PIT	76	77	+1
CIN	71	70	-1
NL West			
SD	89	89	0
ARI	84	82	-2
LAN	82	85	+3
COL	77	81	+4
SF	77	76	-1

	Projected pre-season wins	Projected wins based on actual playing time	Projected wins based on actual underlying performance	Diff
AL East				
NYA	93	95	96	+1
BOS	90	89	101	+12
TOR	84	82	86	+4
BAL	78	75	75	0
TB	74	79	71	-8
AL Central				
CLE	89	91	91	0
MIN	84	84	75	-9
DET	79	80	86	+6
CHA	77	76	72	-4
KC	71	72	66	-6
AL West				
OAK	86	82	84	+2
LAA	84	83	82	-1
TEX	80	78	80	+2
SEA	77	81	80	-1
NL East				
ATL	85	85	85	0
PHI	85	83	87	+4
NYN	84	84	92	+8
FLA	79	78	71	-7
WAS	69	74	70	-4
NL Central				
STL	85	83	74	-9
MIL	84	82	85	+3
CHN	81	79	91	+12
HOU	78	76	68	-8
PIT	76	77	68	-9
CIN	71	70	76	+6
NL West				
SD	89	89	90	+1
ARI	84	82	79	-3
LAN	82	85	86	+1
COL	77	81	89	+8
SF	77	76	76	0

If the projected wins based on actual playing time are significantly fewer than the preseason projected wins, this could reflect injuries (and missed playing time) to one or more impact players, or it could represent poor roster or playing time decisions on the part of the front office or manager. Conversely, if the second win projection is substantially higher than the first, that could indicate some good personnel decisions by the manager or GM. Of course, either situation could also suggest bad preseason playing time estimates.

As I said earlier, if you look at the table, you will probably be surprised by how similar the two win totals are, even for teams that were considered to have had lots of impact injuries this year. The average difference is less than two wins per team.

Only four teams, Tampa Bay, Washington, Colorado, and Seattle, had projections that were more than three wins greater than their preseason projections

Only one team, Oakland, had a projection more than three wins worse than before the season started. This was probably due to injuries to key players, like Rich Harden, Bobby Crosby, and Eric Chavez.

In the next table, I am adding a third projected win column. This represents the number of wins (again, using a Pythagorean formula for each team and simulating 10,000 seasons) that each team "should have" accumulated given the actual park and context-neutral linear weights (again, offensive, defensive, and baserunning) performance of their hitters and the park and context-neutral component ERAs of their pitchers. The difference between column three and column four is strictly the collective difference between a team's projected and actual underlying context-neutral component performance:

Here is where we find lots of substantial differences between what we expected from all the individual player performances and what they actually produced (again, in context and park-neutral component stats). Some of these difference are "errors" in our preseason projections for one or more players, some of it is fluctuation or luck in the performance itself (It is possible for an entire team to substantially over- or underperform its collective individual player projections, due to chance alone, even if those projections were pretty accurate given the information we had at the time they were made.) And of course some may be good or bad managing, coaching, team chemistry or player development.

Looking at the above chart, the teams that moderately outperformed their preseason performance projections were:

- Detroit
- Toronto
- Philly
- Cincinnati

Teams that far outperformed their player projections were:

- Boston
- New York (N)
- Cubs
- Colorado

Should we give these teams' managers credit for this performance overachievement? Perhaps. Or perhaps we should first look at their actual records, or at least their Pythagorean records (based on runs scored and runs allowed), before we start handing out any awards. After all, what good is great context-neutral performance if it does not lead to lots of runs scored or fewer runs allowed, and more wins?

On the flip side, these teams' players moderately underperformed as compared to their preseason projections:

- Chicago (A)
- Washington
- Kansas City

The six teams that really did badly, compared to what a forecaster might have expected, were:

- Tampa Bay
- St. Louis
- Houston
- Pittsburgh

- Florida
- Minnesota

As you can see, many teams significantly over or underperformed their projections. Let's take a look at some underlying data to see if we can figure out where some teams may have gone wrong and others may have gone right. The table below presents each team's expected and actual pitching, batting, defense (UZR) and baserunning.

	Projected Offense	Actual Offense	Projected Pitching	Actual Pitching	Projected Defense	Actual Defense	Projected Baserunning	Actual Baserunning
AL East								
NYA	98	174	54	16	-19	-38	3	7
BOS	72	77	50	154	-20	-23	-11	-8
TOR	0	-53	6	90	13	12	1	-11
BAL	-19	-10	-41	-14	2	-55	-1	-1
TB	-14	13	-9	-12	-14	-102	3	4
AL Central								
CLE	73	50	5	0	5	18	0	-10
MIN	-29	-92	30	0	7	11	-3	2
DET	-6	93	-41	-106	18	41	-1	5
CHA	-40	-108	-8	6	0	6	-9	-10
KC	-44	-126	-70	-98	10	62	-1	-4
AL West								
OAK	-22	-24	9	26	5	20	2	-5
LAA	-56	-20	44	-2	1	12	8	12
TEX	-23	-8	-25	-38	-24	-1	2	15
SEA	-8	67	-5	-25	-3	-70	-1	-1
NL East								
ATL	41	51	-2	3	13	19	1	-6
PHI	23	130	-31	-88	17	25	1	13
NYN	46	45	-8	1	-6	57	5	9
FLA	21	55	-25	-47	-11	-67	4	-3
WAS	-32	-61	-41	-20	2	-28	5	9
NL Central								
STL	-3	-24	-1	-37	24	25	3	-9
MIL	-6	48	15	15	3	-26	-2	1
CHN	-4	-3	-5	13	-9	81	-6	-4
HOU	-19	-49	5	-15	-14	-21	-5	-17
PIT	-8	-53	-24	-51	-2	-5	-1	-4
CIN	-46	23	12	2	-51	-52	-2	-11
NL West								
SD	26	-40	45	73	12	72	2	1
ARI	-18	-57	36	59	3	2	0	11
LAN	-4	22	48	43	-7	1	3	9
COL	-2	48	-21	23	25	13	3	8
SF	-21	-46	-6	20	4	-1	-3	2

Note: While I did present each team's expected and actual baserunning linear weights, I am not going to discuss them any further. As you can see, and contrary to the opinions of some mainstream commentators and analysts, baserunning is not a significant part of a team's success or failure. Other than a few outliers, the difference between the best and worst baserunning teams in any one season is around two wins.

Remember that columns two, four, six, and eight are what a good forecaster might have expected the team to do performance-wise (each column represents runs above/below average, where plus is always good), assuming that forecaster knew who was going to play and how often. Columns three, five, seven, and nine are how those same players actually performed in park and context-neutral linear weights and component ERA.

First, let's bust a myth that has been hanging around the media (and fans I guess, and perhaps, sadly, the team itself) for several years. Texas does not have, nor did it field this year, a good offense! I am probably preaching to the choir here, but I assume that this myth exists and persists because Texas' stadium is the best hitter's park in the AL and perhaps in baseball.

Another thing that has to jump out at you is how bad across the board three organizations are: the Rangers, Pirates, and Nationals. I guess both Washington and Pittsburgh have an excuse—the former being a "new" team, once league-owned, and the latter being part of a small market, in terms of population and local revenue. What is Texas' excuse? Every year, the Rangers are a few pitchers away from contending, according to their fans, front office, management and the local media. It looks to me like they are a lot more than a few pitchers, hitters and defenders away from contending. Kansas City is also a pretty bad organization other than its defense, which unfortunately is only a small part of a team's total package.

Let's look at some other teams and discuss how and why their projections and actual performance were so divergent.

The Overachievers:

Toronto

Interestingly, the Jays' offense far underperformed their projections while their pitching outperformed to an even greater degree, even without B.J. Ryan, a supposed key loss for them. A.J. Burnett pitched brilliantly, better than expected, Roy Halladay was the ace he was supposed to be, and their two young starters, Dustin McGowan and Shaun Marcum, were pleasant

surprises. Their bullpen without Ryan was quite good as well. I have no idea why their hitters performed so poorly. (I rarely know why we, as forecasters, miss the mark on players the way we sometimes do. It is an occupational hazard, I guess.)

Detroit

I really missed the boat with their offense (again, even having the luxury of knowing who played and how often), and I have no idea why. Certainly the stellar performances of Magglio Ordonez and Curtis Granderson did not help my cause. Speaking of the Tigers, can we also get rid of the myth that the Tigers have good pitching? They don't. Their pitching, overall, was not supposed to be good, nor was it, despite the great year, and wonderful talent, of Justin Verlander, and a couple of good young relievers. Do you think that the fact that Detroit is a great pitcher's park has anything to do with this myth, much like the one in Texas? Plus, their good defense bolsters their pitching staff.

Oakland

Oakland did indeed have a poor offense this year, partly as a result of injuries to some key players. Their pitching, however, far exceeded their pitcher projections. (Losing Harden for much of the season was not their problem, although that certainly did not help.) Their problem, as you will see later, was that they could not turn their marginally poor offensive performance, excellent pitching and good defense into wins.

Mets

Other than their hitting (which was good to begin with), the Mets overachieved substantially across the board. Not much else to say. Anyone who says that the Mets were a fantastically talented team that underachieved is grossly misinformed. They are a fairly talented team that tremendously overachieved. Of course, after their historic collapse in '07, try telling that to a Mets fan!

Cubs

The Cubs get a lot of bad press and criticism, at least when they are losing, and sometimes even when they are winning. Maybe it is because of their 99-year World Series drought. In any case, they outpitched their pitching projections, especially Jason Marquis (I still expect him to be the bad pitcher he always was and probably is, from this point hence), and substantially outperformed their defensive projection. Offensively, they were projected to be about average, and performed the same. It is a minor miracle that they ended up winning their division. I would not expect much more than a league-average team next year, unless they make some substantial improvements.

San Diego

One of my favorite teams, and I think one of the best-run in baseball, did not fare well in its actual hitting as compared to their offensive projection. Of course, the Padres weren't nearly as bad offensively as the media made them out to be (they play in an extreme pitcher's park—what a surprise!). Their pitching and defense, though, is what got them to within one game of a wild card berth, even after taking the park out of the equation. They simply destroyed their pitching and defensive projections (which were good to begin with), with the likes of Jake Peavy and Chris Young, another good year for Greg Maddux, unusually good performances from several other lesser-known pitchers, and good defense from just about everyone but Kevin Kouzmanoff.

Colorado

The Rockies, a legitimately good team (finally), simply outdid themselves in hitting and in pitching. It is probably not too likely that they will perform nearly as well next year, given the same personnel.

What about some of the underperformers?

Seattle

It is hard to think of the M's as underachievers since they ended up winning a lot more games than most people, including me, expected. Remember that I am talking here about underlying component performance (not actual runs or wins) as compared to expected performance. Anyway, while the Mariners significantly overachieved offensively, their pitching and defense, especially the latter, were a lot worse than expected. The saving grace for the M's this year was that their actual win total far exceeded their expected win total based on their underlying performance. Unfortunately for M's fans, that is something that is probably not repeatable. Don't expect much from them next year unless they substantially change their personnel. As currently configured, they are a below-average team.

Florida

The Marlins actually had a good offense that did even better than expected. On the other hand, their pitching was not expected to be particularly good, and it really stunk. So did their defense, with the likes of Miguel Cabrera and Hanley Ramirez anchoring (or should I say anchored to) the left side of the infield. They should be a lot better next year, especially if they upgrade or "fix" (Scott Olsen, for example) their pitching staff.

St. Louis

While I am sure that some of their woes had to do with players being hurt, other than defensively, they simply underperformed across the board. Looking at their line in the above table, it is hard to like the re-upping of La Russa for another two years, or think that he did a good job managing the team this year.

Houston

Like the Cardinals, but even worse, they pretty much underachieved across the board, which they could hardly afford to do, given that their overall talent was pretty bad to begin with. They need to do a lot more than get more guys like Carlos Lee (overpaid, good-hit, bad-field corner outfielder) to improve their team. On the other hand, their pitching is and should be decent next year, but they need to do a lot to upgrade their offense and defense.

Pittsburgh

Similar to Houston and even the Cards, they are a bad team that played even worse than expected. They need a lot of help across the board. A lot. The hiring of ex-Indians executive and saber-friendly Neal Huntington as their new GM should help.

Cincinnati

Again, partly because of their hitter's park, and partly because their hitters overachieved this year, there is the illusion that they have a good offense. They don't. And they seem to be unaware of the fact that they have a truly horrendous defensive team. Defense is a lot easier to upgrade than offense—if you know what you are doing (see San Diego). I don't think the Reds do. They are a long way from contending.

Tampa Bay

You can easily see the reason why the Devil Rays' performance this year was far, far below their expected performance: defense, defense, and defense. I don't know how any major league team can place its fielders in such a way as to produce a -102 runs in defense. They clearly need to start moving players around the field or replace some of their bad defenders altogether. Maybe just randomly assign everyone a position, or ask everyone where he wants to play, like the last game of the season in Little League.

Because of their historically poor defense, there was the illusion that the Rays pitching was very bad. It wasn't. It was actually around league average. I hope they realize that. Given their young talent, new management, and new-look uniforms, I think there are some brighter days ahead for the team formerly known as the Devil Rays.

Next let's see how each team's performance translated into runs scored and allowed. There should be, in the long run, an almost perfect correlation between offensive linear weights plus baserunning, and runs scored, and component ERA plus defense, and runs allowed, given that we don't think that clutch hitting or pitching as a skill is significant or pervasive.

Of course, in the short run, in this case one season, the relationship between component performance and runs, like runs (Pythagorean record) and actual record, will not be nearly perfect. Anyway, we're going to add a column to our projected wins table on the right. It is the team's Pythagorean record, based on its actual runs scored and runs allowed.

The difference between the fourth and fifth columns is basically a result of clutch or leveraged play. If you want, you can attribute that to the players themselves. Or you can attribute it to the manager. Or you can attribute it to the alignment of the planets and stars. Anything is fine with me.

Remember that Pythagorean win percentage is a proxy for runs scored and runs allowed. So the difference between columns four and five represents the actual number of runs scored and allowed as compared to what each team should have scored and allowed based on its underlying context (and park) neutral performance. Again, most baseball analysts think that the latter represents a team's true talent and is more predictive of future runs scored and runs allowed than the former. It's similar to the thinking that a team's Pythagorean record is more predictive of a team's true talent and future record than its actual record in the past.

The two teams that significantly overperformed in terms of actual runs scored and allowed (as reflected by their Pythagorean win total) as compared to their underlying offensive and defensive component performance were:

- Los Angeles (A)
- Kansas City

Teams that moderately overperformed in this regard were:

- Minnesota
- Detroit
- Atlanta
- Houston

	Projected pre-season wins	Projected wins based on actual playing time	Projected wins based on actual underlying performance	Pythago-rean Wins	Diff
AL East					
NYA	93	95	96	97	+1
BOS	90	89	101	101	0
TOR	84	82	86	86	0
BAL	78	75	75	71	-4
TB	74	79	71	67	-4
AL Central					
CLE	89	91	91	92	+1
MIN	84	84	75	79	+4
DET	79	80	86	90	+4
CHA	77	76	72	67	-5
KC	71	72	66	75	+9
AL West					
OAK	86	82	84	79	-5
LAA	84	83	82	90	+8
TEX	80	78	80	80	0
SEA	77	81	80	78	-2
NL East					
ATL	85	85	85	89	+4
PHI	85	83	87	87	0
NYN	84	84	92	87	-5
FLA	79	78	71	72	+1
WAS	69	74	70	71	+1
NL Central					
STL	85	83	74	72	-2
MIL	84	82	85	83	-2
CHN	81	79	91	86	-5
HOU	78	76	68	73	+5
PIT	76	77	68	70	+2
CIN	71	70	76	74	-2
NL West					
SD	89	89	90	88	-2
ARI	84	82	79	79	0
LAN	82	85	86	81	-5
COL	77	81	89	90	+1
SF	77	76	76	78	+2

On the flip side, there were no large underperformers. The moderate underachievers were:

- Baltimore
- Tampa Bay
- White Sox
- Oakland

- New York (N)
- Chicago (N)
- Los Angeles (N)

Finally, let's look at each team's actual record at the end of the season. We'll add that to the previous table, resulting in the master table on the right.

The significance of the difference between a team's Pythagorean win total and its actual number of wins has been dissected ad nauseam lately, given the Diamondbacks' situation (best record in the NL and a negative run differential). I won't reiterate the various positions other than to say that a significant difference is likely due mostly to chance, but could also be a "talent" inherent in managerial skill, bullpen prowess, players being able to leverage their skills, etc.

The teams that significantly outperformed their Pythagorean win projections were:

- Chicago (A)
- St. Louis
- Seattle

And of course, Arizona, which won 11 more games than its (negative) run differential suggests!

The teams that won significantly fewer (five or more) games than their Pythagorean win totals were:

- New York (A)
- Kansas City
- San Francisco

Surprise teams like the Rockies or Mariners make baseball interesting to follow, but it is useful to understand why teams did better or worse than expected. While I left many things untouched in terms of the above data and analysis, I think I have presented some useful numbers that can help separate the signal from the noise in evaluating your favorite team's performance this past season and in the near future.

	Projected pre-season wins	Projected wins based on actual playing time	Projected wins based on actual underlying performance	Pythagorean Wins	Actual wins
AL East					
NYA	93	95	96	97	94
BOS	90	89	101	101	96
TOR	84	82	86	86	83
BAL	78	75	75	71	69
TB	74	79	71	67	66
AL Central					
CLE	89	91	91	92	96
MIN	84	84	75	79	79
DET	79	80	86	90	88
CHA	77	76	72	67	72
KC	71	72	66	75	69
AL West					
OAK	86	82	84	79	76
LAA	84	83	82	90	94
TEX	80	78	80	80	75
SEA	77	81	80	78	88
NL East					
ATL	85	85	85	89	84
PHI	85	83	87	87	89
NYN	84	84	92	87	88
FLA	79	78	71	72	71
WAS	69	74	70	71	73
NL Central					
STL	85	83	74	72	78
MIL	84	82	85	83	83
CHN	81	79	91	86	85
HOU	78	76	68	73	73
PIT	76	77	68	70	68
CIN	71	70	76	74	72
NL West					
SD	89	89	90	88	89
ARI	84	82	79	79	90
LAN	82	85	86	81	82
COL	77	81	89	90	90
SF	77	76	76	78	71

The Best Fielding Teams of 2007

by John Dewan

The National League champion Colorado Rockies received plenty of hype for their team defense after they finished the regular season with a record team fielding percentage of .989 (.98925 when taken to the extra decimal points needed to determine their No. 1 ranking). They broke the mark set only a year earlier by the Boston Red Sox, .98909.

Are these two teams, then, two of the best team defenses of all time? Not by any stretch of the imagination. Certainly, making all the plays that you are expected to make is a tremendous asset. But the No. 1 underlying skill needed for great defense is great speed, and neither team has it.

The Rockies and the Red Sox, who squared off in the World Series this past season, finished 14th and 11th, respectively, among the 30 teams in baseball in Team Baserunning (from *The Bill James Handbook 2008*). Correspondingly, neither team has great defense. On our Team Defense plus/minus chart, shown here, the BoSox were slightly below average with a -14 team score while Colorado was right at average with -3.

If you don't have speed, it sure helps to be surehanded and that's exactly what played an important part in getting the Red Sox and Rockies to the World Series. Colorado set the team fielding percentage record, while Boston followed up its record-breaking 2006 season with a .986 percentage, good for second place in the American League (behind the Baltimore Orioles).

If not the Rockies or Red Sox, which 2007 team really threw the leather? The Toronto Blue Jays! They had the best team defense in 2007 by a significant margin over the second-place New York Mets, when measured using the Plus/Minus System. The system, developed for my book *The Fielding Bible* (released in February 2006), is based on videotape reviews by Video Scouts at Baseball Info Solutions. They record the exact direction, distance, speed and type of every batted ball into a computer, allowing for tremendously detailed analysis of defense (see more on the system below).

Why plus/minus and not fielding percentage? The best way I can describe it is by analogy. On-base percentage plus slugging percentage (OPS) has become well accepted as the best, easily calculable statistic for measuring offensive ability. Before OPS, there was batting average as the best stat to use to analyze hitting. Now we know

it's not. Fielding percentage is like batting average. It tells part of the story, but nowhere near what you need to know. The Plus/Minus System is like OPS. Fielding percentage is, in essence, a subset of plus/minus. If you have a better batting average, you have a better OPS. Likewise, if you have a better fielding percentage, you have a better plus/minus.

Back to the Blue Jays. They had a team plus/minus figure of +92 in 2007. That means they made 92 more plays than could be expected of an average defense. They were 19 plays ahead of the second-place Mets. Over the last four years that we've been doing this analysis, the Blue Jays' defense has been consistently good, posting scores of +92, +65, +31 and +47. That's impressive. They turned it up another notch this past year as the double-play combination of Aaron Hill and John McDonald sparkled in the field.

The best defensive outfield plus/minus score was posted by the Atlanta Braves for the third year in a row. They scored a +69 in 2007 after their +63 and +61 in 2006 and 2005. Now that's consistent!

For 2007 they had the Fielding Bible Award winner Andruw Jones at +24 in center field. Jeff Francouer was the runner-up for the award in right field and had a +10 plus/minus figure. Willie Harris was absolutely awesome (+21) after securing the bulk of the left field job in May. Now look at their throwing arms: They ranked No. 1 in the majors in intimidation factor by allowing just 45.4% of runners to attempt an extra base on a single or double. Also, they had 21 baserunner kills as a unit, tied for sixth best in baseball. Combine all these elements and they easily win this year's title: Best Outfield Defense for 2007.

A year ago, we gave the title of Best Infield Defense to the Detroit Tigers. They scored a +46, beating the competition with their superb performance in turning double plays and handling bunts. But that's no comparison to the incredible plus/minus figure of +81 turned in by the infield of the 2007 Toronto Blue Jays. We already mentioned the tremendous job done by Hill, who won the Fielding Bible Award at second base, and by McDonald, who finished third in the voting for the shortstop award. Now add in Lyle Overbay's +13 at first base and another +9 by third-baseman Troy Glaus, and you have an unbeatable combination—and the title of Best Infield Defense for 2007.

Team Totals and Rankings - 2007

Team	PLUS/MINUS Middle Infield	Corner Infield	Outfield	Total	Rank	GROUND DP GDP Opps	GDP	Pct	Rank	BUNTS Opps	Score	Grade	Rank	THROWING Opps To Advance	Extra Bases	Kills	Pct	Rank
Toronto Blue Jays	+56	+25	+11	+92	1	346	146	.422	9	22	.461	C-	30	418	203	18	.486	9
New York Mets	+15	+11	+47	+73	2	319	110	.345	29	54	.622	B+	2	407	219	16	.538	27
Atlanta Braves	-5	+4	+69	+68	3	330	119	.361	28	59	.529	C+	17	449	204	21	.454	1
Kansas City Royals	+25	+24	+17	+66	4	295	138	.468	1	25	.466	C-	26	460	234	21	.509	21
Arizona Diamondbacks	+19	-18	+53	+54	5	327	138	.422	8	41	.562	B-	10	416	211	18	.507	19
Detroit Tigers	0	+29	+16	+45	6	297	125	.421	10	24	.515	C+	19	470	229	18	.487	10
Chicago Cubs	+3	+13	+20	+36	7	303	117	.386	26	61	.534	C+	14	402	194	26	.483	8
St Louis Cardinals	-17	+58	-5	+36	7	334	131	.392	23	35	.734	A+	1	497	243	18	.489	12
Oakland Athletics	+14	+8	+3	+25	9	318	135	.425	7	33	.480	C	22	465	250	12	.538	26
San Diego Padres	0	-6	+30	+24	10	324	126	.389	25	68	.607	B+	4	434	238	14	.548	28
Philadelphia Phillies	+25	-2	-4	+19	11	339	135	.398	21	55	.589	B	6	478	218	29	.456	2
San Francisco Giants	+1	+46	-31	+16	12	328	130	.396	22	63	.618	B+	3	442	220	9	.498	15
Cleveland Indians	+5	-9	+12	+8	13	334	136	.407	18	49	.530	C+	16	474	240	14	.506	18
Washington Nationals	-33	-8	+45	+4	14	320	134	.419	12	55	.580	B	7	474	254	13	.536	25
Texas Rangers	-9	-14	+21	-2	15	366	143	.391	24	37	.470	C	24	495	261	19	.527	24
Milwaukee Brewers	-5	-41	+44	-2	15	299	125	.418	13	51	.545	B-	12	489	244	14	.499	16
Colorado Rockies	+46	-16	-33	-3	17	344	154	.448	4	44	.518	C+	18	465	233	12	.501	17
Minnesota Twins	+14	+16	-36	-6	18	299	128	.428	6	29	.469	C-	25	428	204	18	.477	6
Los Angeles Angels	+8	+27	-47	-12	19	294	133	.452	3	30	.465	C-	27	460	228	17	.496	14
Boston Red Sox	+3	+14	-31	-14	20	276	115	.417	14	31	.577	B	8	378	192	13	.508	20
Baltimore Orioles	+3	-5	-12	-14	20	331	133	.402	19	49	.462	C-	28	520	269	19	.517	23
Los Angeles Dodgers	-8	-20	+13	-15	22	338	142	.420	11	46	.593	B	5	447	265	9	.593	30
New York Yankees	-20	+17	-34	-37	23	331	151	.456	2	39	.462	C-	29	463	218	25	.471	4
Seattle Mariners	-11	-14	-24	-49	24	339	140	.413	15	34	.472	C	23	502	238	16	.474	5
Pittsburgh Pirates	-4	-18	-28	-50	25	368	163	.443	5	52	.575	B	9	527	260	21	.493	13
Houston Astros	-5	-17	-29	-51	26	332	112	.337	30	52	.547	B-	11	438	243	18	.555	29
Cincinnati Reds	+7	-29	-37	-59	27	317	130	.410	16	49	.490	C	21	482	235	17	.488	11
Chicago White Sox	-38	-15	-23	-76	28	344	138	.401	20	55	.536	C+	13	528	271	15	.513	22
Florida Marlins	-54	-44	+10	-88	29	347	128	.369	27	56	.530	C+	15	554	267	26	.482	7
Tampa Bay Devil Rays	-51	-17	-39	-107	30	314	128	.408	17	49	.491	C	20	546	256	24	.469	3

Description of the 2007 Team Totals and Rankings

The team totals and rankings are broken into four groups: Plus/Minus, Ground DP, Bunts and Throwing. In the columns under the heading Plus/Minus we've broken down the data further into three groupings: Middle Infield (second base and shortstop), Corner Infield (first and third base), and Outfield (left, center and right).

The next three main column headings are associated with one of those position groupings. Ground DP tells you how often the team turned double plays given its opportunities (groundball with a man on first and less than two outs) and primarily applies to the middle infielders, though all GDPs are included in these team totals. Bunts apply primarily to the corner infielders, though all bunts are included in the team totals, regardless of who fielded them. You'll see letter grades based on the traditional system in schools of A through F, so you can get an idea of how well a team performed on bunts. The entire bunt grading system is described in *The Fielding Bible*. Throwing applies to outfielders only.

The Plus/Minus System

My book *The Fielding Bible* goes into great length describing the new fielding system we developed at Baseball Info Solutions—the Plus/Minus System. (I'll be bringing out a new edition in February of 2009.) Video Scouts at Baseball Info Solutions review video of every play of every major league game and record detailed information on each play, such as the location of each batted ball, the speed, the type of hit, etc.

Using this in-depth data, we're able to figure out how each player compares to his peers at his position. For example, how often does Derek Jeter field that ball hit softly 20 feet to the right of the normal shortstop position compared to all other major league shortstops?

A player gets credit (a "plus" number) if he makes a play that at least one other player at his position missed during the season, and he loses credit (a "minus" number) if he misses a play that at least one player made. The credit is directly related to how often players make the play. Each play is considered individually and receives its own score.

Sum up all the plays for each player at each position and you get his total plus/minus for the season. A total plus/minus score near zero means the player is average. A positive score is above average, and a negative score is below average. Albert Pujols turned in the highest total in 2007 with +37. That means he made 37 more plays than the average MLB first baseman would make if he had the same types of batted balls to handle that Pujols had.

The Bill James Handbook 2008 has the final plus/minus leader boards (and trailer boards) for the 2007 season, plus the announcement of the second annual Fielding Bible Awards (which, just for the record, come out each year **before** the Gold Gloves!).

A Random Walk Through a Markov Model in 2007

by John Beamer

The reason I love baseball is because it is perhaps the most multi-faceted sport there is. To an uninformed fan, the game is about hitting a small white ball with a cylindrical lump of wood. However, an astute observer quickly realizes that unlike other sports, baseball makes it possible to precisely quantify many aspects of the game. This allows us to produce advanced statistics such as linear weights, run expectancy, win probability and leverage index.

The creation of these metrics is possible because of the discrete nature of the game. In addition, there are run estimators and simulators to model in-game situations and answer precise strategic and tactical questions. All that and more can be done through the application of a Markov chain. This is because a Markov is the most mathematically perfect way to model baseball, as it reflects the precise way that the game is played.

Why is this? In a nutshell, a Markov chain splits a process into discrete states and records the possible transitions between those states. In baseball, the states are the 24 different base-out combinations. At the start of an inning, the bases are empty and there are no outs: This is our starting state. Provided we know the odds of the batter reaching a base or making an out, we can calculate the probability of entering any future base-out state. The logic is best illustrated through example.

Imagine a very simple game of baseball where there are only two events: singles, which occur one-third of the time, and outs, which occur two-thirds of the time. From our starting state ("bases empty, no out") we transition into "man on first, no out" 33% of the time, and "no men on, one out" 67% of the time. We repeat this for the remaining 23 states to complete what is called the transition matrix. Some transitions will result in runs being scored and we must log those.

In this simplified example, each start state has only two possible transitions (a single and an out). In a real game of baseball, there are many transitions based on how a batter hits and how aggressive any base runners are. These transitions form the centerpiece of the Markov chain.

Once we have a final transition matrix, we can work out how many runs are scored from any start state to the end of an inning by multiplying the probabilities of moving through every combination of states and noting the number of runs scored, if any, as we jump through the transitions. This generates a run expectancy matrix, which is the primary output of a Markov. The calculations are computationally intense (moving from any state requires a minimum of 24 multiplications) so we use matrix algebra to simplify life.

Having the run expectancy chart opens a universe of possibilities for a baseball analyst. From it we can produce custom linear weights, win probabilities and leverage indexes for any run environment. We can calculate the optimal lineup for a team, or the validity of a bunt strategy with two on, one out in the eighth, or the change in leverage of bringing in a pinch hitter.

I have built an Excel-based Markov model, which is available to you as a purchaser of the *Annual*; the details are at the end of this chapter. I want to use it to take a more analytical look at the 2007 season and see the extent to which a team's batting and pitching line reflects its runs scored and allowed. Then I want to spend some time using the Markov to look into how we can quantify bench level performance precisely. To finish, we'll apply the Markov at a player level to look at how three individuals contributed to the success of their teams.

First, let's focus on the regular season.

The 2007 Season

The season ended in the most spectacular fashion with Matt Holliday sliding head-first into home plate to secure a 13th- inning 9-8 win after Jamey Carroll's shallow fly ball. That was the last at-bat of the regular season. In total in 2007 there were 167,783 at-bats, 44,977 hits, 4,857 home runs, 2,918 stolen bases and 3,985 double plays. There were also 1,755 hit by pitches, 1,323 intentional walks and a slew of other, less noteworthy, statistical categories.

The Markov model suggests that under those conditions the average team scored 4.83 runs per game. The actual runs per game score adjusting for home wins (no bottom ninth) and extra innings was 4.83—a perfect match.

As mentioned above, the core output of the Markov model is the run expectancy matrix. And here it is for 2007:

	0 out	1 out	2 out
xxx	0.537	0.285	0.107
1xx	0.941	0.550	0.236
x2x	1.219	0.743	0.359
xx3	1.422	0.979	0.397
12x	1.591	0.994	0.486
1x3	1.800	1.209	0.510
x23	2.056	1.439	0.635
123	2.415	1.669	0.805

If this is the first run expectancy table you have seen, don't fret. It is easy to read. Each number represents the expected number of runs that will be scored from that state to the end of the inning. For instance, with a man on third and one out we'd expect 0.97 runs to be scored. If the hitter jacked a home run to empty the bases, his team would score two runs and, with the bases empty and one out, we'd expect a further 0.387 runs to cross home plate.

From this we can work out the values of the various offensive events for 2007. Here are the values of the more common batting and running events in 2007, denominated in runs and wins:

Event	Run value	Win value
1B	0.479	0.047
2B	0.822	0.081
3B	1.060	0.104
HR	1.433	0.140
BB	0.353	0.035
SB	0.190	0.019
Out	-0.303	-0.030

To the uninitiated this says that, on average, each walk is worth 0.35 runs or 0.035 wins while a single is worth 0.48 runs or 0.047 wins. Unsurprisingly, the more destructive the event, the greater its worth. Those familiar with linear weights will note that the 2007 run values are similar to commonly used historical numbers. In fact these numbers change only slightly each year, which is why analysts usually stick with the same weights.

The Markov also gives a perfect match at the league level: In the NL it predicts an average of 4.80 adjusted runs per game, bang in line with the data. Ditto in the AL with 4.86 runs per game. However, when we look at more micro level data (for instance, the performance of individual teams), we start to detect differences between actual and expected performance. This is because of sample size issues and strategic choices made by some teams that invalidate some of the model's assumptions.

Let's dig a bit further and see how each ballclub's runs scored and allowed jibes with predicted runs scored and allowed from the Markov. The objective is to understand how lucky (or unlucky) each team was to score the number of runs it did.

You may wonder why we need a Markov to do this instead of a run estimator. True, we could use a run estimator—Base Runs would be best as it works over different run environments. Markov analysis isn't necessarily superior to Base Runs, but it does allow us to better control the hitting and running assumptions if we wish. Also the Markov can give us custom win expectancy and leverage index charts and also calculate optimal lineup, which Base Runs can't.

Here are the 2007 Markov runs scored and allowed along with actual runs scored and allowed.

Team	RS	Markov RS	Diff	RA	Markov RA	Diff
LAA	822	790	-32	731	734	3
ARI	712	720	8	732	753	21
ATL	810	813	3	733	747	14
BAL	756	759	3	868	809	-59
BOS	867	897	30	657	662	5
CHA	693	687	-6	839	807	-32
CHN	752	782	30	690	704	14
CIN	783	792	9	853	850	-3
CLE	811	812	1	704	712	8
COL	860	862	2	758	757	-1
DET	887	874	-13	797	797	0
FLA	790	814	24	891	897	6
HOU	723	736	13	813	857	44
KC	706	653	-53	778	822	44
LAN	735	762	27	727	701	-26
MIL	801	815	14	776	774	-2
MIN	718	706	-12	725	748	23
NYA	968	952	-16	777	781	4
NYN	804	835	31	750	746	-4
OAK	741	754	13	758	733	-25
PHI	892	913	21	821	850	29
PIT	724	707	-17	846	843	-3

Team	RS	Markov RS	Diff	RA	Markov RA	Diff
SDN	741	735	-6	666	661	-5
SEA	794	783	-11	813	808	-5
SF	683	683	-0	720	738	18
STL	725	728	3	829	795	-34
TB	782	785	3	944	911	-33
TEX	816	753	-63	844	830	-14
TOR	753	749	-4	699	682	-17
WAS	673	676	3	783	812	29

As expected there are differences between Markov runs and actual runs. There are four major reasons for this.

First, certain events are situation-dependent and require assumptions when modeling to avoid over-complexity. The obvious example is the intentional walk, which most times would be issued with first base open. Walks and stolen bases are likewise—the model does make some situational adjustments to limit these effects.

Second, the running game is based on 2000-2005 data and hasn't been updated for 2007.

Third, we assume teams all run the bases identically. Of course this isn't true. So-called small ball teams are more aggressive in taking the extra base.

And fourth, the model assumes that all events are randomly distributed. One reason that teams over- or underperform Markov runs is because they cluster hits together (or not), which means they score more (or fewer) runs than predicted. Although these errors cancel at the league level, at the team level they do not. As we'll see with a couple of examples, the last two have a bigger effect than the first two.

Let's get back to the data and look at some of the standouts, starting with runs scored. The team with the largest discrepancy between actual and Markov runs scored is the Texas Rangers—they scored 63 runs more than expected based on their batting line. Why? The main reason is clustering of hits and runs. With runners in scoring position, Rangers batters had an OPS of .834, compared to the league average of .780. With the bases empty, the Rangers' OPS was .719 compared to the league average of .742. Simply put, they were able to generate a lot more runs than expected because of the sequencing of their hits.

The Los Angeles Angels also are an interesting team. Behind Vladimir Guerrero, the Halos bashed 822 runs; yet enter their batting line into the Markov and they should have scored only 790. The Angels have a reputation as an aggressive running team and ogling their stolen base record you can see that: They led the majors in stolen base attempts and caught stealing.

Closer examination shows how stark this is: When the Angels are in a tie game or within a run, they attempt to steal twice as often as the average team. The Markov captures this, but what it misses is increased aggressiveness on the base paths—for instance, taking the extra base on an out or single, which, if executed well, creates more runs. If we adjust the running matrix to reflect the Angels' more aggressive base running, the run difference almost disappears.

Turning our attention to pitching, the team with the largest discrepancy between actual and Markov runs allowed is Baltimore. According to the Markov, the O's conceded 59 more runs than they should have. The difference in baserunning is less pronounced when analyzing pitching, as hurlers have limited control over the running game and, over the course of a season, face teams with contrasting running styles. Clustering hits and runs likely accounts for most of the gap.

Sure enough, with men on base Baltimore's OPS against was .821, compared to a league average of .779. With bases empty, Baltimore's OPS against was .719, more than 20 points better than the league average.

We can take this a step further and use Markov runs scored and allowed to calculate expected wins and compare that to actual wins. For instance, based on Markov runs the Angels should have finished 86-76. Well short of their 94-68 record, the Angels would have finished two games behind Seattle in the AL West.

Perhaps the most interesting example is the Kansas City Royals who, for the first time in four years, avoided a 100-loss season with a 69-93 record. The Markov believes they punched above their weight and should have ended 64-98, perilously close to the 100-loss mark. What is going on?

Two factors explain why they outperformed expectations. First, Kansas City hit very well with runners in scoring position, which was amplified by having the worst OPS in the league. Second the strong bullpen (3.89 ERA against 4.33 league average ERA) helped them win a lot of close games—their record in one-run affairs was 21-22. However, the astute among you will note that based on actual runs scored and allowed they should have been 10 wins better off than Markov predicted, with a 74-88 record.

The Royals were in a funny position: They scored a lot more runs than expected, but couldn't convert those runs to wins. That is because the Royals were involved on the right side of some monstrous blowouts—they scored 17 runs three times, which padded the runs scored column.

Wins Above Bench

The beauty of the Markov is that its flexibility allows us to analyze many different aspects of the game. One application is to define replacement level for hitters. The Markov is especially well suited to this task because we can select different combinations of hitters and see how many runs they would have scored. So, provided we can identify replacement players, we can define replacement level.

Regular readers of *The Hardball Times* will know that we have a mild a fascination with bench level—you'll see this in our Win Shares Above Bench (WSAB) data presented at the back of the *Annual*. I want to use it to define a base level for performance.

There are a couple of reasons. First, defining replacement level is not trivial. Many define replacement as a Quad-A player, but the problem with that is that Quad-A doesn't actually exist. For hitters, a commonly accepted replacement level is 70-75% of league average performance, but again it feels slightly arbitrary. The beauty of bench level is that it is easier to quantify: a glance down a team's roster at playing time (accounting for injuries and trades) can discriminate between bench and first-choice players. Second, building a capable bench is a strategic requirement of the front office whether through acquiring handy low-level talent or by promoting young players. Assessing how each organization manages its resources to build a good bench is an intriguing question and one that the Markov model can help answer.

The process for defining bench level is relatively straightforward. We identify each team's first choice lineup by looking at who had the most starts at each field position; everyone else is classified as bench. For instance, Julio Lugo racked up the most appearances at shortstop for the Red Sox so he is classified as a Boston regular; someone like Alex Cora, who on occasion stood in for Lugo, is classified as bench.

This approach sounds fine in theory but does mean some first choice players, like Jack Cust, slip through the cracks. Cust was called up late and then split time between the corner positions and DH. Although he had the fifth most plate appearances on the team, he didn't play enough at any one position to be classified as a regular.

Other victims include players who were traded midseason, for instance Mark Teixiera, who went from Texas to the Braves. Although Teixiera does make the first choice Texas lineup, he is a bench player for the Braves because he didn't appear enough at first base to unseat incumbent Scott Thorman, who is your more typical bench player. We adjust to fix these issues.

We must make a few other assumptions, too. First, platooning is a problem, so our approach is to assign the player with the least playing time to the bench. Second, in the NL we assume that pitchers hit at the league-average rates for pitchers and do not give teams credit for having good hitting pitchers. This is because the pitcher is not in the lineup for his hitting ability (Micah Owings excepted) and rotates every day. Third, we adjust for park to ensure a fair comparison. And fourth, in all win calculations we assume that pitching is league average.

Let's walk through an example: Take the Atlanta Braves. Their most common lineup was Kelly Johnson (2B), Edgar Renteria (SS), Chipper Jones (3B), Andruw Jones (CF), Brian McCann (C), Jeff Francoeur (RF), Matt Diaz (LF), Scott Thorman (1B) and a league average hitting pitcher. To handle the Teixiera issue we create a blended starting first baseman with four months of Thorman and two months of Teixiera. Had this combo played every inning of every game, according to the Markov, the Braves would have won 95 games against a league average pitching staff. If you do the same for the bench, they'd have won just 63.

Once we have established the bench for each team, we can calculate bench level for each league. Processing the math tells us that 2007 bench level in the NL was 66 wins and in the AL 59 wins. In other words, pick a random selection of bench players and they'll win 66 games in the NL and 59 in the AL. The reason for the gap is that the presence of the pitcher in NL lineups reduces the difference in production between the starting nine and the bench

Following is the data for 2007. The first column reports how many wins the starting lineup would have recorded if it had batted in every plate appearance of every game. The second column is the same for bench players.

	Starter Wins	Bench Wins
LAA	95	59
ARI	78	59
ATL	92	60
BAL	87	52
BOS	96	53
CHA	79	47
CHN	88	62
CIN	91	63
CLE	91	62
COL	92	47
DET	105	52
FLA	93	70
HOU	83	66
KC	73	54
LAN	87	67
MIL	92	64
MIN	85	46
NYA	105	66
NYN	95	72
OAK	86	65
PHI	96	76
PIT	78	72
SDN	84	76
SEA	88	64
SF	76	61
STL	82	75
TB	92	62
TEX	80	67
TOR	82	57
WAS	79	60

So, which team had the best bench? The distinction is comfortably held by the San Diego Padres, whose reserves were an astonishing 10 wins above league-bench–the starting lineup was only eight wins better! Hitters like Scott Hairston, Milton Bradley and Rob Bowen contributed strongly from the bench.

Perhaps more surprising is that the Colorado Rockies had the worst supporting cast at 18 wins below the average NL bench! How does that tally with their wild card victory? A quick glance at the Rockies' roster shows that the only half-decent bench hitter is Ryan Spilborghs. The Rox' strength was the second best starting lineup in the NL (at 92 wins) and also above average pitching.

Turning attention to the starters, no one will rub their eyes in disbelief when they see that the Kansas City Royals have the least effective starting nine, but may when seeing that the Diamondbacks' first-choice batters would only have won 78 games against league average pitching. How the Snakes managed to secure the best record in the National League continues to defy logic and befuddle analysts. In the NL, the Phillies had the best lineup with 96 wins, but pound for pound the New York Yankees have the best starters in baseball, and would have won 105 games had A-Rod and company begun and finished every game.

Other 2007 Tales

One other cool application of the Markov is the ability to play with batting lineups and churn through some what-if scenarios. Let's kick off by looking at the impact that Alfonso Soriano had on the Chicago Cubs. Even those with short memories won't need reminding that Soriano signed the richest contract of the 2006-07 offseason, signing a $136 million/eight-year deal. We can use the Markov to assess the impact of this trade on the Cubs.

According to the Markov, the Cubs' record should have been 89-73; they actually ended 85-77. The Markov predicts that the Cubs score 4.86 runs per game, which is more than the 4.68 they actually scored.

Let's see what happens when subtracting Soriano's offensive contribution. Without Soriano leading off, the Cubs' leadoff man, mostly shortstop Ryan Theriot, hit a respectable .286/.332/.429. That lineup (sans Soriano) would have been good for 4.70 runs per game—a deficit of 0.16 runs compared to when Soriano started. Play that forward over the 162 games and it equates to 27 runs or 2.7 wins. Losing those wins would have made enough of a difference to send the NL Central division 90 miles north to Wisconsin.

Of course, there is a chaining issue, as Theriot can't bat in two spots in the order. How many additional wins do the Cubs cede if we promote a bench player to left field? On average the Cubs' bench scored 3.87 runs per game. A bench player probably wouldn't be leading off, so assume he'd bat at number eight. That would have cost the Cubs another three wins and nudged them below .500. At least year one of Soriano's deal was worth the money.

We can also use this approach to look at pitchers, so we'll turn the microscope on whether the $55 million posting fee that the Red Sox put up for Daisuke Matsuzaka was the difference maker in their AL East triumph over the Yankees.

It is fair to say that Dice-K didn't live up to the lofty expectations that many set when he came over from Japan. His ERA was 4.40, which was only marginally ahead of the league average mark of 4.56 but behind the 4.21 mark set by Red Sox starters. If we replace Dice-K with a league average starter, the Markov reports that the Red Sox would have allowed 4.17 runs per game instead of 4.08 runs per game. Over the course of the 205 innings that Dice-K threw, that is 20 runs or two wins, which would give the Sox the same record as the Yankees.

Had Boston not secured the services of Dice-K, he would have probably ended up playing in pinstripes. How many wins would Matsuzaka have added to the Yankees? According to the Markov, Yankees pitchers collectively allowed 4.78 runs per game. A look at the Yankees rotation indicates that Andy Pettitte, Chien-Ming Wang, Mike Mussina and Roger Clemens filled four of the five starting slots for the year. Behind them was a slew of dross like Kei Igawa and Jeff Karstens, who collectively recorded an ERA of 5.84 while throwing 188 innings. If we add 188 innings of Dice-K, the Yankees would have been 49 runs (five wins) better off! They'd have won 99 games and beaten the Red Sox by five games.

Finally, consider Barry Bonds, who played for a godawful Giants team that mustered only 71 wins and yet hit an age-defying .276/.480/.565. Just how bad would the Giants have been without Bonds? The Markov will tell us. With Bonds in the lineup batting cleanup, the Giants generate 64 Markov wins. Take him out and bat a bench player in his stead and it costs you five wins. Were it not for Bonds, the Giants would be perilously close to 100 losses. Someone that good deserves to play in 2008.

I hope I have demonstrated the power and potential of the Markov approach. The beauty is that you can control almost every aspect of the game and assess the impact in any run environment. Want to see what a baseball game that has only wild pitches looks like? The Markov will tell you.

You can download your Markov spreadsheet from http://www.hardballtimes.com/THT2008Annual/. The username is "tht08" and the password is "utley." This is a service to book purchasers only.

One neat feature of this spreadsheet is the ability to choose your own lineup, change the batting order and play around with base running; it also gives win probabilities for any two teams of your choosing. As yet it can't make coffee or complete tax returns—that's for version 2.0.

Happy analyzing.

Mr. Clutch

by Bill James

Back in the early days of sabermetrics, when dinosaurs roamed the American League Western Division, we made a very fundamental mistake. A friend of mine wrote an article asserting, essentially, that clutch hitters don't exist. At the time, we lacked any real ability to study the issue. We didn't have access to play by play of the games. No one could plausibly assert that clutch hitting *did* exist, because we couldn't document it without access to the game accounts, but Dick Cramer had finagled access to a couple of seasons of old data, studied the data and concluded that it didn't. There was nowhere for the discussion to go.

It was about seven years after that before we *began* to have access to play by play, long before the data began to come on line, the discussion had stalled out at the assertion that clutch hitting did not exist.

In retrospect, this may not have been the best place to begin the discussion. A logical path for the discussion, it seems to me, would have been more like this:

1. Do you think clutch-hitting ability exists?
2. I don't know, what do you think?
3. I don't know. How would we study that?
4. Define a clutch situation and accumulate data on how players perform over a period of years? That would seem to work.
5. How would you define a clutch situation?

We would then proceed to debate the definition of a clutch situation, and gradually we would develop data, and perhaps even an understanding of the data.

Instead, the discussion went more like this:

(A) Clutch hitting doesn't exist.
(B) Umm … OK.
(C) I don't know … I think maybe it could exist.
(A & B in unison) Prove it.
(C) I can't prove it.
(A) OK then, it doesn't exist.

(B) If you can't prove it exists, we have to assume that it doesn't.

The discussion has been premised upon an assertion, rather than flowing from the question itself. What I have been trying to do for the last couple of years is to back up, define a clutch situation, begin accumulating data, and gradually go down the other path.

Some people find this confusing. "Why are you publishing this clutch data," they will ask, "when you don't have any reason to believe that there is such a thing as a clutch hitter?" But that's the thing: We're publishing the data because we *don't* know.

The other question everybody asks now is "How do you determine what is a clutch at bat?" I'll have to stiff you on that one for right now. I'll explain it generally and leave the details for some other time.

"Clutch" is a complicated concept, containing at least seven elements:

1. The score,
2. The runners on base,
3. The outs,
4. The inning,
5. The opposition,
6. The standings,
7. The calendar.

Sometimes people look at things like batting average with runners in scoring position, batting average with runners in scoring position and two out, batting average in the late innings of close games. Those things are all interesting, but Tampa Bay playing Texas in April is not the same as San Diego playing Los Angeles in September.

We made up a system giving weight to each of these seven factors; not saying it's perfect, but you have to start somewhere. Baseball's most famous clutch hitter is David Ortiz, so let's start with him. The Big Papi's batting record in clutch situations, over the last six years, is at the top of the next page.

David Ortiz

Season	Avg	OBP	Slg	OPS	AB	H	2B	3B	HR	RBI	BB	SO	GIDP
2002	.280	.345	.680	1.025	50	14	3	1	5	19	5	9	1
2003	.307	.376	.640	1.016	75	23	10	0	5	38	9	13	3
2004	.339	.413	.726	1.139	62	21	3	0	7	33	9	14	2
2005	.333	.422	.750	1.172	72	24	6	0	8	37	13	12	3
2006	.370	.475	.696	1.170	46	17	3	0	4	28	11	7	1
2007	.315	.435	.607	1.042	89	28	8	0	6	29	17	17	4
Totals	.322	.413	.678	1.090	394	127	33	1	35	184	64	72	14

That's the regular season; I understand he's had a couple of hits in postseason as well. It's a pretty good record; in fact, you kind of have to see more data to understand how good it is. We've started an award for the major leagues' clutch hitter of the year, based on the data, and David could pretty much win it any year. Only a handful of players a year drive in 30 runs in clutch situations. As to whether these data **prove** that David is a clutch hitter ... I ain't going there. This discussion has been messed up for 30 years because we got our shoulders way out in front of our shoelaces. From now on, I'm holding back.

One thing you just have to accept in order to study this: "Clutch" is not an equal opportunity employer. Mike Sweeney has hit very well in the clutch, too—arguably better than Ortiz—but few people have noticed because the canvas is so small:

Mike Sweeney

Season	Avg	OBP	Slg	OPS	AB	H	2B	3B	HR	RBI	BB	SO	GIDP
2002	.344	.462	.594	1.055	32	11	2	0	2	10	7	4	0
2003	.368	.467	.553	1.019	38	14	4	0	1	13	7	4	2
2004	.382	.432	.735	1.168	34	13	3	0	3	18	2	4	1
2005	.310	.364	.483	.846	29	9	2	0	1	9	3	7	4
2006	.429	.500	.786	1.286	14	6	2	0	1	8	1	3	1
2007	.333	.429	.833	1.262	12	4	0	0	2	3	1	2	0
Totals	.358	.440	.629	1.069	159	57	13	0	10	61	21	24	8

Ortiz has had more than twice as many clutch at bats as Sweeney – again, not counting the postseason. The statistician's tendency is to want to adjust that difference out of existence, but you can't. It's a fact of a life: The Royals don't play as many critical games as the Red Sox do. When the Red Sox wiped out in August of 2006, Ortiz' clutch at bats for the 2006 season dropped sharply because the Red Sox September games just did not mean as much as they have in the other years. The same thing happened to Albert Pujols in 2007. The Cardinals were out of it early, so Pujols did not have nearly as many clutch opportunities as he has had in other seasons. This is not a statistical artifact. That's the way it really is.

Who **hasn't** hit well in the clutch? Juan Pierre hasn't done great.

Juan Pierre

Season	Avg	OBP	Slg	OPS	AB	H	2B	3B	HR	RBI	BB	SO	GIDP
2002	.111	.111	.111	.222	27	3	0	0	0	1	0	3	0
2003	.318	.434	.364	.798	44	14	0	1	0	8	9	2	2
2004	.233	.327	.349	.675	43	10	1	2	0	10	5	3	0
2005	.309	.367	.382	.748	55	17	2	1	0	14	5	6	2
2006	.229	.289	.314	.604	35	8	1	1	0	4	2	4	2
2007	.190	.246	.206	.453	63	12	1	0	0	10	3	4	1
Totals	.240	.311	.296	.607	267	64	5	5	0	47	24	22	7

Nobody would confuse Juan Pierre with David Ortiz anyway, but that's not a great clutch record for a guy who gets 200 hits a year. Ken Griffey Jr.'s clutch record is not impressive:

Ken Griffey Jr.

Season	Avg	OBP	Slg	OPS	AB	H	2B	3B	HR	RBI	BB	SO	GIDP
2002	.235	.400	.412	.812	17	4	0	0	1	4	6	5	1
2003	.105	.217	.263	.481	19	2	0	0	1	4	2	7	0
2004	.273	.342	.394	.736	33	9	1	0	1	11	4	3	1
2005	.353	.419	.647	1.066	34	12	1	0	3	22	6	8	0
2006	.233	.313	.550	.863	60	14	4	0	5	27	7	11	2
2007	.205	.319	.462	.781	39	8	1	0	3	12	7	9	2
Totals	.243	.337	.485	.823	202	49	7	0	14	80	32	43	6

But it may be better than his teammate Adam Dunn's:

Adam Dunn

Season	Avg	OBP	Slg	OPS	AB	H	2B	3B	HR	RBI	BB	SO	GIDP
2002	.196	.439	.478	.918	46	9	1	0	4	16	17	19	0
2003	.189	.412	.459	.871	37	7	1	0	3	8	13	14	0
2004	.275	.393	.686	1.080	51	14	0	0	7	18	9	17	0
2005	.189	.434	.351	.785	37	7	0	0	2	8	15	12	0
2006	.206	.345	.471	.816	68	14	3	0	5	22	14	29	1
2007	.244	.368	.467	.835	45	11	1	0	3	13	10	18	1
Totals	.218	.395	.493	.888	284	62	6	0	24	85	78	109	2

What Griffey's record would have been in his salad days, I don't know; we'll get to that, praise Retrosheet, but we haven't figured it yet. One guess from the little bit of data I have had the opportunity to study is that there may be a decentralization under pressure, the good hitters getting better and the weaker hitters struggling to stay where they are. This might be suggested by the clutch-hitting record of, for example, Chipper Jones:

Chipper Jones

Season	Avg	OBP	Slg	OPS	AB	H	2B	3B	HR	RBI	BB	SO	GIDP
2002	.356	.465	.610	1.075	59	21	3	0	4	17	12	9	2
2003	.354	.457	.615	1.072	65	23	5	0	4	18	14	7	1
2004	.211	.363	.423	.785	71	15	3	0	4	23	17	20	2
2005	.393	.506	.787	1.293	61	24	6	0	6	27	15	8	3
2006	.263	.400	.447	.847	38	10	1	0	2	14	10	6	1
2007	.333	.436	.652	1.087	66	22	6	0	5	27	12	13	6
Totals	.319	.438	.594	1.032	360	115	24	0	25	126	80	63	15

Chipper's clutch-hitting record, apart from the RBI count, is close to a match for Ortiz'. It may be that most outstanding hitters tend to be even more outstanding when the game or the season is on the line. Albert Pujols certainly doesn't contest the point:

Albert Pujols

Season	Avg	OBP	Slg	OPS	AB	H	2B	3B	HR	RBI	BB	SO	GIDP
2002	.310	.416	.507	.923	71	22	5	0	3	26	14	6	3
2003	.364	.478	.673	1.151	55	20	5	0	4	19	12	7	2
2004	.317	.452	.730	1.183	63	20	8	0	6	27	18	11	6
2005	.278	.363	.506	.869	79	22	3	0	5	19	10	7	7
2006	.383	.524	.827	1.351	81	31	1	1	11	38	24	9	3
2007	.400	.527	.650	1.177	40	16	5	1	1	18	13	3	5
Totals	.337	.456	.648	1.104	389	131	27	2	30	147	91	43	26

Eleven clutch homers in the Cardinals' championship season. David Ortiz' career high is eight.

One reason that I have been reluctant to write about clutch hitting, in the absence of hard data, is that I am reluctant to interpret sporting events as tests of character. If you write that Johnny Baseball is a poor clutch hitter, what you are implicitly saying is that Johnny Baseball lacks courage. I am extremely reluctant to impugn the character of any player based on what could be a random data outcome.

And, in all candor, I am reluctant to buy into the other side of that, too. There is a strain of journalism as hero worship, a strain that asks us to believe that sports are tests of character, that those who come through at key moments of the game have reached down deep inside themselves and found the strength and courage to succeed. I don't want to get into that. I am willing to look at the data and see what they have to tell us, but I want to keep at arms' length any judgments about the character of the athletes. Sports talk show hosts may be comfortable doing that, but that's their job, it's not mine. This discussion has been fouled up for a long time, and my only goal is to straighten it out just a little bit.

Editor's note: Bill James is working on a new book (The Bill James Gold Mine 2008) and website (Bill James Online) to explore baseball issues such as this one at more length based on new data only now becoming available from Baseball Info Solutions.

With or Without You

by Tom M. Tango

Geno Petralli led the American League in passed balls in 1987, with 35. And he was the third-string catcher! He followed that up with a league-leading 20 passed balls in 1988. And another league-leading performance of 20 in 1990. Was Petralli really that bad a catcher?

A quick look at the Rangers' pitchers shows a staff with 61 wild pitches in 1987 (with the Rangers' opponents having 62 wild pitches). Nothing special there. But we have two indications that something strange was going on. The first is that the regular catcher, Don Slaught, had 20 passed balls, and the other backup, Mike Stanley, had 18. All told, that's 73 passed balls. The pitcher on the mound when 65 of them went past the catchers was none other than notable knuckleballer Charlie Hough. Furthermore, while Petralli caught fewer than 30% of all Rangers innings in 1987, he caught 50% of Hough's.

It is sometimes easy to forget that baseball statistics don't exist in a vacuum. There are some stats that are heavily teammate dependent, and passed balls are one of them. But, what to do? As we saw, in 1987, it wasn't just Petralli who was saddled with Hough's knuckler, but all the Rangers' catchers. So, the context for Petralli is his pitchers. And Hough, while horrible to his catchers in 1987, was pretty tough on them throughout his career. Jim Sundberg was his main catcher, followed by Petralli and Steve Yeager. In all, Hough had 35 catchers. Why don't we compare how Hough did with and without Petralli?

Hough, with Petralli as his catcher, was involved in 53 passed balls over the years, while facing 2,482 batters. That's 107 passed balls per 5,000 batters faced (5,000 batters is about 130 complete games). Here is how Hough did with the other 34 catchers:

Catcher	PA	PB	Rate
Jim Sundberg	2,803	37	66
Steve Yeager	1,662	20	60
Don Slaught	1,475	27	92
Ron Karkovice	1,296	5	19
Joe Ferguson	944	19	101
Benito Santiago	884	12	68
Mike Stanley	665	20	150
Donnie Scott	639	13	102

Catcher	PA	PB	Rate
Chad Kreuter	420	12	143
Ned Yost	365	9	123
Orlando Mercado	359	3	42
Ron Tingley	352	9	128
Johnny Oates	332	5	75
Glenn Brummer	297	3	51
Don Wakamatsu	284	3	53
Other 19 catchers	894	26	145
ALL 34 catchers	13,671	223	82

The Rate column is passed balls per 5,000 batters. As you can see, while Petralli allowed plenty of passed balls (a rate of 107), so did most of Hough's catchers. One enormous exception is Ron Karkovice. Overall, the non-Petralli catchers allowed passed balls at the rate of 82 per 5,000 batters. And, with 34 catchers, this gives us a decent cross-section to compare Petralli against.

Remember, all these catchers are not just other catchers on the team when Petralli was there (like Slaught with the Rangers), but all catchers that had ever caught Charlie Hough (like Yeager with the Dodgers). So, we get this comparison point:

- Petralli (with Hough): 107 passed balls per 5,000 batters faced
- All others (with Hough): 82 passed balls per 5,000 batters faced

While Petralli wasn't that good with Hough (allowed 25 more passed balls), what about all the other pitchers he's caught? We repeat this process with:

- Petralli and Mitch Williams (and his catchers, like Darren Daulton, Slaught again, Joe Girardi, et al);
- Petralli and Jose Guzman (and his catchers: Ivan Rodriguez, Rick Wilkins, et al);
- And on and on.

Petralli has caught 94 pitchers, and we are comparing how each of those pitchers did with and without Petralli as his catcher. With such a large number of pitchers, who essentially span every single team, across decades, we are hoping to capture an excellent baseline to compare to Petralli.

Overall, Petralli was behind the plate for 16,649 batters, working with 94 different pitchers, who themselves had a total of 359 unique catchers. As a point of comparison, in the Retrosheet years (1957-2006, except for 1999, which is where all these data are coming from), there were 828 catchers. Of course, not each catcher is equally represented (Ivan Rodriguez makes up 8% of the catcher pool of Petralli's pitchers).

But we'll get to that a bit later. Petralli had 80 passed balls with 16,649 batters, or a rate of 24 passed balls per 5,000 batters. His peers, with the exact same set of pitchers, had a rate of 21 passed balls per 5,000 batters. Petralli therefore allowed three more passed balls per 5,000 batters than his peers.

And, there's no reason that we need to limit ourselves to just passed balls. Non-batter events also include stolen bases, caught stealings, balks, pickoffs and wild pitches. We can repeat our passed balls process for each of these events. And of course, we don't just do this for Petralli, but all 828 men who have caught in the Retrosheet years. So, that's what I did. Listed below and on the next three pages

are the results of the 167 catchers who have been behind the plate for at least 15,000 batters in the Retrosheet years:

To read the fifth line: Ivan Rodriguez has been behind the plate for effectively 13.1 seasons of 5,000 batters (a total of 65,566). Per 5,000 batters, he has allowed 46 fewer stolen bases than his baseline group. That is, by far, the best total of all catchers. His arm is legendary, and deservedly so. His caught-stealings are close to the average in his group (one fewer than average). If no one is stealing, it's hard to throw anyone out, and still, Rodriguez managed to throw out his fair share. Why runners tried to steal on him, who knows?

In the rest of the categories, Rodriguez and his pitchers picked off runners at the average rate. His pitchers allowed one fewer balks. Rodriguez had problems with wild pitches, allowing eight more than his peer group, but allowed two fewer passed balls. The LWTS column is the linear weights run value, which essentially is figured this way: Every positive event for Rodriguez (caught stealing, pickoffs) is worth 0.50 runs, and every negative event (stolen base, balk, wild pitch, passed ball) is worth -0.25 runs. (Think of a run being worth four bases, meaning each base is worth 0.25 runs. An out would be worth an additional 0.25 runs.)

CATCHER	LWTS	Years	SB	CS	PK	BK	WP	PB
Charlie O'Brien	15.3	5.0	12	6	11	1	-10	-5
Clay Dalrymple	11.3	6.6	-20	7	2	-1	-7	0
Bob Kearney	10.6	3.1	-18	6	1	3	-11	-1
Brian Schneider	10.6	4.1	-19	6	1	0	-6	-3
Ivan Rodriguez	10.4	13.1	-46	-1	0	-1	8	-2
Marc Hill	10.1	4.1	-14	9	0	-3	-1	-5
Henry Blanco	10.1	3.8	-24	9	-3	-2	-3	-1
Rick Dempsey	10.0	10.4	-17	3	3	0	-9	-3
Jim Sundberg	9.8	13.5	-14	5	4	-1	-4	-4
Steve Yeager	9.2	7.9	-13	1	4	-2	-9	-3
Gary Carter	8.9	14.5	-4	10	-1	0	-8	-5
Ron Karkovice	8.8	6.0	-22	4	-3	-1	-4	-7
Tom Pagnozzi	8.6	5.7	-9	11	-3	-2	-5	-3
Johnny Bench	8.2	12.2	-22	-3	4	0	-7	-1
Bruce Benedict	8.0	6.6	5	6	-2	-3	-17	-8
Bob Boone	7.8	15.6	-17	4	2	1	-1	-3
Yogi Berra	7.3	3.3	-6	7	-2	1	-10	-5
Jason LaRue	7.1	4.7	-20	4	1	-1	-2	3
Brad Ausmus	7.1	11.0	-15	0	0	-1	-8	-6
Jake Gibbs	6.9	3.2	-6	-3	-1	-1	-21	-6
Lance Parrish	6.8	12.9	-24	2	0	0	-4	4
Dan Wilson	6.8	8.1	-19	-3	-1	-3	-8	-6
Chris Cannizzaro	6.7	4.5	-17	-1	3	-1	-1	-5
Bob Rodgers	6.6	6.2	-9	3	0	-3	-4	-4

CATCHER	LWTS	Years	SB	CS	PK	BK	WP	PB
Del Crandall	6.5	5.7	-10	3	-1	0	-7	-6
Rick Wilkins	6.5	4.3	-7	11	0	0	3	0
Glenn Borgmann	6.5	3.1	-1	1	6	-1	-5	-5
Mike Ryan	6.3	4.3	-19	-1	-4	0	-11	-4
Mike Matheny	6.2	8.3	-12	-1	0	-3	-8	-3
Johnny Oates	6.0	3.3	-11	4	0	0	-3	-2
Mike LaValliere	5.9	5.5	-1	9	1	2	-2	-4
Sherm Lollar	5.9	4.5	-10	2	-3	-1	-6	-9
Charles Johnson	5.9	7.6	-18	1	-4	-1	-7	-4
Thurman Munson	5.7	9.3	-14	8	0	-3	7	2
Alex Trevino	5.5	4.7	-9	7	-1	1	-3	0
Jody Davis	5.1	7.3	5	14	5	4	4	3
Mike Redmond	5.1	3.0	9	4	1	-1	-15	-2
Dave Valle	5.1	6.0	-21	2	-4	2	-4	-1
John Stearns	5.0	5.0	0	6	4	1	0	-3
Bill Freehan	4.9	11.4	-3	-1	-1	-2	-13	-5
Rod Barajas	4.9	3.5	-23	-5	-3	1	-12	-2
Paul Casanova	4.9	5.6	-22	-6	0	-2	-4	-4
Randy Hundley	4.5	7.1	-20	-2	-2	-1	-1	-6
Joe Oliver	4.4	6.7	-2	5	3	-1	0	0
Jeff Torborg	4.4	3.3	1	-3	6	0	-10	-2
Buck Martinez	4.4	6.2	-6	-3	3	-4	-7	-1
Hal Smith	4.4	3.2	-8	-1	2	0	-3	-5
Ellie Rodriguez	4.3	5.0	-11	3	2	-1	3	2
Jim Essian	4.2	4.1	13	14	0	-1	1	-2
Joe Azcue	4.0	5.8	-24	-1	2	1	5	6
Bob Brenly	4.0	4.5	-10	10	3	1	11	7
Toby Hall	4.0	4.4	-30	-1	-6	1	2	-2
Smoky Burgess	3.8	4.0	7	2	3	-3	-4	-5
Ray Fosse	3.8	6.0	-1	7	0	0	0	1
Paul LoDuca	3.7	5.4	3	4	0	-4	-6	0
Barry Foote	3.7	4.3	-13	-2	2	-1	0	-1
Brian Downing	3.3	4.7	19	3	5	1	-11	-7
Jorge Fabregas	3.1	3.4	-5	3	2	-1	5	-1
Jerry Grote	3.0	9.1	-21	-3	-2	0	1	-3
Phil Roof	3.0	5.0	-11	-1	-1	0	-4	-2
Joe Torre	2.8	6.0	-8	1	1	-1	4	-1
Tony Pena	2.8	13.5	-8	3	0	-2	6	-2
Darrell Porter	2.8	10.7	-5	4	4	-1	7	3
Pat Borders	2.8	6.6	-1	11	-2	0	9	-1
Butch Wynegar	2.6	9.0	-7	1	-4	-1	-3	-4
Geno Petralli	2.6	3.3	2	5	4	2	1	3
Kirt Manwaring	2.4	6.3	-5	2	-4	2	-10	-1
Elston Howard	2.3	7.7	-14	-3	-2	0	-2	-3
Joe Girardi	2.2	8.3	-4	-1	5	-1	4	-1
Jeff Reed	2.1	6.1	3	0	4	1	-1	-3
Carlton Fisk	2.0	15.7	-5	-1	-1	-1	-3	-1
Ed Bailey	2.0	6.2	-9	-3	-2	0	-3	-6

CATCHER	LWTS	Years	SB	CS	PK	BK	WP	PB
Manny Sanguillen	1.9	8.0	-6	-3	-2	0	-10	-1
Bob Melvin	1.9	3.9	-2	-1	-1	4	-11	-1
Greg Myers	1.8	5.1	3	0	0	0	-7	-2
Einar Diaz	1.7	3.7	0	6	-1	0	5	-3
Sandy Alomar Jr.	1.5	9.0	-9	-3	-3	-2	-4	-3
Ramon Hernandez	1.5	6.2	-2	-1	-1	0	-7	-1
Ed Herrmann	1.4	5.5	2	1	0	0	-7	2
Earl Battey	1.4	7.4	-15	-3	3	-2	9	3
Brian Harper	1.4	4.7	12	8	-3	-2	-6	0
Tom Lampkin	1.3	3.1	-11	0	-4	0	-4	0
Joe Ferguson	1.3	5.1	-1	-1	4	2	-2	1
Brent Mayne	1.2	7.0	0	0	-1	-2	-4	-2
Gus Triandos	1.1	5.8	-19	0	-3	0	6	2
Johnny Edwards	1.1	9.6	-7	1	-2	1	1	-2
Jason Varitek	0.8	6.1	-3	-5	-1	-3	-8	-1
Andy Etchebarren	0.8	5.7	-4	-5	-2	-2	-7	-5
Paul Bako	0.8	3.2	1	5	-1	-3	6	1
Rick Cerone	0.8	8.6	-10	1	0	0	6	2
Ted Simmons	0.7	12.8	6	4	3	-1	2	4
Terry Steinbach	0.6	9.1	-14	3	-6	0	7	0
Benito Santiago	0.4	12.8	-13	-3	1	1	5	1
Damian Miller	0.4	5.7	-10	0	-4	-1	-1	1
Fred Kendall	0.3	5.3	3	-3	2	1	-3	-3
Gregg Zaun	0.2	5.0	5	-2	2	0	-6	-1
Rich Gedman	0.1	6.5	6	0	-2	2	-1	1
Terry Kennedy	0.1	9.5	13	4	0	2	-6	-3
Joel Skinner	0.0	3.4	-17	-6	-5	-2	-1	-3
Alan Ashby	-0.2	8.9	17	3	1	1	-6	-3
Jeff Newman	-0.4	3.1	-1	-2	0	-2	3	-2
George Mitterwald	-0.4	5.3	7	8	-1	1	8	1
Duke Sims	-0.5	4.2	5	-2	-1	-1	-6	0
Bengie Molina	-0.5	5.4	-8	-2	-2	1	1	0
Darren Daulton	-0.6	6.9	0	-2	0	0	-1	-2
B.J. Surhoff	-0.7	5.0	-1	-3	-1	0	-4	1
Chad Kreuter	-0.7	4.9	-4	2	1	2	9	0
Tim McCarver	-0.7	9.7	3	-6	3	-2	-4	0
John Roseboro	-0.8	10.0	-10	-2	0	1	8	1
Dick Brown	-0.8	4.0	-8	-3	-2	-1	0	1
Mike Heath	-0.9	7.3	-14	-6	-5	0	-3	0
Kelly Stinnett	-1.2	3.7	15	-1	0	-1	-8	-1
Mike Lieberthal	-1.2	7.3	-4	-1	-2	1	5	-2
Damon Berryhill	-1.3	3.9	-1	2	0	1	8	1
Johnny Estrada	-1.4	3.1	5	-8	1	0	-8	-4
Chris Hoiles	-1.5	5.8	10	-3	0	-1	-6	-3
Jason Kendall	-1.6	10.5	7	-1	-1	2	-1	-7
Gene Tenace	-1.6	5.6	12	2	5	4	1	3
Bo Diaz	-1.6	6.5	9	6	-3	4	-2	2
Mike Scioscia	-1.6	9.4	14	1	3	4	-3	-1

CATCHER	LWTS	Years	SB	CS	PK	BK	WP	PB
Scott Servais	-1.7	4.9	9	1	-2	0	-6	0
Charlie Moore	-1.7	5.8	5	3	0	-2	7	2
Dave Rader	-1.8	5.0	-2	-2	-1	0	5	-2
Jorge Posada	-1.8	7.9	-7	1	-3	-3	7	4
Gary Bennett	-1.9	3.2	-6	-9	-2	0	-7	-1
Don Slaught	-1.9	8.3	1	-4	-3	3	-5	-3
Bill Haselman	-2.1	3.1	16	-4	-1	-4	-11	-2
Mike Macfarlane	-2.1	6.7	-13	-6	1	-1	10	3
Duffy Dyer	-2.1	4.2	7	1	-2	2	1	-3
John Flaherty	-2.2	6.4	9	-1	-2	-1	-1	-4
Steve Swisher	-2.2	3.2	-3	-10	4	5	-4	-1
Ernie Whitt	-2.3	8.0	4	1	-3	0	-1	1
John Romano	-2.4	5.6	2	-5	1	0	-1	1
Javy Lopez	-2.4	9.0	-3	-5	0	0	1	1
Matt Walbeck	-2.7	3.8	10	0	-1	-4	4	1
Russ Nixon	-2.9	4.7	2	-8	1	0	-5	3
Andy Allanson	-3.0	3.4	-6	-7	-3	8	-6	-2
Ron Hassey	-3.2	6.3	-4	-9	1	1	1	0
Todd Pratt	-3.3	3.1	-5	-9	-1	-3	-2	3
Tom Haller	-3.4	8.0	1	-4	-1	-1	-2	4
J.C. Martin	-3.6	3.7	-13	-7	-1	-1	10	2
Jamie Quirk	-3.6	3.1	14	8	0	2	12	3
Todd Hundley	-3.8	6.6	-1	-6	-1	0	0	2
Dave Duncan	-3.8	6.1	7	-5	-1	-2	-1	0
Junior Ortiz	-4.0	4.3	8	4	0	2	14	2
Ellie Hendricks	-4.2	3.8	9	-7	5	1	-1	5
John Bateman	-4.5	6.6	-6	-10	-1	0	3	0
John Wathan	-4.5	3.8	0	-10	0	0	2	-3
Victor Martinez	-4.6	3.3	6	-8	-6	-2	-10	-2
Jim Pagliaroni	-4.8	4.9	3	-4	-7	1	-2	-4
Tim Laudner	-4.8	4.3	3	-7	3	4	8	-2
Brook Fordyce	-4.9	3.3	24	-6	1	-3	-10	-1
Darrin Fletcher	-5.1	6.8	25	-3	2	-1	-3	-3
Bob Tillman	-5.6	4.9	6	-10	-2	1	-4	-4
Mickey Tettleton	-5.8	6.0	4	0	-7	-4	7	2
A.J. Pierzynski	-5.9	5.6	1	-8	-2	-1	5	-2
Chris Widger	-6.6	3.1	14	1	-4	-1	6	2
Matt Nokes	-6.7	4.5	19	-2	-1	2	-2	1
Ozzie Virgil	-7.3	4.7	23	3	-5	3	-2	0
Mike Stanley	-7.4	4.9	8	-12	1	2	-6	2
Earl Williams	-8.1	3.1	18	1	2	1	12	6
Bob Stinson	-8.3	3.7	21	-3	-3	-2	0	1
Michael Barrett	-8.5	5.0	8	-9	0	1	6	1
Mike Fitzgerald	-9.2	4.8	36	-1	-1	1	-2	-1
Eddie Taubensee	-9.4	4.8	21	-2	1	2	9	3
Mike Piazza	-9.6	10.5	36	-6	1	1	-6	-1
Dick Dietz	-13.2	3.6	16	-11	2	-3	11	10

So, there we have it. The best catcher of the Retrosheet years in holding runners at bay was Charlie O'Brien. And behind him was Clay Dalrymple. Who? He played with the Phillies in the '60s, and ended his career as a backup with the Orioles in the early '70s. All told, he caught almost 1,000 games, while hitting around average for a catcher. He also forced a rule change:

It was a sultry summer night at Memorial Stadium in 1969, but home plate umpire John Rice expected things to reach a boil after spotting Oriole Clay Dalrymple with his customary catcher's mitt on his hand and a fielder's glove hanging out of his back pocket.

Rice immediately questioned Dalrymple as to the purpose of the extra glove. The catcher replied matter-of-factly that if a play at the plate occurred, he would simply switch to his fielder's glove.

After huddling with his fellow umpires, Rice could not find a rule forbidding the use of a second glove. But he extracted a promise from Dalrymple that he would not attempt to use the fielder's mitt until the league office made a formal decision.

Expectedly, Oriole Manager Earl Weaver protested. He argued, "If there is nothing covered in the rules, why rule against, why not for it."

Eventually, Weaver's two-glove ploy led to Rule 1.12, which allows the catcher to wear "only a leather mitt."

Source: "New Rule on Size of Gloves Is Catching On"; [Bulldog Edition] ALAN GOLDSTEIN. *Los Angeles Times.* Los Angeles, Calif.: May 6, 1990. pg. 15

After O'Brien, very little separates the top catchers; they are all worth close to 10 runs each. Among the catchers with at least 10 effective seasons, here are the leaders: Rodriguez, Rick Dempsey, Jim Sundberg,

Gary Carter, Johnny Bench, Bob Boone, Brad Ausmus, Lance Parrish and Bill Freehan. Rodriguez has received the most Gold Gloves (12, as of 2006). Bench is next at 10, Boone with seven, Sundberg six, and Freehan with five. Carter did win three, as did Lance Parrish and Brad Ausmus.

It's nice to see that their reputations were earned. But among these leaders each with at least three Gold Gloves, Dempsey was shut out. Dempsey's full seasons lasted from 1978 through 1986, when Gold Gloves were won by Sundberg, Boone and Parrish. Just bad luck for Dempsey.

Among the catchers with four Gold Gloves (Charles Johnson, Del Crandall, Mike Matheny, Tony Pena), only Pena doesn't come out with a high score in this system. Bill James once noted that a system that always surprises is probably wrong, and one that never surprises is probably useless. The careers of Pena and Dempsey overlapped, but in different leagues. As a result, 20 years from now, Pena's four Gold Gloves may indicate he was a better catcher than Dempsey, who had zero. But, now we know better. And guys with shorter careers, like O'Brien and Dalrymple, can be given their due respect.

Also, let's not forget the worst catchers: right near the bottom is Mike Piazza. As much as Rodriguez, et. al., helped, Piazza has hurt his team. There is a 20-run gap between these star catchers, just on the running game. Note that we are not considering how catchers handle their pitchers.

Now, even though we did this whole network of peers, as we noted earlier, Petralli's peers include 8% of Ivan Rodriguez, which is hardly fair to Petralli. As it turns out, if we take the run value of each of Petralli's peers, their overall run value is two runs. And that is as bad as it gets. Every catcher is compared to a peer worth plus or minus two runs (and most of them were within one). It is reasonable to consider that, for catchers, their peer group is representative of the typical league average catcher.

Pitchers

Now, let's invert this, and look at it from the pitcher's perspective. Here are the top 10 and bottom 10 following the same process. All rate stats are per 1,000 batters faced (roughly 35 starts).

Pitcher		LWTS	Years
Don	Elston	6.6	3.1
Jesse	Jefferson	6.3	4.8
Armando	Reynoso	6.2	4.0
Ron	Robinson	5.9	3.4
Bob	Shirley	5.5	6.1
Brian	Anderson	5.0	6.0
Geoff	Zahn	5.0	7.8
Mark	Buehrle	5.0	5.9
Greg	Swindell	4.9	9.0
Kirk	Rueter	4.6	7.4

Those were the top 10. Next up is a list of the bottom 10…

Pitcher		LWTS	Years
Joe	Niekro	-4.9	15.2
Charlie	Hough	-5.3	16.2
Jason	Isringhausen	-5.3	3.1
Ron	Davis	-5.3	3.2
Hector	Carrasco	-5.6	3.3
Jason	Grimsley	-5.9	3.9
Tim	Stoddard	-6.0	3.2
Bruce	Berenyi	-6.2	3.4
Hoyt	Wilhelm	-8.2	6.6
Mark	Clear	-11.1	3.6

At the bottom of the list are noted knuckleballers Hoyt Wilhelm and Charlie Hough. Wilhem had 27 more wild pitches and passed balls than his peers, easily outpacing Hough's 19, to lead the Retrosheet years.

While it looks like the range in runs is narrower for pitchers, remember that the pitchers' totals are per 1,000 batters, while those for catchers are per 5,000 batters. As bad as you think Piazza was with runners on base, Mark Clear was far worse.

With or Without ... Derek Jeter

by Tom M. Tango

"They think they have a mathematical equation that figures everything out," Jeter said. "Like every single person is out there with the same runner and the same pitcher and the ball is hit in the same exact place. It seems like once somebody says one thing about you, people tend to run with it and we never hear the end of it."

Source: "Extra Practice for Jeter, But No Hint of Doubt"; Jack Curry. *New York Times*. (Late Edition (East Coast)). New York, N.Y.: Apr 18, 2007. pg. D.5

Derek Jeter is right.

Ultimate Zone Rating (UZR) by Mitchel Lichtman (who is also co-author of *The Book*) is regarded by many to be the best fielding system around. And since 2003, UZR says that Jeter makes about 16 fewer plays than the average shortstop (that's 13 runs worse than average) per 162 games. That puts him near the bottom of the pile with Angel Berroa (no one's idea of a good shortstop). At the bottom is Michael Young. In short, he is to shortstop what Mike Piazza is to catcher.

Being 16 plays worse than average works out to getting .03 fewer outs per play, compared to an average shortstop. But, as Jeter correctly and sarcastically pointed out, "the ball is hit in the same exact place." The way UZR works is to establish a set of parameters, among others:

- Location of batted ball
- Hardness of hit (slow, medium, fast)
- Trajectory (ground, pop, fly)
- Tendency of pitcher to allow ground ball
- Runners on base and outs
- Park

The first three are subjective, and depend on multiple human data recorders. UZR looks at all balls hit in or through the infield, and classifies them by the above parameters. By combining the various parameters, UZR determines how often a shortstop converted that specific play into an out. So a medium hit ball, hit halfway between second and third bases, with a groundball pitcher on the mound, and runner on first with one out at Camden Yards was converted into an out, say, 90% of the time. If for that combination Jeter actually converted the play into an out 86% of the time, he gets -.04 (.90 - .86) outs per play, relative to the average shortstop. UZR goes through every possible combination of actual results by all shortstops and compares it to Jeter's results. And overall, Jeter is .03 outs per play worse than average. And over 162 games, that's 16 outs.

But what if the human data recorder noted the play as being halfway between second base and third base (45 feet), but it was really 40 feet off third base? Under that combination, maybe the average shortstop made the play 88% of the time. And maybe the ball was hit hard, not medium, lowering the likelihood of making the play to 85%. Suddenly, in a play that Jeter made an out 86% of the time, he's now better than average, compared to our new 85%.

Even in "sure out" situations, where the average shortstop makes the play 99% of the time, UZR and its sister systems (David Pinto's PMR, John Dewan's Plus/Minus), would only be able to classify the play to say around 95%. That is, there is enough uncertainty in the classification of a ball; in a play that you and I, as fans, would be able to spot as a "99%" play, the advanced fielding systems, with their limited data input, can only classify it as a "95%" play. That's pretty good with only a .04 error range here. But, as we saw, the difference between a bad fielder and an average one is .03 outs per play.

Jeter can fairly say that because of the uncertainty in the data being recorded, it may be biased against him. Never mind that obvious super fielders, like Adam Everett and Scott Rolen, come out smelling like roses in these advanced fielding systems. It's always possible, Jeter will assert, that he's in the minority of players being biased against, even after several years and many different human data recorders. It's a tenuous position, but not one we can disregard, especially since the fielding systems themselves are somewhat proprietary.

"Like every single person is out there with ... the same pitcher," Jeter said. It would be fair to say that Roger Clemens and Andy Pettitte, whether they have

Everett or Jeter behind him, will give up the same kind of distribution of balls in play. Jeter has been behind 124 different pitchers in his career. And if we focus only on seasons since 1993, Jeter's pitchers have had, in all, 308 different shortstops (starting with Mike Bordick, Alex Gonzalez, Omar Vizquel, Miguel Tejada, Cal Ripken, Orlando Cabrera, and so on).

See where I'm going here? Just as we looked at various events for combinations of pitchers and catchers in our last article, we can look at results of balls in play for various combinations of pitchers and shortstops. Here then is how Clemens and Jeter paired up:

- 1,966: number of balls in play to all fielders (BIP)
- 209: number of plays with an out recorded by the shortstop (Out6)
- 10.6%: percentage of all plays that the shortstop recorded for an out, or Out6/BIP (Rate6)

The above excludes all bunts and home runs. So, of all fieldable balls in play, Jeter made an out on 10.6% of them.

And since 1993, here's a list of all the other shortstops that Clemens has had:

SHORTSTOP	PA	OUT6	RATE6
John Valentin	1,689	199	11.8%
Adam Everett	1,081	152	14.1%
Alex S. Gonzalez	1,061	127	12.0%
Jose Vizcaino	232	27	11.6%
Tomas Perez	130	10	7.7%
Erick Almonte	128	15	11.7%
Other 16	582	70	12.0%
ALL	4,903	600	12.2%

Let's recap here. Clemens, with Jeter as his shortstop for 1,966 balls in play (anywhere in the park), had Jeter turn 10.6% of them into outs. Clemens, with 22 other shortstops since 1993, for 4,903 balls in play, had those shortstops, collectively, turn 12.2% of them into outs. (And check out the wonderful Adam Everett.)

And we're not going to stop with just Clemens. Jeter had a total of 118 pitchers (out of 124) whom each also had at least one other shortstop. Here's how each of those pitchers did with and without Jeter as his shortstop:

PITCHER	JETER PA	JETER RATE6	OTHER PA	OTHER RATE6
Andy Pettitte	3,980	12.7%	2,411	13.9%
Mike Mussina	3,081	9.8%	4,591	11.6%
David Wells	2,411	13.0%	5,037	13.3%
Roger Clemens	1,966	10.6%	4,903	12.2%
Mariano Rivera	1,895	11.3%	315	10.2%
Ramiro Mendoza	1,761	12.5%	451	13.1%
Orlando Hernandez	1,632	9.9%	1,051	10.1%
David Cone	1,589	9.0%	2,388	11.2%
Randy Johnson	1,168	12.1%	5,124	12.6%
Chien-Ming Wang	1,067	15.7%	61	14.8%
Dwight Gooden	1,045	10.3%	1,271	13.1%
Mike Stanton	999	9.6%	1,360	11.5%
Kenny Rogers	974	16.7%	7,054	13.7%
Jeff Nelson	663	12.7%	980	12.1%
Kevin Brown	607	12.0%	5,590	15.2%
Jaret Wright	599	12.0%	1,956	12.6%
Jon Lieber	569	13.0%	5,234	13.0%
Ted Lilly	564	10.1%	2,046	10.7%
OTHER 100	12,974	11.4%	134,819	12.6%

Mariano Rivera and Kenny Rogers like Derek Jeter. A couple of other pitchers are ambivalent. The rest don't like him. Overall, with 39,544 balls in play with Jeter as shortstop, he converted 11.6% of them into outs. The other shortstops with Jeter's pitchers (prorated to the number of balls in play with Jeter as his shortstop), converted 12.5% of their balls in play into outs. So, Jeter does make fewer plays than his peers. With around 4,000 balls in play per season, that difference of almost 1% comes out to 38 fewer plays made by Derek Jeter. That is not good.

Why don't we do this for all shortstops? Here are all 46 shortstops with at least 12,000 balls in play (three full seasons) since 1993:

SHORTSTOP	PA	RATE6	OTHER RATE6	DIFF_ PER_4000
Rey Sanchez	17,695	13.5%	12.0%	59
Adam Everett	13,169	13.6%	12.2%	57
Greg Gagne	16,416	13.0%	11.8%	45
Orlando Cabrera	27,695	12.4%	11.6%	34
Mark Grudzielanek	12,522	12.8%	12.1%	29
Jack Wilson	21,614	13.3%	12.5%	29
Cesar Izturis	13,811	12.8%	12.1%	29
Julio Lugo	20,413	12.8%	12.1%	26
Jose Valentin	28,390	13.0%	12.5%	22

SHORTSTOP	PA	RATE6	OTHER RATE6	DIFF_ PER_4000
Neifi Perez	23,235	13.0%	12.5%	20
Rey Ordonez	19,825	12.9%	12.4%	19
Jose Hernandez	14,864	12.70%	12.20%	18
Juan Uribe	15,968	13.2%	12.7%	17
Jimmy Rollins	23,693	12.2%	11.8%	15
John Valentin	13,507	12.6%	12.2%	15
Walt Weiss	21,260	12.1%	11.8%	13
Alex Gonzalez	21,655	12.3%	12.0%	11
Cal Ripken	15,097	12.2%	11.9%	10
Kevin Stocker	19,417	12.3%	12.1%	9
Pat Meares	22,801	12.2%	12.0%	8
Ozzie Guillen	18,337	11.8%	11.7%	5
Jose Vizcaino	18,443	12.6%	12.5%	5
Rafael Furcal	23,884	12.9%	12.8%	4
Omar Vizquel	46,202	12.4%	12.4%	2
Edgar Renteria	36,409	12.2%	12.2%	1
Rich Aurilia	22,898	12.0%	12.0%	0
Alex S. Gonzalez	30,949	12.1%	12.1%	0
Carlos Guillen	17,965	12.3%	12.3%	0
Angel M. Berroa	16,895	12.0%	12.1%	-1
Miguel Tejada	33,020	12.8%	12.9%	-2
Royce Clayton	45,315	12.6%	12.6%	-3
Jay Bell	21,886	13.0%	13.1%	6
Cristian Guzman	22,090	11.9%	12.0%	-5
Nomar Garciaparra	22,973	12.4%	12.5%	-5
Barry Larkin	27,771	12.3%	12.5%	-8
Deivi Cruz	24,668	11.8%	12.1%	-13
Gary DiSarcina	21,201	12.2%	12.5%	-13
Mike Bordick	32,609	12.2%	12.6%	-14
Alex Rodriguez	29,366	12.0%	12.4%	-17
Jeff Blauser	17,018	12.3%	12.8%	-21
Ricky Gutierrez	18,454	11.8%	12.4%	-22
Chris Gomez	23,912	11.7%	12.3%	-24
David Eckstein	20,649	11.9%	12.6%	-29
Felipe Lopez	12,403	11.2%	12.0%	-33
Derek Jeter	39,544	11.6%	12.5%	-38
Mike Young	12,955	11.8%	13.1%	-51

And there's Derek Jeter, right near the bottom. You'll also note that the Rate6 for each player's other shortstop has quite a range, from Orlando Cabrera's 11.6% to Michael Young's 13.1%. So Jeter was right that it matters who the pitcher is. Cabrera's pitchers didn't give any help, since his pitchers allowed their shortstops (outside of Cabrera) to only convert 11.6% of the balls in play into outs. That Cabrera managed to convert 12.4% into outs is a testament

to Cabrera himself. Michael Young on the other hand had it easy, as his pitchers made life easy for all their shortstops. And still, Young converted far fewer than his peers.

"...and the ball is hit in the same exact place," Jeter said. This is what UZR and the other fielding systems try to get a handle on. But let's take a slightly different approach. What if we look at who the batters are? Johnny Damon has hit the ball in play 398 times when Derek Jeter was on the field. Jeter turned 43 of those into outs, or 10.8%. Of the other 4,859 times that Damon has hit the ball without Jeter on the field, the shortstop turned 529 of them into an out, or 10.9%. So far as Damon is concerned, Jeter is as good as any other shortstop.

Jeter has had 993 different batters come to the plate with him on the field, and 992 of them have also come to bat when someone other than Jeter was a shortstop. While Jeter's batters had 11.6% of their balls in play converted into an out by Jeter, his batters had 12.2% of their balls in play turned into outs by a shortstop other than Jeter. Let's see how all shortstops fared. Everett and Sanchez again are at the top. Jeter is near the bottom once more:

SHORTSTOP	PA	RATE6	OTHER RATE6	DIFF_ PER_4000
Adam Everett	13,238	13.6%	12.2%	53
Rey Sanchez	17,711	13.5%	12.3%	48
Jose Valentin	28,554	13.0%	12.2%	34
Juan Uribe	15,968	13.2%	12.4%	32
Jack Wilson	21,774	13.3%	12.6%	30
Miguel Tejada	33,057	12.8%	12.1%	29
Greg Gagne	16,554	13.0%	12.3%	28
Neifi Perez	23,313	13.0%	12.3%	28
Julio Lugo	20,413	12.8%	12.2%	22
Rafael Furcal	23,872	12.9%	12.4%	21
Jay Bell	22,409	13.0%	12.6%	14
Nomar Garciaparra	23,078	12.4%	12.0%	14
Rey Ordonez	19,815	12.9%	12.5%	13
Cesar Izturis	13,863	12.8%	12.5%	11
Omar Vizquel	46,293	12.4%	12.1%	11
John Valentin	13,513	12.6%	12.3%	11
Carlos Guillen	17,998	12.3%	12.1%	8
Mark Grudzielanek	12,591	12.8%	12.7%	6
Mike Bordick	32,677	12.2%	12.1%	5
Royce Clayton	45,449	12.6%	12.4%	5
Orlando Cabrera	28,072	12.4%	12.3%	4
Jose Vizcaino	18,532	12.6%	12.5%	4

SHORTSTOP	PA	RATE6	OTHER RATE6	DIFF_ PER_4000
Jose Hernandez	14,947	12.6%	12.6%	3
Pat Meares	22,801	12.2%	12.2%	-1
Alex Gonzalez	31,028	12.1%	12.2%	-3
Kevin Stocker	19,459	12.4%	12.5%	-5
Alex Gonzalez	21,659	12.3%	12.4%	-6
Alex Rodriguez	29,927	12.0%	12.2%	-9
Cristian Guzman	22,089	11.9%	12.1%	-10
Angel Berroa	16,923	12.0%	12.3%	-11
David Eckstein	20,648	11.9%	12.2%	-11
Edgar Renteria	36,582	12.2%	12.5%	-12
Gary DiSarcina	21,275	12.2%	12.5%	-13
Walt Weiss	21,278	12.2%	12.5%	-13
Cal Ripken	15,200	12.2%	12.5%	-13
Barry Larkin	27,849	12.3%	12.6%	-14
Deivi Cruz	24,748	11.8%	12.2%	-15
Michael Young	12,976	11.8%	12.2%	-16
Jeff Blauser	17,025	12.3%	12.7%	-17
Jimmy Rollins	24,330	12.1%	12.6%	-19
Rich Aurilia	22,894	12.0%	12.5%	-21
Chris Gomez	24,001	11.7%	12.3%	-23
Derek Jeter	39,657	11.6%	12.2%	-25
Ozzie Guillen	18,340	11.8%	12.4%	-26
Ricky Gutierrez	18,542	11.8%	12.5%	-28
Felipe Lopez	12,410	11.2%	12.4%	-47

SHORTSTOP	PA	RATE6	OTHER RATE6	DIFF_ PER_1300
Adam Everett	3,958	14.2%	12.3%	24
Jack Wilson	6,934	13.6%	12.2%	19
Mark Grudzielanek	3,667	13.5%	12.3%	15
Juan Uribe	4,892	13.3%	12.2%	14
Rey Sanchez	5,523	13.3%	12.3%	13
John Valentin	4,484	13.1%	12.1%	13
Jose Valentin	8,912	13.0%	12.2%	11
Greg Gagne	4,971	13.1%	12.3%	10
Miguel Tejada	10,599	12.8%	12.1%	10
Rafael Furcal	7,368	13.0%	12.3%	9
Omar Vizquel	14,680	12.7%	12.1%	8
Jose Hernandez	4,733	12.9%	12.3%	7
Carlos Guillen	5,736	12.6%	12.1%	6
Neifi Perez	7,385	12.7%	12.2%	6
Mike Bordick	10,430	12.4%	12.0%	5
Jay Bell	6,818	12.8%	12.5%	4
Jeff Blauser	4,921	12.8%	12.5%	3
Rey Ordonez	5,928	12.6%	12.4%	3
Walt Weiss	6,655	12.7%	12.5%	3
Orlando Cabrera	8,476	12.3%	12.3%	1
Jimmy Rollins	7,209	12.4%	12.4%	1
Cesar Izturis	4,081	12.2%	12.2%	0
Barry Larkin	8,456	12.4%	12.5%	-1
Cal Ripken	4,723	12.1%	12.2%	-1
Royce Clayton	14,505	12.1%	12.3%	-2
Deivi Cruz	7,813	12.0%	12.2%	-2
Rich Aurilia	7,314	12.1%	12.3%	-3
Pat Meares	7,234	11.9%	12.2%	-3
Jose Vizcaino	5,665	12.2%	12.5%	-3
Alex Rodriguez	9,832	11.9%	12.1%	-3
Alex Gonzalez	9,876	11.9%	12.2%	-4
Kevin Stocker	6,162	12.2%	12.5%	-4
Julio Lugo	6,573	12.0%	12.3%	-4
Alex Gonzalez	6,664	12.0%	12.3%	-5
Ozzie Guillen	5,973	11.9%	12.2%	-5
Cristian Guzman	6,749	11.6%	12.1%	-6
David Eckstein	6,383	11.6%	12.2%	-8
Michael Young	4,297	11.6%	12.1%	-8
Edgar Renteria	11,390	11.9%	12.5%	-8
Nomar Garciaparra	7,169	11.5%	12.2%	-9
Ricky Gutierrez	5,818	11.8%	12.5%	-9
Gary DiSarcina	6,855	11.4%	12.1%	-10
Angel Berroa	5,530	11.4%	12.3%	-11
Chris Gomez	7,730	11.4%	12.2%	-11
Derek Jeter	12,193	11.3%	12.2%	-11
Felipe Lopez	3,907	10.9%	12.2%	-17

"Like every single person is out there with the same runner," Jeter said. Uh, that's a tall order isn't it? We looked at how Jeter converted a ball in play into an out based on the pitcher and the batter, clearly the two largest influences. But Jeter is now suggesting that the runner on first base is an influence? He may be right. After all, if you have a threat at first base, Jeter may move a few more steps closer to second base.

Let's leave no stone unturned. Most of the time, first base is unoccupied (27,465 plate appearances for Jeter, which is almost 70% of the time). He turned 11.7% of those times into an out. All other shortstops have a 12.4% out rate. But let's keep going. Manny Ramirez was on first base 123 times with Jeter as shortstop. The batter, with Ramirez on first base and Jeter at short, made an out to Jeter seven times (only 5.7% of the time). With Ramirez on first base, but without Jeter at short, the out was made by the shortstop 10.3%. Focusing only on when there was a runner on first base, here is a list of how all the shortstops did based on the identity of the runner:

The rate is per 1,300 runners on first base, which is a season's worth. And who is number two from the bottom? Derek Jeter. At the top is our old friend Adam Everett.

"I play half my games at Yankee Stadium," Jeter could have said, but didn't. Well let's take a look, shall we? At Yankee Stadium, 20,237 balls were hit when Derek Jeter was on the field, and he turned 11.4% of them into an out. When Derek Jeter was not on the field (meaning other Yankee shortstops since 1993, and all Yankee opponents), 11.8% of them were converted into an out.

At Fenway, he's at 10.8% and other shortstops are at 12.1%. If we go through all the parks, Jeter converted 11.6% of the balls in play into an out. And, if we weight each park based on how often Jeter played at that park, the non-Jeter shortstop converted 12.0% of them into an out. From this measure, this makes Jeter "only" 18 plays worse than average. Here is the entire list of shortstops:

SHORTSTOP	PA	RATE6	OTHER RATE6	DIFF_PER_ 4000
Rey Sanchez	17,716	13.5%	12.4%	44
Adam Everett	13,239	13.6%	12.6%	39
Jose Valentin	28,556	13.0%	12.1%	37
Juan Uribe	15,972	13.2%	12.4%	31
Miguel Tejada	33,059	12.8%	12.1%	28
Greg Gagne	16,559	13.0%	12.4%	25
Rafael Furcal	23,884	12.9%	12.3%	23
Neifi Perez	23,323	13.0%	12.5%	22
John Valentin	13,514	12.6%	12.0%	22
Jack Wilson	21,786	13.3%	12.8%	21
Jay Bell	22,423	13.0%	12.6%	15
Julio Lugo	20,413	12.8%	12.4%	15
Nomar Garciaparra	23,079	12.4%	12.0%	14
Rey Ordonez	19,827	12.9%	12.5%	13
Jimmy Rollins	24,338	12.1%	11.8%	13
Cesar Izturis	13,864	12.8%	12.5%	10
Gary DiSarcina	21,275	12.2%	12.0%	8
Kevin Stocker	19,462	12.4%	12.2%	7
Royce Clayton	45,463	12.6%	12.4%	6
Carlos Guillen	17,998	12.3%	12.2%	6
Mark Grudzielanek	12,593	12.8%	12.8%	3
Jeff Blauser	17,029	12.3%	12.2%	2
Jose Hernandez	14,952	12.6%	12.6%	2
Barry Larkin	27,855	12.3%	12.2%	2
Mike Bordick	32,678	12.2%	12.2%	1
Alex Gonzalez	21,663	12.3%	12.3%	0

SHORTSTOP	PA	RATE6	OTHER RATE6	DIFF_PER_ 4000
Jose Vizcaino	18,537	12.6%	12.6%	0
Cal Ripken	15,200	12.2%	12.2%	-2
Omar Vizquel	46,306	12.4%	12.4%	-2
Orlando Cabrera	28,081	12.4%	12.5%	-3
Alex Gonzalez	31,033	12.1%	12.2%	-4
Alex Rodriguez	29,929	12.0%	12.1%	-4
Edgar Renteria	36,600	12.2%	12.5%	-11
Angel Berroa	16,923	12.0%	12.4%	-14
David Eckstein	20,649	11.9%	12.3%	-15
Walt Weiss	21,291	12.2%	12.5%	-15
Michael Young	12,976	11.8%	12.2%	16
Derek Jeter	39,659	11.6%	12.0%	-18
Pat Meares	22,801	12.2%	12.6%	-18
Deivi Cruz	24,752	11.8%	12.3%	-21
Rich Aurilia	22,898	12.0%	12.5%	-22
Ozzie Guillen	18,340	11.8%	12.3%	-22
Chris Gomez	24,006	11.7%	12.3%	-26
Cristian Guzman	22,090	11.9%	12.5%	-26
Ricky Gutierrez	18,551	11.8%	12.6%	-32
Felipe Lopez	12,414	11.2%	12.4%	-48

Everett and Sanchez are there at the top again, but this time, Jeter is catapulted from the terrible range into just the poor range. He makes 18 fewer plays than the average shortstop, based on the park in which he plays. Note that Jeter (just behind Jimmy Rollins) has had the second-toughest park to field in. All other fielders were only able to convert 12.0% of the balls in play in Jeter's parks (half of them at Yankee Stadium) into an out. This is why when we looked at the pitchers and batters Jeter has had, he came out looking pretty bad. A lot of that influence was because of the park. But even accounting for the park, Jeter is still 18 plays worse than average.

Jeter is right. The pitcher, the batter, the runner and the park each influence how well a shortstop converts a ball in play into an out. Because of Jeter's insight, we can now appreciate the great fielding of Adam Everett.

I know Derek Jeter looks good. And fans at my annual Fans' Scouting Report (www.tangotiger.net/scouting) see him as an overall average shortstop. (That same report sees Adam Everett as the best fielding shortstop in baseball.) But where is the evidence to support the claim that Jeter is average or better?

Bill James, in his comparison of Everett and Jeter in Dewan's fine *The Fielding Bible*, looked for it in a myriad of ways and couldn't find it. Lichtman, Dewan and

Pinto have their processes, seemingly unbiased, and couldn't find it. And I've shown a few different open source ways, and I couldn't find it. Since fewer outs are being recorded when Derek Jeter is playing than when he is not, and I couldn't find any evidence of bias that Jeter himself offered (batter, pitcher, runner, park), then the reason is clear: Derek Jeter is simply not making the plays others are making. And it's enough to make him one of the worst fielding shortstops in baseball today. But, he is better than Felipe Lopez.

The Dollar Value of Player Development

by Vince Gennaro

The quality of a team's player development system has a far-reaching impact on any major league franchise. It's the key to controlling payroll, winning efficiently, becoming a pennant contender and even building a deeper emotional connection with a team's fans.

While any MLB team executive will tell you that player development is the lifeblood of any baseball organization, how many teams move beyond the platitudes and treat it like a financial imperative—the key to being competitive at a modest payroll? To elevate player development beyond a cliché to a core business strategy, teams need in-depth understanding of their financial parameters, including the return on investment equation for investing in scouting and player development.

The best way to deepen our understanding may be to answer four key questions:

1. What is the asset value of an internally developed star player to his team?

2. What are the implications of the drastic cost differential between homegrown players and free agents?

3. Which teams seem to devote the most resources to player development; i.e., which teams were most aggressive in the 2007 amateur draft and in the international market?

4. What is the dollar value of the annual amateur draft?

Beyond these four questions, some policy changes might enable MLB to further use player development as a major tool in the ongoing quest for competitive balance.

Internally Developed Players as a Team Asset

As free agent wages continue to rise, there is an ever-increasing value placed on pre-arbitration and arbitration-eligible players, most of whom come from a team's own farm system. A productive player development system that can provide a steady flow of young, inexpensive talent to the major league club is the key to winning efficiently: controlling payroll while staying competitive.

Looking at the relative cost of talent by years of major league service shows the value of developing players internally. The dramatic example of Washington Nationals third baseman Ryan Zimmerman illustrates the point.

In his rookie year, 2006, Zimmerman was runner-up to Hanley Ramirez for NL rookie of the year and a four-marginal win player (i.e., he contributed 12 Win Shares Above Bench (WSAB) to his team). He made $327,000, the major league minimum salary. If the Nationals were to *buy* four marginal wins in the free agent market, they would have expected to pay about $17.6 million ($4.4 million per marginal win), for this hypothetical All-Star caliber player.[1] (The calculation matches salary dollars to salary dollars. Later, we'll incorporate the signing bonus of an early draft pick.)

Let's make a more conservative assumption about Zimmerman's remaining years before he attains free agency—that he returns to earth and plays at his 2007 performance level (three marginal wins) over years two through six of service. Based on a study by Professors Stephen Walters and John Burger of Loyola College that analyzed arbitration awards, we can estimate pay for arbitration- eligible players, based on performance and years of service. Under this scenario, Zimmerman's salary begins at the major league minimum in 2006 and escalates to $12.7 million for 2011, his final arbitration-eligible season.

Now let's compare the cost of Zimmerman to the price of three marginal wins in the free agent market. If we assume free agent costs increase by 6% per year, the 2007 price tag for three marginal wins would have been $14 million, but should rise to $17.7 million by 2011. A free agent would be paid $96 million for the six years of performance we're projecting, compared to the $28 million cumulative compensation we can expect for Zimmerman.

Even when we add back Zimmerman's $2.975 million signing bonus as the fourth overall pick in the 2005 amateur draft and allocate a share of the cost of running a scouting and player development organization, and account for the time value of money, he's more than $65 million cheaper than the free agent alternative.

That $65 million is the asset value of Zimmerman to the Washington Nationals—the difference between what we expect him to be paid and the cost of replacing his production in the free agent market. Zimmerman is a poster child for why the player development system is the economic key to any baseball franchise. The following graph compares how his compensation is likely to grow, including his arbitration years, vs. the comparable free agent pay rate, including a factor for inflation.

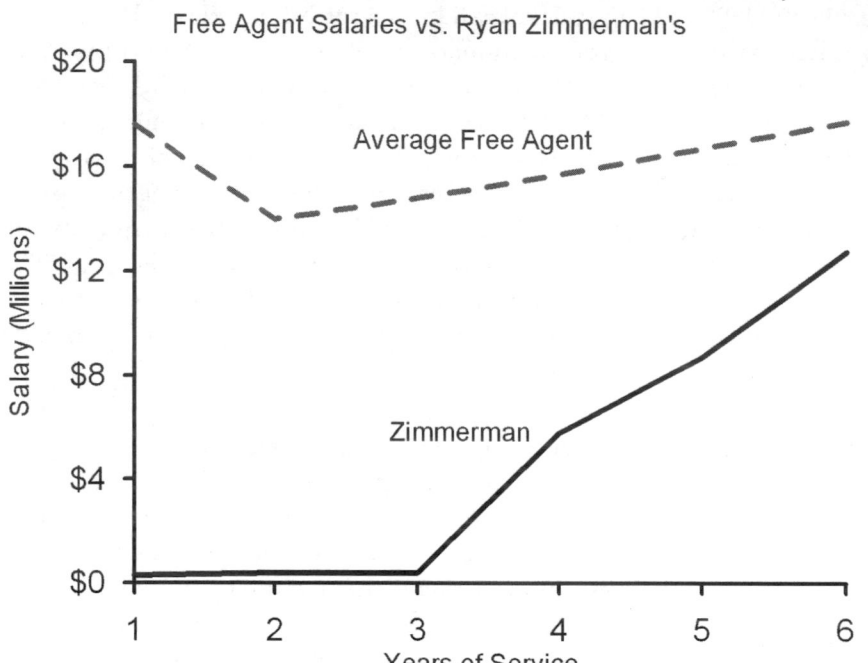

Free Agent Salaries vs. Ryan Zimmerman's

Rookie stars like Zimmerman, Ramirez or Justin Verlander don't come along every day, but lesser players —Toronto's Jesse Litsch or Baltimore's Daniel Cabrera, for example—still save their teams money, even if it is proportionally less. A $20 million differential is still a big saving, particularly to a small market club on a tight budget.

When a player development system fails to produce major league talent, a team has only two alternatives: purchase wins in the free agent market, or go with unready farmhands and turn in a subpar season. Teams with unproductive farm systems seldom can afford to buy 10 or 15 wins in the free agent market, so they often try a little of each—adding a few Triple-A players to the major league roster and dabbling in the free agent market. Even five or six marginal wins at the going rate in the free agent market can cost a team upward of $20 million.

Implications of the Cost Differential

The economic realities of baseball's pay scale and the resulting financial benefit of superior player development have several important implications:

Improving the player development system is handsomely rewarded financially.

It pays (literally) to dissect and understand every aspect of finding, developing and maintaining the health of your talent to improve the "yield"—the number of internally developed players who graduate to the major league club. By improving the yield of its farm system, a team can manage the mix of its roster toward inexpensive, pre-arbitration and arbitration eligible players in an effort to stay competitive at a modest payroll.

In 2005, the Indians delivered 93 wins with a $42 million payroll, while the Yankees spent $208 million to win 95 games. The Indians' roster consisted mainly of inexpensive homegrown talent, still playing at a discount to free agent wages, while the Yankees had only a handful of young former farmhands and were dominated by pricey free agents.

It's nearly impossible to "overspend" on player development.

If the price (signing bonus) of first-round draft picks doubled, it would still be dramatically cheaper than the alternative —buying talent in the free agent market. Investing in player development is a key to success for teams that can't afford to consistently engage in the free agent market. The Minnesota Twins of recent years are an example of a team that, despite tightly managing their payroll, focused on securing the best talent available in the amateur draft and spared no expense in the process.

In 2001, while the Twins had the lowest major league payroll in baseball, they had the overall No. 1 pick in the amateur draft. They signed catcher Joe Mauer to a near record $5.15 million signing bonus—more than 20% of their entire major league payroll. Had the Twins spent the $5.15 million in the free agent market, allowing Mauer to go unsigned, they potentially would have added two wins to their 2001 record, but passed on *24* future wins—Mauer's four marginal wins per year over his first six years of ML service.

Teams with different economic characteristics should use different sources of players to feed into their player development system.

There are two primary sources of playing talent for a team's minor league system—the amateur draft (which includes the United States, Canada and Puerto Rico) and international talent. International players are not eligible for the draft and can be signed as "free agents." Teams that are flush with financial resources, such as the Yankees, Red Sox, Mets and Cubs, can leverage their financial superiority by fishing in international waters. Any team willing to invest in academies, scouting and training resources and signing bonuses can have a leg up when it comes to signing prized teenagers from the Dominican Republic and Venezuela.

The Pacific Rim, particularly Korea, Taiwan and, more recently, China are also fertile ground for finding emerging talent. Conversely, teams at the low end of the economic food chain, such as the Royals and Pirates, need to supplement their international signings by capitalizing on the amateur draft. Their often-low finish in the standings yields the highest value, early draft picks, allowing them to select the prime domestic talent. To fully capitalize, they need to draft and sign the best players available, instead of passing up players for reasons of "signability"—a code word for not wanting to meet a draftee's bonus demand.

The 2007 Draft

By examining the early rounds of the 2007 amateur draft, we can get some sense of how teams capitalize on the opportunity to infuse talent into their organization. Which teams draft the best talent available and which teams view the draft as yet another opportunity to "save money?"

While there is no foolproof methodology to determine if a team had a successful draft until many years later, we can devise a test of aggressiveness by looking at which teams paid "over slot" bonuses—by exceeding MLB's recommended bonus scale based on draft position. While a draftee's bonus demands don't always indicate the caliber of the prospect (some multi-sport stars use competing sports or college scholarship offers to raise the ante) we still can use those demands as a proxy for "prospect quality." Figure 2 shows each team's draft aggressiveness in 2007 (signing bonuses relative to slot recommendations) compared to their major league payroll.

Experts insisted that New Jersey high school pitcher Rick Porcello, who was represented by super-agent Scott Boras, was among the top five prospects in the 2007 draft. Nevertheless, Porcello sunk to the 27th pick, where the aggressive Detroit Tigers selected him and promptly agreed to a $7 million deal, second in value only to that given Tampa Bay's No. 1 overall pick, David Price. While it's not fair to indict every team between say, the fourth and 26th pick for passing on Porcello—a high schooler, when some teams clearly prefer college pitchers—we can question the way some look at the math. By making some assumptions about Porcello's future, we can estimate a "break even" signing bonus and a rate of return on Detroit's $7 million deal.

Baseball America's Jim Callis analyzed the draft from 1990 to 1997 to determine where the flops, everyday players and stars come from—the round, high school vs.

Figure 2
Who Was Aggressive in the 2007 MLB Draft?

MLB Payroll	Low	Medium	High
High	NYM LAA LAD	SEA CWS	NYY DET BOS BAL CHC
Medium	STL PHI ATL CIN MIN HOU	OAK MIL TOR	SFG
Low	COL	TEX PIT FLA CLE SDP	TBA WAS KC ARI

Draft Aggressiveness

college and position. He concluded that more than 27% of the high schoolers drafted in the first round became major league regulars or better. We would expect the percentage to be even higher for early first-round picks.

Let's examine what might have been a "maximum bonus" for Porcello, by assuming he had a 50% chance of "making it" and a 50% chance of being a bust. Furthermore, **if** he makes it to the big leagues, let's assume he produces three marginal wins for each of his first six years of service, before becoming a free agent. (This places his performance somewhere comparable to the 2007 seasons of Cubs Ted Lilly and Rich Hill, or Arizona's Micah Owings and Doug Davis —comparable to a typical third starter.) With these conservative estimates of both Porcello's probability of making it and his ceiling, the drafting team still could justify a *$10 million signing bonus.*[2] In other words, the dollar value of Porcello's expected performance, when measured by the cost of buying his conservatively projected wins in the free agent market, is about $10 million more than his cumulative salary over his first six years of major league service.

Another metric to evaluate the Porcello signing is to measure the Tigers' internal rate of return on the bonus. By looking at the expected future savings Porcello generates, offset by the initial commitment of $7 million, we can calculate the interest rate the project delivers—the rate of return the Tigers expect to generate on their investment. Using the same assumptions for the draftee's performance, the rate is estimated at 19%, which certainly tops many traditional investments.

This aggressive approach to the draft has been a theme of the Tigers under Dave Dombrowski, who clearly believes the draft is his primary source of reasonably priced talent. He has made his club a consistent playoff contender by supplementing key free agent signings with early-first-round caliber draft picks who were selected later in the round, but paid as if they were among the top picks. In a couple of years, we may be looking at a starting rotation of Verlander, Andrew Miller and Porcello, three first-rounders who were paid well in excess of MLB's recommended slot value.

Other teams that see the draft as a prime opportunity to add to their talent base are the Yankees and Red Sox. The Red Sox have been aggressive in the draft since GM Theo Epstein's arrival and the Yankees have recommitted to the draft after several years of

neglecting it and focusing on international signings and free agent players.

Of the teams at the low end of major league economics, Tampa Bay and Washington stepped up in the 2007 draft with an aggressiveness that acknowledges the draft as an efficiently priced, primary source of future talent. Tampa Bay's GM, Andrew Friedman, gladly signed overall No. 1 pick Price, a lefthanded pitcher from Vanderbilt, for more than $7 million—a commitment worth nearly 30% of the Rays' 2007 team payroll. The Orioles made the most of their lone draft choice in the top 100 picks, the fifth overall, selecting highly touted Georgia Tech catcher Matt Wieters and signing him to a $6 million contract, more than 2.5 times the recommended slot value of the pick.

International Player Sourcing

Not long ago, young, talented prospects could be found at bargain prices in the Dominican Republic, Venezuela and the Far East. While the hot prospects still abound, the price tag is rising fast.

In 2006, the Giants signed Angel Villalona, a highly touted Dominican third baseman, for $2.1 million, an amount comparable to the eighth or ninth pick in the first round of the draft. The 2007 market is as hot as ever and many teams are realizing that it's no longer possible to find a "steal" internationally. The top prospect, (who remained unsigned through October), 16-year old Dominican shortstop Edward Salcedo, may exceed a $2 million signing bonus.

Among the most active teams in 2007 international signings are the Yankees, Mets, Mariners, Red Sox and Rangers. The Yankees have divided signing bonuses totaling $3.75 million among five 16-year-olds from the Dominican Republic and Venezuela, all among the top 20 international players signed. Seattle and the Mets each signed three position players for a total of $2.25 million and $1.65 million in bonuses, respectively. Boston and Texas also invested more than $1 million in signing bonuses to Latin American youngsters.

Even with inflated international signing bonuses, teams can create significant value by scouring the globe for raw talent. Let's say a team can produce a modest three wins over the first six years of a player's major league service from each year's crop of international signees. If a team pays $3 million in signing bonuses, and takes four or five years to develop the young prospects, it still may save upwards of $10 million in payroll by avoiding paying premium prices for wins in the free agent market.

While teams believe that the competition and escalating signing bonuses in the international market are eliminating a cheap source of talent, they must realize it's the *relative costs* that really determine whether the international market can still create value. The days of signing a top prospect for $50,000 may be history, but significant financial value still can be created, thanks to ever-escalating free agent salaries.

The High Stakes of a High Draft Pick

The Atlanta Braves have the distinction of allowing the highest-value draft slot get away unsigned—Joshua Fields, a right-handed pitcher at the overall 69th pick (fifth in the second round). Based on *Baseball America's* analysis of what we can expect from a college pitcher drafted in the second round, converted into WSAB, the Braves failed to bring in an expected 3.7 marginal wins, cumulatively over the first six years of Fields' major league service. To replace those wins in the free agent market, the Braves can expect to spend $16.4 million in today's dollars. Even if they offered a signing bonus of $1 million, a bit more than twice the MLB slot recommendation, their expected return on investment would have been substantial: 23%.

The real question is whether teams view the draft as a high-stakes business process that has a profound impact on their financial success. On average, how much is the amateur draft worth to a team?

If we take the same analysis we applied to the Braves 69th pick to the first 10 rounds of the draft and convert the expected performance into WSAB, the average team delivers about 3.25 marginal wins per year for players' six years before free agency. If we apply the average bonuses paid after the 2007 draft and compare them with the cost of replacing those 19-plus cumulative wins the draft generates, the 2007 draft is worth about $56 million to each team. In other words, the average draft produces future wins that "save" a team $56 million in future free agent wages.

MLB Policy

The player development system has the potential to be the "great equalizer" in the MLB competitive balance debate. Teams with the highest revenues, particularly the highest marginal revenues from winning, have a distinct advantage in the free agent market. They can rationally bid for players who would make no economic sense to teams that have lower revenues. But if these lesser teams have a productive scouting and player development process, they can lessen their dependency on high-priced free agents. They can be competitive at a lower cost. Could major league baseball implement some policies or rules to further enable player development and level the playing field between the "haves" and the "have-nots?"

For one, MLB should abandon its hard-line recommendations on bonuses based on draft slot. While those recommendations may keep downward pressure on ever-escalating costs, they also create the illusion that above-slot bonuses may be bad business. In reality, they still represent one of the lowest-cost sources of future major league talent.

Another idea may be to permit teams to trade draft picks, currently prohibited. I'll make no excuses for teams that fail to draft the caliber of player worthy of a draft slot just to save money. However, if draft picks could be traded, the Tigers might have traded up to ensure that they could draft Porcello. Maybe the Brewers (with the seventh overall pick) could have secured two or three additional draft picks in exchange for their first-round slot instead of drafting Matt LaPorta, who likely would have been available later in the round.

Taking the idea one step further, maybe the Rays or Royals (first and second overall picks, respectively) could have *sold* their picks for cash—big cash—and invested those dollars in international free agents, possibly signing two or three top Latin American players for the price of the top picks in the draft. (Any policy changes that permit trading of draft choices would need to deal with the added complication of draft picks that change hands as a result of free agent compensation.)

What if MLB allowed money to be exchanged for players? This would provide a powerful incentive for some teams—those that don't have the strongest revenue base—to invest heavily in player development, possibly turning it into a profit center and source of capital, which could fuel all aspects of a team's competitiveness. Developing players to field a competitive team is surely ample motivation to build a first-rate scouting and player development process, but allowing teams to sell their highest value assets—young players who are ML-ready and are paid a fraction of free agent wages—could turn an important competency into a source of cash for otherwise cash-starved teams.

For perspective, at the time of his trade to the Marlins, Ramirez was a young star with a full six years of below-market wages ahead of him. That gave him an economic value of more than $50 million—the gap between his expected pay and the cost of replacing his wins in the free agent market. There are many issues with cash transactions, including ensuring the team owner does not deplete his team's talent and pocket the cash. Certainly any such policy would need to come equipped with safeguards from abuse.

The player development system is undoubtedly the lifeblood of an MLB franchise. It has the potential to create more economic value than anything else an MLB team does, short of convincing taxpayers to pay for a new ballpark. It has greater potential impact than any marketing program, shrewd trade or efficient free agent signing. For teams that treat scouting and player development like a prime investment opportunity,

giving it the money, attention, scrutiny and accountability it deserves, October baseball can become a regular occurrence.

References

1. Dave Studenmund, *The Hardball Times Baseball Annual 2007,* Net Win Shares Value 2006, p. 131.

2. This assumes the bonus is paid as a lump sum in 2007, the player spends three years in the minor leagues, and the cost of 1.5 wins in the free agent market increases by 6% per year.

Do Managers Matter?

by David Gassko

It takes a special person to be hired and fired from the same job five different times. Billy Martin, who managed the New York Yankees from 1975 to 1978 and then again in 1979, 1983, 1985 and 1988, was a very special manager. He was temperamental, reckless, a force of nature. He clashed with players, management, and umpires. He never lasted long at one job. But Martin was a tremendously gifted manager.

On average, Martin's teams improved by 19 games in his first full season on the job. He won 1,253 games during his career with just 1,013 losses and two World Series rings. There is no way to make an even somewhat comprehensive short list of players who improved significantly under Martin because so many did, but to name just a few: Jim Perry, Rod Carew, Mickey Lolich, Ron Guidry.

But now here's the question: How can we quantify Martin's influence as a manager? Surely, he was an able man and surely, it was no coincidence that every team he ever took over improved so significantly, but how can we decide how much of the credit for that belongs to Martin? Was he really worth a 19-game improvement to the teams he took over, or was some of that due to other causes? And to balance the books, so to speak, how much did Martin's temperament cost his teams after the initial honeymoon wore off?

I was inspired to tackle this question by Chris Jaffe's "Evaluating Managers," published in 2006. In his study, Jaffe assigns the five following statistical categories to managerial influence:

- How much a team's hitters outperformed their projections
- How much a team's pitchers outperformed their projections
- How many more runs a team scored than we would expect based on its component statistics
- How many more runs a team allowed than we would expect based on its component statistics
- The difference between a team's wins and its expected wins based on runs scored and allowed

I don't believe that there is much reason to think that a manager would affect whether his team scores or allows more or fewer runs than expected, so I'll focus this study on how players perform versus expectations under different managers.

I considered including the difference between a team's actual and expected record based on runs scored and allowed as well, but didn't for two reasons: First, that difference is mostly attributable to variables that the manager does not control, such as the team's distribution of runs scored and allowed, the quality of its closer, and its hitting in the clutch. Secondly, I want to focus this study on whether a manager can make his players better, and if so by how much, rather than strategic aspects of managing, which is really what would be reflected in the variance between a team's expected and actual record.

Methodology

So the question is, how do we determine the impact a manager had on his players' performance? Jaffe approached this question by essentially creating a projection for each player season based on that player's performance in the two years before and after that season. That is a solid approach, but I believe it might underestimate managerial effects, as that projection often will be based completely or mostly on the statistics put up by a player under the same manager. In other words, if a manager makes a player great this year and if that manager doesn't get fired, the player is probably going to be great again next year, but our projection for him will already be really high because of his performance this season.

We can never totally get rid of that issue—in this study, a player who plays his whole career under the same manager will end up counted as a 0, even if the manager did make him better—but I do think that it helps to use a player's whole career, so as to better isolate the influence of any one manager.

I handle hitters and pitchers using a similar method, but I'll explain the process for each separately. Let's start with the hitters. First, we need a metric that can easily be converted into runs and then wins and applied to hitters from every era. I chose to use Weighted On-Base Average (wOBA), a statistic invented by the authors of *The Book: Playing the Percentages in Baseball*, which takes into account all major offensive events and converts them into a rate statistic that approximates the more well-known on-base percentage. The formula I used was:

$$(.72*(BB - IBB) + .75*HBP + .90*1B + 1.24*2B + 1.56*3B + 1.95*HR)/PA$$

Note that the official formula also includes reached on error, but that's not going to make a big difference. I then adjusted all statistics for park and league effects so that an average wOBA was equal to .335. The nice thing about wOBA is that it can easily be converted into runs above average by subtracting the average wOBA (in this case, .335) from a player's wOBA, multiplying by plate appearances and dividing by 1.15. So for example, in 2001, Barry Bonds had an adjusted wOBA of .561 in 664 plate appearances, which converts to:

$$(.561 - .335)*664/1.15 = 130 \text{ runs above average.}$$

I then calculated each player's career adjusted wOBA, and used the above formula to calculate how many more runs a player created in a given season than we would expect based on his career statistics. Through 2006, for example, Bonds had a career wOBA of .435, and therefore created 72 "runs above self" in 2001. There is, of course, one obvious issue with this approach, which is that it does not adjust for age. But that's a problem that is easily correctable. I summed "runs above self" for every player at every age in baseball history, which yielded the following aging pattern:

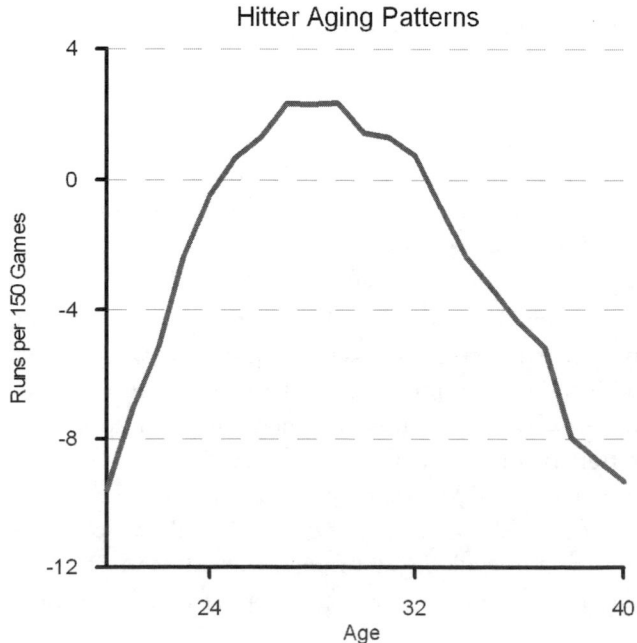

The graph corresponds with other studies on aging patterns, showing that players improve rapidly in their early 20s, peak between the ages of 27 and 29, and then decline throughout their 30s, albeit more slowly. To use Bonds as an example again, age-adjusted, he was 81 "runs above self" in 2001. Once I had calculated "runs above self" for every player-season in the history of baseball, the rest was easy.

First, I excluded teams that had more than one manager because there exists no way to correctly split the credit. Once I'd done that, I summed the "runs above self" that hitters had posted for every manager in baseball history. For example, Martin's hitters were 364 runs better playing for him than they were in their overall careers. That's pretty damn good, seventh all-time to be exact.

OK, but the question still is, what does that mean? Is that number in any way significant? Or was Martin just extraordinarily lucky? I'll get back to that in a second.

First, let's quickly go over how I handled the pitchers. I decided to use wOBA for pitchers as well, in part so that I was using the same metric throughout this study and in part because random noise can make runs allowed numbers less meaningful. There are certain minuses to this approach—if a manager makes pitchers much better at pitching from the stretch, this study will not reflect that—but overall, I think it's the way to go.

Because doubles and triples allowed numbers are not available for much of baseball history, I simply multiplied the league average of doubles per hit and triples per hit by the hits allowed for each pitcher. This may underrate those pitchers who give up fewer doubles or triples per hit than the average hurler, but since we're looking at players relative to *themselves*, it won't matter. Anyway, after estimating doubles and triples, I applied the same formula to pitchers as I used for hitters, with all the same adjustments.

Aging patterns are calculated the same way, though they're not quite as smooth for pitchers, as you can see on the next page.

Overall, the adjustments for pitchers in their early 20s are small enough to make the rough variations inconsequential. The steady decline after 28 mirrors other studies on pitcher aging. Again we calculate age-adjusted "runs above self" for pitchers and look at how pitchers have performed under each manager. Martin does well here, too, at 113 runs above average.

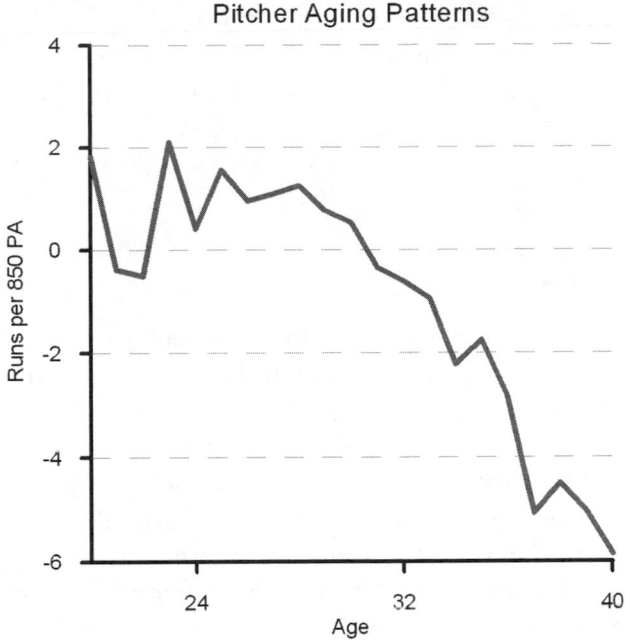

Pitcher Aging Patterns

So now we return to the most important question: Are these numbers meaningful or simply the result of a lot of random variation?

To obtain the answer, I first split players into two groups, those whose last names begin with A-L and those whose last names begin with M-Z. I took this method from James Click, who applied it in a study similar to this one in *Baseball Between the Numbers*. The idea is that managers should have the same impact on players no matter what letter their last name starts with, so we can compare their effects on each group. If there is a significant correlation, that would provide direct evidence that managers do in fact have an impact on

player performance; if the observed impact is due only to random chance, there should be no correlation.

Let's look at all managers with at least 1,000 career games managed, with their overall impact (hitters and pitchers combined) on players based on the player's last name (the graph is below).

The dotted line shows an overall positive relationship between the two variables, meaning that managers do appear to have an impact on player performance. For the statistically minded, the correlation is .31 and the T-value 3.17. There is almost no chance that this result could occur due to random chance alone. So the question now becomes, how large an impact have we found? Can a great manager be worth 20 games a year, as Martin's turnarounds suggest, or is he worth some number so small that it is pretty much meaningless?

To answer that question, we have to employ a statistical concept known as "regression to the mean." Basically, every statistic is subject to random chance, but we can estimate its true value by adding a given amount of average performance.

So if a player hits .330 in 500 at-bats, we might add 700 at-bats of average performance and project that he is most likely a .295 hitter. If you look at all players in baseball history with a .330 batting average in about 500 at-bats in one season, they will likely have hit .295 as a group the next year. With managerial performance, we find that we have to add about 2,260 games worth of average managing to estimate true talent. In the next section of this article, I will present estimated true talents for the best and worst managers in baseball history as well as currently active skippers.

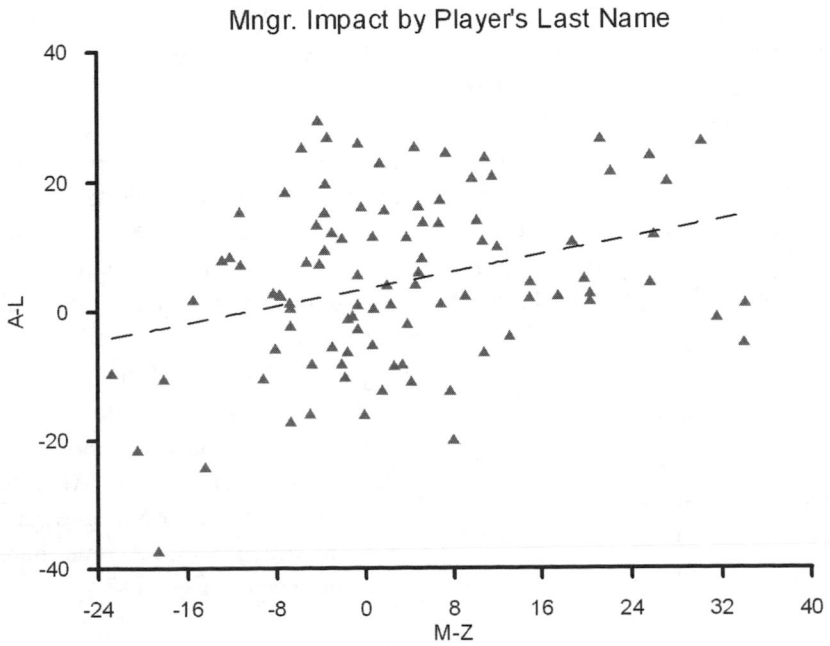

Mngr. Impact by Player's Last Name

The Results

Since everyone loves a good top 10 ranking, let's start by looking at the 10 greatest managers in baseball history. I should note once more that I am trying only to estimate these managers' effects on players, ignoring their strategic abilities and other things a manager might be responsible for. These numbers are presented in terms of wins added per 162 games.

Name	Skill
Bobby Cox	2.29
Earl Weaver	2.16
Billy Martin	1.96
Jim Mutrie	1.80
Billy Southworth	1.77
Al Lopez	1.75
Dusty Baker	1.65
Gus Schmelz	1.57
Pop Snyder	1.46
Jimmie Dykes	1.45

Bobby Cox tops the list on the strength of his effect on pitchers. Overall, pitchers have outperformed their expected numbers by 1,063 runs under Cox; his hitters have actually been somewhat worse with Cox than elsewhere. Immediately, an issue with this study becomes obvious: There is no way to split credit between coaches and managers. Many previous studies have attributed the Braves' great pitching to pitching coach Leo Mazzone; this study gives the credit to Cox. Who actually deserves it? I don't know, but here, any improvements made due to good coaches will be credited to the manager.

Martin is third on the list and while some of the older managers' names here are not very well-known, overall these rankings match our general intuition. Expanding this list to the top-20 managers, we find respected names like Whitey Herzog, Bobby Valentine, Lou Piniella, Sparky Anderson, Cap Anson and Larry Dierker. So far, so good. Now let's look at the 10 worst managers of all-time:

Name	Skill
Art Howe	-1.88
Terry Francona	-1.82
Mike Hargrove	-1.55
Fred Haney	-1.45
Jim Marshall	-1.27
Joe Torre	-1.23
Horace Phillips	-1.22
Nick Leyva	-1.17
Nixey Callahan	-1.14
Billy Barnie	-1.09

You may be surprised to find some highly respected names on this list, like Francona, Hargrove and Torre. At first, I was too. And it's possible, of course, that these numbers are wrong about one or all of these managers. After all, we can only estimate how good they are.

However, I do think I have a few plausible explanations for why these managers are listed among the all-time worst. First, the effects we're finding here are not that significant—fewer than two wins a year. Now are two wins important? Of course. Teams pay about $5 million a win on the free agent market these days. But will they crush the playoff chances of a good team? Generally not. So these managers could be doing bad jobs with good teams and still not be exposed.

That said, there are plenty of aspects of a manager's job that this study doesn't cover. Torre, for example, is well-known for keeping together teams that could easily splinter and fall apart. Even if he isn't the best coach in the world, the alternatives could be even worse. Torre actually measures as above-average with hitters but awful with pitchers. It's possible that we're simply measuring the Mel Stottlemyre effect here. Of course, given how long Torre kept Stottlemyre around even after it became clear that he was not an effective pitching coach, maybe we should be debiting Torre for that.

That's the thing: A counterargument can be made for each of these rankings. And then an argument counter to that and so forth. While I think that these numbers are mostly "right," I do acknowledge that they are of limited scope and meant only to quantify a question that will always require some subjectivity. With that said, let's look at a few of the more surprising results:

Joe McCarthy (-0.36 "Skill"): Seventh all-time in wins, McCarthy ranked first in Jaffe's study, and by a large margin: The difference between McCarthy and the second-place finisher (Al Lopez) was greater than the gap between Lopez and the 48th-best manager (Gabby Street). So how come there is such a big difference between our results?

Jaffe found that McCarthy was better than any other manager in the history of the game at handling hitters and at handling pitchers. I have McCarthy rated as slightly above average with hitters and a bit more below average with pitchers. Overall, that adds up to a slightly below average score. Is that a fair evaluation of a manager who is among the all-time leaders in wins? I don't know, but it sounds more reasonable than rating McCarthy head and shoulders (and torso) above everybody else. Perhaps the right answer is somewhere in-between.

Casey Stengel (-0.78 "Skill"): How can the legendary Yankees manager, a six-time World Series winner, rank 25th from the bottom? Well, the simple answer is there's more to Stengel's career than just his time with the Yankees. As successful as his Yankee teams were, none of Stengel's other teams ever won the pennant, and the Mets under his direction barely won 30% of their games. Overall, Stengel's career winning percentage was a very average .508. The question that arises, then, is whether Stengel made the Yankees good or whether the Yankees made him look good. The numbers suggest it was the latter, though the overall effect still isn't very large.

Dusty Baker (+1.65 "Skill"): Baker is regarded by many as an awful manager. He is often blamed for the demise of Mark Prior and Kerry Wood and almost anything else that has ever gone wrong with the Cubs. But the fact is, Baker has turned around the careers of many players, and while my numbers indicate that he hasn't been very good with pitchers, Baker scores as the greatest manager of all time with hitters. That actually matches anecdotal evidence: The Giants were always known for getting a lot more than expected out of veteran hitters when Baker was at the helm. The Reds, who just hired him for the 2008 season, hope he can repeat that performance with Ken Griffey Jr.

Finally, for some numbers that are pertinent to today's game, let's peek at all 2007 managers with a least one full season at the helm of a team through 2006 (I've removed teams with more than one manager in 2007):

Team	Name	Skill
Angels	Mike Scioscia	-0.45
Blue Jays	John Gibbons	0.45
Braves	Bobby Cox	2.29
Brewers	Ned Yost	0.51
Cardinals	Tony La Russa	0.35
Cubs	Lou Piniella	1.24
Devil Rays	Joe Maddon	-0.27
Diamondbacks	Bob Melvin	-0.59
Dodgers	Grady Little	0.38
Giants	Bruce Bochy	0.87
Indians	Eric Wedge	-0.41
Mets	Willie Randolph	-0.05
Phillies	Charlie Manuel	0.01
Pirates	Jim Tracy	1.04
Red Sox	Terry Francona	-1.82
Rockies	Clint Hurdle	-0.64
Royals	Buddy Bell	-0.02
Tigers	Jim Leyland	-0.42
Twins	Ron Gardenhire	0.72
White Sox	Ozzie Guillen	0.06
Yankees	Joe Torre	-1.23

Conclusions

So what have we learned? We've learned that:

- Manager impact on player performance can be quantified.
- There is a lot of random chance inherent in managerial ratings and they need to be regressed to accurately gauge the size of managerial effect.
- The difference between the best and worst managers at impacting player performance is about four wins a year. That's not on par with the value of a great player, but the impact of a great manager on player performance can be worth quite a bit to a team.

Appendix

The following table is estimated managerial skill ratings through the 2006 season for all managers with at least 1,000 career games managed:

Name	Skill	Name	Skill	Name	Skill
Felipe Alou	0.86	Bucky Harris	-0.29	Lou Piniella	1.24
Walter Alston	-0.21	Jack Hendricks	0.74	Paul Richards	0.86
Sparky Anderson	1.21	Whitey Herzog	1.39	Branch Rickey	-0.47
Cap Anson	1.20	Gil Hodges	1.04	Jim Riggleman	0.68
Dusty Baker	1.65	Ralph Houk	0.01	Bill Rigney	0.30
Billy Barnie	-1.09	Art Howe	-1.88	Frank Robinson	-0.30
Don Baylor	1.04	Miller Huggins	-0.99	Wilbert Robinson	0.09
Bruce Bochy	0.87	Fred Hutchinson	-0.42	Buck Rodgers	0.74
Lou Boudreau	-0.26	Hughie Jennings	-0.49	Gus Schmelz	1.57
Dave Bristol	-0.53	Davey Johnson	0.39	Red Schoendienst	0.39
Frank Chance	0.11	Fielder Jones	0.51	Mike Scioscia	-0.45
Fred Clarke	-0.15	Tom Kelly	-0.24	Frank Selee	-0.38
Charlie Comiskey	0.88	Gene Lamont	0.99	Burt Shotton	0.17
Bobby Cox	2.29	Tony La Russa	0.35	Buck Showalter	-0.17
Roger Craig	-0.46	Tommy Lasorda	0.62	Mayo Smith	0.37
Joe Cronin	0.65	Jim Leyland	-0.42	Billy Southworth	1.77
Alvin Dark	0.13	Al Lopez	1.75	Tris Speaker	0.91
Patsy Donovan	0.28	Connie Mack	0.80	George Stallings	-0.44
Chuck Dressen	-0.19	Billy Martin	1.96	Casey Stengel	-0.78
Hugh Duffy	0.31	Gene Mauch	1.02	Chuck Tanner	-0.47
Leo Durocher	1.11	Jimmy McAleer	-0.25	Birdie Tebbetts	0.36
Jimmie Dykes	1.45	Joe McCarthy	-0.36	Patsy Tebeau	-0.77
Lee Fohl	0.81	John McGraw	0.95	Bill Terry	-0.19
Terry Francona	-1.82	Bill McKechnie	0.24	Joe Torre	-1.23
Jim Fregosi	-0.22	Jack McKeon	0.82	Bobby Valentine	1.34
Frankie Frisch	0.65	John McNamara	0.18	Bill Virdon	0.75
Phil Garner	-0.23	Fred Mitchell	0.28	Earl Weaver	2.16
Clark Griffith	0.66	Pat Moran	1.17	Dick Williams	0.11
Charlie Grimm	0.04	Danny Murtaugh	1.10	Jimy Williams	0.80
Fred Haney	-1.45	Jim Mutrie	1.80	Jimmie Wilson	-0.16
Ned Hanlon	1.22	Johnny Oates	-0.07	Harry Wright	-0.18
Mike Hargrove	-1.55	Steve O'Neill	0.67	Don Zimmer	0.32

The Origin of the Platoon Advantage

by John Walsh

The platoon advantage—the fact that right-handed hitters tend to perform better against left-handed pitchers, and vice versa—is an essential part of baseball. It dictates strategy (such as left-right-left sequences in batting orders) and it influences roster construction (there would be no such thing as lefty relief specialists and 13-man pitching staffs, without the platoon advantage). It leads to numerous pitching changes, pinch hitters who never get to bat (because they are replaced to counter a pitching change) and disgruntled players who are shifted from full-time roles to being "platoon" players.

Given its importance in the game, how much do we really know about the platoon advantage? Well, we know that there is not much difference among hitters—once you examine enough plate appearances to get the statistical fluctuations down, hitters all exhibit roughly the same increase in performance when facing an opposite-hand pitcher. We also know that this is not true of pitchers—some consistently show large platoon splits, while others show very small, or even negative, splits.

On the other hand, do we understand what causes the platoon advantage? Well, I don't know about you, but I don't. Here's the story that I have generally heard: When a right-handed batter faces a righty pitcher, the breaking ball is tough to hit. It might start out headed straight for the ol' noggin and while the instinct of self-preservation causes you to jerk away from the onrushing danger, the pitch swerves over the plate for a called strike. Or maybe you manage to swing at the pitch, but can't do much with it.

Robert K. Adair, who once held the position of "Physicist to the National League," addressed the causes of the platoon advantage in his classic book *The Physics of Baseball*:

Many, if not most, batters attribute the small but significant hitting difference solely to the different break of the curveball. I have had players tell me that they do not care whether the fastball is thrown left or right. But they find it more difficult to hit the curve that breaks out than the curve that breaks in.

Adair goes on to speculate about the "physics" behind this notion. He explains how hitters start out looking for a medium-fast pitch over the center of the plate and then make adjustments to account for different pitches. Often, though, batters undercorrect, so, for example, they will swing under a "hopping" fastball and be out in front of a changeup. Adair talks of two corrections the batter must make on the curveball:

Batting against the curveball, the batter tends to swing too quickly at the relatively slow pitch, and he tends to underestimate the in-out curve deviation. These errors tend to add up for the out-curves but cancel for the in-curves. Thus the in-curves may be a little easier to hit, accounting for the small advantage batters have when they face a pitcher throwing from the opposite side.

Baseball researcher Peter Morris, in his fabulous work, *A Game of Inches*, noted that the platooning of players did not occur until around 1880 for two reasons: "There were few left-handed pitchers in early baseball, and the curveball did not become a major force in most pitchers' arsenals until the late 1870s."

Morris also described the emergence of the switch-hitter as a way of countering the devilish curveball: "Almost as soon as the left-handed curveball pitcher emerged, left-handed batters seized upon switch-hitting as a way to strike back."

So it *is* the curveball that causes the platoon split. Or is it?

The thing is, we no longer have to assume or speculate on the origins of the platoon split; we can study the issue and figure it out. One way to do that is to look at historical data on platoon splits for pitchers and see if there are certain types of pitchers, perhaps throwing certain types of pitches, that consistently have extreme platoon splits, either large or small. This approach is made possible by the play-by-play data from Retrosheet going back 50 years (1957-2006, excluding 1999). These data allow us to compute the platoon splits for anybody who played in this era.

Perhaps even more exciting is the possibility of comprehensively studying the platoon differentials for specific pitch types. This kind of investigation is made possible by detailed pitch data collected and made available this year by mlb.com, the so-called Pitch f/x data. This data allows us to classify every single pitch by type (e.g. fastball, slider, etc.) and to study the outcomes for each pitch type, taking note of whether the batter enjoyed the platoon advantage or not.

There's a lot to do, so let's get to it.

Historical Platoon Splits

One way to get a handle on what leads to the platoon advantage is to look at pitchers who had extreme splits, either positive or negative, and to see what traits they might have in common. I've already mentioned that pitchers seem to have more variance than hitters in how much platoon advantage they enjoy, so it makes sense to focus on them.

The Retrosheet play-by-play data allows us to calculate pitcher splits going back about 50 years, so that's exactly what I did. A quick note on switch-hitters: I have removed all plate appearances by switch-hitters for this study. Switch-hitters always hit with the platoon advantage, of course, but as a group they are worse hitters than non-switchers with the platoon advantage. Thus, they tend to dilute the kinds of effects we are looking for.

Once you remove the switchers, the average platoon advantage for the period 1957-2006 is .065 of OPS—I'm going to be looking for pitchers who have a much larger advantage or a much smaller, and possibly negative,

one. I'm also going to be careful to select only pitchers who have faced enough batters from both sides of the plate to give us confidence in the results. The exact number of plate appearances required will depend on how big the platoon advantage is—basically I'm going to be looking at the pitchers with the most statistically convincing deviations from the average.

Once I have my lists of pitchers with large and small platoon splits, I'm going to look at what kind of pitches they threw, in the hopes that a pattern will emerge. Sounds easy, right? Well, it turns out Doc Medich had quite a large platoon split. Do you remember the pitch repertoire of Doc Medich? Do you remember Doc Medich?

Fortunately, there is the perfect resource for this kind of research, the incomparable *Neyer/James Guide to Pitchers*. Therein we can find that Medich threw a sinker, slider and changeup. We also learn that Dennis Eckersley abandoned his curveball when he became a reliever, that Brad Clontz was a submariner and that Gary Nolan's changeup had "screwball action." It's a fabulous reference (and it's fun to read, too).

OK, enough accolades for Rob Neyer and Bill James. Let's get back to the business at hand. For each of my extreme pitchers, I've noted their top two or three pitches

Table 1: Pitchers with Large Platoon Splits, 1957-2006

Name	Years	delOPS	Top 3 Pitches	Notes
Lieber_Jon	1994-2006	.234	FB SL CU	
Kison_Bruce	1971-1985	.230	FB SL	sidearm
Gibson_Bob	1959-1975	.163	FB SL CB	
Eckersley_Dennis	1975-1998	.164	FB CB SL	as starter; semi-sidearm
Reed_Steve	1992-2005	.287	FB CB SL	submarine
Shirley_Bob	1977-1987	.224	FB SL CU	
Hunter_Catfish	1965-1979	.154	FB SL CU	
Clontz_Brad	1995-2000	.467	FB SL	submarine
Tekulve_Kent	1974-1989	.214	FB SL CU	sidearm/submarine
Medich_Doc	1972-1982	.173	FB SL CU	
Roberts_Robin	1954-1966	.164	FB CB	
Looper_Braden	1998-2006	.295	FB SL CU	
Webb_Brandon	2003-2006	.236	FB CB CU	
Puleo_Charlie	1981-1989	.258	FB SL CB	
Holt_Chris	1996-2001	.263	FB CB SL	
Fossas_Tony	1988-1998	.298	SL FB	
Swift_Bill	1985-1998	.184	FB SL CB	
Pappas_Milt	1957-1973	.145	FB SL CU	
Pattin_Marty	1968-1980	.165	FB CB	different source: SL
Reuschel_Rick	1972-1991	.142	FB SL CU	
Myers_Mike	1995-2006	.276	FB SL	low sidearm/submarine
Urbina_Ugueth	1995-2005	.248	FB SL CU	

and I've jotted down any other comments that might be relevant to a study of platoon splits. The most important of these is arm angle—pitchers who throw from a low angle, sidearmers and submariners, generally will have a greater split than average, usually much greater.

Table 1 shows the pitchers with the largest platoon splits since 1957. More precisely, these are the 22 pitchers whose large platoon splits are the most significant, which is almost the same thing, but not quite. I started with 30 pitchers, but removed a handful on whom even Neyer and James could not get scouting reports.

Just to be clear, by "platoon split," I mean "OPS surrendered against opposite-hand hitters minus OPS surrendered against same-hand hitters". This is labeled "delOPS" in the table and remember the average value for all pitchers of delOPS is .065. Here is the key to pitch abbreviations: FB fastball, CB curveball, SL slider, CU changeup, SC screwball, KB knuckleball. Oh, one other

thing: I've simplified the pitch types somewhat: rising, sinking and tailing fastballs are all called fastballs, for example.

Quite a mixed bunch we have there. Several Hall of Famers, including the great Gibson, and then guys named Brad Clontz and Charlie Puleo. How do we make sense of this list? First, let's concentrate on pitch types. Well, virtually all these guys (and the large majority of all pitchers) throw the fastball as their primary pitch.

So, let's see what they throw when they aren't throwing the heater. If you stare at the list for a few minutes, you see rather a preponderance of sliders, especially when compared to the curveball. Of the 22 pitchers listed here, 16 prefer the slider to the curveball, while only six prefer the curve.

Another key feature seen in a number of these high-split pitchers is a sidearm delivery: six drop down, a

Table 2: Pitchers with Negative Platoon Splits, 1957-2006

Name	Years	delOPS	Top 3 Pitches			Notes
Trachsel_Steve	1993-2006	-.110	FB	CU	CB	
Hanson_Erik	1988-1998	-.133	CB	CU	FB	big CB
Mussina_Mike	1991-2006	-.059	FB	CB		knuckle curve
McGraw_Tug	1965-1984	-.111	SC	FB	CB	
Norris_Mike	1975-1990	-.116	SC	FB	CB	suspected of spitter
Boyd_Oil Can	1982-1991	-.089	FB	CB	SL	variety of arm angles
Blyleven_Bert	1970-1992	-.015	CB	FB	CU	3rd best CB all-time
Olson_Gregg	1988-2001	-.167	CB	FB	CU	
Marichal_Juan	1960-1975	-.026	SL	FB	CU	also screwball; variety of arm angles
Moyer_Jamie	1986-2006	-.040	FB	CU	CB	
Neagle_Denny	1991-2003	-.072	FB	CU	CB	overhand CB
Reynolds_Shane	1992-2004	-.059	CU	FB	CB	CU is splitter
Sutton_Don	1966-1988	-.002	CB	FB	SL	occasional screwball
Burdette_Lew	1954-1967	-.031	FB	SL	CU	spitter; screwball
Wakefield_Tim	1992-2006	-.032	KB	FB	CB	these are my opinions
Ortega_Phil	1960-1969	-.076	FB	SL		
Adams_Terry	1995-2005	-.091	FB	SL	CB	
Hampton_Mike	1993-2005	-.050	FB	CU		also: SL, sweeping CB
Herbert_Ray	1958-1966	-.040	FB	CB	CU	
Jones_Bobby	1993-2002	-.048	FB	CB	CU	
Rau_Doug	1972-1981	-.074	CU	FB	CB	
Jarvis_Pat	1966-1973	-.060	FB	CB		
Portugal_Mark	1985-1998	-.042	CB	SL	FB	
Nolan_Gary	1967-1977	-.038	CU	CB	FB	CU has screwball action
Nomo_Hideo	1995-2005	-.034	FB	CU	CB	CU is forkball
Williams_Woody	1993-2006	-.033	FB	CB	SL	
Abbott_Jim	1989-1998	-.063	FB	CB	CU	
Deshaies_Jim	1984-1995	-.066	FB	CU	SL	
Palmer_Jim,	1965-1984	.002	FB	CB	SL	

relatively high proportion. It is well-known that side-arm pitchers tend to suffer from large platoon splits.

Let's look at the other extreme—pitchers who have small or even negative platoon splits are listed in Table 2. As before, I started with 30, but removed a few due to lack of scouting information.

Again, the list includes a couple of all-time greats (Marichal and Palmer), another Hall of Famer (Sutton) and a guy who should be in (Blyleven), a number of other solid performers and a few guys you probably never heard of.

Now we see a lot more curveballs and changeups and far fewer sliders. We can do a quick-and-dirty measure of the difference in pitch type between the high- and low-split pitchers by using a 5-3-1 point system: a No. 1 pitch gets five points, a No. 2 two pitch gets three and a No. 3 pitch gets one. Totaling up the points (and ignoring fastballs), we see the following pattern:

Pitch Usage Points

	Slider	Curveball	Changeup
High-split	53	21	10
Low-split	22	62	43

It really appears that pitchers who depend on the slider are more susceptible to having a large platoon differential, compared to pitchers who prefer the curveball or changeup. Now, I knew that the changeup is often used against opposite-hand batters; in fact, most changeups tend to tail away from such hitters. But who would have thought that a reliance on the curveball was good for your platoon split?

Another thing to note about the low-split pitchers: five of these guys were mentioned as throwing a screwball, at least occasionally. Of course, the whole point of the screwball is to be effective against opposite-side batters, so it's not too surprising to see a few on this list.

As far as I can tell, none of these guys were full-time sidearmers, although Marichal and The Can were known to throw from a variety of angles, including sidearm. I think the ability to throw from a low angle, in *specific situations* is qualitatively different from throwing sidearm 100 percent. Guys like Marichal and Boyd would drop down against same-hand hitters, but would not do so against batters of the opposite-hand, thus leaving themselves less susceptible to a large platoon split.

I would like to note here that in *The Book,* authors Tom Tango, Mitchel Lichtman and Andrew Dolphin looked at pitchers with extreme platoon splits during the period 2000-2004. They noted that a number of the pitchers with low platoon splits showed "a variety of styles that lend themselves to facing either-handed hitters, such as Wakefield's knuckler and Zito's 12-to-6 curve." And among the high-split pitchers, they found that roughly three-quarters of them "rely on a slider or a non-overhand curve." I don't really have consistent information on how "overhanded" the historical curveballs in my study were, so I can't comment on that, but we certainly agree on the effect of the slider.

The Platoon Split According to Pitch f/x

The trends that we have seen in the historical data are telling, but can we get more specific? Can we confirm our idea that a preference for the slider over the curveball and changeup leads to large platoon splits? The answer is yes, thanks to some fabulous new pitch data that has been collected by MLB this year and is available for studies like this.

The system, known as Pitch f/x, uses a set of high-speed cameras and sophisticated software to record the detailed trajectories of pitches from the pitcher's hand to home plate. The system also records lots of other good stuff: whether the umpire called a ball or a strike, the result of balls hit into play and things like that. Taken together, we can use these data to see how the platoon split varies for different pitch types.

The type of any given pitch can be deduced to a fairly good degree of confidence using three Pitch f/x quantities: the speed of the pitch and what I call its horizontal and vertical movement. These movements are defined as the deviation of the pitch, horizontally and vertically, from the calculated position of the same pitch thrown without spin. You can think of the horizontal and vertical movements as due to the spin imparted to the ball by the pitcher (and nothing else, including gravity).

The graphic below shows the vertical and horizontal movement for about 400 pitches from several different right-handed pitchers. The view is that of the catcher, so pitches with negative horizontal movement are moving in on a right-handed batter. Fastballs, although they often appear to go straight, generally tail into a right-handed batter (when the pitcher is right-handed) and they almost always have positive vertical movement. (The positive vertical movement does not mean they are truly "rising." It means they drop less than they otherwise would due to the force of gravity). Fastballs are also thrown hard, of course. The pitches that land in the left-most box on the graphic and are thrown above 90 mph are labeled fastballs.

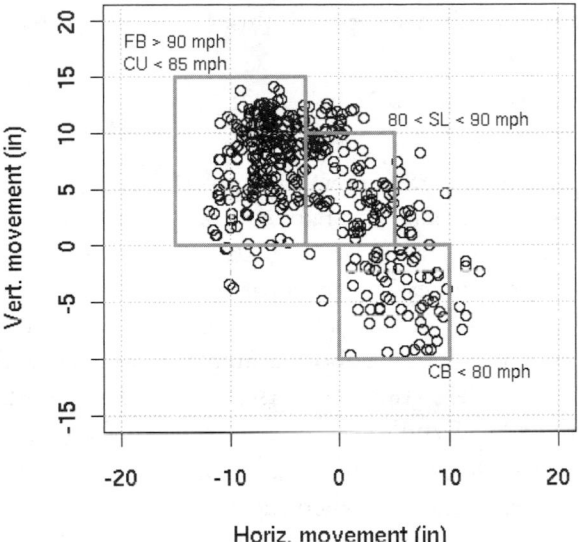

Selected Pitch Types

Adv	Pitch	NP	Speed	Horiz	Vert
B	CB	8,680	74.5	5.2	-4.9
P	CB	9,739	75.6	5.1	-4.4
B	CU	19,459	80.6	-7.6	6.5
P	CU	7,910	80.8	-7.2	6.5
B	FB	33,772	92.8	-7.1	9.3
P	FB	44,291	93.0	-7.0	9.2
B	SL	13,190	85.1	0.5	4.9
P	SL	24,222	85.1	1.0	4.3

B - platoon advantage to batter, P - advantage to pitcher
CB - curveball, CU - changeup, FB - fastball, SL - slider

The pitch variables shown are the average for the selected pitches. As above, I've removed switch-hitters from the sample. I've also avoided sidearmers and submariners by removing pitches released below 4.7 feet from the ground (the release point is part of the Pitch f/x data).

Getting back to the table, we see that pitchers prefer changeups when the batter enjoys the platoon advantage, while sliders are employed more often when batter and pitcher are of the same hand. You can also see that, for each pitch type, pitch speed and movement are similar, regardless of who has the platoon advantage.

Changeups tend to have the same movement as fastballs, with perhaps a bit less vertical movement. I call anything in the upper-left box thrown under 85 mph a changeup.

Curveballs break down and to the right and are generally thrown less than 80 mph. The lower right box shows how I select curveballs. Sliders fall in between fastballs and curves, both in speed and movement. Any pitch thrown between 80 and 90 mph with movement that puts it in the middle box, I call a slider. For a lefty pitcher, the requirements on the horizontal movement are inverted.

Bear in mind that these classifications are only approximate. Every pitcher is different and has slightly different movements on his pitches. As just one example, some pitchers throw a *slurve*, which is something between a slider and a curve and would straddle the middle and lower-right boxes. Furthermore, there are pitches that don't fall into any box at all. To all this I say—that's OK. I don't need my pitch identification to be perfect or comprehensive. I just need to be able to identify correctly a good number of fastballs, changeups, sliders and curves, and I'm confident that I've managed to do that.

OK, now that we're able to identify pitch types, we can start to look at platoon splits for each kind of pitch. First, let's see how many pitches we have of each type.

Our goal is to determine the platoon split for each kind of pitch. To do that, it's easiest to split the pitches into two categories: those that are put into play (including home runs) and those that aren't. In-play pitches are easier to handle, so let's deal with them first.

The next table shows some key results for the different pitch types when the ball is put into play.

Platoon Splits for Balls in Play

Adv	Pitch	NP	BABIP	HR%	OPS	delOPS
B	CB	1,327	.332	.035	.859	.038
P	CB	1,815	.320	.035	.821	
B	CU	4,191	.325	.037	.844	-.015
P	CU	1,488	.325	.047	.859	
B	FB	6,105	.351	.041	.920	.120
P	FB	8,880	.318	.032	.800	
B	SL	2,427	.340	.049	.905	.130
P	SL	4,744	.304	.034	.775	

BABIP - batting average for balls put in play
HR% - percentage of in-play balls that are home runs
OPS - OBP plus slugging percentage
delOPS - the platoon split in OPS (batter minus pitcher)

Now this is interesting: ranking the pitches from largest to smallest platoon split, we have 1) slider, 2) fastball, 3) curveball and 4) changeup. And note that there is a big separation between the first two and the second two. Well, based on the historical results presented above, we were sort of expecting the slider to exhibit a large platoon split. And, likewise, we were expecting the curveball and changeup to show a smaller split. But I had no idea that the fastball is also a major culprit in causing large platoon splits.

But this isn't the whole story, for we still must deal with pitches that were not put into play. Here is a table that shows what happened to pitches that were not put into play. The numbers represent the fraction of pitches for each possible not-in-play outcome.

Platoon Effects for Balls Not in Play

Adv	Pitch	NP	Ball	Called	Foul	Swinging
B	CB	8,680	.408	.210	.134	.090
P	CB	9,739	.391	.195	.118	.102
B	CU	19,459	.404	.116	.134	.124
P	CU	7,910	.382	.128	.167	.115
B	FB	33,772	.374	.169	.206	.065
P	FB	44,291	.343	.184	.200	.067
B	SL	13,190	.357	.143	.212	.100
P	SL	24,222	.364	.144	.146	.141

Called, Foul, Swinging - types of strikes

As you can see, interpreting all these numbers in terms of a platoon split for each pitch type is not straightforward. There are platoon differences for balls, foul balls and called and swinging strikes for each different pitch type. How can we make sense of all that?

Well, if you could assign a run value to a ball and another run value to a strike, then you could boil all the not-in-play pitch results into a single run value for each pitch type/platoon situation. So, let's try to do that. It's best to go through the thinking on this with an example. What is the value of a ball thrown on a 1-0 count? And what about a strike thrown on the same count? Here's how to figure that out.

This season, the average batter put up the following line *after* reaching a count of one ball and zero strikes (AVG/OBP/SLG):

After 1-0: .282/.394/.459

Now, let's say the next pitch is a ball. Mr. Average now hit like this:

After 2-0: .294/.516/.496

That one ball led to an increase in OPS from .853 to 1.012. But, what if the second pitch had been a strike? Then we would have expected this:

After 1-1: .250/.322/.394

…and your OPS is now down to .716. Now, I want to assign a run value to a ball or strike, so I'm going to ditch OPS and start working with batting runs above average (sometimes known as batting linear weights). I won't go into the details of batting runs, just tell you the answer: The ball in the above example is worth around .07 runs (to the batter, of course), while a strike costs him roughly .05 runs.

Still with me? Good. These values (.07 and -.05 runs) are relevant only when the count is 1-0, though. So the next step involves doing this calculation for all possible counts and then weighting by plate appearances that "go through" each count. Again, I'll cut to the chase and just give you the answer: On average, a ball is worth about .065 runs and a strike is worth -.097 runs.

Now that we have this information, we can calculate the platoon splits, in runs above average, for not-in-play pitches for each pitch type. While we're at it, let's express the in-play splits in runs, as well. The next table shows the results:

Platoon Splits in Runs per 100 Pitches

	Not In Play		In Play		Total
Pitch	NP	RunsDiff	NP	RunsDiff	RunsDiff
FB	56,260	0.5	14,985	4.2	1.2
SL	26,897	0.0	7,171	4.5	0.9
CU	19,836	0.4	5,679	-0.6	0.3
CB	13,819	0.0	3,142	1.3	0.1

RunsDiff - Platoon split in runs (batter advantage minus pitcher advantage)

For each pitch type, you can see 1) the number of not-in-play pitches, 2) the not-in-play platoon split (advantage batter minus advantage pitcher) expressed in runs, 3) number of in-play pitches and 4) the in-play platoon split and finally 5) the total platoon split, taking into account both not-in-play and in-play pitches. Whew, that's a lot to keep in mind. While you're taking a few seconds to digest this table, I'll just mention that to get rid of a lot of zeros, I show the platoon splits per

100 pitches. (The number of pitches shown in this table does not agree with the previous tables because I've now removed two-strike foul balls, which don't have any value either way.)

So, we can see for not-in-play pitches, fastballs and changeups have the biggest platoon splits, while curveballs and sliders are essentially platoon-neutral when they are not put into play. Take note that the platoon splits for not-in-play pitches, on a per-pitch basis, are much smaller than the splits for balls in play. However, there are many more not-in-play pitches, so in the end they play an important role.

Finally, when you sum everything up, you get the right-hand column in the table above, which shows the overall platoon split for each pitch type. The fastball has now taken over the lead and the curveball has slipped to the very bottom. The large difference between the fastball/slider and changeup/curveball remains, however.

One last comment on the Pitch f/x study: I consider these results *qualitatively* correct, which is how you should view them, too. I went to the trouble of assigning run values to pitches so we'd have a way to rank pitches according to platoon split, but I wouldn't put too much emphasis on the actual values. To get reliable *quantitative* results, you'd have to take into account the correlation of ball-strike count and pitch type (e.g., 3-0 pitches are usually fastballs) and possibly other effects, as well.

Conclusions

What I've found in this study is that, perhaps contrary to conventional wisdom, it is primarily the fastball and slider that contribute to large platoon splits, while the curveball and changeup are much more platoon-neutral.

If you go back to the first part of this article and look at the historical lists of high- and low-platoon split pitchers, you do in fact see less reliance on the fastball among the low-split hurlers. Indeed, while only one of the high-split group did not throw the fastball as his primary pitch, there were 12 such pitchers in the low-split group.

There remain unanswered questions. *Why* do the fastball and slider lead to large platoon splits? One moves in towards a right-handed batter (if thrown by a righty pitcher), the other moves slightly away. Actually, the slider does not really have much horizontal movement at all (they fall near the center of the plot above), so you might think the movement wouldn't cause a large platoon split.

Maybe the answer lies not in the *movement* of pitches, but in their *speed*. After all, if you rank the pitch types by speed, you get exactly the same ranking that we got for platoon splits. That's curious, isn't it? Let's speculate on this just a minute before wrapping up.

You can imagine that the true reason for the platoon split is simply the fact that the batter gets a "better look" at an opposite-handed delivery. This makes sense, actually, because the opposite-side batter gets a bit more of a "side view" of the pitch, which likely helps the perception of where the pitch is headed and its speed. It's logical to hypothesize that this "side-view" advantage is greater when the pitch is coming in faster, hence the larger platoon splits for the faster pitches.

In any case, I think this might be a good subject for further research. For example, one could repeat the Pitch f/x study, observing how platoon splits vary with pitch speed, independent of the break of the pitch. Additionally, a study of sidearmers, or more generally, the variation of platoon split with arm angle, would certainly shed additional light on the subject.

Resources:

- *The Physics of Baseball,* Robert K. Adair, published by Harper Perrenial.
- *A Game of Inches,* Peter Morris, published by Ivan R. Dee.
- *The Book,* Tom Tango, Mitchel Lichtman, Andrew Dolphin, published by Potomac Books.
- *Retrosheet*: www.retrosheet.org — The information used here was obtained free of charge from and is copyrighted by Retrosheet. Interested parties may contact Retrosheet at "www.retrosheet.org".

Of Home Runs and Free Agents

by Greg Rybarczyk

Hit Tracker has provided trajectory analysis of every home run hit in the major leagues since April 2006. It accomplishes this by combining an aerodynamic model with observation data from home run events to recreate the precise trajectory the ball followed in flight, including the initial velocity of the ball as it left the bat, as described by three parameters: the speed off the bat (SOB), the horizontal launch angle (HLA), and the vertical launch angle (VLA). Hit Tracker also calculates the impact of altitude, wind and temperature on the flight of the ball.

In this article we will recap who hit home runs where in 2007, we'll dig deeper into the year's crop of homers with Hit Tracker's exclusive metrics, including several metrics new to Hit Tracker in 2007, and we'll examine why home runs were down in 2007 from the prior year. Finally, we'll extend the reach of Hit Tracker through a case study that analyzes not just home runs, but every batted ball struck in 2007 by two top free agent center fielders, Torii Hunter and Andruw Jones. This unprecedented analysis will provide insight not only into the comparative skill and value of these two top players, but into the fundamental relationship between batted ball trajectories, defensive positioning and the outcomes of those batted balls.

2007 Home Run Demographics

In 2007, 4,957 home runs were hit, a rate of 2.04 per game. The Milwaukee Brewers led with 231, while four other teams exceeded 200 homers (Philadelphia, Cincinnati, Florida and the New York Yankees). Kansas City brought up the rear with only 102 homers. Citizens Bank Park in Philadelphia saw 241 home runs clear the fences to lead the league, while PETCO Park had the fewest long balls with only 117 homers (with only 45 allowed by the Padres' pitchers!)

Five hundred different players hit home runs in 2007, led by Alex Rodriguez with 54 homers, and rounded out by 84 players who hit exactly one homer each. Seventy-five different players hit their first career homer in 2007, led by Milwaukee's Ryan Braun, who hit 34, fifth-most in the National League.

Houston's Woody Williams and Arizona's Livan Hernandez each allowed a major league-high 34 home runs; they were among the 605 different pitchers who served up long balls in 2007. Tampa Bay's Al Reyes led the majors with 13 home runs allowed in relief, including 11 in the ninth inning or later, and two walk-offs. Seventy-one pitchers allowed exactly one homer in 2007, including Washington's Saul Rivera, who served up his one homer on April 24 and then racked up 87 consecutive homerless innings to finish the season.

There were 15 inside-the-park homers in 2007, 27 homers hit by pitchers (led by Arizona's Micah Owings with four, including 886 feet worth of homers on Aug. 18 at Turner Field), 81 extra-inning homers and 60 walk-off homers (Minnesota's Justin Morneau led with three walk-off homers). Alex Rodriguez led the league with eight homers in the ninth inning and tallied the most homers against a single opponent: eight vs. Tampa Bay. On the mound, Boston's Curt Schilling allowed 21 homers in 151 innings, but amazingly 10 of those were hit by one team, the Yankees. Schilling started five games against New York and gave up two home runs in each one.

How Far:

The Year's Longest

The year's longest home run belongs to Chicago Cub Aramis Ramirez, who picked a good day (85 degrees and 15-mph tail wind) to hit a ball out of Wrigley Field. The ball landed 495 feet later, well past the ballhawks on Waveland Avenue and a good 60 feet down Kenmore Avenue. Ramirez's homer picked up a total of 57 feet from the warm air, wind and Chicago's 600-foot altitude, so on a "standard" 70 degree, no-wind day at sea level, his homer would have traveled "only" 438 feet—a blast, but not nearly the biggest of the year.

Quite a few hitters hit homers that under standard conditions would have outdistanced Ramirez's homer. Arizona's Chris Young belted the year's longest homer by standard distance, a 476-foot rocket at Chase Field on Sept. 22 off San Diego's David Wells. In total, 122 home runs were hit in 2007 with a longer standard distance than Ramirez's Wrigley Field homer, including four each by Carlos Delgado, Mark Teixeira and Alex Rodriguez, but the honors go to Milwaukee's Prince Fielder, who hit an amazing nine home runs with a standard distance longer than 438 feet. Fielder's power earned him the 2007 Golden Sledgehammer, awarded to the hitter with the longest average standard distance; in 2007, Fielder's 50 home runs averaged 408 feet of standard distance. The door opened for Fielder in 2007 when 2006 winner Alex Rodriguez traded raw distance (416 feet average standard distance for 35 home runs in 2006) for quantity (54 in 2007 at 400 feet each).

Easiest and Toughest Homers

While Aramis Ramirez benefited greatly from a warm wind at Wrigley Field, there were other home runs hit in even more favorable conditions. In 2007, Hit Tracker began listing a Home Run Park Factor (HRPF) for each home run, based on the physical configuration of the ballpark and the wind and temperature conditions that prevailed at the time of the hit. (The Hit Tracker HRPF method was described in detail in a THT article entitled "Home Run Park Factor—A New Approach.")

The HRPF for Ramirez's homer was 151, primarily due to a strong wind blowing out left field, where his homer eventually landed. The highest HRPF for the 2007 season was 177, for Colorado's Kaz Matsui's Sept. 7 homer at Coors Field. Many other homers hit at Coors Field had HRPFs above 150. The lowest HRPF of the year was 20, for New York's Robinson Cano, who hit a homer over the center field fence at Comerica Park on Aug. 26, cutting through an 11-mph crosswind.

Home Run Types

In 2007, Hit Tracker began classifying home runs into three categories, based on how far past the fence they flew. The three categories are as follows:

- "Just Enough" or JE: cleared the fence by 10 vertical feet or fewer, or landed within one fence height past the fence.
- "No Doubt" or ND: cleared the fence by at least 20 vertical feet, and landed at least 50 feet past the fence.
- "Plenty" or PL: all other home runs.

The 2007 leaders in No Doubt homers tend to look like the league's biggest sluggers. In the NL:
- Adam Dunn (15)
- Prince Fielder (14)
- Lance Berkman (10)

In the AL:
- Alex Rodriguez (10)
- Frank Thomas (10)
- Carlos Pena (9)

The 2007 leaders in Just Enough homers, on the other hand, reads more like a list of MVP contenders. The NL leaders:
- Brandon Phillips (14)
- Matt Holliday (13)
- David Wright (12)
- Chipper Jones (12)
- Prince Fielder (12)
- Ryan Braun (12)
- Jimmy Rollins (10)

There weren't as many AL MVP contenders as in the NL, but the right name is certainly here:
- Jim Thome (15)
- Alex Rodriguez (13)
- David Ortiz (13)
- Jack Cust (12)
- Carlos Pena (10)

One other metric that was new to Hit Tracker in 2007 is the "lucky" designation. A homer is called "lucky" if it would not have been a home run in 70-degree, no-wind conditions. The individual lucky lists are more cluttered than the JE lists because the sample size is smaller, but the top three teams for lucky homers suggest a correlation between team wins and lucky homers (though it seems strange to include the Mets on a 2007 list that involves good luck...)
- Colorado (35)
- New York Mets (27)
- Philadelphia (26)

NL Power

The National League significantly outdistanced the American League in long distance homers in 2007; remarkably, 31 of the 35 longest home runs by true (actual) distance, including the top 11, were hit by NL sluggers. While the NL features quite a few tape-measure artists, undoubtedly the optimal slugging conditions in Denver and Phoenix have something to do with the NL's dominance of the distance leader board. 14 of the year's 35 longest homers were hit in Coors Field and Chase Field (seven each).

The mile-high altitude at Coors Field and its salutary effect on long fly balls is well documented, but less well known is the fact that Chase Field is the second-highest ballpark in the major leagues at almost 1,100 feet above sea level. A typical 400-foot fly ball at sea level will travel about 408 feet at Chase Field.

Another important factor at both Coors and Chase is the humidity (or lack thereof). The average afternoon/evening relative humidity in Phoenix is 18% during baseball season; in Denver, it's 35%. No other baseball park averages lower than 53%. Baseballs stored in dry air become lighter and smaller, and thus will fly farther when struck than a ball kept in moist air.

Colorado implemented a humidor in 2002 to try to keep baseballs closer to their "as-manufactured" state, but to date the Diamondbacks have not. Tests would have to be performed to see if the balls used at Chase are more resilient than balls used elsewhere, but one piece of data makes me wonder: of the 20 hardest-hit home runs of 2007 by Diamondbacks hitters (as measured by SOB), 17 were hit at Chase Field. The odds of that happening if the baseballs were the same at Chase as elsewhere are the same as the odds of flipping 20 coins and getting 17 heads: 1 in 5,000. It might be time for Arizona to install a humidor…

Fewer Homers in 2007: Why?

While in historic terms home runs were still quite common in 2007 (4,957 or 2.04 per game), there was an 8% decline from 2006. A home run is not a fundamentally different event in a game; it is simply a fly ball that has enough distance to carry to the fence. So, if we accept that the number of fly balls in 2007 was not significantly different from 2006, then we can conclude that fly balls must not have flown as far, on average, in 2007 as compared to the prior year. So, let's try to determine how large this distance reduction was.

The graph below is a plot of 2007 home runs, broken out by home run type.

This chart is meant to illustrate that the home run population (here showing 2007 data) is made up of three different home run types. Of those three types, the ones in the "Just Enough" category are the ones that could potentially stay in the park if fly balls were to fly slightly less distance from one year to the next, while the "Plenty" and "No Doubt" homers would still clear the fence.

Let's put this in perspective. From 2006 to 2007, total home runs decreased by 429. In 2006, there were 1,454 home runs in the "Just Enough" category. So the total decrease works out to be 29.5% of all Just Enough homers. To change 429 of the 2006 homers to non-homers would require an average distance reduction of 29.5% times 10 feet (since JE homers clear the fence by 1-10 feet), or three feet.

Looking at the problem from another angle, the average true home run distance from 2006 to 2007 as calculated by Hit Tracker went down, with the average homer in '07 covering 395.4 feet, a 1.8-foot reduction from 2006. So it would seem at first that we have a contradiction, with one approach suggesting a three-foot difference, and the other 1.8 feet. However, the reduction in average distance for each fly ball would not simply be the difference in average true distance (1.8 feet), because when all homers from 2006 are reduced by some amount, the distance distribution for homers shifts: some homers in the "JE" part of the population become non-homers and drop out of the population we are averaging, thus pushing the average back up somewhat. In other words, the reduction in fly ball distance would have to be greater than 1.8 feet. But how much greater?

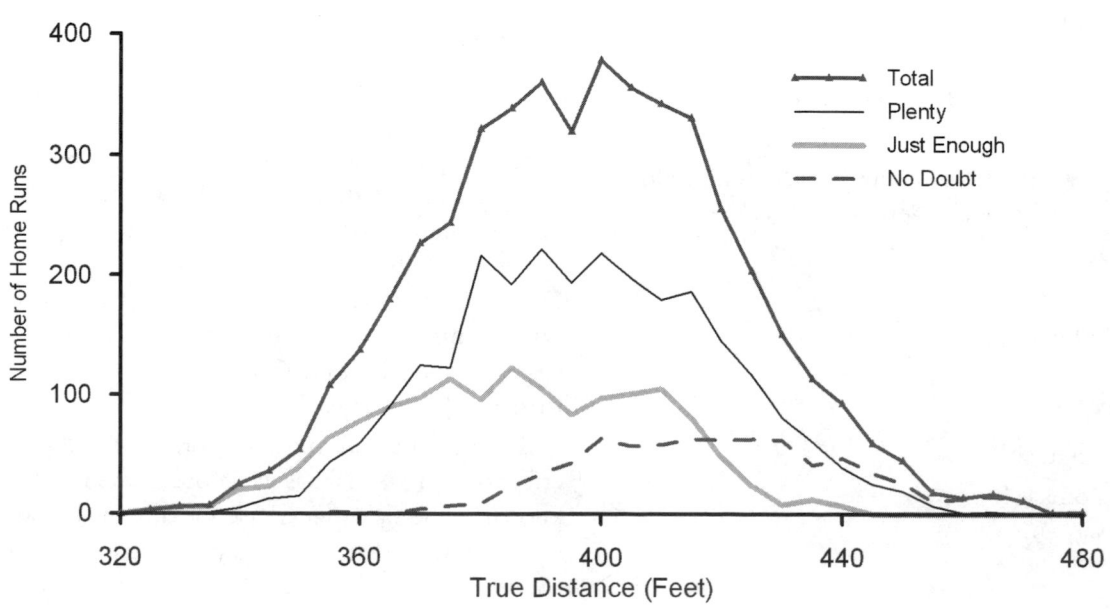

Our other method points to a three-foot reduction, so let's consider that. To model a reduction in all fly balls by three feet, we need to do two things: remove 30% of the JE homers from 2006, and then reduce the distance for each remaining homer by three feet. When these steps are taken, the remaining home runs have an average true distance of exactly 395.4 feet, which exactly matches the results from 2007! So, the two methods are not in conflict after all: we can confidently conclude that long fly balls flew three fewer feet on average in 2007 than they did in 2006. But why?

The primary explanation for this drop in fly ball distance is the weather. The weather in 2007 was significantly less favorable than that in 2006: in 2007, the average homer was hit in a temperature of 72.4 degrees, 1.3 degrees lower than in 2006. This colder air collectively robbed 2007 fly balls of about 0.6 feet of distance. Winds were less favorable as well, adding only 1.1 feet of distance per homer in 2007, while in 2006 the wind had added 2.1 feet per homer. The combined difference in weather impact from 2006 to 2007 was about 1.6 feet per homer.

It is important to note that this is the impact on each homer, not on each fly ball; we need to adjust that number, just as earlier we had to adjust the 1.8 foot difference. Unfortunately, it's not possible to adjust this weather impact number the same way we did for true distance, because true distance is only weakly correlated to weather impact. So, the fly ball distance reduction from weather was probably more than 1.6 feet in magnitude, but we can't know for sure how much larger.

Ballpark Owners: Longest Home Runs in Each Park

Loyal fans and announcers alike are quick to recognize and honor the longest (or at least the most visually impressive) home runs in their home ballpark. Hit Tracker maintains a list of these homers and the players who hit them (termed the ballpark "owner") in the section of the site labeled "Ballparks".

The 2007 list includes some familiar names:

- Alex Rodriguez, who hit the longest 2007 homers in Yankee Stadium (456 feet on June 16), the Metro-dome (449 feet on April 10) and AT&T Park (456 feet on June 23).

- Prince Fielder, proud owner of Dodger Stadium (452 feet on May 21) and Minute Maid Park (470 feet on Aug. 10), but not Miller Park where he plays his home games. Cincinnati's Adam Dunn (467 feet on Aug. 17) topped him there.

- Vladimir Guerrero, owner of Angels Stadium for the second straight year with his 457-foot bomb on April 6, as well as Kauffman Stadium, where he launched a 468-foot homer on May 1.

- Mark Teixeira, who owns three ballparks from 2007: his home fields of Rangers Ballpark in Arlington (457 feet on May 27) and Turner Field (476 feet on Sept. 21), as well as Safeco Field (456 feet on June 2).

Some other 2007 ballpark owners are less well known nationally, though their long-distance homers come as no surprise to those who watch them daily:

- Florida Marlins teammates Cody Ross, who knocked the longest homer of 2007 at Busch Stadium (445 feet on Aug. 23), and Dan Uggla, who blasted the year's longest at RFK Stadium (463 feet on April 2).

- Chicago's Josh Fields, who picked up ownership of PNC Park in Pittsburgh during interleague play with his 443-foot homer on June 16.

- Arizona's Mark Reynolds temporarily assumed the lead at Turner Field with his 467-foot homer on Aug. 17 (later passed by Mark Teixeira as described earlier), but it must have had a bad influence on him, as the next day the rookie slugger began a record-tying streak of strikeouts in nine consecutive plate appearances. Fortunately, by Aug. 30 he had recovered enough to launch the longest homer of the year at PETCO Park, a 445-foot blast on Aug. 30.

- Minnesota's Garrett Jones, whose 456-foot homer in the center field bleachers at Fenway Park on Sept. 27 provided a spark in the Twins' final series of the year. Let's hope Jones doesn't suffer the fate of last year's biggest surprise long-distance home run artist, Florida's Reggie Abercrombie, who went 481 feet into the upper deck at Great American Ball Park in April 2006, but hit poorly overall and spent only 35 games in the major leagues in 2007.

"Did Anyone Order a Center Fielder?" Case Study: All Batted Balls by Torii Hunter and Andruw Jones

For its first two years Hit Tracker has primarily been used to analyze home runs, but the trajectory modeling methodology works equally well for all fly balls. Studying all batted balls can provide some very interesting insights, as you're about to see.

The outcomes of all 2007 plate appearances by Minnesota's Torii Hunter and Atlanta's Andruw Jones are listed in the table below.

Hit Type	T. Hunter	A. Jones
1B - Grounder	62	31
1B - Fly	36	41
2B - Grounder	4	4
2B - Fly	41	23
3B - Grounder	0	1
3B - Fly	1	1
HR	28	26
Out - Grounder	178	133
Out - Fly	101	123
Error - Grounder	5	9
Error - Fly	0	1
Popups & Foulouts	36	49
Strikeout	101	138
BB - Unintentional	30	66
BB - Intentional	10	4
HBP	5	8

Fly Balls

The fly balls listed above were analyzed using Hit Tracker, with the exception of the popups and foulouts; the trajectories of those batted balls are both difficult to accurately analyze and statistically uninteresting. One of Hunter's home runs was not observed as well, due to video being unavailable. The remaining hits, in and out of the park, were analyzed to determine the "launch parameters" of the ball: Speed Off Bat (SOB) in miles per hour; Vertical Launch Angle (VLA) in degrees, and Horizontal Launch Angle (HLA) in degrees, with the right field line equal to 45, straightaway center field at 90 and the left field line at 135.

The next page contains plots of Hunter's and Jones' fly balls: the horizontal axis shows the direction of the hit (HLA), with left field at the left side, center field in the center and right field at the right; the vertical axis shows the vertical angle (VLA) of the ball off the bat, with line drives at the bottom of the plot and high fly balls at the top.

Hit Tracker provides continuous data on VLA, without any need for an observer to qualitatively assign a trajectory category, and thus one possible source of observer bias is avoided. However, it is still convenient to examine the data in groups, so let's divide the batted balls into three VLA categories: line drives (VLA < 20 degrees), fly balls (VLA 20-40 degrees) and high fly balls (VLA > 40 degrees).

It is immediately apparent that line drives are frequently base hits, with Hunter achieving a single or double on 44 of 53 line drives (83%). Jones fared slightly worse, with only 35 of 57 line drives going for hits (61%), but both of these figures are well above the overall league average BABIP of about 30%. Note: neither Hunter nor Jones hit a homer on a line drive, as line drives are defined here. Homers on balls hit with VLA < 20 degrees are exceedingly rare, accounting for only 10 out of 4,942 homers that cleared the fence, or one out of every 494 homers.

At the other end of the spectrum, high fly balls (VLA > 40 degrees) are most often outs: Hunter reached safely on 12 of 53 balls shown in the plot above, but if we factor in his popups and foulouts, his results are 12 hits out of 89 high fly balls, or 13%. Jones' results are even more unfavorable, with only seven hits out of 121 high fly balls, or a dreadful 6%.

In between the liners and the high fly balls are the regular fly balls (VLA between 20 and 40 degrees). Hunter reached safely on 49 out of 100 fly balls (49%), while Jones scored a hit on 49 of 86 fly balls (57%).

Overall, Hunter tallied 105 hits on 242 total balls hit in the air, hitting safely 43% of the time. Jones achieved 91 hits on 264 total balls in the air, which is 34%.

Grounders

Hit Tracker's primary analytical engine uses an aerodynamic model to recreate the trajectory of baseballs flying through air, but it cannot be used to model ground balls, which not only don't fly through the air but also collide repeatedly with the ground in ways that are difficult to accurately model.

To model ground ball trajectories (which will necessarily be less accurate than those determined from the main Hit Tracker engine), we will use a model based on dynamic friction, with an assumed coefficient of friction. Ground balls slow down as they pass through the infield, from air resistance and from friction with the dirt and grass during bounces. The following chart

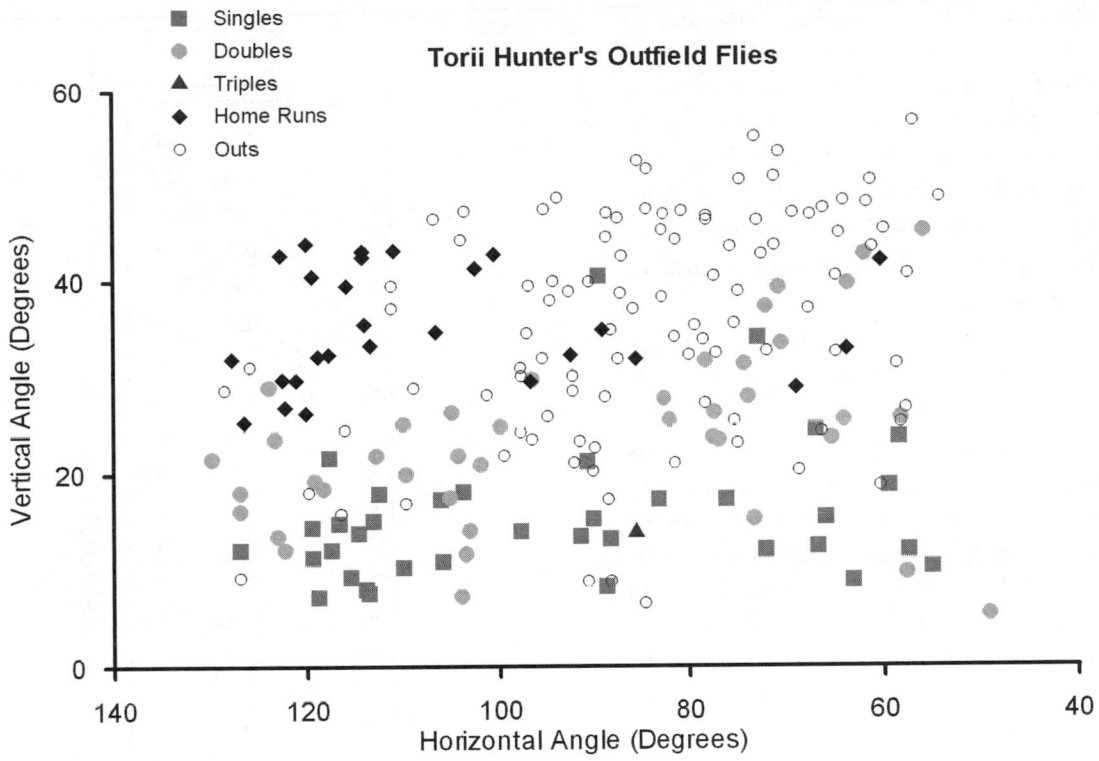

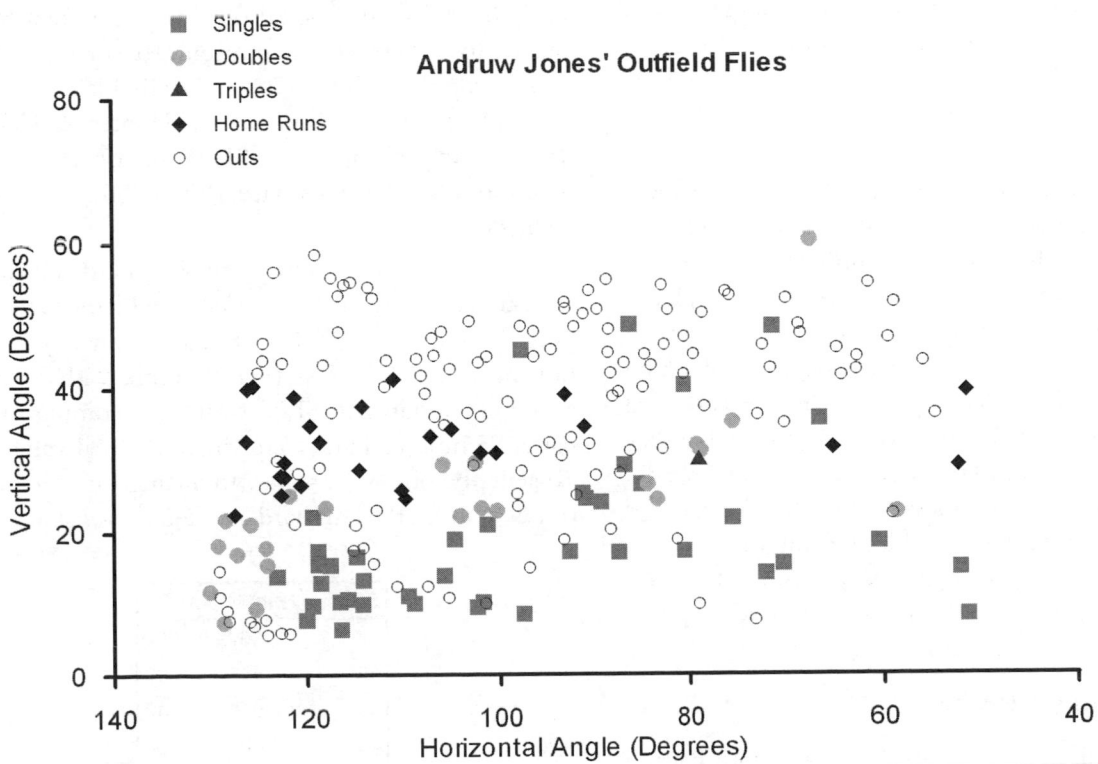

shows the relationship between time and distance that will be used for grounders. By timing the ground balls to the point where they are fielded or leave the infield, and measuring the distance to the final point, we can calculate an SOB for the grounder. Note: we are not attempting to differentiate between infields: this will introduce some additional uncertainty in the SOB numbers for grounders, but not so much as to preclude using the data.

On the next page, you can see the plots for Hunter's and Jones' ground balls.

The first thing that jumps off these plots is the distinct lack of hard-hit ground balls to the right side of the infield by Jones. John Dewan's Stat of the Week at ACTA Sports for April 27, 2007 described Andruw Jones as a candidate for an infield shift, and this plot certainly supports that: the combination of directional and SOB data shows that in 154 games during the 2007 season, during which he hit 178 ground balls, Jones hit only three balls that would have required a second baseman in the normal spot, with the other balls on the right side of the chart being easily gobbled up by the first baseman or pitcher.

Moving the second baseman to HLA = 95 and the shortstop to HLA = 118 would have eliminated as many as 15 of Jones' hits, while surrendering at most half that many in the vacated spots. And if Jones were to respond by hitting grounders to the right side, he would certainly compromise his power potential in doing so. Certainly a strong infield shift should be applied when Andruw Jones is at bat, and when it is applied, his batting average on grounders is going to suffer.

Hunter presents a much more balanced assortment of hit directions, and thus is not vulnerable to an infield shift, except that the first baseman need not cover the line. One other interesting point on Hunter's plot is the large number of soft grounders to the left side of the infield. These are swinging bunts, eight of which resulted in infield hits. The opposing pitcher and third baseman would do well to be ready to come in, but they can't afford to play too far in, as Hunter also ripped a large number of fast grounders to the left side, many of which would skip past an infielder playing in.

Overall, Jones achieved 36 hits on 178 total ground balls, which is 20% hits. Hunter tallied 66 hits on 249 total grounders, for a hit percentage of 27%.

Speed Off Bat vs. BABB

Earlier, we discussed how VLA interacts with Batting Average on Batted Balls (BABB), which includes all batted balls except popups and foulouts: line drives are best, fly balls still highly favorable, and high fly balls extremely poor. Next let's look at how SOB correlates with BABB.

SOB	Hunter	Jones
30	.167	.000
35	.444	.500
40	.000	.143
45	.000	.000
50	.143	.200
55	.000	.000
60	.100	.100
65	.176	.067
70	.121	.148
75	.188	.263
80	.296	.241
85	.235	.163
90	.264	.189
95	.346	.318
100	.523	.370
105	.775	.600
110	.765	.842
115	.769	.739

Both Hunter and Jones display a similar pattern: very softly hit balls (intentional or swinging bunts) have a chance to be hits; softly hit grounders or fly balls are mostly converted into outs, and balls hit harder than 100 mph are overwhelmingly hits. Hunter hit 123 balls harder than 100 mph, and 91 of them (74%) became hits. Jones hit 108 balls harder than 100 mph and got 69 hits (64%).

The importance of hitting the ball hard is displayed even more clearly in the next table, which shows Slugging Percentage vs. SOB. There is hardly any distinction between SOBs less than 95 mph, with such hits averaging about .250 SLG, while hits coming off the bat at 95 mph or harder are where the real value is at. To state the obvious, the key to hitting for average and power is to hit the ball hard as often as possible.

SOB	Hunter	Jones
30	.167	.000
35	.444	.500
40	.000	.143
45	.000	.000
50	.143	.200
55	.000	.000

Continued on page 180

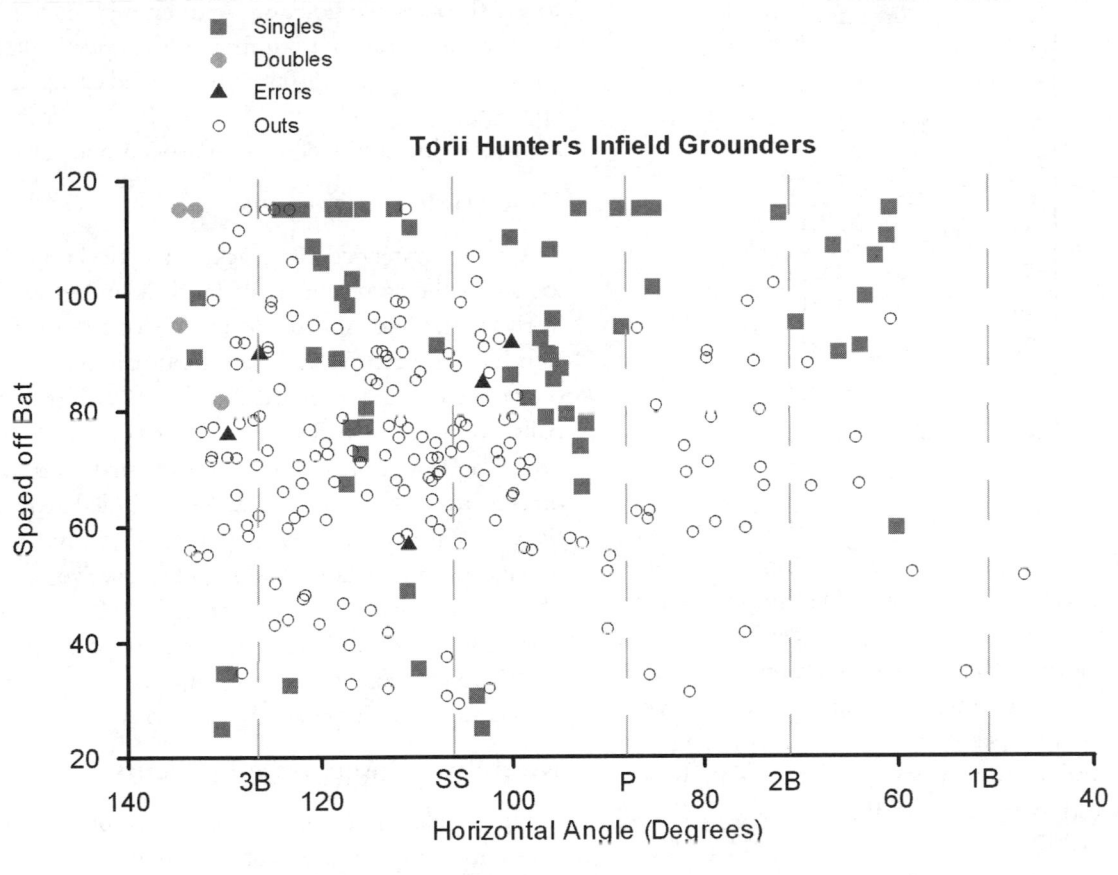

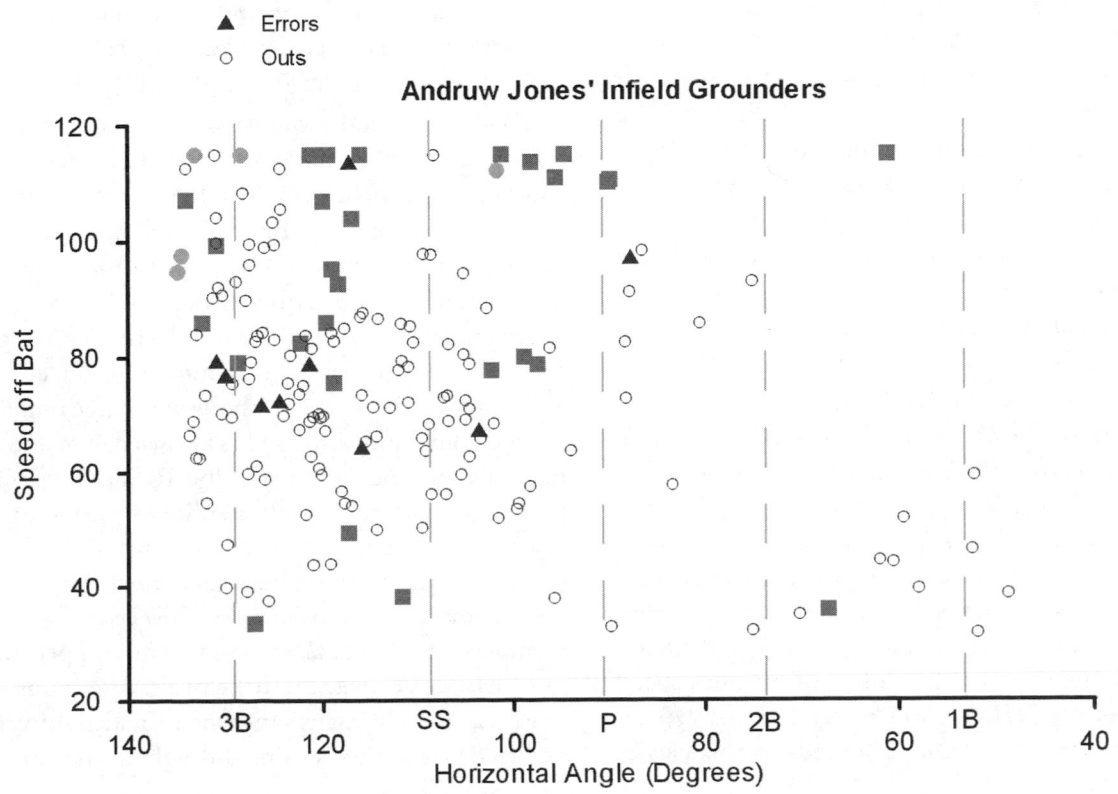

SOB	Hunter	Jones
60	.150	.200
65	.176	.067
70	.152	.148
75	.188	.316
80	.370	.241
85	.235	.163
90	.283	.243
95	.615	.432
100	1.000	.717
105	1.875	1.533
110	1.765	2.158
115	1.154	1.478

Pitch Type

Hit Tracker metrics can also be combined with pitch type data to yield further insights. One thing that can be analyzed is how hard, on average, a player hits one type of pitch vs. another. In the case of Hunter and Jones, there aren't any SOB trends vs. pitch type, but when we examine their scatter graphs on the facing page, we do see some interesting things. Note: the data is only partial, as not all ballparks had Pitch f/x data collected for the entire 2007 season.

Earlier we saw that overall, Hunter hit most of his grounders to the left side, but he also hit enough grounders to the right side to obligate the defense to play him straight up. But there is a difference to the right of HLA = 75 (which is approximately the "normal" position of the second baseman): Against fastballs in 2007—Hunter hit 20% of his grounders to the right of HLA = 75 (9 of 45, including four for hits through the HLA = 60-65 hole), while against off-speed pitches, he hit only 2% (one of 54) there (as seen on the graph). Clearly, if the second baseman is reading the signs from the catcher, he should cheat hard up the middle when he knows a breaking ball or change is coming—at least as much as he can manage without giving the pitch away to Hunter at the plate!

We saw earlier that in 2007 Jones hit nearly all of his grounders to the left side of the infield, and that trend persists across the split in pitch types, so there is no additional positioning effect to exploit for Jones. However, there is a game-state trend here that is potentially exploitable: against fastballs, Jones' grounders are well-spread across the left side and across the spectrum of SOB, from slow to fast. But against off-speed pitches in the graph, there is a large cluster of medium-speed grounders between HLA = 105 (normal shortstop position) and the third base line. The balls in this cluster are almost all perfect double-play balls: not fast enough to get through the hole, but with enough pace to make the turn and beat Jones to first. This is particularly true when the anti-Jones shift recommended earlier has been applied. So, if you need a double-play ball from Jones, apply the shift and feed him off-speed pitches!

Case Study Conclusions

With the extended Hit Tracker analytical model, we've looked at the complete set of fly balls and grounders by Torii Hunter and Andruw Jones. We've studied the relationship between VLA and batted-ball outcomes, and quantified the value of line drives and fly balls over high fly balls. We've reaffirmed the importance of hard-hit balls in achieving favorable outcomes from batted balls, whether on the ground or in the air. We've identified some potentially profitable strategies involving defensive positioning and pitch selection. And hopefully, we've established Hit Tracker analysis as a potentially valuable method for providing deeper understanding of the underlying factors that drive the game of baseball, and making practical use of that understanding in game situations.

Wrap-up and Acknowledgements

Hit Tracker remains the most complete and accurate home run measurement system available, but when extended to all batted-ball types, in can provide even more valuable information. Complete analysis of all batted balls is a time-consuming endeavor, but it remains the ultimate goal. Meanwhile, individual queries or suggestions for analytical projects are welcome; feel free to contact the author at grybar@hittrackeronline.com.

I'd like to extend my most sincere thanks and appreciation to a number of people who have helped make Hit Tracker a success in 2007. Top honors go to site volunteers Brenton Blair and Brian O'Malley, who each gave an enormous amount of effort and time in providing observations for home runs throughout the year, as well other contributions to the overall Hit Tracker project too numerous to list. Tim Lammers provided invaluable support for some of the year's longest and most elusive home runs through his knowledge of and access to home run video footage. Joe P. Sheehan provided pitch type data for the Hunter/Jones case study. Sean Forman provided important data for the home run demographics section, both personally and through his incomparable website *Baseball-Reference.com*. Various members of the *Hardball Times* team chipped in with information, feedback and helpful suggestions. Many thanks also to the many fans who provided information and feedback on home runs throughout the year.

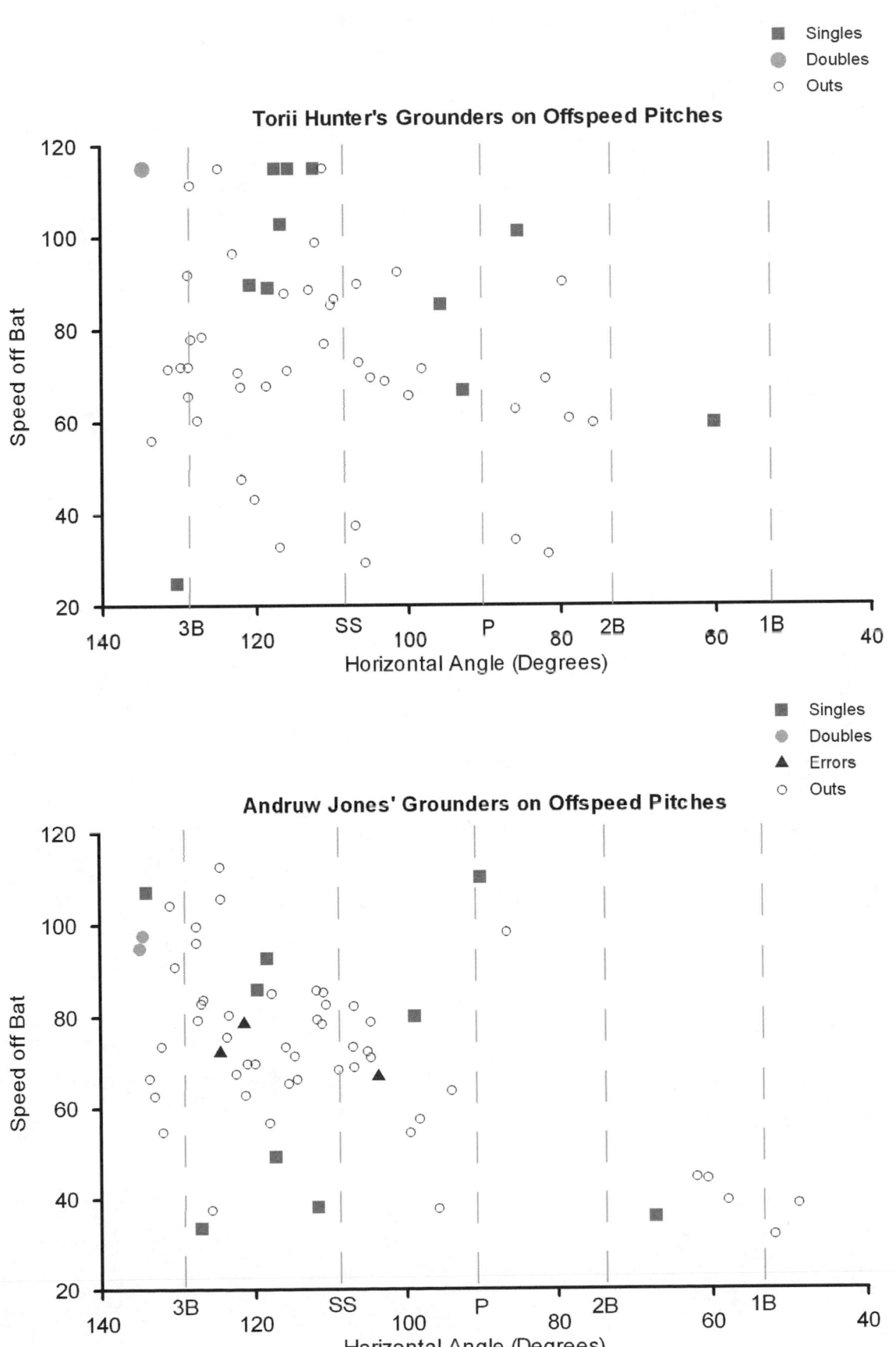

Statistics

Now You Has Stats

This is where the real fun begins: the first of pages and pages of baseball statistics. At THT, we take great pride in not just listing baseball stats, but presenting them in a way that helps you see both the big picture and the fine detail. The forest and the trees, if you will.

That's why you'll find graphs and numbers side-by-side on the following pages. We think numbers alone are okay, and graphs alone are okay too. But pictures and numbers, when presented next to each other, tell you what happened on the ballfield in a way nothing else can.

That's also why you'll find lots of traditional stats and, on the same page, a table of our (not really) "patented" batted ball statistics. A fuller picture emerges when you gaze at both types of stats side-by-side. What do I mean? Let me give you an example.

The White Sox's Jose Contreras had an awful 2007. Take a look at his traditional pitching stats (table below): a 10-17 record and a 5.57 ERA. Among all American League pitchers who qualified for the ERA title, Contreras' was the worst. 232 hits and only 113 strikeouts in 189 innings pitched? That's pretty bad.

But there are some clues that Contreras might not really have been as bad as all that. Even among those "traditional" stats, you can see that his FIP was a respectable 4.84, a little worse than average, but not terrible. This indicates that his pitching basics—strikeouts, walks and home runs allowed—weren't horribly out of line.

You can also see that his defenders apparently gave him little support: his .657 DER was the third-worst in the league.

By the way, DER and FIP are defined in the glossary at the end of the book. If you're not sure what they are, stick your finger in this page and go look them up. We'll still be here.

To better understand what happened to Jose, take a look at the second table, his batted ball statistics (for reference, the major league averages are also listed). As you can see, his strikeout rate was low, his walk rate was average, and his batted ball distribution (ground balls, line drives and fly balls) was about average. This is key—sometimes pitchers have low DER's because they've given up a lot of line drives, but this didn't happen in Contreras' case.

The next batted ball stats break down fly balls into infield flies and home runs on outfield flies. These are both important "secondary" batted ball stats that tell you a lot about a pitcher's effectiveness. Contreras, again, looks average.

Then, a little further to the right, we see the most fundamental difference between Jose and the average major league pitcher: only 68% of his ground balls were fielded successfully for outs; the major league average is 74%. That's a big difference. If you look further to the right, you also see that Jose gave up more runs per ground ball (.08 vs. .05) and, when compared to the average major league pitcher overall, gave up 16 more runs on ground balls over the entire season.

For every other type of batted ball, Contreras was about average. It was the ground ball that did Jose in.

There's no doubt that a decent proportion of Contreras' ground balls were sharply hit. I also assume that a good number of his ground balls just happened to find an infield hole. But there's also no doubt that the White Sox infield didn't always do their job when Contreras was on the mound.

Now, I don't expect Contreras to suddenly bounce back in 2008, assuming his infield improves and he's luckier with the ground balls. His declining strikeout rate (it was 16% in 2006) is an indicator that his stuff wasn't as nasty this year, a bad omen for the future. But I do expect him to be much closer to average.

Player	PRC	IP	BFP	G	GS	K	BB	IBB	HBP	H	HR	DP	DER	SB	CS	PO	W	L	Sv	Op	Hld	H-A	R^L	RA	ERA	FIP
Contreras J	55	189.0	858	32	30	113	62	1	15	232	21	21	.657	25	6	1	10	17	0	0	0	.013	-.051	6.38	5.57	4.84

	% of PA		% of Batted Balls					Out %		Runs Per Event				Total Runs vs. Avg.				
Player	K%	BB%	GB%	LD%	FB%	IF/F	HR/OF	GB	OF	NIP	GB	LD	OF	NIP	GB	LD	FB	Tot
Contreras J	13	9	45	19	36	.11	.10	68	82	.07	.08	.35	.18	3	16	-0	1	20
MLB Average	17	9	43	19	38	.10	.10	74	83	.05	.05	.40	.18	--	--	--	--	--

This is the sort of information you'll find in our pages. If you've purchased previous *Annuals*, you're already familiar with our format. But before you dig into the numbers, I'd like to highlight the few changes we have made this year. For newcomers, I'll then explain how our stats are organized.

Splits

The biggest change we've made is that we are now including "split" information for every batter and pitcher. There are two types of splits embedded in each table of "traditional" stats:

1. Home/Away splits (labeled "H-A"), and

2. Lefty/Righty splits (labeled "L^R" for batters and "R^L" for pitchers)

Both statistics are simply computed as the difference in Gross Production Average (GPA—it's in the glossary) for each split. For instance, look at Jose Contreras' splits on the previous page. His home/away split last year was .013, which means that his GPA was 13 points higher at U.S. Cellular (the White Sox's home park) than on the road. Specifically, his home GPA was .282 and his road GPA was .270 (rounding makes the difference between the two equal to 13).

The average pitcher pitches slightly better at home, just as the average batter bats better at home. The difference is nine points in GPA (.261 vs. .252). So the difference between Contreras' home/away split and the average pitcher's was .022 (.013 plus .009). That's a significant difference, but U.S. Cellular is known as a hitter's park. If you look at the White Sox's pitching page, you'll see that Mark Buehrle had an even more extreme home/away split, although starters Jon Garland and Javier Vazquez actually pitched better at home.

The impact of parks on specific players is often unpredictable within a given year; that's why we're listing the splits for you.

The lefty/right splits are a little more difficult to present in a simple table, but we were determined to make it work. Here's how we did it:

1. We put a "handedness" label next to each batter and pitcher in the table. Each lefthanded batter or pitcher has an asterisk (*) next to his name, while switch hitters have a plus sign (+) next to theirs. Righthanded players have no label.

2. We vary the lefty/righty calculation according to the player's handedness. For righty batters, the calculation is L-R (average versus lefthanded pitch-

ers minus average versus righthanded pitchers). For lefty batters, the calculation is R-L. For switch hitters, we stuck to the more conventional L-R.

3. For pitchers, we switched the calculations—for righthanded pitchers, it's R-L, for southpaws, it's L-R.

This is why we use the label "L^R." The exact calculation depends on the player's natural handedness and whether he was a pitcher or batter.

Why do we do this? To make the tables easier to read. Remember this rule: **natural splits for batters are positive, and natural splits for pitchers are negative** (said another way: more offense is good for batters, and less offense is good for pitchers).

A couple of examples: Lefthanded batter Jim Thome crushes righthanded pitching (as you might expect), and his lefty/right split is .143, one of the biggest splits in the majors. On the other hand, LOOGY Ray King handles lefthanded batters extremely well (again, as expected) and his lefty/right split is -.151.

Lefty/Righty splits are more extreme than the average home/road splits of nine points. Here is a table of the splits for each type of batter in 2007:

	Righty Pitchers	Lefty Pitchers	L^R
Righty Batters	.245	.273	.028
Lefty Batters	.270	.242	.028
Switch Hitters	.256	.258	.002

Not surprisingly, switch hitters don't have much of a handedness split, but isn't it interesting that the average split for righty and lefty batters was virtually even?

The average pitcher had a slightly different set of splits, because switch hitters are listed as lefty or righty batters. Here's a table of the differences:

	Righty Batters	Lefty Batters	R^L
Righty Pitchers	.246	.265	-.020
Lefty Pitchers	.270	.241	-.028

Remember, these are the average major league GPA splits for all batters and pitchers in 2007.

Admittedly, this is a bit awkward, but we think you'll get used to it pretty quickly. You might begin with the leaderboards, which include the most lopsided splits for each league. That's where you'll see that Curtis Granderson had the most lopsided lefty/righty split in the majors.

A lefthanded batter, Granderson batted 164 points better off righthanded pitchers than lefthanded ones! That's .332 vs. an abysmal .168. Although Granderson had a tremendous season, that split was his Achilles' heel and one of the key reasons he batted only .184 in "late and close" situations.

See? That's why we included split statistics.

Base Runs

In the past, the *Annuals* have included the Runs Created of every batter. Runs Created, invented by Bill James, was one of the first "run estimation" formulas (formulas that estimate how many runs a batter contributed to the offense). We used Runs Created because it is the best-known of all the formulas, and it is used in Win Shares (which we also include in the *Annual*).

However, there are many formulas like Runs Created, and some of them are clearly, if marginally, better. Since we like to present the most accurate stats, we decided to switch to David Smyth's Base Runs this year.

For those of you who would like to better understand why Base Runs is more accurate than Runs Created, we refer you to http://www.tangotiger.net/#Baseruns.

When calculating Base Runs for the *Annual*, we decided to include some of the same features we (and Bill James) previously included in Runs Created:

- Each batter's Base Runs is calculated in the context of a league-average team.
- Base Runs is adjusted for ballpark, so you can compare players on different teams.
- Our version of Base Runs includes the impact of "situational hitting" that Bill James built into Runs Created. This is described in our Glossary.

You can still find Runs Created for every player in the *Bill James Handbook*. In fact, another reason we decided to drop Runs Created is that our results have always differed a bit from those in the *Handbook*, and we figure that the *Handbook* should serve as the authoritative source for Runs Created.

A Few Other Changes...

In our batted balls statistics, we've added the number of outs recorded for each ground ball and for each outfield fly (not including home runs). As the Contreras example shows, this information can be very useful.

We've also added batted ball stats to our leaderboards, expanding the size of our leaderboard section 50%. These leaderboards will provide more context to the batted ball stats of your favorite players.

On another note, the *Annual* contains a few different descriptions of team fielding statistics, which might be a bit confusing. Please be aware of each statistic and when we use it:

- Defense Efficiency Ratio, or DER, is the number of batted balls successfully fielded for outs (not including home runs). It is listed for every team and every pitcher, and its batting equivalent, Batting Average on Balls in Play (or BABIP) is listed for every team.

- "Fielding Plays" is our simple plus/minus statistic. It's similar to DER, but it adjusts by the number of batted ball types given up by each pitcher. Since line drives are much harder to catch than infield flies, for instance, this statistic factors that in. This statistic is only used in each league pitching/fielding graph.

- Plus/Minus is the system developed by John Dewan of Baseball Info Solutions, and it is based on the type of ball hit, where it was hit and how hard it was hit. This statistic is only included in John's article, "Team Defense." It is the best metric in this book for judging fielding.

Additionally, our player fielding statistics now include BIS's Revised Zone Rating (RZR), as well as plays made out of zone. Revised Zone Ratings were first introduced by John Dewan in the *Fielding Bible,* and THT is the only place you can find it on a daily, updated basis.

RZR is like Zone Rating, except that plays made out of zone are not forced into the formula—they're listed separately. Not all RZR's are the same, as the following table shows:

POS	BIZ	Plays	RZR	OOZ
1B	6697	4965	0.741	1048
2B	12192	10120	0.830	1412
SS	13019	10625	0.816	1912
3B	10623	7221	0.680	1717
LF	9373	8014	0.855	1614
CF	12264	10886	0.888	1944
RF	9597	8418	0.877	1575

(BIZ stands for "balls in zone"; OOZ stands for plays made "out of zone.")

Corner infielders tend to have lower RZR's than other fielders, and you should keep this in mind when reading your team's fielding stats.

And that is all the new stuff there is to print. Following is the general description of how our stats section is laid out.

League/Team Statistics

We've laid out graphs and stats that show the relative position of each team, separated into the American and National Leagues. The first graph is a display of how many runs each team scored and allowed, and how that relates to the number of games it won.

Below the graph is a table that gives more detail regarding how each team scored runs, gave up runs and turned their run differential into victories.

In the far right column of that table, PWINS stands for "Projected Wins" or "Pythagorean Wins" depending on how technical you want to get. VAR stands for variance, the difference between each team's actual wins and its projected wins. You can read more about Pythagorean Wins in the Glossary.

On the next two pages, we repeat the graphs and stats format for runs scored and allowed. The graph and stats are pretty standard.

You'll find some unique statistics on the following two pages.

- Miscellaneous batting, base running, pitching and fielding stats. The definitions of all of these are contained in the Glossary.
- Win Stats. These include Win Probability Stats for batters, starters and relievers, as well as the Leverage Index for each bullpen. Plus, we've included Win Shares for batting, pitching and fielding, as well as some miscellaneous Win Share stats (average team age, weighted by Win Share contribution, and career Win Shares on the team).
- Batted Ball Stats. We have compiled our one-of-a-kind batted ball information for all teams.

League Leaderboards

Leaderboards are a popular item, so we've listed the top 10 players for a bunch of statistics in each league. You can find the definition of all the leaderboard stats in our Glossary.

There are also complete player listings of all stats on our website, at http://www.hardballtimes.com/main/stats.

Team/Player Stats

Specific stats for players are laid out by team in alphabetical order. Each team section begins with a graphical review of that team's wins and losses during the year, shown as running 10-game totals. The graphs also include each team's 10-game average in runs scored and allowed, so you can visualize how the team's batters and pitchers performed throughout the year.

In addition, we've listed some of the season's highlights below the graph. There's also a table under the graph that displays the team's monthly vital stats (wins, losses, runs scored and allowed per game, OBP and SLG for the offense and FIP and DER for the defense).

On the following three or four pages, individual player stats are listed for batters, pitchers and fielders. Most of these are relatively straightforward stats, and you can find the definitions in the Glossary. If a statistic is italicized, that means it was adjusted for the home park.

Each team section also has detailed batted ball information for each batter who appeared in at least 100 plate appearances for that team, and each pitcher who faced at least 100 batters for that team. The batted ball stats are:

- Percent of plate appearances that resulted in a strikeout or walk (including intentional walks and HBP's).
- The proportion of all batted balls, not including bunts, that were ground balls, line drives and fly balls.
- Two breakdown stats: the percent of fly balls that were infield flies (caught in the infield) and the percent of outfield flies that were home runs.
- The percent of ground balls and outfield flies that were outs (home runs not included in the outfield fly category).
- The average run value of each type of batted ball. This is calculated by assigning linear weights to each batted ball outcome (such as singles, doubles, home runs, and double plays) and averaging them over the total number of each batted ball type.
- Finally, a comparison of how many total runs each player contributed, relative to the major league average, over the entire season. This is a function of both batted ball frequency and run value. The denominator is the number of outs made by each batter or pitcher.

In the leaderboards, the total runs compared to the major league average are labeled "RAA," as in Runs Above Average.

As with our split stats, a positive run contribution by a batter is desired, as is a negative "run contribution" result by a pitcher. In those cases, the individual player is better than the major league average.

As you can imagine, the different team statistics take up a lot of pages, 4-5 per team depending on the layout.

Appendices

Just like last year, we've included two appendices of statistics. The first appendix contains the win stats (Win Shares and Win Probability Added) for all 2007 players.

We've included the basics in these tables: batting and pitching WPA, as well as batting, pitching and fielding Win Shares.

The second appendix contains thirty unique graphs contributed by John Burnson of *Heater Magazine*. These are called "Playing Time Constellations," and they are graphical representations of who played which position for each team throughout the year. Yes, that's a mouthful, but if you check out the appendix, we think you'll be impressed.

That's the layout. We've had fun developing these graphs and tables for you, and we hope you find enough baseball stuff in these pages to keep you occupied and happy the entire offseason.

American League Team Stats

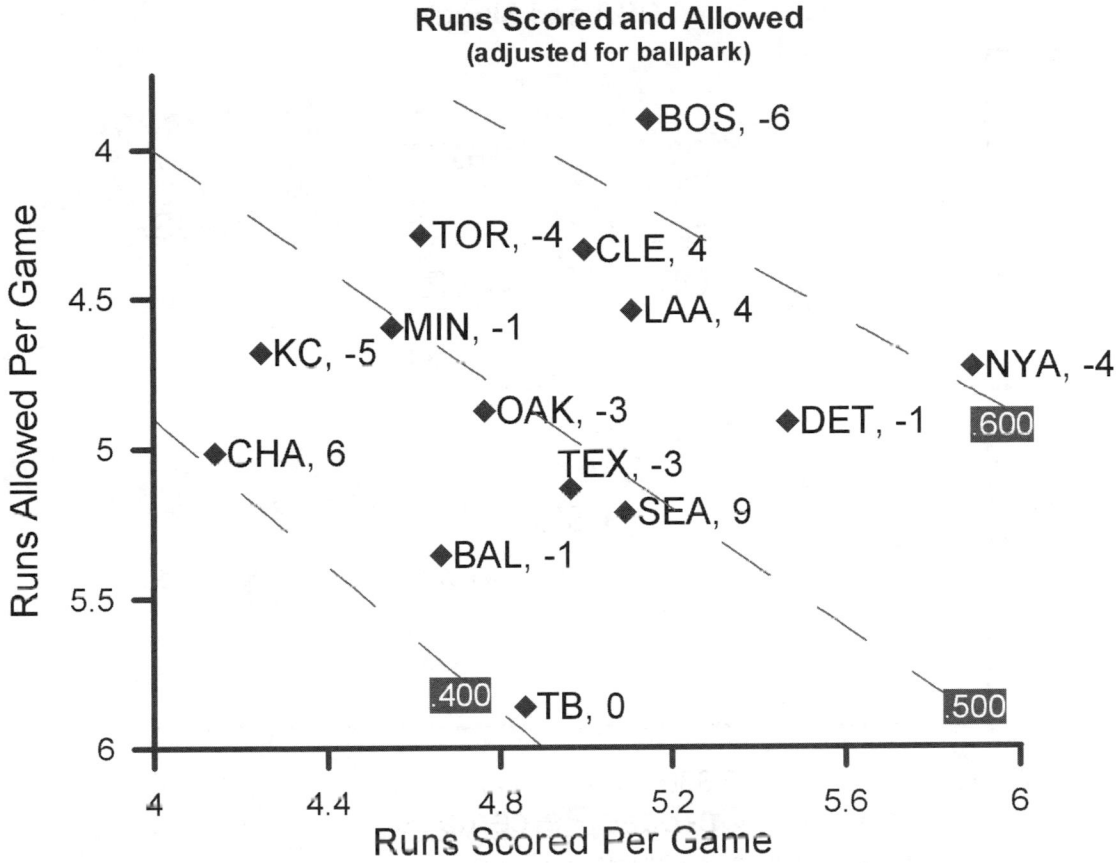

Runs Scored and Allowed
(adjusted for ballpark)

Notes: The dotted lines represent winning percentage based on run differential. The number after each team name represents the difference between the team's actual record and its run differential record.

	Team Record					Scoring Runs			Preventing Runs				Projection	
Team	W	L	RS	RA	RS-RA	AB/RSP	BA/RSP	HR	ERA	HRA	K	DER	PWINS	VAR
BAL	69	93	756	868	-112	1,452	.269	142	5.18	161	1,087	.688	70	-1
BOS	96	66	867	657	210	1,548	.284	166	3.87	151	1,149	.706	102	-6
CHA	72	90	693	839	-146	1,261	.243	190	4.77	174	1,015	.684	66	6
CLE	96	66	811	704	107	1,468	.255	178	4.05	146	1,047	.687	92	4
DET	88	74	887	797	90	1,533	.311	177	4.57	174	1,047	.693	89	-1
KC	69	93	706	778	-72	1,420	.278	102	4.48	168	993	.685	74	-5
LAA	94	68	822	731	91	1,494	.284	123	4.23	151	1,156	.681	90	4
MIN	79	83	718	725	-7	1,430	.276	118	4.16	185	1,094	.689	80	-1
NYA	94	68	968	777	191	1,627	.293	201	4.49	150	1,009	.690	98	-4
OAK	76	86	741	758	-17	1,430	.246	171	4.28	138	1,036	.694	79	-3
SEA	88	74	794	813	-19	1,452	.284	153	4.73	147	1,020	.675	79	9
TB	66	96	782	944	-162	1,415	.265	187	5.54	199	1,194	.657	66	0
TEX	75	87	816	844	-28	1,426	.285	179	4.75	155	976	.683	78	-3
TOR	83	79	753	699	54	1,398	.276	165	4.00	157	1,067	.706	87	-4
Average	82	80	794	781	13	1,454	.276	161	4.51	161	1,064	.687	81	1

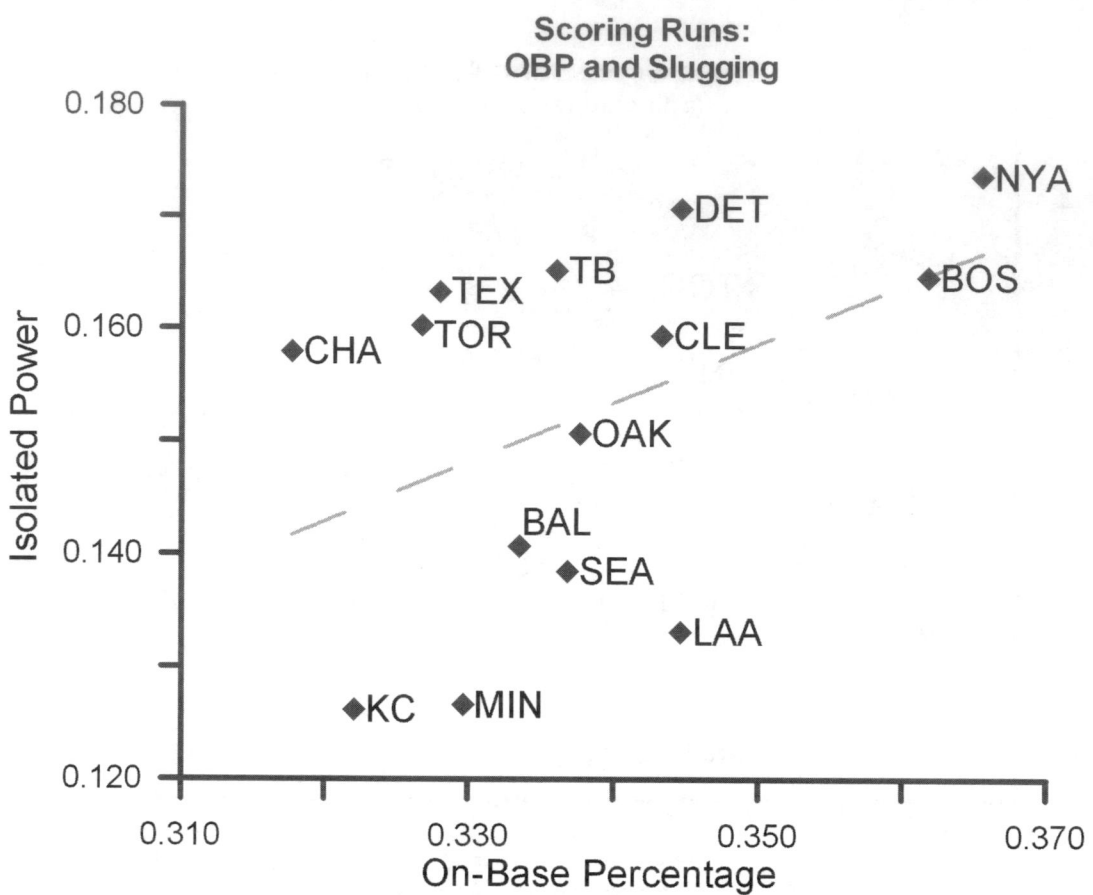

Scoring Runs:
OBP and Slugging

The dotted line shows the relationship between ISO and OBP.

Team	Runs	PA	H	1B	2B	3B	HR	TB	SO	BB	HBP	SH	SF	BA	OBP	SLG	GPA	ISO
BAL	756	6,264	1,529	1,051	306	30	142	2,321	939	500	47	38	47	.272	.333	.412	.253	.141
BOS	867	6,426	1,561	1,008	352	35	166	2,481	1,042	689	64	30	54	.279	.362	.444	.274	.165
CHA	693	6,103	1,341	882	249	20	190	2,200	1,149	532	52	41	35	.246	.318	.404	.244	.158
CLE	811	6,367	1,504	994	305	27	178	2,397	1,202	590	80	32	59	.268	.343	.428	.261	.159
DET	887	6,364	1,652	1,073	352	50	177	2,635	1,054	474	56	31	45	.287	.345	.458	.269	.171
KC	706	6,140	1,447	999	300	46	102	2,145	1,069	428	89	41	47	.261	.322	.388	.242	.126
LAA	822	6,198	1,578	1,108	324	23	123	2,317	883	507	40	32	65	.284	.345	.417	.259	.133
MIN	718	6,161	1,460	1,033	273	36	118	2,159	839	512	48	34	45	.264	.330	.391	.246	.127
NYA	968	6,528	1,656	1,097	326	32	201	2,649	991	637	78	41	54	.290	.366	.463	.280	.174
OAK	741	6,365	1,430	948	295	16	171	2,270	1,119	664	49	18	56	.256	.338	.407	.254	.151
SEA	794	6,209	1,629	1,170	284	22	153	2,416	861	389	62	33	40	.287	.337	.425	.258	.138
TB	782	6,280	1,500	986	291	36	187	2,424	1,324	545	53	34	52	.268	.336	.433	.260	.165
TEX	816	6,214	1,460	947	298	36	179	2,367	1,224	503	56	57	42	.263	.328	.426	.254	.163
TOR	753	6,197	1,434	901	344	24	165	2,321	1,044	533	47	33	48	.259	.327	.419	.252	.160
Average	794	6,273	1,513	1,014	307	31	161	2,364	1,053	536	59	35	49	.271	.341	.423	.259	.152

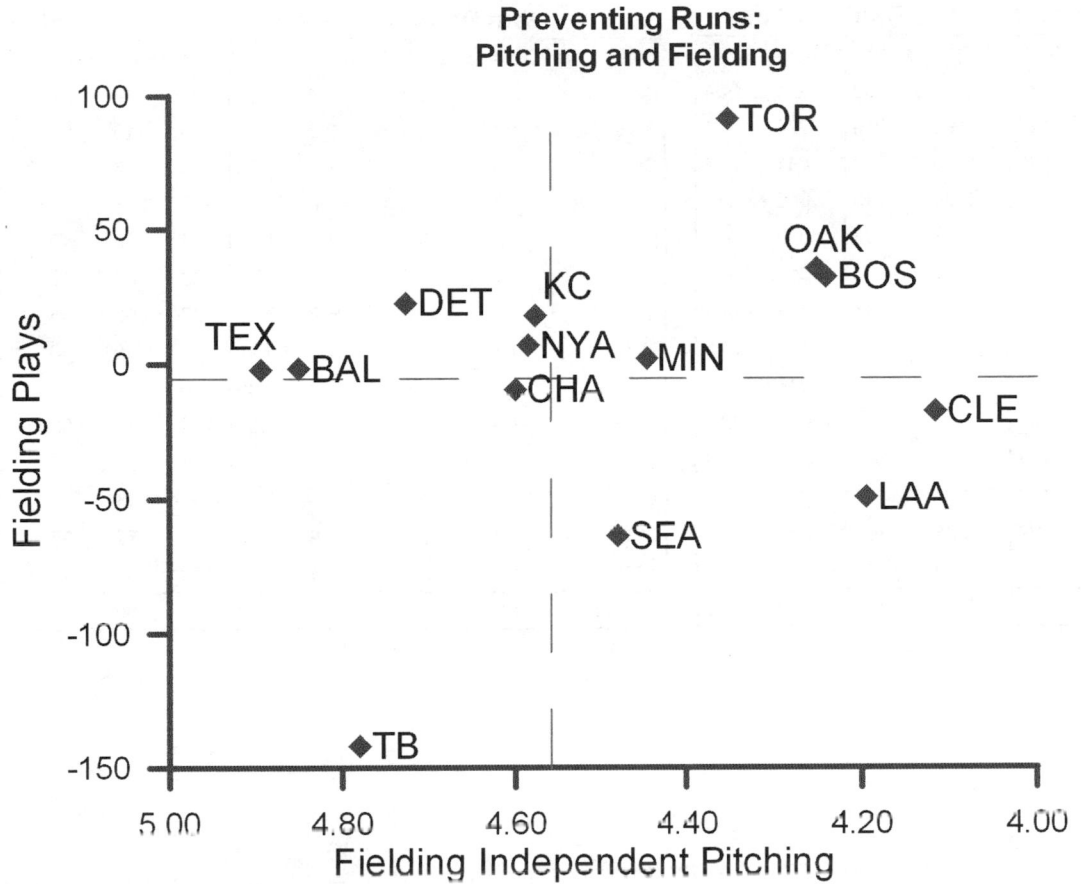

**Preventing Runs:
Pitching and Fielding**

The dotted lines represent the league averages.

Team	RA	IP	BFP	H	HRA	TBA	K	BB	ShO	Sv	Op	%Save	Holds	ERA	FIP	UERA	DER
BAL	868	1438	6,418	1,491	161	2,291	1,087	696	9	30	55	55%	78	5.18	4.85	0.26	.688
BOS	657	1438	6,071	1,350	151	2,138	1,149	482	13	45	56	80%	78	3.87	4.24	0.24	.706
CHA	839	1440	6,293	1,556	174	2,447	1,015	499	9	42	65	65%	73	4.77	4.60	0.48	.684
CLE	704	1462	6,206	1,519	146	2,307	1,047	410	9	49	63	78%	71	4.05	4.12	0.28	.687
DET	797	1447	6,345	1,498	174	2,400	1,047	566	9	44	65	68%	73	4.57	4.73	0.39	.693
KC	778	1437	6,253	1,547	168	2,491	993	520	6	36	54	67%	74	4.48	4.58	0.39	.685
LAA	731	1435	6,161	1,480	151	2,290	1,156	477	9	43	57	75%	74	4.23	4.20	0.36	.681
MIN	725	1436	6,133	1,505	185	2,411	1,094	420	8	38	52	73%	65	4.16	4.45	0.39	.689
NYA	777	1450	6,308	1,498	150	2,329	1,009	578	5	34	55	62%	71	4.49	4.59	0.33	.690
OAK	758	1448	6,247	1,468	138	2,254	1,036	530	9	36	61	59%	66	4.28	4.25	0.43	.694
SEA	813	1434	6,313	1,578	147	2,418	1,020	546	12	43	58	74%	74	4.73	4.48	0.37	.675
TB	944	1429	6,403	1,649	199	2,656	1,194	568	2	28	49	57%	58	5.54	4.78	0.41	.657
TEX	844	1430	6,389	1,525	155	2,354	976	668	6	42	56	75%	80	4.75	4.89	0.56	.683
TOR	699	1448	6,108	1,383	157	2,154	1,067	479	9	44	69	64%	64	4.00	4.35	0.34	.706
Average	781	1,440	6,261	1,503	161	2,353	1,064	531	8	40	58	68%	71	4.51	4.51	0.37	.687

Running and Miscellaneous Batting Stats

Team	SB	CS	SB%	GDP	P/PA	BABIP	H-A	L-R
BAL	144	42	77%	139	3.72	.302	.014	.004
BOS	96	24	80%	146	3.95	.315	.026	.001
CHA	78	45	63%	138	3.86	.278	.011	.004
CLE	72	41	64%	114	3.94	.310	.015	.013
DET	103	30	77%	128	3.73	.323	.012	.010
KC	78	44	64%	151	3.66	.305	.013	.009
LAA	139	55	72%	146	3.66	.315	.034	-.001
MIN	112	30	79%	149	3.73	.291	-.006	-.005
NYA	123	40	75%	138	3.89	.318	.018	-.015
OAK	52	20	72%	142	3.91	.290	-.019	.015
SEA	81	30	73%	154	3.63	.313	-.003	.014
TB	131	48	73%	119	3.81	.318	-.009	.019
TEX	88	25	78%	129	3.88	.305	.024	.004
TOR	57	22	72%	127	3.84	.290	.011	.043
Average	97	35	73%	137	3.80	.305	.010	.010

Win Probability Added   Win Shares

Team	Bat	Starters	Bullpen	LI	Bat	Pitch	Field	WSAge	CWS
BAL	-5.4	0.2	-6.8	1.01	107	66	34	29.6	1,825
BOS	1.8	4.9	8.2	0.97	125	110	52	30.2	2,611
CHA	-8.2	0.7	-1.6	1.10	88	87	40	29.4	1,863
CLE	1.9	5.3	7.8	1.14	127	113	48	27.5	1,763
DET	4.9	0.2	1.9	1.07	144	80	40	30.1	2,444
KC	-12.1	-3.7	3.8	0.96	82	83	42	27.4	1,370
LAA	4.3	2.9	5.8	0.99	137	100	45	28.6	1,800
MIN	-10.3	2.3	6.0	0.97	101	90	46	28.2	1,617
NYA	11.6	-0.4	1.7	0.96	160	83	39	31.2	3,501
OAK	-8.5	3.1	0.3	1.03	105	84	38	27.7	2,125
SEA	3.5	-3.9	7.4	0.94	144	82	37	29.9	1,692
TB	-2.3	-4.6	-8.1	0.95	126	45	27	25.8	803
TEX	0.2	-12.1	5.9	1.00	119	72	35	29.3	1,975
TOR	-4.5	6.0	0.4	1.21	100	104	45	29.1	1,990
Average	-1.6	0.1	2.4	1.02	119	86	41	28.9	1,956

Leverage Index (LI) for bullpen only.

Fielding and Miscellaneous Pitching Stats

Team	DER	Fld %	UER	SBA	CS	%CS	PO	E	TE	FE	DP	GIDP	H-A	R-L
BAL	.688	.987	41	141	32	23%	8	79	37	41	155	133	.007	-.032
BOS	.706	.986	39	139	32	23%	5	81	39	42	145	115	.013	.003
CHA	.684	.982	76	121	23	19%	13	108	53	52	168	138	.002	-.013
CLE	.687	.985	46	139	46	33%	10	92	38	52	167	136	.004	-.008
DET	.693	.984	62	104	31	30%	11	99	47	51	148	125	.001	.006
KC	.685	.982	62	96	26	27%	10	106	49	54	160	138	.006	.002
LAA	.681	.983	57	138	31	22%	6	101	44	55	154	133	-.015	-.003
MIN	.689	.984	62	106	41	39%	10	95	48	45	151	128	-.026	-.037
NYA	.690	.985	53	180	44	24%	6	88	31	55	174	151	-.012	-.021
OAK	.694	.985	69	127	26	20%	7	90	46	42	153	135	-.026	-.004
SEA	.675	.985	59	114	45	39%	20	90	43	46	167	140	-.012	-.004
TB	.657	.980	65	140	44	31%	9	117	56	60	155	128	-.015	-.012
TEX	.683	.980	89	145	47	32%	5	124	59	65	179	143	-.026	-.005
TOR	.706	.984	55	158	24	15%	6	102	52	49	160	146	-.019	-.027
Average	.687	.984	60	132	35	27%	9	98	46	51	160	135	-.008	-.011

Batted Ball Batting Stats

Team	% of PA		% of Batted Balls			IF/F	HR/OF	Out %		Runs Per Event				Total Runs vs. Avg.				
	K%	BB%	GB%	LD%	FB%			GB	OF	NIP	GB	LD	OF	NIP	GB	LD	FB	Tot
BAL	15	9	44	18	38	.11	.09	75	82	.06	.04	.41	.16	-1	-4	3	-22	-24
BOS	16	12	42	18	40	.09	.10	73	79	.08	.05	.39	.20	60	11	-11	61	121
CHA	19	10	44	17	39	.11	.13	77	84	.04	.02	.39	.20	-12	-43	-44	16	-83
CLE	19	11	41	18	41	.07	.10	74	81	.05	.04	.40	.20	12	-11	-13	51	38
DET	17	8	42	20	38	.09	.10	72	82	.04	.06	.41	.19	-20	27	53	29	89
KC	17	8	47	19	34	.10	.08	74	83	.04	.04	.30	.15	-25	0	-5	-75	-98
LAA	14	9	47	17	36	.10	.08	72	81	.06	.06	.41	.16	7	39	3	-34	14
MIN	14	9	50	17	33	.09	.08	75	84	.07	.04	.39	.15	15	7	-22	-71	-71
NYA	15	11	46	19	35	.08	.12	73	82	.08	.05	.42	.21	52	17	50	56	175
OAK	18	11	40	19	40	.11	.10	76	84	.07	.03	.39	.17	35	-35	-1	-12	-14
SEA	14	7	47	18	35	.10	.10	71	85	.04	.06	.39	.16	-24	54	19	-31	18
TB	21	10	43	19	39	.10	.12	72	83	.03	.06	.41	.21	-27	12	2	34	20
TEX	20	9	42	19	39	.09	.11	74	83	.03	.04	.41	.20	-29	-5	3	21	-10
TOR	17	9	40	20	40	.11	.10	76	84	.05	.03	.39	.17	-2	-28	10	-8	-28
MLB Average	*17*	*9*	*43*	*19*	*38*	*.10*	*.10*	*74*	*83*	*.05*	*.05*	*.40*	*.18*	--	--	--	--	--

Batted Ball Pitching Stats

Team	% of PA		% of Batted Balls			IF/F	HR/OF	Out %		Runs Per Event				Total Runs vs. Avg.				
	K%	BB%	GB%	LD%	FB%			GB	OF	NIP	GB	LD	OF	NIP	GB	LD	FB	Tot
BAL	17	12	45	18	37	.08	.10	74	83	.08	.04	.39	.18	59	2	-17	-6	37
BOS	19	9	43	17	40	.10	.10	76	82	.03	.03	.38	.18	-26	-37	-50	1	-112
CHA	16	9	43	19	38	.09	.10	73	82	.05	.05	.38	.19	-6	20	-9	24	29
CLE	17	8	45	18	37	.10	.09	73	84	.03	.05	.41	.16	-42	13	7	-45	-68
DET	16	10	44	18	37	.09	.11	74	86	.06	.04	.43	.17	16	-4	27	-16	23
KC	16	9	41	20	39	.09	.10	74	84	.05	.04	.42	.17	-2	-7	56	-0	47
LAA	19	9	42	18	40	.10	.09	74	81	.03	.05	.40	.18	-32	-3	-9	4	-39
MIN	18	8	43	18	39	.09	.12	74	82	.03	.04	.38	.21	-45	-9	-22	50	-25
NYA	16	10	43	19	39	.10	.09	74	83	.06	.04	.40	.16	23	-3	6	-20	6
OAK	17	9	45	19	37	.10	.09	76	83	.05	.03	.39	.17	-4	-17	-2	-32	-54
SEA	16	10	44	18	38	.11	.09	72	80	.06	.06	.40	.19	12	25	4	9	50
TB	19	10	42	18	40	.10	.12	69	81	.05	.08	.42	.22	0	62	10	78	149
TEX	15	12	47	19	35	.09	.10	73	84	.08	.05	.40	.17	62	23	20	-25	80
TOR	17	9	49	18	33	.09	.11	78	83	.04	.02	.39	.19	-20	-41	-20	-26	-107
MLB Average	*17*	*9*	*43*	*19*	*38*	*.10*	*.10*	*74*	*83*	*.05*	*.05*	*.40*	*.18*	--	--	--	--	--

American League Leaderboards
Batting Leaders

Base Runs			
1 A. Rodriguez	NYA	161
2 M. Ordonez	DET	150
3 D. Ortiz	BOS	135
4 G. Sizemore	CLE	124
5 I. Suzuki	SEA	121
6 V. Guerrero	LAA	120
7 C. Pena	TB	120
8 C. Granderson	DET	112
9 D. Jeter	NYA	109
10 B. Roberts	BAL	108

Runs Scored			
1 A. Rodriguez	NYA	143
2 B. Abreu	NYA	123
3 C. Granderson	DET	122
4 G. Sizemore	CLE	118
5 M. Ordonez	DET	117
6 D. Ortiz	BOS	116
7 A. Rios	TOR	114
8 I. Suzuki	SEA	111
9 G. Sheffield	DET	107
10 P. Polanco	DET	105

Runs Batted In			
1 A. Rodriguez	NYA	156
2 M. Ordonez	DET	139
3 V. Guerrero	LAA	125
4 C. Pena	TB	121
5 M. Lowell	BOS	120
6 D. Ortiz	BOS	117
7 V. Martinez	CLE	114
8 N. Markakis	BAL	112
9 J. Morneau	MIN	111
10 T. Hunter	MIN	107

Gross Production Average (GPA)			
1 A. Rodriguez	NYA	.355
2 M. Ordonez	DET	.351
3 C. Pena	TB	.348
4 D. Ortiz	BOS	.342
5 J. Posada	NYA	.331
6 V. Guerrero	LAA	.325
7 J. Cust	OAK	.319
8 J. Thome	CHA	.316
9 B. Upton	TB	.307
10 C. Granderson	DET	.306

Batting Average			
1 M. Ordonez	DET	.363
2 I. Suzuki	SEA	.351
3 P. Polanco	DET	.341
4 J. Posada	NYA	.338
5 D. Ortiz	BOS	.332
6 C. Figgins	LAA	.330
7 M. Lowell	BOS	.324
7 V. Guerrero	LAA	.324
9 D. Jeter	NYA	.322
10 D. Pedroia	BOS	.317

On-Base Percentage			
1 D. Ortiz	BOS	.445
2 M. Ordonez	DET	.434
3 J. Posada	NYA	.426
4 A. Rodriguez	NYA	.422
5 C. Pena	TB	.411
6 J. Thome	CHA	.410
7 J. Cust	OAK	.408
8 V. Guerrero	LAA	.403
9 I. Suzuki	SEA	.396
10 C. Figgins	LAA	.393

Slugging Percentage			
1 A. Rodriguez	NYA	.645
2 C. Pena	TB	.627
3 D. Ortiz	BOS	.621
4 M. Ordonez	DET	.595
5 J. Thome	CHA	.563
6 C. Granderson	DET	.552
7 V. Guerrero	LAA	.547
8 J. Posada	NYA	.543
9 B. Upton	TB	.508
10 V. Martinez	CLE	.505

OPS (On-Base Plus Slugging)			
1 A. Rodriguez	NYA	1.067
2 D. Ortiz	BOS	1.066
3 C. Pena	TB	1.037
4 M. Ordonez	DET	1.029
5 J. Thome	CHA	.973
6 J. Posada	NYA	.970
7 V. Guerrero	LAA	.950
8 C. Granderson	DET	.913
9 J. Cust	OAK	.912
10 B. Upton	TB	.894

Plate Appearances			
1 G. Sizemore	CLE	748
2 I. Suzuki	SEA	736
3 B. Roberts	BAL	716
4 D. Jeter	NYA	714
5 A. Rios	TOR	711
6 N. Markakis	BAL	710
7 A. Rodriguez	NYA	708
8 D. DeJesus	KC	703
9 O. Cabrera	LAA	701
10 B. Abreu	NYA	699

Outs			
1 D. Young	TB	485
2 N. Markakis	BAL	474
3 G. Sizemore	CLE	467
4 A. Rios	TOR	465
5 O. Cabrera	LAA	462
5 D. Jeter	NYA	462
5 M. Young	TEX	462
5 D. DeJesus	KC	462
9 B. Roberts	BAL	456
10 I. Suzuki	SEA	455

Hits			
1 I. Suzuki	SEA	238
2 M. Ordonez	DET	216
3 D. Jeter	NYA	206
4 M. Young	TEX	201
5 P. Polanco	DET	200
6 O. Cabrera	LAA	192
7 N. Markakis	BAL	191
7 M. Lowell	BOS	191
7 A. Rios	TOR	191
10 R. Cano	NYA	189

Total Bases			
1 A. Rodriguez	NYA	376
2 M. Ordonez	DET	354
3 D. Ortiz	BOS	341
4 C. Granderson	DET	338
5 A. Rios	TOR	320
6 V. Guerrero	LAA	314
7 N. Markakis	BAL	309
8 C. Pena	TB	307
9 T. Hunter	MIN	303
10 R. Cano	NYA	301

Singles			
1 I. Suzuki	SEA	203
2 M. Young	TEX	154
3 P. Polanco	DET	152
4 D. Jeter	NYA	151
5 O. Cabrera	LAA	148
6 J. Vidro	SEA	140
7 D. Young	TB	135
8 M. Ordonez	DET	134
9 S. Stewart	OAK	132
10 M. Lowell	BOS	131

Doubles			
1 M. Ordonez	DET	54
2 D. Ortiz	BOS	52
3 A. Hill	TOR	47
4 T. Hunter	MIN	45
4 V. Guerrero	LAA	45
6 N. Markakis	BAL	43
6 A. Rios	TOR	43
8 J. Posada	NYA	42
8 B. Roberts	BAL	42
10 A. Beltre	SEA	41
10 R. Cano	NYA	41

Triples			
1 C. Granderson	DET	23
2 A. Iwamura	TB	10
3 C. Crawford	TB	9
3 D. DeJesus	KC	9
3 C. Guillen	DET	9
6 M. Byrd	TEX	8
6 M. Teahen	KC	8
6 M. Cabrera	NYA	8
9 6 tied with		7

Home Runs			
1 A. Rodriguez	NYA	54
2 C. Pena	TB	46
3 D. Ortiz	BOS	35
3 J. Thome	CHA	35
5 J. Morneau	MIN	31
5 P. Konerko	CHA	31
7 M. Ordonez	DET	28
7 T. Hunter	MIN	28
7 J. Dye	CHA	28
10 V. Guerrero	LAA	27

Rate stats include only players with at least 502 plate appearances.

Strikeouts

1	J. Cust	OAK	164
2	G. Sizemore	CLE	155
3	B. Upton	TB	154
4	B. Inge	DET	150
5	J. Peralta	CLE	146
6	C. Pena	TB	142
7	C. Granderson	DET	141
8	A. Gordon	KC	137
9	J. Thome	CHA	134
10	N. Swisher	OAK	131

Walks

1	D. Ortiz	BOS	111
2	J. Cust	OAK	105
3	C. Pena	TB	103
4	T. Hafner	CLE	102
5	G. Sizemore	CLE	101
6	N. Swisher	OAK	100
7	A. Rodriguez	NYA	95
7	J. Thome	CHA	95
9	B. Roberts	BAL	89
10	G. Sheffield	DET	84
10	B. Abreu	NYA	84

Intentional Walks

1	V. Guerrero	LAA	28
2	T. Hafner	CLE	17
3	M. Ramirez	BOS	13
3	I. Suzuki	SEA	13
5	V. Martinez	CLE	12
5	N. Swisher	OAK	12
5	D. Ortiz	BOS	12
8	S. Casey	DET	11
8	J. Morneau	MIN	11
8	A. Rodriguez	NYA	11
8	J. Thome	CHA	11

Hit By Pitch

1	D. DeJesus	KC	23
2	A. Rodriguez	NYA	21
3	R. Garko	CLE	20
4	J. Guillen	SEA	19
5	G. Sizemore	CLE	17
6	K. Youkilis	BOS	15
7	D. Jeter	NYA	14
8	A. Gordon	KC	13
9	5 tied with		11

Stolen Bases

1	C. Crawford	TB	50
1	B. Roberts	BAL	50
3	C. Figgins	LAA	41
4	C. Patterson	BAL	37
4	I. Suzuki	SEA	37
6	G. Sizemore	CLE	33
6	J. Lugo	BOS	33
8	J. Owens	CHA	32
9	C. Crisp	BOS	28
10	R. Willits	LAA	27
10	J. Damon	NYA	27

Caught Stealing

1	C. Figgins	LAA	12
2	G. Sizemore	CLE	10
2	C. Crawford	TB	10
4	J. Uribe	CHA	9
4	C. Patterson	BAL	9
4	T. Hunter	MIN	9
7	9 tied with		8

Net Stolen Bases

1	B. Roberts	BAL	36
2	C. Crawford	TB	30
3	C. Granderson	DET	24
4	I. Suzuki	SEA	21
4	J. Damon	NYA	21
4	J. Lugo	BOS	21
7	C. Patterson	BAL	19
7	I. Kinsler	TEX	19
9	C. Figgins	LAA	17
9	J. Bartlett	MIN	17

Sacrifice Hits

1	C. Patterson	BAL	13
2	R. Vazquez	TEX	12
2	J. McDonald	TOR	12
4	R. Willits	LAA	11
5	J. Gathright	KC	10
5	M. Cabrera	NYA	10
7	C. Crisp	BOS	9
7	J. Lopez	SEA	9
9	4 tied with		8

BA on Balls in Play (BABIP)

1	B. Upton	TB	.393
2	C. Figgins	LAA	.391
3	I. Suzuki	SEA	.389
4	J. Posada	NYA	.386
5	M. Ordonez	DET	.381
6	C. Crawford	TB	.374
7	D. Jeter	NYA	.367
8	M. Young	TEX	.366
9	C. Granderson	DET	.360
10	M. Teahen	KC	.359

BA with RISP

1	M. Ordonez	DET	.429
2	I. Suzuki	SEA	.397
3	M. Young	TEX	.376
4	P. Polanco	DET	.364
5	D. Ortiz	BOS	.362
6	M. Lowell	BOS	.356
6	V. Martinez	CLE	.356
8	V. Guerrero	LAA	.354
8	D. Jeter	NYA	.354
10	C. Figgins	LAA	.348

Situational Hitting Runs

1	M. Ordonez	DET	14
2	D. Young	TB	13
3	M. Young	TEX	11
4	A. Rodriguez	NYA	10
5	T. Hunter	MIN	10
6	K. Youkilis	BOS	8
7	R. Ibanez	SEA	7
8	Y. Betancourt	SEA	7
9	M. Teahen	KC	7
10	B. Inge	DET	7

Sacrifice Flies

1	O. Cabrera	LAA	11
1	V. Martinez	CLE	11
3	H. Matsui	NYA	10
4	A. Rodriguez	NYA	9
4	M. Cabrera	NYA	9
4	J. Morneau	MIN	9
4	N. Swisher	OAK	9
8	7 tied with		8

Home/Away Split (Home)

1	C. Figgins	LAA	.094
2	T. Pena	KC	.088
3	J. Cust	OAK	.088
4	C. Patterson	BAL	.087
5	I. Kinsler	TEX	.078
6	M. Lowell	BOS	.072
7	J. Lugo	BOS	.071
8	J. Peralta	CLE	.066
9	J. Uribe	CHA	.062
10	B. Abreu	NYA	.061

Home/Away Split (Away)

1	S. Stewart	OAK	-.065
2	C. Blake	CLE	-.041
3	C. Crawford	TB	-.041
4	R. Ibanez	SEA	-.041
5	B. Upton	TB	-.033
6	K. Youkilis	BOS	-.032
7	A. Beltre	SEA	-.029
8	T. Hafner	CLE	-.028
9	C. Granderson	DET	-.028
10	A. Pierzynski	CHA	-.025

Lefty/Righty Split (Positive)

1	C. Granderson	DET	.164
2	J. Thome	CHA	.143
3	B. Inge	DET	.103
4	M. Ramirez	BOS	.099
5	J. Guillen	SEA	.098
6	D. Ortiz	BOS	.096
7	I. Kinsler	TEX	.085
8	M. Ellis	OAK	.083
9	F. Thomas	TOR	.081
10	R. Ibanez	SEA	.078

Lefty/Righty Split (Negative)

1	G. Matthews	LAA	-.074
2	C. Patterson	BAL	-.050
3	N. Punto	MIN	-.043
4	A. Iwamura	TB	-.043
5	A. Rodriguez	NYA	-.032
6	M. Cabrera	NYA	-.029
7	B. Roberts	BAL	-.026
8	V. Martinez	CLE	-.023
9	P. Polanco	DET	-.018
10	S. Stewart	OAK	-.018

Rate stats include only players with at least 502 plate appearances.

Strikeout % (Lowest)

	Player	Team	
1	P. Polanco	DET	5
2	D. Pedroia	BOS	7
3	K. Johjima	SEA	8
4	C. Kotchman	LAA	8
5	Y. Betancourt	SEA	9
6	J. Vidro	SEA	9
7	O. Cabrera	LAA	9
8	V. Guerrero	LAA	9
9	S. Stewart	OAK	10
10	M. Tejada	BAL	10

Strikeout % (Highest)

	Player	Team	
1	J. Cust	OAK	32
2	B. Upton	TB	28
3	B. Inge	DET	26
4	J. Thome	CHA	25
5	J. Varitek	BOS	24
6	C. Pena	TB	23
7	A. Gordon	KC	23
8	J. Peralta	CLE	23
9	M. Teahen	KC	21
10	G. Sizemore	CLE	21

Walk % (Highest)

	Player	Team	
1	J. Cust	OAK	21
2	J. Thome	CHA	19
3	C. Pena	TB	18
4	D. Ortiz	BOS	17
5	N. Swisher	OAK	17
6	T. Hafner	CLE	16
7	A. Rodriguez	NYA	16
8	G. Sizemore	CLE	16
9	G. Sheffield	DET	16
10	J. Varitek	BOS	15

Walk % (Lowest)

	Player	Team	
1	I. Rodriguez	DET	2
2	T. Pena	KC	3
3	Y. Betancourt	SEA	3
4	D. Young	TB	4
5	J. Lopez	SEA	4
6	C. Patterson	BAL	5
7	K. Johjima	SEA	5
8	C. Crawford	TB	6
9	A. Hill	TOR	6
10	A. Beltre	SEA	6

Ground ball % (Lowest)

	Player	Team	
1	K. Millar	BAL	29
2	F. Thomas	TOR	30
3	M. Ellis	OAK	32
4	G. Sizemore	CLE	33
5	C. Granderson	DET	34
6	K. Youkilis	BOS	34
7	I. Kinsler	TEX	35
8	J. Dye	CHA	35
9	J. Uribe	CHA	35
10	M. Lowell	BOS	36

Ground ball % (Highest)

	Player	Team	
1	T. Pena	KC	56
2	I. Suzuki	SEA	56
3	D. Jeter	NYA	56
4	I. Rodriguez	DET	52
5	R. Cano	NYA	52
6	M. Tejada	BAL	52
7	M. Cabrera	NYA	51
8	N. Punto	MIN	51
9	J. Vidro	SEA	51
10	G. Matthews Jr.	LAA	51

Line Drive % (Highest)

	Player	Team	
1	M. Young	TEX	27
2	C. Figgins	LAA	26
3	P. Polanco	DET	24
4	J. Cust	OAK	23
5	R. Willits	LAA	23
6	J. Posada	NYA	22
7	B. Inge	DET	22
8	M. Ramirez	BOS	22
9	S. Stewart	OAK	21
10	B. Harris	TB	21

Line Drive % (Lowest)

	Player	Team	
1	G. Matthews Jr.	LAA	13
2	T. Hunter	MIN	14
3	N. Punto	MIN	15
4	J. Uribe	CHA	15
5	C. Patterson	BAL	15
6	V. Guerrero	LAA	16
7	J. Morneau	MIN	16
8	J. Guillen	SEA	16
9	C. Kotchman	LAA	16
10	A. Huff	BAL	16

Infield Fly/Fly balls (Lowest)

	Player	Team	
1	M. Young	TEX	.02
2	B. Abreu	NYA	.02
3	K. Youkilis	BOS	.03
4	J. Vidro	SEA	.03
5	C. Figgins	LAA	.03
6	J. Cust	OAK	.04
7	D. Jeter	NYA	.04
8	J. Peralta	CLE	.04
9	J. Posada	NYA	.05
10	C. Crawford	TB	.05

HR/OF (Highest)

	Player	Team	
1	J. Cust	OAK	.33
2	C. Pena	TB	.32
3	A. Rodriguez	NYA	.29
4	J. Thome	CHA	.29
5	B. Upton	TB	.21
6	D. Ortiz	BOS	.18
7	J. Morneau	MIN	.17
8	P. Konerko	CHA	.17
9	T. Hafner	CLE	.17
10	J. Dye	CHA	.17

Out per Ground ball % (Lowest)

	Player	Team	
1	B. Upton	TB	63
2	I. Suzuki	SEA	63
3	A. Iwamura	TB	65
4	J. Guillen	SEA	66
5	M. Lowell	BOS	66
6	O. Cabrera	LAA	67
7	D. Jeter	NYA	67
8	R. Ibanez	SEA	67
9	P. Polanco	DET	67
9	J. Posada	NYA	67

Out per Outfield Fly % (Lowest)

	Player	Team	
1	D. Ortiz	BOS	72
2	D. Drew	BOS	73
3	C. Crawford	TB	73
4	J. Cust	OAK	74
5	J. Posada	NYA	74
6	M. Ordonez	DET	74
7	R. Garko	CLE	75
8	C. Kotchman	LAA	75
9	C. Granderson	DET	75
10	K. Johjima	SEA	78

Runs per NIP

	Player	Team	
1	P. Polanco	DET	.17
2	C. Kotchman	LAA	.15
3	G. Sheffield	DET	.15
4	V. Guerrero	LAA	.15
5	D. Pedroia	BOS	.15
6	J. Vidro	SEA	.13
7	D. Ortiz	BOS	.13
8	D. DeJesus	KC	.12
9	H. Matsui	NYA	.12
10	M. Ordonez	DET	.11

Runs per Ground ball

	Player	Team	
1	I. Suzuki	SEA	.12
2	A. Iwamura	TB	.11
3	B. Upton	TB	.09
4	P. Polanco	DET	.09
5	O. Cabrera	LAA	.09
6	J. Guillen	SEA	.09
7	M. Ellis	OAK	.08
8	M. Lowell	BOS	.08
9	D. Jeter	NYA	.08
10	Y. Betancourt	SEA	.08

Runs per Line Drive

	Player	Team	
1	A. Rodriguez	NYA	.51
2	T. Hunter	MIN	.50
3	J. Thome	CHA	.49
4	B. Upton	TB	.48
5	C. Granderson	DET	.48
6	A. Huff	BAL	.47
7	C. Kotchman	LAA	.46
8	C. Figgins	LAA	.46
9	N. Swisher	OAK	.45
10	J. Posada	NYA	.45

Runs per Outfield Fly

	Player	Team	
1	J. Cust	OAK	.54
2	C. Pena	TB	.47
3	J. Thome	CHA	.43
4	A. Rodriguez	NYA	.42
5	D. Ortiz	BOS	.36
6	B. Upton	TB	.35
7	M. Ordonez	DET	.30
8	V. Guerrero	LAA	.28
9	J. Morneau	MIN	.28
10	J. Dye	CHA	.27

Rate stats include only players with at least 502 plate appearances.

Not in Play RAA			
1	D. Ortiz	BOS	21
2	A. Rodriguez	NYA	18
3	G. Sheffield	DET	17
4	T. Hafner	CLE	17
5	C. Pena	TB	16
6	N. Swisher	OAK	15
7	G. Sizemore	CLE	14
8	J. Thome	CHA	13
9	V. Guerrero	LAA	13
10	K. Youkilis	BOS	12

Ground ball RAA			
1	I. Suzuki	SEA	32
2	D. Jeter	NYA	15
3	P. Polanco	DET	14
4	O. Cabrera	LAA	14
5	A. Iwamura	TB	12
6	L. Castillo	MIN	12
7	J. Guillen	SEA	11
8	J. Owens	CHA	10
9	Y. Betancourt	SEA	10
10	D. Pedroia	BOS	9

Line Drive RAA			
1	C. Figgins	LAA	19
2	M. Young	TEX	15
3	P. Polanco	DET	15
4	J. Posada	NYA	14
5	D. Young	TB	13
6	C. Granderson	DET	13
7	M. Ordonez	DET	12
8	I. Suzuki	SEA	12
9	V. Martinez	CLE	11
10	A. Hill	TOR	11

Fly ball RAA			
1	C. Pena	TB	46
2	D. Ortiz	BOS	46
3	A. Rodriguez	NYA	45
4	M. Ordonez	DET	32
5	J. Thome	CHA	28
6	C. Granderson	DET	24
7	J. Cust	OAK	23
8	V. Guerrero	LAA	21
9	J. Morneau	MIN	20
10	R. Garko	CLE	19

Total Batted Ball RAA			
1	A. Rodriguez	NYA	70
2	D. Ortiz	BOS	67
3	M. Ordonez	DET	61
4	C. Pena	TB	54
5	V. Guerrero	LAA	46
6	J. Posada	NYA	44
7	J. Thome	CHA	38
8	C. Granderson	DET	35
9	G. Sizemore	CLE	31
10	D. Jeter	NYA	30

WPA (Win Probability Added)			
1	Rodriguez, A	NYA	7.51
2	Ordonez, M	DET	6.27
3	Guerrero, V	LAA	5.94
4	Ortiz, D	BOS	4.81
5	Pena, C	TB	3.85
6	Crawford, C	TB	3.50
7	Cust, J	OAK	2.99
8	Thome, J	CHA	2.90
9	Polanco, P	DET	2.89
10	Figgins, C	LAA	2.88

WPA/LI			
1	Rodriguez, A	NYA	6.41
2	Ortiz, D	BOS	6.29
3	Ordonez, M	DET	5.20
4	Pena, C	TB	4.61
5	Thome, J	CHA	3.68
6	Guerrero, V	LAA	3.52
7	Granderson, C	DET	3.14
8	Posada, J	NYA	3.01
9	Jeter, D	NYA	2.77
10	Upton, B	TB	2.70

Pitching Leaders

Pitching Runs Created			
1	C. Sabathia	CLE	131
2	J. Santana	MIN	123
3	J. Beckett	BOS	120
3	J. Lackey	LAA	120
5	F. Carmona	CLE	116
6	D. Haren	OAK	115
7	E. Bedard	BAL	114
7	J. Vazquez	CHA	114
9	S. Kazmir	TB	107
10	R. Halladay	TOR	104

Earned Run Average (ERA)			
1	J. Lackey	LAA	3.01
2	F. Carmona	CLE	3.06
3	D. Haren	OAK	3.07
4	E. Bedard	BAL	3.16
5	C. Sabathia	CLE	3.21
6	J. Beckett	BOS	3.27
7	J. Santana	MIN	3.33
8	K. Escobar	LAA	3.40
9	S. Kazmir	TB	3.48
10	M. Buehrle	CHA	3.63

Runs Allowed Per 9 (RA)			
1	E. Bedard	BAL	3.26
2	F. Carmona	CLE	3.27
3	J. Beckett	BOS	3.41
4	J. Lackey	LAA	3.50
5	C. Sabathia	CLE	3.51
6	J. Santana	MIN	3.62
7	K. Escobar	LAA	3.63
8	D. Haren	OAK	3.68
9	C. Wang	NYA	3.79
10	M. Buehrle	CHA	3.85

Fielding Independent Pitching (FIP)			
1	J. Beckett	BOS	3.22
2	C. Sabathia	CLE	3.27
3	E. Bedard	BAL	3.33
4	K. Escobar	LAA	3.50
5	S. Kazmir	TB	3.58
6	J. Blanton	OAK	3.59
7	R. Halladay	TOR	3.65
8	J. Lackey	LAA	3.66
9	D. McGowan	TOR	3.82
9	D. Haren	OAK	3.82

Innings Pitched			
1	C. Sabathia	CLE	241.0
2	J. Blanton	OAK	230.0
3	R. Halladay	TOR	225.3
4	J. Lackey	LAA	224.0
5	D. Haren	OAK	222.7
6	J. Santana	MIN	219.0
7	J. Vazquez	CHA	216.7
8	G. Meche	KC	216.0
9	A. Pettitte	NYA	215.3
10	F. Carmona	CLE	215.0
10	J. Shields	TB	215.0

Games			
1	J. Walker	BAL	81
1	S. Downs	TOR	81
3	C. Bradford	BAL	78
4	L. Vizcaino	NYA	77
5	J. Gobble	KC	74
5	P. Neshek	MIN	74
7	M. Guerrier	MIN	73
7	G. Sherrill	SEA	73
9	S. Shields	LAA	71
10	J. Benoit	TEX	70
10	C. Janssen	TOR	70

Batters Faced			
1	C. Sabathia	CLE	975
2	J. Blanton	OAK	950
3	D. Haren	OAK	935
4	J. Lackey	LAA	929
5	R. Halladay	TOR	927
6	D. Cabrera	BAL	922
7	A. Pettitte	NYA	916
8	G. Meche	KC	906
9	S. Kazmir	TB	887
10	C. Gaudin	OAK	886

Pitches			
1	D. Haren	OAK	3,635
2	S. Kazmir	TB	3,609
3	C. Sabathia	CLE	3,581
4	G. Meche	KC	3,579
5	D. Cabrera	BAL	3,565
6	J. Blanton	OAK	3,481
7	D. Matsuzaka	BOS	3,480
8	J. Vazquez	CHA	3,465
9	J. Lackey	LAA	3,396
10	A. Pettitte	NYA	3,395

Rate stats include only pitchers with at least 162 innings pitched.

Strikeouts

1	S. Kazmir	TB	239
2	J. Santana	MIN	235
3	E. Bedard	BAL	221
4	J. Vazquez	CHA	213
5	C. Sabathia	CLE	209
6	D. Matsuzaka	BOS	201
7	J. Beckett	BOS	194
8	D. Haren	OAK	192
9	J. Shields	TB	184
10	J. Verlander	DET	183

Walks (Most)

1	D. Cabrera	BAL	108
2	C. Gaudin	OAK	100
3	S. Kazmir	TB	89
4	E. Jackson	TB	88
5	M. Batista	SEA	85
6	D. Matsuzaka	BOS	80
7	S. Trachsel	BAL	69
7	A. Pettitte	NYA	69
9	J. Washburn	SEA	67
9	J. Verlander	DET	67

Strikeouts Per Game

1	E. Bedard	BAL	11.7
2	S. Kazmir	TB	10.4
3	J. Santana	MIN	10.3
4	A. Burnett	TOR	9.8
5	J. Vazquez	CHA	9.3
6	J. Beckett	BOS	9.1
7	D. Matsuzaka	BOS	8.9
8	C. Sabathia	CLE	8.3
9	J. Verlander	DET	8.2
10	J. Shields	TB	8.1

Walks Per Game (Fewest)

1	P. Byrd	CLE	1.3
2	C. Sabathia	CLE	1.5
3	J. Shields	TB	1.6
3	J. Blanton	OAK	1.6
3	C. Silva	MIN	1.6
6	J. Beckett	BOS	1.9
7	R. Halladay	TOR	2.0
8	M. Buehrle	CHA	2.1
9	J. Lackey	LAA	2.2
9	J. Vazquez	CHA	2.2

Wins

1	J. Beckett	BOS	20
2	F. Carmona	CLE	19
2	C. Wang	NYA	19
2	C. Sabathia	CLE	19
2	J. Lackey	LAA	19
6	K. Escobar	LAA	18
6	J. Verlander	DET	18
8	T. Wakefield	BOS	17
9	M. Batista	SEA	16
9	R. Halladay	TOR	16

Losses

1	D. Cabrera	BAL	18
2	J. Contreras	CHA	17
3	J. Washburn	SEA	15
3	E. Jackson	TB	15
5	C. Silva	MIN	14
5	K. Millwood	TEX	14
5	E. Santana	LAA	14
8	7 tied with		13

Saves

1	J. Borowski	CLE	45
2	F. Rodriguez	LAA	40
2	J. Putz	SEA	40
2	B. Jenks	CHA	40
5	T. Jones	DET	38
6	J. Nathan	MIN	37
6	J. Papelbon	BOS	37
8	M. Rivera	NYA	30
8	J. Accardo	TOR	30
10	A. Reyes	TB	26

Save Opportunities

1	J. Borowski	CLE	53
2	B. Jenks	CHA	46
2	F. Rodriguez	LAA	46
4	T. Jones	DET	44
5	J. Putz	SEA	42
6	J. Nathan	MIN	41
7	J. Papelbon	BOS	40
8	J. Accardo	TOR	35
9	M. Rivera	NYA	34
10	A. Reyes	TB	30

Holds

1	R. Betancourt	CLE	31
1	S. Shields	LAA	31
3	H. Okajima	BOS	27
4	S. Downs	TOR	24
4	J. Speier	LAA	24
4	C. Janssen	TOR	24
7	G. Sherrill	SEA	22
8	F. Francisco	TEX	21
8	J. Walker	BAL	21
10	3 tied with		19

Home Runs Allowed

1	J. Santana	MIN	33
2	J. Vazquez	CHA	29
3	J. Danks	CHA	28
3	J. Shields	TB	28
5	P. Byrd	CLE	27
5	B. Bonser	MIN	27
5	S. Marcum	TOR	27
8	E. Santana	LAA	26
9	D. Matsuzaka	BOS	25
9	D. Cabrera	BAL	25

Home Runs Per Game

1	C. Wang	NYA	0.42
2	K. Escobar	LAA	0.52
3	R. Halladay	TOR	0.63
4	J. Blanton	OAK	0.65
5	A. Pettitte	NYA	0.68
6	F. Carmona	CLE	0.70
7	J. Lackey	LAA	0.75
8	D. McGowan	TOR	0.77
9	S. Kazmir	TB	0.78
10	C. Sabathia	CLE	0.79

Slugging Average Against

1	E. Bedard	BAL	.337
2	D. McGowan	TOR	.348
3	F. Carmona	CLE	.352
4	J. Verlander	DET	.358
4	K. Escobar	LAA	.358
6	A. Burnett	TOR	.362
7	C. Wang	NYA	.368
8	R. Halladay	TOR	.373
9	J. Lackey	LAA	.375
10	J. Beckett	BOS	.377

Stolen Bases Allowed

1	T. Wakefield	BOS	41
2	A. Burnett	TOR	31
3	D. McGowan	TOR	29
4	J. Contreras	CHA	25
5	D. Cabrera	BAL	24
5	M. Mussina	NYA	24
7	D. Haren	OAK	20
7	R. Halladay	TOR	20
9	4 tied with		19

Caught Stealing

1	C. Sabathia	CLE	10
2	M. Batista	SEA	9
3	A. Sonnanstine	TB	8
3	T. Wakefield	BOS	8
3	A. Pettitte	NYA	8
3	S. Kazmir	TB	8
7	6 tied with	TOR	7

Pick Offs

1	M. Buehrle	CHA	5
1	A. Pettitte	NYA	5
1	R. Feierabend	SEA	5
4	M. Maroth	DET	4
4	J. Santana	MIN	4
4	J. Washburn	SEA	4
7	S. Trachsel	BAL	3
7	D. Reyes	MIN	3
7	H. Ramirez	SEA	3
7	S. Kazmir	TB	3

Net Stolen Bases

1	R. Feierabend	SEA	-16
2	A. Sonnanstine	TB	-15
3	M. Buehrle	CHA	-14
3	J. Garland	CHA	-14
5	M. Maroth	DET	-13
6	C. Sabathia	CLE	-12
7	J. Washburn	SEA	-11
7	D. Reyes	MIN	-11
7	J. Santana	MIN	-11
10	3 tied with		-10

Rate stats include only pitchers with at least 162 innings pitched.

Defense Efficiency Ratio (Highest)				Defense Efficiency Ratio (Lowest)				Double Plays				Hit By Pitch		
1	B. Bannister	KC	.739	1	K. Millwood	TEX	.643	1	F. Carmona	CLE	36	1	J. Verlander	DET	19
1	A. Burnett	TOR	.739	2	S. Kazmir	TB	.648	2	A. Pettitte	NYA	34	2	D. Cabrera	BAL	15
3	J. Guthrie	BAL	.730	3	J. Contreras	CHA	.657	2	C. Wang	NYA	34	2	J. Contreras	CHA	15
4	J. Santana	MIN	.729	4	F. Hernandez	SEA	.658	4	K. Escobar	LAA	33	4	D. Matsuzaka	BOS	13
5	D. McGowan	TOR	.727	5	A. Pettitte	NYA	.665	5	R. Halladay	TOR	30	5	J. Lackey	LAA	12
6	J. Verlander	DET	.721	6	B. Bonser	MIN	.668	6	L. DiNardo	OAK	29	5	A. Burnett	TOR	12
7	F. Carmona	CLE	.720	7	J. Bonderman	DET	.670	6	C. Sabathia	CLE	29	7	F. Carmona	CLE	11
8	T. Wakefield	BOS	.718	8	M. Batista	SEA	.675	8	C. Gaudin	OAK	27	8	J. Shields	TB	10
8	J. Shields	TB	.718	9	K. Escobar	LAA	.678	9	M. Buehrle	CHA	26	9	V. Padilla	TEX	9
10	E. Bedard	BAL	.717	10	P. Byrd	CLE	.679	9	F. Hernandez	SEA	26	10	Many tied with		8
								9	C. Silva	MIN	26				

Home/Away Split (Home)				Home/Away Split (Away)				Lefty/Righty Split (Negative)				Lefty/Righty Split (Positive)			
1	J. Blanton	OAK	-.069	1	B. Bannister	KC	.077	1	B. Bonser	MIN	-.106	1	M. Buehrle	CHA	.053
2	C. Wang	NYA	-.041	2	P. Byrd	CLE	.046	2	D. McGowan	TOR	-.074	2	E. Bedard	BAL	.037
3	K. Millwood	TEX	-.034	3	J. Guthrie	BAL	.040	3	J. Washburn	SEA	-.071	3	A. Pettitte	NYA	.032
4	C. Silva	MIN	-.034	4	D. Cabrera	BAL	.033	4	F. Hernandez	SEA	-.069	4	T. Wakefield	BOS	.024
5	A. Burnett	TOR	-.033	5	M. Buehrle	CHA	.028	5	B. Bannister	KC	-.065	5	A. Burnett	TOR	.019
6	M. Batista	SEA	-.032	6	J. Washburn	SEA	.024	6	D. Cabrera	BAL	-.063	6	G. Meche	KC	.017
7	J. Garland	CHA	-.031	7	J. Lackey	LAA	.019	7	C. Sabathia	CLE	-.061	7	J. Shields	TB	.013
8	D. McGowan	TOR	-.029	8	J. Bonderman	DET	.016	8	J. Contreras	CHA	-.051	8	D. Haren	OAK	.012
9	D. Haren	OAK	-.029	9	J. Beckett	BOS	.016	9	S. Kazmir	TB	-.049	9	J. Garland	CHA	.003
10	C. Sabathia	CLE	-.021	10	J. Contreras	CHA	.013	10	C. Wang	NYA	-.046	10	J. Bonderman	DET	-.001

Strikeout % (Lowest)				Strikeout % (Highest)				Walk % (Highest)				Walk % (Lowest)			
1	C. Silva	MIN	10	1	E. Bedard	BAL	30	1	D. Cabrera	BAL	13	1	P. Byrd	CLE	4
2	P. Byrd	CLE	11	2	S. Kazmir	TB	27	2	C. Gaudin	OAK	12	2	C. Sabathia	CLE	5
3	J. Garland	CHA	11	3	J. Santana	MIN	27	3	A. Burnett	TOR	11	3	J. Blanton	OAK	5
4	B. Bannister	KC	11	4	A. Burnett	TOR	25	4	S. Kazmir	TB	11	4	C. Silva	MIN	5
5	C. Wang	NYA	13	5	J. Vazquez	CHA	24	5	M. Batista	SEA	11	5	J. Shields	TB	5
6	J. Contreras	CHA	13	6	J. Beckett	BOS	24	6	D. Matsuzaka	BOS	11	6	J. Beckett	BOS	5
7	J. Washburn	SEA	14	7	D. Matsuzaka	BOS	23	7	J. Verlander	DET	10	7	R. Halladay	TOR	6
8	T. Wakefield	BOS	14	8	C. Sabathia	CLE	21	8	K. Millwood	TEX	10	8	M. Buehrle	CHA	6
9	M. Buehrle	CHA	14	9	J. Shields	TB	21	9	B. Bonser	MIN	9	9	D. Haren	OAK	6
10	J. Blanton	OAK	15	10	J. Verlander	DET	21	10	J. Contreras	CHA	9	10	J. Santana	MIN	6

Ground ball % (Lowest)				Ground ball % (Highest)				Line Drive % (Highest)				Line Drive % (Lowest)			
1	J. Washburn	SEA	37	1	F. Carmona	CLE	64	1	J. Garland	CHA	23	1	F. Carmona	CLE	14
2	J. Santana	MIN	38	2	F. Hernandez	SEA	61	2	K. Millwood	TEX	21	2	A. Burnett	TOR	15
3	P. Byrd	CLE	38	3	C. Wang	NYA	58	3	P. Byrd	CLE	21	3	S. Kazmir	TB	16
4	D. Matsuzaka	BOS	38	4	A. Burnett	TOR	55	4	J. Blanton	OAK	21	4	J. Beckett	BOS	16
5	T. Wakefield	BOS	39	5	R. Halladay	TOR	53	5	A. Pettitte	NYA	19	5	D. Cabrera	BAL	16
6	J. Garland	CHA	39	6	D. McGowan	TOR	53	6	C. Gaudin	OAK	19	6	D. McGowan	TOR	16
7	J. Vazquez	CHA	40	7	C. Gaudin	OAK	51	7	J. Guthrie	BAL	19	7	F. Hernandez	SEA	16
8	B. Bannister	KC	41	8	D. Cabrera	BAL	50	8	B. Bannister	KC	19	8	J. Shields	TB	16
9	J. Verlander	DET	41	9	J. Bonderman	DET	48	9	J. Lackey	LAA	19	9	M. Batista	SEA	17
10	J. Guthrie	BAL	42	10	E. Bedard	BAL	48	10	J. Verlander	DET	19	10	J. Vazquez	CHA	17

Rate stats include only pitchers with at least 162 innings pitched.

Infield Fly/Fly balls (Highest)				HR/OF (Lowest)				Out per Ground ball % (Highest)				Out per Outfield Fly % (Highest)			
1	J. Washburn	SEA	.15	1	K. Escobar	LAA	.06	1	B. Bannister	KC	82	1	J. Verlander	DET	87
2	J. Beckett	BOS	.14	2	C. Wang	NYA	.07	2	J. Lackey	LAA	80	2	P. Byrd	CLE	87
3	B. Bannister	KC	.13	3	R. Halladay	TOR	.07	3	J. Garland	CHA	80	3	N. Robertson	DET	86
4	T. Wakefield	BOS	.12	4	A. Pettitte	NYA	.07	4	J. Guthrie	BAL	79	4	T. Wakefield	BOS	85
5	J. Garland	CHA	.12	5	J. Blanton	OAK	.07	5	J. Santana	MIN	79	5	J. Bonderman	DET	85
6	A. Burnett	TOR	.12	6	J. Garland	CHA	.08	6	D. McGowan	TOR	79	6	B. Bonser	MIN	85
7	K. Escobar	LAA	.11	7	B. Bannister	KC	.08	7	E. Bedard	BAL	78	7	A. Burnett	TOR	85
8	J. Bonderman	DET	.11	8	M. Batista	SEA	.08	8	C. Gaudin	OAK	78	8	B. Bannister	KC	85
9	D. Haren	OAK	.11	9	J. Lackey	LAA	.08	9	R. Halladay	TOR	78	9	S. Kazmir	TB	84
10	G. Meche	KC	.11	10	C. Sabathia	CLE	.08	10	A. Burnett	TOR	78	10	K. Millwood	TEX	83

Runs per NIP				Runs per Ground ball				Runs per Line Drive				Runs per Outfield Fly			
1	C. Sabathia	CLE	-.03	1	B. Bannister	KC	.00	1	J. Verlander	DET	.32	1	K. Escobar	LAA	.14
2	J. Beckett	BOS	-.03	2	J. Lackey	LAA	.00	2	J. Guthrie	BAL	.32	2	B. Bannister	KC	.14
3	J. Santana	MIN	-.02	3	J. Guthrie	BAL	.01	3	J. Garland	CHA	.34	3	R. Halladay	TOR	.14
4	J. Shields	TB	-.02	4	J. Garland	CHA	.01	4	F. Carmona	CLE	.34	4	J. Blanton	OAK	.14
5	J. Vazquez	CHA	-.02	5	C. Gaudin	OAK	.01	5	A. Burnett	TOR	.35	5	J. Verlander	DET	.14
6	E. Bedard	BAL	-.01	6	J. Santana	MIN	.01	6	C. Wang	NYA	.35	6	P. Byrd	CLE	.15
7	D. Haren	OAK	-.01	7	A. Burnett	TOR	.01	7	J. Washburn	SEA	.35	7	T. Wakefield	BOS	.16
8	J. Blanton	OAK	-.00	8	D. McGowan	TOR	.02	8	J. Contreras	CHA	.35	8	S. Kazmir	TB	.16
9	F. Hernandez	SEA	.00	9	E. Bedard	BAL	.02	9	J. Blanton	OAK	.36	9	J. Garland	CHA	.16
10	J. Bonderman	DET	.01	10	D. Matsuzaka	BOS	.02	10	D. Haren	OAK	.37	10	N. Robertson	DET	.17

Not in Play RAA				Ground ball RAA				Line Drive RAA				Fly ball RAA			
1	C. Sabathia	CLE	-22	1	J. Lackey	LAA	-12	1	F. Carmona	CLE	-17	1	R. Halladay	TOR	-16
2	J. Santana	MIN	-20	2	J. Guthrie	BAL	-10	2	A. Burnett	TOR	-15	2	R. Betancourt	CLE	-14
3	J. Beckett	BOS	-18	3	J. Santana	MIN	-10	3	J. Vazquez	CHA	-12	3	J. Blanton	OAK	-14
4	J. Shields	TB	-17	4	B. Bannister	KC	-10	4	J. Verlander	DET	-12	4	C. Wang	NYA	-13
5	J. Vazquez	CHA	-17	5	D. Matsuzaka	BOS	-10	5	J. Shields	TB	-12	5	J. Westbrook	CLE	-13
6	D. Haren	OAK	-15	6	J. Garland	CHA	-10	6	J. Beckett	BOS	-12	6	J. Accardo	TOR	-12
7	E. Bedard	BAL	-14	7	C. Gaudin	OAK	-8	7	E. Bedard	BAL	-11	7	R. Jenks	CHA	-11
8	J. Blanton	OAK	-14	8	E. Bedard	BAL	-8	8	D. McGowan	TOR	-10	8	B. Tallet	TOR	-11
9	C. Schilling	BOS	-12	9	J. Putz	SEA	-8	9	D. Haren	OAK	-10	9	K. Escobar	LAA	-11
10	J. Lackey	LAA	-11	10	A. Burnett	TOR	-7	10	J. Santana	MIN	-10	10	J. Soria	KC	-10

Total Batted Ball RAA				WPA (Relievers)				WPA (Starters)				WPA/LI (All)			
1	E. Bedard	BAL	-40	1	Putz, J	SEA	6.17	1	Carmona, F	CLE	4.38	1	Carmona, F	CLE	3.94
2	C. Sabathia	CLE	-33	2	Betancourt, R	CLE	5.38	2	Bedard, E	BAL	3.87	2	Bedard, E	BAL	3.56
3	R. Betancourt	CLE	-31	3	Soria, J	KC	3.85	3	Sabathia, C	CLE	3.66	3	Beckett, J	BOS	3.47
4	J. Putz	SEA	-31	4	Papelbon, J	BOS	3.72	4	Halladay, R	TOR	3.38	4	Sabathia, C	CLE	3.24
5	J. Blanton	OAK	-31	5	Nathan, J	MIN	3.63	5	Lackey, J	LAA	3.12	5	Lackey, J	LAA	3.19
6	J. Santana	MIN	-30	6	Rodriguez, F	LAA	2.95	6	Escobar, K	LAA	3.11	6	Halladay, R	TOR	3.06
7	F. Carmona	CLE	-29	7	Okajima, H	BOS	2.93	7	Beckett, J	BOS	3.02	7	Santana, J	MIN	2.91
8	R. Halladay	TOR	-29	8	Neshek, P	MIN	2.83	8	Shields, J	TB	2.83	8	Betancourt, R	CLE	2.91
9	J. Beckett	BOS	-29	9	Benoit, J	TEX	2.48	9	Haren, D	OAK	2.77	9	Blanton, J	OAK	2.78
10	J. Lackey	LAA	-27	10	Perez, R	CLE	2.41	10	Wang, C	NYA	2.28	10	Escobar, K	LAA	2.58

National League Team Stats

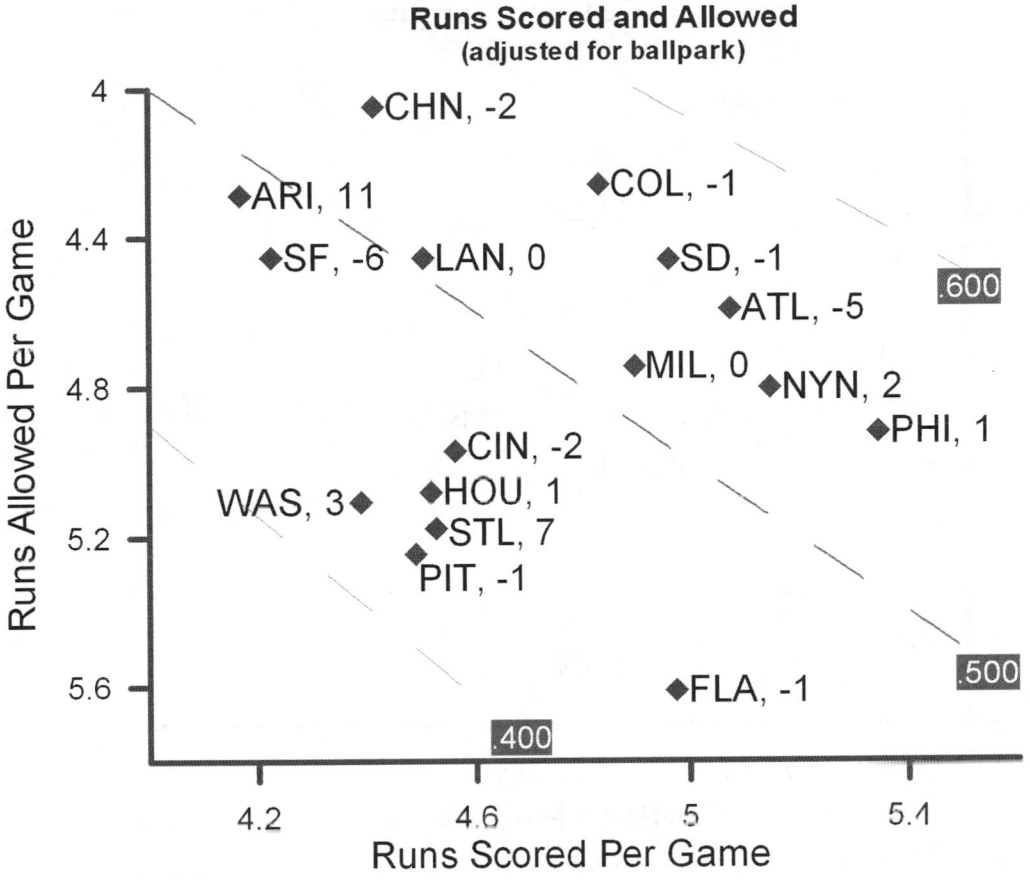

Runs Scored and Allowed
(adjusted for ballpark)

Notes: The dotted lines represent winning percentage based on run differential. The number after each team name represents the difference between the team's actual record and its run differential record.

Team	Team Record					Scoring Runs			Preventing Runs				Projection	
	W	L	RS	RA	RS-RA	AB/RSP	BA/RSP	HR	ERA	HRA	K	DER	PWINS	VAR
ARI	90	72	712	732	-20	1,306	.249	171	4.13	169	1,088	.694	79	11
ATL	84	78	810	733	77	1,452	.291	176	4.11	172	1,106	.700	89	-5
CHN	85	77	752	690	62	1,468	.279	151	4.05	165	1,211	.707	87	-2
CIN	72	90	783	853	-70	1,382	.263	204	4.94	198	1,068	.679	74	-2
COL	90	73	860	758	102	1,586	.276	171	4.32	164	967	.702	91	-1
FLA	71	91	790	891	-101	1,439	.268	201	4.95	176	1,142	.663	72	-1
HOU	73	89	723	813	-90	1,404	.266	167	4.68	206	1,109	.686	72	1
LAN	82	80	735	727	8	1,459	.278	129	4.20	146	1,184	.685	82	0
MIL	83	79	801	776	25	1,358	.261	231	4.41	161	1,174	.680	83	0
WAS	73	89	673	783	-110	1,366	.261	123	4.58	187	931	.700	70	3
NYN	88	74	804	750	54	1,454	.276	177	4.26	165	1,134	.702	86	2
PHI	89	73	892	821	71	1,577	.259	213	4.73	198	1,050	.687	88	1
PIT	68	94	724	846	-122	1,369	.272	148	4.93	174	997	.675	69	-1
STL	78	84	725	829	-104	1,368	.274	141	4.65	168	945	.690	71	7
SD	89	74	741	666	75	1,335	.271	171	3.71	119	1,136	.701	90	-1
SF	71	91	683	720	-37	1,349	.264	131	4.19	133	1,057	.698	77	-6
Average	80	82	763	774	-11	1,417	.269	169	4.43	169	1,081	.691	81	-1

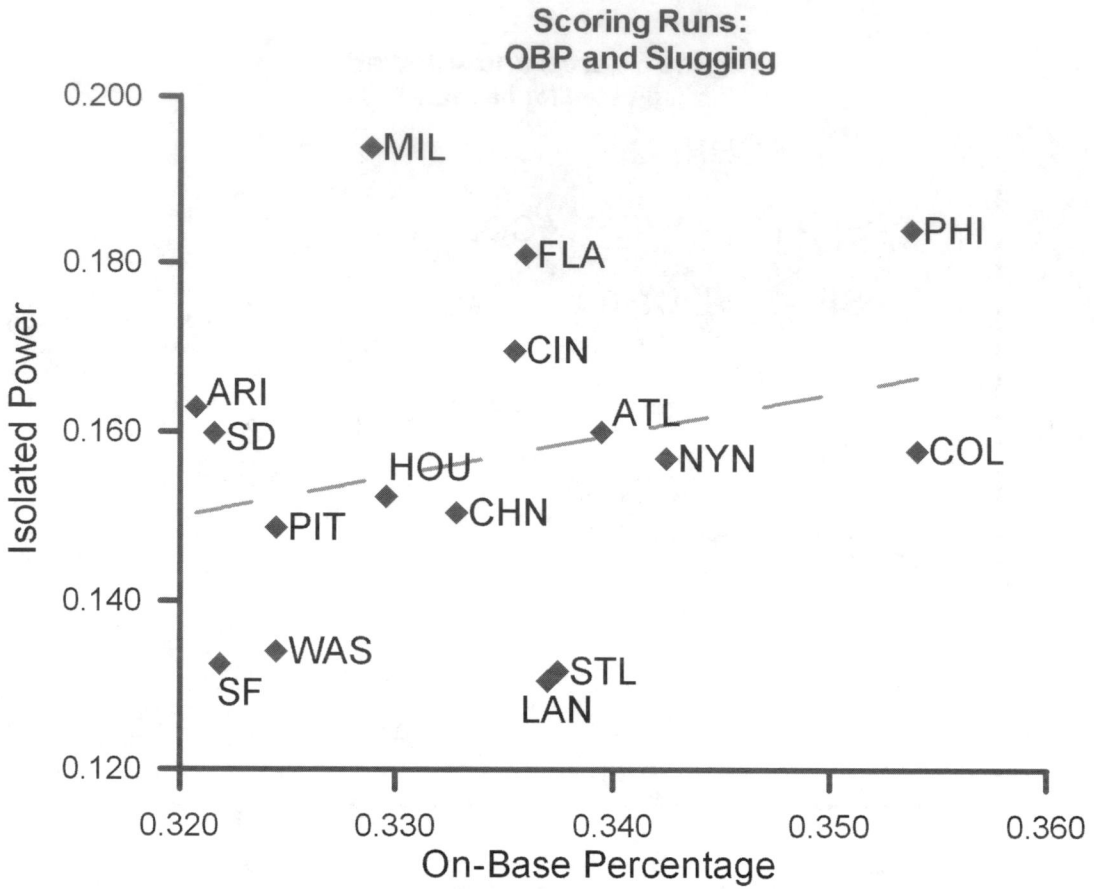

Scoring Runs:
OBP and Slugging

The dotted line shows the relationship between ISO and OBP.

Team	Runs	PA	H	1B	2B	3B	HR	TB	SO	BB	HBP	SH	SF	BA	OBP	SLG	GPA	ISO
ARI	712	6,101	1,350	853	286	40	171	2,229	1,111	532	57	55	58	.250	.321	.413	.248	.163
ATL	810	6,374	1,562	1,031	328	27	176	2,472	1,149	534	49	55	47	.275	.339	.435	.261	.160
CHN	752	6,268	1,530	1,011	340	28	151	2,379	1,054	500	40	48	37	.271	.333	.422	.255	.150
CIN	783	6,332	1,496	976	293	23	204	2,447	1,113	536	66	73	46	.267	.335	.436	.260	.170
COL	860	6,498	1,591	1,071	313	36	171	2,489	1,152	622	58	83	44	.280	.354	.437	.269	.158
FLA	790	6,344	1,504	925	340	38	201	2,523	1,332	521	82	72	42	.267	.336	.448	.263	.181
HOU	723	6,324	1,457	967	293	30	167	2,311	1,043	547	55	77	40	.260	.330	.412	.251	.152
LAN	735	6,282	1,544	1,104	276	35	129	2,277	864	511	41	58	55	.275	.337	.406	.253	.131
MIL	801	6,238	1,455	877	310	37	231	2,532	1,137	501	76	60	47	.262	.329	.456	.262	.194
WAS	673	6,201	1,415	952	309	31	123	2,155	1,128	524	53	63	41	.256	.325	.390	.244	.134
NYN	804	6,344	1,543	1,045	294	27	177	2,422	981	549	54	77	58	.275	.342	.432	.262	.157
PHI	892	6,537	1,558	978	326	41	213	2,605	1,205	641	90	65	52	.274	.354	.458	.274	.184
PIT	724	6,214	1,463	962	322	31	148	2,291	1,135	463	71	60	51	.263	.325	.411	.249	.149
STL	725	6,211	1,513	1,080	279	13	141	2,241	909	506	54	68	54	.274	.337	.405	.253	.132
SD	741	6,326	1,408	884	322	31	171	2,305	1,229	557	49	64	44	.251	.322	.411	.247	.160
SF	683	6,213	1,407	972	267	37	131	2,141	907	532	39	67	36	.254	.322	.387	.241	.133
Average	763	6,300	1,487	981	306	32	169	2,364	1,091	536	58	65	47	.266	.334	.423	.256	.157

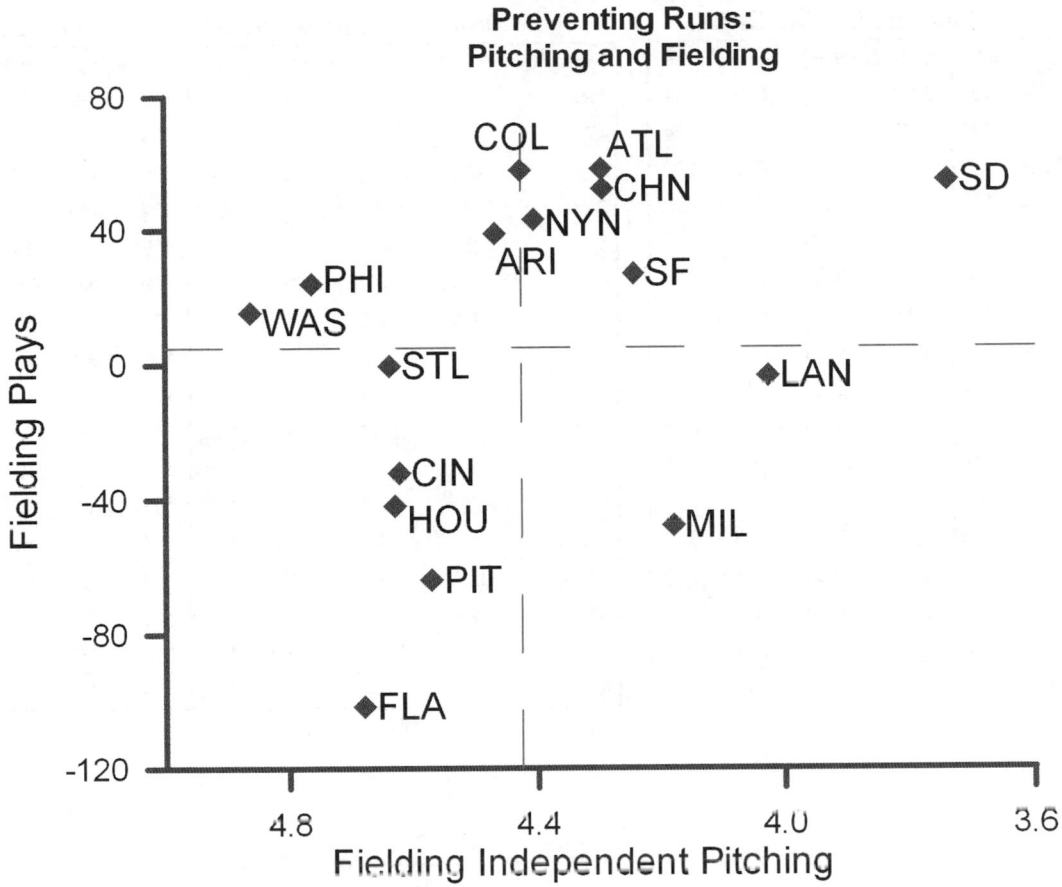

Preventing Runs:
Pitching and Fielding

The dotted lines represent the league averages.

Team	RA	IP	BFP	H	HR	TBA	K	BB	ShO	Sv	Op	%Save	Holds	ERA	FIP	UERA	DER
ARI	732	1441	6,216	1,446	169	2,314	1,088	546	12	51	66	77%	85	4.13	4.47	0.44	.694
ATL	733	1456	6,263	1,442	172	2,308	1,106	537	6	36	51	71%	64	4.11	4.30	0.42	.700
CHN	690	1446	6,186	1,340	165	2,173	1,211	573	10	39	53	74%	67	4.05	4.29	0.25	.707
CIN	853	1449	6,354	1,605	198	2,596	1,068	482	7	34	62	55%	59	4.94	4.62	0.35	.679
COL	758	1472	6,293	1,497	164	2,377	967	504	7	39	68	57%	80	4.32	4.43	0.32	.702
FLA	891	1443	6,544	1,617	176	2,509	1,142	661	4	40	64	63%	106	4.95	4.68	0.61	.663
HOU	813	1464	6,417	1,566	206	2,603	1,109	510	6	38	63	60%	65	4.68	4.63	0.32	.686
LAN	727	1450	6,196	1,443	146	2,204	1,184	518	6	43	60	72%	73	4.20	4.03	0.31	.685
MIL	776	1444	6,285	1,513	161	2,369	1,174	507	6	49	69	71%	95	4.41	4.18	0.42	.680
WAS	783	1446	6,333	1,502	187	2,417	931	580	6	46	73	63%	95	4.58	4.86	0.29	.700
NYN	750	1452	6,293	1,415	165	2,272	1,134	570	10	39	56	70%	78	4.26	4.41	0.39	.702
PHI	821	1458	6,385	1,555	198	2,546	1,050	558	5	42	63	67%	90	4.73	4.76	0.33	.687
PIT	846	1447	6,374	1,627	174	2,528	997	518	5	32	51	63%	68	4.93	4.57	0.33	.675
STL	829	1435	6,283	1,514	168	2,413	945	509	8	34	45	76%	63	4.65	4.64	0.55	.690
SD	666	1484	6,254	1,406	119	2,109	1,136	474	20	45	67	67%	76	3.71	3.74	0.33	.701
SF	720	1453	6,299	1,442	133	2,243	1,057	593	10	37	60	62%	86	4.19	4.24	0.27	.698
Average	774	1452	6,311	1,496	169	2,374	1,081	540	8	40	61	66%	78	4.43	4.43	0.37	.691

Running and Miscellaneous Batting Stats

Team	SB	CS	SB%	GDP	P/PA	BABIP	H-A	L-R
ARI	109	24	82%	121	3.80	.282	.026	-.004
ATL	64	30	68%	137	3.77	.314	-.010	-.004
CHN	86	33	72%	127	3.74	.308	.019	-.002
CIN	97	31	76%	140	3.73	.298	.011	-.020
COL	100	31	76%	140	3.88	.322	.038	-.007
FLA	105	34	76%	107	3.74	.315	.014	.010
HOU	65	33	66%	142	3.78	.291	.012	.018
LAN	137	50	73%	116	3.64	.303	.007	.005
MIL	96	32	75%	112	3.72	.289	.018	.035
WAS	69	23	75%	143	3.79	.300	-.002	.020
NYN	200	46	81%	114	3.73	.303	-.007	.017
PHI	138	19	88%	125	3.88	.311	.011	.011
PIT	68	30	69%	130	3.76	.303	.008	.022
STL	56	33	63%	154	3.72	.303	.007	.006
SD	55	24	70%	113	3.72	.291	-.026	.018
SF	119	33	78%	142	3.65	.281	.001	-.006
Average	98	32	76%	129	3.75	.301	.008	.008

Win Probability Added / Win Shares

Team	Bat	Starters	Bullpen	LI	Bat	Pitch	Field	WSAge	CWS
ARI	-1.2	2.7	7.5	1.07	102	116	52	27.2	1,693
ATL	0.1	-1.9	4.8	0.97	124	87	41	28.9	2,315
CHN	-2.2	3.4	2.7	1.05	99	106	50	29.1	2,120
CIN	-0.8	-3.5	-4.7	1.07	104	76	36	29.3	1,995
COL	9.5	-1.2	0.2	1.10	119	102	49	27.6	1,745
FLA	1.2	-13.2	2.0	1.03	129	56	28	26.4	958
HOU	-8.2	-2.5	2.7	1.11	107	76	36	30.1	2,172
LAN	-5.0	-0.3	6.3	0.97	105	99	41	29.3	2,870
MIL	1.5	-0.4	0.9	1.09	126	86	37	26.9	1,403
NYN	3.9	1.7	1.4	1.02	138	86	41	30.3	3,948
PHI	10.8	-3.7	0.9	1.10	145	82	39	28.5	1,910
PIT	-9.1	-4.7	0.8	1.00	103	66	35	26.9	1,006
SD	-6.6	6.2	7.9	1.12	125	101	40	29.8	2,566
SF	-11.0	2.8	-1.8	1.17	83	89	41	31.3	2,715
STL	-2.9	-6.8	6.8	0.82	121	76	37	30.0	2,436
WAS	-9.7	-3.6	5.3	1.14	104	73	42	27.7	1,234
Average	-1.9	-1.6	2.7	1.05	115	86	40	28.7	2,068

Leverage Index (LI) for bullpen only.

Fielding and Miscellaneous Pitching Stats

Team	DER	Fld %	UER	SBA	CS	%CS	PO	E	TE	FE	DP	GIDP	H-A	R-L
ARI	.694	.983	70	130	42	32%	18	106	44	60	157	138	.007	-.029
ATL	.700	.983	68	128	30	23%	9	107	50	56	141	119	-.005	-.010
CHN	.707	.984	40	140	24	17%	11	94	40	52	134	117	.009	-.011
CIN	.679	.984	57	119	31	26%	9	95	35	59	155	130	-.011	.009
COL	.702	.989	52	121	25	21%	8	68	38	30	180	154	.006	.000
FLA	.663	.977	98	127	33	26%	10	137	68	69	159	128	-.005	.015
HOU	.686	.983	52	112	28	25%	9	103	39	64	128	112	-.021	.002
LAN	.685	.981	50	142	46	32%	10	114	58	54	160	142	-.004	.017
MIL	.680	.982	68	123	24	20%	10	109	50	53	144	125	-.023	-.002
WAS	.700	.982	47	117	37	32%	11	109	58	47	153	134	-.029	.004
NYN	.702	.983	63	134	29	22%	9	101	50	50	124	110	-.014	-.027
PHI	.687	.986	54	123	39	32%	9	89	34	54	162	135	.008	-.017
PIT	.675	.986	53	145	35	24%	12	83	26	55	190	163	-.022	-.003
STL	.690	.980	88	92	34	37%	11	121	47	72	155	131	-.017	-.006
SD	.701	.985	55	209	20	10%	8	92	39	50	147	126	-.034	-.013
SF	.698	.986	43	110	33	30%	7	88	32	54	148	130	.003	-.005
Average	.691	.984	60	130	32	25%	10	101	44	55	152	131	-.009	-.005

Batted Ball Batting Stats

Team	% of PA K%	BB%	% of Batted Balls GB%	LD%	FB%	IF/F	HR/OF	Out % GB	OF	Runs Per Event NIP	GB	LD	OF	Total Runs vs. Avg. NIP	GB	LD	FB	Tot
ARI	18	10	41	18	41	.13	.11	75	84	.05	.04	.39	.18	-6	-17	-40	0	-63
ATL	18	9	44	19	37	.09	.11	72	82	.04	.06	.41	.19	-13	17	17	15	37
CHN	17	9	45	19	36	.08	.10	73	82	.04	.05	.39	.18	-17	18	9	-3	7
CIN	18	10	42	19	39	.12	.13	74	85	.05	.05	.40	.20	-3	-4	1	18	13
COL	18	10	43	21	36	.08	.11	74	82	.06	.04	.39	.20	20	5	28	19	73
FLA	21	10	40	19	41	.10	.12	73	81	.03	.05	.42	.22	-27	-3	8	61	39
HOU	16	10	43	18	39	.12	.10	73	84	.06	.05	.38	.18	5	-2	-33	-15	-44
LAN	14	9	40	19	35	.10	.08	73	84	.07	.05	.38	.15	9	22	-3	-59	-32
MIL	18	9	41	18	41	.10	.14	74	86	.04	.05	.43	.21	-13	-3	3	56	42
NYN	15	10	45	19	36	.10	.11	74	84	.06	.05	.41	.18	13	7	30	-12	38
PHI	18	11	41	19	40	.09	.13	72	82	.06	.06	.40	.22	32	9	9	76	125
PIT	18	9	42	19	39	.09	.09	75	82	.03	.04	.40	.17	-28	-22	-6	-7	-64
SD	19	10	40	18	41	.08	.10	77	82	.04	.03	.40	.18	-16	-44	-25	14	-71
SF	15	9	46	17	37	.11	.08	76	84	.06	.03	.38	.15	9	-21	-35	-62	-109
STL	15	9	44	19	37	.10	.09	73	85	.06	.05	.39	.14	8	11	7	-62	-36
WAS	18	9	46	19	35	.10	.09	75	82	.04	.04	.39	.17	-13	-22	-15	-52	-101
MLB Average	*17*	*9*	*43*	*19*	*38*	*.10*	*.10*	*74*	*83*	*.05*	*.05*	*.40*	*.18*	--	--	--	--	--

Batted Ball Pitching Stats

Team	% of PA K%	BB%	% of Batted Balls GB%	LD%	FB%	IF/F	HR/OF	Out % GB	OF	Runs Per Event NIP	GB	LD	OF	Total Runs vs. Avg. NIP	GB	LD	FB	Tot
ARI	18	10	44	19	37	.09	.11	73	83	.05	.05	.37	.19	3	-0	-19	4	-12
ATL	18	9	45	19	36	.08	.11	74	86	.04	.05	.40	.17	10	0	-9	-27	-46
CHN	20	10	41	18	41	.11	.10	75	85	.04	.04	.39	.17	-3	-22	-36	-21	-83
CIN	17	9	40	20	40	.11	.12	72	83	.04	.06	.39	.20	-13	21	22	45	74
COL	15	9	46	18	35	.09	.11	77	82	.06	.02	.40	.20	-0	-42	-5	13	-34
FLA	17	11	42	20	38	.10	.11	69	82	.07	.07	.39	.19	42	46	26	16	130
HOU	17	9	44	17	39	.09	.12	74	81	.04	.05	.42	.22	-13	19	-8	67	65
LAN	19	9	45	19	35	.11	.10	73	85	.03	.05	.40	.17	-26	8	-2	-51	-71
MIL	19	9	42	19	39	.10	.10	71	84	.04	.07	.40	.17	-24	30	4	-21	-11
NYN	18	10	41	19	40	.10	.10	75	84	.05	.04	.41	.16	5	-20	0	-30	-45
PHI	16	10	43	20	36	.10	.12	75	82	.06	.04	.40	.22	15	-13	32	43	78
PIT	16	9	44	19	37	.09	.11	72	81	.06	.05	.39	.20	9	17	6	41	73
SD	18	8	46	18	36	.09	.08	77	83	.03	.03	.40	.15	-35	-31	-24	-70	-160
SF	17	10	43	19	38	.10	.08	76	82	.06	.04	.39	.16	17	-22	-14	-27	-47
STL	15	9	43	19	38	.10	.10	75	82	.06	.04	.40	.19	11	-23	23	26	37
WAS	15	10	40	18	42	.10	.10	73	86	.07	.05	.39	.16	25	7	4	-3	34
MLB Average	*17*	*9*	*43*	*19*	*38*	*.10*	*.10*	*74*	*83*	*.05*	*.05*	*.40*	*.18*	--	--	--	--	--

National League Leaderboards
Batting Leaders

Base Runs

1	D Wright	NYN	131
2	M Cabrera	FLA	129
3	P Fielder	MIL	124
4	H Ramirez	FLA	124
5	M Holliday	COL	121
6	J Rollins	PHI	119
7	A Gonzalez	SD	118
8	A Pujols	STL	117
9	R Howard	PHI	116
10	C Jones	ATL	112

Runs Scored

1	J. Rollins	PHI	139
2	H. Ramirez	FLA	125
3	M. Holliday	COL	120
4	J. Reyes	NYN	119
5	D. Uggla	FLA	113
5	D. Wright	NYN	113
7	P. Fielder	MIL	109
8	C. Jones	ATL	108
9	B. Phillips	CIN	107
10	A. Rowand	PHI	105

Runs Batted In

1	M. Holliday	COL	137
2	R. Howard	PHI	136
3	M. Cabrera	FLA	119
3	C. Lee	HOU	119
3	P. Fielder	MIL	119
6	B. Hawpe	COL	116
7	C. Beltran	NYN	112
8	G. Atkins	COL	111
9	D. Wright	NYN	107
10	A. Dunn	CIN	106

Gross Production Average (GPA)

1	C. Jones	ATL	.346
2	A. Pujols	STL	.342
3	M. Cabrera	FLA	.331
3	D. Wright	NYN	.331
5	P. Fielder	MIL	.329
6	H. Ramirez	FLA	.324
7	C. Utley	PHI	.317
8	R. Howard	PHI	.313
9	A. Gonzalez	SD	.306
10	D. Young	WAS	.305

Batting Average

1	M. Holliday	COL	.340
2	C. Jones	ATL	.337
3	E. Renteria	ATL	.332
3	C. Utley	PHI	.332
3	H. Ramirez	FLA	.332
6	A. Pujols	STL	.327
7	D. Wright	NYN	.325
8	T. Helton	COL	.320
8	D. Young	WAS	.320
8	M. Cabrera	FLA	.320

On-Base Percentage

1	T. Helton	COL	.434
2	A. Pujols	STL	.429
3	C. Jones	ATL	.425
4	D. Wright	NYN	.416
5	C. Utley	PHI	.410
6	M. Holliday	COL	.405
7	M. Cabrera	FLA	.401
8	D. Lee	CHN	.400
8	P. Burrell	PHI	.400
10	P. Fielder	MIL	.395

Slugging Percentage

1	P. Fielder	MIL	.618
2	M. Holliday	COL	.607
3	C. Jones	ATL	.604
4	R. Howard	PHI	.584
5	A. Pujols	STL	.568
6	C. Utley	PHI	.566
7	M. Cabrera	FLA	.565
8	H. Ramirez	FLA	.562
9	A. Soriano	CHN	.560
10	A. Dunn	CIN	.554

OPS (On-Base Plus Slugging)

1	C. Jones	ATL	1.029
2	P. Fielder	MIL	1.013
3	M. Holliday	COL	1.012
4	A. Pujols	STL	.997
5	C. Utley	PHI	.976
5	R. Howard	PHI	.976
7	M. Cabrera	FLA	.965
8	D. Wright	NYN	.963
9	H. Ramirez	FLA	.948
10	A. Dunn	CIN	.940

Plate Appearances

1	J. Rollins	PHI	778
2	J. Reyes	NYN	765
3	J. Pierre	LAN	729
4	D. Uggla	FLA	728
5	R. Zimmerman	WAS	722
6	A. Gonzalez	SD	720
7	M. Holliday	COL	713
8	D. Wright	NYN	711
9	H. Ramirez	FLA	706
10	B. Phillips	CIN	702

Outs

1	J. Rollins	PHI	521
2	J. Reyes	NYN	517
3	R. Zimmerman	WAS	506
4	B. Phillips	CIN	497
4	J. Pierre	LAN	497
6	D. Uggla	FLA	488
7	F. Lopez	WAS	475
8	A. Gonzalez	SD	470
8	J. Francoeur	ATL	470
10	C. Lee	HOU	469

Hits

1	M. Holliday	COL	216
2	J. Rollins	PHI	212
2	H. Ramirez	FLA	212
4	J. Pierre	LAN	196
4	D. Wright	NYN	196
6	J. Reyes	NYN	191
7	C. Lee	HOU	190
8	A. Rowand	PHI	189
9	M. Cabrera	FLA	188
9	J Francoeur	ATL	188

Total Bases

1	M. Holliday	COL	386
2	J. Rollins	PHI	380
3	H. Ramirez	FLA	359
4	P. Fielder	MIL	354
5	M. Cabrera	FLA	332
6	C. Lee	HOU	331
7	D. Wright	NYN	330
8	A. Gonzalez	SD	324
8	A. Soriano	CHN	324
10	A. Pujols	STL	321

Singles

1	J. Pierre	LAN	164
2	J. Reyes	NYN	131
3	J. Francoeur	ATL	129
3	H. Ramirez	FLA	129
5	F. Sanchez	PIT	126
6	B. Phillips	CIN	125
7	J. Rollins	PHI	124
7	M. Holliday	COL	124
7	R. Furcal	LAN	124
10	D. Wright	NYN	123

Doubles

1	M. Holliday	COL	50
2	D. Uggla	FLA	49
3	C. Utley	PHI	48
3	H. Ramirez	FLA	48
5	A. Gonzalez	SD	46
6	A. Rowand	PHI	45
7	K. Greene	SD	44
8	R. Zimmerman	WAS	43
8	C. Lee	HOU	43
8	R. Church	WAS	43

Triples

1	J. Rollins	PHI	20
2	J. Reyes	NYN	12
3	K. Johnson	ATL	10
4	A. Amezaga	FLA	9
4	H. Pence	HOU	9
4	C. Hart	MIL	9
4	O. Hudson	ARI	9
4	D. Roberts	SF	9
9	E. Byrnes	ARI	8
9	J. Pierre	LAN	8

Home Runs

1	P. Fielder	MIL	50
2	R. Howard	PHI	47
3	A. Dunn	CIN	40
4	M. Holliday	COL	36
5	M. Cabrera	FLA	34
5	L. Berkman	HOU	34
5	R. Braun	MIL	34
8	C. Beltran	NYN	33
8	A. Soriano	CHN	33
10	3 tied with		32

Rate stats include only players with at least 502 plate appearances.

Strikeouts				Walks				Intentional Walks				Hit By Pitch			
1	R. Howard	PHI	199	1	B. Bonds	SF	132	1	B. Bonds	SF	43	1	C. Utley	PHI	25
2	D. Uggla	FLA	167	2	T. Helton	COL	116	2	R. Howard	PHI	35	2	A. Rowand	PHI	19
3	A. Dunn	CIN	165	3	P. Burrell	PHI	114	3	M. Cabrera	FLA	23	3	J. Willingham	FLA	16
4	M. Cameron	SD	160	4	R. Howard	PHI	107	4	A. Pujols	STL	22	4	R. Weeks	MIL	14
5	J. Bay	PIT	141	5	A. Dunn	CIN	101	5	P. Fielder	MIL	21	4	P. Fielder	MIL	14
5	C. Young	ARI	141	6	A. Pujols	STL	99	6	T. Helton	COL	16	4	E. Encarnacion	CIN	14
7	A. Gonzalez	SD	140	7	L. Berkman	HOU	94	7	K. Griffey Jr.	CIN	14	7	D. Uggla	FLA	13
8	A. Jones	ATL	138	7	D. Wright	NYN	94	8	J. Reyes	NYN	13	7	A. Boone	FLA	13
9	B. Hawpe	COL	137	9	P. Fielder	MIL	90	9	A. Ethier	LAN	12	7	C. Hart	MIL	13
10	A. LaRoche	PIT	131	10	K. Griffey Jr.	CIN	85	10	L. Berkman	HOU	11	10	4 tied with		12
								10	B. Hawpe	COL	11				

Stolen Bases				Caught Stealing				Net Stolen Bases				Sacrifice Hits			
1	J. Reyes	NYN	78	1	J. Reyes	NYN	21	1	E. Byrnes	ARI	36	1	J. Pierre	LAN	20
2	J. Pierre	LAN	64	2	J. Pierre	LAN	15	1	J. Reyes	NYN	36	2	O. Vizquel	SF	14
3	H. Ramirez	FLA	51	3	H. Ramirez	FLA	14	3	J. Pierre	LAN	34	3	K. Matsui	COL	8
4	E. Byrnes	ARI	50	4	W. Harris	ATL	11	4	J. Rollins	PHI	29	3	C. Burke	HOU	8
5	J. Rollins	PHI	41	5	F. Lopez	WAS	9	4	S. Victorino	PHI	29	3	R. Theriot	CHN	8
6	S. Victorino	PHI	37	5	W. Taveras	COL	9	6	D. Wright	NYN	24	6	D. Eckstein	STL	7
7	D. Wright	NYN	34	5	R. Martin	LAN	9	6	K. Matsui	COL	24	6	C. Biggio	HOU	7
8	W. Taveras	COL	33	8	B. Phillips	CIN	8	8	H. Ramirez	FLA	23	6	W. Taveras	COL	7
9	K. Matsui	COL	32	8	R. Freel	CIN	8	9	R. Weeks	MIL	21	6	L. Castillo	NYN	7
9	B. Phillips	CIN	32	10	3 tied with		7	9	D. Roberts	SF	21	6	J. Wilson	PIT	7

BA on Balls in Play (BABIP)				BA with RISP				Situational Hitting Runs				Sacrifice Flies			
1	M. Holliday	COL	.377	1	M. Cabrera	FLA	.378	1	J. Willingham	FLA	13.6	1	C. Lee	HOU	13
2	E. Renteria	ATL	.375	2	D. Lee	CHN	.364	2	J. Francoeur	ATL	9.3	2	K. Greene	SD	11
3	D. Lee	CHN	.364	3	E. Encarnacion	CIN	.360	3	M. Cabrera	FLA	8.7	2	D. Uggla	FLA	11
4	C. Utley	PHI	.362	4	J. Willingham	FLA	.345	4	E. Encarnacion	CIN	8.4	4	C. Beltran	NYN	10
5	D. Young	WAS	.356	5	F. Sanchez	PIT	.344	5	R. Howard	PHI	7.7	4	P. Lo Duca	NYN	10
6	D. Wright	NYN	.356	6	J. Francoeur	ATL	.341	6	F. Sanchez	PIT	7.4	4	G. Atkins	COL	10
7	M. Cabrera	FLA	.355	7	A. Ramirez	CHN	.340	7	P. Feliz	SF	6.8	7	R. Durham	SF	9
8	H. Ramirez	FLA	.353	8	C. Hart	MIL	.339	8	A. Kearns	WAS	6.1	7	K. Griffey Jr.	CIN	9
9	C. Jones	ATL	.348	9	M. Holliday	COL	.333	9	A. Ramirez	CHN	6.0	7	A. Jones	ATL	9
10	A. Rowand	PHI	.345	10	E. Renteria	ATL	.331	10	B. Molina	SF	5.9	7	F. Sanchez	PIT	9

Home/Away Split (Home)				Home/Away Split (Away)				Lefty/Righty Split (Positive)				Lefty/Righty Split (Negative)			
1	D. Lee	CHN	.102	1	A. Pujols	STL	-.064	1	R. Zimmerman	WAS	.132	1	C. Jones	ATL	-.117
2	M. Holliday	COL	.087	2	A. Soriano	CHN	-.064	2	A. Ramirez	CHN	.122	2	J. Willingham	FLA	-.081
3	A. Ramirez	CHN	.082	3	B. Giles	SD	-.057	3	B. Hawpe	COL	.108	3	D. Young	WAS	-.042
4	T. Tulowitzki	COL	.073	4	C. Delgado	NYN	-.055	4	R. Martin	LAN	.094	4	L. Berkman	HOU	-.038
5	C. Biggio	HOU	.072	5	K. Greene	SD	-.055	5	M. Cabrera	FLA	.088	5	L. Gonzalez	LAN	-.037
6	P. Burrell	PHI	.067	6	R. Martin	LAN	-.054	6	H. Ramirez	FLA	.084	6	A. Soriano	CHN	-.032
7	D. Young	WAS	.065	7	A. Gonzalez	SD	-.047	7	R. Howard	PHI	.080	7	G. Atkins	COL	-.029
8	C. Lee	HOU	.064	8	A. Kearns	WAS	-.044	8	K. Kouzmanoff	SD	.080	8	O. Hudson	ARI	-.027
9	C. Utley	PHI	.061	9	L. Berkman	HOU	-.043	9	T. Helton	COL	.079	9	M. Holliday	COL	-.023
10	D. Uggla	FLA	.059	10	J. Francoeur	ATL	-.038	10	P. Fielder	MIL	.078	10	M. DeRosa	CHN	-.018

Rate stats include only players with at least 502 plate appearances.

Strikeout % (Lowest)

1	J. Pierre	LAN	5
2	M. Loretta	HOU	8
3	O. Vizquel	SF	8
4	R. Theriot	CHN	8
5	A. Pujols	STL	9
6	J. Wilson	PIT	9
7	C. Lee	HOU	9
8	J. Reyes	NYN	10
9	B. Molina	SF	10
10	R. Furcal	LAN	11

Strikeout % (Highest)

1	R. Howard	PHI	31
2	A. Dunn	CIN	26
3	B. Hall	MIL	25
4	M. Cameron	SD	25
5	J. Bay	PIT	23
6	D. Uggla	FLA	23
7	R. Weeks	MIL	23
8	B. Hawpe	COL	23
9	C. Young	ARI	23
10	A. Soriano	CHN	21

Walk % (Highest)

1	P. Burrell	PHI	20
2	R. Weeks	MIL	18
3	T. Helton	COL	17
4	R. Howard	PHI	17
5	A. Dunn	CIN	17
6	A. Pujols	STL	16
7	P. Fielder	MIL	15
8	L. Berkman	HOU	15
9	D. Wright	NYN	14
10	B. Hawpe	COL	14

Walk % (Lowest)

1	B. Molina	SF	3
2	C. Biggio	HOU	5
3	P. Feliz	SF	5
4	J. Pierre	LAN	5
5	K. Greene	SD	6
6	A. Soriano	CHN	6
7	F. Sanchez	PIT	6
8	R. Belliard	WAS	6
9	B. Phillips	CIN	6
10	J. Hardy	MIL	6

Ground ball % (Lowest)

1	P. Burrell	PHI	30
2	G. Atkins	COL	31
3	R. Howard	PHI	31
4	A. Soriano	CHN	34
5	D. Uggla	FLA	34
6	A. Dunn	CIN	35
7	P. Fielder	MIL	35
8	K. Greene	SD	35
9	K. Griffey Jr.	CIN	35
10	E. Byrnes	ARI	35

Ground ball % (Highest)

1	J. Pierre	LAN	53
2	O. Hudson	ARI	52
3	R. Winn	SF	51
4	R. Furcal	LAN	50
5	F. Lopez	WAS	50
6	R. Theriot	CHN	49
7	R. Martin	LAN	48
8	S. Victorino	PHI	47
9	B. Phillips	CIN	47
10	A. Ethier	LAN	46

Line Drive % (Highest)

1	G. Atkins	COL	24
2	R. Howard	PHI	24
3	T. Helton	COL	24
4	D. Wright	NYN	23
5	B. Hall	MIL	23
6	E. Renteria	ATL	23
7	F. Sanchez	PIT	22
8	R. Church	WAS	22
9	M. DeRosa	CHN	22
10	M. Loretta	HOU	22

Line Drive % (Lowest)

1	R. Durham	SF	13
2	C. Young	ARI	15
3	P. Feliz	SF	15
4	D. Uggla	FLA	16
5	K. Griffey Jr.	CIN	16
6	J. Bautista	PIT	16
7	C. Lee	HOU	16
8	S. Drew	ARI	16
9	J. Bay	PIT	17
10	S. Victorino	PHI	17

Infield Fly/Fly balls (Lowest)

1	O. Hudson	ARI	.02
2	M. DeRosa	CHN	.03
2	R. Howard	PHI	.03
4	A. Ethier	LAN	.03
5	F. Lopez	WAS	.03
6	C. Jones	ATL	.04
7	K. Kouzmanoff	SD	.04
8	D. Wright	NYN	.04
9	M. Holliday	COL	.04
10	A. Soriano	CHN	.05

HR/OF (Highest)

1	R. Howard	PHI	.30
2	A. Dunn	CIN	.26
3	P. Fielder	MIL	.25
4	L. Berkman	HOU	.23
5	M. Cabrera	FLA	.19
6	C. Beltran	NYN	.19
7	M. Holliday	COL	.19
8	B. Hawpe	COL	.19
9	P. Burrell	PHI	.19
10	C. Jones	ATL	.18

Out per Ground ball % (Lowest)

1	C. Hart	MIL	63
2	E. Byrnes	ARI	65
3	M. Holliday	COL	67
4	R. Weeks	MIL	67
5	H. Ramirez	FLA	67
6	B. Phillips	CIN	68
7	S. Victorino	PHI	68
8	E. Encarnacion	CIN	68
9	C. Utley	PHI	69
10	D. Lee	CHN	69

Out per Outfield Fly % (Lowest)

1	A. Rowand	PHI	74
2	D. Young	WAS	75
3	C. Jones	ATL	75
4	H. Ramirez	FLA	76
5	O. Hudson	ARI	77
6	B. Hawpe	COL	77
7	R. Church	WAS	77
8	R. Belliard	WAS	78
9	D. Wright	NYN	78
10	C. Utley	PHI	78

Runs per NIP

1	A. Pujols	STL	.18
2	T. Helton	COL	.17
3	M. Loretta	HOU	.13
4	B. Giles	SD	.13
5	C. Jones	ATL	.13
6	L. Gonzalez	LAN	.12
7	J. Pierre	LAN	.12
8	J. Kent	LAN	.12
9	J. Reyes	NYN	.12
10	P. Burrell	PHI	.12

Runs per Ground ball

1	C. Hart	MIL	.13
2	E. Byrnes	ARI	.10
3	R. Weeks	MIL	.10
4	E. Encarnacion	CIN	.09
5	H. Ramirez	FLA	.09
6	C. Utley	PHI	.09
7	S. Victorino	PHI	.08
8	A. Soriano	CHN	.08
9	K. Johnson	ATL	.08
10	J. Wilson	PIT	.08

Runs per Line Drive

1	C. Hart	MIL	.50
2	A. Dunn	CIN	.48
3	M. Cabrera	FLA	.48
4	A. Soriano	CHN	.48
5	M. Holliday	COL	.48
6	R. Church	WAS	.47
7	J. Reyes	NYN	.47
8	E. Encarnacion	CIN	.47
9	D. Lee	CHN	.47
10	H. Ramirez	FLA	.46

Runs per Outfield Fly

1	R. Howard	PHI	.47
2	A. Dunn	CIN	.40
3	P. Fielder	MIL	.38
4	C. Jones	ATL	.35
5	B. Hawpe	COL	.34
6	M. Holliday	COL	.34
7	L. Berkman	HOU	.32
8	A. Rowand	PHI	.31
9	M. Cabrera	FLA	.30
10	D. Wright	NYN	.28

Rate stats include only players with at least 502 plate appearances.

Not in Play RAA		
1 B. Bonds	SF	36
2 T. Helton	COL	25
3 A. Pujols	STL	22
4 P. Burrell	PHI	20
5 P. Fielder	MIL	14
6 D. Wright	NYN	13
7 C. Jones	ATL	13
8 L. Berkman	HOU	13
9 R. Weeks	MIL	12
10 K. Griffey Jr.	CIN	11

Ground ball RAA		
1 W. Taveras	COL	21
2 N. Hopper	CIN	15
3 C. Hart	MIL	14
4 M. Kemp	LAN	13
5 H. Pence	HOU	12
6 J. Reyes	NYN	11
7 H. Ramirez	FLA	11
8 Y. Escobar	ATL	10
9 J. Diaz	ATL	10
10 B. Phillips	CIN	9

Line Drive RAA		
1 E. Renteria	ATL	17
2 J. Rollins	PHI	15
3 M. Holliday	COL	15
4 T. Helton	COL	14
5 D. Wright	NYN	14
6 M. Cabrera	FLA	14
7 D. Lee	CHN	13
8 A. Pujols	STL	12
9 F. Sanchez	PIT	12
10 R. Church	WAS	11

Fly ball RAA		
1 P. Fielder	MIL	46
2 R. Howard	PHI	42
3 A. Dunn	CIN	35
4 C. Jones	ATL	33
5 M. Holliday	COL	33
6 R. Braun	MIL	32
7 B. Hawpe	COL	27
8 A. Gonzalez	SD	24
9 A. Rowand	PHI	24
10 D. Wright	NYN	24

Total Batted Ball RAA		
1 C. Jones	ATL	59
2 M. Holliday	COL	59
3 A. Pujols	STL	57
4 P. Fielder	MIL	55
5 D. Wright	NYN	53
6 B. Bonds	SF	52
7 T. Helton	COL	47
8 C. Utley	PHI	46
9 H. Ramirez	FLA	46
10 M. Cabrera	FLA	44

WPA (Win Probability Added)		
1 Fielder, P	MIL	5.24
2 Holliday, M	COL	5.06
3 Helton, T	COL	4.80
4 Pujols, A	STL	4.65
5 Cabrera, M	FLA	4.61
6 Ramirez, A	CHN	4.55
7 Bonds, B	SF	4.33
8 Jones, C	ATL	4.23
9 Hawpe, B	COL	4.11
10 Wright, D	NYN	4.09

WPA/LI		
1 Holliday, M	COL	5.56
2 Fielder, P	MIL	5.17
3 Utley, C	PHI	4.86
4 Wright, D	NYN	4.86
5 Jones, C	ATL	4.69
6 Bonds, B	SF	4.41
7 Pujols, A	STL	4.37
8 Helton, T	COL	3.81
9 Lee, D	CHN	3.80
10 Cabrera, M	FLA	3.79

Pitching Leaders

Pitching Runs Created		
1 J. Peavy	SD	143
2 B. Webb	ARI	129
3 A. Harang	CIN	119
4 J. Smoltz	ATL	112
5 R. Oswalt	HOU	110
6 T. Hudson	ATL	108
6 B. Penny	LAN	108
8 C. Hamels	PHI	101
9 J. Francis	COL	100
9 T. Lilly	CHN	100

Earned Run Average (ERA)		
1 J. Peavy	SD	2.54
2 B. Webb	ARI	3.01
3 B. Penny	LAN	3.03
4 J. Smoltz	ATL	3.11
5 C. Young	SD	3.12
6 R. Oswalt	HOU	3.18
7 T. Hudson	ATL	3.33
8 C. Hamels	PHI	3.39
9 O. Perez	NYN	3.56
10 M. Cain	SF	3.65

Runs Allowed Per 9 (RA)		
1 J. Peavy	SD	2.70
2 B. Penny	LAN	3.25
3 R. Oswalt	HOU	3.40
4 J. Smoltz	ATL	3.41
5 C. Young	SD	3.43
6 B. Webb	ARI	3.47
7 T. Hudson	ATL	3.49
8 C. Hamels	PHI	3.53
9 M. Cain	SF	3.78
10 A. Harang	CIN	3.88

Fielding Independent Pitching (FIP)		
1 J. Peavy	SD	2.80
2 J. Smoltz	ATL	3.10
3 B. Webb	ARI	3.19
4 T. Hudson	ATL	3.38
5 C. Young	SD	3.46
6 R. Oswalt	HOU	3.54
7 G. Maddux	SD	3.56
8 B. Penny	LAN	3.63
9 A. Harang	CIN	3.70
10 M. Cain	SF	3.76

Innings Pitched		
1 B. Webb	ARI	236.3
2 A. Harang	CIN	231.7
3 T. Hudson	ATL	224.3
4 J. Peavy	SD	223.3
5 C. Zambrano	CHN	216.3
6 J. Francis	COL	215.3
7 R. Oswalt	HOU	212.0
8 B. Arroyo	CIN	210.7
9 B. Penny	LAN	208.0
9 I. Snell	PIT	208.0

Games		
1 J. Rauch	WAS	88
2 S. Rivera	WAS	85
3 J. Broxton	LAN	83
3 J. Beimel	LAN	83
5 A. Heilman	NYN	81
5 H. Bell	SD	81
7 C. Meredith	SD	80
7 P. Moylan	ATL	80
9 C. Qualls	HOU	79
10 3 tied with		78

Batters Faced		
1 B. Webb	ARI	975
2 A. Harang	CIN	948
3 D. Willis	FLA	942
4 C. Zambrano	CHN	925
4 T. Hudson	ATL	925
6 J. Francis	COL	922
7 B. Arroyo	CIN	921
8 J. Suppan	MIL	919
9 L. Hernandez	ARI	913
10 R. Oswalt	HOU	910

Pitches		
1 C. Zambrano	CHN	3,692
2 J. Peavy	SD	3,610
3 A. Harang	CIN	3,591
4 D. Willis	FLA	3,491
5 J. Francis	COL	3,485
6 B. Webb	ARI	3,437
7 B. Arroyo	CIN	3,432
8 B. Zito	SF	3,411
9 L. Hernandez	ARI	3,361
10 D. Davis	ARI	3,356

Rate stats include only pitchers with at least 162 innings pitched.

Strikeouts

1	J. Peavy	SD	240
2	A. Harang	CIN	218
3	J. Smoltz	ATL	197
4	B. Webb	ARI	194
5	R. Hill	CHN	183
6	J. Maine	NYN	180
7	I. Snell	PIT	177
7	C. Zambrano	CHN	177
7	C. Hamels	PHI	177
10	O. Perez	NYN	174
10	T. Lilly	CHN	174

Walks (Most)

1	C. Zambrano	CHN	101
2	D. Davis	ARI	95
3	D. Willis	FLA	87
3	N. Lowry	SF	87
5	S. Olsen	FLA	85
6	B. Zito	SF	83
7	O. Perez	NYN	79
7	L. Hernandez	ARI	79
7	M. Cain	SF	79
10	K. Wells	STL	78

Strikeouts Per Game

1	J. Peavy	SD	10.4
2	C. Hamels	PHI	9.3
3	C. Young	SD	9.2
4	J. Smoltz	ATL	9.0
4	A. Harang	CIN	9.0
6	O. Perez	NYN	8.9
7	R. Hill	CHN	8.8
8	J. Maine	NYN	8.7
9	T. Lilly	CHN	8.0
10	W. Rodriguez	HOU	7.9

Walks Per Game (Fewest)

1	G. Maddux	SD	1.2
2	D. Bush	MIL	2.1
2	A. Harang	CIN	2.1
2	J. Smoltz	ATL	2.1
5	M. Belisle	CIN	2.2
5	T. Hudson	ATL	2.2
7	C. Hamels	PHI	2.3
8	A. Cook	COL	2.5
8	W. Williams	HOU	2.5
8	P. Maholm	PIT	2.5

Wins

1	J. Peavy	SD	19
2	C. Zambrano	CHN	18
2	B. Webb	ARI	18
4	J. Francis	COL	17
5	T. Hudson	ATL	16
5	B. Penny	LAN	16
5	A. Harang	CIN	16
8	J. Maine	NYN	15
8	O. Perez	NYN	15
8	C. Hamels	PHI	15

Losses

1	K. Wells	STL	17
2	M. Cain	SF	16
3	B. Arroyo	CIN	15
3	D. Willis	FLA	15
3	P. Maholm	PIT	15
3	S. Olsen	FLA	15
3	W. Williams	HOU	15
8	D. Lowe	LAN	14
8	A. Reyes	STL	14
10	3 tied with		13

Saves

1	J. Valverde	ARI	47
2	F. Cordero	MIL	44
3	T. Hoffman	SD	42
4	T. Saito	LAN	39
5	C. Cordero	WAS	37
6	B. Wagner	NYN	34
7	D. Weathers	CIN	33
8	J. Isringhausen	STL	32
8	K. Gregg	FLA	32
10	R. Dempster	CHN	28

Save Opportunities

1	J. Valverde	ARI	54
2	F. Cordero	MIL	51
3	T. Hoffman	SD	49
4	C. Cordero	WAS	46
5	T. Saito	LAN	43
6	B. Wagner	NYN	39
6	D. Weathers	CIN	39
8	K. Gregg	FLA	36
9	J. Isringhausen	STL	34
10	R. Dempster	CHN	31

Holds

1	B. Lyon	ARI	35
2	H. Bell	SD	34
3	J. Rauch	WAS	33
3	D. Turnbow	MIL	33
5	J. Broxton	LAN	32
6	T. Pena	ARI	30
7	R. Franklin	STL	25
8	J. Romero	PHI	22
8	B. Howry	CHN	22
8	A. Heilman	NYN	22

Home Runs Allowed

1	W. Williams	HOU	35
2	L. Hernandez	ARI	34
3	C. James	ATL	32
4	J. Moyer	PHI	30
4	A. Eaton	PHI	30
6	D. Willis	FLA	29
6	S. Olsen	FLA	29
8	A. Harang	CIN	28
8	B. Arroyo	CIN	28
8	T. Lilly	CHN	28

Home Runs Per Game

1	B. Penny	LAN	0.41
2	T. Hudson	ATL	0.42
3	B. Webb	ARI	0.48
4	C. Young	SD	0.55
5	J. Peavy	SD	0.56
6	A. Wainwright	STL	0.57
7	R. Oswalt	HOU	0.60
8	M. Cain	SF	0.66
8	G. Maddux	SD	0.66
10	J. Suppan	MIL	0.76

Slugging Average Against

1	C. Young	SD	.297
2	J. Peavy	SD	.312
3	B. Webb	ARI	.334
4	T. Hudson	ATL	.352
5	B. Penny	LAN	.360
6	M. Cain	SF	.366
7	C. Zambrano	CHN	.372
8	J. Smoltz	ATL	.375
9	O. Perez	NYN	.382
10	D. Lowe	LAN	.384

Stolen Bases Allowed

1	C. Young	SD	44
2	G. Maddux	SD	37
3	B. Webb	ARI	26
4	R. Hill	CHN	23
5	B. Sheets	MIL	21
5	B. Kim	FLA	21
5	J. Peavy	SD	21
8	J. Marquis	CHN	20
8	L. Hernandez	ARI	20
10	J. Germano	SD	18

Caught Stealing

1	D. Lowe	LAN	12
2	B. Webb	ARI	9
2	W. Rodriguez	HOU	9
2	A. Eaton	PHI	9
5	A. Harang	CIN	8
5	T. Glavine	NYN	8
5	A. Wainwright	STL	8
8	D. Bush	MIL	7
9	Many tied with		6

Pick Offs

1	D. Davis	ARI	8
2	W. Rodriguez	HOU	6
3	J. Simontacchi	WAS	5
3	J. Beimel	LAN	5
5	J. Moyer	PHI	4
5	J. Francis	COL	4
5	R. Hill	CHN	4
8	O. Perez	NYN	3
8	T. Gorzelanny	PIT	3
10	Many tied with		2

Net Stolen Bases

1	D. Davis	ARI	-21
2	W. Rodriguez	HOU	-17
3	J. Simontacchi	WAS	-16
4	T. Glavine	NYN	-15
5	A. Eaton	PHI	-14
6	B. Arroyo	CIN	-13
7	J. Beimel	LAN	-12
7	A. Wainwright	STL	-12
9	J. Moyer	PHI	-11
9	C. Billingsley	LAN	-11
9	T. Tankersley	FLA	-11

Rate stats include only pitchers with at least 162 innings pitched.

Defense Efficiency Ratio (Highest)				Defense Efficiency Ratio (Lowest)				Double Plays				Hit By Pitch			
1	C. Young	SD	.751	1	S. Olsen	FLA	.635	1	T. Hudson	ATL	31	1	C. Zambrano	CHN	14
2	T. Lilly	CHN	.733	2	K. Wells	STL	.661	2	B. Penny	LAN	30	1	D. Willis	FLA	14
3	B. Zito	SF	.727	3	M. Belisle	CIN	.663	2	A. Cook	COL	30	1	M. Owings	ARI	14
4	C. Zambrano	CHN	.723	4	D. Willis	FLA	.665	4	P. Maholm	PIT	29	1	B. Kim	FLA	14
5	J. Maine	NYN	.721	5	D. Bush	MIL	.668	5	Z. Duke	PIT	28	5	B. Arroyo	CIN	13
6	M. Cain	SF	.720	6	J. Suppan	MIL	.669	6	D. Davis	ARI	27	5	J. Fogg	COL	13
7	R. Hill	CHN	.719	7	D. Davis	ARI	.670	6	J. Suppan	MIL	27	5	J. Marquis	CHN	13
8	J. Peavy	SD	.718	8	P. Maholm	PIT	.672	8	D. Lowe	LAN	26	5	B. Thompson	STL	13
9	B. Looper	STL	.716	9	R. Oswalt	HOU	.677	9	J. Francis	COL	25	9	W. Williams	HOU	12
10	J. Marquis	CHN	.708	10	A. Wainwright	STL	.677	9	N. Lowry	SF	25	9	R. Hill	CHN	12
								9	L. Hernandez	ARI	25				

Home/Away Split (Home)				Home/Away Split (Away)				Lefty/Righty Split (Negative)				Lefty/Righty Split (Positive)			
1	W. Rodriguez	HOU	-.064	1	B. Webb	ARI	.038	1	D. Willis	FLA	-.176	1	D. Bush	MIL	.056
2	B. Looper	STL	-.061	2	R. Hill	CHN	.032	2	B. Webb	ARI	-.081	2	B. Penny	LAN	.045
3	P. Maholm	PIT	-.060	3	J. Fogg	COL	.031	3	T. Gorzelanny	PIT	-.072	3	T. Glavine	NYN	.036
4	R. Oswalt	HOU	-.059	4	C. Zambrano	CHN	.030	4	J. Peavy	SD	-.069	4	A. Cook	COL	.029
5	S. Olsen	FLA	-.055	5	D. Davis	ARI	.028	5	P. Mahold	PIT	-.063	5	J. Moyer	PHI	.024
6	C. Young	SD	-.048	6	M. Cain	SF	.018	6	C. Young	SD	-.059	6	A. Wainwright	STL	.021
7	D. Bush	MIL	-.026	7	T. Hudson	ATL	.018	7	C. Zambrano	CHN	-.058	7	C. Hamels	PHI	.016
8	J. Smoltz	ATL	-.024	8	W. Williams	HOU	.017	8	J. Suppan	MIL	-.053	8	G. Maddux	SD	.012
9	J. Maine	NYN	-.024	9	A. Cook	COL	.016	9	J. Marquis	CHN	-.053	9	A. Harang	CIN	.011
10	T. Glavine	NYN	-.023	10	A. Wainwright	STL	.015	10	R. Hill	CHN	-.050	10	B. Arroyo	CIN	.006

Strikeout % (Lowest)				Strikeout % (Highest)				Walk % (Highest)				Walk % (Lowest)			
1	A. Cook	COL	9	1	J. Peavy	SD	27	1	C. Zambrano	CHN	12	1	G. Maddux	SD	4
2	L. Hernandez	ARI	10	2	C. Hamels	PHI	24	2	D. Davis	ARI	12	2	J. Smoltz	ATL	6
3	T. Glavine	NYN	10	3	C. Young	SD	24	3	K. Wells	STL	12	3	C. Hamels	PHI	6
4	B. Looper	STL	12	4	J. Smoltz	ATL	23	4	O. Perez	NYN	11	4	A. Harang	CIN	6
5	W. Williams	HOU	12	5	A. Harang	CIN	23	5	C. Young	SD	11	5	M. Belisle	CIN	6
6	J. Suppan	MIL	12	6	O. Perez	NYN	23	6	D. Willis	FLA	11	6	T. Hudson	ATL	7
7	G. Maddux	SD	13	7	R. Hill	CHN	23	7	M. Chico	WAS	11	7	D. Bush	MIL	7
8	M. Chico	WAS	13	8	J. Maine	NYN	22	8	J. Marquis	CHN	11	8	T. Lilly	CHN	7
9	J. Fogg	COL	13	9	T. Lilly	CHN	21	9	S. Olsen	FLA	10	9	A. Cook	COL	7
10	J. Marquis	CHN	13	10	W. Rodriguez	HOU	20	10	B. Zito	SF	10	10	P. Maholm	PIT	7

Ground ball % (Lowest)				Ground ball % (Highest)				Line Drive % (Highest)				Line Drive % (Lowest)			
1	C. Young	SD	29	1	D. Lowe	LAN	65	1	S. Olsen	FLA	24	1	D. Lowe	LAN	16
2	O. Perez	NYN	33	2	T. Hudson	ATL	62	2	M. Belisle	CIN	22	2	R. Oswalt	HOU	16
3	M. Chico	WAS	33	3	B. Webb	ARI	62	3	T. Glavine	NYN	21	3	M. Cain	SF	16
4	T. Lilly	CHN	34	4	A. Cook	COL	58	4	B. Looper	STL	21	4	W. Williams	HOU	16
5	B. Arroyo	CIN	35	5	P. Maholm	PIT	53	5	D. Willis	FLA	21	5	C. Young	SD	16
6	R. Hill	CHN	36	6	R. Oswalt	HOU	53	6	J. Moyer	PHI	21	6	T. Hudson	ATL	17
7	J. Maine	NYN	37	7	G. Maddux	SD	51	7	R. Hill	CHN	21	7	I. Snell	PIT	17
8	S. Olsen	FLA	38	8	J. Marquis	CHN	50	8	L. Hernandez	ARI	21	8	C. Zambrano	CHN	17
9	L. Hernandez	ARI	38	9	B. Penny	LAN	49	9	B. Arroyo	CIN	21	9	O. Perez	NYN	17
10	B. Zito	SF	39	10	A. Wainwright	STL	48	10	B. Penny	LAN	20	10	P. Maholm	PIT	17

Rate stats include only pitchers with at least 162 innings pitched.

Infield Fly/Fly balls (Highest)

#	Player	Team	
1	B. Arroyo	CIN	.16
2	O. Perez	NYN	.13
3	C. Young	SD	.13
4	C. Zambrano	CHN	.13
5	C. Hamels	PHI	.13
6	J. Maine	NYN	.13
7	J. Moyer	PHI	.13
8	R. Hill	CHN	.12
9	W. Williams	HOU	.12
10	T. Lilly	CHN	.12

HR/OF (Lowest)

#	Player	Team	
1	B. Penny	LAN	.04
2	C. Young	SD	.05
3	J. Peavy	SD	.06
4	T. Hudson	ATL	.06
5	M. Cain	SF	.06
6	A. Wainwright	STL	.07
7	R. Oswalt	HOU	.07
8	T. Gorzelanny	PIT	.07
9	G. Maddux	SD	.08
10	J. Suppan	MIL	.08

Out per Ground ball % (Highest)

#	Player	Team	
1	B. Looper	STL	82
2	T. Glavine	NYN	81
3	B. Zito	SF	80
4	A. Cook	COL	79
5	G. Maddux	SD	79
6	C. Zambrano	CHN	79
7	C. Young	SD	78
8	J. Peavy	SD	78
9	R. Hill	CHN	78
10	T. Hudson	ATL	77

Out per Outfield Fly % (Highest)

#	Player	Team	
1	B. Penny	LAN	89
2	O. Perez	NYN	89
3	C. Young	SD	89
4	B. Zito	SF	88
5	B. Looper	STL	88
6	D. Davis	ARI	86
7	R. Hill	CHN	86
8	M. Chico	WAS	85
9	J. Maine	NYN	85
10	T. Gorzelanny	PIT	85

Runs per NIP

#	Player	Team	
1	J. Smoltz	ATL	-.02
2	C. Hamels	PHI	-.02
3	A. Harang	CIN	-.01
4	G. Maddux	SD	-.01
5	J. Peavy	SD	-.00
6	T. Lilly	CHN	.00
7	B. Webb	ARI	.02
8	M. Belisle	CIN	.02
9	D. Lowe	LAN	.02
10	R. Hill	CHN	.02

Runs per Ground ball

#	Player	Team	
1	T. Glavine	NYN	-.00
2	B. Looper	STL	-.00
3	A. Cook	COL	.01
4	B. Zito	SF	.01
5	C. Young	SD	.01
6	C. Zambrano	CHN	.01
7	G. Maddux	SD	.02
8	J. Peavy	SD	.02
9	T. Hudson	ATL	.02
10	R. Hill	CHN	.03

Runs per Line Drive

#	Player	Team	
1	A. Cook	COL	.34
2	B. Webb	ARI	.34
3	L. Hernandez	ARI	.34
4	T. Lilly	CHN	.34
5	M. Belisle	CIN	.35
6	R. Hill	CHN	.35
7	A. Harang	CIN	.36
8	D. Lowe	LAN	.37
9	M. Chico	WAS	.37
10	C. Hamels	PHI	.37

Runs per Outfield Fly

#	Player	Team	
1	B. Penny	LAN	.04
2	C. Young	SD	.07
3	J. Peavy	SD	.10
4	O. Perez	NYN	.12
5	M. Cain	SF	.12
6	T. Gorzelanny	PIT	.13
7	T. Hudson	ATL	.13
8	B. Zito	SF	.13
9	B. Looper	STL	.15
10	J. Smoltz	ATL	.15

Not in Play RAA

#	Player	Team	
1	A. Harang	CIN	-18
2	J. Smoltz	ATL	-17
3	C. Hamels	PHI	-15
4	J. Peavy	SD	-15
5	G. Maddux	SD	-13
6	T. Lilly	CHN	-12
7	B. Webb	ARI	-9
8	D. Lowe	LAN	-7
9	B. Sheets	MIL	-7
10	M. Hendrickson	LAN	-7

Ground ball RAA

#	Player	Team	
1	T. Glavine	NYN	-13
2	J. Hirsh	COL	-13
3	B. Looper	STL	-13
4	M. Owings	ARI	-10
5	B. Zito	SF	-10
6	C. Zambrano	CHN	-10
7	C. Young	SD	-10
8	J. Peavy	SD	-9
9	A. Cook	COL	-8
10	R. Hill	CHN	-7

Line Drive RAA

#	Player	Team	
1	O. Hernandez	NYN	-17
2	T. Lilly	CHN	-14
3	B. Webb	ARI	-13
4	T. Lincecum	SF	-13
5	A. Harang	CIN	-12
6	A. Pena	ARI	-11
7	D. Lowe	LAN	-10
8	T. Saito	LAN	-10
9	J. Peavy	SD	-10
10	H. Bell	SD	-10

Fly ball RAA

#	Player	Team	
1	B. Penny	LAN	-31
2	J. Peavy	SD	-23
3	C. Young	SD	-21
4	T. Hudson	ATL	-21
5	B. Webb	ARI	-18
6	C. Marmol	CHN	-13
7	Y. Gallardo	MIL	-13
8	K. Cameron	SD	-12
9	L. Gardner	FLA	-12
10	M. Cain	SF	-11

Total Batted Ball RAA

#	Player	Team	
1	J. Peavy	SD	-57
2	C. Young	SD	-41
3	B. Webb	ARI	-40
4	T. Hudson	ATL	-35
5	H. Bell	SD	-33
6	J. Smoltz	ATL	-28
7	B. Penny	LAN	-28
8	T. Saito	LAN	-27
9	A Harang	CIN	-27
10	T. Lilly	CHN	-27

WPA (Relievers)

#	Player	Team	
1	Saito, T	LAN	4.27
2	Bell, H	SD	4.12
3	Marmol, C	CHN	2.80
4	Lyon, B	ARI	2.80
5	Isringhausen, J	STL	2.75
6	Corpas, M	COL	2.71
7	Pena, T	ARI	2.56
8	Moylan, P	ATL	2.40
9	Soriano, R	ATL	2.32
10	Valverde, J	ARI	2.20

WPA (Starters)

#	Player	Team	
1	Peavy, J	SD	4.79
2	Webb, B	ARI	3.35
3	Oswalt, R	HOU	3.05
4	Young, C	SD	2.75
5	Penny, B	LAN	2.72
6	Hamels, C	PHI	2.53
7	Harang, A	CIN	2.42
8	Cain, M	SF	2.34
9	Smoltz, J	ATL	2.18
10	Zambrano, C	CHN	2.09

WPA/LI (All)

#	Player	Team	
1	Peavy, J	SD	4.52
2	Webb, B	ARI	3.37
3	Young, C	SD	3.25
4	Hudson, T	ATL	3.02
5	Bell, H	SD	2.83
6	Cain, M	SF	2.60
7	Smoltz, J	ATL	2.55
8	Penny, B	LAN	2.44
9	Oswalt, R	HOU	2.27
10	Saito, T	LAN	2.15

Arizona Diamondbacks

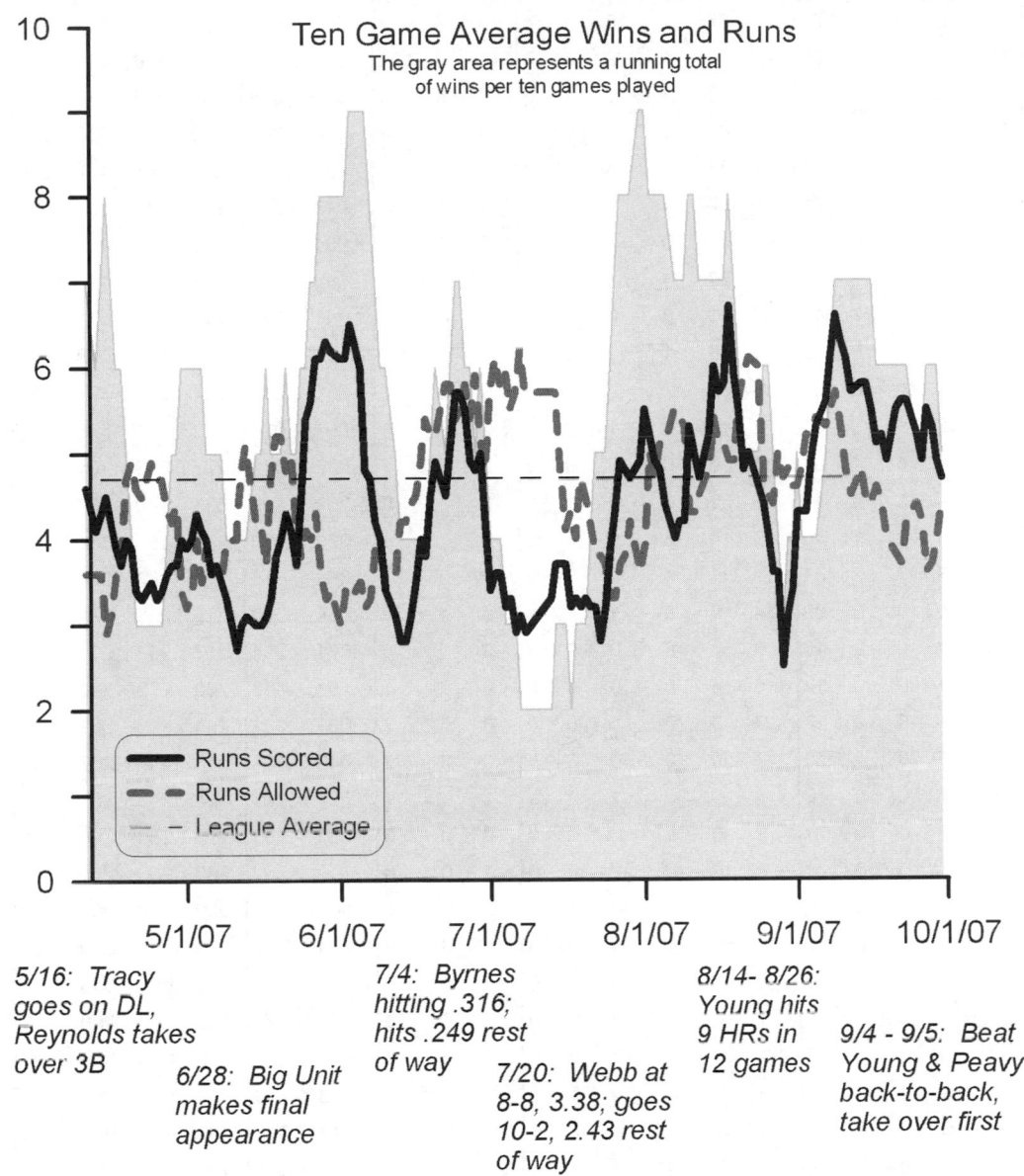

Ten Game Average Wins and Runs
The gray area represents a running total
of wins per ten games played

Legend:
— Runs Scored
– – Runs Allowed
– – League Average

5/16: Tracy goes on DL, Reynolds takes over 3B

6/28: Big Unit makes final appearance

7/4: Byrnes hitting .316; hits .249 rest of way

7/20: Webb at 8-8, 3.38; goes 10-2, 2.43 rest of way

8/14- 8/26: Young hits 9 HRs in 12 games

9/4 - 9/5: Beat Young & Peavy back-to-back, take over first

Stat Facts:
- Eric Byrnes stole 50 bases in 57 attempts
- Juan Cruz struck out 33% of the batters he faced
- Randy Johnson, in his brief 10-game season, struck out 31% of the batters he faced
- Jose Valverde struck out 29% of the batters he faced
- Mark Reynolds struck out in 31% of his PAs
- 27% of Byrnes's fly balls were infield pop-ups
- 62% of the batted balls off Brandon Webb were ground balls
- 32% of Tony Clark's fly balls were home runs
- Chris Young started four double plays from center field
- Micah Owings hit 14 batters in 153 innings
- Owings' GPA of .312 was by far the best on the roster — second best was .269
- Carlos Quentin was hit by 11 pitches in 263 PAs

Team Batting and Pitching/Fielding Stats by Month						
	April	May	June	July	Aug	Sept/Oct
Wins	16	16	14	13	16	15
Losses	11	12	13	13	12	11
RS/G	4.3	4.4	4.0	3.8	4.5	5.3
RA/G	4.0	4.1	4.7	4.7	5.0	4.5
OBP	.331	.324	.306	.302	.309	.354
SLG	.384	.434	.395	.404	.407	.457
FIP	4.31	3.97	4.55	4.41	4.81	4.33
DER	.698	.694	.681	.697	.712	.683

Batting Stats

Player	BR	Runs	RBI	PA	Outs	H	2B	3B	HR	TB	K	BB	IBB	HBP	SH	SF	SB	CS	GDP	H-A	L^R	BA	OBP	SLG	GPA
Byrnes E	98	103	83	699	466	179	30	8	21	288	98	57	5	10	1	4	50	7	12	.026	-.014	.286	.353	.460	.261
Hudson O +	75	69	63	601	388	152	28	9	10	228	87	70	1	2	5	7	10	2	21	.041	-.027	.294	.376	.441	.266
Young C	70	85	68	624	445	135	29	3	32	266	141	43	1	6	1	5	27	6	5	.017	.008	.237	.295	.467	.238
Drew S *	67	60	60	619	418	129	28	4	12	201	100	60	5	3	5	8	9	0	4	-.014	.002	.238	.313	.370	.222
Jackson C	63	56	60	477	307	118	29	1	15	194	50	53	2	4	2	3	2	2	8	.021	.055	.284	.368	.467	.269
Reynolds M	59	62	62	414	270	102	20	4	17	181	129	37	4	5	1	5	0	1	5	.013	-.009	.279	.349	.495	.267
Snyder C	46	37	47	380	254	82	20	0	13	141	67	40	3	7	3	4	0	1	9	.004	.074	.252	.342	.433	.250
Tracy C *	32	30	35	260	175	60	18	2	7	103	43	29	4	1	0	3	0	0	8	.048	.161	.264	.346	.454	.256
Clark T +	28	31	51	245	174	55	5	1	17	113	59	21	3	0	0	0	0	0	8	.111	-.034	.249	.310	.511	.255
Quentin C	27	29	31	263	187	49	16	0	5	80	54	18	1	11	1	4	2	2	5	.139	-.026	.214	.298	.349	.211
Montero M *	19	30	37	244	173	48	7	0	10	85	35	20	2	3	1	6	0	0	7	.051	.025	.224	.292	.397	.220
Hairston S	18	21	16	199	141	39	13	1	3	63	37	19	0	1	3	0	2	0	4	-.001	-.021	.222	.301	.358	.214
Salazar J *	15	13	10	103	69	26	6	1	1	37	19	9	0	0	0	0	2	0	1	.027	.018	.277	.340	.394	.239
Owings M	14	9	15	64	40	20	7	1	4	41	16	2	0	0	1	1	0	0	0	-.254	-.109	.333	.349	.683	.312
Ojeda A +	14	16	12	132	83	31	2	2	1	40	13	15	3	0	2	2	1	0	1	-.059	-.039	.274	.354	.354	.236
Upton J	13	17	11	152	112	31	8	3	2	51	37	11	4	1	0	0	2	0	3	.060	.015	.221	.283	.364	.208
Callaspo A +	7	10	7	156	122	31	8	0	0	39	14	9	0	1	1	1	1	1	8	-.004	.036	.215	.265	.271	.178
Bonifacio E	4	2	2	27	19	5	1	0	0	6	3	4	0	0	0	0	0	1	0	-.071	-.093	.217	.333	.261	.205
Cirillo J	4	6	6	44	33	8	4	0	0	12	6	4	0	0	0	0	0	0	1	.198	-.083	.200	.273	.300	.188
Hammock R	4	5	0	49	37	11	2	0	0	13	7	3	0	1	0	0	0	0	3	-.061	.031	.244	.306	.289	.200
Hernandez L	3	9	5	79	62	16	1	0	1	20	7	0	0	0	3	1	0	0	3	-.040	.061	.213	.211	.267	.154
DaVanon J +	1	5	1	33	24	4	2	0	0	6	8	5	0	1	0	1	1	1	1	.067	-.123	.154	.303	.231	.185
Pena T	1	1	1	4	3	1	0	0	0	1	2	0	0	0	0	0	0	0	0	.350	-.233	.250	.250	.250	.167
Smith J *	0	0	0	4	3	1	0	0	0	1	2	0	0	0	0	0	0	0	0	--	--	.250	.250	.250	.167
Eveland D *	0	0	0	1	0	0	0	0	0	0	0	0	0	0	1	0	0	0	0	.000	--	.000	.000	.000	.000
Kim B	-0	0	0	1	1	0	0	0	0	0	0	0	0	0	0	0	0	0	0	.000	--	.000	.000	.000	.000
Sadler D	-0	0	0	1	1	0	0	0	0	0	0	0	0	0	0	0	0	0	0	--	--	.000	.000	.000	.000
Cruz J	-0	0	0	2	2	0	0	0	0	0	2	0	0	0	0	0	0	0	0	.000	--	.000	.000	.000	.000
Nippert D	-0	0	0	2	2	0	0	0	0	0	1	0	0	0	0	0	0	0	0	.000	--	.000	.000	.000	.000
Barden B	-1	0	0	12	11	1	0	0	0	1	3	0	0	0	0	0	0	0	0	-.070	-.100	.083	.083	.083	.056
Johnson R	-1	0	0	18	14	1	0	0	0	1	7	1	0	0	2	0	0	0	0	.013	.005	.067	.125	.067	.069
Gonzalez E	-1	0	0	24	17	4	0	0	0	4	4	0	0	0	3	0	0	0	0	-.175	.193	.190	.190	.190	.127
Petit Y	-1	2	0	18	16	1	0	0	0	1	8	0	0	0	2	0	0	0	1	.233	.175	.063	.063	.063	.042
Davis D	-3	3	1	68	54	4	0	0	0	4	21	1	0	0	9	0	0	0	0	.074	-.038	.069	.085	.069	.053
Webb B	-3	1	3	82	70	6	2	0	0	8	31	1	0	0	8	0	0	0	3	.041	.037	.082	.095	.110	.067

Italicized stats have been adjusted for home park.

Batted Ball Batting Stats

Player	% of PA		% of Batted Balls					Out %		Runs Per Event				Total Runs vs. Avg.				
	K%	BB%	GB%	LD%	FB%	IF/F	HR/OF	GB	OF	NIP	GB	LD	OF	NIP	GB	LD	FB	Tot
Byrnes E	14	10	35	19	46	.27	.11	65	83	.07	.10	.41	.19	3	9	5	-2	15
Jackson C	10	12	38	20	43	.10	.11	75	84	.13	.05	.39	.17	8	-1	4	3	15
Hudson O	14	12	52	20	28	.02	.08	76	77	.09	.03	.38	.22	7	-2	3	2	10
Reynolds M	31	10	36	20	44	.14	.18	67	72	-.00	.09	.40	.38	-6	3	-3	16	10
Tracy C	17	12	37	18	45	.07	.09	88	74	.08	-.05	.46	.23	2	-7	2	7	3
Snyder C	18	12	40	15	45	.15	.11	73	83	.08	.05	.45	.18	4	-0	-2	1	2

Batted Ball Batting Stats continued at end of fielding stats

Pitching Stats

Player	PRC	IP	BFP	G	GS	K	BB	IBB	HBP	H	HR	DP	DER	SB	CS	PO	W	L	Sv	Op	Hld	H-A	R^L	RA	ERA	FIP
Webb B	129	236.3	975	34	34	194	72	6	5	209	12	21	.698	26	9	2	18	10	0	0	0	.038	-.081	3.47	3.01	3.19
Davis D *	79	192.7	862	33	33	144	95	7	5	211	21	27	.670	6	6	8	13	12	0	0	0	.028	-.020	4.67	4.25	4.64
Hernandez L	68	204.3	913	33	33	90	79	1	6	247	34	25	.693	20	5	2	11	11	0	0	0	-.010	.004	5.11	4.93	5.78
Owings M	60	152.7	651	29	27	106	50	2	14	146	20	16	.720	4	3	0	8	8	0	0	0	-.002	-.042	4.78	4.30	4.80
Valverde J	44	64.3	265	65	0	78	26	1	3	46	7	7	.709	4	2	1	1	4	47	54	0	.021	-.008	2.94	2.66	3.56
Pena T	42	85.3	344	75	0	63	31	4	5	63	8	11	.755	1	0	2	5	4	2	5	30	-.014	-.070	3.80	3.27	4.14
Lyon B	41	74.0	307	73	0	40	22	2	1	70	2	8	.707	5	1	0	6	4	2	5	35	-.039	.054	3.04	2.68	3.39
Gonzalez E	35	102.0	437	32	12	62	28	4	4	110	18	12	.705	2	3	1	8	4	0	0	0	.023	-.088	5.38	5.03	5.17
Cruz J	32	61.0	262	53	0	87	32	3	5	45	7	5	.695	2	2	0	6	1	0	0	4	-.016	-.134	4.13	3.10	3.58
Johnson R *	29	56.7	233	10	10	72	13	3	4	52	7	3	.657	4	4	2	4	3	0	0	0	.164	-.045	4.13	3.81	3.08
Petit Y	23	57.0	243	14	10	40	18	1	0	58	12	4	.728	4	0	0	3	4	0	0	0	-.024	-.085	4.74	4.58	5.50
Slaten D *	18	36.3	163	61	0	28	14	0	0	41	4	4	.667	3	0	0	3	2	0	1	7	.004	-.029	3.72	2.72	4.32
Nippert D	15	45.3	196	36	0	38	16	1	0	48	5	5	.679	1	0	0	1	1	0	0	2	-.038	.032	5.96	5.56	4.02
Medders B	12	29.3	128	30	0	23	16	1	1	30	9	2	.722	0	5	0	1	2	0	1	1	-.121	.066	4.91	4.30	7.43
Wickman B	4	6.7	28	8	0	2	1	0	1	6	0	1	.708	1	0	0	0	1	0	0	1	-.030	-.376	2.70	1.35	3.57
Peguero J	3	14.7	71	18	0	9	13	1	1	17	2	2	.674	0	1	0	1	0	0	0	3	-.016	.092	9.20	9.20	6.47
Murphy B *	2	6.3	34	10	0	2	7	2	1	9	0	1	.625	0	0	0	0	0	0	0	1	.026	.156	5.68	5.68	5.48
Eveland D *	0	5.0	28	5	1	3	5	0	0	8	0	0	.600	1	0	0	1	0	0	0	0	.218	.222	14.40	14.40	5.07
Kennedy J *	0	2.7	19	3	0	1	2	0	4	4	1	0	.583	0	0	0	0	0	0	0	1	-.435	.049	23.63	20.25	9.27
Kim B	0	2.7	22	2	2	3	2	0	1	11	1	0	.267	2	1	0	0	1	0	0	0	-.174	.002	30.38	23.63	9.27
Durbin J	0	0.7	10	1	0	1	1	0	0	7	0	0	.125	0	0	0	0	0	0	0	0	--	-.025	94.50	94.50	4.77
Ojeda A	0	1.0	3	1	0	0	0	0	0	0	0	0	1.000	0	0	0	0	0	0	0	0	--	.000	0.00	0.00	3.27
Choate R *	0	0.0	3	2	0	0	0	0	0	3	0	0	0.000	0	0	0	0	0	0	0	0	--	--	0.00	0.00	3.27
Cirillo J	0	1.0	5	1	0	1	2	0	0	0	0	0	1.000	0	0	0	0	0	0	0	0	--	.075	0.00	0.00	7.27
Gonzalez E	0	2.0	11	1	0	0	1	0	0	4	0	1	.500	1	0	0	0	0	0	0	0	.023	-.088	18.00	13.50	4.77
Schultz M	0	1.0	3	1	0	1	0	0	0	1	0	1	.500	0	0	0	0	0	0	0	0	--	-.700	0.00	0.00	1.27

Italicized stats have been adjusted for home park.

Batted Ball Pitching Stats

Player	% of PA		% of Batted Balls					Out %		Runs Per Event				Total Runs vs. Avg.				
	K%	BB%	GB%	LD%	FB%	IF/F	HR/OF	GB	OF	NIP	GB	LD	OF	NIP	GB	LD	FB	Tot
Webb B	20	8	62	18	20	.04	.08	77	78	.02	.03	.34	.20	-9	1	-13	-18	-40
Pena A	18	10	48	12	40	.09	.08	76	83	.05	.02	.31	.16	0	-2	-11	-2	-15
Valverde J	29	11	36	17	47	.14	.11	75	81	.01	.03	.37	.20	-3	-2	-5	-0	-10
Lyon B	13	7	43	19	38	.11	.02	75	78	.05	.03	.31	.12	-1	-1	-3	-5	-10
Johnson R	31	7	40	19	40	.13	.14	61	90	-.03	.13	.34	.18	-6	4	-4	-2	-8
Cruz J	33	14	35	19	47	.08	.12	68	86	.02	.09	.42	.18	-1	0	-4	-1	-6
Owings M	16	10	37	20	42	.12	.11	81	83	.06	-.00	.38	.21	1	-10	1	6	-2
Nippert D	19	8	38	28	34	.04	.11	74	90	.02	.03	.34	.15	-1	-1	3	-2	-1
Slaten D	17	9	44	17	39	.04	.09	70	83	.04	.07	.41	.16	-0	1	-0	0	1
Petit Y	16	7	33	15	52	.11	.12	70	84	.03	.08	.42	.21	-2	1	-2	6	4
Gonzalez E	14	7	45	15	40	.09	.15	72	86	.04	.06	.40	.22	-2	2	-3	8	6
Medders B	18	13	28	20	52	.09	.22	75	91	.08	.04	.35	.29	2	-0	-1	6	7
Davis D	17	12	47	19	34	.11	.10	71	86	.07	.06	.45	.16	7	4	9	-8	12
Hernandez L	10	9	38	21	41	.06	.12	71	83	.11	.06	.34	.20	7	2	4	14	27
MLB Average	17	9	43	19	38	.10	.10	74	83	.05	.05	.40	.18	--	--	--	--	--

Fielding Stats

Name	INN	SBA/G	CS%	ERA	WP+PB/G	PO	A	TE	FE
Catcher									
Snyder C	891.3	0.71	26%	3.73	0.374	722	58	1	0
Montero M	510.7	0.78	20%	4.81	0.405	340	30	3	2
Hammock R	39.0	0.92	75%	4.62	0.692	41	6	0	0

Name	Inn	PO	A	TE	FE	FPct	DPS	DPT	RZR	OOZ
First Base										
Jackson C	867.7	859	48	5	6	.988	1	0	.727	14
Clark T	452.7	432	32	0	2	.996	4	0	.721	8
Tracy C	114.7	122	5	0	1	.992	1	0	.789	2
Cirillo J	3.0	1	1	0	0	1.000	0	0	1.000	0
Snyder C	2.0	1	0	0	0	1.000	0	0	--	--
Hammock R	1.0	1	0	0	0	1.000	0	0	0.000	0
Second Base										
Hudson O	1183.0	258	387	3	7	.985	45	54	.798	58
Ojeda A	164.7	29	70	0	0	1.000	9	8	.786	5
Bonifacio E	46.0	9	15	1	0	.960	2	4	.833	1
Callaspo A	41.0	4	12	0	0	1.000	4	0	1.000	2
Cirillo J	3.0	0	0	0	0	0.000	0	0	--	--
Reynolds M	2.0	1	0	0	0	1.000	0	0	--	--
Sadler D	1.0	1	0	0	0	1.000	0	0	--	--
Shortstop										
Drew S	1283.0	212	409	5	12	.973	42	51	.777	57
Ojeda A	75.7	18	23	0	0	1.000	0	3	.762	4
Callaspo A	75.0	11	25	2	0	.947	2	0	.833	4
Smith J	7.0	0	2	0	0	1.000	0	0	1.000	0

Name	Inn	PO	A	TE	FE	FPct	DPS	DPT	RZR	OOZ
Third Base										
Reynolds M	842.3	55	157	8	3	.951	20	1	.657	30
Tracy C	374.0	29	73	3	1	.962	7	0	.733	8
Callaspo A	119.3	11	23	0	1	.971	5	0	.714	2
Cirillo J	58.0	5	13	0	0	1.000	1	0	.786	2
Barden B	17.0	0	2	0	0	1.000	1	0	0.000	1
Ojeda A	14.7	0	3	0	0	1.000	0	0	1.000	0
Hammock R	13.7	0	2	0	1	.667	0	0	1.000	1
Jackson C	2.0	1	0	0	0	1.000	0	0	--	--
Left Field										
Byrnes E	970.7	239	9	0	4	.984	0	0	.923	48
Hairston S	380.0	90	3	0	3	.969	2	0	.857	19
Hammock R	32.0	6	0	0	0	1.000	0	0	.800	2
Callaspo A	19.0	3	0	0	0	1.000	0	0	.750	0
Salazar J	17.0	3	0	0	0	1.000	0	0	.667	1
Jackson C	9.0	3	0	0	0	1.000	0	0	1.000	0
Quentin C	7.3	3	0	0	0	1.000	0	0	1.000	0
DaVanon J	5.0	1	0	0	0	1.000	0	0	0.000	1
Snyder C	1.0	0	0	0	0	0.000	0	0	--	--
Center Field										
Young C	1263.0	354	6	1	5	.984	4	0	.875	66
Byrnes E	169.0	50	0	0	0	1.000	0	0	.956	7
Salazar J	8.0	2	0	0	0	1.000	0	0	1.000	0
Hairston S	1.0	0	0	0	0	0.000	0	0	--	--
Right Field										
Quentin C	577.0	138	2	0	1	.993	0	0	.891	24
Upton J	315.3	65	1	1	3	.930	0	0	.877	8
Byrnes E	250.3	62	3	1	0	.985	2	0	.875	6
Salazar J	178.0	47	3	0	0	1.000	2	0	.894	5
Callaspo A	61.0	12	1	0	0	1.000	0	0	.857	0
DaVanon J	52.0	10	0	0	1	.909	0	0	1.000	0
Hammock R	4.3	1	0	0	0	1.000	0	0	1.000	0
Reynolds M	3.0	1	0	0	0	1.000	0	0	1.000	0

Continued from Batting section

Batted Ball Batting Stats

	% of PA		% of Batted Balls					Out %		Runs Per Event				Total Runs vs. Avg.				
Player	K%	BB%	GB%	LD%	FB%	IF/F	HR/OF	GB	OF	NIP	GB	LD	OF	NIP	GB	LD	FB	Tot
Clark T	24	9	49	17	34	.05	.32	80	97	.01	.01	.37	.41	-3	-3	-3	10	1
Young C	23	8	37	15	48	.13	.17	73	85	.01	.06	.39	.26	-8	1	-10	16	-1
Ojeda A	10	11	43	21	36	.00	.03	71	91	.13	.07	.34	-.00	2	2	0	-6	-2
Montero M	14	9	39	14	47	.10	.13	70	90	.07	.06	.27	.16	1	-0	-6	1	-5
Upton J	24	8	36	16	48	.17	.05	78	84	-.00	.02	.51	.11	-2	-1	-1	-3	-7
Hairston S	19	10	36	18	46	.14	.05	78	81	.05	.03	.33	.14	-0	-2	-3	-2	-7
Quentin C	21	11	43	16	41	.15	.08	79	86	.05	.02	.41	.12	0	-2	-3	-5	-10
Callaspo A	9	6	47	21	32	.12	.00	82	89	.08	-.02	.35	-.01	-0	-4	0	-8	-12
Drew S	16	10	38	16	46	.11	.07	75	86	.06	.05	.38	.11	2	-2	-6	-9	-15
Webb B	38	1	68	10	22	.22	.00	86	86	-.10	-.02	.42	-.01	-5	-3	-4	-5	-17
MLB Average	17	9	43	19	38	.10	.10	74	83	.05	.05	.40	.18	--	--	--	--	--

Atlanta Braves

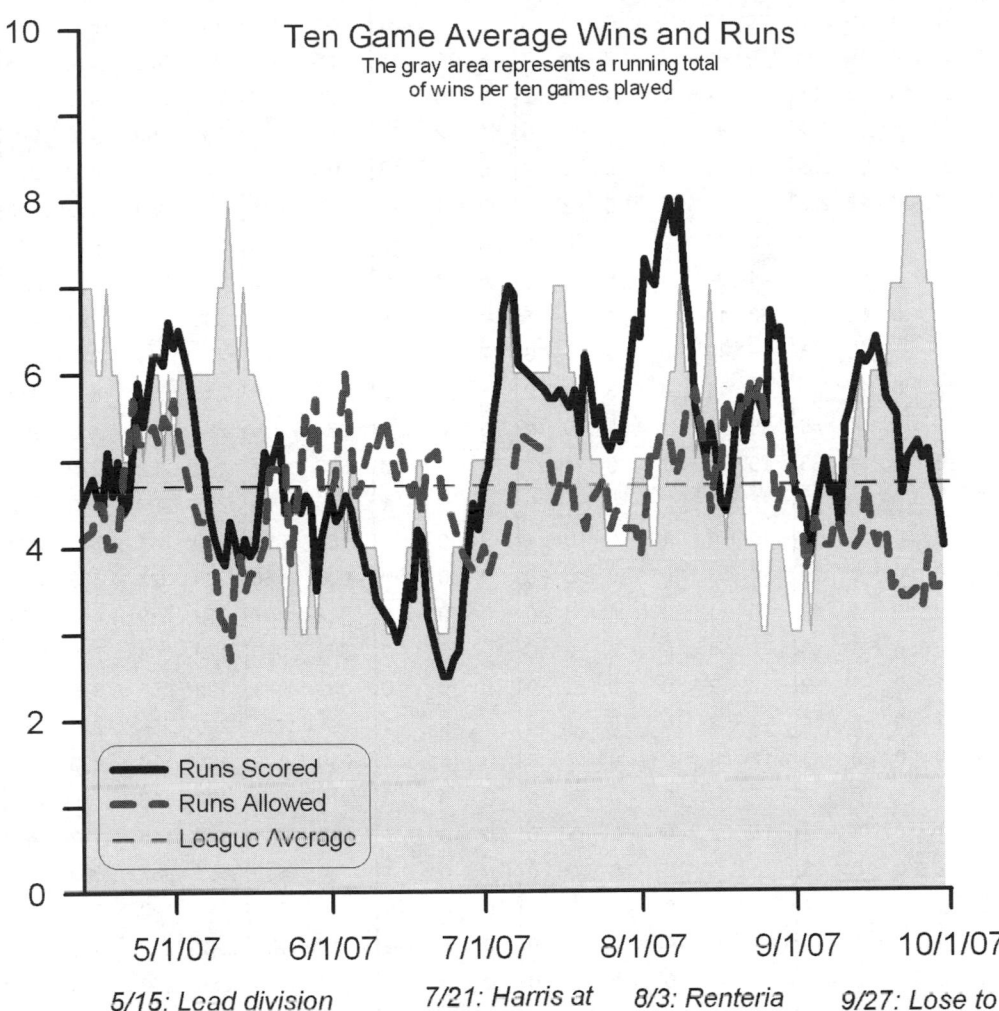

Ten Game Average Wins and Runs
The gray area represents a running total of wins per ten games played

Legend:
- Runs Scored
- Runs Allowed
- League Average

5/15: Lead division at 25-15. Go 59-64 rest of way

7/21: Harris at .339/.403/.441 after 6-hit game; Goes .190/.288/.335 rest of way

7/31: Teixeira acquired for prospects; hits .317/.404/.615 for ATL

8/3: Renteria on DL for month

8/15: Cox sets all-time ejection record

9/27: Lose to PHI; eliminated from playoff picture

Stat Facts:

- Switch-hitter Chipper Jones had the most extreme negative L^R in the league, at -.117
- Chipper led the league with a .346 GPA
- Tim Hudson led the league with 31 double plays induced
- 62% of the balls in play against Hudson were ground balls
- Chuck James's FIP (5.41) was much worse than his ERA (4.24)
- James allowed 32 homers in 161 innings
- Lance Cormier allowed 16 homers in 46 innings
- 37% if the fly balls against Cormier were home runs
- 51% of the batted balls off Rafael Soriano were fly balls
- Chad Paronto struck out just 8% of the batters he faced
- Andruw Jones had a .921 RZR and 80 plays OOZ

Team Batting and Pitching/Fielding Stats by Month

	April	May	June	July	Aug	Sept/Oct
Wins	16	14	13	13	13	15
Losses	9	14	15	13	15	12
RS/G	5.4	4.3	4.0	5.8	5.7	4.9
RA/G	4.7	4.3	4.5	4.6	5.3	3.8
OBP	.354	.319	.324	.357	.349	.332
SLG	.457	.414	.394	.452	.488	.398
FIP	4.11	4.00	4.27	3.99	4.68	4.27
DER	.687	.702	.699	.694	.703	.717

Batting Stats

Player	BR	Runs	RBI	PA	Outs	H	2B	3B	HR	TB	K	BB	IBB	HBP	SH	SF	SB	CS	GDP	H-A	L^R	BA	OBP	SLG	GPA
Jones C +	112	108	102	600	362	173	42	4	29	310	75	82	10	0	0	5	5	1	21	-.026	-.117	.337	.425	.604	.346
Francoeur J	99	84	105	696	470	188	40	0	19	285	129	42	5	5	0	7	5	2	14	-.038	.035	.293	.338	.444	.266
Johnson K *	89	91	68	608	390	144	26	10	16	238	117	79	3	4	2	2	9	5	8	-.029	.024	.276	.375	.457	.286
Renteria E	81	87	57	543	346	164	30	1	12	232	77	46	0	1	2	0	11	2	14	-.001	.031	.332	.390	.470	.296
Jones A	78	83	94	659	463	127	27	2	26	236	138	70	4	8	0	9	5	2	16	-.013	.031	.222	.311	.413	.246
McCann B *	71	51	92	552	388	136	38	0	18	228	74	35	7	5	2	6	0	1	19	.024	.014	.270	.320	.452	.260
Teixeira M +	59	38	56	240	144	66	9	1	17	128	46	27	3	4	0	1	0	0	2	-.028	-.024	.317	.404	.615	.339
Escobar Y	51	54	28	355	224	104	25	0	5	144	44	27	1	5	2	2	5	3	6	.005	.023	.326	.385	.451	.289
Diaz M	51	44	45	384	245	121	21	0	12	178	63	16	3	4	1	5	4	0	8	.012	.059	.338	.368	.497	.293
Harris W *	49	56	32	391	265	93	20	8	2	135	71	40	0	3	1	3	17	11	3	.040	.076	.270	.349	.392	.258
Thorman S *	28	37	36	307	232	62	18	0	11	113	70	14	3	3	1	2	1	1	6	-.026	.076	.216	.258	.394	.217
Saltalamacch	12	11	12	153	105	40	6	0	4	58	28	10	1	1	0	1	0	0	4	.031	.039	.284	.333	.411	.255
Woodward C	9	16	8	151	112	27	6	1	1	38	29	10	1	0	4	1	1	0	3	-.020	.071	.199	.252	.279	.185
Hudson T	8	6	9	83	57	20	3	0	0	23	18	3	0	0	4	0	0	0	1	.008	-.085	.263	.291	.303	.209
Franco J	6	1	8	45	31	10	3	0	0	13	10	4	1	0	0	1	0	0	1	-.162	.091	.250	.311	.325	.223
Prado M	6	5	2	62	42	17	3	0	0	20	6	3	0	0	0	0	0	0	0	-.006	-.165	.288	.323	.339	.232
Miller C	4	3	4	29	21	7	2	0	1	12	5	1	0	1	0	0	0	0	1	.012	-.107	.259	.310	.444	.253
Wilson C	4	6	2	69	48	10	2	0	1	15	25	8	0	3	0	0	0	0	0	.044	.090	.172	.304	.259	.204
Davies K	3	3	4	30	21	5	1	0	1	9	12	2	0	0	2	0	0	0	0	-.009	-.043	.192	.250	.346	.201
Orr P *	3	11	2	69	53	13	1	0	0	14	14	3	0	0	1	0	1	0	1	-.051	.126	.200	.235	.215	.161
Carlyle B *	2	4	3	43	32	5	0	0	0	5	12	0	0	0	7	0	0	0	1	-.039	.028	.139	.139	.139	.098
Reyes J *	1	1	0	23	16	3	0	0	0	3	7	0	0	0	4	0	0	0	0	.210	-.009	.158	.158	.158	.112
James C *	1	3	2	63	48	6	1	0	0	7	16	2	0	0	8	0	0	0	1	-.072	.048	.113	.145	.132	.099
Sammons C	1	0	0	3	2	2	1	0	0	3	0	0	0	0	0	0	0	0	1	--	.600	.667	.667	1.000	.556
Jones B *	1	0	4	21	16	3	1	0	0	4	8	0	0	1	0	1	0	0	0	-.168	-.343	.158	.190	.211	.140
Pena B +	0	2	3	33	29	7	0	0	1	10	3	0	0	0	0	0	0	1	2	.013	.057	.212	.212	.303	.173
Villarreal O	-0	0	0	5	3	1	0	0	0	1	1	0	0	0	1	0	0	0	0	.233	-.233	.250	.250	.250	.177
Mahay R *	-0	0	0	1	1	0	0	0	0	0	0	0	0	0	0	0	0	0	0	.000	--	.000	.000	.000	.000
Yates T	-0	0	0	1	1	0	0	0	0	0	1	0	0	0	0	0	0	0	0	.000	--	.000	.000	.000	.000
Redman M *	-0	1	0	6	5	0	0	0	0	0	3	1	0	0	0	0	0	0	0	-.225	.225	.000	.167	.000	.076
Lerew A *	-0	0	0	3	3	0	0	0	0	0	0	0	0	0	0	0	0	0	0	.000	--	.000	.000	.000	.000
Moylan P	-0	0	0	5	5	0	0	0	0	0	3	1	0	0	0	0	0	0	1	.225	-.225	.000	.200	.000	.091
Bennett J	-0	0	0	4	4	0	0	0	0	0	2	0	0	0	0	0	0	0	0	.000	--	.000	.000	.000	.000
Smoltz J	-1	1	2	68	49	5	1	0	0	6	19	1	0	0	13	0	0	0	0	-.067	-.005	.093	.109	.111	.078
Langerhans R	-1	3	1	52	45	3	1	0	0	4	16	6	1	1	0	1	0	1	3	-.010	.124	.068	.192	.091	.110
Cormier L	-1	0	0	17	16	0	0	0	0	0	7	1	0	0	0	0	0	0	0	-.045	.075	.000	.059	.000	.027

Italicized stats have been adjusted for home park.

Pitching Stats

Player	PRC	IP	BFP	G	GS	K	BB	IBB	HBP	H	HR	DP	DER	SB	CS	PO	W	L	Sv	Op	Hld	H-A	R^L	RA	ERA	FIP
Smoltz J	112	205.7	853	32	32	197	47	9	4	196	18	10	.685	11	4	1	14	8	0	0	0	-.024	-.034	3.41	3.11	3.10
Hudson T	108	224.3	925	34	34	132	53	8	8	221	10	31	.699	9	4	2	16	10	0	0	0	.018	-.011	3.49	3.33	3.38
James C *	67	161.3	691	30	30	116	58	5	1	164	32	10	.727	9	5	1	11	10	0	0	0	-.008	-.012	4.30	4.24	5.41
Moylan P	55	90.0	359	80	0	63	31	12	7	65	6	16	.754	9	2	1	5	3	1	2	8	.065	-.057	2.70	1.80	3.60
Soriano R	41	72.0	276	71	0	70	15	2	2	47	12	5	.785	7	2	0	3	3	9	12	19	.034	.000	3.25	3.00	4.12
Carlyle B	33	107.0	462	22	20	74	32	8	2	117	19	13	.687	4	2	0	8	7	0	0	0	.031	-.098	5.64	5.21	4.92
Villarreal O	29	76.3	336	51	0	58	32	8	4	75	6	5	.695	3	0	0	2	2	1	2	2	.002	-.096	4.72	4.24	3.87
Davies K	23	86.0	389	17	17	59	44	3	2	92	12	8	.699	9	2	0	4	8	0	0	0	-.002	.005	6.38	5.76	5.21
Yates T	21	66.0	294	75	0	69	31	8	3	64	6	2	.676	7	1	0	2	3	2	3	13	-.030	-.112	6.00	5.18	3.54
Mahay R *	19	28.0	117	30	0	23	16	2	0	19	1	3	.753	1	0	0	1	0	0	1	6	-.022	-.178	2.57	2.25	3.59
Wickman B	18	43.7	204	49	0	35	20	4	2	48	4	1	.671	7	0	0	3	3	20	26	0	-.149	.005	4.53	3.92	4.09
Acosta M	18	23.7	93	21	0	22	14	1	0	13	2	5	.782	4	0	1	1	1	0	0	4	.082	-.115	2.28	2.28	4.16
Gonzalez M *	16	17.0	70	18	0	13	8	0	0	15	0	2	.694	1	1	0	0	0	2	2	5	-.145	.088	1.59	1.59	3.15
Paronto C	14	40.3	180	41	0	14	19	5	3	47	1	10	.664	6	2	0	3	1	1	2	2	-.022	-.042	4.46	3.57	4.16
Reyes J *	12	50.7	230	11	10	27	30	2	1	55	9	9	.699	2	1	1	2	2	0	0	0	-.068	-.121	6.93	6.22	6.23
Devine J	10	8.3	39	10	0	7	8	2	0	7	0	1	.708	0	0	0	1	0	0	0	0	.047	-.068	1.08	1.08	3.75
Cormier L	10	45.7	210	10	9	27	22	3	0	56	16	7	.717	4	0	0	2	6	0	0	0	-.042	.079	7.49	7.09	7.89
Bennett J	7	13.0	57	3	2	14	3	1	0	14	3	0	.703	0	0	0	2	1	0	0	0	-.011	-.163	3.46	3.46	4.58
McBride M *	5	15.0	75	18	0	17	15	1	0	14	1	1	.659	1	0	0	1	0	0	0	0	.075	-.138	5.40	3.60	5.07
Ascanio J	5	16.0	74	13	0	13	6	2	0	17	3	0	.673	0	0	0	1	1	0	0	0	.160	-.042	6.19	5.06	4.83
Dotel O	3	7.7	30	9	0	12	1	0	0	5	1	0	.688	0	0	0	0	0	0	1	1	.266	.047	5.87	4.70	2.23
Lerew A	3	11.7	57	3	3	9	7	1	0	14	4	1	.703	1	0	0	0	2	0	0	0	-.266	.039	7.71	7.71	7.73
Redman M *	2	21.7	116	6	5	13	11	2	2	38	4	0	.605	1	1	0	0	4	0	0	0	-.115	-.225	12.05	11.63	5.99
Boyer D	2	5.3	26	5	0	3	1	1	0	10	0	0	.545	1	0	0	0	0	0	0	1	-.162	-.063	5.06	3.38	2.14
Colyer S *	1	3.7	22	7	0	4	4	0	0	9	1	0	.385	0	2	2	0	1	0	0	1	.185	-.113	4.91	4.91	7.91
Ledezma W *	1	9.3	45	12	0	7	4	0	0	12	1	1	.667	1	0	0	0	2	0	0	2	-.174	-.136	9.64	7.71	4.45
Barry K	0	2.0	14	1	0	4	2	0	0	6	0	0	.250	0	0	0	0	0	0	0	0	--	-.027	22.50	22.50	2.27
Ring R *	0	5.0	19	11	0	4	3	0	0	2	0	0	.833	0	1	0	0	0	0	0	0	.014	-.071	0.00	0.00	3.47

Italicized stats have been adjusted for home park.

Batted Ball Pitching Stats

Player	% of PA		% of Batted Balls					Out %		Runs Per Event				Total Runs vs. Avg.				
	K%	BB%	GB%	LD%	FB%	IF/F	HR/OF	GB	OF	NIP	GB	LD	OF	NIP	GB	LD	FB	Tot
Hudson T	14	7	62	17	22	.03	.06	77	82	.03	.02	.41	.13	-7	-4	-3	-21	-35
Smoltz J	23	6	45	20	35	.09	.09	73	84	-.02	.06	.39	.15	-17	2	-3	-11	-28
Moylan P	18	11	62	13	25	.05	.10	81	91	.06	-.01	.48	.12	1	-7	-5	-9	-20
Soriano R	25	6	33	16	51	.13	.14	73	99	-.02	.05	.35	.13	-6	-2	-6	-4	-17
Mahay R	20	14	45	24	32	.08	.05	79	90	.07	.00	.31	.02	1	-2	-1	-5	-6
Villarreal O	17	11	44	23	33	.08	.08	83	86	.06	.00	.43	.13	1	-5	5	-6	-3
Yates T	23	12	46	17	37	.07	.10	63	88	.04	.14	.32	.15	0	8	-6	-4	-1
Paronto C	8	12	51	15	34	.08	.02	65	84	.17	.09	.36	.07	4	4	-1	-4	2
Wickman B	17	11	43	17	39	.11	.04	66	88	.06	.11	.51	.08	1	4	2	-5	2
James C	17	9	31	20	49	.10	.14	75	87	.04	.04	.33	.21	-2	-2	-5	13	4
Davies K	15	12	41	20	39	.11	.13	74	88	.09	.04	.43	.17	4	-0	4	-1	7
Reyes J	12	13	45	15	40	.05	.13	72	82	.13	.05	.40	.22	5	1	-2	5	9
Carlyle E	16	7	32	23	44	.07	.13	75	84	.03	.05	.40	.21	-3	-2	7	10	12
Cormier L	13	10	51	19	30	.09	.37	79	78	.09	.02	.33	.58	2	-2	-1	16	15
MLB Average	*17*	*9*	*43*	*19*	*38*	*.10*	*.10*	*74*	*83*	*.05*	*.05*	*.40*	*.18*	--	--	--	--	--

Fielding Stats

Name	INN	SBA/G	CS%	ERA	WP+PB/G	PO	A	TE	FE
Catcher									
McCann B	1139.0	0.69	20%	3.89	0.332	907	53	8	5
Saltalamacchia J	187.0	1.25	19%	4.72	0.481	138	12	1	0
Miller C	62.0	0.44	33%	4.50	0.435	49	3	0	0
Pena B	59.3	0.91	33%	6.07	0.455	52	2	0	0
Sammons C	9.0	2.00	50%	4.00	0.000	5	1	0	0

Name	Inn	PO	A	TE	FE	FPct	DPS	DPT	RZR	OOZ
First Base										
Thorman S	608.3	571	56	2	4	.991	2	1	.720	23
Teixeira M	474.0	494	30	1	3	.992	3	1	.746	13
Wilson C	141.7	133	10	1	0	.993	0	0	.800	6
Saltalamacchia	103.3	96	9	2	0	.981	0	0	.667	2
Franco J	91.3	101	10	0	0	1.000	3	1	.882	4
Woodward C	35.0	28	1	1	0	.967	1	0	.600	0
Diaz M	2.7	3	1	0	0	1.000	0	1	--	--
Second Base										
Johnson K	1153.0	227	383	4	10	.978	38	45	.813	34
Escobar Y	164.3	28	49	2	1	.963	3	7	.826	5
Prado M	64.3	14	34	0	3	.941	1	3	.839	4
Woodward C	54.3	12	16	0	0	1.000	3	0	.786	4
Orr P	20.0	9	3	0	0	1.000	0	2	1.000	0

Name	Inn	PO	A	TE	FE	FPct	DPS	DPT	RZR	OOZ
Shortstop										
Renteria E	1019.0	147	322	6	5	.977	40	28	.815	49
Escobar Y	363.0	59	113	2	2	.977	8	13	.848	11
Woodward C	67.0	7	20	1	1	.931	2	3	.895	0
Jones C	7.0	1	1	0	0	1.000	0	0	1.000	0
Third Base										
Jones C	1080.0	75	226	3	5	.971	16	1	.662	57
Escobar Y	159.3	20	28	2	2	.923	2	0	.559	10
Woodward C	100.3	5	16	0	3	.875	2	0	.600	4
Orr P	63.0	4	13	1	0	.944	1	0	.647	3
Prado M	44.0	4	7	0	0	1.000	0	0	.500	3
Harris W	9.0	0	4	0	1	.800	0	0	.667	1
Left Field										
Diaz M	678.3	155	4	1	1	.988	1	0	.869	42
Harris W	620.3	138	4	2	1	.979	2	0	.872	29
Langerhans R	114.0	18	0	0	0	1.000	0	0	.800	6
Jones B	43.0	5	0	0	0	1.000	0	0	.800	1
Orr P	0.7	0	0	0	0	0.000	0	0	0.000	0
Center Field										
Jones A	1346.0	396	3	1	1	.995	2	0	.921	80
Harris W	110.3	35	0	0	0	1.000	0	0	.933	7
Right Field										
Francoeur J	1440.0	327	19	1	4	.986	4	0	.893	62
Diaz M	15.7	3	0	0	0	1.000	0	0	1.000	0

Batted Ball Batting Stats

Player	% of PA		% of Batted Balls					Out %		Runs Per Event				Total Runs vs. Avg.				
	K%	BB%	GB%	LD%	FB%	IF/F	HR/OF	GB	OF	NIP	GB	LD	OF	NIP	GB	LD	FB	Tot
Jones C	13	14	44	19	37	.04	.18	71	75	.13	.06	.43	.35	13	4	9	33	59
Renteria E	14	9	46	23	31	.07	.09	70	81	.06	.07	.46	.17	1	5	17	-1	23
Johnson K	19	14	43	19	39	.06	.11	70	82	.08	.08	.42	.20	8	6	2	5	21
Teixeira M	19	13	38	17	45	.08	.24	66	86	.07	.09	.43	.36	3	3	0	15	20
Escobar Y	12	9	56	21	23	.03	.08	68	73	.08	.09	.34	.23	2	10	2	0	14
Diaz M	16	5	46	21	34	.03	.11	63	86	-.00	.11	.44	.17	-5	10	8	1	14
Francoeur J	19	7	43	19	37	.15	.11	69	85	.01	.07	.46	.17	-8	6	10	-4	4
Harris W	18	11	42	21	37	.06	.02	75	80	.06	.05	.47	.10	2	1	7	-7	2
Saltalamacchia J	18	7	36	19	45	.06	.08	76	82	.02	.03	.39	.15	-1	-1	0	1	-2
McCann B	13	7	39	19	43	.10	.09	77	84	.05	.02	.45	.14	-2	-5	6	-1	-2
Jones A	21	12	39	17	44	.11	.14	77	82	.05	.02	.33	.23	2	-6	-11	10	-5
Woodward C	19	7	35	17	48	.16	.02	70	88	.00	.07	.26	.04	-2	0	-4	-6	-13
Thorman S	23	6	41	14	45	.12	.13	75	87	-.02	.04	.42	.19	-7	-2	-6	1	-13
MLB Average	*17*	*9*	*43*	*19*	*38*	*.10*	*.10*	*74*	*83*	*.05*	*.05*	*.40*	*.18*	*--*	*--*	*--*	*--*	*--*

Baltimore Orioles

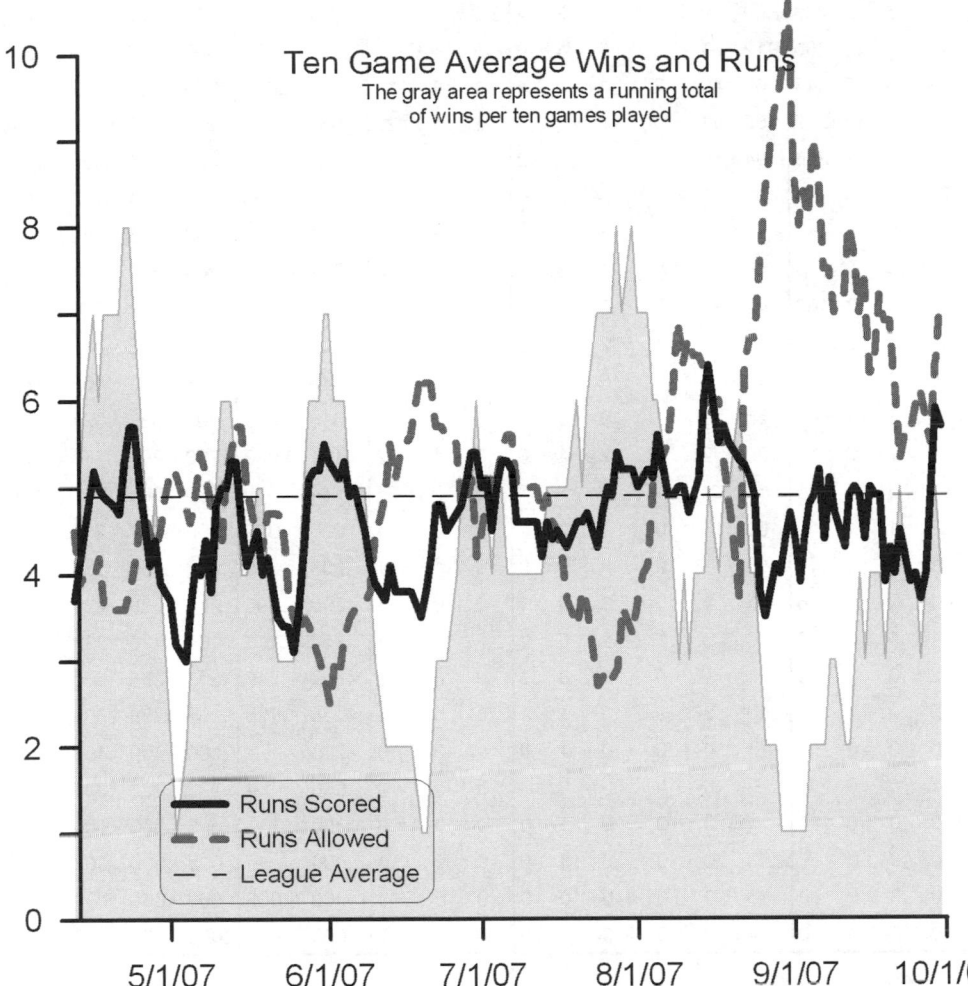

Ten Game Average Wins and Runs
The gray area represents a running total
of wins per ten games played

Legend:
— Runs Scored
- - Runs Allowed
— — League Average

6/8: Last day of 2007 in second place

6/21: Broken wrist ends Tejada's 1152 consecutive game streak

7/27: Guthrie is 6-2, 2.47 ERA over first 16 starts

9/16: Markakis hits 20th HR and 100th RBI of the season

9/11: A 10-5 loss to LAA guarantees 10th straight losing year

Stat Facts:
- Brian Roberts stole 50 bases in 57 attempts
- Corey Patterson led the league with 13 sacrifice bunts
- Patterson's negative L^R of -.050 was second strongest in the league
- Kevin Millar's GB% of 29% was lowest in the league
- 51% of Millar's batted balls were fly balls
- Miguel Tejada's GB% of 52% was among the highest in the league
- Only 31% of Tejada's batted balls were fly balls
- Erik Bedard was third in the league in FIP at 3.33
- Bedard struck out 30% of the batters he faced, leading major league starters
- Steve Trachsel struck out only 7% of the batters he faced
- The DER of .730 behind Jeremy Guthrie was third-highest in the league

Team Batting and Pitching/Fielding Stats by Month						
	April	May	June	July	Aug	Sept/Oct
Wins	12	15	8	15	9	10
Losses	14	13	17	11	19	19
RS/G	4.35	4.64	4.38	4.88	4.96	4.76
RA/G	4.62	3.89	5.23	4.08	7.11	6.97
OBP	.322	.344	.333	.346	.332	.324
SLG	.392	.398	.401	.431	.437	.413
FIP	4.12	4.32	4.61	4.61	5.01	5.27
DER	.694	.726	.697	.719	.650	.659

Batting Stats

Player	BR	Runs	RBI	PA	Outs	H	2B	3B	HR	TB	K	BB	IBB	HBP	SH	SF	SB	CS	GDP	H-A	L^R	BA	OBP	SLG	GPA
Roberts B +	108	103	57	716	456	180	42	5	12	268	99	89	6	0	2	4	50	7	8	-.021	-.026	.290	.377	.432	.280
Markakis N *	107	97	112	710	474	191	43	3	23	309	112	61	5	5	1	6	18	6	22	.013	.039	.300	.362	.485	.287
Huff A *	80	68	72	603	410	154	34	5	15	243	87	48	2	1	0	4	1	1	13	.022	-.006	.280	.337	.442	.265
Tejada M	76	72	81	569	385	152	19	1	18	227	55	41	9	10	0	3	2	1	22	.036	.050	.296	.357	.442	.274
Millar K	74	63	63	562	364	121	26	1	17	200	94	76	2	8	0	2	1	1	8	.024	.007	.254	.365	.420	.272
Mora M	63	67	58	527	364	128	23	1	14	195	83	47	3	3	5	5	9	3	22	-.017	.006	.274	.341	.418	.260
Hernandez R	57	40	62	409	282	94	18	0	9	139	59	36	1	6	0	3	1	3	9	.024	.012	.258	.333	.382	.248
Patterson C	53	65	45	503	349	124	26	2	8	178	65	21	1	4	13	4	37	9	3	.087	-.050	.269	.304	.386	.236
Payton J	50	48	58	470	334	111	21	5	7	163	42	22	0	3	5	6	5	2	9	-.006	.055	.256	.292	.376	.228
Gibbons J *	24	28	28	290	213	62	14	0	6	94	52	15	1	2	0	3	0	0	5	-.039	-.039	.230	.272	.348	.212
Redman T *	22	23	16	139	93	42	9	2	2	61	18	5	0	0	1	1	7	1	2	.043	.193	.318	.341	.462	.272
Gomez C	19	17	16	185	125	51	10	1	1	66	20	10	1	0	5	1	1	2	5	-.016	-.013	.302	.339	.391	.253
Bynum F *	14	21	11	101	74	25	8	2	2	43	30	2	0	2	1	0	8	1	2	-.151	0.000	.260	.290	.448	.245
Hernandez L	6	5	7	71	52	20	2	0	1	25	10	1	0	0	1	0	2	2	1	.144	.070	.290	.300	.362	.228
Bako P *	6	13	8	174	129	32	3	1	1	40	50	15	0	1	1	1	0	1	4	.020	.022	.205	.277	.256	.191
Moore S *	6	2	11	50	37	12	2	0	1	17	15	1	0	0	0	2	0	1	1	.203	.226	.255	.260	.362	.210
Knott J	4	3	4	19	12	3	0	0	1	6	3	4	0	0	0	1	0	0	1	-.290	-.496	.214	.368	.429	.276
Fahey B *	2	10	1	56	47	9	1	1	0	12	9	2	0	0	0	0	2	1	1	.120	.172	.167	.196	.222	.145
House J	2	5	3	41	30	8	2	0	3	19	11	1	0	2	0	0	0	0	0	-.062	-.246	.211	.268	.500	.248
Castillo A	2	5	3	36	27	5	2	0	1	10	10	3	0	0	1	1	0	0	1	-.138	.196	.161	.229	.323	.185
Bedard E *	1	0	1	6	3	2	0	0	0	2	1	0	0	0	1	0	0	0	0	-.280	--	.400	.400	.400	.283
Molina G	1	1	0	9	7	2	1	0	0	3	3	0	0	0	0	0	0	0	0	-.098	--	.222	.222	.333	.185
Burres B *	0	0	1	3	1	1	0	0	0	1	1	0	0	0	0	0	0	0	0	-.350	--	.500	.500	.500	.354
Cabrera D	-0	0	0	3	3	0	0	0	0	0	3	0	0	0	0	0	0	0	0	.000	--	.000	.000	.000	.000
Trachsel S	-1	0	0	5	5	0	0	0	0	0	3	0	0	0	0	0	0	0	0	.000	.000	.000	.000	.000	.000
Guthrie J	-1	0	0	7	7	0	0	0	0	0	4	0	0	0	0	0	0	0	0	.000	.000	.000	.000	.000	.000

Italicized stats have been adjusted for home park.

Batted Ball Batting Stats

Player	% of PA		% of Batted Balls					Out %		Runs Per Event				Total Runs vs. Avg.				
	K%	BB%	GB%	LD%	FB%	IF/F	HR/OF	GB	OF	NIP	GB	LD	OF	NIP	GB	LD	FB	Tot
Markakis N	16	9	45	18	37	.07	.12	73	79	.06	.04	.43	.24	1	0	4	15	20
Roberts B	14	12	36	20	45	.05	.05	72	81	.10	.06	.40	.13	10	2	4	-1	16
Millar K	17	15	29	20	51	.14	.10	83	80	.10	-.02	.40	.19	11	-10	1	7	10
Tejada M	10	9	52	17	31	.10	.13	73	85	.11	.05	.41	.18	4	3	2	-1	8
Redman T	13	4	47	18	35	.03	.05	67	78	-.01	.11	.38	.16	-2	4	1	1	3
Huff A	14	8	46	16	38	.09	.09	77	81	.05	.03	.47	.19	-1	-3	3	4	2
Bynum F	30	4	42	15	44	.11	.08	77	73	-.06	.04	.62	.25	-3	0	-0	1	-2
Gomez C	11	5	53	21	26	.11	.03	77	76	.04	.02	.42	.13	-1	-1	3	-4	-2
Mora M	16	9	40	19	42	.08	.10	73	86	.06	.03	.38	.15	1	-1	-2	-2	-3
Hernandez R	14	10	49	16	35	.12	.09	75	81	.08	.04	.35	.17	2	-1	-5	-2	-5
Payton J	9	5	50	17	33	.18	.06	73	85	.06	.06	.39	.09	-3	5	-0	-13	-12
Patterson C	13	5	44	15	41	.16	.06	73	82	.01	.06	.42	.12	-6	7	-4	-9	-12
Bako P	28	9	56	23	21	.00	.05	83	86	-.00	-.01	.39	.06	-3	-4	-1	-7	-14
Gibbons J	18	6	40	19	41	.19	.08	80	87	.00	.02	.36	.12	-4	-3	-2	-7	-15
MLB Average	17	9	43	19	38	.10	.10	74	83	.05	.05	.40	.18	--	--	--	--	--

Pitching Stats

Player	PRC	IP	BFP	G	GS	K	BB	IBB	HBP	H	HR	DP	DER	SB	CS	PO	W	L	Sv	Op	Hld	H-A	R^L	RA	ERA	FIP
Bedard E *	114	182.0	733	28	28	221	57	0	5	141	19	16	.710	5	2	0	13	5	0	0	0	-.007	.037	3.26	3.16	3.33
Guthrie J	81	175.3	723	32	26	123	47	2	4	165	23	21	.719	4	5	1	7	5	0	1	0	.040	-.023	4.00	3.70	4.52
Cabrera D	67	204.3	922	34	34	166	108	6	15	207	25	22	.683	24	4	0	9	18	0	0	0	.033	-.063	5.86	5.55	5.06
Trachsel S	47	140.7	623	25	25	45	69	0	2	151	16	14	.715	17	6	3	6	8	0	0	0	-.027	.013	4.67	4.48	5.73
Burres B *	38	121.0	559	37	17	96	66	1	5	140	14	13	.659	11	5	1	6	8	0	0	0	.012	.018	6.02	5.95	5.03
Walker J *	30	61.3	258	81	0	41	17	4	2	57	6	5	.724	2	1	0	3	2	7	13	21	.003	-.036	3.67	3.23	4.05
Bradford C	28	64.7	289	78	0	29	16	3	6	77	1	7	.667	4	1	0	4	7	2	7	19	.086	-.056	3.90	3.34	3.57
Ray C	19	42.7	179	43	0	44	18	2	2	35	5	3	.727	2	1	0	5	6	16	20	0	-.048	-.019	4.64	4.43	4.11
Bell R	14	53.0	251	30	0	28	24	5	0	73	7	4	.651	9	1	0	4	3	0	0	1	.000	-.085	6.28	5.94	5.12
Parrish J *	14	41.7	199	45	0	36	33	4	2	41	2	3	.683	0	0	1	2	2	0	2	9	.062	-.021	5.62	5.40	4.51
Loewen A *	14	30.3	143	6	6	22	26	0	3	27	1	7	.692	0	0	0	2	0	0	0	0	-.051	-.025	4.15	3.56	5.23
Baez D	14	50.3	233	53	0	29	29	5	7	50	8	6	.738	6	0	0	0	6	3	5	14	-.009	-.105	6.44	6.44	6.14
Birkins K *	8	34.3	170	19	2	30	14	0	3	52	3	2	.583	1	0	0	1	2	0	0	0	-.055	-.020	8.13	8.13	4.25
Olson G *	8	32.3	162	7	7	28	28	1	2	42	4	6	.620	3	1	1	1	3	0	0	0	-.036	-.066	7.79	7.79	5.95
Leicester J	7	32.0	145	10	5	16	13	0	3	36	3	3	.700	2	0	0	2	3	0	0	0	.038	.000	7.59	7.59	5.10
Liz R	6	24.7	122	9	4	24	23	1	0	25	3	0	.676	3	1	0	0	2	0	0	0	-.184	.019	7.66	6.93	5.81
Williamson S	6	14.3	61	16	0	16	8	0	0	12	1	1	.694	7	0	0	1	0	0	1	1	-.119	-.111	5.02	4.40	3.73
Hoey J	6	24.7	115	23	0	18	18	1	1	25	2	3	.684	3	0	0	3	4	0	3	4	-.026	-.118	7.66	7.30	5.16
Shuey P	4	25.7	126	25	0	22	21	0	0	33	3	5	.613	2	1	0	0	1	1	1	6	.043	-.145	9.82	9.82	5.64
Cherry R	4	16.3	79	10	0	10	13	1	2	17	3	2	.725	0	0	0	0	0	0	0	0	-.050	.134	7.71	7.71	7.12
Williams T	3	14.3	64	14	0	9	4	0	1	19	2	2	.646	0	0	0	0	2	0	1	3	.101	-.136	7.53	7.53	4.99
Santos V	2	14.3	68	4	3	4	10	1	1	20	5	6	.688	0	0	0	0	2	0	0	0	.052	.035	8.18	8.18	9.45
Zambrano V	2	12.3	63	5	2	11	11	0	4	12	1	1	.667	2	1	0	0	1	0	0	0	.269	-.121	9.49	9.49	6.30
Wright J	2	10.3	48	3	3	7	9	0	0	12	1	2	.645	2	1	1	0	3	0	0	0	-.189	-.062	9.58	6.97	5.90
Cabrera F	1	10.0	50	9	0	9	9	0	0	12	2	1	.667	0	1	0	0	0	1	1	0	-.076	-.136	12.60	12.60	6.88
Johnson J	0	2.0	11	1	0	1	2	0	0	3	0	0	.625	0	0	0	0	0	0	0	0	--	-.103	9.00	9.00	5.38
Doyne C	0	3.7	22	5	0	2	3	0	1	7	1	0	.600	0	0	0	0	0	0	0	0	.315	-.083	14.73	14.73	9.11

Italicized stats have been adjusted for home park.

Batted Ball Pitching Stats

Player	% of PA		% of Batted Balls			IF/F	HR/OF	Out %		Runs Per Event				Total Runs vs. Avg.				
	K%	BB%	GB%	LD%	FB%			GB	OF	NIP	GB	LD	OF	NIP	GB	LD	FB	Tot
Bedard E	30	8	48	17	35	.08	.13	78	83	-.01	.02	.41	.20	-14	-8	-11	-6	-40
Guthrie J	17	7	42	19	38	.07	.12	79	82	.02	.01	.32	.22	-6	-10	-7	9	-15
Walker J	16	7	34	21	46	.16	.08	76	86	.03	.03	.34	.11	-2	-2	-1	-5	-9
Ray C	25	11	45	18	38	.07	.13	67	91	.03	.11	.24	.14	-1	3	-5	-2	-5
Bradford C	10	8	62	15	23	.04	.00	74	78	.09	.04	.46	.05	1	3	0	-9	-5
Loewen A	15	20	52	18	30	.04	.04	70	84	.15	.06	.33	.06	6	1	-2	-4	1
Hoey J	16	17	38	19	42	.06	.06	77	83	.12	.02	.41	.13	3	-1	0	-0	2
Parrish J	18	18	49	17	34	.19	.06	73	79	.11	.06	.39	.15	6	1	-2	-3	2
Leicester J	11	11	35	19	45	.04	.06	72	84	.12	.08	.35	.12	2	2	-0	-0	3
Liz R	20	20	23	25	52	.11	.09	71	90	.12	.09	.40	.11	4	-0	1	-1	4
Baez D	12	15	51	17	32	.04	.16	81	88	.14	.00	.42	.23	6	-4	-0	2	4
Shuey P	17	17	54	11	35	.04	.11	59	75	.11	.12	.43	.29	3	4	-2	3	8
Trachsel S	7	11	42	18	41	.06	.08	79	84	.17	.01	.38	.14	11	-4	1	-0	8

Batted Ball Pitching Stats continued after Fielding Stats.

Fielding Stats

Name	INN	SBA/G	CS%	ERA	WP+PB/G	PO	A	TE	FE
Catcher									
Hernandez R	855.0	0.89	20%	5.20	0.379	636	44	5	2
Bako P	421.0	0.73	18%	4.96	0.513	324	24	4	0
Castillo A	91.7	1.28	31%	4.71	0.785	92	7	0	0
House J	46.0	0.78	25%	7.83	0.783	31	2	0	0
Molina G	25.0	0.36	0%	5.40	0.720	12	2	0	0

Name	Inn	PO	A	TE	FE	FPct	DPS	DPT	RZR	OOZ
First Base										
Millar K	873.0	852	66	0	1	.999	8	1	.707	22
Huff A	421.0	424	24	1	2	.993	5	0	.630	10
Gomez C	116.7	131	9	0	0	1.000	0	0	.720	3
Moore S	25.0	19	2	0	0	1.000	0	0	.667	1
House J	2.0	2	0	0	0	1.000	0	0	--	--
Hernandez R	1.0	0	0	0	0	0.000	0	0	--	--
Second Base										
Roberts B	1329.0	278	457	2	5	.991	49	60	.840	47
Gomez C	43.0	8	20	0	0	1.000	3	3	.824	2
Fahey B	31.0	10	15	0	0	1.000	1	3	1.000	4
Bynum F	18.0	2	7	0	0	1.000	0	0	.750	1
Hernandez L	17.0	4	3	0	0	1.000	0	1	.667	0
Shortstop										
Tejada M	1068.0	149	358	6	9	.971	32	41	.830	48
Hernandez L	139.0	31	52	1	2	.965	7	7	.930	7
Fahey B	94.0	11	24	0	0	1.000	4	1	.826	5
Gomez C	71.0	13	31	0	0	1.000	5	4	.846	6
Bynum F	66.0	13	16	0	1	.967	0	1	.933	1

Name	Inn	PO	A	TE	FE	FPct	DPS	DPT	RZR	OOZ
Third Base										
Mora M	1051.0	79	260	6	4	.971	16	1	.689	48
Gomez C	177.0	13	42	2	1	.948	9	0	.709	4
Huff A	122.0	9	24	0	1	.971	1	0	.656	1
Moore S	83.0	6	12	0	0	1.000	2	0	.647	1
Fahey B	3.3	0	1	1	0	.500	0	0	--	--
House J	2.0	0	0	0	0	0.000	0	0	--	--
Left Field										
Payton J	904.0	232	2	1	4	.979	2	0	.835	34
Gibbons J	326.3	75	1	0	1	.974	2	0	.892	9
Bynum F	100.0	27	2	0	0	1.000	0	0	.875	7
Redman T	58.3	16	0	0	0	1.000	0	0	.813	3
Fahey B	20.0	7	0	0	0	1.000	0	0	.833	2
Millar K	15.0	1	0	0	0	1.000	0	0	1.000	0
Knott J	12.0	4	0	0	0	1.000	0	0	1.000	0
Moore S	2.0	0	0	0	0	0.000	0	0	--	--
Hernandez L	1.0	0	0	0	0	0.000	0	0	--	--
Center Field										
Patterson C	1057.0	281	8	1	2	.990	2	0	.904	37
Redman T	231.0	78	1	1	0	.988	2	0	.875	1
Payton J	107.3	41	1	0	2	.955	2	0	.895	7
Bynum F	41.0	9	0	0	0	1.000	0	0	.750	0
Stern A	2.0	0	0	0	0	0.000	0	0	--	--
Right Field										
Markakis N	1399.0	303	13	0	2	.994	8	0	.843	45
Payton J	25.0	8	0	0	0	1.000	0	0	.889	0
Gibbons J	14.0	3	0	0	0	1.000	0	0	.750	0

Batted Ball Pitching Stats

Player	% of PA		% of Batted Balls					Out %		Runs Per Event				Total Runs vs. Avg.				
	K%	BB%	GB%	LD%	FB%	IF/F	HR/OF	GB	OF	NIP	GB	LD	OF	NIP	GB	LD	FB	Tot
Olson G	17	19	34	17	49	.04	.08	60	80	.12	.11	.39	.16	5	2	-0	2	9
Birkins K	18	10	49	23	28	.12	.10	69	78	.05	.09	.49	.22	0	4	6	-0	10
Bell R	11	10	48	14	38	.09	.10	71	78	.10	.08	.48	.21	2	5	1	4	11
Cabrera D	18	13	50	16	35	.10	.13	72	82	.08	.05	.42	.22	12	3	-6	3	11
Burres B	17	13	38	22	40	.12	.10	73	81	.08	.05	.39	.19	7	-1	6	2	14
MLB Average	17	9	43	19	38	.10	.10	74	83	.05	.05	.40	.18	--	--	--	--	--

Boston Red Sox

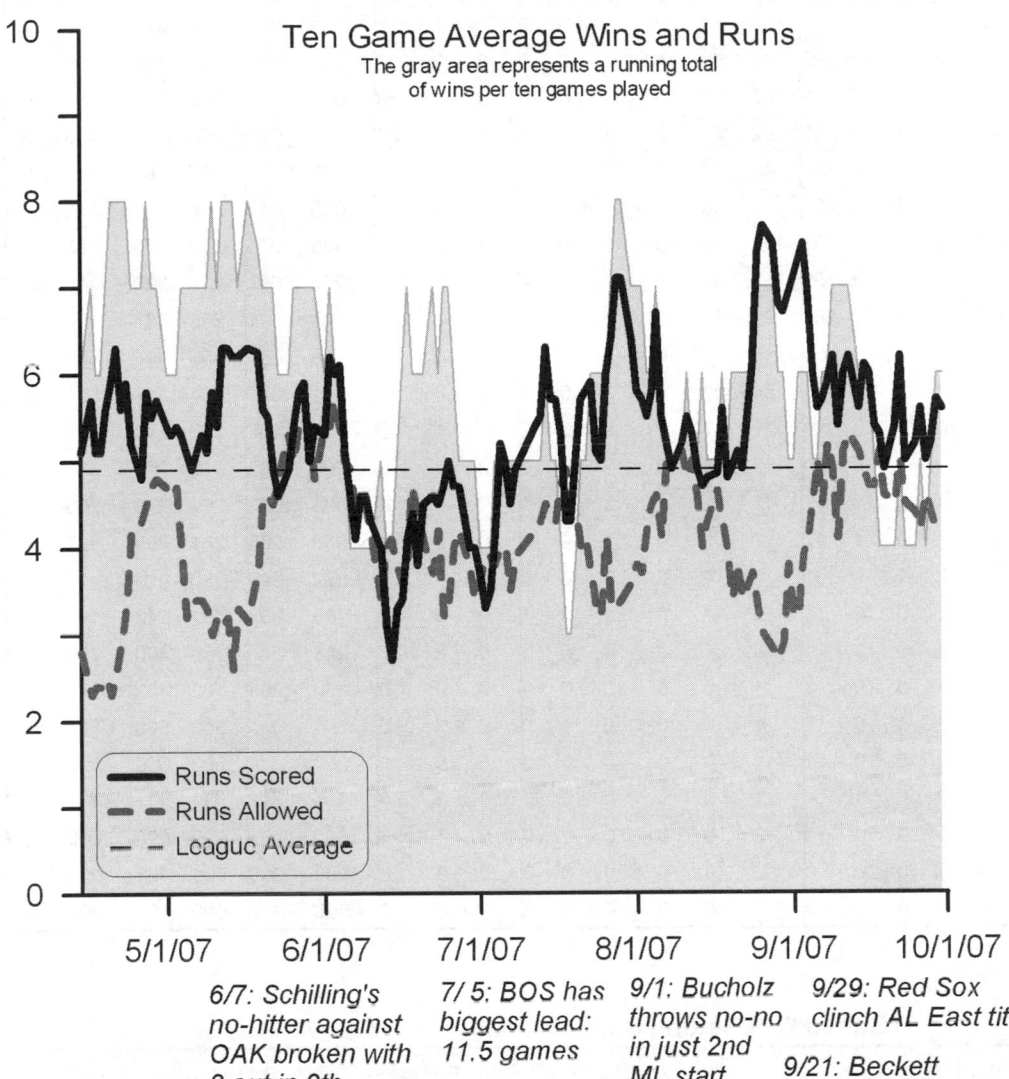

Ten Game Average Wins and Runs
The gray area represents a running total
of wins per ten games played

Legend:
— Runs Scored
- - Runs Allowed
- - League Average

6/7: Schilling's
no-hitter against
OAK broken with
2 out in 9th

7/5: BOS has
biggest lead:
11.5 games

9/1: Bucholz
throws no-no
in just 2nd
ML start

9/29: Red Sox
clinch AL East title

9/21: Beckett
beats TB for
20th win

Stat Facts:

- Julio Lugo's GPA was .211
- David Ortiz's .445 OBP led the major leagues
- 36% of Ortiz's outfield flies produced a run
- Dustin Pedroia struck out in just 7% of his plate appearances
- Only 3% of Kevin Youklis's fly balls were infield pop-ups
- Youkilis committed zero errors
- Josh Beckett's 3.22 FIP led the league
- Beckett tied for third in the league with 120 PRC
- 14% of the fly balls Beckett allowed were infield pop ups
- Tim Wakefield led the league with 41 stolen bases allowed
- Jonathan Papelbon struck out 38% of the batters he faced
- 55% of the batted balls off Papelbon were fly balls

Team Batting and Pitching/Fielding Stats by Month						
	April	May	June	July	Aug	Sept/Oct
Wins	16	20	13	15	16	16
Losses	8	8	14	12	13	11
RS/G	5.2	5.5	4.1	5.7	5.8	5.7
RA/G	3.5	4.2	4.1	4.0	4.1	4.4
OBP	.353	.365	.348	.367	.371	.366
SLG	.426	.465	.413	.446	.439	.472
FIP	3.77	3.91	4.17	3.97	4.07	4.45
DER	.715	.686	.706	.710	.708	.714

Batting Stats

Player	BR	Runs	RBI	PA	Outs	H	2B	3B	HR	TB	K	BB	IBB	HBP	SH	SF	SB	CS	GDP	H-A	L^R	BA	OBP	SLG	GPA
Ortiz D *	135	116	117	667	384	182	52	1	35	341	103	111	12	4	0	3	3	1	16	.041	.096	.332	.445	.621	.342
Lowell M	102	79	120	653	419	191	37	2	21	295	71	53	4	3	0	8	3	2	19	.072	-.009	.324	.378	.501	.284
Youkilis K	99	85	83	625	387	152	35	2	16	239	105	77	0	15	0	5	4	2	9	-.032	-.005	.288	.390	.453	.278
Ramirez M	77	84	88	569	361	143	33	1	20	238	92	71	13	7	0	8	0	0	21	.011	.099	.296	.388	.493	.287
Pedroia D	75	86	50	581	364	165	39	1	8	230	42	47	1	7	5	2	7	1	8	.058	.029	.317	.380	.442	.271
Crisp C +	67	85	60	591	403	141	28	7	6	201	84	50	1	1	9	5	28	6	12	.035	.018	.268	.330	.382	.235
Drew J *	67	84	64	552	354	126	30	4	11	197	100	79	10	1	0	6	4	2	12	.025	.075	.270	.373	.423	.263
Lugo J	67	71	73	630	450	135	36	2	8	199	82	48	0	0	8	4	33	6	9	.071	.007	.237	.294	.349	.211
Varitek J +	60	57	68	518	335	111	15	3	17	183	122	71	9	8	0	4	1	2	9	.001	.011	.255	.367	.421	.260
Ellsbury J *	25	20	18	127	77	41	7	1	3	59	15	8	0	1	0	2	9	0	2	.056	.036	.353	.394	.509	.293
Hinske E *	24	25	21	218	155	38	12	3	6	74	54	28	2	3	0	1	3	0	7	.111	-.023	.204	.317	.398	.233
Cora A *	19	30	18	232	162	51	10	5	3	80	23	7	2	9	7	2	1	1	5	-.052	.107	.246	.298	.386	.222
Pena W	12	18	17	172	128	34	9	1	5	60	58	14	0	2	0	0	3	1	5	-.160	.083	.218	.291	.385	.218
Mirabelli D	12	9	16	127	95	23	3	0	5	41	41	11	0	1	1	0	0	0	4	-.003	.052	.202	.278	.360	.207
Kielty B +	5	6	9	61	43	12	2	0	1	17	17	5	0	1	0	3	0	0	3	-.058	.085	.231	.295	.327	.206
Moss B *	3	6	1	29	19	7	2	1	0	11	6	4	0	0	0	0	0	0	1	.072	.045	.280	.379	.440	.270
Cash K	2	2	4	33	26	3	1	0	0	4	13	4	0	1	0	1	0	0	2	-.185	-.032	.111	.242	.148	.141
Tavarez J *	1	0	0	5	3	1	0	0	0	1	3	1	0	0	0	0	0	0	0	-.243	--	.250	.400	.250	.233
Beckett J	1	1	1	11	9	2	1	0	0	3	1	0	0	0	0	0	0	0	0	-.150	-.206	.182	.182	.273	.144
Murphy D *	1	1	0	2	1	1	0	1	0	3	1	0	0	0	0	0	0	0	0	--	--	.500	.500	1.500	.577
Schilling C	0	0	0	2	1	1	0	0	0	1	1	0	0	0	0	0	0	0	0	-.350	--	.500	.500	.500	.337
Bailey J	0	1	1	9	8	1	0	0	1	4	1	0	0	0	0	0	0	0	0	--	.242	.111	.111	.444	.155
Wakefield T	-0	0	0	2	2	0	0	0	0	0	2	0	0	0	0	0	0	0	0	.000	--	.000	.000	.000	.000
Matsuzaka D	-0	0	0	4	4	0	0	0	0	0	2	0	0	0	0	0	0	0	0	.000	.000	.000	.000	.000	.000
Clayton R	-1	1	0	6	8	0	0	0	0	0	3	0	0	0	0	0	0	0	2	.000	.000	.000	.000	.000	.000

Italicized stats have been adjusted for home park.

Batted Ball Batting Stats

Player	% of PA		% of Batted Balls			IF/F	HR/OF	Out %		Runs Per Event				Total Runs vs. Avg.				
	K%	BB%	GB%	LD%	FB%			GB	OF	NIP	GB	LD	OF	NIP	GB	LD	FB	Tot
Ortiz D	15	17	38	17	45	.05	.18	71	72	.13	.06	.39	.36	21	1	0	46	67
Lowell M	11	9	36	18	46	.09	.10	66	79	.09	.08	.40	.19	3	7	5	13	29
Youkilis K	17	15	34	21	45	.03	.09	71	79	.10	.06	.37	.19	12	1	2	11	26
Ramirez M	16	14	38	22	41	.05	.12	79	81	.10	-0.00	.44	.22	10	-8	10	12	23
Pedroia D	7	9	43	18	38	.13	.05	69	81	.15	.08	.41	.12	7	9	7	-6	17
Drew D	18	14	46	18	37	.11	.09	74	73	.09	.05	.35	.25	9	1	-5	7	13
Varitek J	24	15	42	18	40	.13	.15	71	88	.07	.07	.43	.21	7	2	-2	0	8
Ellsbury J	12	7	52	19	29	.10	.12	68	70	.06	.10	.38	.29	-0	3	1	3	7
Hinske E	25	14	45	11	44	.16	.12	83	72	.05	-.02	.54	.29	2	-4	-4	4	-3
Pena W	34	9	47	17	36	.11	.16	76	77	-.01	.02	.44	.31	-3	-2	-2	2	-6
Mirabelli D	32	9	37	16	47	.15	.17	70	92	-.01	.06	.34	.21	-2	-0	-3	-0	-6
Cora A	10	7	43	20	37	.15	.05	82	81	.08	-0.00	.32	.15	-0	-4	-2	-3	-9
Crisp C	14	9	47	17	36	.08	.04	74	84	.06	.06	.38	.10	0	5	-4	-11	-10
Lugo J	13	8	46	17	37	.11	.05	77	82	.06	.03	.33	.11	-2	1	-9	-12	-22
MLB Average	17	9	43	19	38	.10	.10	74	83	.05	.05	.40	.18	--	--	--	--	--

Pitching Stats

Player	PRC	IP	BFP	G	GS	K	BB	IBB	HBP	H	HR	DP	DER	SB	CS	PO	W	L	Sv	Op	Hld	H-A	R^L	RA	ERA	FIP
Beckett J	120	200.7	822	30	30	194	40	0	5	189	17	16	.684	14	6	1	20	7	0	0	0	.016	-.020	3.41	3.27	3.22
Matsuzaka D	98	204.7	874	32	32	201	80	1	13	191	25	21	.694	18	7	0	15	12	0	0	0	.012	-.008	4.40	4.40	4.35
Wakefield T	72	189.0	800	31	31	110	64	1	4	191	22	19	.710	41	8	0	17	12	0	0	0	.010	.024	4.95	4.76	4.79
Schilling C	72	151.0	633	24	24	101	23	1	2	165	21	12	.700	5	1	1	9	8	0	0	0	.023	-.008	4.05	3.87	4.33
Papelbon J	60	58.3	224	59	0	84	15	0	4	30	5	1	.776	4	0	0	1	3	37	40	2	.063	.052	1.85	1.85	2.59
Okajima H *	56	69.0	272	66	0	63	17	2	1	50	6	6	.746	5	0	5	3	2	5	7	27	.038	.045	2.22	2.22	3.38
Tavarez J	42	134.7	604	34	23	77	51	4	7	151	14	18	.677	0	0	0	7	11	0	0	1	-.008	.032	5.95	5.15	4.79
Delcarmen M	36	44.0	176	44	0	41	17	1	2	28	4	3	.786	2	2	0	0	0	1	2	11	.080	-.016	2.25	2.05	3.93
Timlin M	27	55.3	222	50	0	31	14	3	3	46	7	8	.754	3	2	0	2	1	1	1	8	-.042	.083	3.74	3.42	4.66
Lester J *	27	63.0	275	12	11	50	31	0	1	61	10	6	.716	4	2	1	4	0	0	0	0	.010	-.014	4.71	4.57	5.38
Snyder K	23	54.3	242	46	0	41	32	2	6	45	7	3	.744	5	2	1	2	3	0	0	1	.008	.031	4.80	3.81	5.53
Lopez J *	21	40.7	174	61	0	26	18	2	4	36	2	5	.718	0	1	0	2	1	0	2	13	.020	.073	3.54	3.10	4.22
Gabbard K *	21	41.0	165	7	7	29	18	0	4	28	3	7	.775	0	0	0	4	0	0	0	0	-.111	-.074	3.73	3.73	4.53
Buchholz C	18	22.7	88	4	3	22	10	0	1	14	0	4	.727	0	0	1	3	1	0	0	0	-.041	-.079	2.38	1.59	2.90
Pineiro J	12	34.0	157	31	0	20	14	0	1	41	3	5	.647	1	0	0	1	1	0	0	1	.085	-.052	5.29	5.03	4.67
Donnelly B	11	20.7	90	27	0	15	5	0	4	19	0	0	.712	2	0	0	2	1	0	0	8	.178	.026	3.48	3.05	3.24
Romero J *	11	20.0	94	23	0	11	15	3	0	24	2	4	.667	1	0	0	1	0	1	1	2	.031	-.062	3.15	3.15	5.38
Corey B	8	9.3	32	9	0	6	4	0	0	6	0	6	.727	1	0	0	1	0	0	0	1	.067	.017	1.93	1.93	3.38
Gagne E	6	18.7	89	20	0	22	9	0	0	26	1	1	.561	1	0	0	2	2	0	3	3	-.044	-.019	6.75	6.75	3.17
Hansack D	3	7.7	38	3	1	5	5	0	0	9	2	0	.692	0	0	0	0	1	0	0	0	.126	-.044	5.87	4.70	7.42

Italicized stats have been adjusted for home park.

Batted Ball Pitching Stats

Player	% of PA		% of Batted Balls			IF/F	HR/OF	Out %		Runs Per Event				Total Runs vs. Avg.				
	K%	BB%	GB%	LD%	FB%			GB	OF	NIP	GB	LD	OF	NIP	GB	LD	FB	Tot
Beckett J	24	5	47	16	37	.14	.09	73	77	-.03	.05	.39	.22	-18	1	-12	0	-29
Papelbon J	38	8	29	16	55	.16	.09	86	84	-.03	-.02	.32	.14	-6	-5	-8	-4	-23
Okajima H	23	7	45	15	41	.08	.09	77	89	-.01	.02	.39	.12	-5	-3	-6	-5	-20
Delcarmen M	23	11	45	17	38	.12	.08	86	86	.03	-.02	.32	.14	-1	-4	-4	-3	-12
Timlin M	14	8	39	16	45	.13	.11	82	85	.05	-.01	.31	.17	-1	-4	-4	-0	-9
Matsuzaka D	23	11	38	18	44	.10	.11	78	78	.03	.02	.40	.22	-2	-10	-6	9	-9
Gabbard K	18	13	54	16	30	.00	.09	85	84	.09	-.03	.35	.14	2	-5	-3	-3	-8
Schilling C	16	4	37	19	44	.11	.10	74	83	-.02	.05	.36	.18	-12	1	-1	5	-7
Lopez J	15	13	53	20	28	.06	.06	86	73	.10	-.03	.39	.21	2	-5	0	-1	-3
Wakefield T	14	9	39	19	42	.12	.10	76	85	.06	.04	.39	.16	0	-3	2	-1	-1
Snyder K	17	16	37	15	48	.05	.10	80	83	.11	.01	.32	.17	5	-3	-5	2	-1
Lester J	18	12	34	19	47	.10	.12	74	90	.07	.05	.38	.15	2	-1	-1	-0	-0
Pineiro J	13	10	54	15	31	.00	.08	71	76	.08	.06	.43	.22	1	2	-0	2	5
Tavarez J	13	10	54	16	30	.06	.11	73	80	.08	.05	.40	.21	4	4	-2	3	9
MLB Average	17	9	43	19	38	.10	.10	74	83	.05	.05	.40	.18	--	--	--	--	--

Fielding Stats

Name	INN	SBA/G	CS%	ERA	WP+PB/G	PO	A	TE	FE
Catcher									
Varitek J	1064.0	0.69	23%	3.80	0.169	937	39	4	2
Mirabelli D	292.7	1.38	22%	4.09	0.677	194	19	1	0
Cash K	82.0	1.21	18%	3.95	0.110	56	8	1	0

Name	Inn	PO	A	TE	FE	FPct	DPS	DPT	RZR	OOZ
First Base										
Youkilis K	1094.0	990	90	0	0	1.000	17	1	.835	22
Hinske E	276.0	256	22	0	3	.989	1	0	.725	5
Ortiz D	48.0	37	3	0	0	1.000	0	0	.571	0
Bailey J	17.7	16	2	0	0	1.000	0	0	1.000	1
Cora A	3.0	1	0	1	0	.500	0	0	0.000	0
Second Base										
Pedroia D	1141.0	259	360	2	4	.990	36	44	.824	34
Cora A	297.3	67	95	0	1	.994	8	12	.870	13
Shortstop										
Lugo J	1228.0	214	360	8	11	.968	25	37	.807	55
Cora A	202.3	25	69	2	1	.969	7	10	.804	11
Clayton R	8.0	0	3	1	0	.750	0	0	.750	0
Third Base										
Lowell M	1324.0	105	264	7	8	.961	34	2	.732	27
Youkilis K	108.0	5	30	1	2	.921	4	0	.735	5
Clayton R	6.3	0	2	0	0	1.000	0	0	1.000	1

Name	Inn	PO	A	TE	FE	FPct	DPS	DPT	RZR	OOZ
Left Field										
Ramirez M	994.7	182	8	1	1	.990	0	0	.684	35
Ellsbury J	144.0	37	0	0	0	1.000	0	0	.816	6
Hinske E	101.0	26	1	0	0	1.000	0	0	.786	4
Pena W	89.0	13	1	0	0	1.000	0	0	.591	0
Kielty B	57.0	14	1	0	0	1.000	0	0	.867	1
Moss B	52.0	11	1	0	0	1.000	0	0	.833	1
Murphy D	1.0	1	0	0	0	1.000	0	0	1.000	0
Center Field										
Crisp C	1216.0	408	7	0	1	.998	8	0	.909	58
Ellsbury J	107.0	38	0	0	0	1.000	0	0	.806	9
Pena W	86.0	23	2	0	2	.926	2	0	.833	3
Drew J	29.3	12	0	1	0	.923	0	0	.857	0
Right Field										
Drew J	1062.0	212	3	0	5	.977	2	0	.864	28
Pena W	205.3	43	0	0	1	.977	0	0	.860	6
Hinske E	82.3	16	0	0	0	1.000	0	0	.875	2
Kielty B	67.0	14	0	0	0	1.000	0	0	1.000	1
Moss B	12.0	1	0	0	0	1.000	0	0	1.000	0
Ellsbury J	6.0	0	0	0	0	0.000	0	0	--	--
Murphy D	4.0	1	0	0	0	1.000	0	0	.500	0

Chicago Cubs

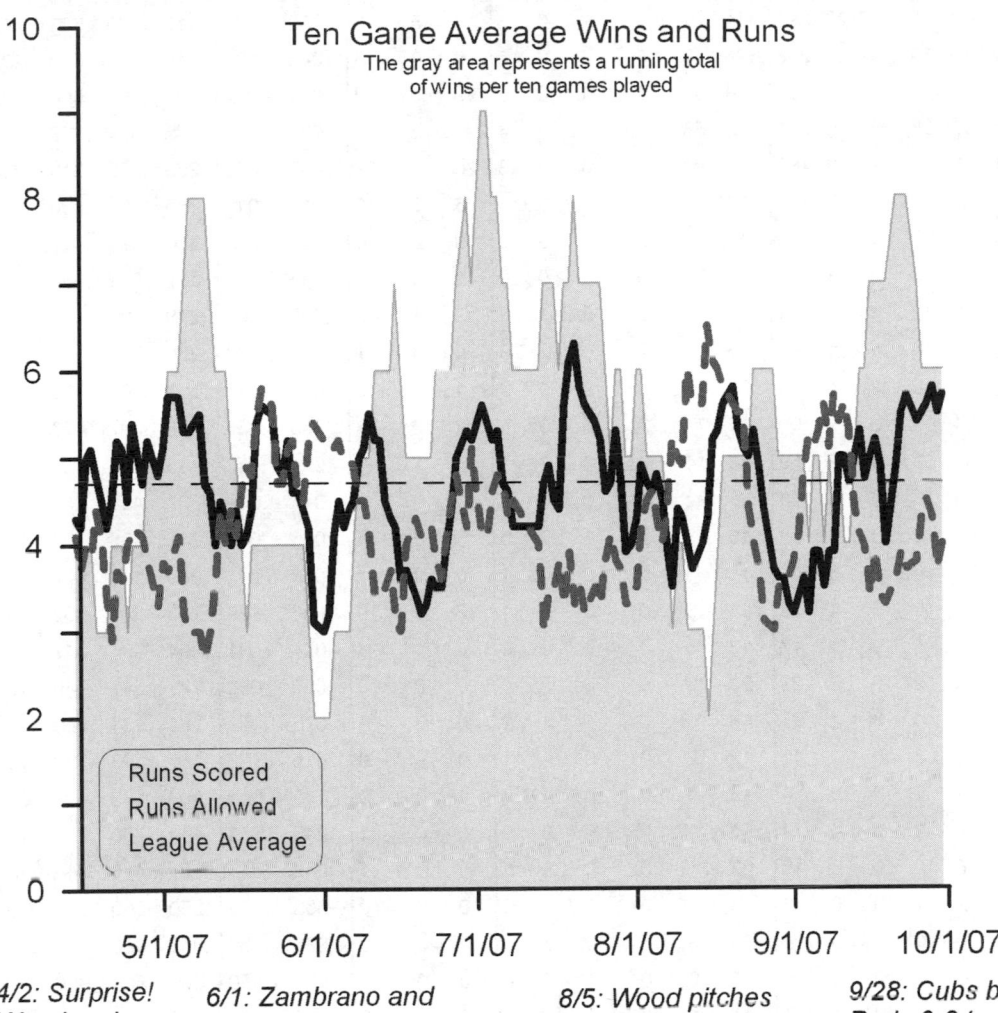

Ten Game Average Wins and Runs
The gray area represents a running total
of wins per ten games played

Runs Scored
Runs Allowed
League Average

4/2: Surprise!
Wood and
Prior on DL

6/1: Zambrano and
Barrett come to blows

8/5: Wood pitches
first game of year
from the pen

9/28: Cubs beat
Reds 6-0 to
clinch division

4/30: Cubs bottom
of division with a
10-14 record

8/28: Soriano returns
from DL to hit 14 HR
in September

Stat Facts:

- Carlos Zambrano walked 12% of the batters he faced, worst in the league
- Zambrano tied for the league lead with 14 hit batters
- Derek Lee's home-away split of .102 was the highest in the league
- Alfonso Soriano's home-away split of -.064 tied for lowest in the league
- Soriano hit a ground ball in just 34% of his batted balls
- 46% of Soriano's batted balls were fly balls
- Aramis Ramirez's L^R of .122 was second in the league
- Carlos Marmol struck out 34% of the batters he faced
- Scott Eyre allowed a line drive in 24% of his batted balls
- Michael Barrett threw out just 6% of base stealers
- Jason Kendall threw out just 4% of base stealers
- Ted Lilly allowed just .34 runs per line drive

Team Batting and Pitching/Fielding Stats by Month						
	April	May	June	July	Aug	Sept/Oct
Wins	10	12	17	17	12	17
Losses	14	15	11	9	16	12
RS/G	4.7	4.4	4.8	4.8	4.2	5.0
RA/G	3.8	4.8	4.3	3.3	4.9	4.3
OBP	.326	.325	.336	.326	.330	.351
SLG	.413	.407	.440	.374	.398	.489
FIP	4.28	4.36	4.13	4.21	4.67	3.71
DER	.732	.704	.701	.725	.697	.689

Batting Stats

Player	BR	Runs	RBI	PA	Outs	H	2B	3B	HR	TB	K	BB	IBB	HBP	SH	SF	SB	CS	GDP	H-A	L^R	BA	OBP	SLG	GPA
Lee D	106	91	82	650	407	180	43	1	22	291	114	71	8	9	0	3	6	5	15	.102	.037	.317	.400	.513	.299
Ramirez A	94	72	101	558	362	157	35	4	26	278	66	43	8	4	0	5	0	0	13	.082	.122	.310	.366	.549	.293
Soriano A	93	97	70	617	421	173	42	5	33	324	130	31	4	4	0	3	19	6	9	-.064	-.032	.299	.337	.560	.283
DeRosa M	73	64	72	574	374	147	28	3	10	211	93	58	2	7	3	4	1	2	17	.021	-.018	.293	.371	.420	.264
Theriot R	62	80	45	597	410	143	30	2	3	186	50	49	1	0	8	3	28	4	12	.036	.048	.266	.326	.346	.226
Jones J *	60	52	66	495	342	129	33	2	5	181	70	34	5	2	3	3	6	3	15	-.017	-.013	.285	.335	.400	.243
Floyd C *	41	40	45	322	208	80	10	1	9	119	47	35	5	5	0	0	0	0	6	-.038	-.012	.284	.373	.422	.265
Murton M	27	35	22	261	173	66	13	0	8	103	39	26	0	0	0	0	1	0	4	-.084	.052	.281	.352	.438	.260
Fontenot M *	26	32	29	260	178	65	12	4	3	94	43	22	0	0	1	3	5	4	5	.076	.069	.278	.336	.402	.244
Kendall J	24	21	19	202	131	47	10	1	1	62	15	19	2	6	3	0	0	3	1	-.015	-.017	.270	.362	.356	.245
Pagan A +	23	21	21	161	110	39	10	2	4	65	32	10	0	0	1	2	4	1	0	.093	-.010	.264	.306	.439	.240
Barrett M	22	23	29	231	164	54	9	0	9	90	36	17	3	0	0	3	2	2	5	.079	.056	.256	.307	.427	.238
Pie F *	21	26	20	194	140	38	9	3	2	59	43	14	0	0	2	1	8	1	0	-.024	.133	.215	.271	.333	.199
Ward D *	19	16	19	133	80	36	13	0	3	58	23	22	8	0	0	1	0	0	6	.042	.059	.327	.436	.527	.319
Izturis C +	12	15	8	207	150	47	11	0	0	58	16	13	2	1	2	0	3	0	6	-.086	-.083	.246	.298	.304	.204
Soto G	12	12	8	60	34	21	6	0	3	36	14	5	0	0	0	1	0	0	1	-.082	.011	.389	.433	.667	.351
Cedeno R	8	6	13	80	60	15	2	0	4	29	18	3	0	0	2	1	2	1	0	.006	-.129	.203	.231	.392	.196
Monroe C	5	6	4	55	43	10	4	0	1	17	13	6	0	0	0	0	0	1	3	.024	.011	.204	.291	.347	.211
Zambrano C +	3	9	5	86	61	20	2	0	2	28	29	0	0	0	5	0	0	0	0	.059	.092	.247	.247	.346	.192
Hill K +	3	7	12	105	82	15	4	0	2	25	18	8	0	1	1	2	0	0	4	.073	-.027	.161	.231	.269	.166
Blanco H	2	3	4	58	45	9	3	0	0	12	12	2	0	0	1	1	0	0	0	.015	-.138	.167	.193	.222	.138
Marshall S *	1	1	0	34	26	3	1	0	0	4	13	1	0	0	4	0	0	0	0	-.140	-.080	.103	.133	.138	.092
Fox J	1	3	1	15	13	2	2	0	0	4	2	1	0	0	0	0	0	0	1	.246	.223	.143	.200	.286	.157
Hill R *	0	0	5	67	56	8	2	0	0	10	33	1	0	0	3	0	0	0	1	.042	-.014	.127	.141	.159	.100
Patterson E	0	0	0	9	6	2	1	0	0	3	3	0	0	0	1	0	0	0	0	.358	--	.250	.250	.375	.200
Fuld S *	0	3	0	9	6	0	0	0	0	0	3	3	0	0	0	0	0	0	0	.096	.169	.000	.333	.000	.146
Gallagher S	0	0	0	2	1	0	0	0	0	0	0	0	0	1	0	0	0	0	0	-.450	-.450	.000	.500	.000	.218
Marquis J *	0	9	4	77	62	10	3	0	1	16	24	1	0	0	4	0	0	0	0	.049	.040	.139	.151	.222	.120
Miller W	-0	0	0	4	3	1	0	0	0	1	0	0	0	0	0	0	0	0	0	.233	-.233	.250	.250	.250	.170
Wood K	-0	0	0	1	1	0	0	0	0	0	1	0	0	0	0	0	0	0	0	.000	--	.000	.000	.000	.000
Dempster R	-0	0	0	1	1	0	0	0	0	0	0	0	0	0	0	0	0	0	0	.000	--	.000	.000	.000	.000
Eyre S *	-0	0	0	1	1	0	0	0	0	0	0	0	0	0	0	0	0	0	0	.000	--	.000	.000	.000	.000
Cherry R	-0	0	0	1	1	0	0	0	0	0	0	0	0	0	0	0	0	0	0	.000	--	.000	.000	.000	.000
Wuertz M	-0	0	0	2	2	0	0	0	0	0	1	0	0	0	0	0	0	0	0	.000	.000	.000	.000	.000	.000
Bowen R +	-0	3	2	36	31	2	1	0	0	3	13	4	0	0	0	1	0	0	2	-.103	-.016	.065	.167	.097	.096
Trachsel S	-0	0	0	7	6	1	0	0	0	1	1	0	0	0	0	0	0	0	0	-.140	-.140	.143	.143	.143	.097
Moore S *	-0	0	0	5	5	0	0	0	0	0	2	0	0	0	0	0	0	0	0	--	--	.000	.000	.000	.000
Marmol C	-1	0	0	7	6	0	0	0	0	0	3	0	0	0	0	0	0	0	0	.000	.000	.000	.000	.000	.000
Lilly T *	-1	5	5	77	64	10	1	0	0	11	32	1	0	0	3	0	1	0	1	.066	.078	.137	.149	.151	.102
Guzman A	-1	0	0	7	7	0	0	0	0	0	2	0	0	0	0	0	0	0	0	.000	.000	.000	.000	.000	.000

Italicized stats have been adjusted for home park.

Batted Ball Batting Stats are listed after Fielding Stats.

Pitching Stats

Player	PRC	IP	BFP	G	GS	K	BB	IBB	HBP	H	HR	DP	DER	SB	CS	PO	W	L	Sv	Op	Hld	H-A	R^L	RA	ERA	FIP
Lilly T *	100	207.0	847	34	34	174	55	2	3	181	28	13	.733	14	4	2	15	8	0	0	0	.011	.003	3.96	3.83	4.16
Zambrano C	99	216.3	925	34	34	177	101	4	14	187	23	22	.723	4	3	1	18	13	0	0	0	.030	-.058	4.16	3.95	4.55
Hill R *	93	195.0	812	32	32	183	63	3	12	170	27	17	.719	23	5	4	11	8	0	0	0	.032	-.050	4.11	3.92	4.30
Marmol C	80	69.3	285	59	0	96	35	3	4	41	3	2	.741	9	0	1	5	1	1	2	16	-.003	-.064	1.43	1.43	2.62
Marquis J	65	191.7	846	34	33	109	76	6	13	190	22	20	.708	20	2	0	12	9	0	0	0	-.022	-.053	5.21	4.60	4.92
Howry B	45	81.3	336	78	0	72	19	3	2	76	8	4	.702	2	0	0	6	7	8	12	22	.012	.054	3.43	3.32	3.44
Marshall S *	42	103.3	446	21	19	67	35	3	1	107	13	11	.697	5	2	1	7	8	0	0	0	.028	-.059	4.53	3.92	4.57
Wuertz M	39	72.3	312	73	0	79	35	6	0	64	8	4	.700	7	1	0	2	3	0	0	8	.020	-.009	3.73	3.48	3.73
Dempster R	26	66.7	282	66	0	55	30	4	1	59	8	6	.723	9	0	0	2	7	28	31	0	-.003	-.054	4.86	4.73	4.39
Eyre S *	23	52.3	240	55	0	45	35	5	1	59	3	12	.635	8	1	0	2	1	0	4	5	-.015	-.038	4.47	4.13	4.07
Hart K	17	11.0	42	8	0	13	4	0	0	7	0	2	.720	1	0	0	0	0	0	0	0	-.064	.249	0.82	0.82	2.00
Guzman A	16	30.3	128	12	3	26	9	0	2	32	2	5	.663	4	0	0	0	1	0	1	0	-.055	-.051	3.56	3.56	3.50
Ohman W *	14	36.3	168	56	0	33	16	4	1	42	3	2	.643	4	0	0	2	4	1	1	12	.218	-.046	4.95	4.95	3.60
Wood K	14	24.3	101	22	0	24	13	1	0	18	0	2	.719	0	1	0	1	1	0	0	0	-.120	.075	3.33	3.33	2.78
Cherry R	8	15.0	66	12	0	13	6	1	1	13	1	0	.689	1	0	0	1	1	0	1	0	-.080	.013	3.60	3.00	3.60
Cotts N *	7	16.7	76	16	0	14	9	0	3	15	1	4	.673	1	1	1	0	1	0	0	2	.065	-.018	4.86	4.86	4.53
Trachsel S	3	17.3	79	4	4	11	7	1	0	25	3	3	.603	2	1	1	1	3	0	0	0	-.167	.171	8.31	8.31	5.29
Petrick B	2	9.7	42	8	0	6	7	0	0	8	3	2	.808	1	1	0	0	0	0	0	1	-.139	.145	7.45	7.45	8.23
Gallagher S	2	14.7	74	8	0	5	12	0	1	19	3	3	.679	0	0	0	0	0	1	1	0	-.016	.098	9.20	8.59	7.91
Miller W	2	13.7	70	3	3	6	6	0	0	24	5	0	.642	1	1	0	0	1	0	0	0	-.093	-.130	10.54	10.54	8.46
Pignatiello	1	2.0	8	4	0	3	0	0	0	3	1	0	.500	0	1	0	0	0	0	0	1	.008	.475	4.50	4.50	6.77
Rapada C *	0	0.3	1	1	0	0	0	0	0	0	0	0	1.000	0	0	0	0	0	0	0	0	--	--	0.00	0.00	3.27

Italicized stats have been adjusted for home park.

Batted Ball Pitching Stats

Player	% of PA		% of Batted Balls					Out %		Runs Per Event				Total Runs vs. Avg.				
	K%	BB%	GB%	LD%	FB%	IF/F	HR/OF	GB	OF	NIP	GB	LD	OF	NIP	GB	LD	FB	Tot
Lilly T	21	7	34	17	49	.12	.11	77	84	.00	.03	.34	.17	-12	-4	-14	3	-27
Marmol C	34	14	31	16	52	.10	.03	74	91	.02	.04	.43	.01	-2	-2	-6	-13	-23
Hill R	23	9	36	21	43	.12	.13	78	86	.02	.03	.35	.19	-6	-7	-6	-1	-20
Zambrano C	19	12	47	17	37	.13	.12	79	84	.07	.01	.42	.18	7	-10	-7	-6	-16
Howry B	21	6	32	20	48	.14	.08	69	87	-.01	.08	.38	.12	-6	0	-1	-5	-12
Wuertz M	25	11	44	15	41	.13	.12	70	83	.03	.08	.41	.21	-1	1	-5	-0	-6
Dempster R	20	11	47	20	32	.11	.15	82	87	.05	.00	.38	.23	1	-5	-1	-0	-5
Wood K	24	13	34	18	48	.03	.00	81	86	.05	-.01	.49	.03	0	-1	-0	-4	-5
Guzman A	20	9	45	19	36	.06	.07	83	68	.02	-.02	.42	.23	-1	-2	0	1	-2
Marshall S	15	8	48	16	36	.08	.12	72	87	.05	.06	.38	.18	-1	4	-4	-1	-2
Marquis J	13	11	50	17	33	.08	.10	77	84	.09	.03	.43	.18	7	-5	2	-2	2
Ohman W	20	10	41	18	42	.15	.08	65	78	.04	.10	.45	.20	-0	2	0	0	3
Eyre S	19	15	39	24	38	.03	.05	67	87	.09	.06	.49	.08	4	0	6	-5	6
MLB Average	17	9	43	19	38	.10	.10	74	83	.05	.05	.40	.18	--	--	--	--	--

Fielding Stats

Name	INN	SBA/G	CS%	ERA	WP+PB/G	PO	A	TE	FE
Catcher									
Barrett M	475.3	0.64	6%	4.17	0.435	389	18	3	1
Kendall J	431.7	1.13	4%	4.29	0.438	362	24	5	0
Hill K	232.3	0.50	23%	2.98	0.155	190	11	1	0
Soto G	122.0	1.03	29%	3.61	0.148	109	10	0	0
Blanco H	109.0	0.83	20%	4.79	0.661	102	4	0	0
Bowen R	76.3	0.59	20%	4.72	0.000	78	3	1	0

Name	Inn	PO	A	TE	FE	FPct	DPS	DPT	RZR	OOZ
First Base										
Lee D	1274.0	1165	87	1	6	.994	5	0	.724	24
Ward D	90.7	90	5	0	1	.990	0	0	1.000	3
DeRosa M	55.7	49	0	0	1	.980	0	0	.571	0
Blanco H	15.0	8	1	0	0	1.000	0	0	1.000	0
Moore S	9.0	10	1	0	0	1.000	0	0	1.000	1
Fox J	2.0	3	0	0	0	1.000	0	0	--	--
Second Base										
DeRosa M	708.7	168	193	3	3	.984	18	24	.869	15
Fontenot M	468.0	112	128	3	3	.976	13	21	.814	9
Theriot R	236.0	47	70	0	1	.992	9	9	.902	3
Cedeno R	33.0	10	14	0	0	1.000	2	1	1.000	0
Soriano A	1.0	0	0	0	0	0.000	0	0	--	--
Shortstop										
Theriot R	859.0	126	260	3	4	.980	32	22	.858	28
Izturis C	450.7	57	130	3	4	.964	11	16	.842	17
Cedeno R	110.0	14	33	0	2	.959	3	2	.800	3
Fontenot M	19.0	2	0	0	2	.500	0	0	0.000	0
DeRosa M	8.0	1	1	0	0	1.000	0	0	1.000	0
Third Base										
Ramirez A	1091.0	88	260	4	6	.972	20	0	.715	37
DeRosa M	287.3	24	68	2	2	.958	3	0	.761	10
Theriot R	54.0	5	7	0	2	.857	0	0	.500	2
Cedeno R	14.0	3	3	0	0	1.000	1	0	.667	1

Name	Inn	PO	A	TE	FE	FPct	DPS	DPT	RZR	OOZ
Left Field										
Soriano A	1064.0	244	19	1	5	.978	8	0	.872	40
Murton M	185.7	50	1	0	0	1.000	0	0	.905	12
Floyd C	132.7	32	0	0	0	1.000	0	0	.967	3
Jones J	18.3	2	0	0	0	1.000	0	0	.667	0
Theriot R	11.0	4	0	0	0	1.000	0	0	.750	1
Monroe C	10.0	4	0	0	0	1.000	0	0	1.000	1
DeRosa M	8.0	2	0	0	0	1.000	0	0	1.000	1
Patterson E	7.0	1	0	0	0	1.000	0	0	.500	0
Pie F	5.0	1	0	0	0	1.000	0	0	1.000	0
Pagan A	3.0	0	0	0	0	0.000	0	0	--	--
Ward D	1.0	0	0	0	0	0.000	0	0	--	--
Fuld S	1.0	0	0	0	0	0.000	0	0	--	--
Center Field										
Jones J	645.0	195	8	0	4	.981	0	0	.925	35
Pie F	424.3	120	1	0	0	1.000	0	0	.937	16
Pagan A	236.0	60	0	0	0	1.000	0	0	.900	6
Soriano A	100.3	29	0	0	0	1.000	0	0	.893	4
Monroe C	39.0	10	0	0	0	1.000	0	0	.900	1
Murton M	1.0	0	0	0	0	0.000	0	0	0.000	0
Fuld S	1.0	0	0	0	0	0.000	0	0	--	--
Right Field										
Floyd C	412.3	69	1	0	0	1.000	0	0	.821	5
Jones J	349.0	75	0	0	0	1.000	0	0	.938	15
Murton M	282.7	65	2	1	3	.944	2	0	.846	10
DeRosa M	138.7	28	1	0	0	1.000	0	0	.870	8
Pagan A	92.0	20	0	0	0	1.000	0	0	.929	7
Ward D	74.0	25	1	0	0	1.000	0	0	.909	6
Monroe C	46.0	8	0	0	0	1.000	0	0	.889	0
Fox J	22.0	2	0	0	0	1.000	0	0	.500	0
Fuld S	22.0	9	1	0	0	1.000	2	0	1.000	2
Theriot R	7.0	1	0	0	0	1.000	0	0	.500	0
Hill K	1.0	0	0	0	0	0.000	0	0	--	--

Batted Ball Batting Stats

Player	% of PA		% of Batted Balls			IF/F	HR/OF	Out %		Runs Per Event				Total Runs vs. Avg.				
	K%	BB%	GB%	LD%	FB%			GB	OF	NIP	GB	LD	OF	NIP	GB	LD	FB	Tot
Lee D	18	12	41	21	38	.06	.13	69	80	.08	.07	.47	.24	7	4	13	15	39
Ramirez A	12	8	39	18	44	.08	.14	70	80	.08	.06	.44	.25	2	4	6	23	34
Soriano A	21	6	34	20	46	.05	.17	70	87	-.02	.08	.48	.25	-11	3	10	22	25
Ward D	17	17	40	22	39	.06	.09	77	59	.11	.01	.46	.32	4	-1	3	5	10
DeRosa M	16	11	42	22	36	.03	.07	74	81	.08	.04	.39	.15	5	-1	7	-2	8
Murton M	15	10	47	16	37	.07	.12	68	78	.07	.08	.30	.24	1	4	-4	5	6
Floyd C	15	12	46	17	37	.19	.13	67	92	.10	.09	.40	.15	4	5	-0	-4	6
Kendall J	7	12	47	18	35	.13	.02	68	77	.17	.10	.22	.11	4	4	-4	-3	2
Barrett M	16	7	40	19	41	.13	.14	73	91	.03	.06	.34	.18	-1	1	-1	1	-1
Pagan A	20	6	36	18	46	.10	.09	76	86	-.00	.04	.48	.14	-2	1	1	-1	-2
Fontenot M	17	8	47	19	34	.03	.05	73	83	.04	.05	.43	.10	-1	2	2	-5	-2
Jones J	14	7	58	19	23	.10	.06	73	76	.04	.05	.36	.19	-2	5	-0	-6	-4
Izturis C	8	7	53	22	25	.07	.00	76	80	.10	.03	.32	.05	0	-0	1	-7	-6
Hill K	17	9	52	8	40	.03	.07	85	86	.04	-.03	.34	.10	-1	-3	-4	-2	-10
Theriot R	8	8	49	21	30	.07	.02	72	87	.11	.06	.32	.03	3	7	0	-21	-11
Pie F	22	7	48	20	32	.12	.05	84	80	-.00	-.00	.39	.15	-3	-3	-1	-4	-11
MLB Average	17	9	43	19	38	.10	.10	74	83	.05	.05	.40	.18	--	--	--	--	--

Chicago White Sox

Stat Facts:

- Jim Thome's L^R of .143 was second highest in the league
- 29% of Thome's outfield flies were home runs
- Thome's BB% of 19% was second highest in the league
- 56% of Rob Mackowiak's batted balls were ground balls
- Josh Fields struck out in 30% of his plate appearances
- Mark Buerhle tied for the league lead with five pickoffs
- Buerhle surrendered just two stolen bases in five attempts
- Buerhle's lefty-righty split of .053 was highest in the league
- Jon Garland allowed only 2 SBs in 8 attempts
- Jose Contreras allowed 25 steals in 31 attempts
- Contreras hit 15 batters
- Gavin Floyd gave up 17 homers in 70 innings

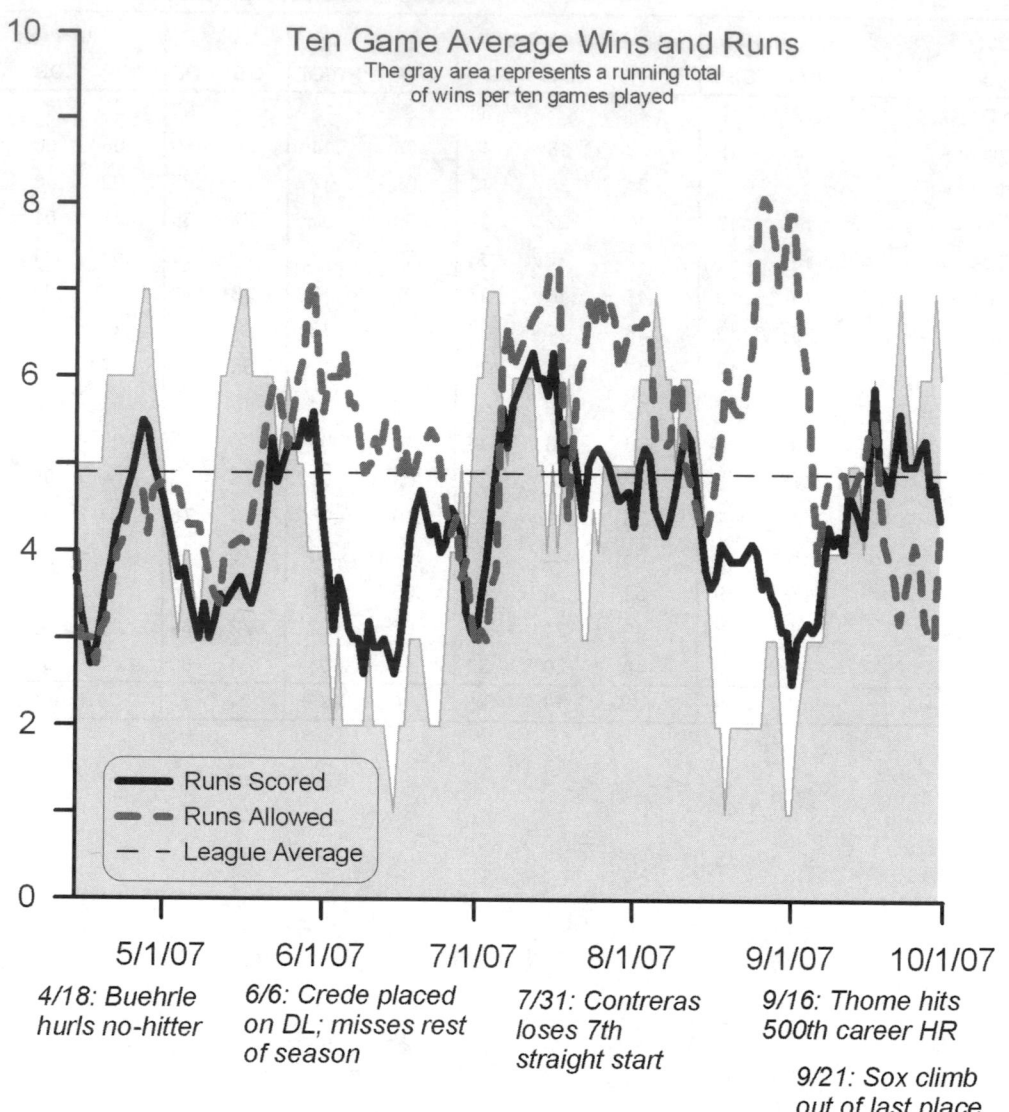

Ten Game Average Wins and Runs
The gray area represents a running total of wins per ten games played

Runs Scored
Runs Allowed
League Average

4/18: Buehrle hurls no-hitter

6/6: Crede placed on DL; misses rest of season

7/31: Contreras loses 7th straight start

9/16: Thome hits 500th career HR

9/21: Sox climb out of last place

Team Batting and Pitching/Fielding Stats by Month						
	April	May	June	July	Aug	Sept/Oct
Wins	12	12	10	14	9	15
Losses	11	14	18	15	20	12
RS/G	4.1	4.0	3.6	5.1	4.1	4.7
RA/G	4.2	5.2	4.5	6.4	6.1	4.2
OBP	.317	.302	.308	.342	.312	.322
SLG	.379	.365	.353	.447	.428	.443
FIP	4.07	4.53	4.20	5.05	4.81	3.76
DER	.734	.697	.677	.659	.682	.671

Batting Stats

Player	BR	Runs	RBI	PA	Outs	H	2B	3B	HR	TB	K	BB	IBB	HBP	SH	SF	SB	CS	GDP	H-A	L^R	BA	OBP	SLG	GPA
Thome J *	100	79	96	536	324	119	19	0	35	243	134	95	11	6	0	3	0	1	10	.005	.143	.275	.410	.563	.316
Konerko P	86	71	90	636	429	142	34	0	31	269	102	78	9	3	0	6	0	1	21	.014	.060	.259	.351	.490	.272
Dye J	67	68	78	561	397	129	34	0	28	247	107	45	2	4	0	4	2	1	17	-.001	.057	.254	.317	.486	.257
Fields J	56	54	67	418	294	91	17	1	23	179	125	35	0	1	6	3	1	1	11	-.011	.115	.244	.308	.480	.251
Uribe J	51	55	68	563	408	120	18	2	20	202	112	34	2	4	7	5	1	9	6	.062	.032	.234	.284	.394	.220
Pierzynski A	46	54	50	509	370	124	24	0	14	190	66	25	5	8	1	3	1	1	21	-.025	.002	.263	.309	.403	.233
Iguchi T	44	45	31	377	251	82	17	4	6	125	65	44	1	2	1	3	8	1	5	.039	-.033	.251	.340	.382	.242
Owens J *	37	44	17	389	274	95	9	2	1	111	63	27	0	3	3	0	32	8	5	-.021	.015	.267	.324	.312	.217
Mackowiak R	35	34	36	268	177	66	11	2	6	99	53	23	1	6	0	2	3	1	5	-.002	.022	.278	.354	.418	.256
Erstad D *	34	33	32	347	239	77	13	1	4	104	44	28	0	0	0	1	7	2	4	.036	.100	.248	.310	.335	.217
Richar D *	21	30	15	206	152	43	9	3	6	76	33	16	0	0	2	1	1	3	5	-.008	-.006	.230	.289	.406	.225
Cintron A +	19	23	19	196	146	45	7	1	2	60	35	9	1	1	0	1	2	1	5	-.046	.001	.243	.281	.324	.201
Terrero L	18	18	12	139	94	27	2	0	5	44	35	12	0	9	1	0	4	3	1	.004	-.000	.231	.348	.376	.243
Podsednik S	18	30	11	235	176	52	13	4	2	79	36	13	0	4	4	0	12	5	9	-.002	-.061	.243	.299	.369	.220
Crede J	17	13	22	178	133	36	5	0	4	53	24	10	0	0	0	1	0	1	1	-.001	-.007	.216	.258	.317	.190
Gonzalez A	12	17	11	215	163	35	6	0	2	47	61	25	1	0	1	0	1	5	4	.025	.013	.185	.280	.249	.183
Ozuna P	5	9	3	85	60	19	3	0	0	22	9	3	0	1	3	0	3	0	1	.077	.005	.244	.280	.282	.191
Hall T	3	8	3	120	94	24	4	0	0	28	12	3	0	0	0	1	0	0	2	-.021	.129	.207	.225	.241	.157
Sweeney R *	3	5	5	49	39	9	3	0	1	15	5	4	0	0	0	0	0	1	2	-.045	.051	.200	.265	.333	.197
Garland J	0	0	0	2	0	0	0	0	0	0	0	0	0	0	0	2	0	0	0	.000	--	.000	.000	.000	.000
Lucy D	-0	0	0	15	12	3	0	0	0	3	6	0	0	0	0	0	0	0	0	-.113	.242	.200	.200	.200	.136
Contreras J	-0	0	0	1	1	0	0	0	0	0	1	0	0	0	0	0	0	0	0	.000	--	.000	.000	.000	.000
Thornton M *	-0	0	0	1	1	0	0	0	0	0	1	0	0	0	0	0	0	0	0	.000	--	.000	.000	.000	.000
Massel N	-0	0	0	2	1	0	0	0	0	0	1	0	0	0	0	1	0	0	0	.000	--	.000	.000	.000	.000
Danks J *	-0	0	0	2	2	0	0	0	0	0	2	0	0	0	0	0	0	0	0	.000	--	.000	.000	.000	.000
Anderson B	-0	3	0	19	17	2	1	0	0	3	7	2	0	0	0	0	0	0	2	.114	-.168	.118	.211	.176	.135
Buehrle M *	-0	0	0	6	5	0	0	0	0	0	4	0	0	0	0	0	0	0	0	.000	.000	.000	.000	.000	.000
Vazquez J	-1	0	0	7	7	0	0	0	0	0	2	0	0	0	1	0	0	0	1	.000	.000	.000	.000	.000	.000
Molina G	-1	0	1	21	17	1	0	0	0	1	4	1	0	0	1	1	0	0	0	.071	-.040	.056	.100	.056	.057

Italicized stats have been adjusted for home park.

Batted Ball Batting Stats

Player	% of PA		% of Batted Balls			IF/F	HR/OF	Out %		Runs Per Event				Total Runs vs. Avg.				
	K%	BB%	GB%	LD%	FB%			GB	OF	NIP	GB	LD	OF	NIP	GB	LD	FB	Tot
Thome J	25	19	43	18	39	.05	.29	78	81	.08	.02	.49	.43	13	-5	1	28	38
Konerko P	16	13	38	17	45	.10	.17	80	87	.09	.00	.41	.25	8	-9	-0	17	16
Dye J	19	9	35	19	46	.13	.17	81	81	.03	-.00	.38	.27	-3	-9	-2	17	3
Mackowiak R	20	11	56	15	29	.09	.12	78	77	.05	.03	.47	.26	1	0	-1	1	1
Terrero L	26	15	51	16	33	.20	.25	71	100	.06	.06	.49	.28	1	0	-2	-1	-1
Fields J	30	9	41	17	43	.07	.23	82	80	-.01	-.01	.47	.38	-8	-6	-5	17	-1
Iguchi T	17	12	43	21	36	.06	.07	81	82	.08	.00	.36	.16	3	-5	-1	-2	-4
Richar D	16	8	45	18	36	.11	.12	84	89	.04	-.02	.44	.19	-1	-4	1	-1	-5
Podsednik S	15	7	53	19	28	.02	.04	74	89	.03	.04	.44	.06	-1	0	1	-8	-7
Erstad D	12	8	53	17	30	.09	.06	75	75	.07	.05	.26	.16	0	2	-7	-4	-9
Hall T	10	3	41	17	41	.14	.00	84	78	-.02	-.01	.34	.04	-2	-3	-1	-5	-11
Cintron A	18	5	43	19	39	.17	.04	77	85	-.01	.03	.39	.08	-3	-1	-0	-6	-11
Pierzynski A	13	6	43	18	39	.13	.10	83	79	.04	-.02	.40	.19	-3	-11	0	2	-12

Batted Ball Batting Stats are continued after Fielding Stats.

Pitching Stats

Player	PRC	IP	BFP	G	GS	K	BB	IBB	HBP	H	HR	DP	DER	SB	CS	PO	W	L	Sv	Op	Hld	H-A	R^L	RA	ERA	FIP
Vazquez J	114	216.7	882	32	32	213	50	2	7	197	29	20	.705	6	4	0	15	8	0	0	0	-.012	-.002	3.95	3.74	3.92
Buehrle M *	95	201.0	835	30	30	115	45	5	5	208	22	26	.704	2	3	5	10	9	0	0	0	.028	.053	3.85	3.63	4.33
Garland J	75	208.3	883	32	32	98	57	3	4	219	19	24	.706	2	6	2	10	13	0	0	0	-.031	.003	4.92	4.23	4.46
Contreras J	55	189.0	858	32	30	113	62	1	15	232	21	21	.657	25	6	1	10	17	0	0	0	.013	-.051	6.38	5.57	4.84
Danks J *	46	139.0	622	26	26	109	54	4	4	160	28	15	.679	10	1	2	6	13	0	0	0	.000	.011	5.96	5.50	5.60
Jenks B	44	65.0	249	66	0	56	13	4	1	45	2	5	.751	5	0	0	3	5	40	46	0	-.013	-.038	2.77	2.77	2.52
Thornton M *	24	56.3	249	68	0	55	26	6	2	59	4	7	.654	1	1	1	4	4	2	7	17	.064	.013	4.95	4.79	3.52
Floyd G	23	70.0	314	16	10	49	19	0	6	85	17	10	.682	12	0	0	1	5	0	0	0	.024	-.032	5.79	5.27	6.21
Logan B *	18	50.7	226	68	0	35	20	3	0	59	7	9	.659	7	1	1	2	1	0	2	11	.057	-.116	5.33	4.97	4.80
Wassermann E	12	23.0	94	33	0	14	7	4	2	20	0	4	.704	2	0	0	1	1	0	1	9	-.035	-.315	3.52	2.74	2.82
Bukvich R	11	35.7	170	45	0	18	24	1	3	36	5	4	.717	1	0	0	1	0	0	1	4	.088	.030	5.80	5.05	6.38
Broadway L	11	10.3	41	4	1	14	5	0	0	5	0	2	.727	0	0	0	1	1	0	0	0	--	-.139	1.74	0.87	2.12
MacDougal M	10	42.3	208	54	0	39	33	3	2	50	3	7	.634	9	0	0	2	5	0	3	19	-.019	-.028	7.87	6.80	4.73
Aardsma D	10	32.3	151	25	0	36	17	3	1	39	4	2	.624	0	0	0	2	1	0	3	3	-.152	.010	6.68	6.40	4.15
Masset N	9	39.3	193	27	1	21	26	5	2	52	2	5	.634	8	1	0	2	3	0	1	2	.037	.003	7.55	7.09	4.73
Sisco A *	3	14.0	74	19	0	13	11	0	1	19	2	0	.617	3	0	0	0	1	0	0	4	.057	-.170	8.36	8.36	5.95
Phillips H *	3	7.3	34	6	0	2	4	1	0	10	1	1	.667	0	0	1	1	1	0	0	0	-.228	.014	3.68	3.68	5.83
Day D	2	12.0	65	13	0	7	9	0	2	19	1	2	.587	1	0	0	0	1	0	0	1	-.111	-.016	11.25	11.25	6.05
Haeger C	1	11.3	59	8	0	1	8	2	1	17	3	2	.674	2	0	0	0	1	0	0	1	.145	-.100	8.74	7.15	8.50
Myers M *	1	13.7	70	17	0	6	7	2	1	21	3	2	.623	2	0	0	1	0	0	1	2	.139	-.207	12.51	11.20	6.67
Prinz B	1	3.3	16	4	0	1	2	1	0	4	1	0	.750	0	0	0	0	0	0	0	0	.520	-.158	8.10	8.10	7.58

Italicized stats have been adjusted for home park.

Batted Ball Pitching Stats

Player	% of PA		% of Batted Balls					Out %		Runs Per Event				Total Runs vs. Avg.				
	K%	BB%	GB%	LD%	FB%	IF/F	HR/OF	GB	OF	NIP	GB	LD	OF	NIP	GB	LD	FB	Tot
Jenks R	22	6	54	16	31	.11	.04	76	89	-.02	.03	.30	.04	-5	-2	-7	-11	-25
Vazquez J	24	6	40	17	43	.09	.12	74	82	-.02	.05	.37	.21	-17	-2	-12	8	-24
Buehrle M	14	6	43	18	39	.08	.09	77	81	.03	.02	.39	.17	-7	-6	0	1	-13
Garland J	11	7	39	23	38	.12	.08	80	81	.06	.01	.34	.16	-2	-10	6	-3	-9
Thornton M	22	11	47	19	34	.07	.08	73	76	.04	.07	.37	.22	0	2	-1	1	2
Logan B	15	9	51	14	35	.09	.13	60	87	.05	.12	.33	.19	0	7	-4	0	4
Bukvich R	11	16	44	11	44	.02	.09	73	84	.16	.04	.45	.16	5	0	-2	2	5
Aardsma D	24	12	37	21	42	.05	.11	66	79	.04	.10	.43	.23	0	1	1	3	5
MacDougal M	19	17	56	18	26	.21	.11	72	71	.10	.06	.47	.28	5	2	1	-1	8
Masset N	11	15	43	17	40	.12	.04	59	79	.15	.13	.32	.13	5	6	-1	-1	8
Floyd G	16	8	42	17	41	.06	.18	71	81	.04	.05	.38	.28	-1	1	-1	12	11
Contreras J	13	9	45	19	36	.11	.10	68	82	.07	.08	.35	.18	3	16	-0	1	20
Danks J	18	9	35	19	46	.09	.15	73	85	.05	.06	.41	.24	-0	1	3	17	21
MLB Average	17	9	43	19	38	.10	.10	74	83	.05	.05	.40	.18	--	--	--	--	--

Fielding Stats

Name	INN	SBA/G	CS%	ERA	WP+PB/G	PO	A	TE	FE
Catcher									
Pierzynski A	1058.0	0.63	16%	4.41	0.391	796	46	2	0
Hall T	292.7	0.89	10%	6.12	0.461	187	10	2	1
Molina G	57.0	0.32	0%	4.26	0.474	41	1	0	0
Lucy D	33.0	2.18	0%	5.18	0.273	27	1	0	0

Name	Inn	PO	A	TE	FE	FPct	DPS	DPT	RZR	OOZ
First Base										
Konerko P	1227.0	1180	71	2	2	.996	17	4	.707	25
Erstad D	173.7	174	14	1	0	.995	2	0	.781	2
Mackowiak R	23.0	23	1	0	0	1.000	0	0	.333	0
Gonzalez A	8.3	7	0	0	0	1.000	0	0	1.000	0
Thome J	8.0	6	0	0	0	1.000	0	0	--	--
Second Base										
Iguchi T	778.0	188	247	1	5	.986	25	43	.824	23
Richar D	491.7	103	139	1	2	.988	16	21	.802	14
Cintron A	117.7	22	24	2	1	.939	1	4	.773	2
Ozuna P	29.3	12	10	0	0	1.000	0	3	1.000	1
Gonzalez A	24.0	4	4	0	0	1.000	1	0	.800	0
Shortstop										
Uribe J	1305.0	245	443	10	7	.976	58	43	.796	49
Cintron A	132.3	34	45	1	1	.975	5	7	.800	4
Gonzalez A	2.0	0	0	0	0	0.000	0	0	--	--
Ozuna P	1.0	0	0	0	0	0.000	0	0	--	--
Third Base										
Fields J	689.7	47	159	1	7	.958	12	1	.668	15
Crede J	388.3	36	97	2	2	.971	15	0	.829	25
Gonzalez A	188.0	15	42	7	2	.864	4	0	.607	7
Cintron A	112.7	9	27	2	3	.878	2	1	.733	5
Ozuna P	61.0	5	9	1	2	.824	0	0	.467	3
Mackowiak R	1.0	0	0	0	0	0.000	0	0	--	--

Name	Inn	PO	A	TE	FE	FPct	DPS	DPT	RZR	OOZ
Left Field										
Podsednik S	460.3	108	4	1	3	.966	2	0	.900	9
Mackowiak R	424.7	90	3	1	1	.979	2	0	.880	9
Fields J	179.3	34	2	0	2	.947	0	0	.750	7
Gonzalez A	121.0	31	1	0	0	1.000	0	0	.700	3
Sweeney R	92.7	19	1	0	0	1.000	2	0	.941	3
Erstad D	43.7	15	0	0	0	1.000	0	0	.933	1
Ozuna P	43.0	13	0	0	1	.929	0	0	.909	3
Owens J	35.7	5	0	0	0	1.000	0	0	.750	2
Terrero L	29.0	2	0	0	0	1.000	0	0	.667	0
Anderson B	11.3	1	0	0	0	1.000	0	0	0.000	1
Center Field										
Owens J	708.7	208	1	1	1	.991	2	0	.920	24
Erstad D	371.3	105	1	0	1	.991	0	0	.896	19
Terrero L	237.7	70	2	0	1	.986	2	0	.918	3
Gonzalez A	53.0	16	1	0	0	1.000	2	0	.875	2
Sweeney R	26.0	6	0	0	0	1.000	0	0	1.000	2
Anderson B	24.0	8	0	0	1	.889	0	0	1.000	1
Podsednik S	20.0	2	0	0	0	1.000	0	0	1.000	1
Right Field										
Dye J	1150.0	284	9	2	1	.990	6	0	.807	38
Mackowiak R	88.7	22	1	0	1	.950	0	0	.833	7
Erstad D	76.3	12	1	0	0	1.000	0	0	.833	2
Gonzalez A	63.0	15	0	0	0	1.000	0	0	.846	4
Terrero L	56.7	12	0	0	0	1.000	0	0	.692	3

Batted Ball Batting Stats

Player	% of PA		% of Batted Balls					Out %		Runs Per Event				Total Runs vs. Avg.				
	K%	BB%	GB%	LD%	FB%	IF/F	HR/OF	GB	OF	NIP	GB	LD	OF	NIP	GB	LD	FB	Tot
Crede J	13	6	32	15	53	.17	.06	65	93	.02	.10	.26	.05	-2	2	-5	-7	-12
Owens J	16	8	62	19	19	.06	.00	70	90	.04	.08	.32	-0.00	-2	10	-4	-17	-13
Gonzalez A	28	12	48	15	37	.15	.05	72	81	.02	.05	.33	.10	-1	-0	-6	-6	-14
Uribe J	20	7	35	15	50	.17	.12	69	89	.00	.08	.40	.16	-8	2	-8	-2	-16
MLB Average	17	9	43	19	38	.10	.10	74	83	.05	.05	.40	.18	--	--	--	--	--

Cincinnati Reds

Stat Facts:

- Matt Belisle had an LD% of 22%, second highest in the league
- Belisle's ERA of 5.32 was much worse than his FIP of 4.54
- The DER behind Belisle was .663, third-lowest in the league
- Bronson Arroyo was second in the league with 13 hit batsmen
- Aaron Harang was third in the league with 119 PRC
- Adam Dunn walked or struck out in 43% of his plate appearances
- 26% of Dunn's fly balls were home runs
- Jeff Keppinger struck out in just 4% of his plate appearances
- 58% of Norris Hopper's batted balls were ground balls
- Dave Ross threw out 39% of base stealers
- Ross had a .209 GPA despite hitting 17 homers in 348 PAs
- Ken Griffey Jr. committed 8 fielding errors

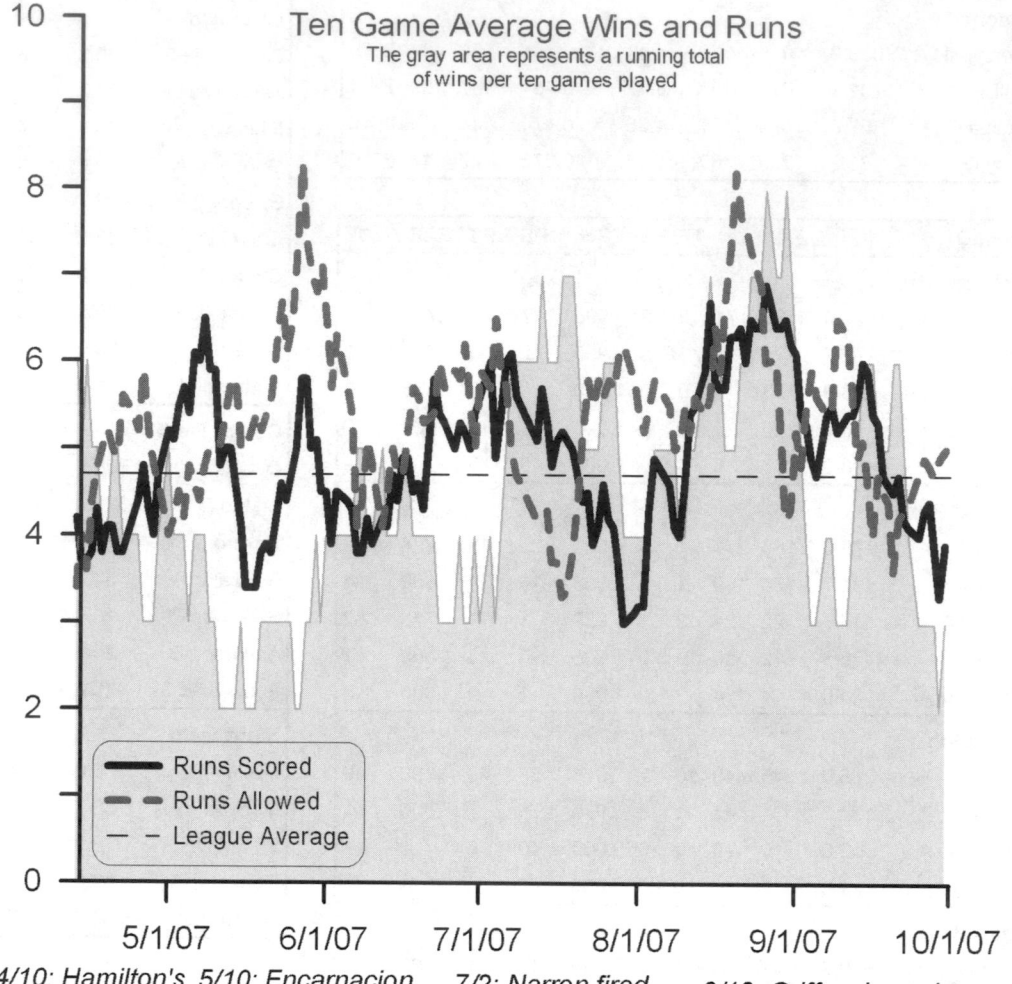

Ten Game Average Wins and Runs
The gray area represents a running total of wins per ten games played

Runs Scored
Runs Allowed
League Average

4/10: Hamilton's 1st career hit: 2-run HR

5/10: Encarnacion sent to AAA for 12 days after slow start

6/8: Bailey wins ML debut

7/2: Narron fired, replaced by MacKanin

8/2: Phillips steals 2 bases in one play as WAS puts shift on Dunn

9/19: Griffey Jr. ends season with strained groin; Dunn hits 40th HR for 4th straight year

Team Batting and Pitching/Fielding Stats by Month						
	April	May	June	July	Aug	Sept/Oct
Wins	12	9	10	14	17	10
Losses	13	21	16	12	11	17
RS/G	4.4	4.7	4.8	4.5	6.0	4.5
RA/G	4.4	5.9	5.2	5.1	5.8	5.1
OBP	.319	.327	.318	.333	.375	.337
SLG	.393	.456	.452	.389	.499	.417
FIP	3.47	4.39	4.58	4.72	5.31	4.75
DER	.684	.671	.679	.670	.684	.687

Batting Stats

Player	BR	Runs	RBI	PA	Outs	H	2B	3B	HR	TB	K	BB	IBB	HBP	SH	SF	SB	CS	GDP	H-A	L^R	BA	OBP	SLG	GPA
Dunn A *	102	101	106	632	398	138	27	2	40	289	165	101	8	5	0	4	9	2	12	.016	.069	.264	.386	.554	.295
Phillips B	85	107	94	702	497	187	26	6	30	315	109	33	4	12	2	5	32	8	26	-.006	.075	.288	.331	.485	.255
Griffey Jr.	82	78	93	623	397	146	24	1	30	262	99	85	14	1	0	9	6	1	14	.045	.069	.277	.372	.496	.276
Encarnacion	80	66	76	560	363	145	25	1	16	220	86	39	4	14	0	1	8	1	5	-.003	.010	.289	.356	.438	.255
Hamilton J *	56	52	47	337	220	87	17	2	19	165	65	33	4	4	0	2	3	3	6	.033	.129	.292	.368	.554	.287
Hatteberg S	56	50	47	417	257	112	27	1	10	171	35	49	6	3	1	3	0	0	8	.089	.114	.310	.394	.474	.279
Gonzalez A	50	55	55	430	300	107	27	1	16	184	75	24	1	8	2	3	0	1	13	-.031	-.044	.272	.325	.468	.249
Keppinger J	38	39	32	276	173	80	16	2	5	115	12	24	0	4	6	1	2	1	11	-.066	.044	.332	.400	.477	.283
Hopper N	38	51	14	335	220	101	14	2	0	119	33	20	1	1	6	1	14	6	8	-.018	.031	.329	.371	.388	.249
Freel R	30	44	16	304	221	68	13	3	3	96	47	18	0	7	2	0	15	8	4	.052	-.140	.245	.308	.347	.213
Conine J	29	23	32	242	162	57	11	1	6	88	28	20	0	0	1	6	4	0	4	.084	.050	.265	.320	.409	.232
Valentin J +	29	19	34	265	183	67	21	0	2	94	25	19	2	1	0	2	0	0	7	-.076	.050	.276	.328	.387	.231
Ross D	28	32	39	348	257	63	10	0	17	124	92	30	4	0	5	2	0	0	9	.057	.043	.203	.271	.399	.209
Votto J *	16	11	17	89	57	27	7	0	4	46	15	5	1	0	0	0	1	0	0	.153	.114	.321	.360	.548	.282
Cantu J	9	8	9	68	43	17	8	0	1	28	10	7	0	2	0	2	0	0	3	.035	-.076	.298	.382	.491	.279
Jorgensen R	4	3	6	15	12	3	0	0	2	9	5	0	0	0	0	0	0	0	0	-.126	-.062	.200	.200	.600	.227
Ellison J	3	7	2	56	39	9	1	0	1	13	15	5	0	1	2	0	1	0	0	-.131	-.093	.188	.278	.271	.182
Coats B *	3	2	2	38	28	7	4	0	0	11	15	3	0	0	0	1	0	0	1	-.231	-.348	.206	.263	.324	.188
Hanigan R	2	3	2	11	7	3	1	0	0	4	2	1	1	0	0	0	0	0	0	.302	-.368	.300	.364	.400	.249
Castro J	2	5	5	98	75	16	5	0	0	21	21	4	0	0	3	2	0	0	2	-.001	.092	.180	.211	.236	.145
Bailey H	1	3	2	12	8	3	1	0	0	4	5	0	0	0	1	0	0	0	0	-.027	.167	.273	.273	.364	.202
Saarloos K	1	1	2	6	4	1	1	0	0	2	1	0	0	0	1	0	0	0	0	.238	-.317	.200	.200	.400	.179
Wise D *	1	1	1	6	4	1	0	1	0	3	1	1	1	0	0	0	0	0	0	--	--	.200	.333	.600	.283
Livingston B	1	3	2	31	19	7	0	0	0	7	7	2	0	0	4	0	0	0	1	-.161	.124	.280	.333	.280	.208
Milton E *	1	0	2	9	6	1	0	0	0	1	2	0	0	0	2	0	0	0	0	.175	-.140	.143	.143	.143	.094
Bellhorn M +	0	2	1	18	13	1	0	0	0	1	5	4	0	0	0	0	0	0	0	-.230	.046	.071	.278	.071	.135
Arroyo B	0	5	3	79	61	10	2	0	1	15	30	2	0	1	6	0	0	0	1	.001	.026	.143	.178	.214	.126
Cruz E	-0	0	0	1	1	0	0	0	0	0	0	0	0	0	0	0	0	0	0	--	--	.000	.000	.000	.000
Ramirez E +	-0	2	0	5	4	1	0	0	0	1	0	0	0	0	0	0	1	0	0	-.175	.350	.200	.200	.200	.132
Stanton M *	-0	0	0	2	2	0	0	0	0	0	0	0	0	0	0	0	0	0	0	.000	--	.000	.000	.000	.000
Majewski G	-0	0	0	2	2	0	0	0	0	0	2	0	0	0	0	0	0	0	0	.000	--	.000	.000	.000	.000
Lohse K	-0	1	1	42	28	5	0	0	0	5	7	1	0	0	7	1	0	0	0	-.073	-.036	.152	.171	.152	.109
Santos V	-0	0	0	4	3	0	0	0	0	0	1	0	0	0	1	0	0	0	0	.000	.000	.000	.000	.000	.000
Gosling M *	-0	0	0	5	5	0	0	0	0	0	3	0	0	0	0	0	0	0	0	.000	.000	.000	.000	.000	.000
Lopez P	-1	1	0	47	37	8	2	0	0	10	10	1	0	1	0	0	0	0	0	-.032	-.098	.178	.213	.222	.143
Dumatrait P	-1	0	0	6	6	0	0	0	0	0	4	0	0	0	0	0	0	0	0	.000	.000	.000	.000	.000	.000
Moeller C	-1	6	2	49	42	8	1	0	1	12	17	0	0	0	1	0	0	0	2	.065	.164	.167	.167	.250	.130
Shearn T	-1	0	0	13	12	0	0	0	0	0	4	1	0	0	1	0	0	0	1	-.064	-.064	.000	.083	.000	.035
Belisle M	-2	2	1	61	48	3	0	0	0	4	32	3	0	0	8	0	1	0	1	-.007	-.070	.060	.113	.080	.067
Harang A	-3	0	2	88	68	7	1	0	0	8	28	1	0	1	11	1	0	0	1	-.049	-.020	.095	.117	.108	.075

Italicized stats have been adjusted for home park.
Batted Ball Batting Stats are listed after Fielding Stats.

Pitching Stats

Player	PRC	IP	BFP	G	GS	K	BB	IBB	HBP	H	HR	DP	DER	SB	CS	PO	W	L	Sv	Op	Hld	H-A	R^L	RA	ERA	FIP
Harang A	119	231.7	948	34	34	218	52	3	8	213	28	17	.702	13	8	0	16	6	0	0	0	.003	.011	3.88	3.73	3.70
Arroyo B	87	210.7	921	34	34	156	63	6	13	232	28	17	.684	3	6	2	9	15	0	0	0	-.012	.006	4.66	4.23	4.51
Belisle M	60	177.7	771	30	30	125	43	4	7	212	26	17	.663	11	6	0	8	9	0	0	0	-.001	-.014	5.62	5.32	4.54
Lohse K	47	131.7	561	21	21	80	33	1	6	143	16	13	.695	6	4	1	6	12	0	0	0	-.065	.003	5.19	4.58	4.50
Weathers D	37	77.7	328	70	0	48	27	4	5	67	4	7	.725	5	1	0	2	6	33	39	0	.005	-.039	3.82	3.59	3.78
Burton J	26	43.0	176	47	0	36	22	4	2	28	2	5	.754	4	1	1	4	2	0	3	11	.076	.004	3.14	2.51	3.59
Santos V	19	49.0	216	32	0	44	23	5	2	51	10	6	.693	4	2	1	1	4	0	0	2	-.056	.030	5.14	5.14	5.35
Stanton M *	18	57.7	263	69	0	40	18	2	5	75	6	8	.634	4	1	1	1	3	0	3	10	-.120	-.044	6.09	5.93	4.33
Livingston B	18	56.3	250	10	10	27	8	0	1	77	8	5	.660	2	0	0	3	3	0	0	0	-.058	.056	5.59	5.27	4.64
Coutlangus J	17	41.0	187	64	0	38	27	4	4	38	3	6	.670	3	1	1	4	2	0	3	9	-.019	-.021	4.83	4.39	4.64
Coffey T	16	51.0	242	58	0	43	19	4	5	70	12	10	.613	6	0	0	2	1	0	3	7	-.008	.005	6.35	5.82	5.82
Bailey H	13	45.3	205	9	9	28	28	1	3	43	3	7	.699	9	0	1	4	2	0	0	0	.049	-.053	6.35	5.76	4.88
Salmon B	12	24.0	101	26	0	22	10	1	1	22	3	3	.708	2	0	0	0	1	0	1	0	.070	-.122	4.13	4.13	4.31
Shearn T	12	32.7	137	7	6	16	13	0	0	32	8	6	.750	0	0	0	3	0	0	0	0	.003	.106	4.96	4.96	6.67
Gosling M *	11	33.0	164	23	0	32	28	8	1	42	5	5	.622	2	1	1	2	0	0	1	0	-.037	-.104	6.00	4.91	5.21
Saarloos K	10	42.7	201	34	3	27	19	1	3	54	8	7	.653	2	0	0	1	5	0	1	4	-.050	-.033	7.59	7.17	5.92
Milton E *	9	31.3	143	6	6	18	9	0	0	39	4	2	.670	2	0	0	0	4	0	0	0	-.032	.011	6.03	5.17	4.64
McBeth M	7	19.7	88	23	0	17	7	1	1	22	2	2	.672	7	0	0	3	2	0	2	3	.119	-.054	5.95	5.95	3.93
Bray B *	5	14.3	63	19	0	14	5	1	0	16	1	1	.651	1	0	0	3	3	1	1	3	.009	-.165	6.28	6.28	3.06
Majewski G	4	23.0	113	32	0	10	3	1	2	43	3	4	.579	1	0	0	0	4	0	3	6	.049	.034	8.61	8.22	4.62
Ramirez E	3	16.3	73	4	3	8	8	0	0	20	5	4	.712	1	0	0	0	2	0	0	0	.101	.001	7.71	7.71	7.74
Guardado E *	3	13.7	62	15	0	8	4	0	1	16	2	0	.702	0	0	0	0	0	0	2	1	.042	.126	7.24	7.24	5.10
Dumatrait P	1	18.0	104	6	6	9	12	0	1	39	6	1	.566	0	0	0	0	4	0	0	0	.065	.010	15.00	15.00	8.77
Stone R	1	5.3	23	5	0	3	0	0	1	7	4	1	.800	0	0	0	0	0	0	0	0	-.042	.579	10.13	10.13	12.46
Cormier R *	0	3.0	14	6	0	1	1	0	1	4	1	1	.700	0	0	0	0	0	0	0	3	.297	-.349	9.00	9.00	8.94

Italicized stats have been adjusted for home park.

Batted Ball Pitching Stats

Player	% of PA		% of Batted Balls					Out %		Runs Per Event				Total Runs vs. Avg.				
	K%	BB%	GB%	LD%	FB%	IF/F	HR/OF	GB	OF	NIP	GB	LD	OF	NIP	GB	LD	FB	Tot
Harang A	23	6	40	18	42	.09	.11	74	84	-.01	.05	.36	.19	-18	-0	-12	3	-27
Burton L	20	14	45	15	40	.02	.04	71	91	.07	.05	.25	.03	2	0	-6	-7	-11
Weathers D	15	10	36	21	43	.11	.04	79	83	.07	.01	.37	.10	1	-4	1	-6	-9
Lohse K	14	7	35	22	43	.13	.10	75	84	.04	.05	.39	.16	-3	-2	5	0	0
Coutlangus J	20	17	48	17	35	.10	.08	65	91	.09	.08	.48	.10	4	1	-0	-4	1
Bailey D	14	15	47	18	35	.14	.05	70	81	.13	.07	.39	.11	5	1	-0	-4	2
Shearn T	12	9	39	13	48	.10	.18	78	89	.09	.02	.43	.24	1	-1	-1	4	3
Milton E	13	6	26	24	50	.11	.08	79	78	.04	.04	.43	.17	-1	-1	4	2	4
Santos V	20	12	45	22	33	.13	.24	78	87	.05	.02	.41	.36	1	-2	2	5	5
Livingston B	11	4	42	23	35	.14	.13	77	75	.00	.04	.37	.26	-3	-0	4	5	6
Arroyo B	17	8	35	21	44	.16	.11	72	84	.04	.06	.40	.18	-4	2	7	2	7
Stanton M	15	9	36	24	40	.10	.08	66	79	.05	.08	.36	.17	0	3	4	1	8
Gosling M	20	18	41	24	35	.14	.17	71	76	.10	.05	.44	.32	5	-1	3	3	10
Saarloos K	13	11	53	17	30	.11	.21	77	58	.09	.02	.44	.46	2	-2	1	10	11
Coffey J	18	10	58	16	27	.02	.24	62	91	.05	.11	.40	.33	1	8	-1	5	13
Belisle M	16	6	42	22	36	.09	.14	70	83	.02	.07	.35	.23	-7	7	4	11	14
MLB Average	17	9	43	19	38	.10	.10	74	83	.05	.05	.40	.18	--	--	--	--	--

Fielding Stats

Name	INN	SBA/G	CS%	ERA	WP+PB/G	PO	A	TE	FE
Catcher									
Ross D	837.3	0.63	39%	4.57	0.408	662	50	3	1
Valentin J	471.7	0.86	11%	5.17	0.458	341	19	1	0
Moeller C	86.7	1.25	8%	7.17	0.415	72	5	0	0
Jorgensen R	34.0	0.00	0%	6.35	0.265	29	1	1	0
Hanigan R	20.0	0.45	0%	4.05	0.450	16	0	0	0

Name	Inn	PO	A	TE	FE	FPct	DPS	DPT	RZR	OOZ
First Base										
Hatteberg S	772.7	657	50	0	3	.996	3	0	.675	12
Conine J	431.7	390	21	1	2	.993	2	1	.688	10
Votto J	137.0	107	11	0	0	1.000	5	0	.467	4
Cantu J	104.3	86	4	0	0	1.000	0	0	.556	3
Valentin J	2.0	3	0	0	0	1.000	0	0	--	--
Keppinger J	2.0	2	0	0	0	1.000	0	0	--	--
Second Base										
Phillips B	1371.0	341	433	2	6	.990	48	67	.863	49
Keppinger J	26.0	10	7	0	0	1.000	2	0	.625	2
Castro J	25.0	6	5	2	0	.846	0	0	.667	1
Freel R	9.0	3	3	0	0	1.000	0	1	1.000	0
Lopez P	9.0	1	1	0	0	1.000	0	1	--	--
Cantu J	8.0	1	3	0	0	1.000	0	0	1.000	0
Bellhorn M	1.7	0	1	0	0	1.000	1	0	1.000	0
Shortstop										
Gonzalez A	872.7	147	264	2	14	.963	45	22	.862	32
Keppinger J	390.7	62	124	2	0	.989	14	13	.845	11
Lopez P	93.3	23	24	0	1	.979	3	7	.941	2
Castro J	89.3	10	27	0	0	1.000	4	1	.800	5
Cruz E	2.7	0	0	0	1	0.000	0	0	0.000	0
Phillips B	1.0	0	1	0	0	1.000	0	0	--	--

Name	Inn	PO	A	TE	FE	FPct	DPS	DPT	RZR	OOZ
Third Base										
Encarnacion E	1168.0	112	212	8	8	.953	19	0	.600	39
Freel R	124.0	17	29	0	2	.958	3	0	.615	10
Keppinger J	75.7	7	23	0	1	.968	2	0	.741	3
Castro J	64.0	8	9	0	1	.944	0	0	.412	1
Bellhorn M	13.0	0	4	0	0	1.000	0	0	.600	1
Cantu J	4.0	0	0	0	0	0.000	0	0	--	--
Conine J	1.0	0	0	0	0	0.000	0	0	--	--
Left Field										
Dunn A	1189.0	244	4	1	5	.976	0	0	.826	31
Hopper N	115.0	37	1	0	0	1.000	0	0	.962	12
Votto J	51.0	14	0	0	1	.933	0	0	.778	0
Ellison J	30.0	10	0	0	0	1.000	0	0	1.000	1
Hamilton J	27.0	5	0	0	0	1.000	0	0	.833	0
Coats B	24.0	10	1	0	0	1.000	0	0	.900	1
Keppinger J	11.0	5	0	0	0	1.000	0	0	.667	1
Freel R	2.0	0	0	0	0	0.000	0	0	--	--
Center Field										
Hamilton J	555.7	168	6	1	3	.978	4	0	.898	18
Freel R	444.3	136	3	2	0	.986	0	0	.824	33
Hopper N	408.3	133	2	1	0	.993	2	0	.898	18
Coats B	17.0	4	0	0	0	1.000	0	0	1.000	0
Wise D	13.3	6	0	0	0	1.000	0	0	1.000	1
Ellison J	11.0	8	0	0	0	1.000	0	0	1.000	2
Right Field										
Griffey Jr. K	1163.0	291	5	0	8	.974	4	0	.880	28
Hopper N	84.7	27	2	0	0	1.000	0	0	1.000	5
Ellison J	82.0	26	1	0	0	1.000	0	0	952	6
Hamilton J	81.0	27	1	0	0	1.000	0	0	.893	2
Coats B	27.7	4	1	0	1	.833	0	0	.750	1
Keppinger J	7.3	1	1	0	0	1.000	0	0	1.000	0
Conine J	4.0	1	0	0	0	1.000	0	0	1.000	0

Batted Ball Batting Stats

Player	% of PA		% of Batted Balls					Out %		Runs Per Event				Total Runs vs. Avg.				
	K%	BB%	GB%	LD%	FB%	IF/F	HR/OF	GB	OF	NIP	GB	LD	OF	NIP	GB	LD	FB	Tot
Dunn A	26	17	35	19	47	.11	.26	82	81	.07	-.01	.48	.40	10	-9	2	35	37
Griffey Jr. K	16	14	35	16	49	.13	.16	72	84	.10	.05	.39	.23	11	-1	-4	16	21
Hamilton J	19	11	45	22	33	.01	.23	74	81	.05	.05	.37	.38	1	0	2	16	19
Hatteberg S	8	12	43	23	34	.11	.10	79	82	.16	.01	.40	.19	9	-4	10	2	16
Encarnacion E	15	9	38	19	43	.15	.10	68	86	.06	.09	.47	.14	2	7	8	-4	12
Phillips B	16	6	47	18	35	.10	.16	68	88	.02	.07	.37	.23	-6	9	-0	8	11
Keppinger J	4	10	47	21	32	.07	.07	69	84	.21	.07	.38	.11	5	4	5	-3	10
Gonzalez A	17	7	34	22	44	.17	.14	80	83	.02	-.01	.42	.23	-3	-7	6	7	2
Hopper N	10	6	58	20	22	.05	.00	68	87	.07	.08	.34	.03	-1	15	-0	-12	2
Conine J	12	8	38	18	44	.10	.07	70	90	.08	.07	.41	.07	0	1	1	-6	-3
Valentin J	9	8	40	19	42	.09	.02	76	80	.09	.04	.38	.08	0	-1	1	-5	-4
Freel R	15	8	49	18	33	.19	.05	73	86	.05	.05	.45	.08	-1	2	2	-9	-7
Castro J	21	4	39	17	43	.00	.00	74	80	-.04	.04	.15	.05	-3	-1	-4	-3	-12
Ross D	26	9	34	19	48	.19	.19	84	91	-.00	-.02	.38	.25	-5	-7	-5	3	-15
Harang A	32	2	60	9	30	.23	.00	88	90	-.08	-.04	.42	-.04	-4	-4	-5	-6	-19
MLB Average	17	9	43	19	38	.10	.10	74	83	.05	.05	.40	.18	--	--	--	--	--

Cleveland Indians

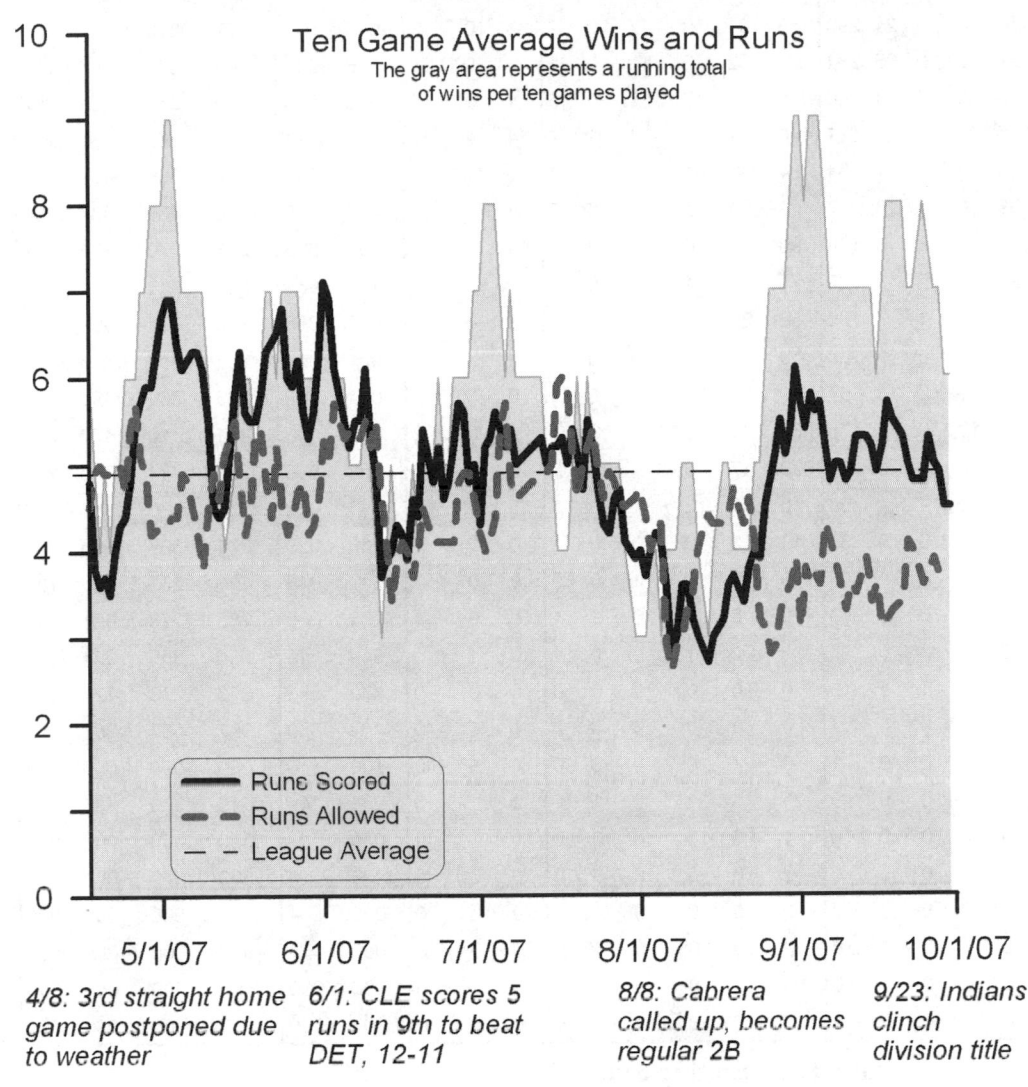

Ten Game Average Wins and Runs
The gray area represents a running total
of wins per ten games played

Legend:
— Runs Scored
– – Runs Allowed
- - League Average

4/8: 3rd straight home game postponed due to weather

6/1: CLE scores 5 runs in 9th to beat DET, 12-11

8/8: Cabrera called up, becomes regular 2B

9/23: Indians clinch division title

8/16: Latest day CLE not in 1st place

Stat Facts:

- Josh Barfield had a GPA of .207
- His OBP was .270
- Grady Sizemore led the league with 748 plate appearances
- Sizemore walked or struck out in 37% of those appearances
- Ryan Garko was third in the league with 20 HBPs
- C.C. Sabathia led the league with 131 PRC
- Sabathia led the league with 241 IP and 975 BFP
- His FIP of 3.27 was second in the league
- Sabathia walked just 5% of the batters he faced
- Paul Byrd walked just 4%
- Rafael Betancourt walked just 3%
- Fausto Carmona induced 36 double plays, most in the majors
- Carmona's GB% of 64% led the league
- His LD% of 14% was lowest in the league

Team Batting and Pitching/Fielding Stats by Month						
	April	May	June	July	Aug	Sept/Oct
Wins	14	19	15	12	17	19
Losses	8	11	13	14	11	9
RS/G	5.2	6.0	4.9	4.7	4.4	4.9
RA/G	4.7	4.6	4.7	4.8	3.7	3.5
OBP	.346	.367	.343	.326	.328	.347
SLG	.406	.475	.426	.419	.395	.437
FIP	4.19	4.51	3.86	3.88	3.78	3.43
DER	.695	.688	.668	.680	.708	.683

Batting Stats

Player	BR	Runs	RBI	PA	Outs	H	2B	3B	HR	TB	K	BB	IBB	HBP	SH	SF	SB	CS	GDP	H-A	L^R	BA	OBP	SLG	GPA
Sizemore G *	124	118	78	748	467	174	34	5	24	290	155	101	9	17	0	2	33	10	3	.044	.017	.277	.390	.462	.297
Martinez V +	107	78	114	645	412	169	40	0	25	284	76	62	12	10	0	11	0	0	19	-.008	-.023	.301	.374	.505	.300
Hafner T *	93	80	100	661	416	145	25	2	24	246	115	102	17	7	0	5	1	1	15	-.028	-.004	.266	.385	.451	.292
Peralta J	86	87	72	647	435	155	27	1	21	247	146	61	2	4	1	7	4	4	12	.066	.024	.270	.341	.430	.266
Garko R	72	62	61	541	357	140	29	1	21	234	94	34	1	20	0	3	0	1	12	.016	.035	.289	.359	.483	.288
Blake C	70	81	78	662	448	159	36	4	18	257	123	54	2	10	5	5	4	5	14	-.041	.026	.270	.339	.437	.267
Barfield J	42	53	50	444	326	102	19	3	3	136	90	14	0	3	3	4	14	5	3	.003	-.023	.243	.270	.324	.207
Gutierrez F	38	41	36	301	209	72	13	2	13	128	77	21	1	1	5	3	8	3	7	.102	.064	.266	.318	.472	.266
Michaels J	36	43	39	295	202	72	11	1	7	106	50	20	1	3	2	3	3	4	3	.033	.056	.270	.324	.397	.250
Nixon T *	33	30	31	354	239	77	17	0	3	103	59	44	7	0	0	3	0	0	9	.023	.045	.251	.342	.336	.243
Cabrera A +	26	30	22	186	121	45	9	2	3	67	29	17	0	2	5	3	0	0	7	-.044	.062	.283	.354	.421	.270
Shoppach K	26	26	30	177	121	42	13	0	7	76	56	11	0	1	3	1	0	0	2	.028	.130	.261	.310	.472	.263
Lofton K *	22	24	15	196	128	49	9	3	0	64	23	17	0	0	4	2	2	3	1	-.029	.090	.283	.344	.370	.252
Dellucci D *	18	25	20	199	142	41	11	2	4	68	40	17	2	1	0	3	2	1	4	-.036	.072	.230	.296	.382	.234
Francisco B	7	10	12	66	49	17	5	0	3	31	19	3	0	0	0	1	0	2	2	.136	-.029	.274	.303	.500	.267
Marte A	5	3	8	60	46	11	4	0	1	18	9	2	0	1	0	0	0	0	0	.117	.040	.193	.233	.316	.188
Gomez C	3	4	5	55	39	15	2	0	0	17	6	0	0	0	1	1	0	0	1	.252	.008	.283	.278	.321	.209
Choo S *	3	5	5	20	13	5	0	0	0	5	5	2	1	0	0	1	0	1	0	.044	.146	.294	.350	.294	.236
Rivas L	2	3	4	11	8	3	0	1	1	8	0	0	0	0	0	0	0	0	0	.670	.567	.273	.273	.727	.311
Sabathia C *	1	0	0	3	1	2	0	0	0	2	0	0	0	0	0	0	0	0	0	-.467	-.350	.667	.667	.667	.476
Sowers J *	1	1	0	2	0	1	0	0	0	1	0	1	0	0	0	0	0	0	0	-.700	--	1.000	1.000	1.000	.714
Rouse M *	0	7	4	76	60	8	1	0	0	9	20	7	1	0	1	1	1	1	0	-.001	.146	.119	.200	.134	.126
Betancourt R	-0	0	0	1	1	0	0	0	0	0	1	0	0	0	0	0	0	0	0	.000	--	.000	.000	.000	.000
Westbrook J	-0	0	0	2	2	0	0	0	0	0	2	0	0	0	0	0	0	0	0	.000	--	.000	.000	.000	.000
Byrd P	-0	0	0	2	2	0	0	0	0	0	0	0	0	0	0	0	0	0	0	.000	--	.000	.000	.000	.000
Stanford J *	-0	0	0	3	2	0	0	0	0	0	2	0	0	0	1	0	0	0	0	.000	--	.000	.000	.000	.000
Carmona F	-0	0	0	5	4	0	0	0	0	0	3	0	0	0	1	0	0	0	0	.000	.000	.000	.000	.000	.000
Lee C *	-1	0	0	5	5	0	0	0	0	0	2	0	0	0	0	0	0	0	0	.000	.000	.000	.000	.000	.000

Italicized stats have been adjusted for home park.

Batted Ball Batting Stats

Player	% of PA		% of Batted Balls			IF/F	HR/OF	Out %		Runs Per Event				Total Runs vs. Avg.				
	K%	BB%	GB%	LD%	FB%			GB	OF	NIP	GB	LD	OF	NIP	GB	LD	FB	Tot
Sizemore G	21	16	33	21	47	.05	.12	73	85	.09	.06	.42	.20	14	2	4	11	31
Martinez V	12	11	42	20	38	.06	.14	79	83	.11	.01	.44	.22	8	-8	11	13	24
Hafner T	17	16	48	17	35	.07	.17	74	85	.11	.04	.39	.26	17	0	-3	10	24
Garko R	17	10	38	19	44	.08	.13	76	75	.06	.03	.39	.27	1	-4	1	19	18
Peralta J	23	10	47	19	35	.04	.15	74	78	.03	.04	.37	.27	-3	-2	-4	11	3
Blake C	19	10	39	18	43	.09	.10	72	83	.04	.06	.41	.18	-1	0	-1	4	3
Gutierrez F	26	7	43	15	42	.07	.17	70	79	-.01	.07	.43	.30	-5	2	-4	9	1
Shoppach K	32	7	46	15	39	.07	.18	67	74	-.03	.10	.40	.36	-5	2	-4	6	-0
Lofton K	12	9	39	20	41	.03	.00	78	79	.08	.04	.40	.06	1	1	2	-5	-1
Cabrera A	16	10	44	20	36	.06	.04	74	81	.07	.03	.40	.14	1	-1	1	-2	-2
Michaels J	17	8	37	17	46	.07	.07	68	86	.03	.08	.38	.12	-2	2	-2	-2	-3
Dellucci D	20	9	43	20	37	.10	.06	87	77	.03	-.04	.40	.20	-1	-5	-0	-0	-7
Nixon T	17	12	39	18	44	.05	.03	74	80	.08	.04	.36	.09	4	-1	-3	-6	-7
Barfield J	20	4	40	17	43	.10	.02	74	79	-.04	.06	.32	.10	-11	1	-8	-8	-27
MLB Average	17	9	43	19	38	.10	.10	74	83	.05	.05	.40	.18	--	--	--	--	--

Pitching Stats

Player	PRC	IP	BFP	G	GS	K	BB	IBB	HBP	H	HR	DP	DER	SB	CS	PO	W	L	Sv	Op	Hld	H-A	R^L	RA	ERA	FIP
Sabathia C *	130	241.0	975	34	34	209	37	1	8	238	20	29	.682	10	10	1	19	7	0	0	0	-.021	-.061	3.51	3.21	3.27
Carmona F	115	215.0	879	32	32	137	61	2	11	199	16	36	.708	13	5	2	19	8	0	0	0	-.009	-.038	3.27	3.06	4.05
Betancourt R	84	79.3	289	68	0	80	9	3	0	51	4	3	.760	4	4	0	5	1	3	6	31	-.011	-.071	1.47	1.47	2.25
Byrd P	65	192.3	835	31	31	88	28	3	6	239	27	18	.679	11	2	2	15	8	0	0	0	.046	-.008	5.01	4.59	4.77
Westbrook J	59	152.0	648	25	25	93	55	5	6	159	13	25	.688	14	7	2	6	9	0	0	0	.025	-.039	4.62	4.32	4.37
Perez R *	49	60.7	236	44	0	62	15	2	0	41	5	7	.727	2	1	0	1	2	1	2	12	.014	-.042	2.23	1.78	3.05
Lee C *	26	97.3	443	20	16	66	36	1	7	112	17	9	.685	4	1	0	5	8	0	0	0	-.005	.035	6.75	6.29	5.59
Mastny T	24	57.7	262	51	0	52	32	9	2	63	6	7	.659	4	2	0	7	2	0	0	7	.019	-.030	4.68	4.68	4.23
Borowski J	24	65.7	292	69	0	58	17	4	2	77	9	3	.655	9	2	1	4	5	45	53	0	-.033	.007	5.35	5.07	4.08
Fultz A *	23	37.0	158	49	0	28	18	2	1	31	2	1	.734	1	2	0	4	3	0	1	11	.069	-.026	2.92	2.92	3.95
Lewis J	23	29.3	125	26	0	34	10	1	1	26	1	0	.671	0	1	1	1	1	0	0	5	.080	.026	2.45	2.15	2.53
Laffey A *	18	49.3	207	9	9	25	12	0	4	54	2	9	.665	1	3	0	4	2	0	0	0	.006	.074	4.74	4.56	3.87
Sowers J *	16	67.3	303	13	13	24	21	2	4	84	10	8	.689	10	2	0	1	6	0	0	0	-.033	-.104	6.55	6.42	5.62
Cabrera F	12	33.7	157	24	0	39	22	3	0	38	7	2	.652	4	3	1	1	2	0	0	1	-.066	-.135	5.88	5.61	5.46
Stanford J *	9	26.3	118	8	2	16	7	0	2	32	1	3	.652	1	0	0	1	1	0	0	0	.079	.149	5.13	4.78	3.68
Hernandez R	6	26.0	125	28	0	18	16	3	1	33	2	4	.625	1	1	0	3	1	0	1	4	.053	.079	7.27	6.23	4.61
Davis J	4	11.3	56	8	0	5	9	1	0	13	0	2	.643	1	0	0	0	0	0	0	0	.082	.159	4.76	4.76	4.62
Mujica E	2	13.0	60	10	0	7	2	0	0	19	3	0	.667	1	0	0	0	0	0	0	0	-.196	.028	8.31	8.31	5.76
Koplove M	2	6.0	26	5	0	4	2	0	1	6	0	1	.684	2	0	0	0	0	0	0	0	-.035	.153	6.00	6.00	3.55
Lara J *	0	1.3	7	1	0	2	1	0	0	2	1	0	.667	0	0	0	0	0	0	0	0	--	.483	13.50	13.50	12.38
Miller M	0	1.0	5	2	0	0	0	0	0	2	0	0	.600	0	0	0	0	0	0	0	0	--	.350	0.00	0.00	3.38

Italicized stats have been adjusted for home park.

Batted Ball Pitching Stats

Player	% of PA		% of Batted Balls			IF/F	HR/OF	Out %		Runs Per Event				Total Runs vs. Avg.				
	K%	BB%	GB%	LD%	FB%			GB	OF	NIP	GB	LD	OF	NIP	GB	LD	FB	Tot
Sabathia C	21	5	45	18	37	.10	.08	75	81	-.03	.04	.42	.17	-22	-2	-1	-8	-33
Betancourt R	28	3	27	20	54	.20	.04	74	91	-.07	.04	.39	.03	-11	-3	-3	-14	-31
Carmona F	16	8	64	14	22	.06	.12	76	79	.05	.03	.34	.22	-3	-0	-17	-9	-29
Perez R	26	6	53	17	30	.15	.10	79	86	-.02	.01	.43	.15	-5	-3	-3	-6	-17
Westbrook J	14	9	54	20	27	.05	.09	77	86	.07	.02	.44	.12	2	-4	8	-13	-7
Lewis J	27	9	32	19	48	.11	.03	72	88	-.00	.08	.47	.06	-2	0	-0	-4	-6
Fultz A	18	12	35	22	43	.10	.05	82	90	.07	.00	.43	.05	1	-2	2	-5	-5
Laffey A	12	8	62	19	19	.06	.07	76	63	.07	.03	.33	.27	0	0	-1	-1	-1
Stanford J	14	8	46	13	41	.24	.04	67	78	.05	.08	.46	.13	-0	2	-1	-2	-1
Borowski J	20	7	33	21	45	.10	.11	59	93	.00	.14	.43	.11	-4	6	3	-4	2
Mastny T	20	13	40	19	41	.13	.10	68	75	.07	.08	.34	.23	3	2	-2	3	5
Hernandez R	14	14	48	17	35	.06	.07	69	74	.11	.07	.49	.21	2	1	1	1	6
Cabrera F	25	14	34	22	44	.10	.18	76	81	.05	.06	.48	.30	1	-0	2	5	8
Sowers J	8	8	40	16	44	.05	.10	69	87	.12	.08	.43	.14	2	5	2	1	10
Byrd P	11	4	38	21	41	.09	.10	72	87	.02	.06	.42	.15	-9	3	17	1	11
Lee C	15	10	35	15	50	.09	.12	70	83	.07	.07	.48	.19	2	2	1	9	14
MLB Average	17	9	43	19	38	.10	.10	74	83	.05	.05	.40	.18	--	--	--	--	--

Fielding Stats

Name	INN	SBA/G	CS%	ERA	WP+PB/G	PO	A	TE	FE
Catcher									
Martinez V	1042.7	0.86	30%	4.01	0.285	779	53	1	3
Shoppach K	420.0	0.77	36%	4.16	0.364	287	28	3	1

Name	Inn	PO	A	TE	FE	FPct	DPS	DPT	RZR	OOZ
First Base										
Garko R	1066.0	1073	71	3	5	.993	6	1	.729	17
Martinez V	221.0	187	13	0	1	.995	2	0	.791	4
Hafner T	91.0	97	4	0	0	1.000	0	0	.846	2
Blake C	49.7	39	5	0	0	1.000	0	0	.800	1
Gomez C	34.7	25	2	0	0	1.000	0	0	.583	0
Second Base										
Barfield J	1032.0	242	338	6	8	.975	32	40	.784	41
Cabrera A	321.0	70	119	0	1	.995	9	18	.850	13
Rouse M	69.7	21	24	1	0	.978	1	3	.720	3
Gomez C	25.0	12	9	0	0	1.000	0	3	.750	0
Rivas L	15.0	3	4	0	0	1.000	0	0	.600	1
Shortstop										
Peralta J	1348.0	249	452	6	13	.974	50	51	.763	65
Rouse M	65.7	10	32	0	1	.977	2	3	.909	6
Cabrera A	42.0	8	21	0	0	1.000	3	1	.900	2
Rivas L	7.0	0	4	0	1	.800	0	0	.667	0
Third Base										
Blake C	1209.0	99	258	7	6	.962	22	2	.708	27
Marte A	135.7	16	27	1	3	.915	2	0	.688	5
Rouse M	58.7	4	11	0	1	.938	3	0	.733	0
Gomez C	58.0	6	16	0	0	1.000	4	0	.722	1
Cabrera A	1.3	0	1	0	0	1.000	0	0	1.000	0

Name	Inn	PO	A	TE	FE	FPct	DPS	DPT	RZR	OOZ
Left Field										
Michaels J	499.7	117	4	0	0	1.000	0	0	.833	27
Lofton K	387.7	82	3	0	0	1.000	2	0	.878	10
Dellucci D	382.3	97	3	0	0	1.000	0	0	.766	15
Francisco B	102.3	26	0	0	0	1.000	0	0	.810	9
Gutierrez F	58.7	7	0	0	0	1.000	0	0	.875	0
Choo S	32.0	10	1	0	0	1.000	2	0	1.000	1
Center Field										
Sizemore G	1408.0	399	4	0	2	.995	4	0	.881	45
Gutierrez F	32.0	11	0	0	0	1.000	0	0	.769	1
Lofton K	21.0	2	0	0	0	1.000	0	0	.667	0
Michaels J	1.0	1	0	0	0	1.000	0	0	1.000	0
Right Field										
Nixon T	675.0	129	4	0	4	.971	4	0	.885	14
Gutierrez F	578.7	136	3	1	0	.993	2	0	.908	28
Michaels J	116.0	29	0	0	1	.967	0	0	.852	6
Blake C	54.0	13	2	0	0	1.000	4	0	.875	6
Francisco B	28.0	6	0	0	0	1.000	0	0	1.000	0
Choo S	11.0	0	0	0	0	0.000	0	0	--	--

Colorado Rockies

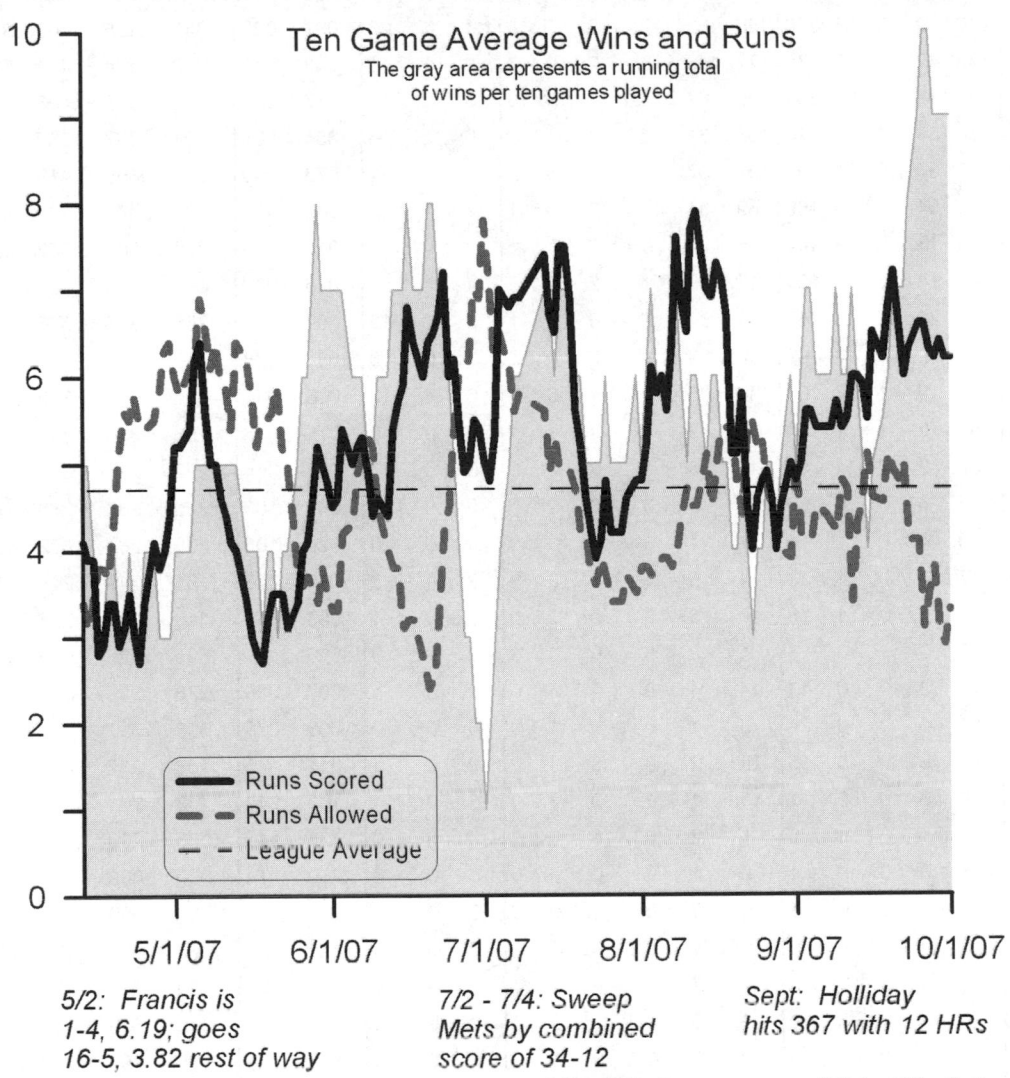

Ten Game Average Wins and Runs
The gray area represents a running total of wins per ten games played

Legend:
— Runs Scored
- - Runs Allowed
- - League Average

5/2: Francis is 1-4, 6.19; goes 16-5, 3.82 rest of way

6/1: Atkins hitting .223; hits .338 with 22 HR rest of way

7/2 - 7/4: Sweep Mets by combined score of 34-12

8/6 - 8/8: Sweep Brewers by combined score of 36-10

Sept: Holliday hits 367 with 12 HRs

9/21: Win 2-1 14-inning thriller to begin sweep in SD

Stat Facts:

- Troy Tulowitzki made 87 OOZ plays, and had an RZR of .861
- Aaron Cook induced 30 DPs in 166 innings
- Garrett Atkins hit only 31% groundballs, and 44% flyballs
- Brad Hawpe had an L^R of .108
- 21% of the flies allowed by Brian Fuentes were infield pop-ups
- Despite just 16 IBBs, Todd Helton drew a walk in 17% of his PAs
- Manuel Corpas allowed a line drive on just 14% of his balls in play
- Kaz Matsui committed only four errors
- Matsui stole 32 bases in 36 attempts
- Matt Holliday had an RZR of .892
- Just 21% of the batted balls against LaTroy Hawkins were fly balls

Team Batting and Pitching/Fielding Stats by Month						
	April	May	June	July	Aug	Sept/Oct
Wins	10	15	14	15	15	21
Losses	16	13	13	9	14	8
RS/G	4.1	4.3	5.6	5.8	5.7	6.2
RA/G	5.0	5.0	4.7	4.4	4.4	4.4
OBP	.345	.328	.359	.351	.363	.373
SLG	.366	.396	.469	.445	.451	.488
FIP	4.23	4.35	4.63	4.10	4.50	4.30
DER	.683	.700	.700	.708	.707	.713

Batting Stats

Player	BR	Runs	RBI	PA	Outs	H	2B	3B	HR	TB	K	BB	IBB	HBP	SH	SF	SB	CS	GDP	H-A	L^R	BA	OBP	SLG	GPA
Holliday M	121	120	137	713	447	216	50	6	36	386	126	63	7	10	0	4	11	4	23	.087	-.023	.340	.405	.607	.304
Helton T *	99	86	91	682	395	178	42	2	17	275	74	116	16	2	0	7	0	1	15	.043	.079	.320	.434	.494	.290
Atkins G	94	83	111	684	440	182	35	1	25	294	96	67	3	2	0	10	3	1	16	.057	-.029	.301	.367	.486	.261
Hawpe B *	94	80	116	606	381	150	33	4	29	278	137	81	11	3	1	5	0	2	13	.054	.108	.291	.387	.539	.281
Tulowitzki T	86	104	99	682	452	177	33	5	24	292	130	57	3	9	5	2	7	6	14	.073	.040	.291	.359	.479	.256
Matsui K +	54	84	37	453	297	118	24	6	4	166	69	34	1	0	8	1	32	4	1	.072	-.022	.288	.342	.405	.232
Taveras W	47	64	24	408	263	119	13	2	2	142	55	21	0	7	7	1	33	9	1	.014	.056	.320	.367	.382	.237
Spilborghs R	43	40	51	300	191	79	14	1	11	128	45	28	1	2	0	6	4	1	5	.026	.080	.299	.363	.485	.259
Torrealba Y	31	47	47	443	315	101	22	1	8	149	73	34	1	6	6	1	2	1	19	.052	.012	.255	.323	.376	.218
Iannetta C	25	22	27	234	157	43	8	3	4	69	58	29	3	5	1	2	0	0	3	-.089	.038	.218	.330	.350	.215
Carroll J	21	45	22	268	180	51	9	1	2	68	34	28	1	4	6	3	6	2	2	-.068	.047	.225	.317	.300	.198
Sullivan C *	17	19	14	153	105	40	6	1	2	54	25	9	1	2	1	1	2	0	5	-.075	-.018	.286	.336	.386	.225
Baker J	7	17	12	159	119	32	2	2	4	50	40	13	1	2	0	0	0	0	7	.082	.064	.222	.296	.347	.200
Quintanilla	5	6	5	75	57	16	4	0	0	20	15	5	0	0	0	0	0	0	3	.041	.106	.229	.280	.286	.179
Stewart I *	5	3	9	46	34	9	4	0	1	16	17	1	0	2	0	0	0	0	0	.026	.103	.209	.261	.372	.191
Finley S *	3	9	2	102	79	17	3	0	1	23	4	8	1	0	0	0	0	0	2	.066	-.018	.181	.245	.245	.156
Mabry J *	3	4	5	39	31	4	1	0	1	8	10	5	0	0	0	0	0	0	1	-.083	.167	.118	.231	.235	.148
Smith S *	2	4	0	8	3	5	0	1	0	7	1	0	0	0	0	0	0	0	0	-.050	--	.625	.625	.875	.455
Cook A	2	8	1	60	33	10	3	0	0	13	14	4	0	1	13	0	0	0	1	-.097	-.058	.238	.319	.310	.201
Morales F *	1	1	1	15	9	4	0	0	0	4	5	1	0	0	1	0	0	0	0	.009	.278	.308	.357	.308	.216
Francis J *	1	2	3	79	53	12	3	0	0	15	20	2	0	0	13	0	0	0	1	-.014	.046	.188	.212	.234	.140
Barmes C	1	5	1	39	30	8	3	0	0	11	13	1	1	0	1	0	0	0	1	.163	.244	.216	.237	.297	.164
Koshansky J	1	0	2	15	11	1	1	0	0	2	5	2	0	0	0	1	0	0	0	.198	.142	.083	.200	.167	.120
Ortiz R	1	1	1	2	0	1	0	0	0	1	0	1	0	0	0	0	0	0	0	.250	--	1.000	1.000	1.000	.636
Harikkala T	0	0	1	1	0	1	0	0	0	1	0	0	0	0	0	0	0	0	0	--	--	1.000	1.000	1.000	.636
Julio J	0	0	0	1	0	0	0	0	0	0	0	1	0	0	0	0	0	0	0	.450	--	.000	1.000	.000	.409
Buchholz T	0	0	1	26	20	3	0	0	0	3	11	2	0	0	1	0	0	0	0	.073	-.070	.130	.200	.130	.111
Barker S	0	0	0	3	2	0	0	0	0	0	1	0	0	1	0	0	0	0	0	.225	--	.000	.333	.000	.136
Dessens E	0	2	0	9	6	0	0	0	0	0	2	0	0	0	1	0	0	0	0	.150	--	.000	.250	.000	.102
Hawkins L	-0	0	0	1	1	0	0	0	0	0	1	0	0	0	0	0	0	0	0	.000	--	.000	.000	.000	.000
Bautista D	-0	0	0	1	1	0	0	0	0	0	1	0	0	0	0	0	0	0	0	.000	--	.000	.000	.000	.000
McClellan Z	-0	0	0	1	1	0	0	0	0	0	1	0	0	0	0	0	0	0	0	.000	--	.000	.000	.000	.000
Kim B	-0	0	0	2	2	0	0	0	0	0	1	0	0	0	0	0	0	0	0	.000	--	.000	.000	.000	.000
Arias A	-0	0	0	2	2	0	0	0	0	0	2	0	0	0	0	0	0	0	0	.000	.000	.000	.000	.000	.000
Martin T *	-0	0	0	2	2	0	0	0	0	0	0	0	0	0	1	0	0	0	1	.000	--	.000	.000	.000	.000
Bellorin E	-0	0	0	2	3	0	0	0	0	0	0	0	0	0	0	0	0	0	1	--	.000	.000	.000	.000	.000
Herges M *	-1	0	0	6	6	0	0	0	0	0	5	0	0	0	0	0	0	0	0	.000	.000	.000	.000	.000	.000
Hirsh J	-1	0	2	34	29	3	0	0	0	3	17	1	0	0	2	0	0	0	1	.136	.182	.097	.125	.097	.073
Redman M *	-1	0	0	8	8	0	0	0	0	0	1	0	0	0	0	0	0	0	0	.000	.000	.000	.000	.000	.000
Jimenez U	-1	0	0	31	22	2	0	0	0	2	6	3	0	0	4	0	0	0	0	-.098	.017	.083	.185	.083	.095
Gil G	-1	1	0	16	14	1	0	0	0	1	5	0	0	0	1	0	0	0	1	-.095	-.131	.071	.133	.071	.071
Fogg J	-1	3	1	63	48	7	0	0	0	7	19	1	0	0	9	0	0	0	2	-.060	.185	.132	.148	.132	.091
Lopez R	-2	0	0	24	22	1	0	0	0	1	13	1	0	0	1	0	0	0	1	.078	.010	.045	.087	.045	.046

Italicized stats have been adjusted for home park.
Batted Ball Batting Stats are listed after Fielding Stats.

Pitching Stats

Player	PRC	IP	BFP	G	GS	K	BB	IBB	HBP	H	HR	DP	DER	SB	CS	PO	W	L	Sv	Op	Hld	H-A	R^L	RA	ERA	FIP
Francis J *	100	215.3	922	34	34	165	63	7	7	234	25	25	.678	9	4	4	17	9	0	0	0	.014	-.041	4.30	4.22	4.12
Cook A	60	166.0	698	25	25	61	44	6	6	178	15	30	.705	8	2	0	8	7	0	0	0	.016	.029	4.72	4.12	4.50
Corpas M	59	78.0	306	78	0	58	20	3	2	63	6	12	.727	0	3	0	4	2	19	22	16	-.007	-.018	2.31	2.08	3.51
Fogg J	58	165.7	745	30	29	94	59	7	13	194	23	17	.685	12	2	0	10	9	0	0	0	.031	.005	5.38	4.94	5.12
Hirsh J	44	112.3	483	19	19	75	48	5	2	103	18	8	.741	4	0	1	5	7	0	0	0	-.000	.006	5.05	4.81	5.22
Buchholz T	40	93.7	396	41	8	61	20	4	2	105	8	12	.679	7	0	0	6	5	0	0	1	.015	.016	4.52	4.23	3.65
Jimenez U	33	82.0	354	15	15	68	37	4	6	70	10	9	.730	16	0	0	4	4	0	0	0	-.002	-.048	5.05	4.28	4.62
Fuentes B *	33	61.3	255	64	0	56	23	0	7	46	6	5	.755	1	1	1	3	5	20	27	8	-.062	-.007	3.82	3.08	4.18
Lopez R	30	79.3	333	14	14	43	21	6	0	83	11	7	.709	8	4	1	5	4	0	0	0	.016	-.021	4.88	4.42	4.55
Affeldt J *	30	59.0	253	75	0	46	33	9	3	47	3	9	.714	7	1	0	4	3	0	4	9	-.111	.021	3.97	3.51	3.74
Hawkins L	29	55.3	225	62	0	29	16	1	0	52	6	8	.736	2	1	0	2	5	0	5	18	-.072	-.014	3.42	3.42	4.44
Herges M	28	48.7	191	35	0	30	15	2	0	34	4	4	.775	0	1	0	5	1	0	2	3	.106	-.025	3.14	2.96	3.91
Julio J	26	52.7	221	58	0	50	20	1	1	50	6	8	.688	10	2	0	0	3	0	5	16	-.052	.081	4.27	3.93	3.99
Morales F *	21	39.3	163	8	8	26	14	1	2	34	2	4	.723	4	1	1	3	2	0	0	0	.068	-.099	3.43	3.43	3.75
Redman M *	10	19.7	84	5	3	14	6	0	0	21	2	2	.694	0	0	0	2	0	0	0	0	.118	.016	3.66	3.20	4.08
Martin T *	9	25.7	117	26	0	10	9	0	1	32	4	1	.699	1	0	0	0	0	0	0	2	-.053	.015	4.91	4.91	5.68
Speier R	9	18.0	77	20	0	13	8	1	1	20	1	7	.630	1	1	0	3	1	0	1	2	.215	-.060	4.00	4.00	3.88
McClellan Z	5	14.0	63	12	0	13	5	2	0	20	0	3	.511	0	1	0	1	0	0	1	0	-.084	-.110	5.79	5.79	2.05
Dessens E	4	19.0	87	5	5	10	9	0	0	21	3	0	.723	0	0	0	1	1	0	0	0	-.174	-.080	7.58	7.58	5.69
Ramirez R	4	17.3	78	22	0	15	6	2	1	21	2	2	.648	3	0	0	2	2	0	0	3	.240	.116	8.31	8.31	3.90
Ortiz R	3	13.0	59	10	0	7	7	0	1	15	4	2	.725	1	1	0	1	0	0	0	0	-.077	-.114	7.62	7.62	8.04
Arias A	3	7.3	32	6	0	3	5	0	0	8	1	2	.696	0	0	0	1	0	0	1	0	.003	-.152	4.91	4.91	6.27
Bautista D	1	8.7	48	9	1	8	4	0	1	18	0	1	.486	1	0	0	2	1	0	0	2	.190	-.089	12.46	12.46	3.15
Newman J *	1	2.0	8	2	0	3	0	0	0	2	0	0	.600	0	0	0	0	0	0	0	0	.330	-.550	4.50	4.50	0.27
Kim B	1	6.0	29	3	1	2	4	0	1	6	2	0	.800	0	0	0	1	2	0	0	0	-.031	-.477	10.50	10.50	9.44
Harikkala T	1	3.3	19	1	1	2	1	0	0	9	0	1	.438	0	0	0	0	0	0	0	0	--	.020	8.10	8.10	2.97
Morillo J	1	3.7	16	4	0	3	1	0	1	3	1	0	.800	1	0	0	0	0	0	0	0	.413	.357	9.82	9.82	6.81
Keppel B	0	4.0	20	4	0	1	3	0	0	6	1	1	.667	0	0	0	0	0	0	0	0	-.056	.093	11.25	11.25	8.27
Serafini D *	0	0.3	4	3	0	0	2	0	1	0	0	0	1.000	0	0	0	0	0	0	0	0	-.150	.338	54.00	54.00	30.27
Clarke D	0	1.3	7	2	0	1	1	0	0	2	0	0	.600	0	0	0	0	0	0	0	0	--	-.500	0.00	0.00	4.02

Italicized stats have been adjusted for home park.
Batted Ball Pitching Stats are listed after Fielding Stats.

Fielding Stats

Name	INN	SBA/G	CS%	ERA	WP+PB/G	PO	A	TE	FE
Catcher									
Torrealba Y	935.3	0.71	18%	4.12	0.260	679	56	7	0
Iannetta C	496.7	0.74	20%	4.71	0.236	301	27	1	0
Gil G	35.0	0.51	0%	4.11	0.771	21	3	0	0
Bellorin E	5.0	0.00	0%	3.60	1.800	3	0	0	0

Name	Inn	PO	A	TE	FE	FPct	DPS	DPT	RZR	OOZ
First Base										
Helton T	1337.0	1448	95	1	1	.999	18	0	.808	42
Baker J	96.7	120	2	1	2	.976	0	0	.857	2
Atkins G	32.3	31	3	0	1	.971	1	0	.889	0
Koshansky J	6.0	9	0	0	0	1.000	0	0	--	--
Second Base										
Matsui K	863.3	200	311	2	2	.992	40	44	.870	22
Carroll J	431.3	81	164	0	2	.992	16	19	.870	14
Quintanilla O	161.3	39	49	0	0	1.000	4	7	.795	8
Barmes C	16.0	1	5	0	0	1.000	0	0	.800	1
Shortstop										
Tulowitzki T	1375.0	262	561	7	4	.987	51	60	.861	87
Carroll J	57.0	10	22	0	0	1.000	2	3	.950	0
Barmes C	35.0	8	12	1	0	.952	1	2	.714	0
Quintanilla O	5.0	1	2	0	0	1.000	0	0	1.000	0
Third Base										
Atkins G	1319.0	84	252	9	4	.963	37	1	.613	40
Carroll J	64.7	5	13	2	0	.900	4	0	.769	3
Stewart I	41.3	5	16	0	0	1.000	0	0	1.000	5
Mabry J	27.0	3	4	0	1	.875	0	0	.800	0
Baker J	18.0	0	3	0	0	1.000	0	0	.750	0
Barmes C	2.0	0	0	0	0	0.000	0	0	--	--

Name	Inn	PO	A	TE	FE	FPct	DPS	DPT	RZR	OOZ
Left Field										
Holliday M	1383.0	296	7	1	2	.990	0	0	.892	47
Spilborghs R	66.3	15	0	0	0	1.000	0	0	1.000	3
Baker J	18.0	5	0	0	0	1.000	0	0	1.000	0
Mabry J	2.0	1	0	0	0	1.000	0	0	1.000	0
Sullivan C	1.0	0	0	0	0	0.000	0	0	--	--
Barker S	1.0	0	0	0	0	0.000	0	0	--	--
Center Field										
Taveras W	714.0	212	7	1	3	.982	0	0	.879	37
Spilborghs R	325.7	75	2	0	1	.987	2	0	.904	9
Sullivan C	257.0	77	1	0	0	1.000	2	0	.859	10
Finley S	155.3	45	1	0	0	1.000	2	0	.854	4
Barmes C	17.0	3	0	1	0	.750	0	0	1.000	1
Barker S	2.0	1	0	0	0	1.000	0	0	--	--
Carroll J	1.0	1	0	0	0	1.000	0	0	1.000	0
Right Field										
Hawpe B	1236.0	246	6	0	6	.977	2	0	.861	37
Spilborghs R	124.3	25	0	0	0	1.000	0	0	.917	3
Baker J	92.0	22	1	0	0	1.000	0	0	.913	1
Carroll J	10.0	1	0	0	0	1.000	0	0	1.000	0
Finley S	6.0	1	0	0	0	1.000	0	0	1.000	0
Smith S	2.0	0	0	0	0	0.000	0	0	--	--
Sullivan C	1.0	0	0	0	0	0.000	0	0	--	--

Batted Ball Batting Stats

Player	% of PA		% of Batted Balls					Out %		Runs Per Event				Total Runs vs. Avg.				
	K%	BB%	GB%	LD%	FB%	IF/F	HR/OF	GB	OF	NIP	GB	LD	OF	NIP	GB	LD	FB	Tot
Holliday M	18	10	44	20	36	.04	.19	67	78	.06	.08	.48	.34	2	9	15	33	59
Helton T	11	17	40	24	36	.06	.10	73	81	.17	.05	.38	.19	25	0	14	7	47
Hawpe B	23	14	36	21	43	.07	.19	75	77	.06	.03	.41	.34	6	-4	3	27	33
Atkins G	14	10	31	24	44	.07	.12	72	87	.08	.04	.36	.17	4	-2	11	7	20
Tulowitzki T	19	10	42	20	38	.12	.14	72	80	.04	.05	.43	.26	-1	1	6	13	19
Spilborghs R	15	10	50	21	30	.05	.17	72	85	.07	.06	.36	.27	1	2	1	5	10
Taveras W	13	7	52	17	32	.08	.03	71	85	.04	.07	.39	.05	-2	21	-3	-13	3
Matsui K	15	8	45	21	34	.08	.03	08	83	.04	.09	.44	.08	-2	8	7	-12	1
Sullivan C	16	7	40	24	36	.05	.03	74	76	.03	.05	.38	.10	-1	0	3	-3	-0
Iannetta C	25	15	41	18	41	.09	.08	70	86	.06	.07	.41	.14	2	0	-2	-3	-3
Baker J	25	9	40	20	39	.05	.08	81	86	.01	-.02	.45	.13	-2	-4	0	-2	-7
Carroll J	13	12	44	25	32	.07	.04	77	89	.11	.04	.26	.03	4	-1	-2	-10	-10
Finley S	4	8	49	11	39	.14	.03	86	90	.19	-.03	.31	.04	1	-3	-3	-4	-10
Torrealba Y	16	9	53	18	29	.11	.10	80	83	.05	.00	.42	.17	-1	-7	-0	-6	-14
MLB Average	17	9	43	19	38	.10	.10	74	83	.05	.05	.40	.18	--	--	--	--	--

Batted Ball Pitching Stats

Player	% of PA		% of Batted Balls					Out %		Runs Per Event				Total Runs vs. Avg				
	K%	BB%	GB%	LD%	FB%	IF/F	HR/OF	GB	OF	NIP	GB	LD	OF	NIP	GB	LD	FB	Tot
Corpas M	19	7	57	14	28	.06	.10	80	79	.01	.00	.32	.21	-3	-5	-7	-2	-18
Fuentes D	22	12	36	21	43	.21	.11	83	88	.05	-.01	.32	.15	0	-5	-3	-4	-12
Herges M	16	8	46	15	38	.06	.08	88	83	.04	-.04	.34	.16	-1	-5	-4	-1	-11
Hawkins L	13	7	63	16	21	.03	.17	80	80	.05	.01	.31	.30	-1	-3	-4	1	-7
Morales F	16	10	55	19	27	.13	.08	77	92	.06	.02	.46	.09	0	-2	1	5	-6
Cook A	9	7	58	19	24	.07	.12	79	75	.09	.01	34	.26	1	-8	-2	3	-6
Buchholz T	15	6	44	17	38	.10	.08	73	81	.01	.05	.42	.16	-5	-0	0	-1	-6
Francis J	18	8	44	18	37	.07	.10	73	83	.02	.05	.41	.18	-7	0	1	2	-5
Julio J	23	10	55	17	28	.07	.15	76	88	.02	.03	.47	.21	-1	-1	-0	-2	-4
Jimenez U	19	12	46	17	37	.08	.11	79	83	.06	.03	.42	.20	2	-3	-3	0	-3
Affeldt J	18	14	53	14	33	.04	.06	78	76	.09	.01	.41	.21	4	-3	-4	0	-3
Lopez R	13	6	47	13	40	.07	.10	76	76	.04	.04	.40	.23	-2	0	-5	7	0
Hirsh J	16	10	30	18	51	.12	.11	90	82	.07	-.06	.45	.20	2	-13	3	9	0
Martin T	9	9	45	23	32	.16	.15	72	100	.12	.07	.40	.14	1	1	3	-2	3
Fogg J	13	10	40	20	40	.11	.11	77	83	.09	.04	.44	.20	5	-1	11	7	23
MLB Average	17	9	43	19	38	.10	.10	74	83	.05	.05	.40	.18	--	--	--	--	--

Detroit Tigers

Stat Facts:

- Curtis Granderson stole 26 bases in 27 attempts
- His 23 triples were more than twice as many as second-best in the league
- Granderson's L^R of .164 was highest in the majors
- Granderson had an RZR of .921 and made 85 OOZ plays
- Placido Polanco committed zero errors in over 1,200 innings at second base
- Polanco struck out in just 5% of his PAs, lowest in the league
- Ivan Rodriguez walked in just 2% of his PAs, lowest in the league
- 52% of Rodriguez's batted balls were ground balls
- Justin Verlander hit 19 batters, most in the majors
- Verlander allowed just four steals in five attempts
- Jeremy Bonderman allowed 19 steals in 23 attempts

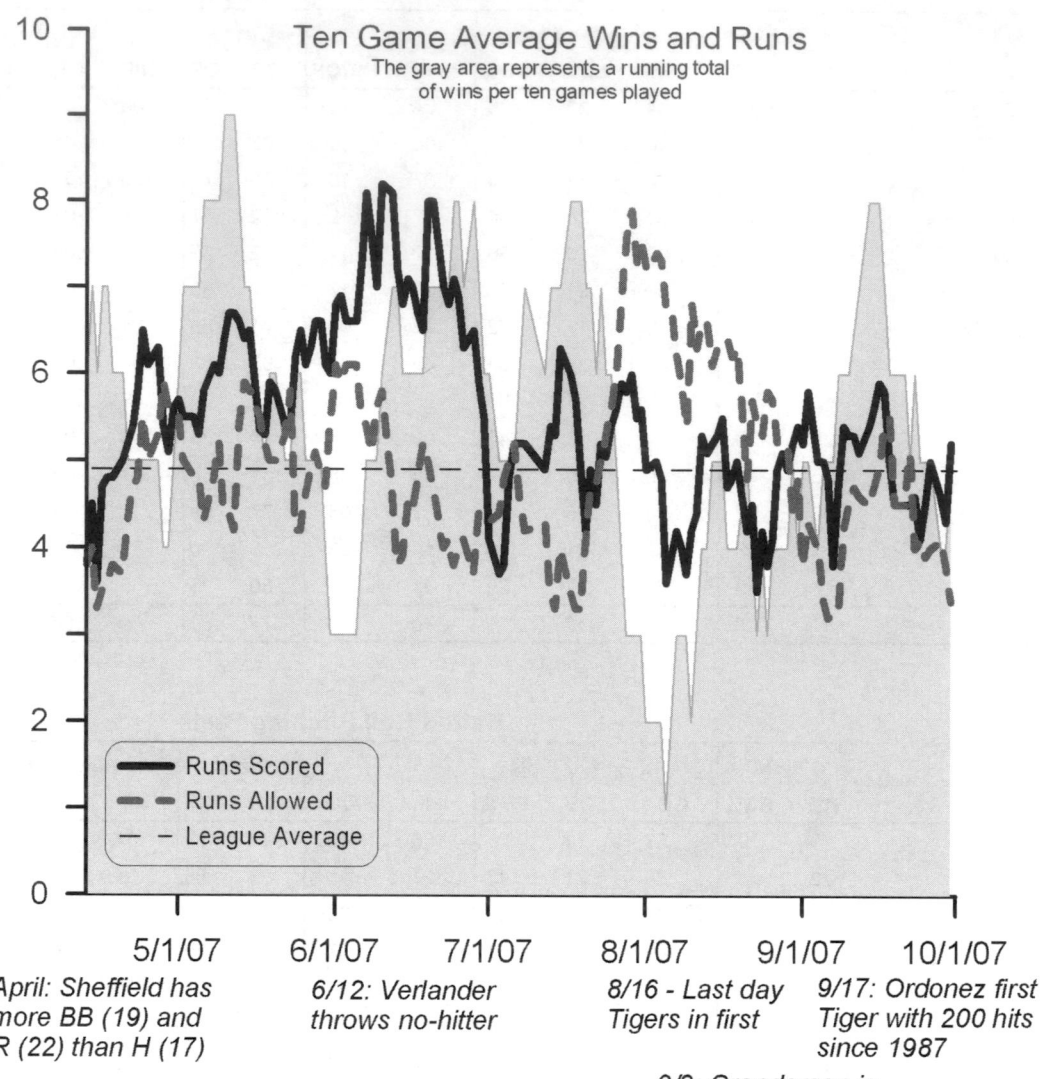

Ten Game Average Wins and Runs
The gray area represents a running total of wins per ten games played

April: Sheffield has more BB (19) and R (22) than H (17)

6/12: Verlander throws no-hitter

8/16 - Last day Tigers in first

9/17: Ordonez first Tiger with 200 hits since 1987

9/9: Granderson is only 3rd person to reach 20-20-20-20

Team Batting and Pitching/Fielding Stats by Month						
	April	May	June	July	Aug	Sept/Oct
Wins	14	16	16	15	11	16
Losses	11	12	10	12	18	11
RS/G	5.1	6.1	6.7	5.3	4.7	5.1
RA/G	4.7	5.1	4.8	5.3	5.4	4.1
OBP	.321	.361	.373	.333	.323	.355
SLG	.405	.527	.477	.449	.432	.450
FIP	4.30	5.03	4.42	4.32	4.58	4.59
DER	.714	.681	.687	.677	.688	.714

Batting Stats

Player	BR	Runs	RBI	PA	Outs	H	2B	3B	HR	TB	K	BB	IBB	HBP	SH	SF	SB	CS	GDP	H-A	L^R	BA	OBP	SLG	GPA
Ordonez M	150	117	139	679	400	216	54	0	28	354	79	76	8	2	0	5	4	1	20	.059	.075	.363	.434	.595	.351
Granderson C*	112	122	74	676	431	185	38	23	23	338	141	52	3	5	5	2	26	1	3	-.028	.164	.302	.361	.552	.306
Guillen C +	99	86	102	630	419	167	35	9	21	283	93	55	10	3	0	8	13	8	14	-.002	.023	.296	.357	.502	.292
Polanco P	99	105	67	641	399	200	36	3	9	269	30	37	3	11	2	4	7	3	9	.012	-.018	.341	.388	.458	.295
Sheffield G	97	107	75	593	378	131	20	1	25	228	71	84	2	9	0	6	22	5	10	.032	-.005	.265	.378	.462	.291
Inge B	70	64	71	577	398	120	25	2	14	191	150	47	5	11	7	4	9	2	8	.035	.103	.236	.312	.376	.239
Rodriguez I	58	50	63	515	379	141	31	3	11	211	96	9	1	1	1	2	2	2	16	.021	.013	.281	.294	.420	.242
Casey S *	56	40	54	496	330	134	30	1	4	178	42	39	11	2	0	2	2	2	9	.036	-.073	.296	.353	.393	.262
Thames M	44	37	54	284	211	65	15	0	18	134	72	13	1	1	0	1	2	1	6	.029	.074	.242	.278	.498	.255
Monroe C	36	47	55	372	280	76	19	0	11	128	94	20	0	2	1	6	0	3	10	-.027	.091	.222	.264	.373	.216
Infante O	23	24	17	178	126	45	6	1	2	59	29	9	0	0	2	1	4	1	4	-.038	.067	.271	.307	.355	.232
Raburn R	23	28	27	148	103	42	12	2	4	70	33	8	1	0	1	1	3	0	7	-.022	-.042	.304	.340	.507	.286
Rabelo M +	17	14	18	185	129	43	10	2	1	60	41	6	0	5	5	1	0	0	4	-.101	.019	.256	.300	.357	.229
Perez T *	17	12	13	96	61	35	9	2	0	48	6	6	0	0	0	0	1	1	5	.020	-.050	.389	.427	.533	.332
Santiago R +	11	10	7	74	48	19	5	1	0	26	10	1	0	3	3	0	3	0	0	-.148	.142	.284	.324	.388	.248
Hessman M	8	7	12	57	39	12	0	0	4	24	17	5	0	0	0	1	0	0	0	.135	-.148	.235	.298	.471	.257
Perez N +	4	5	6	71	55	11	3	0	1	17	8	4	0	0	3	0	0	0	2	-.067	.070	.172	.221	.266	.169
Maybin C	3	8	2	53	42	7	3	0	1	13	21	3	0	1	0	0	5	0	0	.032	-.220	.143	.208	.265	.163
Maroth M *	0	1	0	4	3	1	1	0	0	2	1	0	0	0	0	0	0	0	0	-.238	-.475	.250	.250	.500	.242
Seay B *	-0	0	0	1	1	0	0	0	0	0	1	0	0	0	0	0	0	0	0	.000	--	.000	.000	.000	.000
Ledezma W *	-0	0	0	1	1	0	0	0	0	0	0	0	0	0	0	0	0	0	0	.000	--	.000	.000	.000	.000
Rogers K *	-0	0	0	2	2	0	0	0	0	0	1	0	0	0	0	0	0	0	0	.000	--	.000	.000	.000	.000
Durbin C	-0	0	1	5	4	0	0	0	0	0	0	0	0	0	0	1	0	0	0	.000	.000	.000	.000	.000	.000
Verlander J	-0	0	0	5	4	0	0	0	0	0	3	0	0	0	1	0	0	0	0	.000	--	.000	.000	.000	.000
Bonderman J	-1	1	0	6	5	1	0	0	0	1	3	0	0	0	0	0	0	0	0	-.117	-.175	.167	.167	.167	.119
Miller A *	-1	0	0	5	5	0	0	0	0	0	5	0	0	0	0	0	0	0	0	.000	.000	.000	.000	.000	.000
Clevlen B	-1	2	0	10	10	1	0	0	0	1	7	0	0	0	0	0	0	0	1	-.117	.117	.100	.100	.100	.071

Italicized stats have been adjusted for home park.

Batted Ball Batting Stats

Player	% of PA		% of Batted Balls					Out %		Runs Per Event				Total Runs vs. Avg.				
	K%	BB%	GB%	LD%	FB%	IF/F	HR/OF	GB	OF	NIP	GB	LD	OF	NIP	GB	LD	FB	Tot
Ordonez M	12	11	42	19	39	.05	.15	68	74	.11	.07	.43	.30	10	7	12	32	61
Granderson C	21	8	34	21	45	.07	.11	72	75	.02	.08	.48	.27	-5	3	13	24	35
Polanco P	5	7	45	24	31	.07	.06	67	83	.17	.09	.35	.11	5	14	15	-8	26
Sheffield G	12	16	41	17	42	.15	.14	71	91	.15	.06	.42	.17	17	3	1	-0	20
Guillen C	15	9	39	20	41	.07	.12	72	83	.06	.06	.40	.21	1	3	4	11	19
Raburn R	22	5	41	19	39	.12	.08	65	82	-.02	.08	.58	.19	-3	2	4	0	3
Casey S	8	8	46	21	33	.09	.03	71	88	.11	.06	.41	.05	3	5	9	-16	1
Thames M	25	5	38	16	46	.16	.22	76	88	-.04	.03	.53	.30	-7	-2	0	9	-1
Infante O	16	5	33	21	47	.16	.04	65	84	-.00	.10	.25	.09	-3	3	-3	-4	-7
Rabelo M	22	6	52	22	27	.12	.03	79	69	-.02	.02	.36	.20	-3	-2	-0	-3	-9
Rodriguez I	19	2	52	19	28	.06	.10	73	80	-.07	.05	.41	.20	-15	2	3	-2	-12
Inge B	26	10	37	22	41	.07	.09	77	82	.02	.04	.40	.16	-5	-5	-0	-4	-14
Monroe C	25	6	35	17	47	.12	.10	79	88	-.03	.00	.46	.14	-9	-6	-2	-4	-20
MLB Average	17	9	43	19	38	.10	.10	74	83	.05	.05	.40	.18	--	--	--	--	--

Pitching Stats

Player	PRC	IP	BFP	G	GS	K	BB	IBB	HBP	H	HR	DP	DER	SB	CS	PO	W	L	Sv	Op	Hld	H-A	R^L	RA	ERA	FIP
Verlander J	100	201.7	866	32	32	183	67	3	19	181	20	12	.711	4	1	2	18	6	0	0	0	-.003	-.013	3.93	3.66	4.09
Robertson N	66	177.7	781	30	30	119	63	2	3	199	22	17	.683	7	4	1	9	13	0	0	0	-.017	-.022	4.96	4.76	4.73
Bonderman J	62	174.3	753	28	28	145	48	6	4	193	23	19	.670	19	4	1	11	9	0	0	0	.016	-.001	5.42	5.01	4.22
Durbin C	44	127.7	561	36	19	66	49	4	8	133	21	11	.729	5	2	0	8	7	1	2	3	.052	-.002	5.01	4.72	5.73
Seay B *	34	46.3	189	58	0	38	15	4	2	38	1	4	.722	1	1	0	3	0	1	2	10	-.093	-.052	2.33	2.33	2.86
Grilli J	29	79.7	352	57	0	62	32	1	5	81	5	7	.685	1	2	0	5	3	0	2	11	.129	-.003	5.20	4.74	4.00
Miner Z	26	53.7	232	34	1	34	22	4	0	56	3	7	.671	4	6	0	3	4	0	2	9	-.013	.089	3.69	3.02	3.85
Jones T	25	61.3	265	63	0	33	23	6	0	64	3	7	.699	1	0	0	1	4	38	44	0	-.047	-.006	4.26	4.26	3.77
Maroth M *	23	78.3	346	13	13	28	33	0	3	97	15	14	.689	1	3	4	5	2	0	0	0	-.003	-.016	5.40	5.06	6.53
Rogers K *	22	63.0	275	11	11	36	25	0	1	65	8	6	.707	0	0	2	3	4	0	0	0	-.044	-.064	5.14	4.43	5.13
Rodney F	22	50.7	223	48	0	54	21	0	3	46	5	3	.679	6	2	0	2	6	1	3	12	.003	-.016	4.80	4.26	3.95
Miller A *	20	64.0	309	13	13	56	39	0	7	73	8	7	.643	10	1	0	5	5	0	0	0	-.022	-.120	6.05	5.63	5.41
Byrdak T *	20	45.0	199	39	0	49	26	4	1	38	3	5	.658	2	1	0	3	0	1	2	8	-.008	-.026	4.60	3.20	3.60
Zumaya J	15	33.7	142	28	0	27	17	2	1	23	3	2	.766	3	0	0	2	3	1	5	8	-.121	-.108	4.28	4.28	4.36
Bazardo Y	15	23.7	96	11	2	15	5	0	3	19	2	4	.732	1	0	0	2	1	0	0	1	-.092	-.127	2.66	2.28	4.23
Ledezma W *	12	35.7	166	23	0	24	26	2	0	38	4	3	.688	4	3	1	3	1	0	2	2	.019	.034	5.30	4.79	5.51
Jurrjens J	11	30.7	122	7	7	13	11	0	1	24	4	6	.774	2	0	0	3	1	0	0	0	.057	-.125	4.70	4.70	5.40
Lopez A	5	17.3	76	10	0	7	6	0	2	18	2	2	.729	0	0	0	0	0	1	1	1	.003	-.028	5.19	5.19	5.46
McBride M *	5	17.7	81	20	0	13	10	0	1	19	3	2	.704	0	0	0	0	1	0	0	4	.090	.072	6.11	6.11	5.98
Tata J	3	14.0	64	3	3	8	8	1	2	16	1	4	.667	0	0	0	1	1	0	0	0	.225	-.168	7.71	7.71	5.09
Capellan J	3	14.0	63	10	0	12	3	1	1	18	5	1	.690	1	1	0	0	1	0	0	1	.068	-.227	8.36	6.43	6.95
Vasquez V	3	16.7	81	5	3	7	5	0	1	27	7	2	.656	1	0	0	0	1	0	0	0	-.126	-.086	8.64	8.64	9.08
Mesa J	1	11.7	59	16	0	9	6	0	0	19	3	1	.610	0	0	0	1	1	0	0	3	-.018	.011	12.34	12.34	6.72
de la Cruz E	1	6.7	32	6	0	5	4	1	0	10	1	2	.545	0	0	0	0	0	0	0	0	.361	.120	10.80	6.75	5.18
Rapada C *	0	2.3	12	4	0	4	2	0	0	3	2	0	.750	0	0	0	0	0	0	0	0	.482	-.265	11.57	11.57	13.67

Italicized stats have been adjusted for home park.

Batted Ball Pitching Stats

Player	% of PA		% of Batted Balls					Out %		Runs Per Event				Total Runs vs. Avg.				
	K%	BB%	GB%	LD%	FB%	IF/F	HR/OF	GB	OF	NIP	GB	LD	OF	NIP	GB	LD	FB	Tot
Verlander J	21	10	41	19	40	.10	.09	72	87	.03	.06	.32	.14	-3	2	-12	-10	-23
Seay B	20	9	38	18	44	.09	.02	78	84	.03	.03	.38	.06	-1	-1	-2	-6	-10
Zumaya J	19	13	36	16	48	.13	.08	80	92	.07	.01	.41	.08	1	-2	-2	-4	-7
Jones T	12	9	46	21	33	.10	.05	79	89	.08	.02	.44	.05	1	-2	5	-9	-5
Grilli J	18	11	45	16	39	.05	.05	75	83	.06	.04	.49	.10	1	-1	1	-6	-4
Rodney F	24	11	45	19	35	.10	.11	75	85	.03	.04	.44	.18	-1	0	-0	-2	-3
Jurrjens J	11	10	38	18	44	.14	.11	84	91	.11	-.03	.46	.13	1	-3	1	-1	-2
Miner Z	15	9	56	16	27	.11	.07	71	90	.07	.07	.47	.09	1	4	1	-6	-1
Byrdak T	25	14	40	21	38	.11	.05	65	85	.05	.10	.46	.11	1	2	1	-4	-0
Rogers K	13	9	48	23	29	.08	.14	84	84	.08	-.01	.38	.25	1	-5	4	2	2
Durbin C	12	10	44	16	40	.10	.13	76	90	.10	.04	.40	.18	5	-1	-3	2	3
Bonderman J	19	7	48	18	34	.11	.13	72	85	.01	.06	.48	.21	-9	5	6	2	4
Ledezma W	14	16	36	20	44	.04	.09	75	84	.13	.04	.41	.15	4	-1	1	0	5
Robertson N	15	8	45	18	37	.06	.11	74	86	.05	.05	.45	.17	-1	1	6	0	7
Miller A	18	15	49	21	30	.11	.15	70	85	.09	.07	.43	.23	6	3	3	0	12
Maroth M	8	10	43	20	37	.09	.15	76	81	.15	.03	.42	.25	5	-1	7	9	20
MLB Average	17	9	43	19	38	.10	.10	74	83	.05	.05	.40	.18	--	--	--	--	--

Fielding Stats

Name	INN	SBA/G	CS%	ERA	WP+PB/G	PO	A	TE	FE
Catcher									
Rodriguez I	1052.7	0.56	29%	4.40	0.513	834	50	4	2
Rabelo M	394.7	0.78	24%	5.06	0.570	246	21	3	2

Name	Inn	PO	A	TE	FE	FPct	DPS	DPT	RZR	OOZ
First Base										
Casey S	989.0	992	42	2	0	.998	2	2	.707	22
Thames M	195.3	180	15	0	2	.990	1	1	.788	3
Guillen C	178.7	185	17	0	0	.995	1	0	.906	6
Hessman M	84.3	74	2	0	0	1.000	0	0	.875	2
Second Base										
Polanco P	1209.0	294	389	0	0	1.000	39	61	.868	39
Infante O	124.3	30	38	0	1	.986	5	3	.771	6
Raburn R	74.0	10	26	0	1	.973	2	3	.688	1
Perez N	40.0	7	14	0	0	1.000	3	2	.909	0
Shortstop										
Guillen C	1074.0	160	352	8	16	.955	38	35	.801	36
Santiago R	186.0	29	62	1	1	.978	6	6	.833	13
Perez N	107.7	13	27	0	2	.952	3	2	.815	3
Infante O	79.7	15	17	0	2	.941	3	2	.619	2
Third Base										
Inge B	1309.0	91	325	8	10	.959	24	0	.712	63
Infante O	72.7	6	22	1	0	.966	1	0	.700	0
Hessman M	28.0	1	5	0	0	1.000	0	0	1.000	0
Perez N	24.0	2	10	0	1	.923	0	0	.875	3
Raburn R	13.0	1	1	0	0	1.000	0	0	1.000	0

Name	Inn	PO	A	TE	FE	FPct	DPS	DPT	RZR	OOZ
Left Field										
Monroe C	795.7	162	6	1	2	.982	2	0	.849	33
Thames M	276.7	67	1	0	2	.971	2	0	.894	8
Perez T	158.0	41	2	1	1	.956	0	0	.814	6
Maybin C	80.0	22	0	0	0	1.000	0	0	.875	1
Raburn R	58.0	16	1	0	0	1.000	2	0	.765	3
Sheffield G	56.0	12	1	0	0	1.000	0	0	1.000	2
Clevlen B	13.0	2	0	0	0	1.000	0	0	1.000	0
Granderson C	5.0	4	0	0	0	1.000	0	0	1.000	1
Hessman M	4.0	1	0	0	0	1.000	0	0	.500	0
Infante O	1.0	0	0	0	0	0.000	0	0	--	--
Center Field										
Granderson C	1285.0	424	10	4	1	.989	8	0	.921	85
Infante O	68.0	19	0	0	0	1.000	0	0	.944	2
Raburn R	63.3	15	0	0	0	1.000	0	0	.933	1
Maybin C	25.0	10	0	0	0	1.000	0	0	.889	2
Clevlen B	6.0	0	0	0	0	0.000	0	0	--	--
Right Field										
Ordonez M	1221.0	261	4	0	1	.996	4	0	.906	29
Raburn R	90.0	24	0	0	0	1.000	0	0	.952	4
Sheffield G	50.0	13	0	0	0	1.000	0	0	.889	5
Thames M	37.0	10	0	0	0	1.000	0	0	1.000	1
Perez T	27.0	3	0	0	0	1.000	0	0	.750	0
Infante O	13.0	4	0	0	0	1.000	0	0	1.000	0
Clevlen B	5.3	2	0	0	0	1.000	0	0	1.000	0
Monroe C	4.0	1	0	0	0	1.000	0	0	1.000	0

Florida Marlins

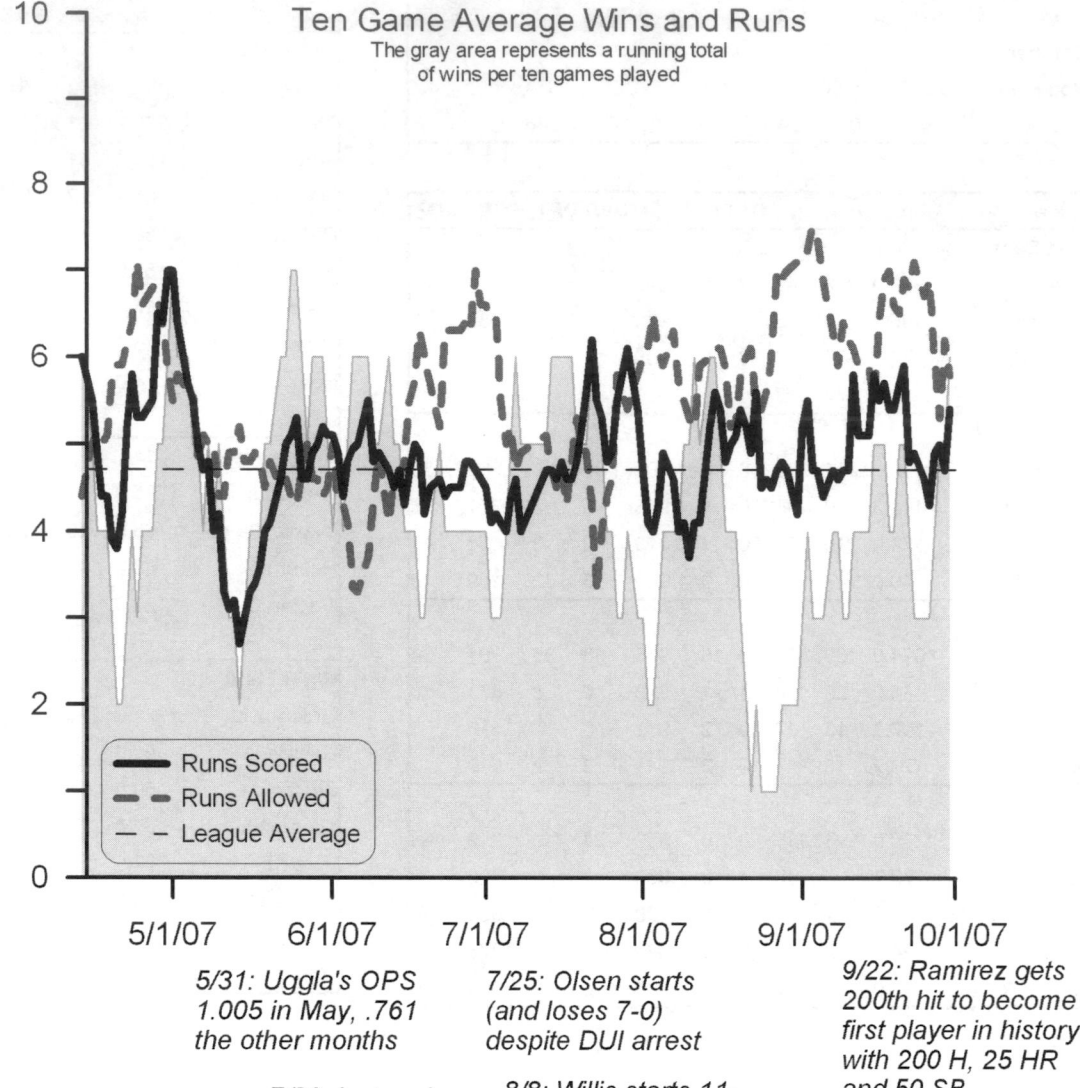

Ten Game Average Wins and Runs
The gray area represents a running total of wins per ten games played

Legend:
— Runs Scored
– – Runs Allowed
– – League Average

5/31: Uggla's OPS 1.005 in May, .761 the other months

7/22: just under .500 (48-51), but 23-40 rest of way

7/25: Olsen starts (and loses 7-0) despite DUI arrest

8/8: Willis starts 11-game stretch of pitching 5.74 ERA and hitting 1.556 OPS

9/22: Ramirez gets 200th hit to become first player in history with 200 H, 25 HR and 50 SB

9/3: Move into NL East basement for good

Team Batting and Pitching/Fielding Stats by Month						
	April	May	June	July	Aug	Sept/Oct
Wins	12	14	11	12	9	13
Losses	13	15	16	14	19	14
RS/G	5.7	4.3	4.6	4.9	4.5	5.3
RA/G	5.6	4.5	5.7	4.9	6.2	6.1
OBP	.355	.319	.321	.351	.331	.342
SLG	.479	.398	.434	.490	.434	.461
FIP	4.68	4.11	4.70	4.41	4.89	4.92
DER	.653	.699	.666	.668	.657	.636

Batting Stats

Player	BR	Runs	RBI	PA	Outs	H	2B	3B	HR	TB	K	BB	IBB	HBP	SH	SF	SB	CS	GDP	H-A	L^R	BA	OBP	SLG	GPA
Cabrera M	129	91	119	680	418	188	38	2	34	332	127	79	23	5	1	7	2	1	17	.034	.088	.320	.401	.565	.331
Ramirez H	124	125	81	706	451	212	48	6	29	359	95	52	3	7	4	4	51	14	10	.016	.084	.332	.386	.562	.324
Willingham J	104	75	89	604	395	138	32	4	21	241	122	66	1	16	0	1	8	1	11	-.013	-.081	.265	.364	.463	.288
Uggla D	92	113	88	728	488	155	49	3	31	303	167	68	0	13	4	11	2	1	10	.059	.007	.245	.326	.479	.275
Hermida J *	75	54	63	484	316	127	32	1	18	215	105	47	2	4	1	3	3	4	10	-.054	.026	.296	.369	.501	.300
Jacobs M *	57	57	54	460	327	113	27	2	17	195	101	31	3	2	0	1	1	2	12	-.007	-.019	.265	.317	.458	.265
Olivo M	49	43	60	469	360	107	20	4	16	183	123	14	2	2	0	1	3	2	13	.055	.065	.237	.262	.405	.226
Ross C	46	35	39	197	117	58	19	0	12	113	38	20	3	3	0	1	2	0	2	.105	.080	.335	.411	.653	.359
Amezaga A +	38	46	30	448	306	105	14	9	2	143	52	35	0	4	4	5	13	7	4	-.004	-.061	.263	.324	.358	.243
Boone A	33	27	28	228	135	54	11	0	5	80	41	21	4	13	1	4	2	0	0	-.032	-.079	.286	.388	.423	.289
Treanor M	27	16	19	198	127	46	7	1	4	67	29	19	1	5	2	1	0	0	2	-.020	-.020	.269	.357	.392	.267
Linden T +	18	15	8	144	98	35	7	1	1	47	36	14	0	1	0	0	4	0	4	.122	-.036	.271	.347	.364	.255
Borchard J +	18	20	19	202	148	35	9	0	4	56	60	21	3	2	0	0	4	0	4	.030	-.045	.196	.287	.313	.214
Wood J	18	11	26	127	90	28	6	0	3	43	38	8	0	0	1	1	0	0	1	.075	-.005	.239	.286	.368	.227
De Aza A *	12	14	8	158	113	33	8	2	0	45	37	6	1	1	5	2	2	0	2	-.093	-.071	.229	.261	.313	.202
Willis D *	11	11	7	80	47	18	1	2	3	32	13	5	0	1	11	0	0	1	1	.008	.040	.286	.348	.508	.292
Abercrombie	4	16	5	80	63	15	3	0	2	24	22	2	0	2	0	0	7	1	1	-.088	-.011	.197	.238	.316	.192
Andino R	1	0	0	13	8	5	1	0	0	6	2	0	0	0	0	0	0	0	0	.074	.037	.385	.385	.462	.297
Sanchez A	1	1	0	14	10	1	0	0	0	1	7	2	0	0	1	0	0	0	0	.093	.012	.091	.231	.091	.130
Julio J	0	0	0	1	0	0	0	0	0	0	0	1	0	0	0	0	0	0	0	-.450	--	.000	1.000	.000	.464
Carroll B	0	10	2	53	41	9	1	0	0	10	15	3	0	0	1	0	0	0	1	.045	.073	.184	.231	.204	.160
Messenger R	-0	0	0	2	1	0	0	0	0	0	1	0	0	0	1	0	0	0	0	.000	--	.000	.000	.000	.000
Martinez C	-0	0	0	1	1	0	0	0	0	0	1	0	0	0	0	0	0	0	0	.000	--	.000	.000	.000	.000
Wolf R	-0	0	0	1	1	0	0	0	0	0	1	0	0	0	0	0	0	0	0	.000	--	.000	.000	.000	.000
Lindstrom M	-0	0	0	1	1	0	0	0	0	0	1	0	0	0	0	0	0	0	0	.000	--	.000	.000	.000	.000
Kensing L	-0	0	0	1	1	0	0	0	0	0	0	0	0	0	0	0	0	0	0	.000	--	.000	.000	.000	.000
Hoover P	-0	1	0	8	5	3	0	0	0	3	2	0	0	0	0	0	0	0	0	.047	.327	.375	.375	.375	.271
Miller J	-0	0	0	2	2	0	0	0	0	0	0	0	0	0	0	0	0	0	0	.000	--	.000	.000	.000	.000
Gregg K	-0	0	0	2	2	0	0	0	0	0	2	0	0	0	0	0	0	0	0	.000	--	.000	.000	.000	.000
Johnson J *	-0	0	0	3	2	0	0	0	0	0	1	0	0	0	1	0	0	0	0	.000	.000	.000	.000	.000	.000
Olsen S *	-0	3	3	61	42	9	3	0	0	12	23	1	0	0	9	0	0	0	0	-.083	.194	.176	.192	.235	.150
Pinto R *	-0	0	0	3	3	0	0	0	0	0	2	0	0	0	0	0	0	0	0	.000	.000	.000	.000	.000	.000
Seddon C *	-0	0	0	5	3	0	0	0	0	0	2	0	0	0	2	0	0	0	0	.000	.000	.000	.000	.000	.000
Gall J	-0	0	0	5	5	0	0	0	0	0	1	0	0	1	0	0	0	0	1	--	.225	.000	.200	.000	.093
Gardner L	-0	0	0	4	4	0	0	0	0	0	3	0	0	0	0	0	0	0	0	.000	.000	.000	.000	.000	.000
Reed E *	-1	3	0	21	18	2	0	0	0	2	6	1	0	0	0	0	1	0	0	-.169	.104	.100	.143	.100	.092
Nolasco R	-1	0	0	7	6	0	0	0	0	0	3	0	0	0	1	0	0	0	0	.000	.000	.000	.000	.000	.000
Barone D	-1	1	0	11	8	1	0	0	0	1	7	0	0	0	2	0	0	0	0	-.100	-.078	.111	.111	.111	.080
Obermueller	-1	1	0	19	15	1	1	0	0	2	4	0	0	0	3	0	0	0	0	.136	-.086	.063	.063	.125	.061
Kim B	-1	0	1	39	28	2	1	0	0	3	11	2	0	0	7	0	0	0	0	.017	-.005	.067	.125	.100	.084
VandenHurk	-2	1	0	27	22	1	0	0	0	1	12	1	0	0	3	0	0	0	0	-.084	.078	.043	.083	.043	.050
Mitre S	-2	0	0	47	36	3	1	0	0	4	19	2	0	0	7	0	0	0	1	.152	.080	.079	.125	.105	.085

Italicized stats have been adjusted for home park.

Batted Ball Batting Stats are listed after Fielding Stats.

Pitching Stats

Player	PRC	IP	BFP	G	GS	K	BB	IBB	HBP	H	HR	DP	DER	SB	CS	PO	W	L	Sv	Op	Hld	H-A	R^L	RA	ERA	FIP
Willis D *	62	205.3	942	35	35	146	87	4	14	241	29	22	.665	6	1	1	10	15	0	0	0	-.014	-.176	5.74	5.17	5.10
Gardner L	51	74.3	311	62	0	52	18	4	3	72	2	7	.678	3	0	0	3	4	2	2	9	.042	-.089	2.30	1.94	2.91
Mitre S	46	149.0	662	27	27	80	41	3	10	180	9	18	.661	12	3	1	5	8	0	0	0	.005	.042	5.32	4.65	3.95
Olsen S *	44	176.7	826	33	33	133	85	4	1	226	29	19	.635	10	6	2	10	15	0	0	0	-.055	-.006	6.83	5.81	5.29
Gregg K	43	84.0	355	74	0	87	40	1	6	63	7	7	.730	3	0	1	0	5	32	36	6	.004	.070	3.64	3.54	3.89
Lindstrom M	34	67.0	284	71	0	62	21	4	3	66	2	5	.668	1	1	0	3	4	0	2	19	-.059	.019	3.63	3.09	2.70
Kim B	33	109.7	511	23	19	102	62	3	14	114	17	10	.674	21	5	0	9	5	0	0	0	.032	-.094	6.07	5.42	5.42
Miller J	31	61.7	259	62	0	74	24	6	0	53	5	5	.679	1	2	1	5	0	0	3	17	.026	-.125	3.94	3.65	2.80
Pinto R *	28	58.7	242	57	0	56	32	2	3	45	7	9	.736	2	3	0	2	4	1	6	16	-.027	-.049	3.84	3.68	4.60
Tankersley T	22	47.3	205	67	0	49	29	3	3	42	4	7	.683	1	4	2	6	1	1	3	16	-.041	-.089	4.18	3.99	4.14
VandenHurk	21	81.7	379	18	17	82	48	5	3	94	15	6	.645	8	3	1	4	6	0	0	0	.011	.000	6.94	6.83	5.34
Kensing L	14	13.3	59	9	0	13	7	2	2	11	0	1	.703	2	0	0	3	0	0	0	0	.002	-.043	1.35	1.35	2.89
Owens H	14	23.0	98	22	0	16	10	1	0	19	3	0	.754	1	0	0	2	0	4	5	5	.050	-.083	2.74	1.96	4.75
Messenger R	13	23.7	103	23	0	12	9	2	0	27	0	5	.659	1	0	0	1	1	0	0	6	.125	-.033	2.66	2.66	3.14
Obermueller	12	59.0	278	18	7	35	36	5	4	72	7	11	.663	6	2	0	2	3	0	0	0	.134	-.024	7.47	6.56	5.40
Barone D	10	41.0	183	16	6	18	19	2	1	50	11	9	.701	1	1	1	1	3	0	0	0	-.040	.098	6.37	5.71	7.20
Sanchez A	9	30.0	151	6	6	14	19	1	2	43	3	3	.646	1	0	0	2	1	0	0	0	-.045	.018	5.10	4.80	5.64
Benitez A	8	33.0	150	36	0	39	20	1	1	32	5	5	.659	4	0	0	2	5	0	5	11	-.008	.005	7.64	5.73	4.69
Garcia H	6	12.3	55	8	0	15	7	1	0	14	3	2	.633	1	0	0	0	1	0	0	0	.178	-.198	4.38	4.38	5.46
Nolasco R	5	21.3	99	5	4	11	9	2	1	26	3	3	.680	2	1	0	1	2	0	0	0	.135	.060	6.75	5.48	5.19
Johnson J	2	15.7	82	4	4	14	12	3	0	26	1	4	.509	1	1	0	0	3	0	0	0	.098	-.098	9.77	7.47	4.04
Seddon C *	2	17.3	91	7	4	10	5	0	1	29	2	0	.589	3	0	0	0	2	0	0	0	.001	-.122	9.87	8.83	4.65
Wolf R	1	12.3	66	14	0	6	3	0	1	24	4	0	.596	0	0	0	0	1	0	0	0	-.123	.128	11.68	11.68	7.49
Ramirez E *	1	3.3	17	4	0	1	2	0	0	4	0	0	.643	0	0	0	0	0	0	0	0	.366	.036	5.40	5.40	4.47
Julio J	1	9.3	59	10	0	6	11	1	2	18	2	1	.553	2	0	0	0	2	0	2	1	-.144	.236	13.50	12.54	8.63
Carvajal M	1	4.0	24	3	0	2	2	0	0	8	0	0	.500	1	0	0	0	0	0	0	0	-.065	-.058	9.00	6.75	3.77
Zarate M	0	5.0	30	4	0	3	1	0	1	11	3	0	.545	0	0	0	0	0	0	0	0	-.125	.039	12.60	10.80	11.07
Martinez C	0	2.7	13	2	0	2	1	0	0	4	3	0	.857	0	0	0	0	0	0	0	0	.026	.126	13.50	13.50	17.52
Field N	0	1.0	7	1	0	2	1	0	0	3	0	0	.250	0	0	0	0	0	0	0	0	--	-.438	27.00	27.00	2.27
Wood J	0	1.0	3	1	0	0	0	0	0	0	0	0	1.000	0	0	0	0	0	0	0	0	--	.000	0.00	0.00	3.27

Italicized stats have been adjusted for home park.
Batted Ball Pitching Stats are listed after Fielding Stats.

Fielding Stats

Name	INN	SBA/G	CS%	ERA	WP+PB/G	PO	A	TE	FE
Catcher									
Olivo M	990.3	0.65	28%	5.04	0.609	787	64	8	4
Treanor M	440.7	0.98	13%	4.70	0.388	385	16	3	0
Hoover P	12.7	0.71	0%	7.11	0.000	12	0	0	0

Name	Inn	PO	A	TE	FE	FPct	DPS	DPT	RZR	OOZ
First Base										
Jacobs M	903.0	793	45	1	6	.992	7	0	.688	23
Boone A	388.0	352	26	4	1	.987	5	0	.613	12
Wood J	145.0	112	10	1	2	.976	1	0	.850	7
Amezaga A	4.7	4	1	0	0	1.000	0	0	1.000	0
Hoover P	3.0	1	0	0	0	1.000	0	0	--	--
Second Base										
Uggla D	1383.0	323	402	6	5	.985	37	72	.776	55
Amezaga A	56.0	21	21	1	1	.955	3	4	.882	0
Wood J	4.0	2	0	0	0	1.000	0	0	--	--
Shortstop										
Ramirez H	1301.0	225	392	13	11	.963	61	34	.773	45
Amezaga A	122.0	16	35	0	1	.981	2	2	.875	4
Andino R	20.0	3	4	0	0	1.000	1	0	.000	1
Third Base										
Cabrera M	1310.0	100	266	10	13	.941	37	0	.627	50
Boone A	68.3	6	9	0	0	1.000	0	0	.455	2
Amezaga A	46.7	11	6	0	0	1.000	0	0	.250	3
Wood J	18.0	1	1	0	0	1.000	0	0	0.000	1

Name	Inn	PO	A	TE	FE	FPct	DPS	DPT	RZR	OOZ
Left Field										
Willingham J	1176.0	211	9	2	1	.987	0	0	.836	23
Linden T	119.0	25	0	0	0	1.000	0	0	1.000	5
Borchard J	67.7	15	0	0	1	.938	0	0	.824	1
Ross C	47.0	16	1	0	1	.944	2	0	.882	1
Carroll B	18.7	3	1	0	0	1.000	2	0	.750	0
Abercrombie R	11.0	3	0	0	0	1.000	0	0	.500	2
Amezaga A	2.0	1	0	0	0	1.000	0	0	--	--
Wood J	2.0	0	0	0	0	0.000	0	0	--	--
Center Field										
Amezaga A	643.7	208	8	1	4	.977	2	0	.923	40
De Aza A	303.7	85	3	0	1	.989	0	0	.888	14
Ross C	239.3	63	2	0	1	.985	2	0	.879	5
Abercrombie R	124.3	54	2	0	1	.982	0	0	.962	4
Carroll B	81.0	29	0	1	1	.935	0	0	.958	6
Linden T	31.7	10	0	0	0	1.000	0	0	.889	2
Reed E	20.0	4	0	0	0	1.000	0	0	.750	1
Right Field										
Hermida J	985.7	247	7	2	7	.966	2	0	.879	43
Borchard J	277.3	78	1	0	1	.988	2	0	.896	18
Ross C	106.3	30	2	1	0	.970	4	0	.897	4
Linden T	34.0	5	0	0	0	1.000	0	0	.667	1
Carroll B	22.0	13	0	0	0	1.000	0	0	.923	1
Abercrombie R	9.3	3	0	0	0	1.000	0	0	1.000	0
Gall J	6.0	1	0	0	0	1.000	0	0	1.000	0
Amezaga A	3.0	2	0	0	0	1.000	0	0	1.000	0

Batted Ball Batting Stats

Player	% of PA		% of Batted Balls					Out %		Runs Per Event				Total Runs vs. Avg.				
	K%	BB%	GB%	LD%	FB%	IF/F	HR/OF	GB	OF	NIP	GB	LD	OF	NIP	GB	LD	FB	Tot
Ramirez H	13	8	40	18	42	.11	.13	67	76	.06	.09	.46	.26	1	11	11	23	46
Cabrera M	19	12	40	21	39	.10	.19	71	83	.07	.06	.48	.30	6	1	14	22	44
Ross C	19	12	41	21	38	.13	.22	66	77	.06	.13	.49	.39	1	4	5	10	20
Hermida J	22	11	44	21	35	.02	.16	73	77	.04	.05	.39	.30	-0	2	2	15	18
Willingham J	20	14	36	21	43	.13	.14	74	83	.07	.04	.42	.23	7	-3	4	8	16
Uggla D	23	11	34	16	51	.10	.14	73	84	.04	.06	.42	.23	-1	-0	-8	18	9
Boone A	18	15	26	26	48	.14	.08	65	86	.10	.11	.39	.11	4	2	4	-3	8
Treanor M	15	12	42	24	34	.06	.07	71	83	.10	.07	.31	.11	2	1	0	-3	1
Jacobs M	22	7	36	18	46	.08	.12	75	80	-.00	.02	.43	.23	-6	-4	-0	11	0
Linden T	25	10	47	18	35	.00	.03	65	74	.02	.08	.32	.16	-1	1	-2	-1	-2
Wood J	30	6	39	22	39	.16	.12	81	74	-.03	.01	.42	.26	-3	-2	-0	1	-5
Borchard J	30	11	39	15	45	.06	.08	79	74	.01	.01	.34	.20	-2	-2	-5	1	-8
De Aza A	23	4	39	26	34	.03	.00	78	79	-.04	.03	.31	.10	-4	-1	-1	-4	-9
Amezaga A	12	9	47	21	33	.12	.02	78	84	.08	.02	.42	.05	1	-1	5	-15	-9
Olivo M	26	3	43	17	40	.17	.12	79	81	-.06	.01	.48	.22	-15	-5	-1	0	-22
MLB Average	*17*	*9*	*43*	*19*	*38*	*.10*	*.10*	*74*	*83*	*.05*	*.05*	*.40*	*.18*	--	--	--	--	--

Batted Ball Pitching Stats

Player	% of PA		% of Batted Balls					Out %		Runs Per Event				Total Runs vs. Avg.				
	K%	BB%	GB%	LD%	FB%	IF/F	HR/OF	GB	OF	NIP	GB	LD	OF	NIP	GB	LD	FB	Tot
Gregg K	25	13	29	16	55	.13	.07	68	88	.05	.08	.36	.09	1	-0	-7	-7	-14
Gardner L	17	7	43	18	40	.14	.01	68	85	.02	.08	.40	.04	-3	3	-0	-12	-12
Lindstrom M	22	9	47	16	36	.10	.03	70	84	.02	.07	.43	.06	-2	2	-2	-9	-11
Miller J	29	9	43	14	43	.10	.08	68	78	-.00	.09	.34	.22	-4	2	-7	1	-8
Pinto R	23	14	37	19	44	.14	.13	85	88	.06	-.04	.40	.17	2	-6	-2	-1	-6
Tankersley T	24	16	37	19	44	.08	.06	70	83	.07	.05	.41	.12	3	-1	-1	-3	-2
Mitre S	12	8	60	17	23	.06	.07	75	70	.07	.04	.40	.22	-0	1	1	-3	-0
Benitez A	26	13	29	19	52	.07	.12	64	83	.04	.08	.47	.22	1	-0	-0	3	3
Sanchez A	9	14	45	15	39	.16	.08	61	77	.17	.13	.40	.19	4	4	-0	1	9
Barone D	10	11	40	22	38	.07	.20	72	93	.13	.04	.38	.25	3	0	3	5	11
Obermueller W	13	14	40	21	39	.12	.10	69	84	.13	.08	.37	.17	7	3	3	0	12
Kim B	20	15	41	19	40	.09	.14	73	81	.08	.06	.41	.25	8	0	-0	8	16
Vanden Hurk H	22	13	27	25	48	.10	.14	63	76	.06	.11	.36	.28	4	1	2	13	20
Willis D	15	11	46	21	32	.07	.12	72	81	.07	.07	.40	.22	6	8	11	5	30
Olsen S	16	10	38	24	39	.09	.14	64	84	.07	.10	.39	.21	4	12	13	10	40
MLB Average	*17*	*9*	*43*	*19*	*38*	*.10*	*.10*	*74*	*83*	*.05*	*.05*	*.40*	*.18*	--	--	--	--	--

Houston Astros

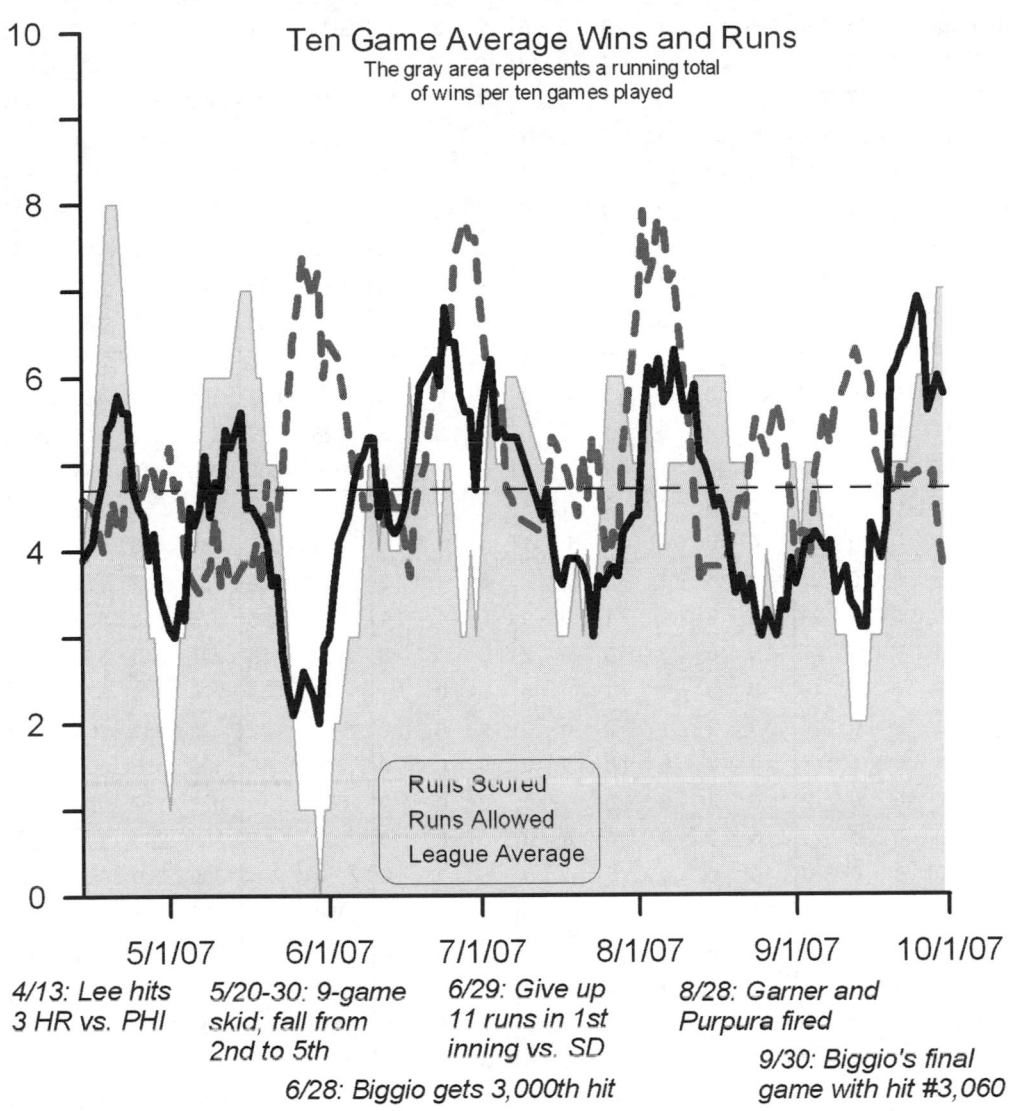

Ten Game Average Wins and Runs
The gray area represents a running total
of wins per ten games played

Runs Scored
Runs Allowed
League Average

4/13: Lee hits
3 HR vs. PHI

5/20-30: 9-game
skid; fall from
2nd to 5th

6/28: Biggio gets 3,000th hit

6/29: Give up
11 runs in 1st
inning vs. SD

8/28: Garner and
Purpura fired

9/30: Biggio's final
game with hit #3,060

Stat Facts:

- Craig Biggio had a GPA of just .223
- Mark Loretta's K% was just 8%, second lowest in the league
- Carlos Lee led the league with 13 sacrifice flies
- Hunter Pence hit a fly ball in just 32% of his batted balls
- 23% of Lance Berkman's fly balls were home runs
- Wandy Rodriguez picked off 6 baserunners
- Rodriguez's H-A split of -.064 led the league
- Brad Lidge struck out 31% of the batters he faced
- Roy Oswalt allowed 53% ground balls, and 31% fly balls
- Chad Qualls allowed 57% ground balls, and 29% fly balls
- Just 9% of Jason Lane's batted balls were line drives
- 28% of Adam Everett's fly balls were infield pop-ups

Team Batting and Pitching/Fielding Stats by Month						
	April	May	June	July	Aug	Sept/Oct
Wins	10	12	12	12	15	12
Losses	14	17	16	13	14	15
RS/G	4.1	3.9	5.2	4.5	4.3	4.7
RA/G	4.3	4.9	5.8	5.2	4.7	5.1
OBP	.327	.311	.345	.326	.325	.342
SLG	.376	.394	.452	.409	.396	.440
FIP	4.30	4.37	5.08	4.15	4.25	5.20
DER	.697	.680	.672	.683	.684	.704

Batting Stats

Player	BR	Runs	RBI	PA	Outs	H	2B	3B	HR	TB	K	BB	IBB	HBP	SH	SF	SB	CS	GDP	H-A	L^R	BA	OBP	SLG	GPA
Berkman L +	109	95	102	668	419	156	24	2	34	286	125	94	11	8	0	5	7	3	11	-.043	-.038	.278	.386	.510	.301
Lee C	108	93	119	697	469	190	43	1	32	331	63	53	10	4	0	13	10	5	27	.064	.038	.303	.354	.528	.291
Pence H	79	57	69	484	324	147	30	9	17	246	95	26	0	1	0	1	11	5	10	.010	.043	.322	.360	.539	.297
Scott L *	59	49	64	425	284	94	28	5	18	186	95	53	4	2	0	1	3	1	8	-.086		.255	.351	.504	.284
Loretta M	58	52	41	511	345	132	23	2	4	171	41	44	0	3	3	1	1	2	15	.014	.042	.287	.352	.372	.251
Biggio C	51	68	50	555	395	130	31	3	10	197	112	23	0	3	7	5	4	3	5	.072	.073	.251	.285	.381	.223
Lamb M *	48	45	40	353	226	90	14	2	11	141	45	36	5	3	1	2	0	0	5	.039	-.087	.289	.366	.453	.278
Burke C	35	39	28	363	259	73	19	2	6	114	52	27	1	8	8	1	9	3	10	.058	.073	.229	.304	.357	.226
Ensberg M	29	36	31	259	179	52	10	0	8	86	48	31	0	0	2	2	0	1	6	-.069	.035	.232	.323	.384	.241
Ausmus B	29	38	25	397	279	82	16	3	3	113	74	37	3	6	4	1	6	1	11	.042	.013	.235	.318	.324	.224
Wigginton T	23	24	18	187	129	48	12	0	6	78	40	13	0	3	0	2	2	0	8	.020	.079	.284	.342	.462	.269
Everett A	22	18	15	236	174	51	11	1	2	70	31	14	0	1	1	0	4	2	3	-.026	-.011	.232	.281	.318	.206
Bruntlett E	19	16	14	165	108	34	5	0	0	39	27	20	1	1	6	0	6	3	1	.006	-.003	.246	.346	.283	.226
Lane J	18	18	27	192	144	30	5	0	8	59	30	16	0	3	1	3	1	1	4	-.062	-.039	.178	.257	.349	.203
Anderson J *	13	10	11	75	44	24	3	0	0	27	6	5	0	2	0	1	1	1	0	.090	-.037	.358	.413	.403	.287
Palmeiro O *	12	12	6	122	82	24	3	0	0	27	8	16	1	1	2	0	0	1	2	-.067	-.025	.233	.342	.262	.219
Towles J	11	9	12	44	27	15	5	0	1	23	1	3	1	1	0	0	0	1	1	-.236	-.096	.375	.432	.575	.338
Munson E *	11	14	15	150	109	31	4	0	4	47	15	16	1	0	0	2	0	0	8	.100	.035	.235	.313	.356	.230
Ransom C	7	9	3	46	28	8	2	0	1	13	9	9	1	2	0	0	0	0	1	.147	.055	.229	.413	.371	.279
Quintero H	3	2	1	57	43	12	2	0	0	14	13	2	1	2	0	0	0	0	2	.041	-.022	.226	.281	.264	.192
Backe B	2	5	1	11	6	4	1	0	1	8	3	1	0	0	0	0	0	0	0	.274	.088	.400	.455	.800	.405
Jennings J *	0	1	1	30	24	2	0	0	0	2	8	3	0	0	1	0	0	0	0	-.089	-.019	.077	.172	.077	.097
Moehler B	0	0	0	5	4	1	0	0	0	1	3	0	0	0	0	0	0	0	0	-.233	--	.200	.200	.200	.140
Driskill T	0	0	0	1	0	0	0	0	0	0	0	0	0	0	1	0	0	0	0	--	--	.000	.000	.000	.000
Patton T +	-0	0	0	3	2	1	0	0	0	1	1	0	0	0	0	0	0	0	0	-.350	--	.333	.333	.333	.233
White R	-0	0	0	1	1	0	0	0	0	0	1	0	0	0	0	0	0	0	0	.000	--	.000	.000	.000	.000
Oswalt R	-0	2	3	79	57	8	1	0	0	9	21	3	0	1	11	0	0	0	1	.072	.004	.125	.176	.141	.115
Borkowski D	-0	0	0	2	2	0	0	0	0	0	1	0	0	0	0	0	0	0	0	.000	--	.000	.000	.000	.000
Sampson C	-0	5	0	34	22	4	0	0	0	4	10	0	0	0	8	0	0	0	0	.125	.040	.154	.154	.154	.108
Gutierrez J	-1	1	0	7	6	0	0	0	0	0	4	0	0	0	1	0	0	0	0	.000	.000	.000	.000	.000	.000
Paulino F	-1	0	0	6	6	0	0	0	0	0	4	0	0	0	0	0	0	0	0	.000	--	.000	.000	.000	.000
Rodriguez W	-1	2	2	63	45	6	1	0	0	7	15	2	0	0	12	0	0	0	2	-.079	.072	.122	.157	.143	.106
Williams W	-2	3	2	64	54	6	0	0	1	9	25	0	0	0	5	0	0	0	1	.004	-.059	.102	.102	.153	.084
Albers M *	-2	0	0	32	27	2	0	0	0	2	17	0	0	0	3	0	0	0	0	-.078	-.140	.069	.069	.069	.048

Italicized stats have been adjusted for home park.

Batted Ball Batting Stats

Player	% of PA		% of Batted Balls					Out %		Runs Per Event				Total Runs vs. Avg.				
	K%	BB%	GB%	LD%	FB%	IF/F	HR/OF	GB	OF	NIP	GB	LD	OF	NIP	GB	LD	FB	Tot
Berkman L	19	15	44	18	38	.14	.23	74	87	.09	.05	.45	.32	13	-0	3	17	33
Pence H	20	6	49	19	32	.10	.17	66	77	-.01	.10	.43	.34	-8	12	5	14	23
Lee C	9	8	38	16	46	.11	.14	74	83	.10	.03	.39	.23	3	-3	1	22	23
Scott L	22	13	41	19	40	.10	.16	81	82	.06	.00	.54	.29	3	-6	5	10	12
Lamb M	13	11	43	18	39	.07	.11	65	87	.10	.11	.32	.17	4	8	-2	2	11
Wigginton T	21	9	44	14	42	.05	.12	62	78	.02	.11	.38	.23	-1	4	-3	4	3
Ensberg M	18	12	35	20	44	.14	.12	73	87	.07	.05	.29	.17	2	-1	-4	-0	-3
Munson E	10	11	37	13	50	.08	.07	77	80	.12	-.01	.25	.14	2	-3	-4	1	-4
Loretta M	8	9	41	22	36	.09	.03	79	79	.13	.01	.35	.09	5	-5	5	-10	-5

Batted Ball Batting Stats continue after Fielding Stats.

Pitching Stats

Player	PRC	IP	BFP	G	GS	K	BB	IBB	HBP	H	HR	DP	DER	SB	CS	PO	W	L	Sv	Op	Hld	H-A	R^L	RA	ERA	FIP
Oswalt R	110	212.0	910	33	32	154	60	6	7	221	14	21	.677	5	1	0	14	7	0	0	1	-.059	-.008	3.40	3.18	3.54
Rodriguez W	69	182.7	782	31	31	158	62	2	5	179	22	11	.686	13	9	6	9	13	0	0	0	-.064	-.025	5.03	4.58	4.17
Williams W	58	188.0	833	33	31	101	53	5	12	216	35	12	.703	11	4	0	8	15	0	0	0	.017	-.018	5.46	5.27	5.57
Qualls C	48	82.7	345	79	0	78	25	5	3	84	10	11	.664	7	5	1	6	5	5	10	21	.036	.073	3.16	3.05	3.79
Sampson C	41	121.7	522	24	19	51	30	2	7	138	20	15	.705	3	1	1	7	8	0	0	0	-.024	-.006	4.73	4.59	5.43
Lidge B	35	67.0	287	66	0	88	30	4	4	54	9	4	.699	3	0	0	5	3	19	27	7	-.017	.038	3.90	3.36	3.73
Albers M	30	110.7	508	31	18	71	50	6	7	127	18	10	.682	11	3	0	4	11	0	0	0	-.030	-.001	6.26	5.86	5.48
Jennings J	26	99.0	445	19	18	71	34	2	2	119	19	8	.677	15	3	1	2	9	0	0	0	-.003	.002	6.64	6.45	5.36
Moehler B	24	59.7	257	42	0	36	17	3	0	67	8	11	.673	3	0	0	1	4	1	1	1	.018	-.062	4.37	4.07	4.51
Borkowski D	23	71.7	325	64	0	63	34	9	4	76	0	7	.071	2	0	0	5	3	1	4	8	-.044	-.060	5.78	5.15	4.18
Wheeler D	20	49.7	205	45	0	56	13	1	2	46	8	4	.698	3	0	0	1	4	11	15	6	.080	.013	5.07	5.07	3.95
Miller T *	18	46.3	211	76	0	46	23	6	4	45	6	2	.697	3	0	0	0	0	1	3	12	-.004	-.080	5.05	4.86	4.33
McLemore M *	16	35.0	161	29	0	35	18	2	1	38	5	0	.667	1	0	0	3	0	0	2	1	.050	.153	4.37	3.86	4.58
Sarfate D	12	8.3	31	7	0	14	1	0	0	5	0	0	.688	0	0	0	1	0	0	0	3	-.054	.007	1.08	1.08	0.27
Backe B	11	28.7	123	5	5	11	11	0	2	27	4	2	.758	0	1	0	3	1	0	0	0	-.037	.102	4.08	3.77	5.68
Gutierrez J	7	21.3	93	7	3	16	6	2	0	25	3	2	.662	1	1	0	1	1	0	0	0	.026	.133	5.91	5.91	4.16
White R	6	29.3	133	23	0	15	14	4	0	36	4	3	.680	0	0	1	1	0	0	1	4	-.107	.037	7.67	7.67	5.04
Patton T *	5	12.7	54	3	2	8	4	0	2	10	3	1	.784	0	0	0	0	2	0	0	0	.084	-.228	4.26	3.55	6.51
Paulino F	4	19.0	85	5	3	11	7	1	0	22	5	2	.710	0	0	0	2	1	0	0	1	-.172	-.073	7.11	7.11	6.48
Randolph S *	1	13.3	78	14	0	22	17	2	1	21	4	1	.500	2	0	0	0	1	0	0	0	.056	.039	12.83	12.15	7.47
Driskill T	1	6.0	29	2	0	4	1	0	0	10	1	1	.565	1	0	0	0	1	0	0	0	--	.025	9.00	4.50	4.60

Italicized stats have been adjusted for home park.

Batted Ball Pitching Stats

Player	% of PA		% of Batted Balls					Out %		Runs Per Event				Total Runs vs. Avg.				
	K%	BB%	GB%	LD%	FB%	IF/F	HR/OF	GB	OF	NIP	GB	LD	OF	NIP	GB	LD	FB	Tot
Oswalt R	17	7	53	16	31	.11	.07	76	76	.03	.04	.45	.18	-7	2	-1	-7	-13
Qualls C	23	8	57	14	29	.06	.16	68	80	.01	.07	.34	.27	-4	4	-7	2	5
Lidge B	31	12	42	15	43	.10	.13	72	81	.01	.07	.52	.25	-2	-0	-4	2	-5
Wheeler D	27	7	36	15	49	.11	.14	74	68	-.02	.04	.21	.33	-4	-1	-7	9	-3
Rodriguez W	20	9	41	19	40	.10	.11	74	84	.02	.06	.42	.19	-5	2	0	2	-1
Backe B	9	11	42	11	46	.09	.10	68	97	.14	.11	.38	.07	2	3	-3	-3	-1
Moehler B	14	7	52	16	32	.03	.13	71	85	.03	.05	.39	.20	-2	2	-1	2	1
Miller T	22	13	34	18	48	.08	.08	76	84	.06	.04	.58	.14	1	-2	3	-1	1
McLemore M	22	12	20	19	61	.17	.09	67	81	.05	.11	.51	.18	1	-0	2	2	4
Borkowski D	19	12	43	19	38	.06	.09	73	76	.06	.06	.40	.21	2	0	-0	3	5
White R	11	11	53	17	30	.10	.14	70	79	.11	.09	.33	.28	1	3	-1	2	5
Sampson C	10	7	47	17	36	.08	.14	79	82	.08	.02	.41	.24	0	-5	1	11	8
Jennings J	16	8	35	21	44	.08	.14	74	85	.04	.05	.43	.21	-1	0	6	9	14
Albers M	14	11	48	17	35	.07	.15	73	82	.09	.06	.39	.26	5	3	-0	10	18
Williams W	12	8	39	16	45	.12	.13	74	81	.07	.06	.39	.23	0	5	-4	20	21
MLB Average	17	9	43	19	38	.10	.10	74	83	.05	.05	.40	.18	--	--	--	--	--

Fielding Stats

Name	INN	SBA/G	CS%	ERA	WP+PB/G	PO	A	TE	FE
Catcher									
Ausmus B	906.7	0.55	15%	4.29	0.169	763	47	4	0
Munson E	309.3	0.84	10%	5.85	0.524	215	14	2	0
Quintero H	151.7	0.77	38%	5.10	0.297	97	13	2	0
Towles J	95.0	0.57	50%	4.26	0.568	65	6	0	0
Biggio C	2.0	0.00	0%	4.50	0.000	1	0	0	0

Name	Inn	PO	A	TE	FE	FPct	DPS	DPT	RZR	OOZ
First Base										
Berkman L	1066.0	1012	103	5	5	.991	7	0	.718	27
Lamb M	225.7	198	29	0	3	.987	5	0	.721	6
Loretta M	153.0	148	15	0	1	.994	0	0	.862	9
Munson E	10.7	11	0	0	0	1.000	0	0	1.000	0
Ausmus B	7.0	6	1	0	0	1.000	1	0	1.000	0
Wigginton T	2.0	3	0	0	0	1.000	0	0	--	--
Second Base										
Biggio C	936.7	191	267	1	9	.979	21	32	.777	32
Burke C	311.0	56	103	2	1	.981	10	8	.804	8
Loretta M	201.0	47	50	0	0	1.000	4	10	.868	5
Ransom C	14.0	3	3	0	0	1.000	0	0	1.000	0
Ausmus B	2.0	0	1	0	0	1.000	0	0	.500	0
Shortstop										
Everett A	535.3	96	197	2	6	.973	14	23	.871	35
Loretta M	486.7	80	157	1	5	.975	15	12	.776	21
Bruntlett E	348.7	62	109	4	3	.961	9	10	.847	15
Ransom C	70.0	16	21	0	2	.949	3	1	.652	4
Burke C	24.0	3	9	0	0	1.000	0	0	1.000	1
Third Base										
Ensberg M	492.3	36	107	5	6	.929	14	0	.637	20
Lamb M	416.3	29	88	2	6	.936	6	1	.619	23
Wigginton T	392.7	34	88	2	1	.976	3	0	.710	15
Loretta M	141.3	11	28	0	0	1.000	0	0	.594	8
Bruntlett E	9.0	1	2	0	0	1.000	0	0	1.000	1
Ransom C	8.0	1	1	0	0	1.000	0	0	.500	0
Ausmus B	5.0	0	0	0	0	0.000	0	0	--	--

Name	Inn	PO	A	TE	FE	FPct	DPS	DPT	RZR	OOZ
Left Field										
Lee C	1369.0	261	8	1	3	.985	4	0	.827	36
Palmeiro O	40.0	13	1	0	0	1.000	0	0	.917	2
Scott L	18.0	4	0	0	0	1.000	0	0	.800	0
Burke C	16.0	5	1	0	0	1.000	0	0	1.000	2
Bruntlett E	8.3	1	0	0	0	1.000	0	0	1.000	0
Lane J	6.0	0	0	0	0	0.000	0	0	--	--
Anderson J	6.0	1	0	0	0	1.000	0	0	.500	0
Wigginton T	1.0	0	0	0	0	0.000	0	0	--	--
Center Field										
Pence H	844.7	260	6	2	2	.985	0	0	.885	45
Lane J	260.7	80	2	0	0	1.000	2	0	.864	10
Burke C	201.0	50	1	0	1	.981	0	0	.851	10
Anderson J	134.0	30	0	0	1	.968	0	0	.871	3
Bruntlett E	12.7	9	0	0	0	1.000	0	0	1.000	2
Scott L	10.7	4	0	0	0	1.000	0	0	.667	0
Berkman L	1.0	0	0	0	0	0.000	0	0	--	--
Right Field										
Scott L	817.0	199	8	1	2	.986	4	0	.918	29
Berkman L	229.7	49	1	0	2	.962	2	0	.884	11
Burke C	132.0	26	1	0	1	.964	2	0	.800	6
Lane J	127.7	43	0	0	0	1.000	0	0	.921	8
Pence H	115.7	36	0	1	1	.947	0	0	.970	4
Palmeiro O	37.0	7	1	0	0	1.000	0	0	1.000	2
Bruntlett E	2.0	0	0	0	1	0.000	0	0	--	--
Anderson J	2.0	1	0	0	0	1.000	0	0	1.000	0
Wigginton T	1.0	0	0	0	0	0.000	0	0	--	--
Lamb M	0.7	0	0	0	0	0.000	0	0	--	--

Batted Ball Batting Stats

	% of PA		% of Batted Balls					Out %		Runs Per Event				Total Runs vs. Avg.				
Player	K%	BB%	GB%	LD%	FB%	IF/F	HR/OF	GB	OF	NIP	GB	LD	OF	NIP	GB	LD	FB	Tot
Palmeiro O	7	14	52	20	29	.08	.00	79	92	.20	.02	.26	-.02	3	-1	-2	-6	-5
Bruntlett E	16	13	46	19	35	.05	.00	76	78	.09	.04	.35	.06	2	-1	-2	-5	-6
Lane J	16	10	35	9	56	.10	.11	80	92	.07	.02	.35	.12	0	-2	-7	-1	-10
Everett A	13	6	45	17	38	.28	.04	77	84	.04	.03	.38	.08	-2	-0	-1	-9	-12
Burke C	14	10	38	17	45	.21	.06	66	89	.07	.09	.28	.10	1	4	-8	-9	-12
Ausmus B	19	11	51	17	31	.08	.03	78	79	.06	.01	.40	.10	1	-5	-3	-10	-16
Biggio C	20	5	45	17	38	.17	.08	71	84	-.03	.07	.45	.14	-12	4	-1	-10	-18
MLB Average	17	9	43	19	38	.10	.10	74	83	.05	.05	.40	.18	--	--	--	--	--

Kansas City Royals

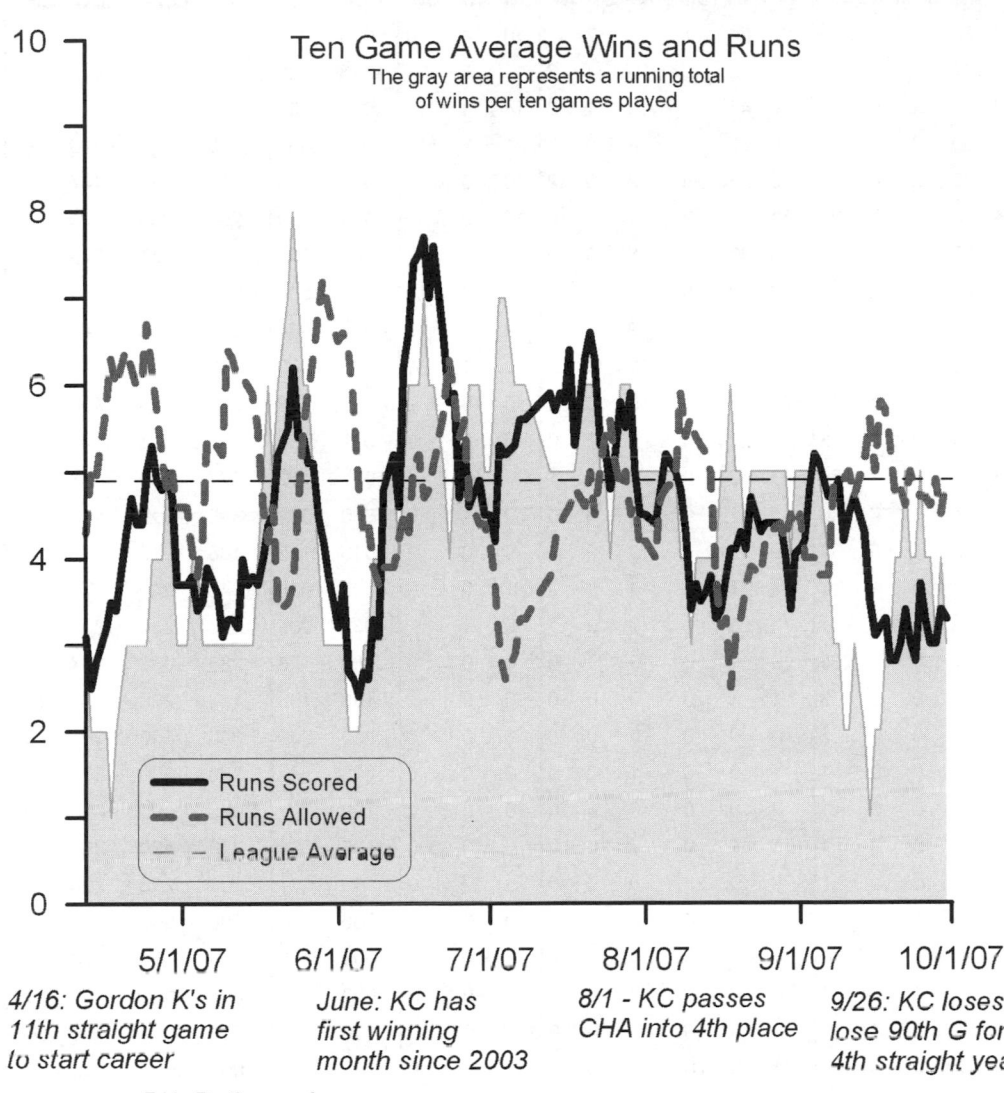

Ten Game Average Wins and Runs
The gray area represents a running total
of wins per ten games played

- Runs Scored
- Runs Allowed
- League Average

4/16: Gordon K's in 11th straight game to start career

5/1: Butler makes major league debut

June: KC has first winning month since 2003

8/1 - KC passes CHA into 4th place

9/26: KC loses lose 90th G for 4th straight year

Stat Facts:

- No Royal with 100 plate appearances had a GPA higher than .268
- Mark Teahen hit a fly ball on just 29% of his batted balls
- Teahen had 17 assists in right field, and started 14 double plays
- David DeJesus led the league with 23 HBPs
- DeJesus had an RZR of .910
- Tony Pena walked in just 3% of his PAs
- Pena's GB% of 56% was highest in the league
- The DER of .739 behind Brian Bannister tied for highest in the league
- Bannister's home away split of .077 was highest in the league
- Just 32% of the batted balls against Zack Greinke were ground balls
- Scott Elarton allowed 12 homers in 37 innings
- Elarton struck out only 7% of the batters he faced

Team Batting and Pitching/Fielding Stats by Month						
	April	May	June	July	Aug	Sept/Oct
Wins	8	11	15	13	13	9
Losses	18	17	12	12	15	19
RS/G	3.8	4.0	5.4	5.5	4.0	3.6
RA/G	5.1	5.7	4.3	4.4	4.5	4.9
OBP	.319	.319	.331	.338	.309	.317
SLG	.381	.380	.397	.426	.361	.383
FIP	4.06	5.00	4.27	4.10	4.36	4.53
DER	.668	.691	.694	.689	.672	.699

Batting Stats

Player	BR	Runs	RBI	PA	Outs	H	2B	3B	HR	TB	K	BB	IBB	HBP	SH	SF	SB	CS	GDP	H-A	L^R	BA	OBP	SLG	GPA
DeJesus D *	84	101	58	703	462	157	29	9	7	225	83	64	7	23	7	4	10	4	10	.030	.028	.260	.351	.372	.251
Teahen M *	80	78	60	608	417	155	31	8	7	223	127	55	8	3	4	2	13	5	23	.043	.039	.285	.353	.410	.261
Gordon A *	71	60	60	601	425	134	36	4	15	223	137	41	4	13	1	2	14	4	12	.035	.026	.247	.314	.411	.244
Grudzielanek	62	70	51	486	332	137	32	3	6	193	60	23	2	8	0	2	1	2	14	-.011	.034	.302	.346	.426	.262
Butler B	49	38	52	360	241	96	23	2	8	147	55	27	5	2	0	2	0	0	8	-.020	.083	.292	.347	.447	.268
Brown E	48	44	62	397	281	94	13	1	6	127	71	24	2	1	0	6	12	2	7	-.005	.099	.257	.300	.347	.222
German E	47	49	37	405	274	92	15	6	4	131	60	43	0	5	6	3	11	7	11	.069	.032	.264	.351	.376	.252
Pena T	45	58	47	536	392	136	25	7	2	181	78	10	0	4	8	5	5	6	13	.088	-.000	.267	.284	.356	.217
Gload R *	45	37	51	346	243	92	22	3	7	141	39	16	2	2	0	8	2	2	13	-.002	-.044	.288	.318	.441	.253
Buck J	40	41	48	399	282	77	18	0	18	149	92	36	0	10	0	6	0	1	11	-.089	.000	.222	.308	.429	.246
Sweeney M	38	26	38	289	205	69	15	1	7	107	29	17	4	5	0	2	0	0	9	-.032	.048	.260	.315	.404	.243
Gathright J	28	28	19	261	168	70	8	0	0	78	36	20	0	3	10	0	9	8	2	-.089	.039	.307	.371	.342	.252
Shealy R	15	18	21	189	138	38	6	0	3	53	53	13	0	3	0	1	0	0	4	-.027	-.112	.221	.286	.308	.206
Sanders R	14	12	11	85	53	23	7	0	2	36	15	11	0	1	0	0	0	1	2	.080	.034	.315	.412	.493	.309
Smith J *	9	9	14	89	71	16	2	1	6	38	29	3	0	0	0	1	0	0	2	-.113	.155	.188	.213	.447	.208
LaRue J	9	14	13	195	150	25	9	0	4	46	66	17	0	4	3	2	1	0	6	.093	.038	.148	.240	.272	.176
Costa S *	8	13	12	109	83	23	6	1	0	31	23	5	0	0	0	1	0	1	2	-.032	.065	.223	.257	.301	.191
Cortez F *	2	3	1	16	10	4	1	0	0	5	0	1	0	0	1	0	0	0	0	.393	-.128	.286	.333	.357	.239
Phillips P	1	2	2	15	13	2	1	0	0	3	1	1	0	0	0	0	0	0	1	-.198	-.108	.143	.200	.214	.144
Peralta J	1	1	2	1	0	1	1	0	0	2	0	0	0	0	0	0	0	0	0	-.950	-.950	1.000	1.000	2.000	.950
Bannister B	1	0	0	4	2	1	0	0	0	1	1	0	0	1	0	0	0	0	0	-.308	--	.333	.500	.333	.308
Duckworth B	1	0	0	1	0	1	0	0	0	1	0	0	0	0	0	0	0	0	0	-.700	--	1.000	1.000	1.000	.700
Brazell C *	0	1	0	5	3	1	0	0	0	1	1	1	0	0	0	0	0	0	0	.425	-.588	.250	.400	.250	.243
Perez O *	-0	1	0	5	4	1	0	0	0	1	2	0	0	0	0	0	0	0	0	-.140	--	.200	.200	.200	.140
Elarton S	-0	0	0	1	1	0	0	0	0	0	1	0	0	0	0	0	0	0	0	.000	--	.000	.000	.000	.000
Greinke Z	-0	0	0	1	1	0	0	0	0	0	1	0	0	0	0	0	0	0	0	.000	--	.000	.000	.000	.000
Musser N *	-0	0	0	1	1	0	0	0	0	0	0	0	0	0	0	0	0	0	0	.000	--	.000	.000	.000	.000
Meche G	-0	0	0	4	4	0	0	0	0	0	2	0	0	0	0	0	0	0	0	.000	--	.000	.000	.000	.000
de la Rosa J	-0	0	0	5	5	0	0	0	0	0	1	0	0	0	0	0	0	0	0	.000	.000	.000	.000	.000	.000
Huber J	-1	2	0	10	9	1	0	0	0	1	2	0	0	0	0	0	0	0	0	.117	.070	.100	.100	.100	.070
Berroa A	-1	0	1	13	12	1	0	0	0	1	4	0	0	1	1	0	0	1	1	-.200	.200	.091	.167	.091	.098

Italicized stats have been adjusted for home park.

Batted Ball Batting Stats

Player	% of PA		% of Batted Balls					Out %		Runs Per Event				Total Runs vs. Avg.				
	K%	BB%	GB%	LD%	FB%	IF/F	HR/OF	GB	OF	NIP	GB	LD	OF	NIP	GB	LD	FB	Tot
Butler B	15	8	47	21	33	.13	.10	74	86	.05	.05	.45	.16	-1	2	7	-3	5
Grudzielanek M	12	6	49	19	31	.03	.05	73	81	.04	.05	.42	.13	-2	4	7	-4	4
DeJesus D	12	12	46	19	36	.09	.04	75	86	.12	.05	.42	.08	12	2	4	-17	1
Teahen M	21	10	50	21	29	.07	.06	71	80	.03	.06	.42	.16	-2	5	5	-7	-0
Gload R	11	5	50	19	31	.10	.09	73	80	.03	.05	.33	.20	-3	2	-1	1	-1
Gathright J	14	9	65	23	12	.15	.00	73	88	.07	.06	.41	-.03	1	6	3	-11	-2
German E	15	12	52	20	27	.00	.05	78	80	.09	.01	.39	.15	4	-4	1	-5	-3
Buck J	23	12	43	13	44	.12	.18	76	86	.04	.03	.33	.27	0	-3	-10	9	-4
Smith J	33	3	37	11	53	.10	.22	81	90	-.07	.01	.39	.29	-4	-1	-3	3	-5
Sweeney M	10	8	35	20	45	.14	.08	73	88	.09	.04	.35	.10	0	-1	1	-5	-5

Batted Ball Batting Stats continue after Fielding Stats.

Pitching Stats

Player	PRC	IP	BFP	G	GS	K	BB	IBB	HBP	H	HR	DP	DER	SB	CS	PO	W	L	Sv	Op	Hld	H-A	R^L	RA	ERA	FIP
Meche G	100	216.0	906	34	34	156	62	2	3	218	22	22	.695	4	5	2	9	13	0	0	0	-.013	.017	4.08	3.67	4.14
Bannister B	68	165.0	683	27	27	77	44	1	6	156	15	15	.726	7	5	2	12	9	0	0	0	.077	-.065	4.15	3.87	4.52
Greinke Z	62	122.0	507	52	14	106	36	5	3	122	12	15	.683	7	3	1	7	7	1	1	12	.006	-.002	3.84	3.69	3.76
Soria J	51	69.0	270	62	0	75	19	3	1	46	3	4	.744	0	0	0	2	3	17	21	9	-.020	.035	2.61	2.48	2.51
Riske D	49	69.7	289	65	0	52	27	4	1	61	8	8	.726	4	1	0	1	4	4	8	16	-.048	.049	2.45	2.45	4.41
Peralta J	42	87.7	366	62	0	66	19	5	2	93	9	10	.681	8	0	1	1	3	1	5	7	-.041	.009	4.00	3.80	3.76
Perez O *	40	137.3	626	26	26	64	50	5	4	178	14	16	.658	9	3	1	8	11	0	0	0	.005	-.019	5.90	5.57	4.84
de la Rosa J	39	130.0	589	26	23	82	53	6	3	160	20	14	.664	6	4	2	8	12	0	0	0	-.017	-.100	6.09	5.82	5.27
Gobble J *	28	53.7	233	74	0	50	23	6	2	56	6	9	.651	2	1	0	4	1	1	3	16	-.052	-.057	3.86	3.02	4.03
Bale J *	20	40.0	179	26	0	42	17	2	1	45	1	3	.627	0	0	0	1	1	0	1	5	-.009	.007	4.05	4.05	2.81
Nunez L	20	43.7	182	13	6	37	10	0	0	44	8	5	.709	5	0	0	2	4	0	0	1	-.063	-.079	4.33	3.92	4.75
Duckworth B	14	46.7	211	26	3	21	23	2	1	51	3	5	.687	1	0	0	3	5	1	1	5	.024	.002	5.79	4.63	4.73
Davies K	12	50.0	239	11	11	40	26	1	3	63	10	2	.656	5	1	0	3	7	0	0	0	-.001	-.012	7.38	6.66	6.06
Dotel O	11	23.0	108	24	0	29	11	4	4	24	3	1	.656	2	0	0	2	1	11	14	0	-.009	-.017	4.30	3.91	3.99
Buckner W	11	34.0	143	7	5	17	16	0	0	37	5	10	.695	1	0	0	1	2	0	0	0	-.054	-.081	5.29	5.29	5.70
Musser N *	10	24.7	116	17	0	19	14	3	0	32	5	3	.654	3	1	0	0	1	0	0	1	.113	.098	4.74	4.38	5.81
Braun R	9	39.3	183	26	0	24	22	1	0	46	4	6	.662	3	1	0	2	0	0	0	1	.158	-.055	7.32	6.64	5.08
Hochevar L	7	12.7	54	4	1	5	4	0	3	11	1	3	.732	0	0	0	0	1	0	0	0	.049	-.059	2.84	2.13	5.28
Elarton S	4	37.0	185	9	9	13	21	0	3	53	12	6	.691	2	0	0	2	4	0	0	0	.084	-.018	10.70	10.46	8.84
Thomson J	4	10.7	46	2	2	3	3	0	0	13	0	2	.675	1	0	0	1	1	0	0	0	.200	.119	4.22	3.38	3.66
Wellemeyer T	2	15.7	84	12	0	9	11	2	1	25	4	1	.610	0	1	0	0	1	0	0	1	-.023	-.154	10.91	10.34	7.47
Standridge J	1	7.7	41	4	0	6	5	2	0	11	2	0	.643	0	0	0	0	1	0	0	0	--	.012	11.74	8.22	6.38
Hudson L	0	2.0	13	1	1	0	4	0	0	2	1	0	.750	0	0	0	0	1	0	0	0	--	.295	22.50	18.00	15.88

Italicized stats have been adjusted for home park.

Batted Ball Pitching Stats

Player	% of PA		% of Batted Balls					Out %		Runs Per Event				Total Runs vs. Avg.				
	K%	BB%	GB%	LD%	FB%	IF/F	HR/OF	GB	OF	NIP	GB	LD	OF	NIP	GB	LD	FB	Tot
Soria J	28	7	39	20	40	.07	.05	76	92	-.02	.03	.30	.05	-6	-2	-6	-10	-24
Meche G	17	7	47	18	35	.11	.10	75	83	.02	.04	.37	.18	-8	0	-6	-4	-17
Bannister B	11	7	41	19	40	.13	.08	82	85	.07	.00	.42	.14	-1	-10	7	-6	-11
Riske D	18	10	41	17	41	.07	.10	74	87	.05	.05	.33	.16	-0	-1	-5	-1	-6
Greinke Z	21	8	32	22	46	.09	.08	75	86	.01	.04	.44	.13	-6	-4	7	-4	-6
Bale J	23	10	43	23	34	.05	.03	63	86	.02	.11	.37	.07	-1	3	0	-5	-3
Peralta J	18	6	36	22	42	.08	.08	75	84	-.00	.04	.45	.13	-5	-2	8	-3	-2
Nunez L	20	5	32	19	49	.12	.12	72	90	-.02	.04	.46	.16	-3	0	1	0	-2
Duckworth B	10	11	45	21	34	.02	.06	76	82	.13	.04	.36	.11	3	-0	2	-3	2
Buckner W	12	11	40	27	33	.14	.16	84	88	.11	-.04	.44	.22	2	-4	6	1	4
Gobble J	21	11	35	21	44	.10	.10	73	82	.04	.04	.47	.19	-0	-1	3	2	4
Braun R	13	12	49	19	32	.07	.08	73	78	.11	.05	.49	.18	3	1	3	-0	6
Musser N	16	12	34	25	41	.06	.16	68	93	.08	.09	.42	.19	1	1	3	1	7
Davies K	17	12	36	21	43	.08	.14	70	84	.08	.08	.49	.24	3	2	5	6	16
Elarton S	7	13	31	18	51	.11	.18	78	84	.18	.00	.48	.29	5	-2	4	12	19
Perez O	10	9	45	20	35	.08	.08	72	84	.10	.06	.46	.14	4	6	14	-3	21
de la Rosa J	14	10	41	20	39	.06	.12	73	83	.07	.06	.42	.20	3	3	8	9	23
MLB Average	17	9	43	19	38	.10	.10	74	83	.05	.05	.40	.18	--	--	--	--	--

Fielding Stats

Name	INN	SBA/G	CS%	ERA	WP+PB/G	PO	A	TE	FE
Catcher									
Buck J	924.3	0.52	17%	4.43	0.331	697	29	5	2
LaRue J	474.3	0.74	33%	4.76	0.455	311	24	3	2
Phillips P	38.7	0.00	0%	3.03	0.698	29	1	0	0

Name	Inn	PO	A	TE	FE	FPct	DPS	DPT	RZR	OOZ
First Base										
Gload R	675.7	623	45	1	2	.996	14	0	.803	15
Shealy R	421.0	402	29	0	0	1.000	3	0	.815	13
Gordon A	154.0	132	8	0	1	.993	2	0	.750	5
Butler B	83.0	79	8	0	2	.978	0	0	.813	5
Teahen M	49.0	45	0	0	0	1.000	0	0	.667	0
Sweeney M	39.3	40	2	1	0	.977	0	0	1.000	0
Smith J	11.3	12	0	0	0	1.000	0	0	--	--
Brazell C	3.0	7	0	0	0	1.000	0	0	--	--
Phillips P	1.0	2	0	0	0	1.000	0	0	--	--
Second Base										
Grudzielanek	947.3	184	300	2	4	.988	35	37	.849	31
German E	406.0	83	105	0	3	.984	10	17	.852	9
Smith J	41.0	9	9	1	0	.947	2	3	.750	0
Cortez F	33.0	12	11	1	0	.958	2	2	.900	0
Pena T	6.0	2	3	0	0	1.000	2	0	1.000	0
Berroa A	4.0	0	0	0	0	0.000	0	0	--	--
Shortstop										
Pena T	1273.0	208	438	10	12	.966	47	48	.848	70
Smith J	120.0	22	39	3	0	.953	2	4	.879	5
Berroa A	21.7	4	11	0	0	1.000	2	4	.857	0
German E	12.0	0	1	0	1	.500	1	0	0.000	1
Gordon A	6.0	2	1	0	0	1.000	0	0	1.000	0
Grudzielanek	4.0	1	2	0	0	1.000	0	0	1.000	0

Name	Inn	PO	A	TE	FE	FPct	DPS	DPT	RZR	OOZ
Third Base										
Gordon A	1135.0	99	247	9	4	.961	20	1	.704	41
German E	281.7	16	49	4	1	.929	5	0	.750	8
Smith J	14.3	1	2	0	1	.750	0	0	0.000	1
LaRue J	6.0	0	1	0	0	1.000	0	0	.500	0
Berroa A	0.3	0	0	0	0	0.000	0	0	--	--
Left Field										
Brown E	606.3	155	7	2	4	.964	4	0	.843	37
Gathright J	519.3	154	3	1	2	.981	0	0	.882	34
Costa S	98.0	31	0	1	0	.969	0	0	.893	6
Sanders R	57.0	11	0	0	0	1.000	0	0	.769	1
Gload R	53.7	10	1	0	0	1.000	0	0	.833	0
Butler B	43.0	4	0	0	1	.800	0	0	.444	0
German E	42.0	6	2	0	0	1.000	0	0	.667	0
Huber J	18.0	2	0	0	0	1.000	0	0	.667	0
Center Field										
DeJesus D	1351.0	401	5	0	4	.990	0	0	.910	46
Gathright J	56.0	16	0	0	1	.941	0	0	.875	2
Teahen M	30.0	8	0	0	0	1.000	0	0	1.000	1
Right Field										
Teahen M	1150.0	318	17	1	5	.982	14	0	.871	48
Brown E	150.7	42	1	0	0	1.000	0	0	.953	1
Costa S	73.0	23	0	0	0	1.000	0	0	.955	2
Sanders R	63.0	27	0	0	0	1.000	0	0	.923	3

Batted Ball Batting Stats

Player	% of PA		% of Batted Balls					Out %		Runs Per Event				Total Runs vs. Avg.				
	K%	BB%	GB%	LD%	FB%	IF/F	HR/OF	GB	OF	NIP	GB	LD	OF	NIP	GB	LD	FB	Tot
Costa S	21	5	49	20	31	.04	.00	82	79	-.03	-.01	.36	.09	-3	-1	-1	-3	-8
Gordon A	23	9	37	19	44	.09	.09	77	81	.02	.03	.39	.19	-5	-5	-2	3	-9
Shealy R	28	8	35	21	44	.25	.08	79	76	-.01	.01	.32	.17	-3	-2	-3	-3	-12
Brown E	18	6	44	17	39	.14	.06	68	86	.01	.08	.39	.09	-5	4	-3	-10	-13
LaRue J	34	11	48	17	35	.11	.12	80	83	-.00	-.00	.23	.21	-3	-4	-8	-3	-17
Pena T	15	3	56	19	25	.08	.02	72	84	-.04	.06	.38	.06	-12	6	-1	-19	-26
MLB Average	*17*	*9*	*43*	*19*	*38*	*.10*	*.10*	*74*	*83*	*.05*	*.05*	*.40*	*.18*	*--*	*--*	*--*	*--*	*--*

Los Angeles Angels of Anaheim

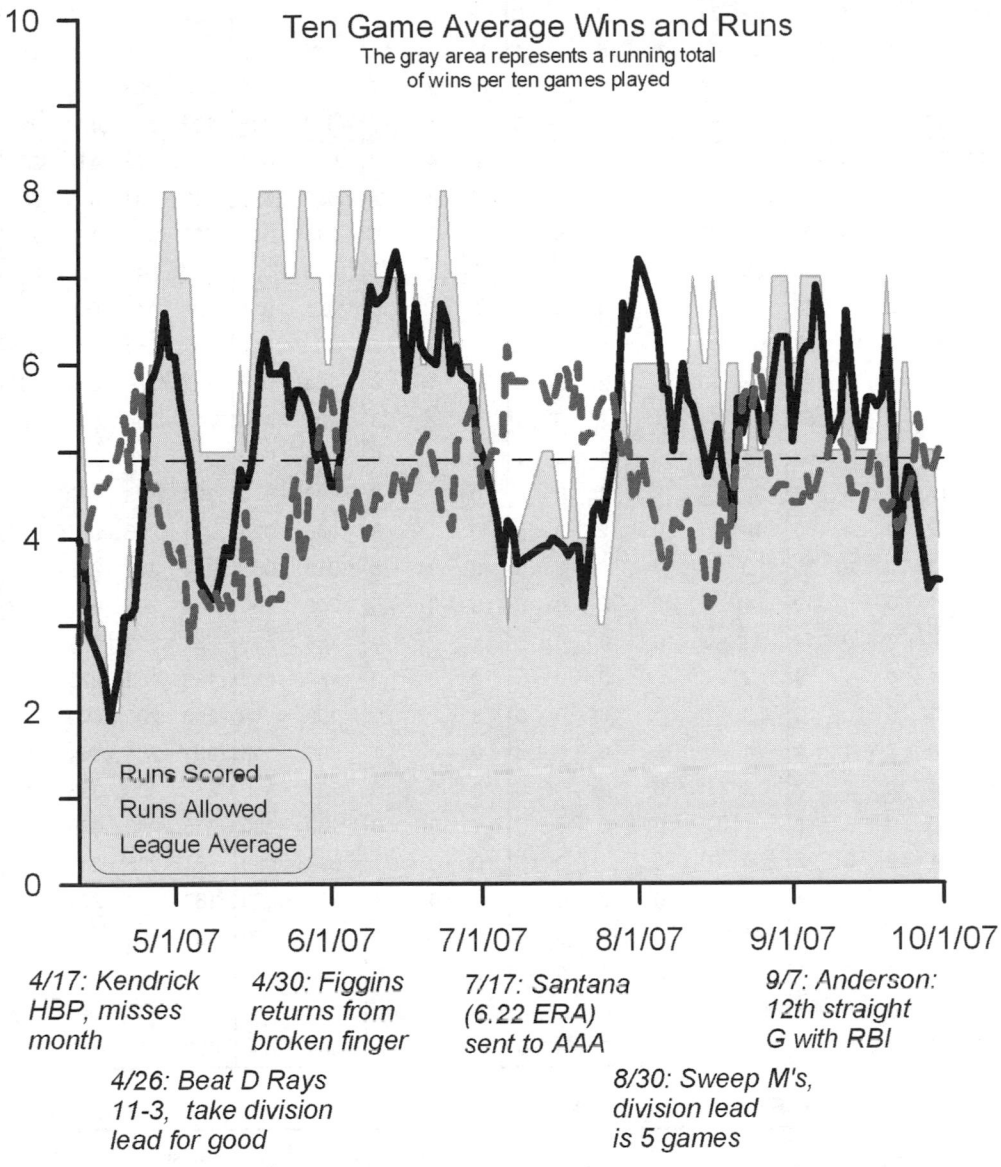

Ten Game Average Wins and Runs
The gray area represents a running total
of wins per ten games played

Runs Scored
Runs Allowed
League Average

5/1/07   6/1/07   7/1/07   8/1/07   9/1/07   10/1/07

4/17: Kendrick
HBP, misses
month

4/30: Figgins
returns from
broken finger

7/17: Santana
(6.22 ERA)
sent to AAA

9/7: Anderson:
12th straight
G with RBI

4/26: Beat D Rays
11-3, take division
lead for good

8/30: Sweep M's,
division lead
is 5 games

Stat Facts:

- 28 of Vladimir Guerrero's 71 walks were intentional
- 51% of Casey Kotchman's batted balls were ground balls
- Chone Figgins's LD% of 26% was second highest in the league
- Figgins's home/away split of .094 was highest in the league
- Gary Matthews's lefty/righty split of -.074 was lowest in the league
- Matthews's LD% of 13% was also lowest in the league
- Kelvim Escobar induced 33 double plays
- Just 6% of Escobar's outfield flies were home runs, lowest in the league
- Francisco Rodriguez struck out 32% of the batters he faced
- Orlando Cabrera tied for the league lead with 11 sacrifice flies
- John Lackey's league-leading 3.01 ERA was much better than his FIP of 3.66

Team Batting and Pitching/Fielding Stats by Month						
	April	**May**	**June**	**July**	**Aug**	**Sept/Oct**
Wins	15	18	17	12	18	14
Losses	11	11	9	12	11	14
RS/G	4.3	4.9	6.1	5.0	5.4	4.8
RA/G	3.9	4.2	4.7	5.0	4.5	4.8
OBP	.331	.337	.374	.328	.342	.353
SLG	.392	.424	.452	.384	.442	.401
FIP	4.03	4.23	4.46	3.95	3.67	3.77
DER	.694	.691	.712	.657	.681	.647

Batting Stats

Player	BR	Runs	RBI	PA	Outs	H	2B	3B	HR	TB	K	BB	IBB	HBP	SH	SF	SB	CS	GDP	H-A	L^R	BA	OBP	SLG	GPA
Guerrero V	120	89	125	660	410	186	45	1	27	314	62	71	28	9	0	6	2	3	19	.003	.017	.324	.403	.547	.325
Cabrera O	89	101	86	701	462	192	35	1	8	253	64	44	0	5	3	11	20	4	12	-.015	.038	.301	.345	.397	.260
Figgins C +	83	81	58	503	315	146	24	6	3	191	81	51	0	0	2	8	41	12	7	.094	.005	.330	.393	.432	.291
Kotchman C *	73	64	68	508	333	131	37	3	11	207	43	53	1	4	3	5	2	4	17	.044	.018	.296	.372	.467	.290
Matthews Jr.	67	79	72	579	402	130	26	3	18	216	102	55	6	2	0	6	18	4	12	.051	-.074	.252	.323	.419	.255
Willits R +	64	74	34	518	319	126	20	1	0	148	83	69	2	3	11	5	27	8	7	.030	.022	.293	.391	.344	.267
Anderson G *	62	67	80	450	301	124	31	1	16	205	54	27	9	0	0	6	1	0	8	.048	.012	.297	.336	.492	.279
Izturis M +	61	47	51	374	244	97	17	2	6	136	39	33	2	0	1	4	7	1	4	.096	-.001	.289	.349	.405	.263
Kendrick H	39	55	39	353	248	109	24	2	5	152	61	9	2	4	1	1	5	4	15	-.021	.014	.322	.347	.450	.274
Napoli M	36	40	34	263	172	54	11	1	10	97	63	33	2	5	1	5	5	2	5	-.005	.017	.247	.351	.443	.274
Aybar E +	15	18	19	211	160	46	5	1	1	56	32	10	0	2	3	2	4	4	8	.054	.077	.237	.279	.289	.202
Quinlan R	15	21	21	194	142	44	9	0	3	62	27	14	1	1	0	1	3	2	6	.000	.034	.247	.304	.348	.229
Hillenbrand	15	19	22	204	155	50	5	0	3	64	18	5	0	1	0	1	0	2	6	.098	.010	.254	.275	.325	.209
Morales K +	15	12	15	126	90	35	10	0	4	57	21	6	2	1	0	0	0	1	5	-.009	-.095	.294	.333	.479	.275
Mathis J	13	24	23	195	139	36	12	0	4	60	49	15	0	2	3	4	0	1	3	.065	.025	.211	.276	.351	.216
Molina J	9	9	10	131	101	28	8	0	0	36	30	3	0	0	3	0	2	1	3	.063	.053	.224	.242	.288	.185
Rivera J	5	3	8	44	36	12	1	0	2	19	4	1	0	0	0	0	0	0	5	-.212	.006	.279	.295	.442	.248
Haynes N *	4	10	1	48	35	12	0	1	0	14	11	3	0	0	0	0	1	2	0	.138	.228	.267	.313	.311	.223
Wood B	1	2	3	33	28	5	1	0	1	9	12	0	0	0	0	0	0	0	0	-.180	.037	.152	.152	.273	.139
Santana E	1	1	2	5	4	1	1	0	0	2	3	0	0	0	0	0	0	0	0	-.190	--	.200	.200	.400	.194
Evans T	1	3	2	13	11	1	0	0	1	4	4	2	0	0	0	0	0	0	1	.508	.113	.091	.231	.364	.199
Escobar K	1	0	0	7	4	2	0	0	0	2	2	0	0	0	1	0	0	0	0	-.233	-.350	.333	.333	.333	.238
Brown M	0	0	0	7	5	0	0	0	0	0	1	2	0	0	0	0	1	0	0	-.180	.180	.000	.286	.000	.131
Murphy T +	0	2	2	39	32	7	1	0	0	8	9	0	0	1	0	0	0	0	1	.008	-.088	.184	.205	.211	.148
Budde R	0	0	1	18	16	3	1	0	0	4	6	0	0	0	0	0	0	0	1	.136	.223	.167	.167	.222	.133
Gorneault N	-0	1	0	5	4	0	0	0	0	0	1	1	0	0	0	0	0	0	0	--	.150	.000	.200	.000	.092
Lackey J	-0	0	0	2	2	0	0	0	0	0	0	0	0	0	0	0	0	0	0	.000	--	.000	.000	.000	.000
Weaver J	-0	0	0	4	3	1	0	0	0	1	1	0	0	0	0	0	0	0	0	-.175	--	.250	.250	.250	.179
Colon B	-1	0	0	3	4	0	0	0	0	0	0	0	0	0	0	0	0	0	1	.000	--	.000	.000	.000	.000

Italicized stats have been adjusted for home park.

Batted Ball Batting Stats

Player	% of PA		% of Batted Balls					Out %		Runs Per Event				Total Runs vs. Avg.				
	K%	BB%	GB%	LD%	FB%	IF/F	HR/OF	GB	OF	NIP	GB	LD	OF	NIP	GB	LD	FB	Tot
Guerrero V	9	12	48	16	36	.10	.16	71	79	.15	.07	.44	.28	13	8	5	21	46
Kotchman C	8	11	51	16	33	.11	.09	79	75	.15	.01	.46	.22	8	-5	4	5	13
Figgins C	16	10	47	26	26	.03	.03	74	80	.06	.04	.46	.11	2	1	19	-9	13
Anderson G	12	6	40	19	41	.13	.12	73	87	.04	.06	.44	.17	-3	2	7	2	8
Kendrick H	17	4	54	16	30	.04	.06	68	64	-.03	.07	.40	.26	-7	6	-1	6	4
Napoli M	24	14	36	19	46	.08	.15	70	84	.06	.07	.31	.23	3	0	-4	4	3
Cabrera O	9	7	43	18	39	.14	.03	67	82	.09	.09	.38	.08	1	14	3	-17	1
Willits R	16	14	49	23	28	.06	.00	72	80	.10	.06	.37	.06	9	5	3	-15	1
Morales K	17	6	47	11	42	.10	.11	67	76	.00	.07	.38	.25	-2	2	-3	4	1
Izturis M	10	9	45	17	38	.11	.06	70	89	.10	.08	.42	.07	2	6	2	-9	0
Matthews Jr. G	18	10	51	13	36	.07	.12	73	80	.05	.05	.40	.22	0	2	-9	6	-0
Quinlan R	14	8	48	14	38	.12	.06	75	85	.05	.03	.42	.11	-1	-1	-2	-4	-7

Batted Ball Batting Stats continue after Fielding Stats.

Pitching Stats

Player	PRC	IP	BFP	G	GS	K	BB	IBB	HBP	H	HR	DP	DER	SB	CS	PO	W	L	Sv	Op	Hld	H-A	R^L	RA	ERA	FIP
Lackey J	119	224.0	929	33	33	179	52	2	12	219	18	23	.692	19	6	2	19	9	0	0	0	.019	-.036	3.50	3.01	3.66
Escobar K	101	195.7	812	30	30	160	66	2	3	182	11	33	.678	17	3	0	18	7	0	0	0	-.015	-.036	3.63	3.40	3.50
Weaver J	69	161.0	695	28	28	115	45	3	2	178	17	10	.678	19	2	1	13	7	0	0	0	.006	-.013	4.30	3.91	4.14
Rodriguez F	46	67.3	285	64	0	90	34	0	1	50	3	3	.688	12	1	0	5	2	40	46	0	.028	.026	2.94	2.81	2.85
Santana E	46	150.0	675	28	26	126	58	3	8	174	26	17	.663	11	3	0	7	14	0	0	0	-.094	-.013	6.18	5.76	5.21
Saunders J *	42	107.3	473	18	18	69	34	1	1	129	11	12	.659	7	4	2	8	5	0	0	0	.041	-.065	4.70	4.44	4.38
Shields S	37	77.0	320	71	0	77	33	0	4	62	7	9	.719	3	1	1	4	5	2	8	31	.012	-.023	4.21	3.86	4.00
Moseley D	37	92.0	383	46	8	50	27	3	3	97	7	14	.696	6	3	0	4	3	0	0	4	.037	.067	4.40	4.40	4.16
Speier J	31	50.0	198	51	0	47	12	1	4	36	6	1	.760	2	3	0	2	3	0	1	24	-.012	-.030	3.06	2.88	3.96
Bootchock C	29	77.3	331	51	0	56	24	3	5	81	7	11	.678	6	2	0	3	3	0	1	4	-.026	-.026	5.00	4.77	4.12
Oliver D *	28	64.3	273	61	0	51	23	2	1	58	5	5	.710	3	0	0	3	1	0	0	8	-.050	.077	4.34	3.78	3.83
Colon B	27	99.3	453	19	18	76	29	1	5	132	15	11	.628	2	2	0	6	8	0	0	1	-.057	-.012	6.70	6.34	4.81
Carrasco H	8	38.3	187	29	1	33	23	1	1	44	8	2	.680	0	0	0	2	1	0	0	2	-.043	.151	7.98	6.57	6.17
Bulger J	4	6.3	25	6	0	8	3	0	0	5	0	2	.643	0	0	0	0	0	0	0	0	.037	-.082	2.84	2.84	2.28
Jones G	2	8.7	42	9	0	5	5	0	1	10	2	0	.724	0	0	0	0	0	0	0	0	-.235	.103	6.23	6.23	7.30
Resop C	2	4.3	17	4	0	2	1	0	0	4	1	1	.769	0	0	0	0	0	0	0	0	--	.097	4.15	4.15	6.15
Thompson R	1	6.7	32	7	0	9	3	0	0	10	4	0	.625	0	1	0	0	0	0	0	0	-.218	.344	10.80	10.80	9.83
Gwyn M	0	5.3	31	3	0	3	5	0	0	9	3	0	.650	0	0	0	0	0	1	1	0	-.182	-.098	15.19	11.81	12.38

Italicized stats have been adjusted for home park.

Batted Ball Pitching Stats

Player	% of PA		% of Batted Balls					Out %		Runs Per Event				Total Runs vs. Avg.				
	K%	BB%	GB%	LD%	FB%	IF/F	HR/OF	GB	OF	NIP	GB	LD	OF	NIP	GB	LD	FB	Tot
Lackey J	19	7	45	19	36	.11	.08	80	79	.01	.00	.39	.18	-11	-12	-1	-3	-27
Escobar K	20	8	44	17	39	.11	.06	74	80	.03	.04	.42	.14	-5	-3	-3	-11	-21
Rodriguez F	32	12	43	17	40	.06	.05	71	79	.02	.08	.33	.14	-2	1	-7	-5	13
Shields S	24	12	45	19	36	.08	.10	77	89	.04	.03	.35	.14	-0	-2	-4	-5	-12
Speier J	24	8	37	12	50	.09	.10	69	87	.00	.09	.27	.15	-3	1	-7	-1	-10
Oliver D	19	9	48	12	40	.10	.07	74	83	.03	.05	.49	.12	-1	-0	-3	-5	-10
Moseley D	13	8	48	18	34	.08	.08	76	74	.06	.02	.27	.23	-0	-2	-6	4	-4
Weaver J	17	7	36	17	47	.11	.07	71	84	.02	.06	.45	.14	-6	2	3	-3	-4
Bootcheck C	17	9	44	19	37	.16	.08	75	80	.05	.04	.45	.15	-0	0	3	-4	-1
Saunders J	15	7	45	21	34	.04	.09	76	81	.04	.03	.44	.17	-2	-1	9	0	6
Carrasco H	18	13	43	20	36	.06	.18	77	81	.08	.03	.41	.31	2	-1	1	6	9
Colon B	17	8	42	18	40	.12	.12	64	78	.03	.10	.43	.22	-3	9	4	6	16
Santana E	19	10	36	19	46	.10	.13	68	82	.04	.08	.40	.23	-0	6	1	16	22
MLB Average	17	9	43	19	38	.10	.10	74	83	.05	.05	.40	.18	--	--	--	--	--

Fielding Stats

Name	INN	SBA/G	CS%	ERA	WP+PB/G	PO	A	TE	FE
Catcher									
Napoli M	598.7	0.93	21%	4.28	0.436	460	32	2	4
Mathis J	467.0	0.93	17%	3.89	0.559	383	42	3	1
Molina J	323.0	0.70	28%	4.60	0.446	283	17	4	0
Budde R	46.3	0.00	0%	4.27	0.583	36	1	1	0

Name	Inn	PO	A	TE	FE	FPct	DPS	DPT	RZR	OOZ
First Base										
Kotchman C	1033.0	978	68	3	0	.997	15	0	.809	32
Quinlan R	234.0	214	16	0	1	.996	4	0	.700	4
Morales K	121.0	119	9	0	0	1.000	0	0	.714	6
Hillenbrand S	47.0	38	2	0	1	.976	1	0	.800	0
Second Base										
Kendrick H	751.3	146	254	3	6	.978	27	30	.825	33
Aybar E	320.3	60	106	1	3	.976	10	16	.819	17
Izturis M	305.3	50	91	0	0	1.000	12	11	.860	6
Figgins C	58.0	9	15	1	0	.960	0	1	1.000	1
Shortstop										
Cabrera O	1330.0	239	415	2	9	.983	49	47	.807	51
Aybar E	79.0	14	24	1	2	.927	1	1	.733	3
Izturis M	19.0	8	3	0	1	.917	0	0	.750	0
Wood B	6.3	0	2	0	0	1.000	0	0	1.000	0
Third Base										
Figgins C	836.7	52	165	7	6	.943	10	0	.676	31
Izturis M	447.0	21	91	1	2	.974	11	0	.742	15
Wood B	75.0	12	14	1	0	.963	2	0	.500	5
Quinlan R	53.3	4	7	1	0	.917	0	0	.600	1
Brown M	14.0	1	3	0	0	1.000	1	0	.800	0
Aybar E	9.0	0	2	0	0	1.000	0	0	.400	0

Name	Inn	PO	A	TE	FE	FPct	DPS	DPT	RZR	OOZ
Left Field										
Anderson G	724.3	143	7	0	2	.987	0	0	.820	20
Willits R	513.3	151	3	1	0	.994	2	0	.895	23
Quinlan R	77.0	17	0	0	0	1.000	0	0	.889	1
Aybar E	29.0	5	0	0	0	1.000	0	0	.750	2
Murphy T	28.0	12	1	0	0	1.000	0	0	.857	6
Haynes N	25.0	5	1	0	0	1.000	0	0	1.000	1
Rivera J	15.0	0	0	0	0	0.000	0	0	--	--
Gorneault N	15.0	5	1	1	0	.857	0	0	1.000	1
Evans T	8.3	2	0	0	0	1.000	0	0	1.000	1
Center Field										
Matthews Jr. G	1144.0	362	7	0	5	.987	3	0	.850	62
Willits R	227.0	68	0	0	1	.986	0	0	.792	7
Haynes N	59.3	10	0	0	0	1.000	0	0	.818	1
Murphy T	4.0	1	0	0	0	1.000	0	0	1.000	0
Right Field										
Guerrero V	930.7	208	5	3	5	.959	5	0	.839	26
Willits R	212.0	41	3	0	1	.978	0	0	.846	8
Figgins C	86.0	17	1	0	0	1.000	0	0	.938	2
Murphy T	55.3	16	0	0	0	1.000	0	0	.917	5
Rivera J	53.0	9	1	0	0	1.000	0	0	.692	0
Haynes N	37.0	11	0	0	0	1.000	0	0	.818	2
Evans T	23.0	2	0	0	0	1.000	0	0	1.000	0
Quinlan R	19.0	3	0	0	0	1.000	0	0	1.000	0
Morales K	16.0	4	0	0	0	1.000	0	0	1.000	1
Aybar E	3.0	0	0	0	0	0.000	0	0	--	--

Batted Ball Batting Stats

Player	% of PA		% of Batted Balls					Out %		Runs Per Event				Total Runs vs. Avg.				
	K%	BB%	GB%	LD%	FB%	IF/F	HR/OF	GB	OF	NIP	GB	LD	OF	NIP	GB	LD	FB	Tot
Hillenbrand S	9	3	47	13	40	.15	.05	74	81	.00	.04	.34	.09	-3	0	-4	-5	-11
Molina J	23	2	49	18	33	.03	.00	76	77	-.07	.03	.35	.08	-4	-1	-2	-4	-11
Mathis J	25	9	42	13	45	.25	.10	71	89	.01	.07	.42	.14	-3	1	-5	-5	-11
Aybar E	15	6	52	12	36	.11	.02	73	86	.01	.04	.36	.04	-3	0	-5	-8	-16
MLB Average	*17*	*9*	*43*	*19*	*38*	*.10*	*.10*	*74*	*83*	*.05*	*.05*	*.40*	*.18*	*--*	*--*	*--*	*--*	*--*

Los Angeles Dodgers

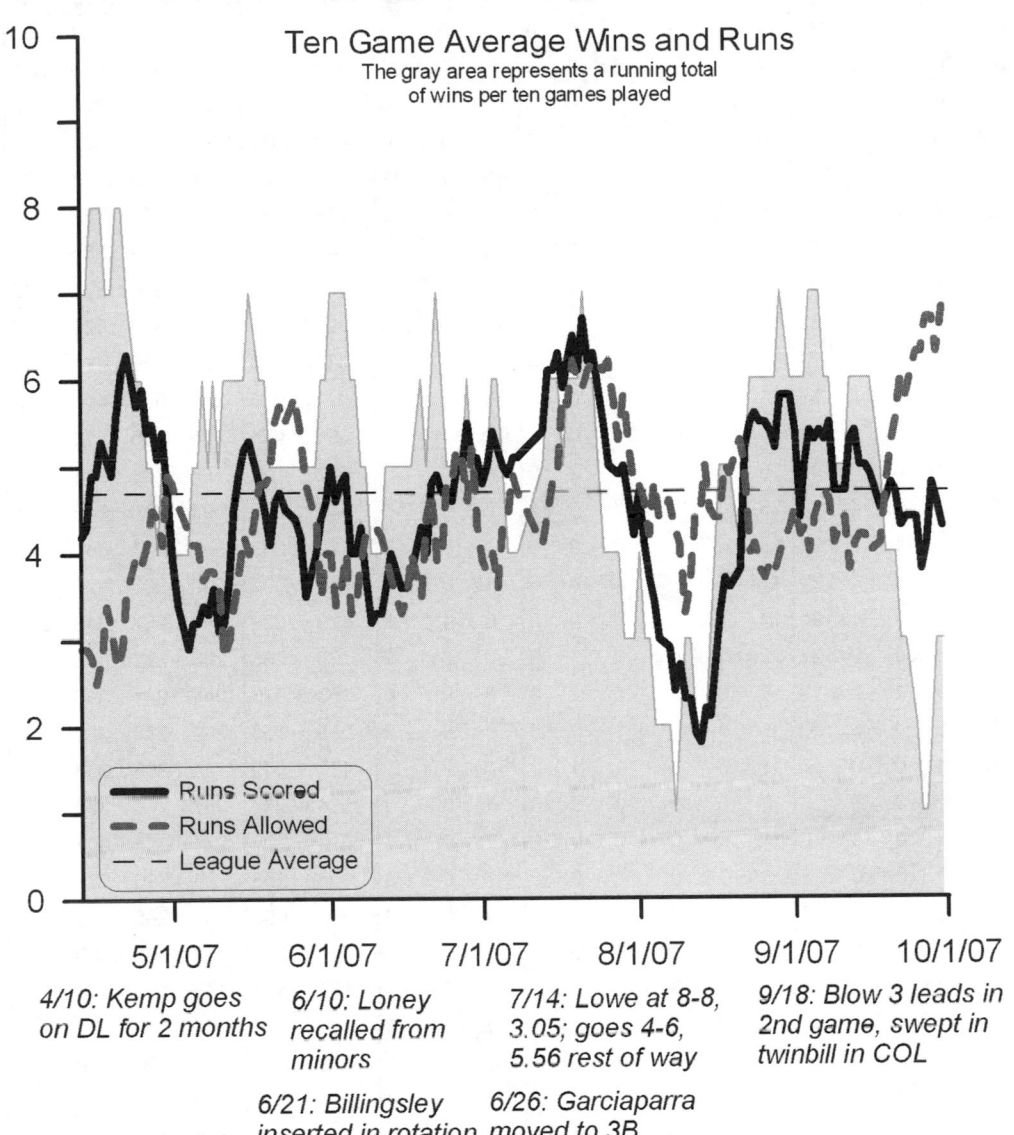

Ten Game Average Wins and Runs
The gray area represents a running total
of wins per ten games played

Legend:
— Runs Scored
- - Runs Allowed
- — League Average

X-axis: 5/1/07, 6/1/07, 7/1/07, 8/1/07, 9/1/07, 10/1/07

4/10: Kemp goes on DL for 2 months

6/10: Loney recalled from minors

6/21: Billingsley inserted in rotation

6/26: Garciaparra moved to 3B

7/14: Lowe at 8-8, 3.05; goes 4-6, 5.56 rest of way

9/18: Blow 3 leads in 2nd game, swept in twinbill in COL

Stat Facts:
- Takashi Saito fanned one-third of the batters he faced
- Jonathan Broxton was close behind, at a 30% K rate
- The Dodgers were the toughest team to strike out in the NL
- 22% of James Loney's batted balls were line drives
- Only 53% of Matt Kemp's groundballs resulted in outs
- Tony Abreu had a .749 RZR at third base, and .949 at second base
- Catcher Russell Martin stole 21 bases
- Wilson Betemit walked or struck out in 43% of his PAs
- Juan Pierre walked or struck out in just 10% of his Pas
- LOOGY Joe Beimel picked off 5 baserunners
- Esteban Loaiza allowed 9 HRs in 22 2/3 innings

Team Batting and Pitching/Fielding Stats by Month						
	April	May	June	July	Aug	Sept/Oct
Wins	15	16	14	12	13	12
Losses	11	11	14	13	15	16
RS/G	4.7	4.3	4.3	5.4	4.1	4.6
RA/G	3.9	4.1	4.2	5.2	4.3	5.2
OBP	.329	.340	.335	.366	.318	.336
SLG	.370	.388	.410	.444	.383	.438
FIP	3.65	3.20	3.56	4.60	3.70	5.05
DER	.689	.673	.705	.670	.691	.682

Batting Stats

Player	BR	Runs	RBI	PA	Outs	H	2B	3B	HR	TB	K	BB	IBB	HBP	SH	SF	SB	CS	GDP	H-A	L^R	BA	OBP	SLG	GPA
Martin R	90	87	87	620	407	158	32	3	19	253	89	67	1	7	0	6	21	9	16	-.054	.094	.293	.374	.469	.291
Kent J	79	78	79	562	365	149	36	1	20	247	61	57	4	5	0	6	1	3	17	.041	.036	.302	.375	.500	.300
Pierre J *	74	96	41	729	497	196	24	8	0	236	37	33	0	6	20	2	64	15	10	.015	.027	.293	.331	.353	.242
Loney J *	72	41	67	375	237	114	18	4	15	185	48	28	5	1	0	2	0	1	6	-.088	.017	.331	.381	.538	.312
Gonzalez L *	67	70	68	526	348	129	23	2	15	201	56	56	4	4	0	2	6	2	11	-.017	-.037	.278	.359	.433	.275
Ethier A *	67	50	64	507	334	127	32	2	13	202	68	46	12	4	0	8	0	4	10	-.013	.037	.284	.350	.452	.276
Furcal R +	66	87	47	643	441	157	23	4	6	206	68	55	3	1	2	3	25	6	11	.049	.026	.270	.333	.355	.243
Garciaparra	60	39	59	466	316	122	17	0	7	160	41	31	5	0	0	4	3	1	6	.089	-.040	.283	.328	.371	.245
Kemp M	50	47	42	311	203	100	12	5	10	152	66	16	0	0	0	3	10	5	6	.020	.060	.342	.373	.521	.304
Betemit W +	28	22	26	192	121	36	8	0	10	74	49	32	0	1	0	3	0	0	1	.089	-.034	.231	.359	.474	.286
Abreu T +	19	19	17	178	126	45	14	1	2	67	21	7	1	3	0	2	0	0	5	-.111	-.008	.271	.309	.404	.245
Laroche A	12	16	10	115	74	21	5	0	1	29	24	20	5	1	0	1	2	1	1	-.068	-.071	.226	.365	.312	.247
Martinez R	12	10	27	147	104	25	4	0	0	29	15	11	0	0	2	5	1	0	0	.032	.022	.194	.248	.225	.171
Saenz O	10	9	18	132	94	21	5	0	4	38	25	16	0	2	0	4	0	0	5	.041	.028	.191	.295	.345	.224
Young D +	7	4	3	36	21	13	1	1	2	22	5	2	0	0	0	0	1	0	0	-.172	-.085	.382	.417	.647	.356
Valdez W	7	12	7	80	58	16	2	1	0	20	12	4	0	1	0	1	1	0	0	-.110	-.002	.216	.263	.270	.189
Hillenbrand	7	6	9	74	57	17	0	2	1	24	12	2	1	0	0	2	0	1	3	.129	.025	.243	.257	.343	.205
Penny B	6	7	7	75	49	16	6	0	0	22	23	1	0	2	7	0	0	0	0	-.196	-.235	.246	.279	.338	.215
Hu C	5	5	5	31	22	7	0	1	2	15	8	0	0	0	2	0	0	0	0	.153	-.073	.241	.241	.517	.243
Lieberthal M	4	6	1	82	61	18	2	0	0	20	11	4	0	1	0	0	0	0	2	.095	-.053	.234	.280	.260	.195
Clark B	4	7	5	66	48	13	4	0	0	17	11	6	0	1	1	0	1	2	1	-.132	.049	.224	.308	.293	.216
Wells D *	2	2	1	15	11	4	1	0	0	5	6	0	0	0	0	0	0	0	0	.524	.277	.267	.267	.333	.207
Sweeney M *	2	2	3	34	24	9	1	0	0	10	11	1	0	0	0	0	0	0	0	.314	.038	.273	.294	.303	.212
Anderson M *	2	3	2	29	20	6	0	0	0	6	5	3	0	0	0	0	1	0	0	.007	.205	.231	.310	.231	.201
Wolf R *	1	1	2	37	25	5	2	0	0	7	13	4	0	0	3	0	0	0	0	.095	.053	.167	.265	.233	.181
Stults E *	1	1	0	12	8	4	2	0	0	6	5	0	0	0	0	0	0	0	0	-.367	-.367	.333	.333	.500	.281
Loaiza E	0	0	2	9	7	1	0	0	0	1	2	0	0	0	2	0	0	0	1	-.175	-.117	.143	.143	.143	.102
Schmidt J	-0	1	1	8	6	1	0	0	1	4	4	0	0	0	1	0	0	0	0	.363	.725	.143	.143	.571	.211
Beimel J *	-0	0	0	1	1	0	0	0	0	0	0	0	0	0	0	0	0	0	0	.000	--	.000	.000	.000	.000
Seanez R	-0	0	0	1	1	0	0	0	0	0	1	0	0	0	0	0	0	0	0	.000	--	.000	.000	.000	.000
Kuo H *	-0	1	1	8	5	1	0	0	1	4	3	0	0	0	2	0	0	0	0	.363	--	.167	.167	.667	.247
Moeller C	-0	2	0	9	8	1	0	0	0	1	1	0	0	1	0	0	0	0	1	.131	-.170	.125	.222	.125	.134
Billingsley	-1	1	2	41	34	4	1	0	0	5	19	1	0	0	4	0	0	0	2	-.046	.092	.111	.135	.139	.097
Hendrickson	-1	1	1	30	26	1	1	0	0	2	10	2	0	0	1	0	0	0	0	-.008	-.067	.037	.103	.074	.066
Lowe D	-2	2	1	71	53	7	0	0	0	7	17	5	0	0	6	1	0	0	1	.032	.123	.119	.185	.119	.115
Tomko B	-2	0	1	30	23	0	0	0	0	0	16	1	0	0	5	0	0	0	0	-.032	.045	.000	.042	.000	.019

Italicized stats have been adjusted for home park.
Batted Ball Batting Stats are listed after Fielding Stats.

Pitching Stats

Player	PRC	IP	BFP	G	GS	K	BB	IBB	HBP	H	HR	DP	DER	SB	CS	PO	W	L	Sv	Op	Hld	H-A	R^L	RA	ERA	FIP
Penny B	108	208.0	865	33	33	135	73	2	5	199	9	30	.701	14	5	0	16	4	0	0	0	-.009	.045	3.25	3.03	3.63
Billingsley	79	147.0	623	43	20	141	64	3	3	131	15	16	.698	5	6	2	12	5	0	1	3	.036	-.034	3.43	3.31	3.98
Lowe D	79	199.3	831	33	32	147	59	2	1	194	20	26	.687	14	12	0	12	14	0	0	1	-.009	-.028	4.52	3.88	3.97
Saito T	71	64.3	234	63	0	78	13	0	3	33	5	9	.785	2	0	0	2	1	39	43	1	-.057	-.070	1.40	1.40	2.60
Broxton J	48	82.0	334	83	0	99	25	3	1	69	6	7	.675	6	3	1	4	4	2	8	32	-.085	.007	3.29	2.85	2.65
Wolf R *	40	102.7	458	18	18	94	39	2	6	110	10	6	.663	4	3	0	9	6	0	0	0	-.049	-.015	4.82	4.73	3.96
Hendrickson	40	122.7	532	39	15	92	29	4	1	142	15	11	.666	11	2	2	4	8	0	1	2	-.026	-.033	5.50	5.21	3.99
Seanez R	37	76.0	329	73	0	73	27	3	4	78	10	7	.679	10	1	0	6	3	1	3	4	.028	.011	3.91	3.79	4.16
Beimel J *	28	67.3	281	83	0	39	24	6	1	63	1	12	.681	2	3	5	4	2	1	1	16	.035	-.089	4.01	3.88	3.15
Tomko B	28	104.0	475	33	15	79	42	1	2	124	13	9	.649	6	4	0	2	11	0	0	0	.028	-.011	6.49	5.80	4.62
Proctor S	15	32.0	137	31	0	27	15	1	3	25	4	2	.761	5	1	0	3	0	0	2	7	.002	.006	3.94	3.38	4.80
Wells D *	12	38.7	162	7	7	19	9	1	0	45	5	3	.690	2	3	1	4	1	0	0	0	-.063	-.113	5.35	5.12	4.59
Stults E *	11	38.7	179	12	5	30	17	2	1	50	5	4	.643	3	0	0	1	4	0	0	1	-.035	.027	6.05	5.82	4.64
Houlton D	11	28.0	113	18	0	21	7	0	0	28	5	4	.700	1	2	0	0	2	0	0	2	-.060	.029	4.50	4.18	4.84
Tsao C	10	24.7	97	21	0	16	8	0	1	18	3	3	.783	2	0	0	0	1	0	1	3	-.099	-.016	4.38	4.38	4.65
Kuo H *	7	30.3	140	8	6	27	14	0	1	35	3	2	.653	3	0	0	1	4	0	0	0	.051	-.069	7.71	7.42	4.26
Schmidt J	6	25.7	125	6	6	22	14	2	1	32	4	1	.643	1	0	0	1	4	0	0	0	.239	.120	7.01	6.31	5.10
Hernandez R	5	20.3	96	22	0	13	9	0	2	26	3	5	.623	1	0	0	0	2	0	0	1	.020	.118	7.08	6.64	5.53
Loaiza E	4	22.7	108	5	5	15	16	1	1	26	9	2	.731	1	0	0	1	4	0	0	0	.050	-.099	8.34	8.34	9.23
Hull E	3	6.7	27	5	0	5	3	0	0	4	0	1	.789	2	0	0	0	0	0	0	0	-.103	.192	4.05	4.05	3.12
Meloan J	1	7.3	38	5	0	7	8	0	1	8	1	0	.667	0	1	0	0	0	0	0	0	.104	.091	11.05	11.05	6.81
Brazoban Y	0	1.7	12	4	0	5	3	1	0	3	0	0		1	0	0	0	0	0	0	0	.215	.523	21.60	16.20	0.87

Italicized stats have been adjusted for home park.

Batted Ball Pitching Stats

Player	% of PA		% of Batted Balls					Out %		Runs Per Event				Total Runs vs. Avg.				
	K%	BB%	GB%	LD%	FB%	IF/F	HR/OF	GB	OF	NIP	GB	LD	OF	NIP	GB	LD	FB	Tot
Penny B	16	9	49	20	31	.10	.04	73	89	.05	.05	.41	.04	-0	-1	5	-31	-28
Saito T	33	7	46	13	41	.11	.10	71	98	-.03	.05	.28	.07	-7	-1	-10	-9	-27
Broxton J	30	8	49	22	29	.07	.09	74	79	-.02	.04	.35	.18	-7	-1	-3	-5	-16
Lowe D	18	7	65	16	19	.04	.18	76	78	.02	.03	.37	.33	-7	3	-10	1	-14
Billingsley C	23	11	41	20	39	.10	.09	73	86	.03	.04	.41	.15	-1	-3	-1	-7	-13
Beimel J	14	9	48	18	35	.10	.02	74	75	.07	.03	.36	.12	0	-1	-2	-5	-8
Proctor S	20	13	34	13	53	.15	.10	67	97	.07	.08	.44	.08	1	0	-2	-4	-5
Tsao C	16	9	39	14	47	.18	.07	85	80	.05	-.02	.47	.15	-0	-2	-1	-1	-4
Seanez R	22	9	36	20	44	.18	.13	70	91	.02	.07	.43	.15	-2	1	1	-4	-3
Hendrickson M	17	6	44	23	33	.13	.13	70	85	-.00	.07	.34	.21	-7	4	2	-1	-1
Houlton D	19	6	36	18	46	.08	.14	74	87	.00	.04	.37	.19	-2	-0	-1	2	-1
Wolf R	21	10	41	19	40	.12	.09	73	81	.04	.06	.46	.17	-1	1	3	-2	1
Wells D	12	6	49	14	37	.08	.11	74	83	.03	.05	.49	.20	-1	1	1	2	2
Kuo H	19	11	31	20	49	.09	.07	62	85	.05	.13	.43	.12	0	1	1	-0	2
Stults E	17	10	39	21	39	.08	.11	68	83	.06	.07	.46	.19	1	1	3	1	6
Schmidt J	18	12	34	19	47	.18	.12	66	76	.07	.11	.40	.26	1	2	0	3	6
Tomko B	17	9	41	21	38	.11	.11	72	79	.05	.06	.42	.21	0	4	6	4	14
MLB Average	*17*	*9*	*43*	*19*	*38*	*.10*	*.10*	*74*	*83*	*.05*	*.05*	*.40*	*.18*	--	--	--	--	--

Fielding Stats

Name	INN	SBA/G	CS%	ERA	WP+PB/G	PO	A	TE	FE
Catcher									
Martin R	1254.0	0.82	28%	3.95	0.323	1065	85	14	0
Lieberthal M	167.0	0.97	22%	6.14	0.216	136	11	2	1
Moeller C	29.0	0.00	0%	4.03	0.000	25	1	0	0

Name	Inn	PO	A	TE	FE	FPct	DPS	DPT	RZR	OOZ
First Base										
Loney J	774.7	725	61	3	5	.989	12	0	.696	21
Garciaparra N	571.0	556	27	0	4	.993	2	0	.691	12
Saenz O	75.0	60	4	0	0	1.000	0	0	.700	0
Sweeney M	12.3	10	0	0	0	1.000	0	0	1.000	0
Anderson M	8.0	9	1	0	0	.909	0	0	1.000	0
Hillenbrand S	6.0	6	0	0	0	1.000	0	0	--	--
Martinez R	3.0	2	0	0	0	1.000	0	0	--	--
Second Base										
Kent J	1084.0	235	328	3	11	.976	30	46	.834	28
Martinez R	178.0	36	38	0	1	.987	5	3	.732	4
Abreu T	115.7	19	48	0	0	1.000	4	5	.949	3
Valdez W	59.0	16	25	0	0	1.000	3	3	.833	0
Betemit W	6.0	1	0	0	0	1.000	0	0	0.000	0
Young D	5.0	3	0	0	0	1.000	0	0	--	--
Anderson M	2.0	0	0	0	0	0.000	0	0	--	--
Shortstop										
Furcal R	1210.0	241	426	11	8	.972	43	51	.823	53
Hu C	70.0	11	22	0	1	.971	4	4	.850	1
Valdez W	64.3	7	26	0	0	1.000	1	3	.944	6
Martinez R	54.7	8	15	0	0	1.000	1	2	.625	2
Abreu T	44.0	7	18	0	1	.962	2	1	.875	2
Betemit W	7.0	0	1	0	0	1.000	0	0	1.000	0

Name	Inn	PO	A	TE	FE	FPct	DPS	DPT	RZR	OOZ
Third Base										
Garciaparra N	354.7	32	64	2	4	.941	4	0	.652	13
Betemit W	353.0	20	60	0	4	.952	6	0	.662	7
Laroche A	237.0	22	48	1	2	.959	8	0	.672	9
Abreu T	198.3	14	57	4	0	.947	5	0	.719	10
Hillenbrand S	154.0	14	35	4	0	.925	4	1	.718	6
Martinez R	104.0	2	33	0	1	.972	2	0	.784	4
Valdez W	43.0	2	9	0	0	1.000	1	1	1.000	2
Saenz O	6.0	0	1	0	0	1.000	0	0	1.000	0
Left Field										
Gonzalez L	996.0	192	4	0	1	.995	0	0	.833	32
Ethier A	306.0	73	2	1	0	.987	0	0	.893	6
Clark B	92.7	14	0	0	0	1.000	0	0	.800	2
Young D	46.0	8	0	0	0	1.000	0	0	1.000	0
Valdez W	8.3	1	0	0	0	1.000	0	0	1.000	0
Laroche A	1.0	0	0	0	0	0.000	0	0	--	--
Center Field										
Pierre J	1416.0	366	4	1	4	.987	0	0	.902	63
Kemp M	17.3	8	0	0	0	1.000	0	0	1.000	1
Clark B	14.0	4	0	0	0	1.000	0	0	1.000	1
Valdez W	2.0	1	0	0	0	1.000	0	0	1.000	0
Right Field										
Ethier A	779.7	176	8	3	1	.979	2	0	.918	31
Kemp M	619.7	129	2	1	3	.970	2	0	.856	16
Clark B	48.0	11	0	0	1	.917	0	0	1.000	3
Betemit W	1.7	0	0	0	0	0.000	0	0	--	--
Loney J	1.0	0	0	0	0	0.000	0	0	0.000	0

Batted Ball Batting Stats

Player	% of PA		% of Batted Balls					Out %		Runs Per Event				Total Runs vs. Avg.				
	K%	BB%	GB%	LD%	FB%	IF/F	HR/OF	GB	OF	NIP	GB	LD	OF	NIP	GB	LD	FB	Tot
Kent J	11	11	38	18	45	.08	.11	71	81	.12	.05	.37	.21	7	1	0	14	22
Loney J	13	8	42	22	36	.13	.15	73	78	.06	.06	.41	.29	-0	2	7	11	21
Martin R	14	12	48	18	34	.12	.14	72	83	.10	.05	.41	.23	8	3	1	6	18
Kemp M	21	5	45	17	37	.05	.12	53	87	-.02	.17	.52	.18	-6	13	5	2	14
Ethier A	13	10	46	18	36	.03	.10	72	82	.08	.06	.36	.18	3	4	-1	4	9
Gonzalez L	11	11	42	19	39	.16	.10	75	85	.12	.04	.39	.16	8	-0	2	-2	8
Betemit W	26	17	43	16	41	.00	.22	79	83	.07	.03	.37	.35	3	-1	-4	8	6
Laroche A	21	18	41	19	40	.14	.04	72	87	.10	.07	.42	.05	3	0	-0	-4	-1
Abreu E	12	6	52	15	32	.04	.04	71	88	.04	.07	.45	.08	-1	2	0	-5	-4
Saenz O	19	14	39	10	51	.16	.08	80	86	.08	-.01	.50	.12	2	-3	-3	-2	-6
Garciaparra N	9	7	43	19	37	.12	.05	70	84	.08	.07	.31	.09	-0	5	-1	-10	-7
Furcal R	11	9	50	19	32	.10	.04	74	85	.09	.05	.34	.08	3	6	-2	-17	-11
Martinez R	10	7	43	21	36	.09	.00	86	82	.08	-.02	.24	.03	-0	-4	-3	-6	-12
Pierre J	5	5	53	21	26	.10	.00	76	86	.12	.04	.38	.01	-1	7	7	-31	-18
MLB Average	*17*	*9*	*43*	*19*	*38*	*.10*	*.10*	*74*	*83*	*.05*	*.05*	*.40*	*.18*	*--*	*--*	*--*	*--*	*--*

Milwaukee Brewers

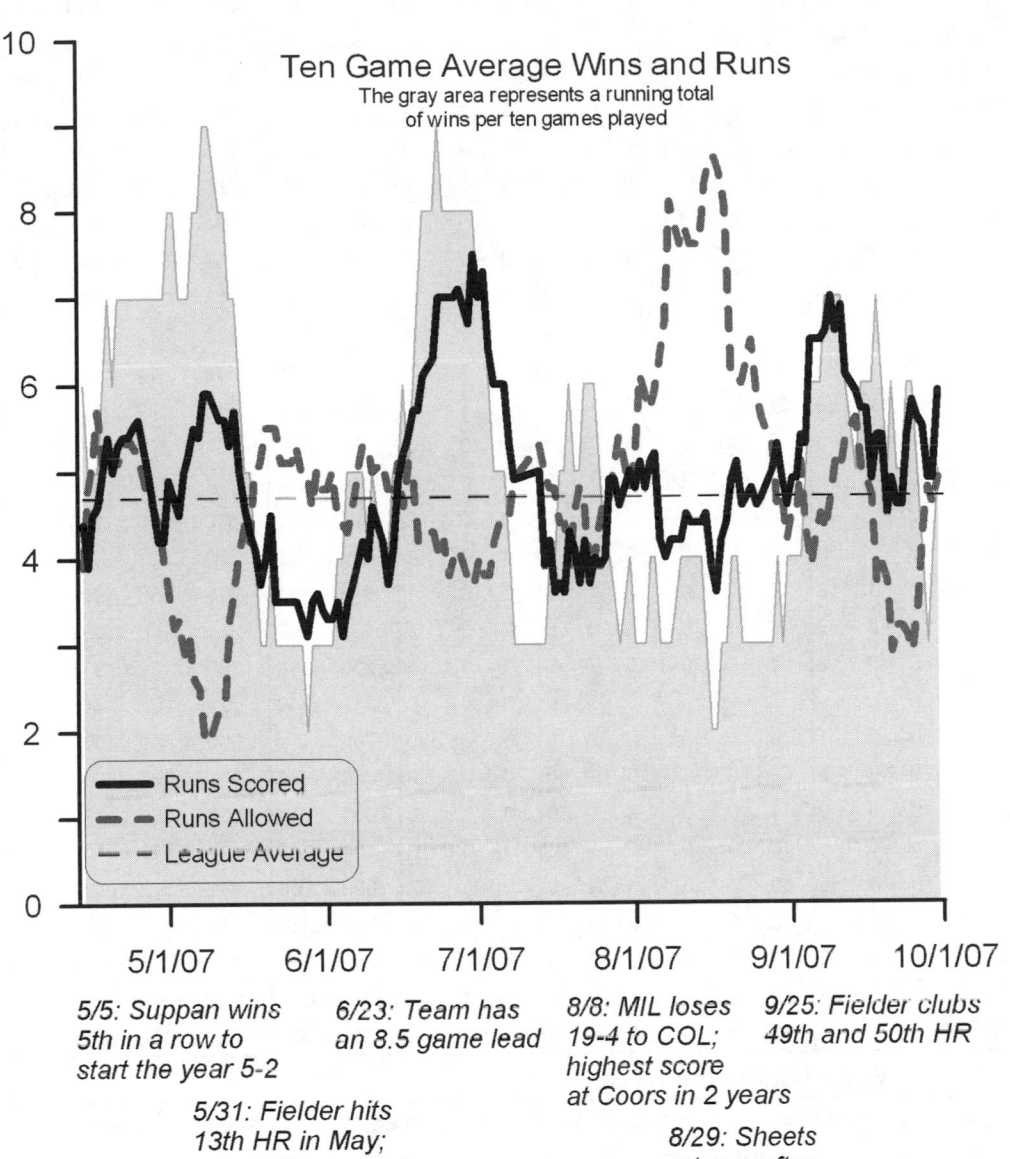

Ten Game Average Wins and Runs

The gray area represents a running total of wins per ten games played

- Runs Scored
- Runs Allowed
- League Average

5/5: Suppan wins
5th in a row to
start the year 5-2

6/23: Team has
an 8.5 game lead

8/8: MIL loses
19-4 to COL;
highest score
at Coors in 2 years

9/25: Fielder clubs
49th and 50th HR

5/31: Fielder hits
13th HR in May;
a franchise record

8/29: Sheets
returns after
6 weeks on DL

Stat Facts:

- Rickie Weeks stole 25 bases in 27 attempts, and hit into just 3 double plays
- Weeks drew a walk in 18% of his plate appearances, second in the league
- 10 of Geoff Jenkins' 32 walks were intentional
- Johnny Estrada put the ball in play in 88% of his PAs
- Estrada threw out just 8% of base stealers
- Bill Hall had a LD% of 23%
- Ben Sheets surrendered 21 stolen bases in 21 attempts
- Francisco Cordero struck out 33% of the batters he faced
- Ryan Braun had an RZR of just .564, and committed 16 throwing errors
- 25% of Prince Fielder's fly balls were home runs
- David Bush's L^R of .056 was highest in the league

Team Batting and Pitching/Fielding Stats by Month						
	April	May	June	July	Aug	Sept/Oct
Wins	16	14	17	11	9	16
Losses	9	15	9	16	18	12
RS/G	4.7	4.3	6.0	4.3	4.4	6.0
RA/G	4.6	4.2	4.4	4.7	6.4	4.5
OBP	.337	.307	.359	.318	.314	.339
SLG	.441	.433	.497	.410	.466	.488
FIP	3.68	4.43	3.80	4.08	4.84	3.80
DER	.678	.707	.695	.688	.636	.673

Batting Stats

Player	BR	Runs	RBI	PA	Outs	H	2B	3B	HR	TB	K	BB	IBB	HBP	SH	SF	SB	CS	GDP	H-A	L^R	BA	OBP	SLG	GPA
Fielder P *	124	109	119	681	419	165	35	2	50	354	121	90	21	14	0	4	2	2	9	.047	.078	.288	.395	.618	.329
Braun R	95	91	97	492	323	146	26	6	34	286	112	29	1	7	0	5	15	5	13	.026	.198	.324	.370	.634	.322
Hart C	94	86	81	566	369	149	33	9	24	272	99	36	3	13	5	7	23	7	6	.038	.072	.295	.353	.539	.291
Hardy J	83	89	80	638	444	164	30	1	26	274	73	40	1	1	4	1	2	3	13	.011	.068	.277	.323	.463	.259
Weeks R	66	87	36	506	318	96	21	6	16	177	116	78	5	14	3	2	25	2	3	-.027	.029	.235	.374	.433	.274
Jenkins G *	61	45	64	464	324	107	24	2	21	198	116	32	10	9	0	3	2	2	9	.064	.036	.255	.319	.471	.259
Hall B	60	59	63	503	351	115	35	0	14	192	128	40	1	3	1	7	4	5	9	.022	.027	.254	.315	.425	.245
Mench K	42	39	37	308	215	77	20	3	8	127	21	16	2	1	0	3	3	1	3	.067	.101	.267	.305	.441	.245
Estrada J +	39	40	54	464	335	123	25	0	10	178	43	12	3	2	1	7	0	0	16	-.037	.027	.278	.296	.403	.232
Counsell C *	28	31	24	334	229	62	12	2	3	87	47	41	4	3	6	2	4	2	7	-.042	.046	.220	.323	.309	.220
Graffanino T	24	34	30	260	184	55	8	0	9	90	44	24	6	3	0	2	0	1	7	.073	-.019	.238	.315	.390	.237
Gross G *	23	28	24	210	142	43	12	2	7	80	37	25	2	1	0	1	3	1	1	.076	.090	.235	.329	.437	.255
Miller D	17	19	24	206	150	44	9	0	4	65	39	14	0	3	0	3	1	0	8	-.033	.011	.237	.296	.349	.218
Gwynn T *	15	13	10	135	92	32	3	2	0	39	24	12	1	0	0	0	8	1	0	-.010	-.012	.260	.326	.317	.224
Dillon J	12	12	10	82	52	26	8	2	0	38	14	5	0	1	0	0	0	0	2	-.094	.242	.342	.390	.500	.298
Gallardo Y	4	5	6	42	31	10	3	0	2	19	10	1	0	0	1	0	0	0	1	.076	.013	.250	.268	.475	.237
Capuano C *	4	2	3	48	33	9	0	0	1	12	16	2	0	0	5	0	0	0	1	.075	-.061	.220	.256	.293	.186
Rivera M	2	2	3	15	10	3	0	0	2	9	3	1	0	0	0	0	0	0	0	-.103	.499	.231	.286	.692	.299
Rottino V	2	0	3	9	7	2	1	0	0	3	1	0	0	0	0	0	0	0	0	.236	.413	.222	.222	.333	.182
Parra M *	2	1	2	10	7	2	2	0	0	4	3	0	0	0	1	0	0	0	0	-.317	.380	.222	.222	.444	.209
Wise M	0	0	0	1	0	1	0	0	0	1	0	0	0	0	0	0	0	0	0	.700	--	1.000	1.000	1.000	.693
Stocker M +	0	0	0	3	3	0	0	0	0	0	0	0	0	0	0	0	4	0	0	.000	.000	.000	.000	.000	.000
Linebrink S	-0	0	0	1	1	0	0	0	0	0	1	0	0	0	0	0	0	0	0	.000	--	.000	.000	.000	.000
Vargas C	-0	1	0	43	33	5	1	0	0	6	10	0	0	0	5	0	0	0	0	.134	.043	.132	.132	.158	.098
Suppan J	-1	4	2	75	55	8	0	0	0	8	16	3	0	0	11	0	0	0	2	.099	.106	.131	.172	.131	.109
Villanueva C	-1	1	0	17	12	1	0	0	0	1	3	0	0	0	4	0	0	0	0	.078	.350	.077	.077	.077	.053
Nix L *	-1	0	0	12	12	0	0	0	0	0	4	0	0	0	0	0	0	0	0	.000	.000	.000	.000	.000	.000
Bush D	-1	2	2	62	50	7	2	0	0	9	11	0	0	1	6	0	0	0	2	-.066	.028	.127	.143	.164	.104
Sheets B	-2	1	0	51	42	3	0	0	0	3	25	0	0	0	6	0	0	0	0	.029	-.066	.067	.067	.067	.046

Italicized stats have been adjusted for home park.

Batted Ball Batting Stats

Player	% of PA		% of Batted Balls					Out %		Runs Per Event				Total Runs vs. Avg.				
	K%	BB%	GB%	LD%	FB%	IF/F	HR/OF	GB	OF	NIP	GB	LD	OF	NIP	GB	LD	FB	Tot
Fielder P	18	15	35	19	46	.08	.25	82	82	.10	-.00	.43	.38	14	-10	5	46	55
Braun R	23	7	39	16	45	.08	.23	64	80	-.00	.09	.55	.37	-6	6	6	32	38
Hart C	17	9	37	17	46	.07	.14	63	89	.04	.13	.50	.19	-1	14	6	9	27
Weeks R	23	18	41	17	41	.17	.16	67	88	.09	.10	.44	.23	12	5	-3	1	15
Jenkins G	25	9	41	21	37	.06	.19	80	83	.01	.01	.44	.29	-5	-6	4	11	4
Hardy J	11	6	41	17	42	.13	.13	71	87	.05	.06	.36	.19	-3	2	-3	6	3
Gross G	18	12	39	20	41	.13	.13	83	84	.08	-.00	.43	.21	2	-3	1	1	1
Mench K	7	6	42	17	41	.07	.08	75	89	.09	.05	.47	.10	-1	1	4	-4	1
Graffanino T	17	10	43	15	42	.16	.14	67	93	.06	.08	.36	.15	1	3	-4	-3	-3
Gwynn A	18	9	53	18	29	.08	.00	72	79	.04	.07	.40	.04	-0	3	-1	-5	-4
Hall B	25	9	36	23	41	.12	.11	71	87	.00	.06	.42	.16	-7	0	4	-4	-7
Miller D	19	8	48	15	37	.09	.08	76	87	.03	.02	.44	.12	-1	-2	-2	-4	-8
Counsell C	14	13	46	15	38	.13	.04	74	86	.11	.06	.26	.04	5	2	-9	-12	-14
Estrada J	9	3	40	20	40	.06	.07	80	86	-.00	.00	.39	.10	-7	-7	6	-6	-14
MLB Average	17	9	43	19	38	.10	.10	74	83	.05	.05	.40	.18	--	--	--	--	--

Pitching Stats

Player	PRC	IP	BFP	G	GS	K	BB	IBB	HBP	H	HR	DP	DER	SB	CS	PO	W	L	Sv	Op	Hld	H-A	R^L	RA	ERA	FIP
Suppan J	72	206.7	919	34	34	114	68	10	11	243	18	27	.669	7	0	0	12	12	0	0	0	-.006	-.053	4.92	4.62	4.30
Sheets B	65	141.3	592	24	24	106	37	2	1	138	17	8	.712	21	0	1	12	5	0	0	0	-.009	.080	3.95	3.82	4.10
Bush D	64	186.3	810	33	31	134	44	1	11	217	27	19	.668	15	7	0	12	10	0	0	0	-.026	.056	5.31	5.12	4.58
Gallardo Y	54	110.3	466	20	17	101	37	2	2	103	8	11	.682	4	1	2	9	5	0	0	0	-.052	-.014	3.92	3.67	3.39
Villanueva C	53	114.3	489	59	6	99	53	3	3	101	16	11	.726	6	3	1	8	5	1	3	16	-.019	-.030	4.09	3.94	4.75
Capuano C *	51	150.0	669	29	25	132	54	2	8	170	20	14	.653	6	0	2	5	12	0	0	0	-.052	-.042	5.58	5.10	4.44
Vargas C	47	134.3	605	29	23	107	54	3	2	153	23	9	.680	11	5	2	11	6	1	2	0	-.006	-.059	5.36	5.09	5.09
Cordero F	39	63.3	261	66	0	86	18	1	1	52	4	3	.664	3	0	0	0	4	44	51	0	-.128	-.041	3.27	2.98	2.23
Turnbow D	29	68.0	292	77	0	84	46	0	2	44	4	7	.737	3	3	1	4	5	1	4	33	.008	-.003	4.76	4.63	3.68
Shouse B *	23	47.7	201	73	0	32	14	5	2	40	0	5	.686	6	2	1	1	1	1	4	21	-.042	-.061	3.59	3.02	2.62
Wise M	20	53.7	236	56	0	43	17	1	1	61	5	6	.653	9	0	0	3	2	1	2	13	-.004	-.005	5.03	4.19	3.83
Spurling C	15	50.0	225	49	0	28	14	3	2	63	6	6	.663	2	0	0	2	1	0	0	2	.074	-.050	5.58	4.68	4.49
Parra M *	12	26.3	116	9	2	26	12	0	2	25	1	4	.653	0	0	0	0	1	0	0	1	.007	-.085	4.44	3.76	3.38
Linebrink S	10	25.3	109	27	0	25	11	2	0	27	3	5	.614	0	3	0	2	3	0	1	6	-.034	.017	4.97	3.55	3.90
Capellan J	5	12.0	52	7	0	8	6	1	0	10	2	0	.778	2	0	0	0	2	0	0	0	.088	.017	4.50	4.50	5.35
Aquino G	5	14.0	59	15	0	12	5	1	0	13	2	1	.725	0	0	0	0	1	0	2	2	-.027	-.078	5.79	4.50	4.27
McClung S	3	12.0	51	14	0	11	5	0	1	11	0	3	.676	0	0	0	0	1	0	0	0	-.144	-.067	6.75	3.75	2.94
Stetter M *	3	5.0	20	6	0	4	2	0	2	2	0	1	.833	0	0	0	1	0	0	0	0	.409	.175	3.60	3.60	4.07
Dessens E	2	15.0	69	12	0	12	3	0	0	24	3	3	.588	1	0	0	1	1	0	0	0	-.163	-.142	9.60	6.60	4.87
King R *	2	6.0	26	12	0	7	3	0	0	6	1	1	.667	1	0	0	0	0	0	0	1	-.071	.115	6.00	6.00	4.60
Balfour G	0	2.7	18	3	0	3	4	0	1	4	1	0	.667	2	0	0	0	2	0	0	0	-.371	.118	20.25	20.25	11.52

Italicized stats have been adjusted for home park.

Batted Ball Pitching Stats

Player	% of PA		% of Batted Balls					Out %		Runs Per Event				Total Runs vs. Avg.				
	K%	BB%	GB%	LD%	FB%	IF/F	HR/OF	GB	OF	NIP	GB	LD	OF	NIP	GB	LD	FB	Tot
Turnbow D	29	16	47	14	40	.16	.08	80	82	.05	.01	.37	.15	3	-4	-8	-6	-15
Cordero F	33	7	41	17	42	.08	.07	65	84	-.03	.10	.44	.11	-7	2	-4	-6	-15
Sheets B	18	6	37	19	45	.12	.10	73	86	.01	.06	.37	.15	-7	-1	-3	-3	-13
Gallardo Y	22	8	38	24	38	.09	.07	73	90	.01	.05	.42	.08	-4	-1	6	-13	-12
Shouse B	16	8	55	21	24	.23	.00	72	93	.04	.06	.38	-.04	-1	2	1	-11	-9
Villanueva C	20	11	36	17	47	.11	.11	69	89	.05	.08	.38	.15	1	2	-6	-2	-5
Parra M	22	12	33	23	44	.13	.04	67	85	.05	.07	.39	.05	0	1	0	-4	-2
Wise M	18	8	35	16	49	.14	.07	65	82	.02	.10	.47	.15	-2	3	1	-0	1
Spurling C	12	7	51	16	33	.07	.11	68	88	.05	.09	.40	.15	-1	6	-0	-1	4
Capuano C	20	9	43	18	39	.10	.12	66	80	.03	.09	.41	.22	-2	7	0	6	11
Vargas C	18	9	34	22	44	.09	.11	71	86	.04	.07	.43	.16	-1	1	10	2	12
Suppan J	12	9	45	20	35	.07	.08	71	82	.08	.06	.40	.15	2	6	8	-4	12
Bush D	17	7	43	19	38	.10	.13	71	80	.02	.08	.38	.23	-7	9	1	12	15
MLB Average	17	9	43	19	38	.10	.10	74	83	.05	.05	.40	.18	--	--	--	--	--

Fielding Stats

Name	INN	SBA/G	CS%	ERA	WP+PB/G	PO	A	TE	FE
Catcher									
Estrada J	961.0	0.74	8%	4.44	0.384	803	37	4	0
Miller D	446.3	0.71	31%	4.46	0.403	359	28	0	0
Rivera M	37.0	0.73	33%	4.38	0.486	33	2	0	0

Name	Inn	PO	A	TE	FE	FPct	DPS	DPT	RZR	OOZ
First Base										
Fielder P	1338.0	1163	99	4	8	.989	5	0	.668	29
Graffanino T	68.3	64	6	0	0	1.000	2	0	.824	1
Dillon J	28.0	25	2	0	0	1.000	0	0	.500	2
Miller D	6.0	4	0	0	1	.800	0	0	0.000	0
Rottino V	4.0	4	0	0	0	1.000	0	0	.500	0
Second Base										
Weeks R	984.0	232	286	6	7	.976	25	45	.785	35
Graffanino T	240.3	65	69	0	1	.993	6	17	.825	3
Counsell C	195.0	46	61	1	0	.991	5	10	.860	10
Dillon J	25.0	10	6	0	0	1.000	0	1	1.000	1
Shortstop										
Hardy J	1271.0	168	397	4	9	.978	51	32	.807	64
Counsell C	170.7	20	55	1	0	.987	10	5	.767	12
Graffanino T	2.0	0	0	0	0	0.000	0	0	--	--
Third Base										
Braun R	945.3	61	161	16	9	.895	12	0	.564	21
Counsell C	297.7	21	73	0	0	1.000	11	0	.789	15
Graffanino T	194.3	28	43	2	0	.973	3	1	.750	9
Dillon J	7.0	1	2	0	0	1.000	1	0	1.000	0

Name	Inn	PO	A	TE	FE	FPct	DPS	DPT	RZR	OOZ
Left Field										
Jenkins G	973.7	242	7	0	3	.988	4	0	.894	41
Mench K	377.7	55	3	0	0	1.000	2	0	.809	17
Dillon J	43.3	13	0	0	0	1.000	0	0	.929	0
Graffanino T	22.0	7	0	0	0	1.000	0	0	.800	3
Gross G	12.3	0	0	0	0	0.000	0	0	--	--
Stocker M	6.0	3	0	0	0	1.000	0	0	1.000	0
Gwynn T	6.0	1	0	0	0	1.000	0	0	1.000	0
Rottino V	2.0	0	0	0	0	0.000	0	0	--	--
Nix L	1.3	0	0	0	0	0.000	0	0	--	--
Center Field										
Hall B	1022.0	295	5	3	6	.971	0	0	.846	54
Hart C	232.3	71	1	1	1	.973	0	0	.904	5
Gwynn T	153.3	34	0	0	1	.971	0	0	.829	5
Gross G	26.0	9	1	0	0	1.000	2	0	1.000	2
Nix L	10.3	1	0	0	0	1.000	0	0	.500	0
Right Field										
Hart C	864.3	253	3	0	1	.996	0	0	.888	39
Gross G	288.7	70	2	2	0	.973	0	0	.875	14
Mench K	219.7	56	3	0	2	.967	2	0	.868	10
Gwynn T	62.7	14	1	0	0	1.000	0	0	1.000	2
Dillon J	6.0	0	1	0	0	1.000	0	0	0.000	0
Stocker M	3.0	0	0	0	0	0.000	0	0	--	--

Minnesota Twins

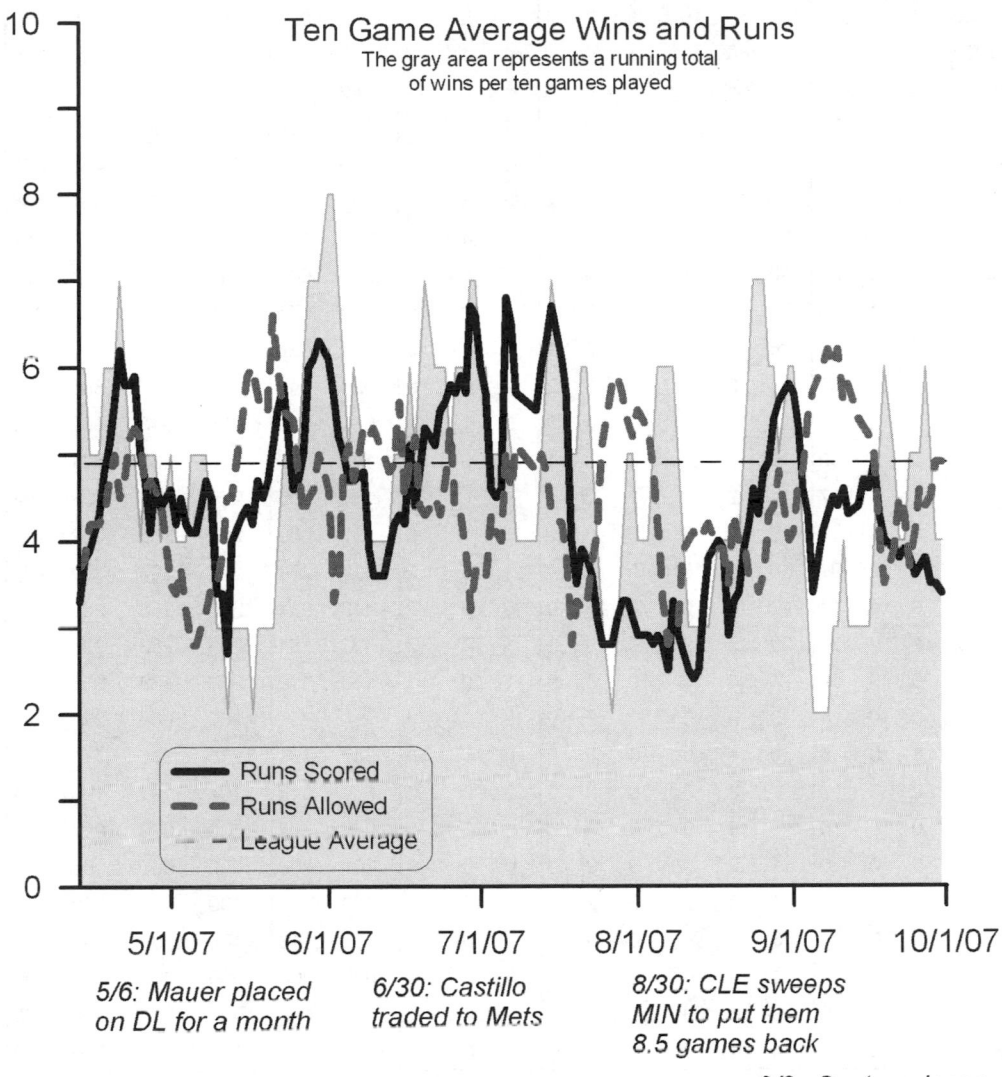

Ten Game Average Wins and Runs
The gray area represents a running total
of wins per ten games played

Runs Scored
Runs Allowed
League Average

5/1/07 6/1/07 7/1/07 8/1/07 9/1/07 10/1/07

*5/6: Mauer placed
on DL for a month*

*6/30: Castillo
traded to Mets*

*8/30: CLE sweeps
MIN to put them
8.5 games back*

*9/3: Santana loses
to CLE for 5th time*

Stat Facts:
- Nick Punto had a GPA of .201
- Punto's SLG was .271
- Joe Mauer threw out 48% of base stealers
- 55% of Mauer's batted balls were grounders, and just 28% were fly balls
- 69% of Luis Castillo's batted balls were grounders
- Carlos Silva walked or struck out just 15% of the batters he faced
- Torii Hunter's LD% of 14% was second-lowest in the league
- Johan Santana was second in the league with 123 PRC
- Santana led the league with 33 home runs allowed
- Santana's GB% of 38% was second-lowest in the league
- Boof Bonser's lefty/righty slit of -.106 was lowest in the league
- Kevin Slowey allowed 16 home runs in 67 innings

Team Batting and Pitching/Fielding Stats by Month						
	April	May	June	July	Aug	Sept/Oct
Wins	14	13	15	13	13	11
Losses	11	14	12	14	16	16
RS/G	4.6	5.0	5.0	4.1	4.0	3.9
RA/G	4.2	4.7	4.5	4.5	4.0	4.9
OBP	.330	.355	.319	.323	.333	.317
SLG	.401	.404	.381	.415	.382	.364
FIP	4.54	4.29	4.21	4.24	4.16	4.17
DER	.698	.697	.697	.705	.698	.646

Batting Stats

Player	BR	Runs	RBI	PA	Outs	H	2B	3B	HR	TB	K	BB	IBB	HBP	SH	SF	SB	CS	GDP	H-A	L^R	BA	OBP	SLG	GPA
Hunter T	105	94	107	650	454	172	45	1	28	303	101	40	10	5	0	5	18	9	17	.018	.029	.287	.334	.505	.279
Morneau J *	98	84	111	668	448	160	31	3	31	290	91	64	11	5	0	9	1	1	17	-.007	.071	.271	.343	.492	.280
Cuddyer M	84	87	81	623	415	151	28	5	16	237	107	64	1	7	0	5	5	0	19	.046	.035	.276	.356	.433	.271
Mauer J *	69	62	60	471	299	119	27	3	7	173	51	57	10	3	2	3	7	1	11	-.094	.059	.293	.382	.426	.281
Kubel J *	67	49	65	466	313	114	31	2	13	188	79	41	2	1	1	5	5	0	9	-.009	.036	.273	.335	.450	.266
Bartlett J	65	75	43	570	386	135	20	7	5	184	73	50	3	8	0	2	23	3	8	-.004	.069	.265	.339	.361	.245
Castillo L +	41	54	18	384	250	106	11	3	0	123	28	29	0	0	5	1	9	4	3	-.008	-.018	.304	.356	.352	.251
Punto N +	38	53	25	536	386	99	18	4	1	128	90	55	1	0	6	3	16	6	7	-.016	-.043	.210	.291	.271	.201
Redmond M	36	23	38	298	201	80	13	0	1	96	23	18	3	5	0	3	0	0	9	.013	.077	.294	.346	.353	.246
Tyner J *	30	42	22	328	232	87	14	2	1	108	26	16	0	5	2	1	8	3	12	-.011	.027	.286	.331	.355	.240
Cirillo J	23	18	21	174	122	40	9	2	2	59	13	15	0	1	3	2	2	0	9	-.025	.048	.261	.327	.386	.246
Ford L	14	13	14	130	94	27	6	0	3	42	24	11	0	3	0	0	3	1	4	.031	.045	.233	.315	.362	.235
White R	13	8	20	119	92	19	4	0	4	35	19	6	0	3	0	1	0	0	2	-.145	-.008	.174	.235	.321	.188
Rodriguez L	11	18	12	173	129	34	5	1	2	47	14	12	0	2	2	2	1	0	8	.067	-.005	.219	.281	.303	.204
Casilla A +	11	15	9	204	153	42	5	1	0	49	29	9	0	0	5	1	11	1	5	-.037	.060	.222	.256	.259	.182
Buscher B *	8	8	10	94	64	20	1	0	2	27	16	10	0	0	1	1	1	0	2	-.028	.074	.244	.323	.329	.230
Heintz C	7	0	7	61	44	14	0	0	0	14	12	3	0	0	2	0	0	0	2	-.118	.037	.250	.288	.250	.194
Jones G *	3	7	5	84	64	16	2	1	2	26	20	6	0	0	0	1	1	1	2	.025	.154	.208	.262	.338	.204
Watkins T	3	2	0	32	19	10	0	0	0	10	4	4	0	0	0	0	1	0	1	.150	.000	.357	.438	.357	.289
Morales J +	2	1	0	3	0	3	1	0	0	4	0	0	0	0	0	0	0	0	0	--	--	1.000	1.000	1.333	.791
Santana J *	1	2	1	8	5	2	1	1	0	5	0	1	0	0	0	0	0	0	0	-.347	.401	.286	.375	.714	.351
Rabe J	0	2	2	31	25	6	0	0	0	6	7	0	0	0	0	0	0	0	0	-.099	.013	.194	.194	.194	.137
Garza M	-0	0	0	3	2	0	0	0	0	0	1	0	0	0	1	0	0	0	0	.000	--	.000	.000	.000	.000
Ortiz R	-0	0	0	3	3	0	0	0	0	0	1	0	0	0	0	0	0	0	0	.000	.000	.000	.000	.000	.000
Bonser B	-0	0	0	5	3	0	0	0	0	0	1	0	0	0	2	0	0	0	0	.000	.000	.000	.000	.000	.000
McDonald D	-0	0	0	11	9	1	0	0	0	1	3	1	0	0	0	0	0	0	0	-.655	-.148	.100	.182	.100	.108
Baker S	-1	0	0	6	6	0	0	0	0	0	1	0	0	0	0	0	0	0	0	.000	.000	.000	.000	.000	.000
Silva C	-1	0	0	6	5	0	0	0	0	0	1	0	0	0	2	0	0	0	1	.000	--	.000	.000	.000	.000
LeCroy M	-1	1	0	20	18	3	1	0	0	4	4	0	0	0	0	0	0	0	1	.072	-.050	.150	.150	.200	.119

Italicized stats have been adjusted for home park.
Batted Ball Batting Stats are listed after Fielding Stats.

Pitching Stats

Player	PRC	IP	BFP	G	GS	K	BB	IBB	HBP	H	HR	DP	DER	SB	CS	PO	W	L	Sv	Op	Hld	H-A	R^L	RA	ERA	FIP
Santana J *	122	219.0	878	33	33	235	52	0	4	183	33	17	.718	6	5	4	15	13	0	0	0	-.003	-.009	3.62	3.33	3.96
Silva C	77	202.0	848	33	33	89	36	2	4	229	20	26	.695	8	7	0	13	14	0	0	0	-.034	-.038	4.41	4.19	4.35
Nathan J	66	71.7	282	68	0	77	19	2	1	54	4	5	.718	7	0	0	4	2	37	41	0	-.030	-.033	1.88	1.88	2.71
Guerrier M	64	88.0	351	73	0	68	21	1	5	71	9	9	.746	6	2	1	2	4	0	4	14	.021	-.070	2.35	2.35	4.02
Baker S	61	143.7	606	24	23	102	29	4	5	162	15	19	.666	11	4	0	9	9	0	0	1	-.009	-.058	4.39	4.26	3.94
Bonser B	59	173.0	772	31	30	136	65	4	5	199	27	14	.668	11	7	1	8	12	0	0	0	-.001	-.106	5.62	5.10	4.98
Neshek P	43	70.3	278	74	0	74	27	5	2	44	7	4	.774	1	2	0	7	2	0	3	15	-.018	-.019	3.20	2.94	3.59
Garza M	34	83.0	367	16	15	67	32	4	4	96	8	14	.645	1	3	1	5	7	0	0	0	.003	-.056	4.77	3.69	4.18
Ortiz R	29	91.0	400	28	10	44	15	1	5	112	12	9	.685	7	2	0	4	4	0	0	0	-.075	-.006	5.34	5.14	4.75
Slowcy K	24	66.7	297	13	11	47	11	0	0	82	16	2	.682	0	0	0	4	1	0	0	0	-.066	.015	5.27	4.73	5.59
Rincon J	20	59.7	272	63	0	49	28	3	3	65	9	6	.689	3	1	0	3	3	0	2	14	-.029	-.077	5.73	5.13	5.11
Perkins G *	16	28.7	115	19	0	20	12	0	2	23	2	7	.734	1	1	0	0	0	0	0	3	.038	.005	3.14	3.14	4.36
Reyes D *	13	29.3	139	50	0	21	21	1	2	34	1	4	.649	1	3	3	2	1	0	0	8	-.025	-.115	4.30	3.99	4.64
Ponson S	9	37.7	181	7	7	23	17	1	3	54	7	4	.626	1	2	0	2	5	0	0	0	.024	.109	7.41	6.93	6.09
Cali C *	8	21.0	101	24	0	14	16	3	2	22	2	2	.701	0	0	0	0	1	0	1	2	-.136	-.050	4.71	4.71	5.43
DePaula J	3	20.0	99	16	0	8	10	1	3	30	5	4	.644	0	0	0	0	1	0	0	1	-.116	.018	9.00	8.55	7.63
Crain J	3	16.3	71	18	0	10	4	0	1	19	4	3	.692	0	1	0	1	2	0	0	6	-.124	.004	8.82	5.51	6.26
Blackburn N	2	11.7	54	6	0	8	2	0	0	19	2	2	.571	0	1	0	0	2	0	1	1	-.261	-.150	9.26	7.71	4.75
Miller J *	0	4.0	22	4	0	2	3	1	0	7	2	0	.667	1	0	0	0	0	0	0	0	-.868	-.163	18.00	18.00	10.38

Italicized stats have been adjusted for home park.

Batted Ball Pitching Stats

	% of PA		% of Batted Balls					Out %		Runs Per Event				Total Runs vs. Avg.				
Player	K%	BB%	GB%	LD%	FB%	IF/F	HR/OF	GB	OF	NIP	GB	LD	OF	NIP	GB	LD	FB	Tot
Santana J	27	6	38	18	44	.10	.14	79	82	-.02	.01	.39	.23	-20	-10	-10	9	-30
Nathan J	27	7	40	21	39	.10	.06	82	88	-.02	-.01	.45	.09	-6	-5	0	-8	-19
Guerrier M	19	7	47	16	36	.10	.11	81	87	.01	.00	.36	.15	-4	-6	-6	-4	-19
Neshek P	27	10	32	16	52	.13	.09	81	84	.02	-.01	.29	.16	-2	-5	-9	-2	-18
Silva C	10	5	48	19	34	.07	.09	77	81	.03	.02	.37	.19	-8	-6	3	3	-8
Perkins G	17	12	39	18	44	.11	.06	71	86	.08	.03	.28	.10	1	-1	-2	-2	-5
Baker T	17	6	35	22	43	.12	.09	70	81	.00	.06	.37	.17	-8	-0	5	2	-2
Reyes D	15	17	64	13	22	.05	.05	70	83	.13	.06	.51	.12	4	2	-0	-3	3
Rincon J	18	11	49	16	36	.10	.15	73	86	.06	.06	.44	.23	2	1	-1	2	4
Garza M	18	10	48	15	38	.09	.09	61	84	.05	.12	.40	.14	0	10	-4	-3	4
Ortiz R	11	5	43	19	37	.08	.11	74	77	.03	.04	.34	.22	-3	-0	0	7	4
Slowey K	16	4	29	21	50	.13	.15	78	78	-.03	.03	.37	.28	-6	-3	2	15	9
Ponson S	13	11	54	18	28	.08	.19	70	69	.10	.06	.38	.40	2	2	1	8	13
Bonser B	18	9	45	17	38	.06	.13	70	85	.04	.07	.43	.22	-1	8	0	10	17
MLB Average	*17*	*9*	*43*	*19*	*38*	*.10*	*.10*	*74*	*83*	*.05*	*.05*	*.40*	*.18*	--	--	--	--	--

Fielding Stats

Name	INN	SBA/G	CS%	ERA	WP+PB/G	PO	A	TE	FE
Catcher									
Mauer J	777.7	0.46	48%	3.78	0.382	598	35	1	0
Redmond M	482.7	0.67	36%	4.38	0.149	385	24	0	0
Heintz C	137.3	0.92	7%	6.03	0.590	106	5	0	0
LeCroy M	35.0	2.06	0%	2.57	0.514	22	0	1	0
Morales J	4.0	0.00	0%	6.75	0.000	5	1	0	0

Name	Inn	PO	A	TE	FE	FPct	DPS	DPT	RZR	OOZ
First Base										
Morneau J	1259.0	1189	102	2	2	.996	9	1	.767	18
Cirillo J	70.0	65	4	1	2	.958	0	0	.667	0
Jones G	63.0	57	4	0	0	1.000	0	0	.571	0
Cuddyer M	39.0	30	4	0	0	1.000	0	0	.800	1
Rodriguez L	3.3	3	1	0	0	1.000	0	0	1.000	0
LeCroy M	2.0	3	0	0	0	1.000	0	0	--	--
Second Base										
Castillo L	726.3	154	220	1	2	.992	21	26	.801	27
Casilla A	421.0	80	147	2	8	.958	16	23	.784	13
Punto N	172.3	46	63	2	1	.973	8	5	.800	5
Rodriguez L	117.0	24	38	0	1	.984	1	8	.857	2
Shortstop										
Bartlett J	1194.0	205	415	11	15	.960	48	43	.804	67
Punto N	210.7	44	70	2	1	.974	9	8	.817	12
Casilla A	30.0	4	8	0	0	1.000	1	1	.889	0
Watkins T	2.0	1	0	0	0	1.000	0	0	1.000	0

Name	Inn	PO	A	TE	FE	FPct	DPS	DPT	RZR	OOZ
Third Base										
Punto N	828.3	83	171	4	2	.973	11	0	.708	29
Rodriguez L	232.0	25	43	1	2	.958	6	0	.653	10
Buscher B	201.3	17	31	1	3	.923	6	0	.512	10
Cirillo J	106.0	6	29	0	0	1.000	3	0	.826	9
Watkins T	69.0	4	15	0	0	1.000	0	0	.800	2
Left Field										
Kubel J	700.3	159	2	2	0	.988	4	0	.873	21
Tyner J	311.0	89	3	0	0	1.000	0	0	.901	16
Ford L	233.3	46	1	1	0	.979	2	0	.927	8
White R	125.0	24	0	0	0	1.000	0	0	.957	2
Rabe J	48.0	12	1	0	0	1.000	0	0	1.000	3
Jones G	19.0	4	0	0	1	.800	0	0	1.000	1
Center Field										
Hunter T	1314.0	387	5	1	1	.995	0	0	.891	47
Tyner J	85.0	19	0	0	0	1.000	0	0	.810	2
Ford L	37.0	7	0	0	0	1.000	0	0	.714	2
Right Field										
Cuddyer M	1224.0	256	19	2	2	.986	3	0	.823	38
Tyner J	144.3	37	0	0	1	.974	0	0	.806	8
McDonald D	25.0	2	1	0	0	1.000	2	0	.500	1
Ford L	23.0	6	0	0	0	1.000	0	0	.800	2
Rabe J	12.0	2	0	0	0	1.000	0	0	.500	0
Jones G	8.0	3	0	0	0	1.000	0	0	1.000	2

Batted Ball Batting Stats

	% of PA		% of Batted Balls					Out %		Runs Per Event				Total Runs vs. Avg.				
Player	K%	BB%	GB%	LD%	FB%	IF/F	HR/OF	GB	OF	NIP	GB	LD	OF	NIP	GB	LD	FB	Tot
Morneau J	14	10	45	16	39	.11	.17	78	82	.08	.02	.38	.28	5	-5	-5	20	15
Hunter T	16	7	49	14	37	.09	.15	74	83	.03	.04	.50	.26	-5	2	-0	15	12
Mauer J	11	13	55	18	28	.01	.07	73	82	.13	.05	.40	.16	9	4	2	-3	11
Cuddyer M	17	11	45	19	36	.15	.11	69	84	.07	.07	.39	.19	4	6	1	-1	10
Kubel J	17	9	43	22	35	.02	.11	78	79	.05	.02	.36	.22	-1	-4	3	6	4
Castillo L	7	8	69	14	16	.04	.00	72	84	.12	.07	.39	.03	2	12	-2	-14	-2
Ford L	18	11	47	16	37	.09	.06	81	83	.06	-.01	.55	.11	0	-2	1	-2	-3
Cirillo J	7	9	49	19	32	.09	.05	80	90	.14	-.00	.46	.04	2	-3	3	-5	-4
Redmond M	7	8	44	21	35	.08	.01	72	86	.12	.05	.39	.02	2	1	5	-11	-4
Bartlett J	13	10	44	20	36	.11	.04	74	84	.09	.05	.36	.09	4	1	1	-12	-6
White R	16	8	51	12	37	.09	.13	85	96	.04	-.02	.46	.13	-1	-3	-2	-2	-8
Tyner J	8	6	60	18	22	.12	.02	77	83	.09	.02	.37	.08	-0	1	-0	-11	-10
Rodriguez L	8	8	54	13	34	.10	.05	75	88	.12	.03	.26	.06	1	-1	-5	-6	-11
Casilla A	14	4	62	16	22	.22	.00	80	84	-.00	.01	.34	.02	-3	-2	-4	-10	-20
Punto N	17	10	51	15	35	.08	.01	77	86	.06	.03	.31	.03	1	1	-14	-22	-34
MLB Average	17	9	43	19	38	.10	.10	74	83	.05	.05	.40	.18	--	--	--	--	--

New York Mets

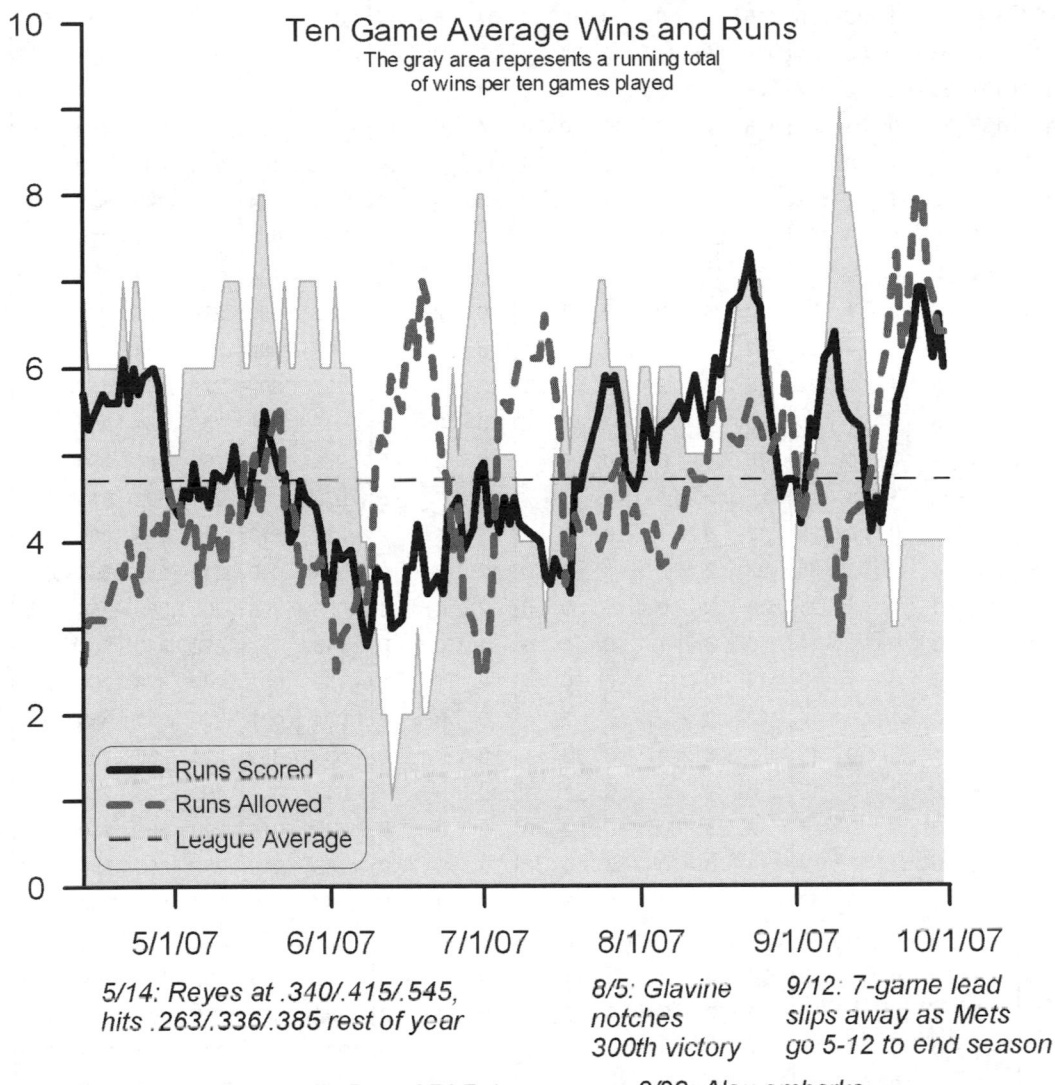

Ten Game Average Wins and Runs
The gray area represents a running total
of wins per ten games played

- Runs Scored
- Runs Allowed
- League Average

5/14: Reyes at .340/.415/.545,
hits .263/.336/.385 rest of year

6/2: Beat ARI 7-1
to go 16 games
over .500

8/5: Glavine
notches
300th victory

8/23: Alou embarks
on 30-game hitting streak

9/12: 7-game lead
slips away as Mets
go 5-12 to end season

9/3: Pedro returns,
gets 3000th career
strikeout

Stat Facts:
- Tom Glavine allowed just 5 stolen bases in 13 attempts
- Glavine struck out just 10% of the batters he faced
- Aaron Sele induced 13 double plays in 54 innings
- Orlando Hernandez allowed just 12% line drives, and 51% fly balls
- Oliver Perez allowed 50% fly balls, and just 33% ground balls
- Carlos Beltran had an RZR of .915
- David Wright had an LD% of 23%
- Just 4% of Wright's fly balls were infield pop-ups
- Wright led the league with 131 Base Runs
- Moises Alou struck out in just 8% of his plate appearances
- 54% of Shawn Green's batted balls were ground balls
- Jose Reyes was second in the league with 517 outs

Team Batting and Pitching/Fielding Stats by Month						
	April	May	June	July	Aug	Sept/Oct
Wins	15	19	12	13	15	14
Losses	9	9	15	14	13	14
RS/G	5.5	4.5	3.9	4.4	5.9	5.6
RA/G	3.5	4.0	4.4	4.9	5.1	5.7
OBP	.361	.341	.308	.325	.366	.351
SLG	.448	.411	.409	.413	.447	.463
FIP	4.29	4.54	4.18	4.48	4.45	4.06
DER	.726	.754	.711	.705	.660	.666

Batting Stats

Player	BR	Runs	RBI	PA	Outs	H	2B	3B	HR	TB	K	BB	IBB	HBP	SH	SF	SB	CS	GDP	H-A	L^R	BA	OBP	SLG	GPA
Wright D	131	113	107	711	427	196	42	1	30	330	115	94	6	6	0	7	34	5	14	.034	.059	.325	.416	.546	.331
Beltran C +	104	93	112	636	411	153	33	3	33	291	111	69	10	2	1	10	23	2	8	-.026	.030	.276	.353	.525	.296
Reyes J +	104	119	57	765	517	191	36	12	12	287	78	77	13	1	5	1	78	21	6	.006	.012	.280	.354	.421	.270
Delgado C *	74	71	87	607	411	139	30	0	24	241	118	52	8	11	0	6	4	0	12	-.055	.033	.258	.333	.448	.267
Green S *	61	62	46	491	331	130	30	1	10	192	62	37	4	5	1	1	11	1	14	.012	.102	.291	.352	.430	.271
Alou M	51	51	49	360	229	112	19	1	13	172	30	27	5	2	0	3	3	0	13	-.075	.064	.341	.392	.524	.314
Lo Duca P	47	46	54	488	342	121	18	1	9	168	33	24	4	6	3	10	2	0	18	-.080	.084	.272	.311	.378	.239
Easley D	35	24	26	218	142	54	6	0	10	90	35	19	1	5	0	1	0	1	2	-.037	.134	.280	.358	.466	.283
Castillo L +	30	37	20	231	144	59	8	2	1	74	17	24	0	0	7	1	10	2	2	.072	.067	.296	.371	.372	.265
Gotay R +	29	25	24	211	139	56	12	0	4	80	42	16	1	1	3	1	3	3	2	-.001	-.098	.295	.351	.421	.269
Milledge L	28	27	29	206	141	50	9	1	7	82	42	13	2	7	1	1	3	2	5	.127	.082	.272	.341	.446	.270
Castro R	25	24	31	157	104	41	6	0	11	80	39	10	0	1	0	2	0	0	1	-.018	.006	.285	.331	.556	.294
Chavez E *	20	20	17	165	114	43	7	2	1	57	16	9	0	0	5	1	5	2	5	.059	.006	.287	.325	.380	.246
Valentin J +	17	18	18	183	132	40	11	1	3	62	28	15	4	0	1	1	2	1	5	.072	.015	.241	.302	.373	.234
Anderson M *	16	14	25	77	50	22	7	0	3	38	12	5	1	0	1	2	3	1	2	-.018	.210	.319	.355	.551	.304
Gomez C	12	14	12	139	99	29	3	0	2	38	27	8	2	3	0	3	12	3	0	.034	.000	.232	.288	.304	.210
Newhan D *	8	9	6	83	60	15	1	1	1	21	19	8	0	1	0	0	2	0	1	.005	.206	.203	.289	.284	.205
Ledee R *	7	6	6	43	28	8	3	0	1	14	10	5	1	0	1	1	1	0	0	.218	--	.222	.310	.389	.241
Franco J	7	7	8	61	42	10	0	0	1	13	13	10	0	0	0	1	2	1	1	-.159	.092	.200	.328	.260	.217
DiFelice M	6	1	5	47	32	10	2	0	1	14	12	2	0	2	2	1	0	0	2	-.084	-.027	.250	.311	.350	.232
Glavine T *	4	3	4	75	44	12	1	0	0	13	5	6	0	0	12	1	0	0	0	-.039	-.051	.214	.286	.232	.190
Conine J	4	2	5	50	34	8	2	0	0	10	8	7	2	0	1	1	0	0	1	-.047	.034	.195	.306	.244	.203
Sosa J	3	0	1	30	20	5	2	0	0	7	9	3	0	0	2	0	0	0	0	-.131	-.014	.200	.286	.280	.203
Lawrence B	2	1	3	12	9	3	0	0	0	3	4	0	0	0	0	0	0	0	0	-.233	-.210	.250	.250	.250	.179
Hernandez O	2	1	3	54	40	8	2	0	0	10	18	0	0	0	6	0	2	0	0	-.067	-.149	.167	.167	.208	.130
Ambres C	1	0	1	3	2	1	0	0	0	1	1	0	0	0	0	0	0	0	0	--	--	.333	.333	.333	.238
Maine J	1	4	3	76	49	6	0	0	1	9	28	5	0	1	14	1	0	0	0	.118	.046	.109	.194	.164	.131
Johnson B	0	2	1	30	22	5	1	0	0	6	11	2	0	0	0	1	0	0	0	.002	-.020	.185	.233	.222	.164
Hernandez A	-0	1	0	3	2	1	0	0	0	1	1	0	0	0	0	0	0	0	0	.233	-.350	.333	.333	.333	.238
Sele A	-0	0	0	6	4	0	0	0	0	0	1	1	0	0	1	0	0	0	0	-.113	-.113	.000	.200	.000	.092
Williams D *	-0	0	0	1	1	0	0	0	0	0	1	0	0	0	0	0	0	0	0	.000	--	.000	.000	.000	.000
Park C	-0	0	0	1	1	0	0	0	0	0	1	0	0	0	0	0	0	0	0	--	--	.000	.000	.000	.000
Mota G	-0	0	0	1	1	0	0	0	0	0	0	0	0	0	0	0	0	0	0	.000	--	.000	.000	.000	.000
Smith J	-0	0	0	1	1	0	0	0	0	0	1	0	0	0	0	0	0	0	0	.000	--	.000	.000	.000	.000
Humber P	-0	0	0	2	1	0	0	0	0	0	0	0	0	0	1	0	0	0	0	.000	.000	.000	.000	.000	.000
Vargas J *	-0	0	0	3	2	0	0	0	0	0	0	0	0	0	1	0	0	0	0	.000	--	.000	.000	.000	.000
Martinez P	-0	1	0	11	8	1	1	0	0	2	6	0	0	0	2	0	0	0	0	.158	-.119	.111	.111	.222	.108
Perez O *	-1	6	1	62	48	9	0	0	0	9	15	0	0	0	6	0	0	1	0	.109	.001	.161	.161	.161	.115
Pelfrey M	-1	1	0	22	19	2	1	0	0	3	9	1	0	0	0	0	0	0	0	.050	.087	.095	.136	.143	.099
Alomar Jr. S	-1	1	0	22	19	3	1	0	0	4	3	0	0	0	0	0	0	0	0	-.107	.043	.136	.136	.182	.109

Italicized stats have been adjusted for home park.
Batted Ball Batting Stats are listed after Fielding Stats.

Pitching Stats

Player	PRC	IP	BFP	G	GS	K	BB	IBB	HBP	H	HR	DP	DER	SB	CS	PO	W	L	Sv	Op	Hld	H-A	R^L	RA	ERA	FIP
Maine J	85	191.0	810	32	32	180	75	3	5	168	23	7	.721	12	5	1	15	10	0	0	0	-.024	-.037	4.24	3.91	4.16
Perez O *	74	177.0	765	29	29	174	79	1	7	153	22	11	.706	13	3	3	15	10	0	0	0	.003	-.030	4.58	3.56	4.36
Glavine T *	70	200.3	855	34	34	89	64	2	4	219	23	23	.704	5	8	2	13	8	0	0	0	-.023	.036	4.58	4.45	4.86
Hernandez O	69	147.7	608	27	24	128	64	4	5	109	23	10	.771	14	6	1	9	5	0	0	0	-.028	-.064	3.90	3.72	4.88
Wagner B *	44	68.3	282	66	0	80	22	4	2	55	6	6	.703	6	0	0	2	2	34	39	0	-.056	.040	2.90	2.63	2.95
Sosa J	42	112.7	481	42	14	69	41	2	0	109	10	10	.712	4	2	0	9	8	0	2	9	.019	-.127	4.63	4.47	4.24
Heilman A	40	86.0	352	81	0	63	20	1	5	72	8	4	.734	8	2	0	7	7	1	6	22	-.061	-.050	3.77	3.03	3.85
Feliciano P	33	64.0	275	78	0	61	31	4	5	47	3	8	.709	3	0	0	2	2	2	3	18	-.012	-.064	3.66	3.09	3.47
Smith J	23	44.3	205	54	0	45	21	4	7	48	3	5	.636	5	1	0	3	2	0	0	10	-.020	-.044	3.65	3.45	3.74
Pelfrey M	21	72.7	342	15	13	45	39	1	9	85	6	8	.671	8	0	1	3	8	0	0	0	.053	-.062	5.82	5.57	5.04
Schoeneweis	19	59.0	265	70	0	41	28	5	3	62	8	7	.697	6	1	1	0	2	2	3	11	.056	-.118	5.49	5.03	4.96
Mota G	18	59.3	261	52	0	47	18	2	2	63	8	2	.699	9	0	0	2	2	0	3	6	-.021	.048	5.92	5.76	4.35
Sele A	15	53.7	250	34	0	29	21	2	2	78	5	13	.611	0	0	0	3	2	0	0	1	.053	-.093	5.70	5.37	4.57
Martinez P	15	28.0	128	5	5	32	7	1	2	33	0	1	.621	3	0	0	3	1	0	0	0	-.071	-.024	3.54	2.57	1.84
Burgos A	11	23.7	98	17	0	19	9	0	2	17	3	2	.769	1	0	0	1	0	0	0	1	.004	-.110	3.00	3.42	4.71
Lawrence B	7	29.0	139	6	6	18	13	1	1	43	4	4	.612	5	1	0	1	2	0	0	0	-.053	-.072	6.83	6.83	5.17
Humber P	1	7.0	32	3	1	2	2	0	0	9	1	0	.704	0	0	0	0	0	0	0	0	.010	-.164	7.71	7.71	5.41
Vargas J *	1	10.3	51	2	2	4	2	1	0	17	4	0	.659	2	0	0	0	1	0	0	0	-.253	-.217	12.19	12.19	7.82
Muniz C	1	2.3	10	2	0	2	2	0	0	1	0	0	.833	1	0	0	0	0	0	0	0	--	.210	7.71	7.71	4.13
Park C	0	4.0	20	1	1	4	2	0	0	6	2	0	.667	0	0	0	0	1	0	0	0	--	-.050	15.75	15.75	9.27
Williams D *	0	4.3	29	2	1	2	5	1	0	12	2	1	.500	0	0	0	0	1	0	0	0	.035	.010	22.85	22.85	11.12
Adkins J	0	1.0	3	1	0	0	0	0	0	0	0	0	1.000	0	0	0	0	0	0	0	0	--	.000	0.00	0.00	3.27
Urdaneta L	0	1.0	5	2	0	0	0	0	0	2	1	0	.750	0	0	0	0	0	0	0	0	--	.538	9.00	9.00	16.27
Collazo W *	0	5.7	27	6	0	0	5	1	0	7	0	2	.682	0	0	0	0	0	0	0	0	-.095	-.216	6.35	6.35	5.39

Italicized stats have been adjusted for home park.

Batted Ball Pitching Stats

Player	% of PA		% of Batted Balls					Out %		Runs Per Event				Total Runs vs. Avg.				
	K%	BB%	GB%	LD%	FB%	IF/F	HR/OF	GB	OF	NIP	GB	LD	OF	NIP	GB	LD	FB	Tot
Maine J	22	10	37	18	45	.13	.11	76	85	.03	.05	.38	.17	-4	-3	-9	-3	-18
Hernandez O	21	11	38	12	51	.15	.13	78	84	.05	.02	.38	.20	1	-7	-17	5	-18
Wagner B	28	9	37	18	45	.13	.09	69	90	-.01	.07	.41	.11	-5	-1	-3	-6	-15
Heilman A	18	7	45	21	34	.09	.10	81	85	.02	.01	.34	.16	-4	-5	-3	-4	-15
Perez O	23	11	33	17	50	.13	.09	65	89	.04	.11	.41	.12	-0	7	-8	-11	-11
Feliciano P	22	13	56	17	27	.11	.07	76	90	.06	.02	.48	.09	2	-2	-0	-9	-9
Sosa J	14	9	38	19	43	.08	.07	76	86	.06	.03	.42	.11	-0	-3	2	-6	-7
Martinez P	25	7	31	24	44	.11	.00	67	76	-.01	.09	.45	.09	-2	0	3	-3	-2
Mota G	18	8	44	18	38	.10	.12	79	82	.02	.03	.43	.20	-2	-2	1	1	-2
Smith J	22	14	62	17	21	0.00	.07	75	64	.06	.03	.53	.26	2	-0	1	-1	2
Glavine T	10	8	42	21	37	.06	.09	81	82	.09	-.00	.40	.16	2	-13	14	1	3
Schoeneweis S	15	12	51	19	30	.05	.13	80	85	.08	.01	.50	.20	3	-3	4	-0	3
Pelfrey M	13	14	48	23	28	.12	.10	73	91	.12	.06	.41	.11	7	2	6	-7	8
Lawrence B	13	10	41	19	41	.14	.11	58	79	.09	.15	.35	.21	1	5	1	2	8
Sele A	12	9	44	23	32	.05	.05	67	73	.09	.09	.45	.19	2	4	8	2	16
MLB Average	17	9	43	19	38	.10	.10	74	83	.05	.05	.40	.18	--	--	--	--	--

Fielding Stats

Name	INN	SBA/G	CS%	ERA	WP+PB/G	PO	A	TE	FE
Catcher									
Lo Duca P	974.0	0.82	19%	4.13	0.240	754	34	9	0
Castro R	330.7	0.79	7%	4.27	0.272	303	12	4	0
DiFelice M	106.7	0.59	14%	4.98	0.338	83	7	0	2
Alomar Jr. S	41.0	0.66	0%	5.71	0.220	29	5	0	0

Name	Inn	PO	A	TE	FE	FPct	DPS	DPT	RZR	OOZ
First Base										
Delgado C	1219.0	1133	74	1	7	.993	14	3	.706	25
Green S	95.0	81	5	0	1	.989	0	0	.818	0
Conine J	77.0	79	2	0	2	.976	0	0	.500	1
Franco J	40.0	22	3	0	0	1.000	0	0	1.000	0
Easley D	14.0	20	0	0	0	1.000	0	0	.667	0
Anderson M	7.0	7	0	0	0	1.000	0	0	1.000	0
Second Base										
Castillo L	432.0	99	95	1	1	.990	11	15	.798	11
Valentin J	380.3	102	116	1	4	.978	11	12	.837	13
Easley D	334.7	79	114	2	2	.980	5	18	.870	7
Gotay R	296.3	72	71	2	1	.979	8	5	.773	6
Newhan D	9.0	1	1	1	0	.667	0	0	.500	0
Shortstop										
Reyes J	1431.0	203	445	8	4	.982	47	36	.871	58
Gotay R	20.0	4	5	0	0	1.000	0	1	1.000	1
Hernandez A	1.0	0	0	0	0	0.000	0	0	--	--
Third Base										
Wright D	1418.0	107	324	11	10	.954	22	1	.689	88
Franco J	18.0	1	4	0	0	1.000	0	0	.333	3
Gotay R	11.0	0	5	0	0	1.000	0	0	.833	0
Easley D	4.0	0	2	0	1	.667	0	0	.667	0
Newhan D	1.0	0	0	0	0	0.000	0	0	--	--

Name	Inn	PO	A	TE	FE	FPct	DPS	DPT	RZR	OOZ
Left Field										
Alou M	703.0	138	7	0	4	.973	0	0	.895	19
Chavez E	195.0	46	1	0	0	1.000	0	0	.829	12
Gomez C	179.3	46	2	0	1	.980	2	0	.974	8
Ledee R	89.0	22	0	0	0	1.000	0	0	.950	3
Milledge L	77.0	20	0	0	0	1.000	0	0	.895	3
Newhan D	67.7	20	0	0	0	1.000	0	0	.882	5
Anderson M	60.3	16	0	0	0	1.000	0	0	.933	2
Johnson B	45.0	12	0	0	0	1.000	0	0	.909	2
Easley D	26.0	4	0	0	0	1.000	0	0	.800	0
Conine J	10.0	0	0	0	0	0.000	0	0	--	--
Center Field										
Beltran C	1240.0	389	6	2	3	.988	4	0	.915	64
Milledge L	120.0	41	2	0	1	.977	0	0	.881	4
Chavez E	58.0	24	0	0	0	1.000	0	0	.955	3
Anderson M	22.0	6	0	0	0	1.000	0	0	.667	2
Gomez C	12.0	4	0	0	0	1.000	0	0	1.000	2
Right Field										
Green S	919.7	203	2	0	3	.986	0	0	.894	26
Milledge L	221.0	51	0	0	1	.981	0	0	.896	8
Gomez C	133.7	35	1	0	1	.947	0	0	.893	10
Chavez E	100.0	31	0	0	0	1.000	0	0	.962	6
Easley D	43.0	9	0	0	0	1.000	0	0	.818	0
Johnson B	23.0	7	0	0	0	1.000	0	0	1.000	1
Anderson M	8.0	2	2	0	0	1.000	0	0	1.000	0
Conine J	2.0	1	0	0	0	1.000	0	0	1.000	0
Ambres C	2.0	0	0	0	0	0.000	0	0	--	--

Batted Ball Batting Stats

Player	% of PA		% of Batted Balls					Out %		Runs Per Event				Total Runs vs. Avg.				
	K%	BB%	GB%	LD%	FB%	IF/F	HR/OF	GB	OF	NIP	GB	LD	OF	NIP	GB	LD	FB	Tot
Wright D	16	14	39	23	38	.04	.16	71	78	.10	.06	.41	.28	13	2	14	24	53
Beltran C	17	11	38	19	43	.13	.19	75	90	.07	.05	.44	.26	4	-1	5	16	24
Alou M	8	8	42	20	38	.05	.10	66	86	.11	.09	.41	.16	2	6	7	3	18
Reyes J	10	10	42	18	40	.14	.05	71	88	.12	.08	.47	.08	8	11	11	-19	11
Green S	13	9	54	18	28	.08	.10	76	80	.07	.03	.44	.20	1	-1	6	-1	6
Easley D	16	11	40	16	44	.13	.17	67	88	.07	.09	.33	.22	2	3	-3	4	5
Castro R	25	7	36	18	46	.10	.23	69	91	-.01	.08	.47	.31	-3	1	0	6	5
Castillo L	7	10	62	16	22	.11	.00	73	76	.16	.06	.48	.08	4	6	2	-6	5
Milledge L	20	10	47	24	29	.17	.18	70	89	.04	.07	.40	.24	-0	1	3	-1	3
Delgado C	19	10	39	18	43	.11	.14	76	87	.05	.03	.42	.20	0	-2	-1	6	2
Gotay R	20	8	46	24	29	.12	.11	71	82	.02	.08	.38	.19	-2	2	3	-2	1
Valentin J	15	8	32	23	45	.16	.06	77	86	.05	.02	.39	.10	-1	-2	2	-4	-4
Chavez E	10	5	60	17	23	.07	.04	77	78	.05	.03	.37	.15	-1	1	-1	-3	-5
Gomez C	19	8	45	16	39	.18	.07	70	92	.02	.10	.28	.05	-1	4	-4	-5	-6
Lo Duca P	7	6	48	23	29	.04	.07	84	83	.11	-.02	.33	.13	0	-12	5	-7	-13
MLB Average	17	9	43	19	38	.10	.10	74	83	.05	.05	.40	.18	--	--	--	--	--

New York Yankees

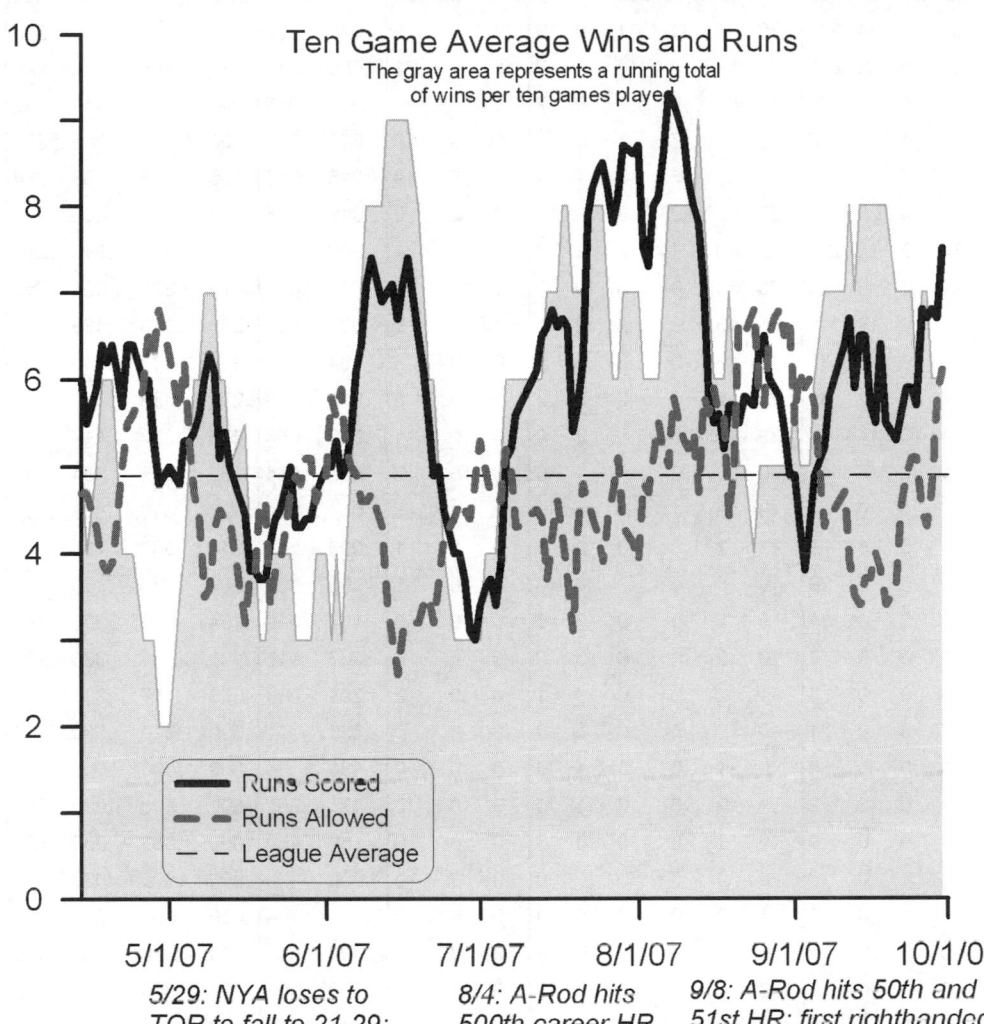

Ten Game Average Wins and Runs
The gray area represents a running total of wins per ten games played

Legend:
- —— Runs Scored
- – – Runs Allowed
- – – League Average

5/1/07 6/1/07 7/1/07 8/1/07 9/1/07 10/1/07

5/29: NYA loses to TOR to fall to 21-29; low point of year

8/4: A-Rod hits 500th career HR

9/8: A-Rod hits 50th and 51st HR; first righthanded Yankee to reach 50

9/19: NYA beats BAL 2-1 and are 1.5 games behind BOS; closest to first all year

9/26: Yankees clinch the AL wild card

Stat Facts:
- Alex Rodriguez led the league with 161 Base Runs and a .355 GPA
- 29% of Rodriguez's outfield flies were home runs
- Rodriguez was second in the league with 21 HBPs
- Jorge Posada was third in the league in OBP, with .426
- Chien-Ming Wang and Andy Pettite each induced 34 double plays
- 59% of the batted balls off Wang were grounders
- Pettite picked off 5 runners, tying for the league lead
- Mike Mussina's ERA of 5.15 was much worse than his FIP of 4.11
- Joba Chamberlain struck out 38% of the batters he faced
- Derek Jeter had an RZR of just .777
- 56% of Jeter's batted balls were grounders, and just 24% were fly balls
- Only 30% of Jason Giambi's batted balls were grounders

Team Batting and Pitching/Fielding Stats by Month						
	April	May	June	July	Aug	Sept/Oct
Wins	9	13	15	20	18	19
Losses	14	15	11	9	11	8
RS/G	5.7	4.9	5.3	7.2	6.1	6.6
RA/G	5.4	4.3	4.2	4.5	5.8	4.7
OBP	.347	.351	.363	.389	.362	.378
SLG	.421	.431	.443	.524	.487	.463
FIP	5.18	4.70	4.31	3.85	4.33	4.21
DER	.703	.720	.697	.670	.665	.687

Batting Stats

Player	BR	Runs	RBI	PA	Outs	H	2B	3B	HR	TB	K	BB	IBB	HBP	SH	SF	SB	CS	GDP	H-A	L^R	BA	OBP	SLG	GPA
Rodriguez A	161	143	156	708	419	183	31	0	54	376	120	95	11	21	0	9	24	4	15	-.024	-.032	.314	.422	.645	.355
Jeter D	109	102	73	714	462	206	39	4	12	289	100	56	3	14	3	2	15	8	21	.008	.017	.322	.388	.452	.291
Abreu B *	102	123	101	699	453	171	40	5	16	269	115	84	0	3	0	7	25	8	11	.061	.055	.283	.369	.445	.280
Posada J +	97	91	90	589	353	171	42	1	20	275	98	74	7	6	0	3	2	0	18	-.022	-.014	.338	.426	.543	.331
Cano R *	93	93	97	669	452	189	41	7	19	301	85	39	5	8	1	4	4	5	19	.016	-.015	.306	.353	.488	.284
Matsui H *	91	100	103	634	402	156	28	4	25	267	73	73	2	3	0	10	4	2	9	.019	.015	.285	.367	.488	.290
Damon J *	84	93	63	605	396	144	27	2	12	211	79	66	1	2	1	3	27	3	4	.006	.014	.270	.351	.396	.260
Cabrera M +	69	66	73	612	415	149	24	8	8	213	68	43	0	5	10	9	13	5	14	-.011	-.029	.273	.327	.391	.247
Giambi J *	42	31	39	303	195	60	8	0	14	110	66	40	2	8	0	1	1	0	1	-.006	.019	.236	.356	.433	.271
Mientkiewicz	25	26	24	192	123	46	12	0	5	73	23	16	0	3	6	1	0	0	3	.134	.054	.277	.349	.440	.270
Phillips A	22	27	25	207	139	54	7	1	2	69	26	12	0	2	6	2	0	3	5	.073	-.026	.292	.338	.373	.248
Betemit W +	16	11	24	92	66	19	4	0	4	35	33	6	0	0	2	0	0	0	1	.079	-.053	.226	.278	.417	.231
Duncan S	14	16	17	83	57	19	1	0	7	41	20	8	0	0	1	0	0	0	2	.105	.064	.257	.329	.554	.290
Cairo M	12	12	10	121	84	27	7	0	0	34	19	8	1	1	4	1	8	1	3	.044	-.021	.252	.308	.318	.220
Molina J	11	9	9	71	46	21	5	0	1	29	13	2	0	0	2	1	0	0	1	.003	.184	.318	.333	.439	.262
Phelps J	8	8	12	88	64	21	2	0	2	29	19	6	0	2	0	0	0	0	5	.006	-.062	.263	.330	.363	.241
Nieves W	4	6	8	66	54	10	4	0	0	14	9	2	0	3	0	0	0	0	3	.137	.018	.164	.190	.230	.145
Thompson K	2	2	2	23	17	4	3	0	0	7	10	2	0	0	0	0	0	0	0	-.167	.017	.190	.261	.333	.203
Sardinha B *	2	6	2	12	8	3	0	0	0	3	1	2	0	0	0	1	0	0	2	-.298	-.099	.333	.417	.333	.274
Clemens R	0	0	0	2	1	1	0	0	0	1	0	0	0	0	0	0	0	0	0	-.350	--	.500	.500	.500	.354
Igawa K *	0	0	0	2	0	0	0	0	0	0	0	1	0	0	1	0	0	0	0	-.450	--	.000	1.000	.000	.455
Clippard T	0	0	0	3	1	1	1	0	0	2	1	0	0	0	1	0	0	0	0	-.475	.950	.500	.500	1.000	.480
Mussina M *	0	0	0	3	2	0	0	0	0	0	0	1	0	0	0	0	0	0	0	-.150	-.450	.000	.333	.000	.152
Myers M *	-0	0	0	1	1	0	0	0	0	0	0	0	0	0	0	0	0	0	0	.000	--	.000	.000	.000	.000
Henn S	-0	0	0	1	1	0	0	0	0	0	1	0	0	0	0	0	0	0	0	.000	--	.000	.000	.000	.000
Basak C	-0	0	0	1	1	0	0	0	0	0	0	0	0	0	0	0	0	0	0	.000	--	.000	.000	.000	.000
Vizcaino L	-0	0	0	2	2	0	0	0	0	0	2	0	0	0	0	0	0	0	0	.000	.000	.000	.000	.000	.000
Proctor S	-0	0	0	3	3	0	0	0	0	0	3	0	0	0	0	0	0	0	0	.000	--	.000	.000	.000	.000
Wang C	-0	0	0	3	3	0	0	0	0	0	3	0	0	0	0	0	0	0	0	.000	--	.000	.000	.000	.000
Pettitte A *	-0	0	0	4	4	0	0	0	0	0	3	0	0	0	0	0	0	0	0	.000	--	.000	.000	.000	.000
Gonzalez A	-2	3	1	15	15	1	0	0	0	1	1	1	0	0	0	0	0	1	1	-.084	.196	.071	.133	.071	.079

Italicized stats have been adjusted for home park.
Batted Ball Batting Stats are listed after Fielding Stats.

Pitching Stats

Player	PRC	IP	BFP	G	GS	K	BB	IBB	HBP	H	HR	DP	DER	SB	CS	PO	W	L	Sv	Op	Hld	H-A	R^L	RA	ERA	FIP
Wang C	91	199.3	823	30	30	104	59	1	8	199	9	34	.698	14	7	0	19	7	0	0	0	-.041	-.046	3.79	3.70	3.92
Pettitte A *	90	215.3	916	36	34	141	69	1	1	238	16	34	.665	18	8	5	15	9	0	0	1	.011	.032	4.43	4.05	4.00
Mussina M	51	152.0	656	28	27	91	35	2	4	188	14	21	.656	24	3	0	11	10	0	0	0	-.049	.006	5.33	5.15	4.11
Rivera M	44	71.3	295	67	0	74	12	2	6	68	4	7	.663	2	1	0	3	4	30	34	0	-.013	.021	3.15	3.15	2.71
Chamberlain	43	24.0	91	19	0	34	6	0	1	12	1	1	.755	1	0	0	2	0	1	1	8	-.078	.022	0.75	0.38	1.96
Clemens R	39	99.0	420	18	17	68	31	0	5	99	9	11	.704	15	4	0	6	6	0	0	0	.008	.012	4.73	4.18	4.28
Vizcaino L	33	75.3	334	77	0	62	43	11	2	66	6	4	.715	5	2	0	8	2	0	3	14	.039	-.040	4.42	4.30	4.12
Hughes P	29	72.7	306	13	13	58	29	0	2	64	8	8	.708	9	3	0	5	3	0	0	0	.094	-.089	4.83	4.46	4.50
Proctor S	23	54.3	245	52	0	37	29	3	3	53	8	3	.714	4	3	0	2	5	0	4	11	.003	-.033	4.47	3.81	5.53
Farnsworth K	22	60.0	266	64	0	48	27	2	2	60	9	3	.711	9	2	0	2	1	0	3	15	-.009	-.053	5.25	4.80	5.08
Myers M *	22	40.7	175	55	0	21	16	0	2	38	3	5	.707	4	2	1	3	0	0	2	4	-.093	.082	3.10	2.66	4.63
Igawa K *	20	67.7	313	14	12	53	37	1	4	76	15	8	.686	1	1	0	2	3	0	0	0	.027	.011	6.38	6.25	6.47
Bruney B	19	50.0	228	58	0	39	37	2	3	44	5	7	.701	4	5	0	3	2	0	2	6	-.033	-.142	5.04	4.68	5.40
Villone R *	18	42.3	176	37	0	25	18	3	3	36	5	9	.744	0	0	0	0	0	0	1	4	-.150	-.011	4.25	4.25	5.01
Kennedy I	12	19.0	77	3	3	15	9	0	0	13	1	1	.769	1	1	0	1	0	0	0	0	.014	.029	2.84	1.89	3.91
Henn S *	8	36.7	181	29	1	28	27	1	3	44	6	4	.658	0	1	0	2	2	0	0	2	-.145	-.060	7.85	7.12	6.35
Rasner D	8	24.7	111	6	6	11	8	0	2	29	4	3	.686	3	1	0	1	3	0	0	0	-.005	-.110	5.11	4.01	5.81
Clippard T	8	27.0	124	6	6	18	17	1	0	29	6	2	.723	5	0	0	3	1	0	0	0	.107	.116	6.33	6.33	6.71
DeSalvo M	7	27.7	135	7	6	10	18	0	3	34	2	4	.686	4	0	0	1	3	0	0	0	-.104	-.101	6.51	6.18	5.87
Britton C	6	12.7	51	11	0	5	4	0	0	9	2	0	.825	1	0	0	0	1	0	0	0	-.002	.096	3.55	3.55	5.59
Ramirez E	5	21.0	103	21	0	31	14	2	3	24	6	0	.633	2	0	0	1	1	1	3	3	.028	-.090	8.14	8.14	6.29
Ohlendorf R	5	6.3	26	6	0	9	2	0	0	5	1	0	.714	0	0	0	0	0	0	0	1	-.243	-.086	2.84	2.84	3.54
Pavano C	3	11.3	48	2	2	4	2	0	0	12	1	3	.692	3	0	0	1	0	0	0	0	.092	.151	5.56	4.76	4.35
Veras J	3	9.3	41	9	0	7	7	1	0	6	0	0	.778	2	0	0	0	0	2	2	1	.044	-.026	5.79	5.79	3.81
Wright C *	3	10.0	49	3	2	8	6	0	2	12	5	1	.750	1	0	0	2	0	0	0	0	-.177	-.046	7.20	7.20	10.68
Karstens J	1	14.7	80	7	3	5	9	0	0	27	4	0	.613	1	0	0	1	4	0	0	0	.011	-.091	12.89	11.05	8.08
Bean C	0	3.0	19	3	0	2	5	0	0	5	0	0	.583	1	0	0	0	1	0	0	0	.562	-.657	12.00	12.00	7.05
Brower J	0	3.3	21	3	0	1	2	0	1	8	0	1	.471	2	0	0	0	0	0	0	1	-.024	.314	18.90	13.50	5.48

Italicized stats have been adjusted for home park.
Batted Ball Pitching Stats are listed after Fielding Stats.

Fielding Stats

Name	INN	SBA/G	CS%	ERA	WP+PB/G	PO	A	TE	FE
Catcher									
Posada J	1111.3	1.05	22%	4.50	0.526	799	54	2	3
Molina J	169.3	0.96	28%	4.62	0.319	153	13	0	0
Nieves W	169.0	1.44	22%	4.37	0.213	111	6	1	1
Phelps J	1.0	0.00	0%	0.00	0.000	0	0	0	0

Name	Inn	PO	A	TE	FE	FPct	DPS	DPT	RZR	OOZ
First Base										
Mientkiewicz D	458.0	482	23	0	2	.996	1	1	.836	19
Phillips A	431.0	380	28	0	0	1.000	4	1	.806	16
Phelps J	162.7	167	9	2	1	.983	1	0	.714	4
Cairo M	156.3	162	9	2	2	.977	3	0	.781	3
Giambi J	121.0	108	6	0	1	.991	1	0	.750	2
Betemit W	74.3	67	4	0	0	1.000	0	0	.750	2
Duncan S	32.0	24	3	0	0	1.000	0	0	1.000	1
Damon J	8.3	9	0	0	1	.900	0	0	--	--
Posada J	6.0	6	0	0	0	1.000	0	0	--	--
Nieves W	1.0	1	0	0	0	1.000	0	0	--	--
Second Base										
Cano R	1408.0	320	497	3	10	.984	60	78	.833	53
Cairo M	23.0	6	7	0	0	1.000	0	0	.778	0
Betemit W	17.0	3	7	0	0	1.000	0	1	.857	0
Phillips A	2.0	0	1	0	0	1.000	0	0	1.000	0
Shortstop										
Jeter D	1318.0	199	390	7	11	.970	51	49	.777	35
Cairo M	52.7	7	22	0	0	1.000	3	1	.769	1
Gonzalez A	39.7	11	12	0	1	.958	2	1	.786	0
Betemit W	39.0	9	9	0	1	.947	1	1	.875	1
Basak C	1.0	0	0	0	0	0.000	0	0	--	--

Name	Inn	PO	A	TE	FE	FPct	DPS	DPT	RZR	OOZ
Third Base										
Rodriguez A	1330.0	106	251	6	5	.965	30	1	.662	47
Betemit W	55.7	1	14	0	2	.882	3	0	.733	2
Cairo M	35.0	1	9	1	0	.909	2	0	.857	2
Phillips A	17.0	1	2	0	0	1.000	0	0	.500	1
Sardinha B	6.0	0	0	0	0	0.000	0	0	0.000	0
Basak C	5.0	0	1	0	0	1.000	0	0	.500	0
Gonzalez A	2.0	0	0	0	0	0.000	0	0	--	--
Left Field										
Matsui H	980.0	213	6	1	2	.986	0	0	.886	28
Damon J	271.0	71	2	0	2	.973	0	0	.877	21
Cabrera M	142.0	34	2	0	0	1.000	0	0	.867	8
Thompson K	22.7	6	0	0	0	1.000	0	0	.833	1
Cairo M	13.0	2	0	0	0	1.000	0	0	1.000	0
Duncan S	12.0	3	0	0	0	1.000	0	0	1.000	0
Sardinha B	9.0	3	0	0	1	.750	0	0	.667	1
Betemit W	1.0	1	0	0	0	1.000	0	0	1.000	0
Center Field										
Cabrera M	1072.0	346	14	1	3	.989	2	0	.910	33
Damon J	377.0	121	1	0	0	1.000	0	0	.928	18
Thompson K	1.0	0	0	0	0	0.000	0	0	--	--
Right Field										
Abreu B	1333.0	313	6	0	4	.988	2	0	.892	25
Duncan S	43.0	11	2	0	0	1.000	2	0	1.000	3
Cabrera M	35.0	5	0	0	0	1.000	0	0	.800	1
Thompson K	24.0	8	0	0	0	1.000	0	0	1.000	1
Sardinha B	12.7	3	0	0	0	1.000	0	0	1.000	1
Damon J	3.0	1	0	0	0	1.000	0	0	.500	0

Batted Ball Batting Stats

Player	% of PA K%	% of PA BB%	% of Batted Balls GB%	% of Batted Balls LD%	% of Batted Balls FB%	IF/F	HR/OF	Out % GB	Out % OF	Runs Per Event NIP	Runs Per Event GB	Runs Per Event LD	Runs Per Event OF	Total Runs vs. Avg. NIP	Total Runs vs. Avg. GB	Total Runs vs. Avg. LD	Total Runs vs. Avg. FB	Total Runs vs. Avg. Tot
Rodriguez A	17	16	41	17	42	.12	.29	74	86	.11	.04	.51	.42	18	-1	8	45	70
Posada J	17	14	40	22	37	.05	.11	67	74	.09	.07	.45	.25	10	5	14	15	44
Jeter D	14	10	56	20	24	.04	.10	67	79	.08	.08	.41	.22	4	15	10	0	30
Matsui H	12	12	43	17	40	.08	.12	75	82	.12	.05	.43	.21	10	1	4	12	26
Cano R	13	7	52	17	31	.05	.11	72	81	.05	.06	.45	.22	-2	6	6	7	17
Abreu B	16	12	45	20	34	.02	.09	76	82	.09	.03	.42	.18	8	-2	6	2	15
Damon J	13	11	48	18	33	.13	.09	70	86	.10	.08	.36	.14	7	8	-1	-8	6
Giambi J	22	16	30	16	53	.06	.15	84	85	.08	-.01	.40	.22	5	-5	-3	8	4
Mientkiewicz D	12	10	36	24	39	.14	.10	79	77	.09	.01	.34	.22	1	-3	2	2	2
Phillips G	13	7	44	19	38	.08	.04	69	83	.05	.07	.42	.09	-1	1	2	-4	-2
Cairo M	16	7	41	14	45	.05	.00	77	78	.03	.02	.44	.07	-1	-1	-2	-3	-7
Cabrera M	11	8	51	20	29	.12	.05	74	88	.08	.04	.42	.08	1	1	6	-18	-10
MLB Average	*17*	*9*	*43*	*19*	*38*	*.10*	*.10*	*74*	*83*	*.05*	*.05*	*.40*	*.18*	*--*	*--*	*--*	*--*	*--*

Batted Ball Pitching Stats

Player	% of PA K%	% of PA BB%	% of Batted Balls GB%	% of Batted Balls LD%	% of Batted Balls FB%	IF/F	HR/OF	Out % GB	Out % OF	Runs Per Event NIP	Runs Per Event GB	Runs Per Event LD	Runs Per Event OF	Total Runs vs. Avg. NIP	Total Runs vs. Avg. GB	Total Runs vs. Avg. LD	Total Runs vs. Avg. FB	Total Runs vs. Avg. Tot
Wang C	13	8	58	18	23	.08	.07	77	79	.07	.02	.35	.17	0	-4	-3	-13	-21
Rivera M	25	6	53	19	29	.14	.08	75	78	-.02	.04	.44	.18	-6	-0	-0	-5	-12
Chamberlain J	38	7	37	22	41	.05	.05	89	89	-.04	-.05	.41	.06	-3	-3	-1	-3	-10
Clemens R	16	9	46	20	34	.09	.09	76	92	.05	.03	.39	.11	-1	0	1	-8	-8
Villone R	14	12	37	19	43	.13	.08	81	87	.10	-.03	.34	.11	2	-3	-1	-3	-5
Hughes P	19	10	37	18	45	.11	.09	71	84	.05	.06	.35	.16	-0	-0	-3	-1	-4
Pettitte A	15	8	48	19	33	.10	.07	74	75	.04	.04	.39	.19	-4	0	4	-2	-2
Vizcaino L	19	14	36	19	45	.11	.07	75	87	.08	.05	.44	.11	4	-1	0	-6	-2
Myers M	12	10	59	16	25	.12	.10	81	69	.10	-0.00	.38	.29	2	-3	-1	1	-2
Farnsworth K	18	11	30	19	51	.07	.10	67	89	.06	.10	.32	.14	1	2	-3	1	-0
Bruney B	17	17	31	17	52	.14	.08	62	92	.12	.10	.43	.08	6	2	-1	-5	3
Proctor S	15	13	25	18	57	.09	.08	73	85	.10	.05	.42	.13	4	-2	0	1	3
Rasner D	10	9	40	20	40	.11	.09	72	83	.11	.08	.41	.16	1	1	2	0	4
Clippard T	15	14	39	7	54	.19	.15	63	88	.11	.11	.70	.21	2	2	-2	2	5
DeSalvo M	7	16	36	18	46	.11	.05	65	85	.20	.10	.45	.09	5	2	2	-2	6
Mussina M	14	6	42	22	36	.11	.08	72	84	.02	.06	.43	.15	-5	3	13	-4	7
Henn S	15	17	38	16	47	.07	.12	71	76	.12	.06	.38	.25	5	1	-1	6	11
Igawa K	17	13	30	20	50	.10	.13	69	87	.09	.07	.47	.20	4	0	5	7	17
MLB Average	*17*	*9*	*43*	*19*	*38*	*.10*	*.10*	*74*	*83*	*.05*	*.05*	*.40*	*.18*	*--*	*--*	*--*	*--*	*--*

Oakland Athletics

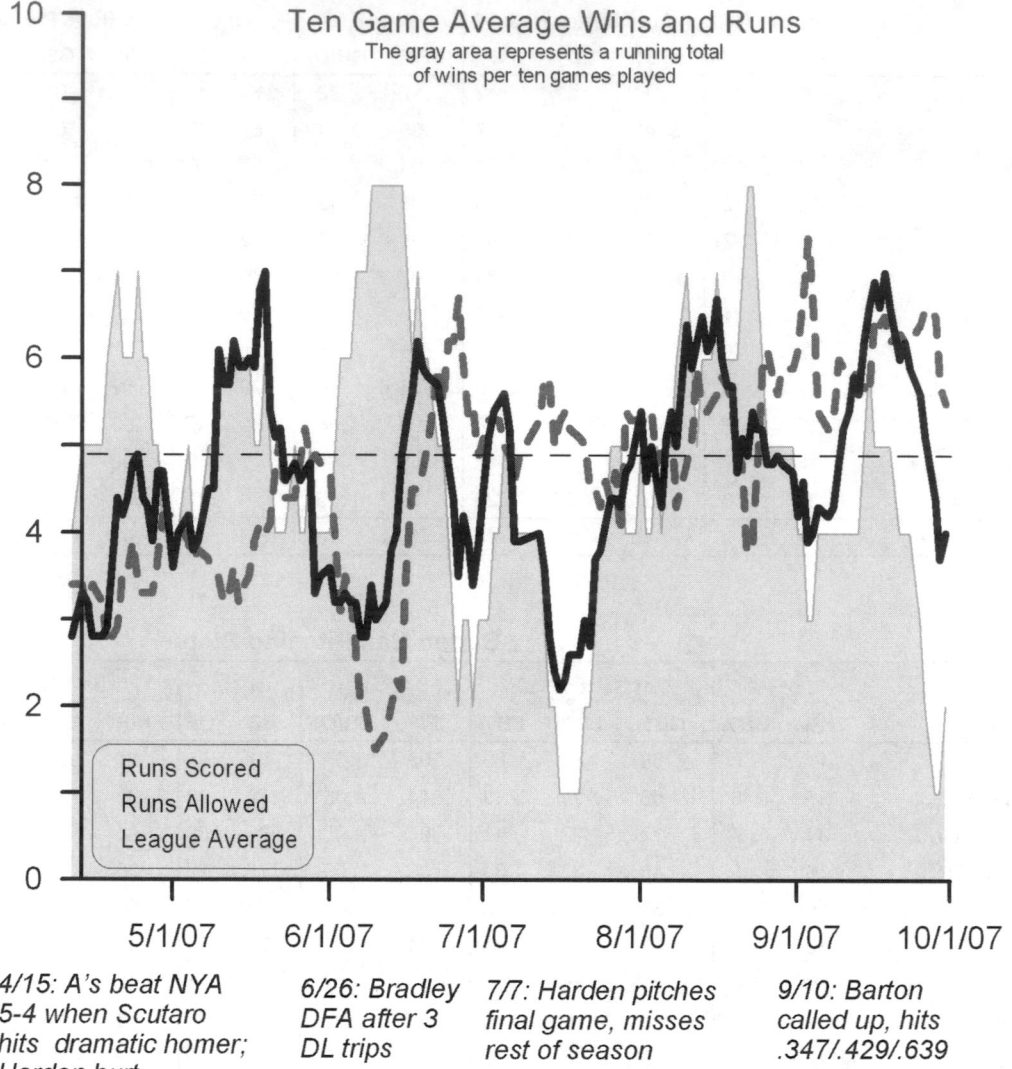

Ten Game Average Wins and Runs
The gray area represents a running total of wins per ten games played

Runs Scored
Runs Allowed
League Average

4/15: A's beat NYA 5-4 when Scutaro hits dramatic homer; Harden hurt

5/3: Cust acquired, hits .256/.408/.504 rest of year

6/26: Bradley DFA after 3 DL trips

7/7: Harden pitches final game, misses rest of season

8/31: Chavez, Buck, Kotsay shut down

9/10: Barton called up, hits .347/.429/.639

Team Batting and Pitching/Fielding Stats by Month						
	April	**May**	**June**	**July**	**Aug**	**Sept/Oct**
Wins	12	14	15	9	17	9
Losses	13	13	13	18	12	17
RS/G	3.8	5.0	4.3	4.0	5.2	5.1
RA/G	3.6	4.1	4.0	5.3	5.3	5.8
OBP	.309	.361	.334	.318	.345	.354
SLG	.349	.432	.426	.363	.440	.420
FIP	3.84	3.89	4.14	3.92	4.23	4.39
DER	.722	.717	.719	.672	.683	.651

Batting Stats

Player	BR	Runs	RBI	PA	Outs	H	2B	3B	HR	TB	K	BB	IBB	HBP	SH	SF	SB	CS	GDP	H-A	L^R	BA	OBP	SLG	GPA
Swisher N +	94	84	78	659	413	141	36	1	22	245	131	100	12	10	1	9	3	2	13	-.005	.053	.262	.381	.455	.294
Cust J *	93	61	82	507	302	101	18	1	26	199	164	105	2	1	0	6	0	2	6	.088	.056	.256	.408	.504	.319
Ellis M	79	84	76	642	436	161	33	3	19	257	94	44	1	10	2	3	9	4	10	-.025	.083	.276	.336	.441	.269
Stewart S	75	79	48	630	427	167	22	1	12	227	60	47	0	3	1	3	11	3	15	-.065	-.018	.290	.345	.394	.262
Johnson D *	63	53	62	495	330	98	20	1	18	174	77	72	4	3	0	4	0	0	12	-.015	-.002	.236	.349	.418	.270
Buck T *	51	41	34	334	213	82	22	5	7	135	66	39	2	4	2	4	4	1	9	-.051	-.058	.288	.377	.474	.297
Scutaro M	43	49	41	379	264	88	13	0	7	122	40	35	1	2	2	2	2	1	13	-.027	.079	.260	.332	.361	.247
Chavez E *	42	43	46	379	270	82	21	2	15	152	76	34	2	0	0	4	4	2	9	.042	.023	.240	.306	.446	.257
Piazza M	38	33	44	329	233	85	17	1	8	128	61	18	0	0	0	2	0	0	9	-.072	.016	.275	.313	.414	.252
Suzuki K	35	27	39	248	164	53	13	0	7	87	39	24	0	3	3	5	0	0	4	-.011	-.059	.249	.327	.408	.257
Crosby B	28	40	31	374	283	79	16	0	8	119	62	23	1	2	0	0	10	2	11	.014	.009	.226	.278	.341	.217
Hannahan J *	24	16	24	169	110	40	12	0	3	61	39	21	0	1	1	2	1	0	6	.012	-.098	.278	.369	.424	.280
Kotsay M *	20	20	20	227	167	44	14	0	1	61	20	19	3	0	0	1	1	1	4	-.066	.103	.214	.279	.296	.206
Murphy D	18	21	21	132	95	26	8	0	6	52	35	10	0	2	1	1	1	0	3	-.038	.109	.220	.290	.441	.248
Kendall J	18	24	22	312	234	66	10	0	2	82	27	12	0	3	2	3	3	1	7	-.051	-.048	.226	.261	.281	.194
Barton D *	15	16	8	84	49	25	9	0	4	46	11	10	0	1	0	1	1	0	2	-.154	.009	.347	.429	.639	.363
Bradley M +	11	6	7	75	49	19	4	0	2	29	14	8	1	1	0	1	2	1	2	-.007	.106	.292	.373	.446	.288
Bowen R +	9	6	5	54	31	12	1	0	2	19	20	10	0	0	1	0	0	0	0	-.238	.025	.279	.415	.442	.306
DaVanon J +	6	9	5	71	50	15	1	1	0	18	19	7	0	0	0	1	0	0	2	.060	.245	.238	.310	.286	.217
Walker T *	4	5	4	52	37	13	1	0	0	14	4	2	0	0	0	2	0	0	2	-.058	.046	.271	.288	.292	.209
Snelling C *	3	4	0	25	13	7	0	0	0	7	4	5	0	0	0	0	0	0	0	--	-.181	.350	.480	.350	.313
Furmaniak J	3	5	1	22	14	3	1	0	0	4	8	3	0	2	0	0	0	0	0	-.269	.108	.176	.364	.235	.229
Melhuse A +	3	2	2	30	20	6	1	0	0	7	8	4	0	0	0	0	0	0	0	.031	.234	.231	.333	.269	.224
Kielty B +	2	4	3	40	29	7	1	0	0	8	9	3	0	1	0	1	0	0	1	-.199	.033	.200	.275	.229	.186
Kennedy J	1	1	2	3	2	1	1	0	0	2	0	0	0	0	0	0	0	0	0	-.317	--	.333	.333	.667	.326
Putnam D *	1	3	2	31	22	6	0	0	1	9	11	3	0	0	0	0	0	0	0	-.137	-.093	.214	.290	.321	.218
Bocachica H	1	2	3	20	17	1	0	0	1	4	5	2	0	0	0	1	0	0	1	-.119	-.055	.059	.150	.235	.130
Melillo K *	0	0	0	1	0	0	0	0	0	0	0	1	0	0	0	0	0	0	0	--	--	.000	1.000	.000	.464
DiNardo L *	0	0	0	4	3	1	0	0	0	1	2	0	0	0	0	0	0	0	0	-.175	.350	.250	.250	.250	.180
Thompson K	0	2	1	15	13	1	0	0	0	1	3	1	0	0	0	0	0	0	0	-.131	.067	.071	.133	.071	.080
Gaudin C	0	1	0	5	3	0	0	0	0	0	2	1	0	0	1	0	0	0	0	-.113	-.150	.000	.250	.000	.116
Langerhans R	-0	0	0	5	4	0	0	0	0	0	2	1	0	0	0	0	0	0	0	--	--	.000	.200	.000	.093
Brown D *	-0	0	0	3	3	0	0	0	0	0	2	0	0	0	0	0	0	0	0	.000	.000	.000	.000	.000	.000
Haren D	-0	0	0	4	4	0	0	0	0	0	1	0	0	0	0	0	0	0	0	.000	.000	.000	.000	.000	.000
Blanton J	-1	0	0	5	5	0	0	0	0	0	3	0	0	0	1	0	0	0	1	.000	--	.000	.000	.000	.000

Italicized stats have been adjusted for home park.

Batted Ball Batting Stats

Player	% of PA		% of Batted Balls					Out %		Runs Per Event				Total Runs vs. Avg.				
	K%	BB%	GB%	LD%	FB%	IF/F	HR/OF	GB	OF	NIP	GB	LD	OF	NIP	GB	LD	FB	Tot
Cust J	32	21	42	23	35	.04	.33	86	74	.07	-.02	.45	.54	12	-9	1	23	27
Swisher N	20	17	37	18	46	.09	.13	78	81	.10	.02	.45	.22	15	-6	0	10	19
Buck T	20	13	44	19	37	.09	.09	74	72	.07	.04	.46	.26	3	-0	2	6	12
Johnson D	16	15	43	18	39	.10	.15	76	87	.11	.03	.32	.21	11	-2	-6	4	7
Ellis M	15	8	32	18	50	.17	.09	68	85	.05	.08	.42	.14	-0	6	2	-2	5
Hannahan J	23	13	37	23	39	.07	.08	78	72	.05	-.00	.41	.22	1	-2	2	2	2
Suzuki K	16	11	39	16	45	.06	.09	72	91	.07	.06	.41	.11	2	1	-2	-2	-1
Stewart S	10	8	45	21	34	.08	.07	74	87	.10	.04	.38	.09	2	-1	9	-13	-2
Murphy D	27	9	35	19	46	.05	.17	83	80	.00	-.01	.33	.29	-2	-3	-2	4	-2
Chavez E	20	9	36	17	46	.24	.15	76	83	.03	.05	.37	.25	-2	-1	-4	4	-3

Batted Ball Batting Stats continue after Fielding Stats.

Pitching Stats

Player	PRC	IP	BFP	G	GS	K	BB	IBB	HBP	H	HR	DP	DER	SB	CS	PO	W	L	Sv	Op	Hld	H-A	R^L	RA	ERA	FIP
Haren D	115	222.7	935	34	34	192	55	1	3	214	24	13	.697	20	6	0	15	9	0	0	0	-.029	.012	3.68	3.07	3.82
Blanton J	98	230.0	950	34	34	140	40	4	4	240	16	25	.695	19	4	2	14	10	0	0	0	-.069	-.027	4.15	3.95	3.59
Gaudin C	77	199.3	886	34	34	154	100	8	8	205	21	27	.685	12	1	0	11	13	0	0	0	.010	-.045	4.88	4.42	4.71
DiNardo L *	43	131.3	555	35	20	59	50	2	3	136	13	29	.702	3	3	0	8	10	0	0	0	-.049	.034	5.07	4.11	4.93
Kennedy J *	35	101.0	450	27	16	42	48	1	5	109	9	15	.702	7	4	2	3	9	0	1	0	.001	-.085	4.72	4.37	5.25
Embree A *	32	68.0	284	68	0	51	19	5	0	67	5	5	.699	4	1	1	1	2	17	21	16	-.069	-.045	3.97	3.97	3.45
Street H	29	50.0	199	48	0	63	12	3	0	35	5	0	.731	5	2	0	5	2	16	21	5	-.026	-.100	3.60	2.88	2.70
Casilla S	23	50.7	219	46	0	52	23	6	1	43	6	1	.723	9	0	0	3	1	2	5	12	-.085	-.011	4.44	4.44	3.93
Harden R	19	25.7	100	7	4	27	11	1	0	18	3	6	.729	1	1	0	1	2	0	0	0	.185	-.118	2.45	2.45	3.96
Brown A	18	41.7	178	33	0	43	17	3	3	38	1	3	.667	3	0	0	3	3	0	2	3	-.020	.009	4.54	4.54	2.85
Braden D *	17	72.3	332	20	14	55	26	1	2	91	9	5	.646	2	1	2	1	8	0	0	1	-.030	-.095	7.34	6.72	4.60
Lugo R	16	37.7	167	27	0	26	24	4	2	31	1	1	.737	2	2	0	4	0	0	0	1	.048	.015	4.30	4.30	4.10
Calero K	13	40.7	185	46	0	31	21	2	2	46	3	4	.664	8	0	0	1	5	1	4	9	.008	.044	5.75	5.75	4.36
Loaiza E	10	14.7	56	2	2	5	4	0	0	10	1	3	.783	0	0	0	1	0	0	0	0	.074	-.046	1.84	1.84	4.40
Lewis C	10	37.7	170	26	1	23	14	3	3	44	7	5	.683	1	0	0	0	2	0	1	3	-.094	-.140	6.69	6.45	5.69
Marshall J *	9	42.0	198	51	0	18	22	6	4	50	3	8	.669	1	0	0	1	2	0	2	9	-.050	-.051	7.07	6.43	4.88
Flores R *	8	17.7	81	17	0	15	12	5	0	16	2	0	.712	0	0	0	0	2	0	1	1	-.141	-.171	4.08	3.57	4.34
Witasick J	7	15.0	65	16	0	10	9	1	1	14	1	2	.705	0	1	0	1	0	0	1	1	-.038	.031	3.60	3.60	4.71
Duchscherer	6	16.3	75	17	0	13	8	3	0	18	3	0	.686	3	0	0	3	3	0	2	5	-.000	-.171	4.96	4.96	5.09
Meyer D *	2	16.3	79	6	3	11	9	0	0	20	2	0	.667	1	0	0	0	2	0	0	0	.099	.129	10.47	8.82	5.28
Komine S	2	7.7	31	2	0	1	1	0	1	6	2	0	.846	0	0	0	0	0	0	0	0	--	-.122	4.70	4.70	7.29
Blevins J *	1	4.7	25	6	0	3	2	0	0	8	1	0	.579	0	0	0	0	1	0	0	0	-.095	-.096	11.57	9.64	6.17
Robertson C	0	2.0	15	3	0	2	2	1	1	6	0	0	.400	0	0	0	0	0	0	0	0	-.155	-.399	18.00	18.00	4.38
Ramirez E *	0	3.0	12	3	0	0	1	0	0	3	0	1	.727	0	0	0	0	0	0	0	0	.043	-.210	0.00	0.00	4.38

Italicized stats have been adjusted for home park.

Batted Ball Pitching Stats

Player	% of PA		% of Batted Balls					Out %		Runs Per Event				Total Runs vs. Avg.				
	K%	BB%	GB%	LD%	FB%	IF/F	HR/OF	GB	OF	NIP	GB	LD	OF	NIP	GB	LD	FB	Tot
Blanton J	15	5	47	21	32	.11	.07	77	82	-.00	.03	.36	.14	-14	-5	2	-14	-31
Haren D	21	6	44	17	38	.11	.10	73	83	-.01	.06	.37	.19	-15	4	-10	-1	-22
Street H	32	6	40	15	45	.13	.11	79	86	-.04	.03	.42	.16	-6	-2	-5	-3	-15
Embree A	18	7	34	20	45	.09	.06	75	84	.01	.04	.39	.11	-3	-2	1	-4	-8
Casilla J	24	11	33	16	51	.10	.09	68	90	.03	.09	.38	.12	-1	1	-4	-3	-6
Harden R	27	11	39	19	42	.08	.13	83	86	.02	-.05	.42	.16	-1	-3	-1	-1	-5
DiNardo L	11	10	56	18	26	.06	.12	76	89	.10	.02	.39	.16	4	-2	0	-7	-4
Brown A	24	11	41	19	41	.09	.02	70	85	.03	.08	.49	.07	-0	1	1	-5	-4
Lugo R	16	16	50	21	29	.12	.03	86	89	.12	-.01	.49	.04	4	-3	3	-6	-3
Kennedy J	9	12	50	15	35	.12	.08	79	79	.14	.01	.43	.17	8	-3	-1	-1	3
Calero K	17	12	34	20	47	.11	.06	66	84	.08	.10	.40	.12	2	2	1	-1	3
Marshall J	9	13	58	19	23	.09	.09	74	76	.16	.04	.38	.20	5	1	1	-1	5
Lewis C	14	10	38	16	46	.10	.13	65	85	.08	.08	.39	.21	1	1	-0	4	6
Gaudin C	17	12	51	19	30	.10	.13	78	82	.08	.01	.43	.24	8	-8	6	1	7
Braden D	17	8	37	18	45	.12	.09	70	75	.04	.08	.41	.22	-1	3	1	6	10
MLB Average	17	9	43	19	38	.10	.10	74	83	.05	.05	.40	.18	--	--	--	--	--

Fielding Stats

Name	INN	SBA/G	CS%	ERA	WP+PB/G	PO	A	TE	FE
Catcher									
Kendall J	714.3	0.88	16%	3.40	0.365	485	34	3	1
Suzuki K	539.0	0.60	19%	5.31	0.468	431	32	1	0
Bowen R	130.7	0.55	13%	5.03	0.482	92	4	1	0
Melhuse A	64.0	1.13	25%	4.36	0.563	42	5	0	0

Name	Inn	PO	A	TE	FE	FPct	DPS	DPT	RZR	OOZ
First Base										
Johnson D	854.7	869	40	0	3	.996	7	0	.767	14
Swisher N	346.7	391	25	0	3	.993	3	0	.703	16
Barton D	157.7	153	7	0	0	1.000	2	0	.826	5
Walker T	89.0	87	8	0	0	1.000	0	0	.625	7
Second Base										
Ellis M	1322.0	302	499	2	3	.994	42	58	.884	45
Scutaro M	110.0	19	44	0	0	1.000	6	4	.878	3
Furmaniak J	13.0	3	4	0	0	1.000	1	1	.667	1
Murphy D	3.0	1	1	0	0	1.000	0	1	--	--
Shortstop										
Crosby B	813.7	131	282	9	5	.967	32	27	.834	40
Scutaro M	348.0	52	111	3	2	.970	10	12	.798	20
Murphy D	265.3	35	91	1	4	.962	10	10	.843	7
Furmaniak J	21.0	5	5	1	0	.909	1	2	1.000	1
Third Base										
Chavez E	774.7	66	169	6	0	.975	17	1	.647	37
Hannahan J	361.7	19	78	3	0	.970	11	0	.716	13
Scutaro M	295.7	23	64	5	4	.906	3	0	.603	15
Furmaniak J	12.0	0	2	0	0	1.000	0	0	1.000	0
Melhuse A	2.0	0	1	0	0	1.000	0	0	1.000	0
Murphy D	2.0	0	1	0	0	1.000	0	0	1.000	0

Name	Inn	PO	A	TE	FE	FPct	DPS	DPT	RZR	OOZ
Left Field										
Stewart S	1154.0	277	4	0	3	.989	3	0	.883	42
Buck T	128.0	26	1	0	0	1.000	0	0	.920	3
Cust J	81.7	14	0	0	1	.933	0	0	.867	1
Scutaro M	19.3	2	0	0	0	1.000	0	0	1.000	0
Thompson K	16.0	2	0	0	0	1.000	0	0	1.000	0
Kielty B	13.0	4	1	0	0	1.000	2	0	1.000	1
Snelling C	9.0	1	0	0	0	1.000	0	0	1.000	0
DaVanon J	8.0	4	0	0	0	1.000	0	0	1.000	0
Putnam D	7.0	4	0	0	0	1.000	0	0	1.000	1
Brown D	5.7	2	0	0	0	1.000	0	0	1.000	0
Furmaniak J	3.0	0	0	0	0	0.000	0	0	--	--
Kendall J	2.3	1	0	0	0	1.000	0	0	1.000	0
Walker T	1.0	0	0	0	0	0.000	0	0	--	--
Center Field										
Swisher N	481.0	139	1	0	2	.986	0	0	.878	17
Kotsay M	472.7	141	5	1	1	.986	6	0	.899	17
DaVanon J	144.7	36	1	0	0	1.000	0	0	.861	5
Bradley M	125.0	29	0	0	0	1.000	0	0	1.000	4
Bocachica H	46.0	10	0	0	1	.909	0	0	.900	1
Putnam D	46.0	7	0	0	0	1.000	0	0	.750	1
Snelling C	38.7	8	1	0	0	1.000	0	0	1.000	0
Stewart S	32.0	12	0	0	1	.923	0	0	.846	1
Buck T	28.0	9	0	0	0	1.000	0	0	1.000	2
Thompson K	18.0	2	0	0	1	.667	0	0	.500	1
Langerhans R	14.0	5	1	0	1	.857	0	0	.833	0
Kielty B	2.0	0	0	0	0	0.000	0	0	--	--
Right Field										
Buck T	509.3	110	2	0	0	1.000	0	0	.918	20
Swisher N	413.7	107	2	0	0	1.000	0	0	.918	19
Cust J	382.0	79	1	1	2	.964	0	0	.855	8
Kielty B	53.0	9	0	0	0	1.000	0	0	.875	2
Putnam D	28.0	8	0	0	1	.889	0	0	.750	2
Scutaro M	26.0	8	0	0	0	1.000	0	0	.875	1
Bradley M	23.0	5	0	0	0	1.000	0	0	1.000	0
Brown D	8.0	1	0	0	0	1.000	0	0	1.000	0
Furmaniak J	3.0	1	0	0	0	1.000	0	0	1.000	0
DaVanon J	1.0	0	0	0	0	0.000	0	0	--	--
Thompson K	1.0	0	0	0	0	0.000	0	0	--	--

Batted Ball Batting Stats

Player	% of PA		% of Batted Balls					Out %		Runs Per Event				Total Runs vs. Avg.				
	K%	BB%	GB%	LD%	FB%	IF/F	HR/OF	GB	OF	NIP	GB	LD	OF	NIP	GB	LD	FB	Tot
Piazza M	19	5	39	21	40	.10	.09	76	81	-.01	.03	.41	.18	-5	-2	3	0	-4
Scutaro M	11	10	39	20	41	.11	.06	71	89	.11	.05	.32	.08	3	-0	-1	-9	-7
Kotsay M	9	8	45	15	41	.05	.01	76	91	.11	.04	.38	-.00	1	-1	-3	-11	-13
Crosby B	17	7	48	20	32	.18	.09	84	87	.02	-.02	.40	.13	-4	-7	0	-9	-19
Kendall J	9	5	42	19	39	.08	.01	80	88	.05	.01	.33	.00	-2	-4	-2	-15	-23
MLB Average	17	9	43	19	38	.10	.10	74	83	.05	.05	.40	.18	--	--	--	--	--

Philadelphia Phillies

Stat Facts:

- Shane Victorino stole 37 bases in 41 attempts
- Geoff Geary induced 17 double plays in 67 innings
- Adam Eaton allowed just 6 stolen bases in 15 attempts
- Kyle Kendrick struck out or walked just 16% of the batters he faced
- Kendrick's FIP of 4.90 was much worse than his ERA of 3.87
- Jimmy Rollins made 65 OOZ plays
- Ryan Howard walked or struck out in 48% of his PAs
- Just 3% of Howard's fly balls were infield pop-ups, and 30% were home runs
- Pat Burrell had a GB% of 30%, lowest in the league
- Burrell's BB% of 20% was highest in the league
- 27% of Jayson Werth's batted balls were line drives
- Chase Utley led the league with 25 HBPs

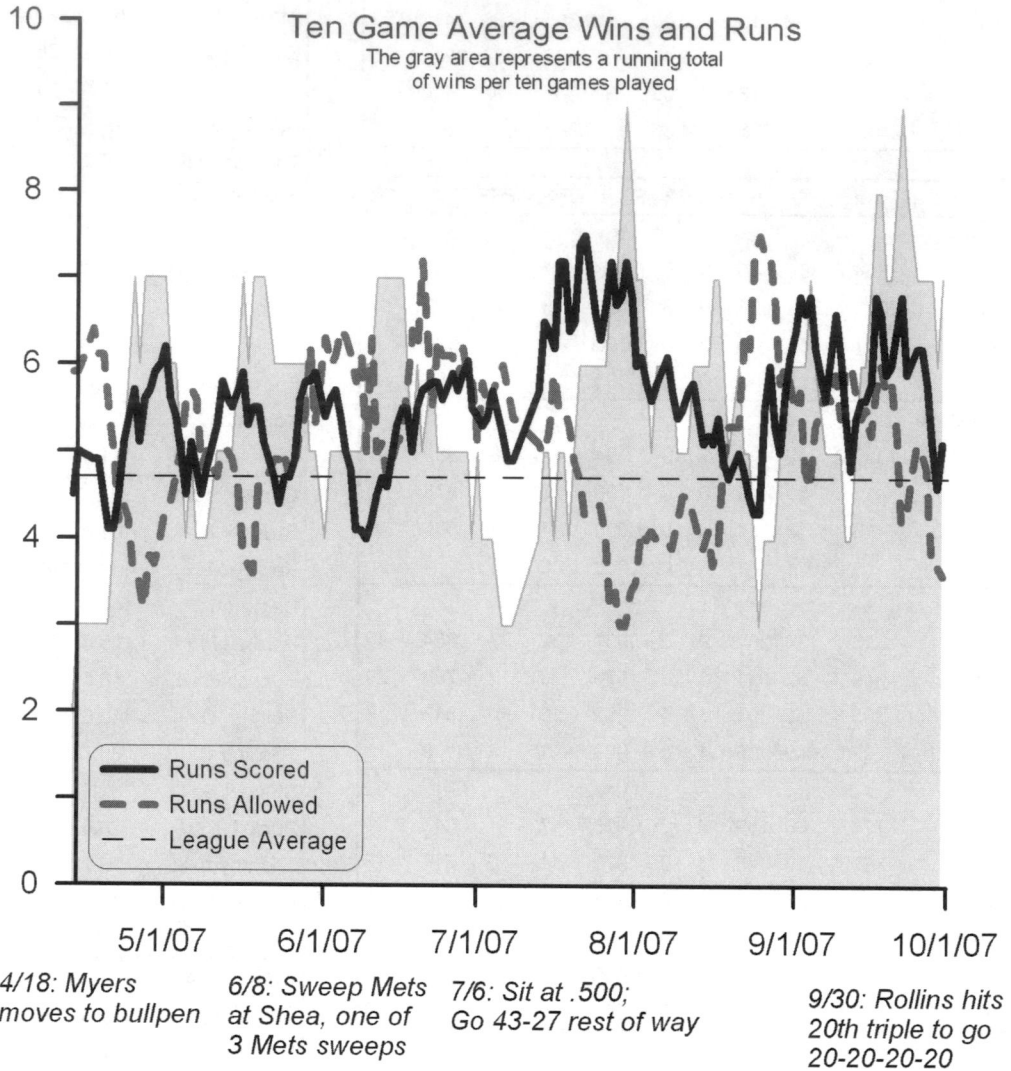

Ten Game Average Wins and Runs

The gray area represents a running total of wins per ten games played

Legend: Runs Scored / Runs Allowed / League Average

4/18: Myers moves to bullpen

6/8: Sweep Mets at Shea, one of 3 Mets sweeps

7/6: Sit at .500; Go 43-27 rest of way

8/26: Utley injured, misses one month

9/12: Start 13-4 run to wrest division crown from Mets

9/30: Rollins hits 20th triple to go 20-20-20-20

Team Batting and Pitching/Fielding Stats by Month						
	April	**May**	**June**	**July**	**Aug**	**Sept/Oct**
Wins	11	15	15	15	16	17
Losses	14	13	13	10	12	11
RS/G	4.9	5.4	5.1	6.4	5.6	5.6
RA/G	4.8	5.0	5.9	4.3	5.2	5.0
OBP	.361	.338	.339	.386	.350	.349
SLG	.427	.431	.450	.527	.467	.444
FIP	4.44	4.64	5.06	4.84	4.72	4.46
DER	.682	.687	.689	.700	.678	.686

Batting Stats

Player	BR	Runs	RBI	PA	Outs	H	2B	3B	HR	TB	K	BB	IBB	HBP	SH	SF	SB	CS	GDP	H-A	L^R	BA	OBP	SLG	GPA
Rollins J +	119	139	94	778	521	212	38	20	30	380	85	49	5	7	0	6	41	6	11	.005	.024	.296	.344	.531	.279
Howard R *	116	94	136	648	400	142	26	0	47	309	199	107	35	5	0	7	1	0	13	-.009	.080	.268	.392	.584	.313
Utley C *	103	104	103	613	362	176	48	5	22	300	89	50	1	25	1	7	9	1	7	.061	.014	.332	.410	.566	.317
Burrell P	96	77	97	598	361	121	26	0	30	237	120	114	1	4	0	8	0	0	10	.067	.023	.256	.400	.502	.296
Rowand A	95	105	89	684	444	189	45	0	27	315	119	47	3	19	2	4	6	3	18	.026	.011	.309	.374	.515	.288
Victorino S	62	78	46	510	342	128	23	3	12	193	62	37	1	10	5	2	37	4	10	-.024	.036	.281	.347	.423	.254
Werth J	53	43	49	304	180	76	11	3	8	117	73	44	1	2	2	1	7	1	0	-.010	.094	.298	.404	.459	.288
Ruiz C	47	42	54	429	295	97	29	2	6	148	49	42	10	5	5	3	6	1	17	.027	-.072	.259	.340	.396	.244
Dobbs G *	40	45	55	358	243	88	20	4	10	146	67	29	4	1	0	4	3	0	7	-.002	.096	.272	.330	.451	.253
Helms W	23	21	39	308	221	69	19	0	5	103	62	19	2	3	2	4	0	0	10	-.094	.071	.246	.297	.368	.219
Iguchi T	20	22	12	156	98	42	10	0	3	61	23	13	0	1	1	3	6	1	1	-.013	.153	.304	.361	.442	.265
Nunez A +	19	24	16	287	203	59	10	1	0	71	48	30	5	1	4	0	2	0	10	.047	.047	.234	.318	.282	.207
Bourn M *	18	29	6	133	88	33	3	3	1	45	21	13	2	0	1	0	18	1	1	.050	.121	.277	.348	.378	.244
Coste C	16	15	22	137	94	36	3	0	5	54	20	4	1	2	2	0	0	0	1	.115	.073	.279	.311	.419	.238
Barajas R	12	16	10	147	100	28	8	0	4	48	24	21	3	2	1	0	0	1	5	-.057	.071	.230	.352	.393	.249
Roberson C +	2	6	1	29	20	8	0	0	0	8	4	1	0	0	0	0	2	0	0	-.015	-.194	.286	.310	.286	.205
Branyan R *	2	2	5	9	7	2	0	0	2	8	6	0	0	0	0	0	0	0	0	-.580	.414	.222	.222	.889	.313
Eaton A	2	4	5	71	49	13	1	0	1	17	22	3	0	0	6	0	0	0	0	-.054	.023	.210	.246	.274	.174
Garcia F	1	1	2	22	14	4	1	0	0	5	7	2	0	0	2	1	0	0	1	.102	.006	.235	.300	.294	.202
Moyer J *	1	4	2	83	65	9	2	0	0	11	26	2	0	0	8	0	0	0	1	.020	.076	.123	.147	.151	.101
Lohse K	1	0	1	23	13	3	0	0	0	3	5	1	0	1	5	0	0	0	0	.042	.582	.188	.278	.188	.167
Kendrick K	1	6	2	50	33	6	0	0	0	6	17	3	0	2	5	1	0	0	0	.042	.010	.154	.244	.154	.144
LaForest P *	1	2	1	13	11	1	0	0	0	1	4	2	0	0	0	0	0	0	1	-.243	.138	.091	.231	.091	.123
Durbin J	0	3	0	22	14	5	1	0	0	6	5	0	0	0	3	0	0	0	0	-.227	.068	.263	.263	.316	.192
Lieber J *	0	2	1	22	16	1	0	0	0	1	8	4	0	0	1	0	0	0	0	.038	.061	.059	.238	.059	.118
Myers B	0	1	0	9	6	0	0	0	0	0	4	2	0	0	1	0	0	0	0	-.060	.060	.000	.250	.000	.109
Rosario F	0	0	0	1	0	0	0	0	0	0	0	0	0	0	1	0	0	0	0	.000	--	.000	.000	.000	.000
Castro F *	0	0	0	1	0	0	0	0	0	0	0	0	0	0	1	0	0	0	0	.000	--	.000	.000	.000	.000
Alfonseca A	-0	0	0	1	1	0	0	0	0	0	0	0	0	0	0	0	0	0	0	.000	--	.000	.000	.000	.000
Romero J +	-0	0	0	1	1	0	0	0	0	0	0	0	0	0	0	0	0	0	0	.000	--	.000	.000	.000	.000
Happ J *	-0	0	0	1	1	0	0	0	0	0	1	0	0	0	0	0	0	0	0	--	--	.000	.000	.000	.000
Segovia Z	-0	0	0	2	2	0	0	0	0	0	0	0	0	0	0	0	0	0	0	--	--	.000	.000	.000	.000
Madson R *	-0	0	0	4	3	0	0	0	0	0	2	0	0	0	1	0	0	0	0	.000	--	.000	.000	.000	.000
Ennis J	-0	0	0	3	3	1	0	0	0	1	1	0	0	0	0	0	0	0	1	--	-.350	.333	.333	.333	.227
Condrey C	-0	0	0	4	4	0	0	0	0	0	3	0	0	0	0	0	0	0	0	.000	--	.000	.000	.000	.000
Geary G	-0	0	0	4	4	0	0	0	0	0	3	0	0	0	0	0	0	0	0	.000	.000	.000	.000	.000	.000
Hamels C *	-2	7	2	72	55	9	2	0	0	11	26	2	0	0	5	1	0	0	0	-.022	-.019	.141	.164	.172	.113

Italicized stats have been adjusted for home park.
Batted Ball Batting Stats are listed after Fielding Stats.

Philadelphia Phillies

Pitching Stats

Player	PRC	IP	BFP	G	GS	K	BB	IBB	HBP	H	HR	DP	DER	SB	CS	PO	W	L	Sv	Op	Hld	H-A	R^L	RA	ERA	FIP
Hamels C *	101	183.3	743	28	28	177	43	4	3	163	25	14	.705	14	2	2	15	5	0	0	0	-.008	.016	3.53	3.39	3.80
Moyer J *	68	199.3	867	33	33	133	66	3	5	222	30	21	.682	9	6	4	14	12	0	0	0	-.012	.024	5.33	5.01	4.91
Kendrick K	50	121.0	499	20	20	49	25	3	7	129	16	18	.709	8	2	0	10	4	0	0	0	.026	-.092	3.94	3.87	4.90
Eaton A	43	161.7	734	30	30	97	71	4	11	192	30	19	.680	6	9	1	10	10	0	0	0	.019	-.054	6.51	6.29	5.93
Romero J *	41	36.3	143	51	0	31	25	2	2	15	1	8	.810	3	2	1	1	2	0	1	22	-.016	-.004	1.24	1.24	3.98
Myers B	33	68.7	293	51	3	83	27	1	1	61	9	2	.699	6	1	0	5	7	21	24	3	-.014	.069	4.33	4.33	3.74
Madson R	33	56.0	237	38	0	43	23	4	2	48	5	2	.713	1	3	0	2	2	1	2	7	-.016	.033	3.05	3.05	4.02
Lieber J	28	78.0	342	14	12	54	22	5	3	91	7	11	.660	2	0	0	3	6	0	0	0	.049	-.035	5.08	4.73	3.82
Lohse K	23	61.0	268	13	11	42	24	2	6	64	6	5	.689	6	4	0	3	0	0	0	0	-.012	.013	4.87	4.72	4.55
Geary G	20	67.3	296	57	0	38	25	6	9	72	8	17	.681	2	2	0	3	2	0	3	9	.092	.056	5.88	4.41	4.93
Durbin J	20	64.7	295	18	10	39	36	4	2	71	6	9	.689	3	1	0	6	5	1	1	0	.091	-.033	5.85	5.15	4.85
Garcia F	18	58.0	264	11	11	50	19	3	5	74	12	5	.652	5	0	1	1	5	0	0	0	.017	.048	6.05	5.90	5.32
Gordon T	16	40.0	170	44	0	32	13	0	2	40	7	6	.698	1	1	0	3	2	6	11	14	.001	-.102	4.73	4.73	5.07
Condrey C	16	50.0	228	39	0	27	16	3	5	61	4	5	.670	1	1	0	5	0	2	2	2	-.035	.007	5.40	5.04	4.31
Alfonseca A	15	49.7	236	61	0	24	27	6	1	65	3	4	.657	7	0	0	5	2	8	13	15	-.014	-.073	5.62	5.44	4.42
Rosario F	10	26.3	127	23	0	25	13	1	4	34	3	2	.622	3	1	0	0	3	1	1	1	-.056	-.005	5.47	5.47	4.67
Mesa J	9	39.0	170	40	0	20	19	2	2	34	6	6	.740	1	0	0	1	2	1	1	4	-.048	.020	7.38	5.54	5.71
Zagurski M *	7	21.3	101	25	0	21	11	2	1	25	3	2	.662	0	0	0	1	0	0	2	5	-.088	-.166	5.91	5.91	4.53
Hernandez Y	6	15.3	67	14	0	13	1	1	0	20	2	0	.647	2	0	0	0	0	0	1	0	.002	.033	5.28	5.28	3.27
Castro F *	4	12.0	56	10	1	14	13	0	0	9	2	2	.741	0	0	0	0	0	0	0	1	.037	-.233	6.00	6.00	6.35
Davis K	4	11.3	59	11	0	10	8	2	0	17	2	1	.590	1	2	0	0	1	0	0	3	.019	-.004	5.56	5.56	5.39
Sanches B	4	14.7	68	12	0	9	12	2	1	13	6	1	.800	1	2	0	1	1	0	0	1	.046	-.006	6.75	5.52	9.61
Ennis J	2	7.7	38	3	1	8	3	0	0	12	1	0	.577	1	0	0	0	0	1	1	0	--	-.083	8.22	8.22	4.05
Segovia Z	1	5.0	23	1	1	2	1	1	0	8	1	1	.632	0	0	0	0	1	0	0	0	--	.142	9.00	9.00	5.07
Happ J *	1	4.0	21	1	1	5	2	0	0	7	3	1	.545	0	0	0	0	1	0	0	0	--	-.028	11.25	11.25	12.02
Smith M *	0	4.0	27	9	0	1	11	1	0	4	0	0	.733	1	0	0	0	0	0	0	3	.060	.162	11.25	11.25	10.27
Garcia A	0	0.7	4	1	0	0	0	0	0	2	0	0	.500	0	0	0	0	0	0	0	0	--	-.467	13.50	13.50	3.27
Bisenius J	0	2.0	9	2	0	3	2	0	0	2	0	0	.500	0	0	0	0	0	0	0	0	.225	.057	0.00	0.00	3.27

Italicized stats have been adjusted for home park.

Batted Ball Pitching Stats

Player	% of PA		% of Batted Balls					Out %		Runs Per Event				Total Runs vs. Avg.				
	K%	BB%	GB%	LD%	FB%	IF/F	HR/OF	GB	OF	NIP	GB	LD	OF	NIP	GB	LD	FB	Tot
Hamels C	24	6	42	19	39	.13	.14	75	84	-.02	.05	.37	.21	-15	-1	-6	1	-21
Romero J	22	19	64	11	25	.05	.05	85	84	.10	-.04	.33	.08	4	-5	-5	-5	-11
Myers B	28	9	46	19	35	.08	.14	75	82	-.00	.04	.38	.25	-4	-1	-4	1	-8
Madson R	18	11	47	21	32	.13	.11	78	83	.06	.03	.37	.18	1	-2	-0	-3	-5
Gordon F	19	9	49	16	35	.05	.17	73	85	.03	.05	.40	.23	-1	0	-2	2	0
Kendrick K	10	6	47	21	32	.10	.13	78	86	.07	.02	.39	.19	-1	-4	6	-1	0
Mesa J	12	12	46	14	39	.14	.14	78	86	.12	.01	.41	.22	3	-2	-2	2	1
Lieber J	16	7	44	28	29	.09	.09	73	85	.03	.04	.36	.17	-2	0	7	-4	2
Condrey C	12	10	46	25	28	.06	.06	71	91	.09	.06	.39	.06	2	2	6	-7	3
Durbin J	13	13	49	14	37	.04	.08	70	83	.11	.07	.38	.16	5	3	-4	-0	4
Lohse K	16	11	40	22	37	.23	.11	79	73	.08	.02	.39	.28	2	-3	3	2	4
Geary G	13	11	49	19	32	.07	.11	71	80	.10	.04	.36	.21	4	1	-1	1	5
Alfonseca A	10	12	53	19	28	.10	.06	76	75	.13	.05	.45	.18	4	1	4	-1	8
Garcia F	19	9	36	27	38	.06	.17	76	81	.04	.04	.44	.27	-1	-1	8	7	13
Moyer J	15	8	39	21	39	.13	.12	75	81	.05	.04	.43	.22	-2	-3	13	10	18
Eaton A	13	11	39	19	42	.10	.14	73	78	.10	.05	.36	.28	8	0	0	25	34
MLB Average	17	9	43	19	38	.10	.10	74	83	.05	.05	.40	.18	--	--	--	--	--

Fielding Stats

Name	INN	SBA/G	CS%	ERA	WP+PB/G	PO	A	TE	FE
Catcher									
Ruiz C	912.7	0.75	25%	4.59	0.316	688	54	2	0
Barajas R	303.0	0.53	33%	5.17	0.505	252	14	0	0
Coste C	242.7	0.78	29%	4.93	0.185	157	12	0	0

Name	Inn	PO	A	TE	FE	FPct	DPS	DPT	RZR	OOZ
First Base										
Howard R	1241.0	1191	103	4	8	.991	16	0	.723	21
Helms W	102.7	93	4	0	1	.990	1	0	.600	1
Dobbs G	97.7	102	0	0	0	1.000	4	0	.786	0
Utley C	8.0	6	0	0	0	1.000	0	0	--	--
Coste C	7.0	6	0	0	0	1.000	0	0	1.000	0
Barajas R	1.0	1	1	0	0	1.000	0	0	.500	0
Werth J	1.0	1	0	0	0	1.000	0	0	--	--
Second Base										
Utley C	1167.0	289	372	6	4	.985	37	46	.859	53
Iguchi T	265.3	72	90	0	0	1.000	9	21	.818	11
Nunez A	19.0	11	4	0	0	1.000	0	2	.400	0
Dobbs G	7.0	0	7	0	0	1.000	0	0	1.000	1
Shortstop										
Rollins J	1441.0	227	479	0	11	.985	61	43	.808	65
Nunez A	17.0	0	3	0	0	1.000	1	0	.667	1

Name	Inn	PO	A	TE	FE	FPct	DPS	DPT	RZR	OOZ
Third Base										
Nunez A	593.7	41	175	5	4	.960	13	0	.711	26
Helms W	441.7	27	97	4	5	.932	2	0	.702	17
Dobbs G	418.0	44	77	5	2	.945	8	0	.644	10
Branyan R	5.0	1	0	0	0	1.000	0	0	--	--
Left Field										
Burrell P	1028.0	176	8	1	8	.948	4	0	.803	21
Bourn M	217.7	52	0	0	0	1.000	0	0	.896	9
Werth J	127.7	35	2	0	0	1.000	2	0	.929	10
Dobbs G	82.7	18	0	0	1	.947	0	0	.778	4
Branyan R	1.0	0	0	0	0	0.000	0	0	--	--
Roberson C	1.0	0	0	0	0	0.000	0	0	--	--
Center Field										
Rowand A	1373.0	392	11	0	2	.995	4	0	.861	69
Bourn M	56.7	16	0	0	0	1.000	0	0	.714	6
Victorino S	16.0	3	0	0	0	1.000	0	0	.600	0
Roberson C	10.0	4	0	0	0	1.000	0	0	1.000	1
Werth J	2.0	3	0	0	0	1.000	0	0	1.000	0
Right Field										
Victorino S	918.7	229	10	1	2	.988	8	0	.892	55
Werth J	446.0	109	7	0	2	.983	2	0	.925	23
Roberson C	54.0	14	1	0	1	.938	2	0	.786	3
Bourn M	29.7	8	0	0	0	1.000	0	0	1.000	2
Dobbs G	10.0	3	0	0	0	1.000	0	0	1.000	0

Batted Ball Batting Stats

	% of PA		% of Batted Balls					Out %		Runs Per Event				Total Runs vs. Avg.				
Player	K%	BB%	GB%	LD%	FB%	IF/F	HR/OF	GB	OF	NIP	GB	LD	OF	NIP	GB	LD	FB	Tot
Utley C	15	12	38	20	42	.06	.12	69	78	.10	.09	.44	.25	9	7	9	21	46
Howard R	31	17	31	24	44	.03	.30	81	81	.05	-.01	.42	.47	8	-10	3	42	43
Rollins J	11	7	36	20	44	.08	.10	71	85	.07	.07	.44	.17	-0	7	15	11	33
Burrell P	20	20	30	18	51	.14	.19	75	87	.12	.04	.40	.27	20	-4	-2	18	32
Rowand A	17	10	43	20	38	.09	.16	70	74	.05	.06	.38	.31	1	3	3	24	31
Werth J	24	15	40	27	33	.10	.15	66	78	.06	.11	.39	.26	4	4	5	2	16
Victorino S	12	9	47	17	36	.11	.09	68	88	.09	.08	.44	.12	3	9	2	-7	7
Iguchi T	15	9	43	19	38	.09	.07	68	87	.06	.09	.42	.11	0	3	1	-2	3
Dobbs G	19	8	38	16	46	.13	.09	69	78	.03	.07	.40	.20	-2	3	-2	4	2
Bourn M	16	10	58	18	24	.05	.05	71	80	.06	.07	.36	.17	0	2	-1	-2	-0
Barajas R	16	16	31	15	54	.12	.09	77	86	.11	.02	.35	.14	3	-2	-2	0	-1
Coste C	15	4	43	17	40	.07	.12	70	86	-.01	.08	.32	.17	-2	1	-2	1	-2
Ruiz C	11	11	46	18	36	.09	.06	74	81	.11	.04	.35	.14	5	-1	-2	-4	-2
Helms W	20	7	39	20	41	.05	.06	76	79	.01	.02	.35	.15	-4	-3	-2	-1	-10
Nunez A	17	11	61	20	18	.05	.00	78	83	.07	.01	.37	.04	1	-3	-1	-11	-14
Moyer J	31	2	61	14	25	.27	.00	89	88	-.08	-.03	.44	-.03	-4	-3	-3	-5	-15
MLB Average	*17*	*9*	*43*	*19*	*38*	*.10*	*.10*	*74*	*83*	*.05*	*.05*	*.40*	*.18*	*--*	*--*	*--*	*--*	*--*

Pittsburgh Pirates

Stat Facts:

- Nate McLouth stole 22 bases in 23 attempts
- 31% of McLouth's batted balls were grounders, and 53% were fly balls
- No Pirate with 100 plate appearances had a GPA better than .275
- Ronny Paulino had an L^R of .154
- Only 3% of Paulino's fly balls were infield pop-ups
- Zach Duke induced 28 double plays in 107 innings
- Paul Maholm had a GB% of 53%
- 50% of the batted balls against Matt Capps were fly balls
- Freddy Sanchez committed just one throwing error
- Jack Wilson made 76 OOZ plays
- Cesar Izturis struck out in just 2% of his plate appearances

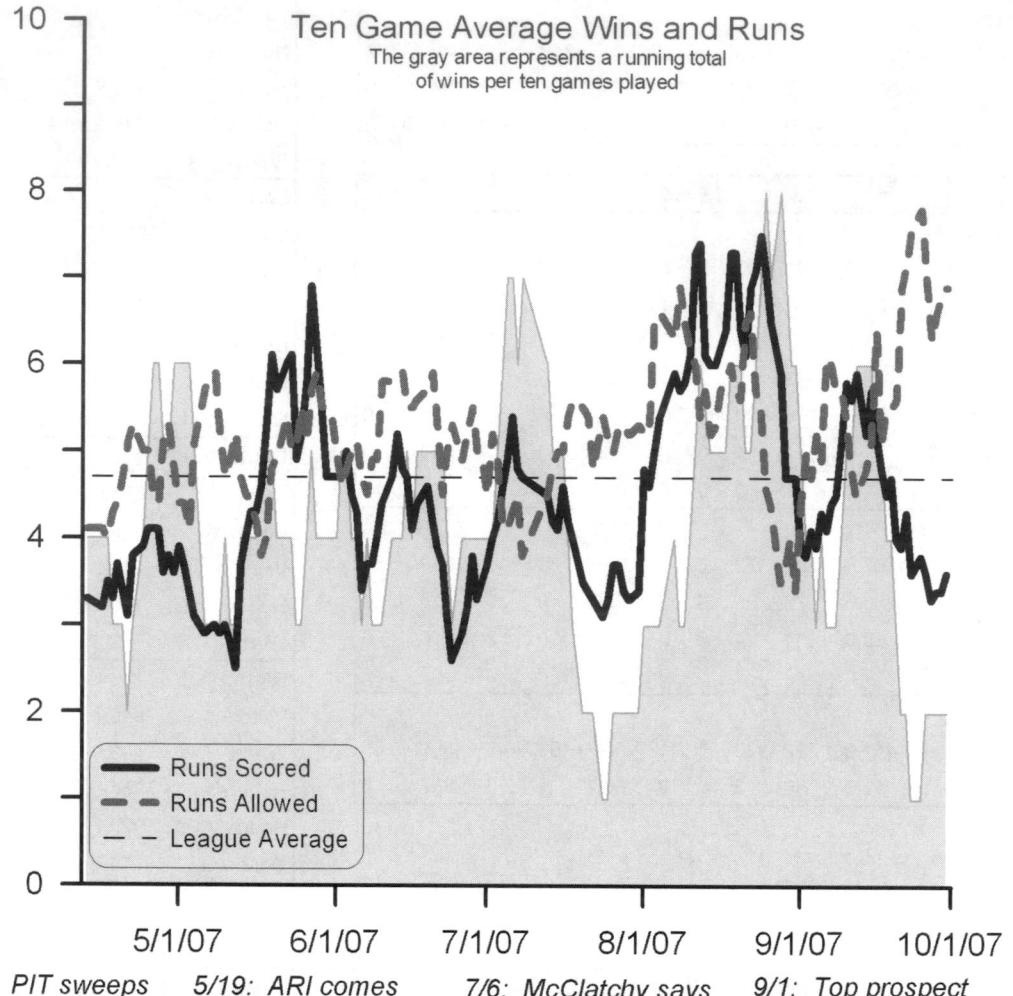

Ten Game Average Wins and Runs
The gray area represents a running total of wins per ten games played

Legend:
— Runs Scored
- - Runs Allowed
- - League Average

4/4: PIT sweeps HOU to start 3-0, alone in first place

5/19: ARI comes back from a 7-1 deficit to beat PIT 9-8

6/7: Southpaw reliever Daniel Moskos is picked 4th overall in draft to the dismay of PIT fans

7/6: McClatchy says he will resign as CEO at season's end

7/31: PIT loses for 14th time in 16 G; 20 games below .500

9/1: Top prospect Pearce makes major-league debut

Team Batting and Pitching/Fielding Stats by Month						
	April	May	June	July	Aug	Sept/Oct
Wins	12	11	12	7	17	9
Losses	12	18	15	17	13	19
RS/G	3.6	4.6	4.1	3.8	6.1	4.4
RA/G	4.4	5.2	5.1	5.3	5.1	6.2
OBP	.295	.326	.322	.293	.353	.343
SLG	.363	.381	.401	.397	.483	.427
FIP	4.06	4.93	4.11	4.17	4.57	5.05
DER	.689	.683	.682	.673	.681	.644

Batting Stats

Player	BR	Runs	RBI	PA	Outs	H	2B	3B	HR	TB	K	BB	IBB	HBP	SH	SF	SB	CS	GDP	H-A	L^R	BA	OBP	SLG	GPA
Sanchez F	91	77	81	653	433	183	42	4	11	266	76	32	2	8	2	9	0	1	13	.004	.076	.304	.343	.442	.267
LaRoche A *	86	71	88	632	429	153	42	0	21	258	131	62	5	3	0	4	1	1	18	.050	-.004	.272	.345	.458	.273
Bay J	75	78	84	614	414	133	25	2	21	225	141	59	3	9	0	8	4	1	8	-.008	.001	.247	.327	.418	.254
Bautista J	73	75	63	614	416	135	36	2	15	220	101	68	1	4	4	6	6	3	16	.002	.018	.254	.339	.414	.259
Wilson J	67	67	56	535	349	141	29	2	12	210	46	38	9	6	7	7	2	5	8	-.021	.071	.296	.350	.440	.270
Nady X	62	55	72	470	328	120	23	1	20	205	101	23	2	12	0	4	3	1	16	-.014	.011	.278	.330	.476	.270
McLouth N *	54	62	38	382	247	85	21	3	13	151	77	39	2	9	3	2	22	1	2	.020	.022	.258	.351	.459	.275
Paulino R	49	56	55	494	353	120	25	0	11	178	79	33	0	2	0	2	2	2	14	.016	.154	.263	.314	.389	.241
Doumit R +	35	33	32	279	190	69	19	2	9	119	59	22	2	4	0	1	1	2	5	.049	-.064	.274	.341	.472	.274
Duffy C *	29	31	22	270	187	60	11	3	3	86	43	21	0	3	2	3	13	4	2	-.006	.032	.249	.313	.357	.233
Phelps J	18	13	19	95	51	27	4	2	5	50	23	14	0	3	0	1	0	0	1	.034	.103	.351	.463	.649	.375
Morgan N *	17	15	7	118	78	32	3	4	1	46	19	9	0	1	1	0	7	3	0	.004	-.015	.299	.359	.430	.272
Castillo J	17	18	24	230	178	54	18	1	0	74	48	6	2	2	0	1	0	0	11	.022	.003	.244	.270	.335	.207
Izturis C +	13	16	8	130	93	34	3	2	0	41	3	6	0	0	1	0	0	3	1	-.065	-.093	.276	.310	.333	.225
Pearce S	9	13	6	73	51	20	5	1	0	27	12	5	0	0	0	0	2	1	2	.110	.103	.294	.342	.397	.256
Kata M +	9	9	10	90	69	22	7	1	1	34	15	0	0	1	1	0	0	0	3	.203	-.104	.250	.258	.386	.215
Davis R	6	6	2	57	38	13	2	1	0	17	3	7	0	0	1	1	5	2	1	.106	.105	.271	.357	.354	.252
Morris M	4	3	2	24	13	6	1	0	1	10	7	0	0	0	5	0	0	0	0	.473	.124	.316	.316	.526	.276
Duke Z *	3	3	3	35	24	8	0	0	0	8	12	0	0	0	3	0	0	0	0	-.242	.154	.250	.250	.250	.177
Cota H	3	1	3	18	10	4	1	0	0	5	2	2	0	1	0	1	0	0	0	.057	-.264	.286	.389	.357	.267
Maldonado C	2	2	4	30	21	5	1	0	2	12	8	5	2	0	0	1	0	0	2	-.172	.244	.200	.333	.500	.278
Maholm P *	1	4	5	62	50	11	1	0	0	12	29	1	0	0	2	0	0	0	2	.082	-.005	.186	.200	.203	.142
Kelly D *	1	2	0	32	24	4	0	0	0	4	3	3	0	2	0	0	0	0	1	.012	.175	.148	.281	.148	.165
Capps M	0	0	0	1	0	1	0	0	0	1	0	0	0	0	0	0	0	0	0	-.700	--	1.000	1.000	1.000	.707
Bullington B	0	1	0	4	2	1	0	0	0	1	0	0	0	0	1	0	0	0	0	-.700	.700	.333	.333	.333	.236
Van Benschot	0	1	0	10	6	1	1	0	0	2	3	1	0	0	2	0	0	0	0	-.125	-.250	.143	.250	.286	.186
Chacon S	0	1	0	13	8	3	0	0	0	3	2	0	0	0	2	0	0	0	0	-.093	.194	.273	.273	.273	.193
Grabow J *	-0	0	0	1	1	0	0	0	0	0	0	0	0	0	0	0	0	0	0	.000	--	.000	.000	.000	.000
Sanchez R	-0	0	0	1	1	0	0	0	0	0	1	0	0	0	0	0	0	0	0	.000	--	.000	.000	.000	.000
Marte D *	-0	0	0	2	2	0	0	0	0	0	1	0	0	0	0	0	0	0	0	.000	.000	.000	.000	.000	.000
McLeary M	-0	0	0	2	2	0	0	0	0	0	0	0	0	0	0	0	0	0	0	.000	.000	.000	.000	.000	.000
Armas Jr. T	-0	0	2	28	23	3	1	0	0	4	12	0	0	0	2	0	0	0	0	-.138	.034	.115	.115	.154	.091
Wasdin J	-0	0	0	4	4	0	0	0	0	0	1	0	0	0	0	0	0	0	0	.000	.000	.000	.000	.000	.000
Osoria F	-0	0	0	5	4	0	0	0	0	0	2	0	0	0	1	0	0	0	0	.000	.000	.000	.000	.000	.000
Snell I	-1	6	2	72	52	5	0	0	0	5	23	3	0	0	12	0	0	0	0	-.029	.025	.088	.133	.088	.083
Youman S *	-1	1	0	15	12	1	0	0	0	1	5	1	0	0	2	0	0	0	1	-.080	.118	.083	.154	.083	.091
Eldred B	-1	3	3	47	42	5	1	0	2	12	16	1	1	0	0	0	0	0	1	-.078	-.026	.109	.128	.261	.124
Gorzelanny T	-3	1	3	72	61	4	0	0	0	4	31	2	0	1	6	0	0	0	2	.040	.026	.063	.106	.063	.064

Italicized stats have been adjusted for home park.
Batted Ball Batting Stats are listed after Fielding Stats.

Pitching Stats

Player	PRC	IP	BFP	G	GS	K	BB	IBB	HBP	H	HR	DP	DER	SB	CS	PO	W	L	Sv	Op	Hld	H-A	R^L	RA	ERA	FIP
Snell I	95	208.0	882	32	32	177	68	4	8	209	22	24	.684	14	6	0	9	12	0	0	0	.007	-.040	4.07	3.76	3.98
Gorzelanny T	88	201.7	874	32	32	135	68	3	11	214	18	20	.685	17	5	3	14	10	0	0	0	-.013	-.072	4.02	3.88	4.22
Maholm P *	54	177.7	765	29	29	105	49	3	6	204	22	29	.672	11	6	1	10	15	0	0	0	-.060	-.063	5.57	5.02	4.58
Capps M	53	79.0	315	76	0	64	16	10	3	64	5	8	.736	1	0	0	4	7	18	21	15	.012	-.098	2.51	2.28	2.81
Chacon S	45	96.0	428	64	4	79	48	11	7	95	9	9	.688	7	4	2	5	4	1	8	12	-.069	-.087	3.94	3.94	4.22
Marte D *	30	45.3	182	65	0	51	18	1	2	32	2	5	.706	0	1	1	2	0	0	0	15	-.072	-.123	2.78	2.38	2.85
Armas Jr. T	27	97.0	442	31	15	73	38	3	8	111	18	5	.689	11	2	0	4	5	0	0	0	-.062	-.024	6.31	6.03	5.51
Duke Z *	26	107.3	482	20	19	41	25	2	3	161	14	28	.622	5	5	2	3	8	0	0	0	-.042	-.022	6.20	5.53	4.93
Grabow J *	20	51.7	228	63	0	42	19	2	1	56	6	5	.681	10	0	0	3	2	1	2	8	-.026	-.071	4.70	4.53	4.20
Torres S	17	52.7	231	56	0	45	17	0	4	57	7	9	.658	2	1	0	2	4	12	18	5	.072	-.026	5.81	5.47	4.48
Morris M	15	62.0	281	11	11	29	22	1	4	78	6	12	.668	8	0	0	3	4	0	0	0	-.040	.059	6.39	6.10	4.80
Youman S *	15	57.3	257	16	8	29	23	1	4	65	5	6	.689	4	1	1	3	5	0	0	0	-.058	.031	6.28	5.97	4.75
Osoria F	9	28.3	126	25	0	13	8	2	4	33	3	6	.684	1	0	0	0	2	0	0	4	.043	-.113	5.08	4.76	4.79
Bayliss J	7	37.7	179	39	0	29	18	2	2	51	5	4	.648	4	1	0	4	3	0	1	4	.102	-.117	8.60	8.36	5.92
Sanchez R	6	18.0	73	16	0	11	8	0	1	16	2	6	.725	0	0	0	1	0	0	0	2	.002	-.027	5.00	5.00	4.99
Wasdin J	5	19.7	93	12	0	10	8	4	0	32	1	3	.581	0	2	1	1	1	0	0	0	-.043	.055	5.95	5.95	3.52
Van Benschot	5	39.0	203	11	9	26	29	1	5	55	4	2	.626	6	1	1	0	7	0	0	0	-.015	.016	10.38	10.15	5.81
Bullington B	5	17.0	76	5	3	7	5	0	0	24	3	4	.639	2	0	0	0	3	0	0	0	-.048	-.234	5.82	5.29	5.62
Perez J *	4	12.3	57	17	0	10	8	0	0	14	2	2	.676	1	0	0	0	0	0	0	0	-.105	-.011	5.11	4.38	5.70
Kuwata M	3	21.0	103	19	0	12	15	4	1	25	6	2	.710	4	0	0	0	1	0	0	3	.070	.066	9.86	9.43	7.55
McLeary M	1	7.7	34	4	0	5	2	0	0	9	4	0	.783	1	0	0	0	0	0	1	0	-.099	-.097	9.39	8.22	9.53
Kolb D	1	3.0	16	3	0	2	2	1	0	6	1	1	.545	0	0	0	0	0	0	0	0	-.028	-.661	9.00	9.00	7.27
Sharpless J	0	4.3	21	6	0	1	1	0	0	7	3	0	.750	0	0	0	0	1	0	0	0	.220	.324	12.46	12.46	12.50
Rogers B	0	2.0	9	3	0	1	1	0	0	3	2	0	.800	1	0	0	0	0	0	0	0	--	.375	13.50	13.50	16.77
Davidson D *	0	2.0	17	2	0	0	2	0	2	6	1	0	.500	0	0	0	0	0	0	0	0	--	.141	27.00	22.50	15.77

Italicized stats have been adjusted for home park.

Batted Ball Pitching Stats

Player	% of PA		% of Batted Balls					Out %		Runs Per Event				Total Runs vs. Avg.				
	K%	BB%	GB%	LD%	FB%	IF/F	HR/OF	GB	OF	NIP	GB	LD	OF	NIP	GB	LD	FB	Tot
Capps M	20	6	31	19	50	.12	.05	73	81	-.01	.05	.24	.12	-5	-2	-9	-4	-21
Snell I	20	9	46	17	37	.06	.10	71	83	.02	.07	.39	.18	-6	5	-8	-0	-9
Marte D	28	11	43	13	44	.10	.05	80	76	.02	.00	.45	.17	-1	-2	-4	-1	-9
Grabow J	18	9	50	17	33	.12	.13	71	88	.03	.06	.37	.18	-1	2	-2	-2	-3
Gorzelanny T	15	9	42	18	40	.10	.07	70	85	.06	.07	.39	.13	0	7	0	-9	-2
Osoria F	10	10	52	19	29	.10	.12	73	78	.11	.03	.24	.21	1	0	-2	0	-0
Torres S	19	9	48	19	34	.07	.14	68	86	.03	.08	.38	.20	-1	3	-1	-0	1
Chacon S	18	13	44	17	39	.15	.10	74	76	.08	.04	.39	.22	5	-1	-3	2	2
Youman S	11	11	38	20	42	.08	.07	71	82	.11	.06	.37	.14	3	1	0	-1	3
Maholm P	14	7	53	17	30	.06	.14	74	81	.04	.04	.40	.24	-3	4	-1	6	6
Morris M	10	9	48	21	31	.12	.10	74	69	.10	.04	.31	.28	2	-0	0	5	6
Bayliss J	16	11	27	16	57	.19	.13	71	75	.07	.06	.58	.26	1	-0	3	7	12
Armas Jr. T	17	10	37	20	43	.13	.13	76	84	.06	.04	.47	.21	2	-2	7	5	12
Van Benschoten J	13	17	39	27	34	.04	.09	69	88	.15	.08	.43	.12	7	2	7	-2	13
Duke Z	9	6	51	20	29	.07	.13	73	66	.07	.04	.39	.34	-1	2	8	18	28
MLB Average	17	9	43	19	38	.10	.10	74	83	.05	.05	.40	.18	--	--	--	--	--

Fielding Stats

Name	INN	SBA/G	CS%	ERA	WP+PB/G	PO	A	TE	FE
Catcher									
Paulino R	1088.0	0.77	20%	4.61	0.323	784	58	3	3
Doumit R	223.7	1.01	16%	5.51	0.523	149	7	0	1
Maldonado C	79.0	0.57	20%	7.06	0.342	64	2	0	0
Cota H	41.0	1.76	13%	5.71	0.439	30	2	0	0
Phelps J	16.0	2.25	0%	7.31	0.563	9	1	0	0

Name	Inn	PO	A	TE	FE	FPct	DPS	DPT	RZR	OOZ
First Base										
LaRoche A	1301.0	1296	81	1	5	.996	21	0	.781	23
Phelps J	96.7	107	5	0	0	1.000	0	0	.818	4
Eldred B	22.0	23	1	0	0	1.000	2	0	1.000	0
Doumit R	18.7	12	0	0	0	1.000	0	0	--	--
Pearce S	9.0	12	0	0	0	1.000	0	0	1.000	0
Second Base										
Sanchez F	1272.0	313	379	1	8	.987	34	80	.834	23
Castillo J	129.0	45	25	1	3	.946	6	5	.591	3
Kata M	34.0	14	14	0	0	1.000	2	5	.833	2
Kelly D	12.0	1	2	0	0	1.000	1	0	.667	0
Shortstop										
Wilson J	1142.0	177	452	4	7	.983	66	44	.816	76
Izturis C	205.0	39	66	1	0	.991	18	6	.895	8
Castillo J	63.0	15	20	1	0	.972	4	2	.941	1
Kelly D	20.0	5	6	0	0	1.000	0	0	1.000	3
Kata M	16.7	2	5	0	0	1.000	1	0	.833	0
Sanchez F	1.0	0	0	0	0	0.000	0	0	--	--

Name	Inn	PO	A	TE	FE	FPct	DPS	DPT	RZR	OOZ
Third Base										
Bautista J	1064.0	95	251	6	9	.958	16	0	.612	36
Castillo J	253.3	23	83	1	3	.964	6	0	.707	12
Kata M	80.7	2	16	1	0	.947	1	0	.579	4
Izturis C	49.0	3	11	0	0	1.000	0	0	.833	0
Left Field										
Bay J	1237.0	265	13	4	4	.972	6	0	.842	47
McLouth N	110.3	19	0	0	0	1.000	0	0	.938	4
Nady X	76.7	14	0	0	0	1.000	0	0	.647	3
Bautista J	12.7	1	0	0	0	1.000	0	0	1.000	0
Kata M	10.0	2	0	0	0	1.000	0	0	1.000	0
Kelly D	1.0	1	0	0	0	1.000	0	0	.500	0
Center Field										
Duffy C	534.7	172	3	0	1	.994	0	0	.902	24
McLouth N	495.3	142	2	0	2	.986	2	0	.862	23
Morgan N	221.7	84	2	0	1	.989	3	0	.907	16
Nady X	83.0	17	0	0	1	.944	0	0	.727	1
Davis R	83.0	27	0	0	0	1.000	0	0	.893	2
Bautista J	30.0	6	0	0	0	1.000	0	0	1.000	1
Right Field										
Nady X	748.0	161	4	0	0	1.000	0	0	.846	26
Doumit R	311.0	62	5	0	1	.985	4	0	.828	10
Pearce S	135.0	31	1	0	0	1.000	0	0	.926	6
Bautista J	130.0	23	1	0	2	.923	0	0	.909	3
McLouth N	68.0	22	0	0	1	.957	0	0	.900	4
Eldred B	51.7	8	0	0	0	1.000	0	0	1.000	1
Castillo J	3.0	3	0	0	0	1.000	0	0	1.000	1
Kata M	1.0	0	0	0	0	0.000	0	0	--	--
Kelly D	0.0	0	0	0	0	0.000	0	0	--	--

Batted Ball Batting Stats

	% of PA		% of Batted Balls					Out %		Runs Per Event				Total Runs vs. Avg.				
Player	K%	BB%	GB%	LD%	FB%	IF/F	HR/OF	GB	OF	NIP	GB	LD	OF	NIP	GB	LD	FB	Tot
McLouth N	20	13	31	16	53	.12	.11	68	83	.06	.10	.41	.20	3	3	-3	6	8
Sanchez F	12	6	39	22	38	.06	.06	73	81	.05	.05	.38	.13	-3	2	12	-2	8
LaRoche A	21	10	36	20	44	.06	.12	79	83	.04	.00	.46	.20	-1	-8	7	8	6
Doumit R	21	9	42	21	38	.08	.13	70	88	.03	.08	.47	.19	-1	2	4	1	6
Nady X	21	7	39	21	40	.08	.15	74	79	.01	.03	.37	.27	-6	-3	1	13	5
Wilson J	9	8	39	19	42	.11	.07	69	83	.11	.08	.34	.12	3	6	-0	-4	4
Morgan N	16	8	57	16	27	.09	.05	74	79	.05	.05	.58	.17	-0	2	1	-2	1
Bay J	23	11	38	17	45	.10	.13	74	84	.04	.05	.44	.20	-1	-2	-3	6	0
Bautista J	16	12	40	16	43	.12	.09	75	84	.08	.04	.41	.16	5	-3	-4	-1	-3
Izturis C	2	5	43	23	33	.18	.00	81	82	.19	.01	.31	.05	-0	-1	1	-5	-4
Duffy C	16	9	56	17	27	.04	.04	73	83	.05	.06	.34	.11	-0	3	-4	-6	-7
Paulino R	16	7	47	17	36	.03	.08	79	79	.03	.01	.42	.17	-4	-6	0	1	-9
Castillo J	21	3	57	18	25	.00	.00	83	72	-.05	-.02	.46	.13	-6	-5	1	-5	-15
MLB Average	17	9	43	19	38	.10	.10	74	83	.05	.05	.40	.18	--	--	--	--	--

San Diego Padres

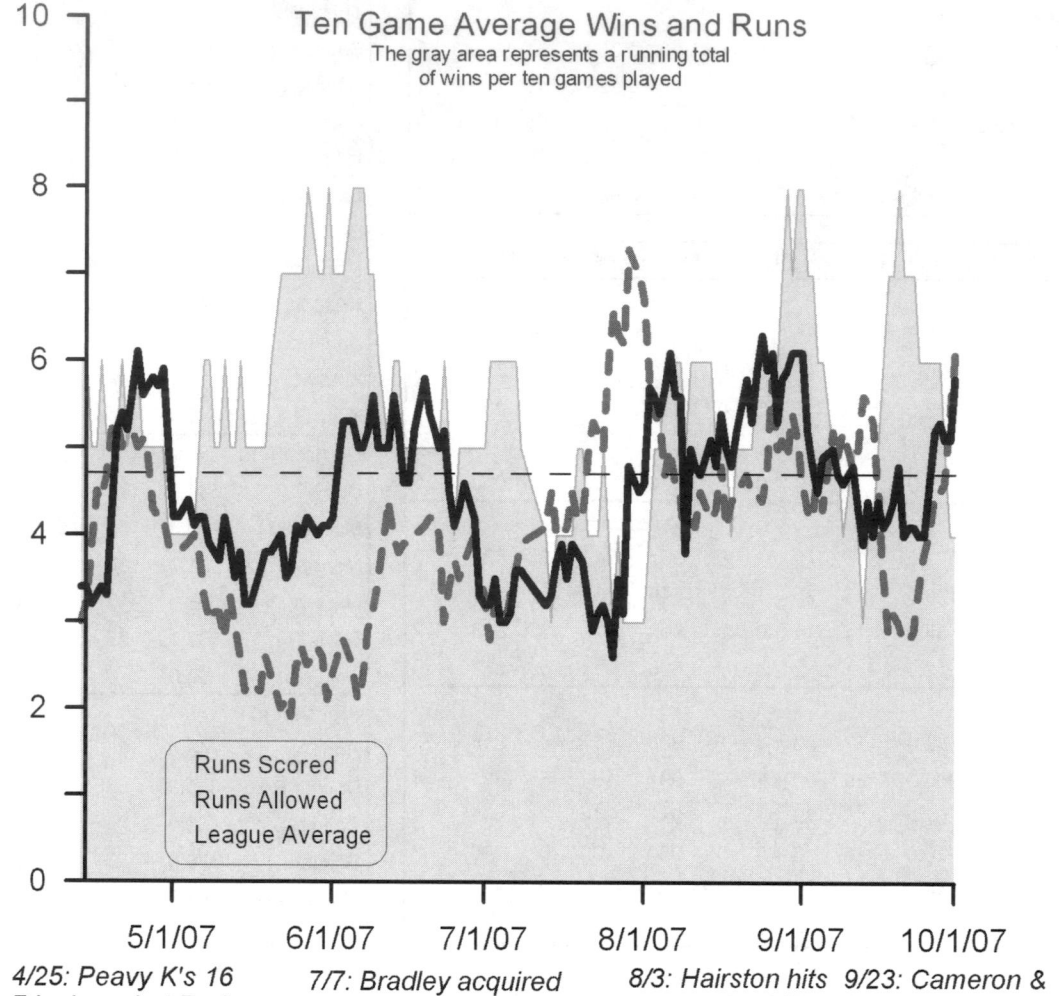

Ten Game Average Wins and Runs
The gray area represents a running total of wins per ten games played

Runs Scored
Runs Allowed
League Average

4/25: Peavy K's 16 7 innings, but Pads lose to Dbacks

7/7: Bradley acquired

7/14: B. Giles finally hits 2nd HR of season

7/24: Young at 9-3, 1.82; goes 0-5, 5.96 rest of way due to injury

8/3: Hairston hits game-tying HR in 8th, walk-off HR in 10th

9/23: Cameron & Bradley lost for season in nightmare sweep by Rockies

Team Batting and Pitching/Fielding Stats by Month						
	April	**May**	**June**	**July**	**Aug**	**Sept/Oct**
Wins	13	18	15	10	18	15
Losses	13	9	11	16	11	14
RS/G	4.4	4.0	4.8	3.7	5.4	4.8
RA/G	4.1	2.5	3.6	5.2	4.6	4.6
OBP	.318	.312	.313	.303	.346	.332
SLG	.397	.383	.404	.369	.470	.428
FIP	3.52	2.94	3.57	4.52	3.65	3.86
DER	.712	.722	.693	.695	.691	.698

Batting Stats

Player	BR	Runs	RBI	PA	Outs	H	2B	3B	HR	TB	K	BB	IBB	HBP	SH	SF	SB	CS	GDP	H-A	L^R	BA	OBP	SLG	GPA
Gonzalez A *	118	101	100	720	470	182	46	3	30	324	140	65	9	3	0	6	0	0	6	-.047	.025	.282	.347	.502	.306
Cameron M	95	88	78	651	447	138	33	6	21	246	160	67	1	8	2	3	18	5	9	-.020	.075	.242	.328	.431	.278
Greene K	88	89	97	659	468	155	44	3	27	286	128	32	3	5	0	11	4	0	12	-.055	.033	.254	.291	.468	.270
Giles B *	79	72	51	552	366	131	27	2	13	201	61	64	5	4	0	1	4	6	8	-.057	.042	.271	.361	.416	.289
Kouzmanoff K	75	57	74	534	360	133	30	2	18	221	94	32	2	10	2	6	1	0	9	-.019	.080	.275	.329	.457	.285
Bard J +	69	42	51	443	295	111	27	2	5	157	58	50	7	0	1	3	0	1	16	-.048	.094	.285	.364	.404	.288
Giles M	50	52	39	476	337	96	19	3	4	133	82	44	0	3	6	3	10	3	10	-.027	.014	.229	.304	.317	.235
Blum G +	40	34	33	370	257	83	21	1	5	121	52	32	4	2	3	3	0	0	10	.058	-.027	.252	.319	.367	.256
Bradley M +	34	31	30	169	103	45	5	1	11	85	27	23	2	2	0	0	3	1	3	-.029	-.050	.313	.414	.590	.363
Cruz J +	29	37	21	293	200	60	12	3	6	96	65	31	1	0	5	1	6	1	3	-.022	.004	.234	.316	.375	.256
Sledge T *	24	22	23	233	167	42	9	0	7	72	60	27	2	3	1	2	1	2	7	-.097	.075	.210	.310	.360	.250
Branyan R *	21	16	19	146	99	24	5	1	7	52	48	21	1	2	0	1	1	0	1	.048	-.066	.197	.322	.426	.273
Hairston S	19	16	20	95	62	25	5	1	8	56	18	7	0	0	0	1	0	0	0	.174	-.037	.287	.337	.644	.340
Bowen R +	13	12	11	98	62	22	8	0	2	36	28	13	3	1	1	1	1	2	0	-.080	.103	.268	.371	.439	.301
Ensberg M	8	11	8	65	46	13	3	0	4	28	19	7	0	0	0	0	0	0	1	-.157	.112	.224	.308	.483	.282
Clark B	7	6	6	57	37	15	1	2	0	20	7	8	2	0	0	0	0	1	2	-.043	.100	.306	.404	.408	.308
Barrett M	7	6	12	136	108	30	8	0	0	38	21	2	0	0	0	1	0	0	5	-.020	-.076	.226	.235	.286	.193
LaForest P *	6	7	3	30	16	9	1	0	1	13	8	5	1	0	0	0	0	0	0	.150	-.455	.360	.467	.520	.370
Bocachica H	6	9	2	68	50	15	4	0	1	22	13	5	0	0	0	0	3	2	0	.070	-.016	.238	.294	.349	.239
Robles O *	4	0	2	33	20	6	0	0	0	6	4	2	1	0	5	0	0	0	0	.000	-.053	.231	.286	.231	.202
Peavy J	4	8	7	84	57	17	4	1	0	23	14	2	0	0	8	1	0	0	1	.072	-.122	.233	.250	.315	.208
McAnulty P *	4	5	5	43	32	8	1	0	1	12	10	3	1	0	0	0	0	0	0	.170	-.158	.200	.256	.300	.207
Young C	4	2	2	58	41	6	1	0	0	7	15	5	0	1	6	0	0	0	1	-.186	.119	.130	.231	.152	.154
Germano J	2	2	2	41	27	5	1	0	0	6	13	3	0	0	6	0	0	0	0	-.052	-.017	.156	.229	.188	.163
Hensley C	2	0	2	16	11	3	0	0	0	3	8	0	0	0	2	0	1	0	0	-.233	-.350	.214	.214	.214	.163
Headley C +	2	1	0	21	16	4	1	0	0	5	4	2	0	1	0	0	0	0	2	.149	-.147	.222	.333	.278	.239
Stansberry C	1	1	1	10	5	2	0	0	0	2	3	0	0	1	2	0	0	0	0	.133	-.009	.286	.375	.286	.261
Myrow D *	1	0	1	12	10	1	1	0	0	2	4	1	0	1	0	0	0	0	1	-.122	--	.100	.250	.200	.177
Stauffer T	1	1	2	5	3	1	0	0	0	1	2	0	0	0	1	0	0	0	0	--	-.233	.250	.250	.250	.190
Mackowiak R	1	6	2	61	47	11	3	0	0	14	18	3	0	2	0	0	1	0	2	.023	-.012	.196	.262	.250	.196
Brocail D *	0	0	0	2	1	1	0	0	0	1	1	0	0	0	0	0	0	0	0	.350	.700	.500	.500	.500	.380
Ledezma W *	-0	1	0	1	1	0	0	0	0	0	0	0	0	0	0	0	0	0	0	.000	--	.000	.000	.000	.000
Morton C	-0	0	0	1	1	0	0	0	0	0	0	0	0	0	0	0	0	0	0	--	--	.000	.000	.000	.000
Meredith C	-0	0	0	1	1	0	0	0	0	0	0	0	0	0	0	0	0	0	0	.000	--	.000	.000	.000	.000
Lane J	-0	0	0	2	2	0	0	0	0	0	1	0	0	0	0	0	0	0	0	--	.000	.000	.000	.000	.000
Thompson M	-0	0	0	2	2	0	0	0	0	0	1	0	0	0	0	0	0	0	0	.000	--	.000	.000	.000	.000
Cameron K	-0	0	0	4	4	0	0	0	0	0	3	0	0	0	0	0	0	0	0	.000	.000	.000	.000	.000	.000
Hampson J *	-1	0	0	4	5	0	0	0	0	0	1	0	0	0	0	0	0	0	1	.000	.000	.000	.000	.000	.000
Cassel J	-1	2	0	8	8	1	0	0	0	1	3	0	0	0	0	0	0	0	1	-.175	-.117	.125	.125	.125	.095
Tomko B	-1	0	0	8	8	0	0	0	0	0	4	0	0	0	0	0	0	0	0	.000	--	.000	.000	.000	.000
Wells D *	-1	1	0	42	34	4	0	0	0	4	12	0	0	0	4	0	0	0	0	.000	.052	.105	.105	.105	.080
Maddux G	-2	2	0	72	55	9	2	0	0	11	19	1	0	0	9	0	1	0	2	-.049	-.060	.145	.159	.177	.126

Italicized stats have been adjusted for home park.
Batted Ball Batting Stats are listed after Fielding Stats.

Pitching Stats

Player	PRC	IP	BFP	G	GS	K	BB	IBB	HBP	H	HR	DP	DER	SB	CS	PO	W	L	Sv	Op	Hld	H-A	R^L	RA	ERA	FIP
Peavy J	143	223.3	898	34	34	240	68	5	6	169	13	18	.718	21	2	1	19	6	0	0	0	.001	-.069	2.70	2.54	2.80
Young C	88	173.0	705	30	30	167	72	0	7	118	10	12	.751	44	0	2	9	8	0	0	0	-.048	-.059	3.43	3.12	3.46
Bell H	75	93.7	363	81	0	102	30	1	2	60	3	10	.739	8	3	1	6	4	2	6	34	-.000	-.061	2.02	2.02	2.50
Maddux G	73	198.0	830	34	34	104	25	3	6	221	14	20	.686	37	2	1	14	11	0	0	0	-.009	.012	4.18	4.14	3.56
Germano J	43	133.3	566	26	23	78	40	3	8	133	14	18	.711	18	2	0	7	10	0	0	0	-.012	.019	4.86	4.46	4.48
Wells D *	32	118.7	532	22	22	63	33	4	3	156	17	13	.651	9	4	2	5	8	0	0	0	-.093	-.008	5.61	5.54	4.88
Meredith C	31	79.7	342	80	0	59	17	4	3	94	6	14	.646	7	2	0	5	6	0	5	10	-.085	-.016	4.29	3.50	3.37
Brocail D	31	76.7	319	67	0	43	24	3	2	66	8	5	.748	3	0	0	5	1	0	0	10	.104	.055	3.87	3.05	4.40
Hampson J *	29	53.3	219	39	0	34	16	4	3	48	1	7	.703	5	2	1	2	3	0	0	4	.010	-.033	2.87	2.70	3.08
Hoffman T	29	57.3	235	61	0	44	15	5	0	49	2	2	.724	3	1	0	4	5	42	49	0	-.094	-.115	3.30	2.98	2.71
Cameron K	27	58.0	263	48	0	50	36	5	0	55	0	6	.667	9	0	0	2	0	0	0	1	-.047	.006	3.72	2.79	3.15
Linebrink S	19	45.0	186	44	0	25	14	1	1	41	9	3	.766	6	0	0	3	3	1	7	15	-.127	.021	3.80	3.80	5.69
Thatcher J *	13	21.0	85	22	0	16	6	2	1	13	1	1	.754	3	0	0	2	2	0	0	2	-.003	.104	2.57	1.29	3.08
Tomko B	11	27.3	113	7	4	26	6	0	0	25	5	1	.711	2	1	0	2	1	0	0	0	-.112	.019	4.61	4.61	4.40
Hensley C	10	50.0	238	13	9	30	32	2	1	62	5	5	.659	10	1	0	2	3	0	0	0	-.116	.033	7.20	6.84	5.23
Cassel J	9	22.7	98	6	4	11	5	0	1	30	1	4	.638	0	0	0	1	1	0	0	0	.080	-.052	3.97	3.97	3.67
Ring R *	6	15.0	69	15	0	17	14	2	0	11	1	3	.703	1	0	0	1	0	0	0	0	-.149	.127	4.80	3.60	4.27
Ledezma W *	4	14.3	69	9	1	16	8	2	0	20	2	2	.581	2	0	0	0	0	0	0	0	-.166	.021	6.91	6.28	4.11
Thompson M	2	15.7	75	7	0	5	7	2	3	19	2	3	.672	1	0	0	0	1	0	0	0	-.083	.021	8.62	6.89	5.82
Stauffer T	0	7.7	45	2	2	6	6	0	1	15	5	0	.630	0	0	0	0	1	0	0	0	--	-.216	21.13	21.13	12.92
Rakers A	0	1.0	4	1	0	0	0	0	0	1	0	0	.750	0	0	0	0	0	0	0	0	--	-.350	0.00	0.00	3.27

Italicized stats have been adjusted for home park.

Batted Ball Pitching Stats

Player	% of PA		% of Batted Balls					Out %		Runs Per Event				Total Runs vs. Avg.				
	K%	BB%	GB%	LD%	FB%	IF/F	HR/OF	GB	OF	NIP	GB	LD	OF	NIP	GB	LD	FB	Tot
Peavy J	27	8	44	17	39	.09	.06	78	84	-.00	.02	.43	.10	-15	-9	-10	-23	-57
Young C	24	11	29	16	54	.13	.05	78	89	.03	.01	.44	.07	-2	-10	-9	-21	-41
Bell H	28	9	59	19	23	.10	.07	82	81	-.00	-.01	.29	.15	-6	-6	-10	-11	-33
Maddux G	13	4	51	20	29	.06	.08	79	80	-.01	.02	.43	.17	-13	-5	10	-6	-14
Hoffman T	19	6	31	18	52	.18	.03	75	80	.00	.04	.36	.12	-3	-1	-3	-4	-11
Brocail D	13	8	42	18	40	.07	.08	79	90	.06	.02	.39	.09	-0	-3	-1	-7	-11
Hampson J	16	9	47	15	38	.13	.02	76	82	.05	.03	.47	.07	-0	-0	-1	-7	-9
Cameron K	19	14	49	19	32	.09	.00	70	86	.08	.07	.37	-.01	3	2	-1	-12	-7
Germano J	14	8	49	17	33	.03	.09	79	80	.06	.01	.40	.18	0	-6	-1	1	-6
Meredith C	17	6	72	14	14	.14	.20	71	67	.00	.06	.32	.41	-4	8	-6	-2	-5
Linebrink S	13	8	39	23	39	.13	.18	86	98	.06	-.02	.33	.20	-0	-3	0	1	-3
Tomko B	23	5	41	17	42	.19	.19	74	90	-.03	.04	.49	.26	-2	-0	-0	1	-2
Hensley C	13	14	49	15	36	.03	.08	73	69	.13	.05	.37	.24	5	1	-2	5	9
Wells D	12	7	42	20	38	.08	.12	70	78	.05	.07	.40	.23	-1	5	6	11	21
MLB Average	17	9	43	19	38	.10	.10	74	83	.05	.05	.40	.18	--	--	--	--	--

Fielding Stats

Name	INN	SBA/G	CS%	ERA	WP+PB/G	PO	A	TE	FE
Catcher									
Bard J	927.3	1.25	6%	3.44	0.291	751	39	2	1
Barrett M	292.7	1.41	13%	4.15	0.308	224	16	1	0
Bowen R	208.0	1.08	8%	3.46	0.389	136	13	1	2
LaForest P	56.7	0.79	0%	7.15	0.318	49	1	1	0

Name	Inn	PO	A	TE	FE	FPct	DPS	DPT	RZR	OOZ
First Base										
Gonzalez A	1462.0	1470	140	2	8	.994	22	1	.722	46
Blum G	9.0	13	1	0	0	1.000	0	0	.500	0
Ensberg M	9.0	7	1	0	0	.889	0	0	1.000	0
LaForest P	4.0	2	2	0	1	.800	0	0	1.000	0
Second Base										
Giles M	947.7	203	332	2	5	.987	32	42	.860	24
Blum G	494.0	86	165	1	1	.992	8	16	.882	14
Robles O	35.7	4	15	0	0	1.000	0	1	.833	1
Stansberry C	7.3	2	2	0	0	1.000	0	1	--	--
Shortstop										
Greene K	1396.0	218	461	7	4	.984	45	51	.848	59
Blum G	88.3	14	26	2	1	.930	2	2	.786	2
Third Base										
Kouzmanoff K	1135.0	91	209	10	11	.932	12	0	.680	36
Branyan R	155.7	10	40	0	0	1.000	8	1	.750	2
Ensberg M	92.7	3	29	0	0	.970	4	0	.808	6
Blum G	54.3	2	8	0	0	1.000	0	0	.833	3
Headley C	38.3	2	3	1	0	.833	0	0	.333	1
Robles O	8.3	2	3	0	0	1.000	0	0	1.000	1

Name	Inn	PO	A	TE	FE	FPct	DPS	DPT	RZR	OOZ
Left Field										
Sledge T	399.3	77	2	0	1	.988	0	0	.827	10
Cruz J	365.3	89	4	0	1	.989	2	0	.875	12
Bradley M	326.3	72	3	1	1	.974	2	0	.891	15
Hairston S	180.3	24	1	0	0	1.000	0	0	.941	8
Branyan R	78.3	14	0	0	1	.933	0	0	.867	1
Blum G	45.0	14	0	0	0	1.000	0	0	1.000	1
Mackowiak R	35.0	8	0	0	1	.889	0	0	.800	0
McAnulty P	22.7	5	0	0	0	1.000	0	0	1.000	1
Clark B	21.3	4	0	0	0	1.000	0	0	1.000	0
Bocachica H	11.0	3	0	0	0	1.000	0	0	.667	1
Center Field										
Cameron M	1329.0	365	7	1	4	.987	4	0	.894	53
Clark B	87.3	26	0	0	0	1.000	0	0	.840	5
Bocachica H	35.0	11	1	0	0	1.000	2	0	.875	4
Cruz J	17.0	4	0	0	0	1.000	0	0	.667	2
Giles B	6.0	1	0	0	0	1.000	0	0	1.000	0
Hairston S	5.0	1	0	0	0	1.000	0	0	--	--
Mackowiak R	4.0	0	0	0	0	0.000	0	0	0.000	0
Lane J	1.3	1	0	0	0	1.000	0	0	1.000	0
Right Field										
Giles B	1062.0	216	2	3	2	.978	2	0	.854	47
Cruz J	178.3	54	1	0	0	1.000	2	0	.886	15
Bocachica H	101.0	21	1	0	0	1.000	0	0	.909	1
Mackowiak R	62.0	16	1	0	0	1.000	0	0	.929	3
McAnulty P	40.3	11	0	0	0	1.000	0	0	1.000	0
Sledge T	21.3	11	0	0	0	1.000	0	0	.900	2
Clark B	11.0	1	0	0	0	1.000	0	0	.500	0
Bradley M	6.0	1	0	0	0	1.000	0	0	1.000	0
Lane J	2.0	0	0	0	0	0.000	0	0	--	--

Batted Ball Batting Stats

Player	% of PA		% of Batted Balls					Out %		Runs Per Event				Total Runs vs. Avg.				
	K%	BB%	GB%	LD%	FB%	IF/F	HR/OF	GB	OF	NIP	GB	LD	OF	NIP	GB	LD	FB	Tot
Gonzalez A	19	9	37	19	44	.06	.14	77	79	.04	.04	.40	.27	-2	-3	2	24	22
Bradley M	16	15	43	16	41	.09	.21	76	79	.11	.03	.55	.35	4	-1	3	8	14
Giles B	11	12	40	19	40	.08	.08	77	83	.13	.03	.36	.14	9	-2	1	-1	7
Kouzmanoff K	18	8	41	18	41	.04	.12	79	80	.03	.02	.38	.22	-3	-4	-2	11	1
Bard J	13	11	52	18	30	.02	.05	76	82	.10	.03	.43	.12	5	-1	3	-6	1
Cameron M	25	12	37	19	44	.11	.12	72	82	.03	.06	.39	.23	-1	-1	-5	7	0
Branyan R	33	16	29	13	57	.07	.18	77	88	.04	.04	.52	.23	1	-1	-3	3	-1
Greene K	19	6	35	18	47	.09	.13	80	82	-.01	.01	.42	.22	-11	-9	-0	16	-4
Sledge T	26	13	41	17	42	.08	.13	75	89	.04	.03	.37	.17	0	-1	-4	-1	-6
Cruz J	22	11	38	16	47	.13	.08	80	80	.03	.02	.41	.17	-1	-2	-5	-1	-8
Blum G	14	9	36	20	44	.07	.04	75	87	.07	.04	.42	.05	1	-2	3	-11	-9
Barrett M	15	1	40	19	42	.15	.00	71	93	-.07	.06	.36	-.03	-4	0	-1	-8	-13
Giles M	17	10	44	20	36	.04	.03	80	85	.05	.00	.40	.07	0	-8	1	-13	-20
MLB Average	17	9	43	19	38	.10	.10	74	83	.05	.05	.40	.18	--	--	--	--	--

San Francisco Giants

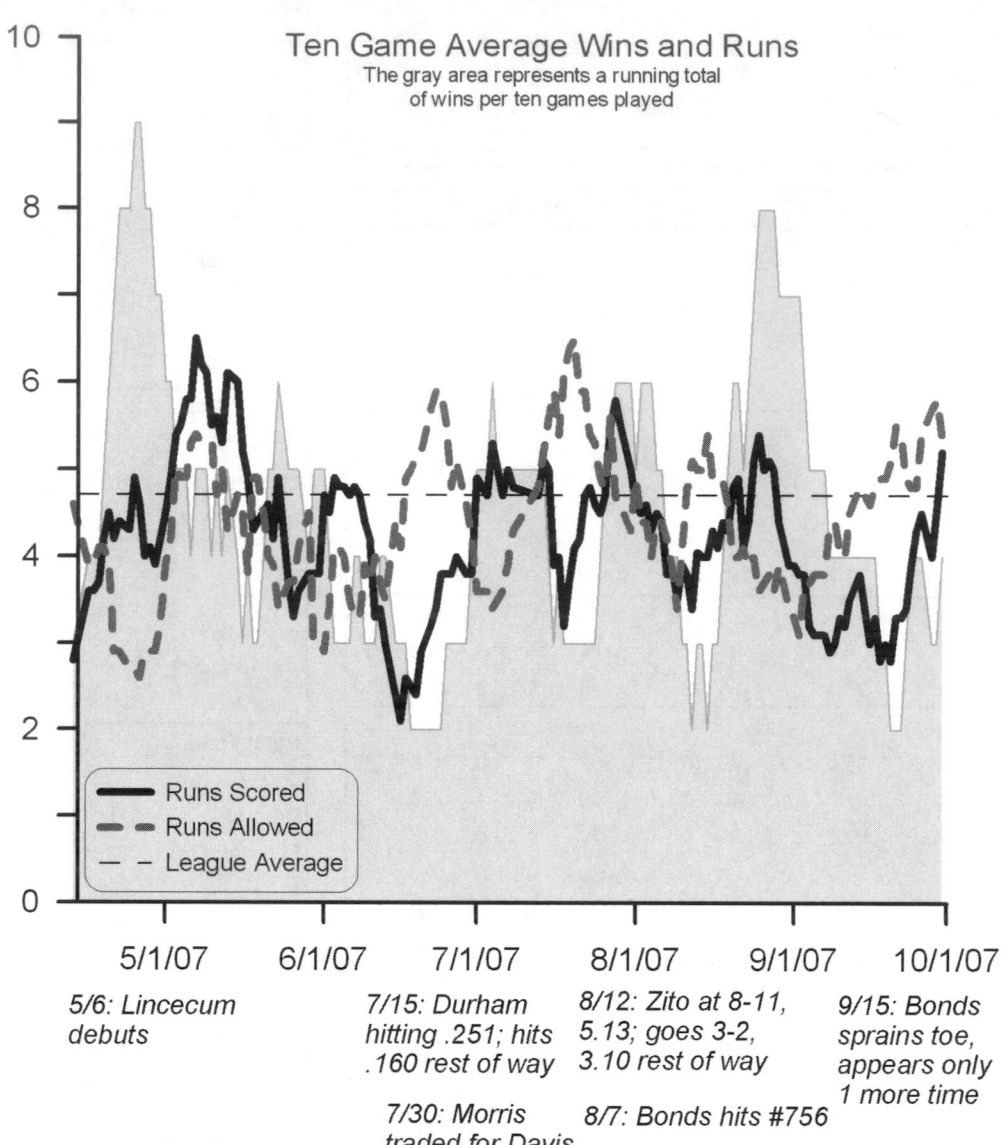

Ten Game Average Wins and Runs
The gray area represents a running total of wins per ten games played

— Runs Scored
– – Runs Allowed
– - League Average

5/6: Lincecum debuts

7/15: Durham hitting .251; hits .160 rest of way

7/30: Morris traded for Davis

8/12: Zito at 8-11, 5.13; goes 3-2, 3.10 rest of way

8/7: Bonds hits #756

9/15: Bonds sprains toe, appears only 1 more time

Team Batting and Pitching/Fielding Stats by Month						
	April	May	June	July	Aug	Sept/Oct
Wins	13	12	9	12	16	9
Losses	11	16	18	13	15	18
RS/G	3.9	4.7	3.8	4.9	4.2	3.9
RA/G	3.8	4.4	4.3	5.2	4.1	5.0
OBP	.312	.314	.324	.346	.327	.306
SLG	.398	.380	.373	.376	.401	.392
FIP	4.19	4.03	4.36	3.92	4.12	4.42
DER	.724	.711	.707	.672	.695	.682

Batting Stats

Player	BR	Runs	RBI	PA	Outs	H	2B	3B	HR	TB	K	BB	IBB	HBP	SH	SF	SB	CS	GDP	H-A	L^R	BA	OBP	SLG	GPA
Bonds B *	87	75	66	477	259	94	14	0	28	192	54	132	43	3	0	2	5	0	13	.012	.024	.276	.480	.565	.357
Winn R +	86	73	65	653	430	178	42	1	14	264	85	44	3	7	4	5	15	3	12	-.012	.063	.300	.353	.445	.270
Feliz P	69	61	72	590	433	141	28	2	20	233	70	29	2	1	0	3	2	2	15	-.016	-.012	.253	.290	.418	.235
Molina B	63	38	81	517	373	137	19	1	19	215	53	15	2	2	1	2	0	0	13	.008	-.001	.276	.298	.433	.242
Roberts D *	51	61	23	443	302	103	17	9	2	144	66	42	1	0	4	0	31	5	4	.008	.115	.260	.331	.364	.240
Vizquel O +	51	54	51	575	407	126	18	3	4	162	48	44	6	1	14	3	14	6	14	.006	-.009	.246	.305	.316	.216
Durham R +	49	56	71	528	383	101	21	2	11	159	75	53	6	2	0	9	10	2	18	.012	.016	.218	.295	.343	.219
Klesko R *	45	51	44	411	283	94	27	3	6	145	68	46	2	1	1	1	5	1	14	.037	-.008	.260	.344	.401	.255
Aurilia R	33	40	33	358	254	83	19	2	5	121	45	22	1	4	0	3	0	0	8	.005	-.011	.252	.304	.368	.229
Frandsen K	29	26	31	296	213	71	12	1	5	100	24	21	3	5	3	3	4	3	17	-.040	-.001	.269	.331	.379	.244
Lewis F *	27	34	19	180	117	45	6	2	3	64	32	19	0	3	1	0	5	1	4	.008	.047	.287	.374	.408	.270
Ortmeier D +	21	20	16	167	115	45	7	4	6	78	41	7	1	1	0	2	2	1	2	-.023	-.002	.287	.317	.497	.267
Davis R	20	26	7	162	106	40	9	1	1	54	25	14	1	4	2	0	17	4	0	-.001	.022	.282	.363	.380	.258
Sweeney M *	14	18	10	107	67	23	8	0	2	37	18	13	0	3	1	0	2	0	0	.007	.102	.256	.368	.411	.268
Rodriguez G	13	10	14	98	69	22	6	0	1	31	17	10	0	0	0	1	0	1	3	.079	.009	.253	.327	.356	.230
Schierholtz	13	9	10	117	79	34	5	3	0	45	19	2	0	1	0	2	3	1	0	-.064	-.177	.304	.316	.402	.243
Alfonzo E	5	5	6	67	52	16	2	1	1	23	23	2	2	1	0	0	0	2	2	.043	-.144	.250	.284	.359	.217
Velez E +	4	5	2	13	8	3	0	2	0	7	3	2	0	0	0	0	4	0	0	-.355	-.363	.273	.385	.636	.332
Linden T +	4	6	3	60	45	10	1	0	0	11	23	5	1	0	0	0	0	0	0	-.011	.097	.182	.250	.200	.163
Ortiz R	1	0	3	19	14	3	1	0	0	4	4	0	0	0	2	0	0	0	0	-.065	.211	.176	.176	.235	.138
Morris M	1	3	1	45	31	7	1	0	0	8	10	1	0	0	6	0	0	0	0	-.140	-.183	.184	.205	.211	.145
Cain M	0	3	4	66	53	4	0	0	2	10	32	2	0	0	7	0	0	0	0	.025	-.118	.070	.102	.175	.090
Sanchez J *	0	0	1	7	5	1	1	0	0	2	3	1	0	0	1	0	0	0	0	.238	--	.167	.167	.333	.158
Blackley T *	0	0	0	3	2	1	0	0	0	1	1	0	0	0	0	0	0	0	0	-.350	.350	.333	.333	.333	.233
Figueroa L +	0	1	0	5	4	1	0	0	0	1	0	0	0	0	0	0	0	0	0	.233	-.175	.200	.200	.200	.140
Chulk V	0	0	0	3	3	1	0	0	0	1	0	0	0	0	0	0	0	0	1	-.350	--	.333	.333	.333	.233
Wilson B	0	0	0	1	0	0	0	0	0	0	0	0	0	0	1	0	0	0	0	.000	--	.000	.000	.000	.000
Kline S +	-0	0	0	1	1	0	0	0	0	0	1	0	0	0	0	0	0	0	0	.000	--	.000	.000	.000	.000
Taschner J *	-0	0	0	2	1	0	0	0	0	0	0	0	0	0	1	0	0	0	0	.000	--	.000	.000	.000	.000
Hennessey B	-0	0	0	1	1	0	0	0	0	0	0	0	0	0	0	0	0	0	0	.000	--	.000	.000	.000	.000
Niekro L	-0	0	0	18	15	3	0	0	0	3	5	1	0	0	0	0	0	0	1	.024	.006	.176	.222	.176	.144
Atchison S	-0	0	0	2	2	0	0	0	0	0	1	0	0	0	0	0	0	0	0	.000	.000	.000	.000	.000	.000
Lowry N	-0	3	5	62	53	5	2	0	1	10	15	1	0	0	4	0	0	1	0	-.020	-.014	.088	.103	.175	.090
McClain S	-0	1	0	11	9	2	0	0	0	2	2	0	0	0	0	0	0	0	0	-.200	-.075	.182	.182	.182	.127
Misch P	-1	0	0	10	8	1	0	0	0	1	3	0	0	0	1	0	0	0	0	.140	-.100	.111	.111	.111	.078
Zito B *	-1	2	3	68	55	7	0	0	0	7	16	2	0	0	4	0	0	0	0	.052	.090	.113	.141	.113	.092
Correia K	-1	0	0	19	14	1	0	0	0	1	4	1	0	0	3	0	0	0	0	.170	-.090	.067	.125	.067	.073
Lincecum T *	-2	2	0	51	40	4	1	0	0	5	21	2	0	0	6	0	0	0	1	-.000	.042	.093	.133	.116	.089

Italicized stats have been adjusted for home park.

Batted Ball Batting Stats

Player	% of PA		% of Batted Balls					Out %		Runs Per Event				Total Runs vs. Avg.				
	K%	BB%	GB%	LD%	FB%	IF/F	HR/OF	GB	OF	NIP	GB	LD	OF	NIP	GB	LD	FB	Tot
Bonds B	11	28	40	17	43	.14	.25	84	85	.21	-.03	.44	.38	36	-9	2	23	52
Winn R	13	8	51	19	31	.05	.09	71	78	.06	.07	.39	.19	-0	9	3	-0	11
Lewis F	18	12	55	15	30	.14	.09	65	83	.07	.10	.44	.17	2	4	-1	-2	2
Davis R	15	11	40	20	40	.16	.03	67	84	.08	.11	.41	.06	1	4	1	-5	1
Ortmeier D	25	5	53	14	32	.13	.18	71	74	-.04	.06	.53	.37	-4	1	-0	4	1

Batted Ball Batting Stats continue after Fielding Stats.

Pitching Stats

Player	PRC	IP	BFP	G	GS	K	BB	IBB	HBP	H	HR	DP	DER	SB	CS	PO	W	L	Sv	Op	Hld	H-A	R^L	RA	ERA	FIP
Cain M	97	200.0	832	32	32	163	79	3	5	173	14	22	.720	8	5	0	7	16	0	0	0	.018	-.018	3.78	3.65	3.76
Zito B *	73	196.7	850	34	33	131	83	4	4	182	24	16	.727	5	1	1	11	13	0	0	0	-.001	-.002	4.81	4.53	4.79
Lincecum T	66	146.3	618	24	24	150	65	5	2	122	12	11	.712	10	2	0	7	5	0	0	0	.024	-.006	4.31	4.00	3.56
Lowry N *	61	156.0	694	26	26	87	87	2	5	155	12	25	.700	7	4	0	14	8	0	0	0	.001	-.079	4.38	3.92	4.88
Correia K	53	101.7	437	59	8	80	40	7	2	94	9	4	.712	10	3	0	4	7	0	3	12	.001	.019	3.45	3.45	3.88
Morris M	44	136.7	603	21	21	73	39	3	5	162	12	17	.671	7	2	0	7	7	0	0	0	.003	-.007	5.20	4.35	4.24
Hennessey B	34	68.3	287	69	0	40	23	1	3	66	7	11	.715	4	1	1	4	5	19	24	13	.004	-.043	3.42	3.42	4.53
Chulk V	26	53.0	222	57	0	41	14	2	2	53	3	6	.685	2	1	1	5	4	0	2	9	.001	-.055	3.74	3.57	3.25
Sanchez J *	18	52.0	238	33	4	62	28	1	5	57	8	5	.630	1	4	1	1	5	0	0	2	-.044	-.093	5.88	5.88	4.73
Taschner J *	17	50.0	222	63	0	51	29	2	1	44	4	2	.708	3	0	0	3	1	0	2	13	-.085	.094	5.58	5.40	3.95
Wilson B	17	23.7	93	24	0	18	7	0	1	16	1	1	.758	0	2	0	1	2	6	7	9	.026	-.225	2.28	2.28	3.31
Misch P *	15	40.3	176	18	4	26	12	2	2	47	3	6	.654	3	1	1	0	4	0	0	2	.053	-.045	4.69	4.24	3.84
Walker T	15	14.3	53	15	0	9	4	1	0	12	0	4	.700	0	1	0	2	0	0	1	7	.098	.078	1.26	1.26	2.64
Kline S *	15	46.0	216	68	0	17	18	3	2	58	2	2	.661	2	2	0	1	2	2	4	9	.078	.003	4.89	4.70	4.20
Ortiz R	14	49.0	223	12	8	27	20	1	6	57	4	4	.675	4	2	0	2	3	0	0	0	.033	-.122	5.88	5.51	4.76
Atchison S	14	30.7	131	22	0	25	10	0	1	32	5	4	.700	4	0	0	0	0	0	1	5	-.054	-.031	4.11	4.11	4.83
Messenger R	14	40.7	188	37	0	22	12	3	1	58	4	4	.638	4	1	1	1	3	1	5	5	-.033	.001	5.09	5.09	4.20
Benitez A	7	17.3	78	19	0	18	9	1	0	17	3	0	.708	2	0	0	0	3	9	11	0	-.034	-.102	4.67	4.67	4.83
Munter S	4	10.7	46	12	0	4	4	0	0	14	0	3	.632	1	0	0	1	1	0	0	0	.026	.058	4.22	4.22	3.64
Giese D	4	9.3	37	8	0	7	2	0	0	8	4	0	.833	0	1	1	0	2	0	0	0	-.310	.153	4.82	4.82	7.98
Blackley T *	2	8.7	40	2	2	5	5	0	0	10	2	1	.714	0	0	0	0	0	0	0	0	-.138	-.274	7.27	7.27	6.85
Threets E *	0	2.3	15	3	0	1	3	0	0	5	0	0	.545	0	0	0	0	0	0	0	0	-.244	.305	19.29	19.29	6.27

Italicized stats have been adjusted for home park.

Batted Ball Pitching Stats

Player	% of PA		% of Batted Balls					Out %		Runs Per Event				Total Runs vs. Avg.				
	K%	BB%	GB%	LD%	FB%	IF/F	HR/OF	GB	OF	NIP	GB	LD	OF	NIP	GB	LD	FB	Tot
Cain M	20	10	39	16	45	.11	.06	76	84	.04	.03	.42	.12	-1	-6	-8	-11	-27
Lincecum T	24	11	47	15	38	.08	.09	74	83	.03	.05	.37	.17	-3	0	-13	-5	-20
Correia K	18	10	45	15	40	.07	.08	77	78	.04	.03	.36	.19	-1	-3	-8	2	-10
Zito B	15	10	39	20	41	.09	.10	80	88	.07	.01	.41	.13	4	-10	4	-7	-9
Chulk V	18	7	31	21	48	.13	.04	69	80	.02	.06	.32	.13	-2	1	-1	-2	-5
Hennessey B	14	9	46	20	34	.10	.11	75	83	.07	.03	.32	.19	1	-2	-2	-0	-4
Taschner J	23	14	33	18	49	.06	.06	78	80	.06	.03	.37	.15	2	-2	-3	-0	-3
Atchison S	19	8	37	23	41	.11	.15	79	76	.03	.01	.27	.29	-1	-1	-1	4	1
Lowry N	13	13	45	20	36	.10	.08	77	82	.12	.02	.37	.15	13	-6	0	-5	2
Misch P	15	8	43	24	33	.05	.07	75	77	.05	.03	.40	.19	-0	-1	4	1	3
Kline S	8	9	48	19	33	.14	.04	67	83	.14	.10	.34	.09	2	6	0	-5	3
Ortiz R	12	11	42	22	35	.12	.08	79	77	.11	.03	.39	.21	3	-2	3	1	5
Sanchez J	26	14	39	22	39	.13	.15	61	88	.05	.11	.45	.21	1	3	2	-0	6
Messenger R	12	7	48	16	36	.11	.08	72	67	.06	.06	.38	.27	-0	2	-0	5	6
Morris M	12	7	49	20	32	.10	.09	77	81	.06	.03	.47	.18	-1	0	11	-3	7
MLB Average	17	9	43	19	38	.10	.10	74	83	.05	.05	.40	.18	--	--	--	--	--

Fielding Stats

Name	INN	SBA/G	CS%	ERA	WP+PB/G	PO	A	TE	FE
Catcher									
Molina B	1104.0	0.57	24%	4.11	0.465	808	61	7	1
Rodriguez G	227.3	0.63	25%	4.87	0.435	179	17	2	1
Alfonzo E	122.0	1.18	31%	3.69	0.148	97	7	2	1
Feliz P	0.3	27.00	0%	27.00	0.000	0	0	0	0

Name	Inn	PO	A	TE	FE	FPct	DPS	DPT	RZR	OOZ
First Base										
Klesko R	804.7	755	66	2	1	.996	11	1	.742	14
Aurilia R	371.0	375	18	1	1	.995	3	0	.853	12
Ortmeier D	171.3	171	11	0	0	1.000	2	1	.882	8
Sweeney M	44.0	51	2	0	0	1.000	0	0	.700	0
Feliz P	31.0	27	2	0	0	1.000	1	0	1.000	1
Niekro L	22.0	24	2	0	0	1.000	0	0	.750	0
McClain S	9.7	8	0	0	0	1.000	0	0	.000	0
Second Base										
Durham R	1028.0	244	300	1	11	.978	31	56	.801	26
Frandsen K	343.3	81	108	1	3	.979	5	18	.853	9
Aurilia R	70.3	18	19	0	1	.974	4	4	.733	2
Velez E	12.0	5	4	1	0	.900	0	2	.400	0
Shortstop										
Vizquel O	1219.0	198	444	3	6	.986	40	38	.806	47
Frandsen K	138.3	28	38	0	1	.985	3	3	.750	5
Aurilia R	94.0	14	35	2	0	.961	3	1	.897	6
Figueroa L	2.0	1	3	0	0	1.000	0	0	1.000	1
Third Base										
Feliz P	1220.0	93	302	1	10	.973	29	0	.747	62
Aurilia R	177.7	15	39	1	3	.931	6	0	.756	4
Frandsen K	55.7	2	11	0	0	1.000	1	0	.357	5
Winn R	0.3	1	0	0	0	1.000	0	0	--	--

Name	Inn	PO	A	TE	FE	FPct	DPS	DPT	RZR	OOZ
Left Field										
Bonds B	842.0	162	2	0	4	.976	0	0	.831	29
Winn R	137.7	27	2	0	0	1.000	0	0	.778	6
Lewis F	115.0	32	0	0	1	.970	0	0	.897	6
Ortmeier D	93.3	29	0	0	0	1.000	0	0	.857	5
Roberts D	83.3	24	0	0	0	1.000	0	0	.870	4
Linden T	49.0	12	0	0	0	1.000	0	0	.900	3
Sweeney M	42.3	6	0	0	0	1.000	0	0	.714	1
Frandsen K	40.3	8	1	0	0	1.000	0	0	.750	2
Davis R	20.7	7	0	0	0	1.000	0	0	.857	1
Feliz P	17.0	5	0	0	0	1.000	0	0	1.000	0
Klesko R	8.0	2	0	0	0	1.000	0	0	1.000	0
Velez E	4.0	0	0	0	0	0.000	0	0	--	--
Figueroa L	1.0	0	0	0	0	0.000	0	0	--	--
Center Field										
Roberts D	756.7	223	6	0	3	.987	0	0	.855	36
Davis R	296.3	97	3	0	0	1.000	0	0	.833	17
Winn R	284.3	82	0	0	0	1.000	0	0	.899	11
Linden T	75.0	23	2	1	1	.926	0	0	.840	2
Lewis F	41.0	12	0	0	0	1.000	0	0	.833	2
Ortmeier D	0.3	0	0	0	0	0.000	0	0	--	--
Right Field										
Winn R	869.0	209	3	0	1	.991	0	0	.916	34
Schierholtz N	229.3	48	0	0	1	.980	0	0	.854	13
Lewis F	205.7	53	0	0	0	1.000	0	0	.875	11
Ortmeier D	89.0	17	0	0	0	1.000	0	0	.810	0
Frandsen K	18.0	5	0	1	0	.833	0	0	.800	1
Linden T	16.0	3	0	0	1	.750	0	0	.500	2
Klesko R	9.0	2	0	0	0	1.000	0	0	.500	0
Davis R	8.0	0	0	0	0	0.000	0	0	--	--
Sweeney M	7.3	1	0	0	0	1.000	0	0	--	--
Feliz P	2.0	0	0	0	0	0.000	0	0	0.000	0
Lowry N	0.3	0	0	0	0	0.000	0	0	--	--

Batted Ball Batting Stats

Player	% of PA		% of Batted Balls					Out %		Runs Per Event				Total Runs vs. Avg.				
	K%	BB%	GB%	LD%	FB%	IF/F	HR/OF	GB	OF	NIP	GB	LD	OF	NIP	GB	LD	FB	Tot
Schierholtz N	16	3	44	15	41	.15	.00	64	76	-.05	.11	.45	.11	-3	3	-0	-2	-2
Klesko R	17	11	47	14	39	.11	.05	72	75	.07	.05	.41	.17	3	0	-5	-1	-3
Roberts D	15	9	48	21	32	.05	.02	73	82	.07	.07	.32	.09	1	6	-3	-11	-7
Frandsen K	8	9	53	21	26	.03	.08	79	95	.13	-.00	.39	.06	2	-5	3	-9	-8
Aurilia R	13	7	39	22	38	.06	.04	82	85	.06	-.01	.41	.08	-1	-5	6	-8	-9
Molina B	10	3	37	19	44	.10	.11	78	89	-.00	.02	.36	.15	-7	-5	2	2	-9
Feliz P	12	5	43	15	42	.17	.10	77	83	.02	.03	.38	.18	-6	-3	-5	2	-13
Durham R	14	10	45	13	41	.10	.07	73	85	.08	.04	.29	.12	3	-0	-14	-7	-18
Vizquel O	8	8	41	18	40	.14	.03	78	87	.11	.02	.33	.04	2	-4	-5	-22	-29
MLB Average	17	9	43	19	38	.10	.10	74	83	.05	.05	.40	.18	--	--	--	--	--

Seattle Mariners

Stat Facts:

- 56% of Ichiro Suzuki's batted balls were ground balls, but only 7 were GIDPs
- Suzuki had 203 singles; second-highest in the league was 154
- Suzuki had an RZR of .893 and made 97 OOZ plays
- Just 3% of Jose Vidro's fly balls were infield pop-ups
- Jarrod Washburn's ground ball % of 37% was lowest in the league
- 15% of the fly balls off Washburn were infield pop-ups, highest in the league
- 61% of the batted balls off Felix Hernandez were grounders, and just 23% were fly balls
- Hernandez induced 26 double plays
- 16% of the outfield flies against Hernandez were home runs
- Horacio Ramirez induced 19 double plays in 98 innings

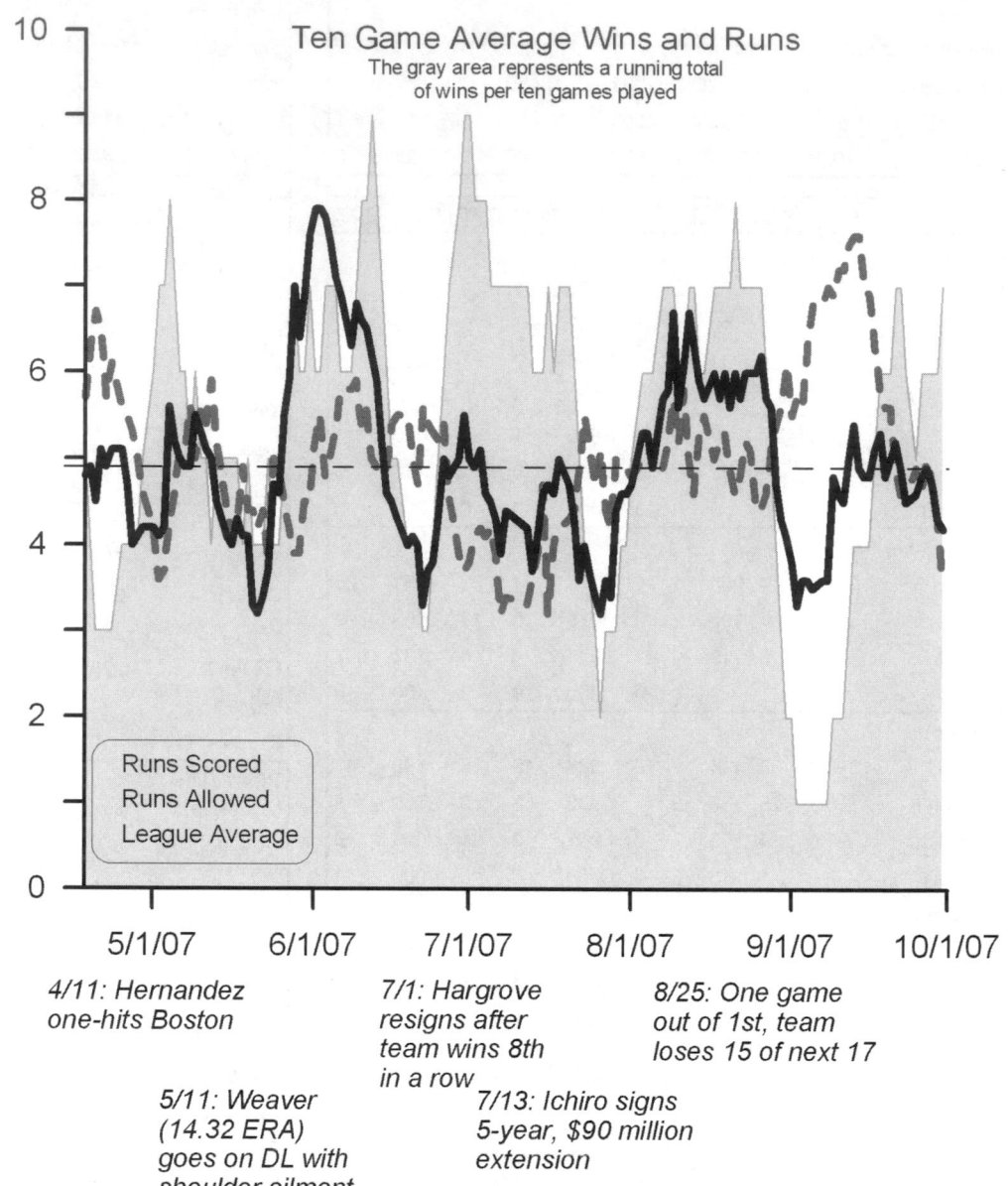

Ten Game Average Wins and Runs
The gray area represents a running total of wins per ten games played

Runs Scored
Runs Allowed
League Average

4/11: Hernandez one-hits Boston

5/11: Weaver (14.32 ERA) goes on DL with shoulder ailment

7/1: Hargrove resigns after team wins 8th in a row

7/13: Ichiro signs 5-year, $90 million extension

8/25: One game out of 1st, team loses 15 of next 17

Team Batting and Pitching/Fielding Stats by Month						
	April	May	June	July	Aug	Sept/Oct
Wins	10	16	18	14	15	15
Losses	10	14	9	14	13	14
RS/G	4.5	5.4	5.3	4.0	5.5	4.6
RA/G	5.2	4.8	4.9	4.5	5.4	5.4
OBP	.310	.345	.348	.320	.358	.330
SLG	.413	.433	.416	.374	.488	.417
FIP	4.29	4.09	3.96	4.53	4.47	4.47
DER	.700	.672	.653	.709	.665	.657

Batting Stats

Player	BR	Runs	RBI	PA	Outs	H	2B	3B	HR	TB	K	BB	IBB	HBP	SH	SF	SB	CS	GDP	H-A	L^R	BA	OBP	SLG	GPA
Suzuki I *	121	111	68	736	455	238	22	7	6	292	77	49	13	3	4	2	37	8	7	.020	.018	.351	.396	.431	.298
Ibanez R *	103	80	105	636	420	167	35	5	21	275	97	53	4	3	0	7	0	0	14	-.041	.078	.291	.351	.480	.289
Guillen J	92	84	99	659	439	172	28	2	23	273	118	41	2	19	0	5	5	1	17	-.017	.098	.290	.353	.460	.285
Beltre A	84	87	99	639	451	164	41	2	26	287	104	38	2	2	0	4	14	2	18	-.029	.030	.276	.319	.482	.275
Vidro J +	79	78	59	625	397	172	26	0	6	216	57	63	5	1	5	8	0	0	21	.020	-.004	.314	.381	.394	.281
Betancourt Y	73	72	67	559	395	155	38	2	9	224	48	15	3	1	3	4	5	4	10	.010	.075	.289	.308	.418	.253
Johjima K	57	52	61	513	370	139	29	0	14	210	41	15	0	11	0	2	0	2	22	-.009	.048	.287	.322	.433	.264
Sexson R	52	58	63	491	357	89	21	0	21	173	100	51	1	5	0	1	1	0	12	-.013	.029	.205	.295	.399	.242
Lopez J	52	58	62	561	411	132	17	2	11	186	64	20	0	5	9	3	2	3	16	-.018	-.003	.252	.284	.355	.226
Broussard B	31	27	29	264	181	66	10	0	7	97	50	17	2	4	0	3	2	0	7	-.001	.022	.275	.330	.404	.260
Bloomquist W	16	28	13	188	137	48	3	0	2	57	35	10	0	1	4	0	7	5	7	.034	.016	.277	.321	.329	.236
Burke J	16	19	12	129	82	34	8	0	1	45	17	7	0	4	5	0	0	1	2	.062	.010	.301	.363	.398	.274
Clement J *	6	4	3	19	10	6	1	0	2	13	3	3	0	0	0	0	0	0	0	.470	.442	.375	.474	.813	.434
Morse M	6	1	3	20	10	8	2	0	0	10	4	1	0	1	0	0	0	0	0	-.354	.173	.444	.500	.556	.379
Jones A	5	16	4	71	50	16	2	1	2	26	21	4	0	1	1	0	2	1	0	-.102	.128	.246	.300	.400	.245
Ellison J	2	9	0	48	37	13	0	0	0	13	12	1	0	0	1	0	3	3	1	-.007	-.114	.283	.298	.283	.213
Jimerson C	2	5	1	2	0	2	0	0	1	5	0	0	0	0	0	0	2	0	0	.750	--	1.000	1.000	2.500	1.120
Balentien W	1	1	4	4	1	2	1	0	1	6	0	0	0	0	0	1	0	0	0	-.300	-1.050	.667	.500	2.000	.755
Hernandez F	1	0	1	4	3	1	0	0	0	1	3	0	0	0	0	0	0	0	0	-.175	-.350	.250	.250	.250	.182
Washburn J *	1	0	1	3	2	1	0	0	0	1	1	1	0	0	0	0	0	0	0	-.425	.100	.500	.667	.500	.443
Weaver J	0	1	0	3	1	0	0	0	0	0	0	0	0	1	1	0	0	0	0	-.225	-.450	.000	.500	.000	.234
Johnson R	0	1	0	3	2	1	0	0	0	1	0	0	0	0	0	0	1	0	0	.350	-.233	.333	.333	.333	.243
Reed J *	0	2	0	17	14	3	0	1	0	5	3	0	0	0	0	0	0	0	0	.006	--	.176	.176	.294	.159
O'Flaherty E	-0	0	0	1	1	0	0	0	0	0	1	0	0	0	0	0	0	0	0	.000	--	.000	.000	.000	.000
Baek C	-0	0	0	1	1	0	0	0	0	0	1	0	0	0	0	0	0	0	0	.000	--	.000	.000	.000	.000
Batista M	-1	0	0	6	6	0	0	0	0	0	1	0	0	0	0	0	0	0	0	.000	.000	.000	.000	.000	.000
Green N	-1	0	0	7	7	0	0	0	0	0	3	0	0	0	0	0	0	0	0	.000	.000	.000	.000	.000	.000

Italicized stats have been adjusted for home park.

Batted Ball Batting Stats

Player	% of PA		% of Batted Balls					Out %		Runs Per Event				Total Runs vs. Avg.				
	K%	BB%	GB%	LD%	FB%	IF/F	HR/OF	GB	OF	NIP	GB	LD	OF	NIP	GB	LD	FB	Tot
Suzuki I	10	7	56	20	24	.09	.04	63	86	.07	.12	.40	.06	0	32	12	-22	22
Guillen J	18	9	48	16	36	.08	.15	66	84	.04	.09	.39	.24	-1	11	-3	10	17
Ibanez R	15	9	42	18	40	.09	.12	67	86	.05	.08	.41	.19	0	8	2	6	16
Beltre A	16	6	44	17	39	.09	.15	73	86	.01	.06	.41	.23	-7	2	-1	11	6
Vidro J	9	10	51	19	30	.03	.04	72	82	.13	.05	.38	.10	8	4	5	-11	6
Burke J	13	9	38	28	34	.06	.03	69	80	.07	.07	.35	.09	0	0	3	-2	1
Johjima K	8	5	46	20	34	.13	.11	82	78	.07	-.01	.42	.19	-2	-10	10	2	-0
Broussard B	19	8	42	20	38	.07	.10	68	87	.02	.07	.37	.15	-2	2	0	-1	-2
Betancourt Y	9	3	43	19	38	.17	.06	69	83	.00	.08	.36	.11	-8	10	3	-11	-5
Bloomquist W	19	6	61	19	20	.07	.08	73	75	-.00	.04	.35	.15	-3	1	-1	-4	-8
Sexson R	20	11	47	15	38	.11	.19	81	91	.05	.00	.40	.25	1	-7	-7	5	-9
Lopez J	11	4	46	17	37	.17	.08	75	91	.02	.04	.40	.08	-7	-2	-1	-16	-26
MLB Average	17	9	43	19	38	.10	.10	74	83	.05	.05	.40	.18	--	--	--	--	--

Pitching Stats

Player	PRC	IP	BFP	G	GS	K	BB	IBB	HBP	H	HR	DP	DER	SB	CS	PO	W	L	Sv	Op	Hld	H-A	R^L	RA	ERA	FIP
Hernandez F	87	190.3	808	30	30	165	53	4	3	209	20	26	.658	10	5	1	14	7	0	0	0	.005	-.069	4.16	3.92	3.83
Putz J	80	71.7	260	68	0	82	13	0	2	37	6	7	.803	3	0	0	6	1	40	42	0	.003	.007	1.38	1.38	2.81
Batista M	74	193.0	860	33	32	133	85	3	8	209	18	19	.675	14	9	1	16	11	0	0	0	-.032	-.038	4.71	4.29	4.61
Washburn J *	71	193.7	839	32	32	114	67	5	8	201	23	21	.702	6	5	4	10	15	0	0	0	.024	-.071	4.74	4.32	4.83
Weaver J	38	146.7	657	27	27	80	35	5	8	190	23	16	.669	9	3	1	7	13	0	0	0	.008	-.050	6.44	6.20	5.11
Sherrill G *	36	45.7	182	73	0	56	17	1	1	28	4	2	.760	0	0	0	2	0	3	7	22	.042	-.023	2.36	2.36	3.18
Green S	31	68.0	304	64	0	53	34	6	3	77	2	12	.632	0	4	1	5	2	0	3	13	-.013	-.068	4.10	3.84	3.57
Morrow B	30	63.3	289	60	0	66	50	5	1	56	3	5	.686	3	2	0	3	4	0	2	18	-.082	-.074	4.12	4.12	4.09
Baek C	24	73.3	321	14	12	49	14	1	3	87	6	5	.667	1	2	0	4	3	0	0	1	-.047	.004	5.52	5.15	3.76
O'Flaherty E	21	52.3	221	56	0	36	20	1	5	45	1	4	.717	2	2	1	7	1	0	1	4	.010	-.077	4.47	4.47	3.63
Ramirez H *	18	98.0	459	20	20	40	42	1	2	139	13	19	.644	9	5	3	8	7	0	0	0	-.053	-.013	7.90	7.16	5.60
Rowland-Smit	18	38.7	168	26	0	42	15	1	2	39	4	4	.638	0	2	2	1	0	0	0	3	.054	-.019	4.42	3.96	3.79
Feierabend R	10	49.3	236	13	9	27	23	2	4	73	10	3	.634	0	3	5	1	6	0	0	0	-.009	-.047	8.03	8.03	6.44
White S	9	35.3	165	15	0	16	20	0	8	35	2	6	.689	2	1	1	1	1	0	0	0	-.148	.001	6.11	5.60	5.59
Davis J	6	25.7	121	16	0	14	16	1	2	29	4	5	.694	1	0	0	2	0	0	0	1	.062	-.031	7.36	6.31	6.30
Mateo J	5	12.0	52	9	0	4	5	1	0	12	0	1	.698	0	1	0	1	0	0	2	0	-.064	.014	3.75	3.75	3.71
Huber J	4	11.3	47	9	0	8	4	0	0	13	1	4	.647	0	0	0	0	0	0	0	3	-.028	-.018	4.76	4.76	4.17
Reitsma C	4	23.7	115	26	0	11	9	1	0	37	3	3	.620	4	0	0	0	2	0	1	6	.119	-.021	8.37	7.61	5.11
Campillo J	3	13.3	63	5	0	9	6	0	1	18	2	3	.622	2	1	0	0	0	0	0	0	-.178	.128	8.10	6.75	5.56
Woods J *	2	10.7	49	4	0	4	7	0	1	9	1	1	.778	2	0	0	0	0	0	0	0	-.051	-.157	6.75	5.91	6.10
Parrish J *	2	10.3	55	8	0	5	4	0	0	22	0	1	.522	0	0	0	0	0	0	0	1	.043	-.048	6.97	6.97	3.57
Lowe M	1	2.7	13	4	0	3	3	0	0	2	1	0	.833	1	0	0	0	0	0	0	2	--	-.804	6.75	6.75	9.38
White R	1	5.3	29	6	0	3	4	1	0	11	0	0	.500	0	0	0	0	1	0	0	0	.117	.082	10.13	8.44	3.94

Italicized stats have been adjusted for home park.

Batted Ball Pitching Stats

Player	% of PA		% of Batted Balls					Out %		Runs Per Event				Total Runs vs. Avg.				
	K%	BB%	GB%	LD%	FB%	IF/F	HR/OF	GB	OF	NIP	GB	LD	OF	NIP	GB	LD	FB	Tot
Putz J	31	6	42	17	41	.11	.10	87	92	-.04	-.04	.35	.10	-8	-8	-7	-8	-31
Sherrill G	31	10	25	21	55	.20	.09	80	85	-.00	.02	.31	.13	-3	-2	-4	-4	-14
O'Flaherty E	16	11	45	18	37	.07	.00	76	84	.08	.03	.36	.03	2	-1	-2	-9	-10
Hernandez F	20	7	61	16	23	.08	.16	73	70	.00	.05	.38	.35	-11	6	-8	7	-5
Morrow B	23	18	35	18	47	.09	.03	72	83	.09	.07	.49	.07	6	0	-1	-8	-2
Baek C	15	5	34	24	42	.09	.06	73	82	.01	.06	.39	.13	-4	1	6	-2	1
Washburn J	14	9	37	18	45	.15	.09	74	81	.07	.04	.35	.18	2	-1	-4	5	1
Rowland-Smith R	25	10	34	21	46	.08	.09	64	78	.02	.10	.38	.20	-1	1	-0	2	2
Green S	17	12	61	20	19	.03	.03	75	68	.08	.04	.43	.20	3	2	3	-4	4
Davis J	12	15	48	20	32	.14	.17	64	95	.15	.08	.28	.18	3	2	-1	-1	4
White S	10	17	53	13	34	.17	.03	73	76	.18	.06	.46	.14	6	2	-1	-2	5
Batista M	15	11	44	17	39	.10	.08	71	80	.08	.06	.42	.17	6	5	-1	-0	9
Feierabend R	11	11	35	21	45	.11	.14	66	82	.12	.10	.44	.24	4	4	5	7	20
Weaver J	12	7	36	17	47	.10	.10	69	82	.05	.08	.43	.19	-3	5	6	14	22
Ramirez H	9	10	48	21	31	.05	.11	74	75	.13	.04	.41	.25	5	1	10	9	25
MLB Average	17	9	43	19	38	.10	.10	74	83	.05	.05	.40	.18	--	--	--	--	--

Fielding Stats

Name	INN	SBA/G	CS%	ERA	WP+PB/G	PO	A	TE	FE
Catcher									
Johjima K	1106.7	0.62	39%	5.07	0.358	805	56	0	1
Burke J	321.7	0.73	12%	3.75	0.644	259	9	0	1
Johnson R	6.0	0.00	0%	3.00	0.000	2	0	0	0

Name	Inn	PO	A	TE	FE	FPct	DPS	DPT	RZR	OOZ
First Base										
Sexson R	991.7	1000	72	0	2	.998	11	2	.655	24
Broussard B	337.0	281	21	2	0	.993	3	0	.780	6
Vidro J	72.0	78	5	0	0	1.000	0	0	.571	1
Morse M	28.0	35	1	0	0	1.000	0	0	.800	1
Bloomquist W	5.7	5	1	0	0	1.000	0	0	--	--
Second Base										
Lopez J	1231.0	280	423	1	7	.989	51	50	.839	44
Bloomquist W	138.0	23	38	3	1	.938	4	3	.824	5
Vidro J	57.0	19	12	0	1	.969	1	1	.733	1
Green N	8.0	2	2	0	0	1.000	0	1	1.000	0
Shortstop										
Betancourt Y	1302.0	239	435	12	11	.967	49	57	.802	46
Bloomquist W	124.0	20	39	1	0	.984	2	2	.865	6
Green N	6.0	0	2	0	0	1.000	0	0	1.000	1
Morse M	2.0	0	0	0	0	0.000	0	0	--	--
Third Base										
Beltre A	1279.0	121	287	12	6	.958	22	1	.668	64
Bloomquist W	128.0	11	29	0	0	1.000	1	0	.594	5
Lopez J	15.0	2	5	0	1	.875	0	0	.800	1
Morse M	12.0	0	5	0	0	1.000	2	0	.667	0

Name	Inn	PO	A	TE	FE	FPct	DPS	DPT	RZR	OOZ
Left Field										
Ibanez R	1114.0	224	10	2	4	.975	4	0	.813	41
Jones A	119.0	24	2	1	0	.963	2	0	.913	3
Broussard B	67.0	14	0	0	0	1.000	0	0	.733	3
Ellison J	63.0	11	0	1	0	.917	0	0	1.000	3
Bloomquist W	60.0	12	0	0	0	1.000	0	0	.846	1
Reed J	10.0	3	0	0	0	1.000	0	0	.429	0
Balentien W	1.0	0	0	0	0	0.000	0	0	--	--
Center Field										
Suzuki I	1339.0	424	8	0	1	.998	6	0	.893	97
Ellison J	40.0	10	0	0	0	1.000	0	0	.818	1
Jones A	34.0	10	0	0	1	.909	0	0	.889	2
Bloomquist W	20.0	8	0	0	0	1.000	0	0	1.000	0
Jimerson C	1.0	0	0	0	0	0.000	0	0	--	--
Right Field										
Guillen J	1273.0	268	9	1	7	.972	6	0	.857	34
Broussard B	82.0	21	0	0	0	1.000	0	0	.905	2
Ellison J	41.0	8	0	0	0	1.000	0	0	1.000	0
Jones A	23.7	5	0	0	0	1.000	0	0	1.000	3
Bloomquist W	4.0	2	0	0	0	1.000	0	0	.667	0
Balentien W	4.0	0	0	0	0	0.000	0	0	--	
Morse M	3.0	0	0	0	0	0.000	0	0	--	--
Jimerson C	2.0	1	0	0	0	1.000	0	0	1.000	0
Reed J	1.0	0	0	0	0	0.000	0	0	--	--

St. Louis Cardinals

Stat Facts:

- Albert Pujols's home-away split of -.064 tied for lowest in the league
- Pujols struck out in just 9% of his plate appearances
- David Eckstein struck out in just 5% of his PAs
- Chris Duncan struck out in 28% of his plate appearances
- Duncan had an RZR of just .781
- 23% of Rick Ankiel's fly balls were home runs
- Scott Spiezio had a line drive % of 25%
- Yadier Molina threw out 50% of base stealers
- Braden Looper struck out just 12% of the batters he faced
- Mike Maroth allowed 71 hits and 11 home runs in 38 innings
- 21% of the fly balls hit against Maroth were home runs

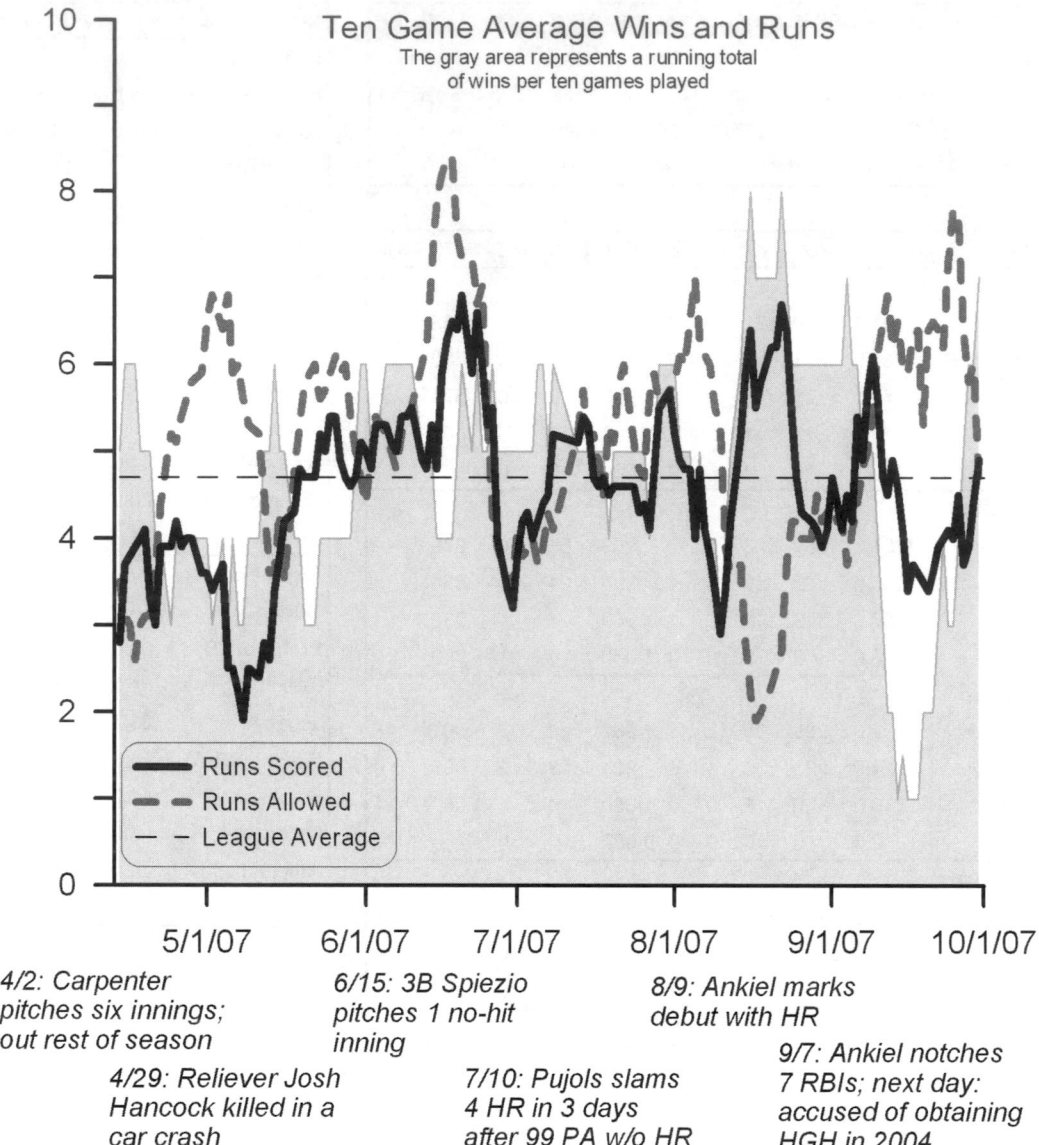

Ten Game Average Wins and Runs
The gray area represents a running total of wins per ten games played

Legend:
— Runs Scored
- - Runs Allowed
- - League Average

4/2: Carpenter pitches six innings; out rest of season

4/29: Reliever Josh Hancock killed in a car crash

6/15: 3B Spiezio pitches 1 no-hit inning

7/10: Pujols slams 4 HR in 3 days after 99 PA w/o HR

8/9: Ankiel marks debut with HR

9/7: Ankiel notches 7 RBIs; next day: accused of obtaining HGH in 2004

Team Batting and Pitching/Fielding Stats by Month						
	April	May	June	July	Aug	Sept/Oct
Wins	10	12	13	15	15	13
Losses	14	15	13	11	13	18
RS/G	3.4	4.1	4.9	5.3	4.5	4.5
RA/G	4.6	5.2	5.6	5.2	4.2	5.8
OBP	.312	.322	.335	.368	.342	.343
SLG	.359	.367	.432	.444	.425	.401
FIP	4.39	4.39	4.68	4.49	4.51	4.89
DER	.719	.678	.695	.660	.706	.685

Batting Stats

Player	BR	Runs	RBI	PA	Outs	H	2B	3B	HR	TB	K	BB	IBB	HBP	SH	SF	SB	CS	GDP	H-A	L^R	BA	OBP	SLG	GPA
Pujols A	117	99	103	679	413	185	38	1	32	321	58	99	22	7	0	8	2	6	27	-.064	.069	.327	.429	.568	.342
Duncan C *	73	51	70	432	283	97	20	0	21	180	123	55	3	1	0	1	2	1	4	-.025	.090	.259	.354	.480	.285
Eckstein D	51	58	31	484	310	134	23	0	3	166	22	24	0	12	7	7	10	1	9	.052	-.015	.309	.356	.382	.261
Rolen S	48	55	58	441	304	104	24	2	8	156	56	37	2	5	0	7	5	3	13	-.028	-.045	.265	.331	.398	.254
Ludwick R	47	42	52	339	227	81	22	0	14	145	72	26	1	7	3	0	4	4	1	.059	-.067	.267	.339	.479	.278
Miles A +	46	55	32	449	306	120	16	1	2	144	40	25	1	1	4	5	2	1	11	.068	.022	.290	.328	.348	.239
Edmonds J *	44	39	53	411	284	92	15	2	12	147	75	41	2	0	2	3	0	2	9	.006	.041	.252	.325	.403	.252
Taguchi S	40	48	30	340	232	89	15	0	3	113	32	23	0	6	3	1	7	4	10	-.006	.030	.290	.350	.368	.255
Molina Y	37	30	40	396	275	97	15	0	6	130	43	34	5	3	2	4	1	1	18	.017	.051	.275	.340	.368	.250
Ankiel R *	33	31	39	190	126	49	8	1	11	92	41	13	0	0	1	4	1	0	3	.124	-.129	.285	.328	.535	.287
Encarnacion	33	43	47	307	216	80	17	1	9	126	43	18	0	1	1	4	2	2	11	.041	-.005	.283	.324	.445	.262
Spiezio S +	32	31	31	257	169	60	14	0	4	86	40	27	2	4	0	3	0	1	5	-.029	.046	.269	.354	.386	.261
Schumaker S	29	19	19	188	124	59	12	2	2	81	20	8	0	0	1	2	1	1	5	.051	-.032	.333	.358	.458	.281
Ryan B	21	30	12	199	131	52	9	0	4	73	19	15	0	1	3	0	7	0	3	.017	.070	.289	.347	.406	.263
Kennedy A *	19	27	18	306	229	61	9	1	3	81	33	22	0	3	1	1	6	2	9	-.018	.071	.219	.282	.290	.204
Bennett G	14	12	17	170	123	39	7	0	2	52	16	8	1	1	2	4	1	1	6	-.110	-.062	.252	.286	.335	.217
Cairo M	9	8	5	72	51	17	2	2	0	23	5	3	0	1	1	0	2	1	0	.069	.028	.254	.296	.343	.223
Wainwright A	7	4	6	74	46	18	3	0	1	24	18	3	0	0	9	0	0	1	1	.144	.107	.290	.323	.387	.247
Wells K	6	7	5	54	36	17	1	0	1	21	19	0	0	0	1	0	0	0	0	-.054	.150	.321	.321	.396	.248
Wilson P	5	6	5	68	53	14	3	0	1	20	17	4	0	0	0	0	2	1	2	-.142	.045	.219	.265	.313	.201
Looper B	4	6	6	63	44	10	2	0	0	12	10	4	0	1	5	0	0	0	1	.020	.065	.189	.259	.226	.177
Branyan R *	4	4	2	39	27	6	0	0	1	9	15	7	0	0	0	0	0	0	1	.085	.172	.188	.333	.281	.225
Stinnett K	3	7	5	87	71	13	3	0	1	19	22	5	2	0	0	0	0	0	2	.028	-.074	.159	.207	.232	.154
Barden B	1	6	0	25	20	5	1	0	0	6	4	2	0	0	0	0	0	0	2	-.043	.235	.217	.280	.261	.195
Maroth M *	0	1	1	11	8	2	0	0	0	2	1	0	0	0	1	0	1	0	0	-.200	-.133	.200	.200	.200	.143
Mulder M *	0	0	0	2	1	1	0	0	0	1	1	0	0	0	0	0	0	0	0	.700	--	.500	.500	.500	.357
Franklin R	0	0	1	2	1	1	0	0	0	1	1	0	0	0	0	0	0	0	0	.350	.700	.500	.500	.500	.357
Jimenez K	0	0	0	3	2	0	0	0	0	0	2	1	0	0	0	0	0	0	0	.225	-.225	.000	.333	.000	.153
Johnson T +	0	0	0	1	0	0	0	0	0	0	0	0	0	0	1	0	0	0	0	.000	--	.000	.000	.000	.000
Carpenter C	-0	0	0	1	1	0	0	0	0	0	0	0	0	0	0	0	0	0	0	--	--	.000	.000	.000	.000
Flores R *	-0	0	0	1	1	0	0	0	0	0	1	0	0	0	0	0	0	0	0	.000	--	.000	.000	.000	.000
Hancock J	-0	0	0	1	1	0	0	0	0	0	0	0	0	0	0	0	0	0	0	.000	--	.000	.000	.000	.000
Springer R	-0	0	0	1	1	0	0	0	0	0	1	0	0	0	0	0	0	0	0	.000	--	.000	.000	.000	.000
Falkenborg B	-0	0	0	1	1	0	0	0	0	0	1	0	0	0	0	0	0	0	0	.000	--	.000	.000	.000	.000
Cate T *	-0	0	0	1	1	0	0	0	0	0	0	0	0	0	0	0	0	0	0	.000	--	.000	.000	.000	.000
Wellemeyer T	-0	1	1	19	14	2	0	0	0	2	9	0	0	0	3	0	0	0	0	-.022	-.127	.125	.125	.125	.089
Keisler R *	-0	1	0	6	5	1	0	0	0	1	2	0	0	0	0	0	0	0	0	.350	.175	.167	.167	.167	.119
Percival T	-0	0	0	4	4	0	0	0	0	0	4	0	0	0	0	0	0	0	0	.000	--	.000	.000	.000	.000
Pineiro J	-1	2	0	24	17	1	0	0	0	1	13	2	0	0	4	0	0	0	0	-.026	-.091	.056	.150	.056	.083
Thompson B	-1	1	0	31	20	4	0	0	0	4	11	0	0	0	7	0	0	0	0	.040	-.147	.167	.167	.167	.119
Reyes A	-1	1	1	32	25	2	0	0	0	2	10	0	0	0	6	0	0	0	1	-.008	.000	.077	.077	.077	.055

Italicized stats have been adjusted for home park.
Batted Ball Batting Stats are listed after Fielding Stats.

Pitching Stats

Player	PRC	IP	BFP	G	GS	K	BB	IBB	HBP	H	HR	DP	DER	SB	CS	PO	W	L	Sv	Op	Hld	H-A	R^L	RA	ERA	FIP
Wainwright A	85	202.0	882	32	32	136	70	4	9	212	13	22	.677	6	8	1	14	12	0	0	0	.015	.021	4.14	3.70	3.87
Looper B	55	175.0	746	31	30	87	51	2	4	183	22	18	.716	5	1	0	12	12	0	0	0	-.061	-.018	5.14	4.94	4.82
Springer R	47	66.0	257	76	0	66	19	1	3	41	3	5	.747	3	3	0	8	1	0	2	11	-.077	-.080	2.45	2.18	2.81
Wells K	44	162.7	750	34	26	122	78	9	9	186	19	16	.661	17	5	2	7	17	0	0	0	-.013	-.017	6.42	5.70	4.73
Franklin R	41	80.0	317	69	0	44	11	0	3	70	8	7	.737	2	2	1	4	4	1	6	25	-.046	-.003	3.15	3.04	3.99
Isringhausen	39	65.3	267	63	0	54	28	3	2	42	4	5	.760	1	0	0	4	0	32	34	0	-.001	-.014	2.89	2.48	3.65
Thompson B	38	129.3	580	44	17	53	40	2	13	157	23	21	.683	4	4	2	8	6	0	0	0	-.015	-.055	5.29	4.73	5.94
Percival T	35	40.0	150	34	1	36	10	0	0	24	3	1	.782	2	3	0	3	0	0	0	3	-.061	-.067	1.80	1.80	3.19
Reyes A	28	107.3	474	22	20	74	43	0	9	108	16	8	.714	4	2	2	2	14	0	0	0	.017	.025	6.46	6.04	5.28
Pineiro J	27	63.7	262	11	11	40	12	0	1	69	11	4	.707	3	2	0	6	4	0	0	0	.009	.075	4.10	3.96	4.87
Wellemeyer T	26	63.7	269	20	11	51	29	0	2	52	7	12	.717	4	0	0	3	2	0	0	1	-.015	-.061	4.38	3.11	4.56
Flores R *	20	55.0	253	70	0	47	15	0	3	71	2	5	.608	2	0	1	3	0	1	2	14	-.016	.028	5.07	4.25	3.01
Johnson T *	15	38.0	164	55	0	24	16	2	3	31	4	2	.761	0	0	0	1	1	0	1	5	.049	.022	4.26	4.03	4.72
Jimenez K	8	42.0	198	34	0	24	17	1	4	56	2	7	.629	4	0	0	3	0	0	0	1	-.057	.026	7.71	7.50	4.17
Cate T *	7	16.0	74	14	0	12	9	0	0	18	1	1	.673	0	0	0	0	0	0	0	2	-.132	-.061	3.94	3.38	4.27
Falkenborg B	7	18.7	84	16	0	16	8	0	1	22	2	3	.649	1	0	0	0	1	0	0	1	.001	-.043	4.82	4.82	4.39
Hancock J	5	12.7	56	8	0	9	5	0	0	14	2	2	.675	0	0	0	0	1	0	0	0	-.100	-.178	4.26	3.55	5.08
Keisler R *	4	17.3	77	4	3	5	5	0	0	21	3	1	.719	0	0	0	0	0	0	0	0	.093	-.142	6.23	5.19	5.81
Maroth M *	3	38.0	203	14	7	23	17	1	2	71	11	6	.553	0	3	2	0	5	0	0	0	-.045	-.100	13.26	10.66	7.24
Cavazos A	2	20.0	104	17	0	15	16	0	2	27	5	3	.636	0	0	0	0	0	0	0	0	.097	.007	12.15	10.35	7.72
Carpenter C	1	6.0	29	1	1	3	1	0	1	9	0	1	.583	0	0	0	0	1	0	0	0	--	-.099	7.50	7.50	3.27
Mulder M *	1	11.0	59	3	3	3	7	0	1	22	4	4	.568	0	1	1	0	3	0	0	0	.037	.046	13.91	12.27	9.63
Dove D	0	3.0	15	3	0	1	1	0	0	5	2	0	.727	0	0	0	0	0	0	0	0	.280	.072	15.00	15.00	12.27
Spiezio S	0	1.0	4	1	0	0	1	0	0	0	0	0	1.000	0	0	0	0	0	0	0	0	--	-.225	0.00	0.00	6.27
Miles A	0	2.0	9	2	0	0	0	0	1	3	1	1	.714	0	0	0	0	0	0	0	0	.600	.051	9.00	9.00	11.27

Italicized stats have been adjusted for home park.

Batted Ball Pitching Stats

Player	% of PA		% of Batted Balls			IF/F	HR/OF	Out %		Runs Per Event				Total Runs vs. Avg.				
	K%	BB%	GB%	LD%	FB%			GB	OF	NIP	GB	LD	OF	NIP	GB	LD	FB	Tot
Springer R	26	9	30	20	51	.18	.03	76	85	.00	.03	.34	.06	-4	-3	-4	-9	-21
Isringhausen J	20	11	45	18	37	.06	.06	81	85	.05	-.00	.26	.11	0	-4	-7	-5	-16
Franklin R	14	4	48	18	34	.10	.10	79	88	-.00	.02	.34	.14	-5	-2	-3	-4	-14
Percival T	24	7	33	12	55	.19	.07	71	93	-.01	.09	.36	.05	-3	1	-5	-6	-13
Wainwright A	15	9	48	18	34	.12	.07	71	80	.06	.06	.38	.15	0	6	-4	-9	-7
Wellemeyer T	19	12	40	17	43	.14	.10	75	87	.06	.02	.37	.15	1	-2	-3	-2	-6
Johnson T	15	12	41	12	47	.09	.08	83	77	.09	-.01	.32	.20	2	-3	-5	2	-4
Looper B	12	7	42	21	36	.09	.10	82	88	.06	-.00	.44	.15	-1	-13	15	-5	-4
Pineiro J	15	5	45	18	36	.11	.16	79	86	-.00	.03	.44	.25	-4	-1	2	5	2
Flores R	19	7	41	23	37	.14	.04	67	71	.01	.09	.43	.16	-2	2	5	-2	3
Jimenez K	12	11	43	26	30	.13	.05	79	76	.10	.01	.46	.16	2	-2	9	-2	7
Reyes A	16	11	35	21	44	.09	.11	77	85	.08	.03	.40	.18	3	-3	3	4	7
Wells K	16	12	48	19	33	.10	.12	76	76	.08	.04	.43	.27	7	-0	6	10	22
Thompson B	9	9	49	17	34	.04	.15	75	81	.12	.03	.42	.27	5	-1	4	16	24
Maroth M	11	9	42	21	37	.09	.21	62	69	.09	.11	.49	.39	2	5	7	13	28
MLB Average	17	9	43	19	38	.10	.10	74	83	.05	.05	.40	.18	--	--	--	--	--

Fielding Stats

Name	INN	SBA/G	CS%	ERA	WP+PB/G	PO	A	TE	FE
Catcher									
Molina Y	861.3	0.48	50%	4.33	0.324	582	63	5	1
Bennett G	370.3	0.63	8%	5.23	0.243	244	9	1	0
Stinnett K	203.0	0.62	21%	5.14	0.355	153	9	4	0
Esposito B	1.0	0.00	0%	0.00	0.000	1	0	0	0

Name	Inn	PO	A	TE	FE	FPct	DPS	DPT	RZR	OOZ
First Base										
Pujols A	1324.0	1325	124	2	6	.995	30	0	.843	51
Spiezio S	61.0	72	2	0	0	1.000	1	0	.714	0
Duncan C	32.0	25	1	0	0	1.000	0	0	1.000	1
Cairo M	9.7	11	1	0	0	1.000	0	0	1.000	0
Branyan R	6.3	6	0	0	0	1.000	0	0	0.000	0
Bennett G	1.0	1	0	0	0	1.000	0	0	--	--
Molina Y	1.0	1	0	0	0	1.000	0	0	0.000	0
Edmonds J	0.0	0	0	0	0	0.000	0	0	--	--
Second Base										
Kennedy A	630.3	156	211	2	5	.981	23	27	.821	26
Miles A	590.7	152	160	2	3	.984	8	28	.820	16
Ryan B	125.0	20	45	0	3	.956	5	4	.795	5
Cairo M	42.7	0	13	0	0	1.000	0	1	.917	1
Spiezio S	36.0	8	8	0	1	.941	1	2	.750	1
Barden B	9.0	2	4	0	0	1.000	0	0	1.000	1
Taguchi S	2.0	1	0	0	1	.500	0	0	--	--
Shortstop										
Eckstein D	943.7	164	310	7	13	.960	26	27	.783	46
Miles A	301.0	73	91	5	4	.948	4	20	.699	12
Ryan B	163.7	31	65	0	3	.970	6	9	.789	11
Barden B	25.3	3	11	0	0	1.000	2	0	1.000	2
Kennedy A	2.0	0	3	0	0	1.000	0	0	1.000	0

Name	Inn	PO	A	TE	FE	FPct	DPS	DPT	RZR	OOZ
Third Base										
Rolen S	935.0	85	226	1	9	.969	21	1	.742	39
Spiezio S	187.7	22	42	2	1	.955	5	0	.720	4
Ryan B	150.0	19	41	2	2	.938	7	0	.644	12
Cairo M	89.0	4	23	0	1	.964	4	0	.870	3
Branyan R	50.0	6	20	1	0	.963	5	0	.773	3
Miles A	19.0	0	8	0	0	1.000	0	0	.857	1
Barden B	5.0	2	0	0	0	1.000	0	0	--	--
Left Field										
Duncan C	747.0	158	5	0	2	.988	0	0	.781	26
Ludwick R	324.0	86	1	0	0	1.000	0	0	.905	19
Taguchi S	212.3	49	2	1	1	.962	2	0	.895	15
Schumaker S	122.7	20	0	1	0	.952	0	0	.938	5
Ankiel R	16.0	6	1	0	0	1.000	0	0	.750	0
Spiezio S	12.0	1	0	0	0	1.000	0	0	1.000	0
Cairo M	1.0	0	0	0	0	0.000	0	0	0.000	0
Miles A	0.7	0	0	0	0	0.000	0	0	--	--
Center Field										
Edmonds J	828.3	244	8	2	3	.981	8	0	.852	48
Taguchi S	380.3	118	1	0	1	.992	2	0	.904	15
Ankiel R	137.0	27	0	0	0	1.000	0	0	.800	3
Schumaker S	64.3	20	1	0	0	1.000	0	0	.762	4
Ludwick R	22.0	7	0	0	0	1.000	0	0	1.000	0
Encarnacion J	3.7	1	0	0	0	1.000	0	0	1.000	0
Right Field										
Encarnacion J	615.3	124	2	1	5	.940	0	0	.873	15
Ludwick R	252.3	60	0	1	0	.984	0	0	.855	13
Ankiel R	197.7	58	2	0	2	.968	0	0	.886	19
Wilson P	123.7	27	0	0	2	.931	0	0	.957	5
Schumaker S	115.3	24	0	0	1	.960	0	0	.905	5
Spiezio S	106.3	17	0	0	1	.944	0	0	.700	3
Taguchi S	23.3	5	0	0	0	1.000	0	0	1.000	0
Kennedy A	1.7	0	0	0	0	0.000	0	0	--	--

Batted Ball Batting Stats

Player	% of PA		% of Batted Balls					Out %		Runs Per Event				Total Runs vs. Avg.				
	K%	BB%	GB%	LD%	FB%	IF/F	HR/OF	GB	OF	NIP	GB	LD	OF	NIP	GB	LD	FB	Tot
Pujols A	9	16	42	19	39	.07	.17	72	86	.18	.05	.45	.25	22	2	12	21	57
Duncan C	28	13	40	18	42	.08	.21	78	75	.03	.03	.42	.37	-0	-4	-3	18	11
Ludwick R	21	10	37	16	47	.17	.16	62	84	.03	.13	.38	.24	-1	6	-4	7	8
Ankiel R	22	7	44	15	41	.13	.23	64	89	-.00	.12	.36	.30	-3	4	-3	6	4
Schumaker J	11	4	54	19	27	.14	.05	74	69	.02	.04	.46	.23	-2	0	4	0	3
Ryan B	10	8	47	19	34	.11	.09	68	91	.10	.09	.40	.09	1	5	1	-5	2
Spiezio S	16	12	36	25	39	.05	.06	86	88	.09	-.03	.48	.06	3	-5	9	-7	-0
Encarnacion J	14	6	44	18	38	.15	.09	69	88	.03	.07	.44	.14	-2	2	2	-3	-0
Eckstein D	5	7	41	22	37	.16	.02	70	87	.17	.07	.36	.03	4	5	8	-18	-1
Taguchi S	9	9	50	20	30	.06	.04	70	92	.11	.07	.38	.02	2	5	3	-13	-3
Edmonds J	18	10	36	19	44	.02	.09	77	87	.05	.02	.38	.14	0	-4	-1	-1	-6
Rolen S	13	10	38	20	43	.14	.06	73	86	.08	.05	.38	.09	2	-0	2	-9	-6
Molina Y	11	9	46	19	35	.07	.06	74	83	.10	.04	.32	.10	3	-1	-2	-7	-8
Bennett G	9	5	43	17	40	.05	.04	82	83	.05	-.02	.37	.07	-1	-4	-1	-4	-10
Miles A	9	6	54	18	28	.10	.02	74	83	.07	.05	.37	.06	-2	5	0	-15	-11
Kennedy A	11	8	43	17	40	.04	.03	76	86	.08	.02	.26	.06	1	-2	-6	-9	-17
MLB Average	17	9	43	19	38	.10	.10	74	83	.05	.05	.40	.18	--	--	--	--	--

Tampa Bay Devil Rays

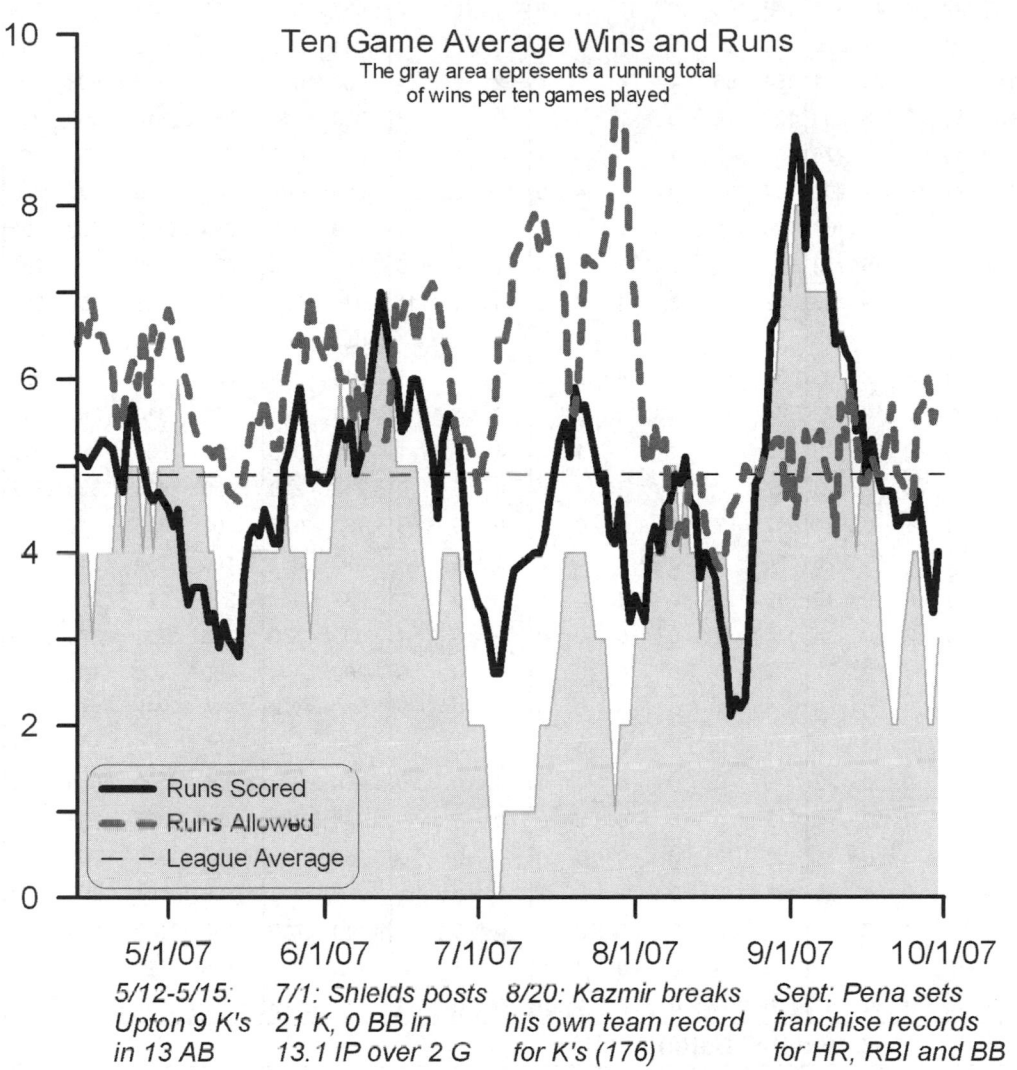

Ten Game Average Wins and Runs
The gray area represents a running total
of wins per ten games played

Runs Scored
Runs Allowed
League Average

5/12-5/15:
Upton 9 K's
in 13 AB

7/1: Shields posts
21 K, 0 BB in
13.1 IP over 2 G

8/20: Kazmir breaks
his own team record
for K's (176)

Sept: Pena sets
franchise records
for HR, RBI and BB

9/4: Rays lose
to O's for loss 82;
10th straight
losing season

Stat Facts:
- 45% of Carlos Pena's batted balls were fly balls, and 32% of his outfield flies were home runs
- Pena's .348 GPA was third in the majors
- Pena committed eight fielding errors
- Delmon Young led the league in outs
- Jonny Gomes struck out in 32% of his plate appearances
- 53% of Gomes's batted balls were fly balls
- Scott Kazmir's K% of 27% was second-highest in the league among starters
- The DER of .648 behind Kazmir was second-lowest in the league
- James Shields's BB% of 5% was fifth-lowest in the league
- Andy Sonnanstine allowed just one stolen base in nine attempts
- Jason Hammel allowed 16 steals in 85 innings

Team Batting and Pitching/Fielding Stats by Month						
	April	May	June	July	Aug	Sept/Oct
Wins	11	11	11	7	15	11
Losses	14	15	17	20	14	16
RS/G	5.0	4.3	5.0	4.3	5.1	5.2
RA/G	6.5	5.7	5.8	7.1	4.6	5.4
OBP	.324	.332	.333	.343	.337	.346
SLG	.434	.411	.447	.424	.430	.454
FIP	5.08	4.89	4.52	4.81	4.12	4.27
DER	.674	.660	.640	.642	.667	.661

Batting Stats

Player	BR	Runs	RBI	PA	Outs	H	2B	3B	HR	TB	K	BB	IBB	HBP	SH	SF	SB	CS	GDP	H-A	L^R	BA	OBP	SLG	GPA
Pena C *	120	99	121	612	359	138	29	1	46	307	142	103	10	10	1	8	1	0	7	.037	.037	.282	.411	.627	.348
Crawford C *	99	93	80	627	421	184	37	9	11	272	112	32	5	5	1	2	50	10	11	-.041	-.005	.315	.355	.466	.282
Upton B	97	86	82	548	354	142	25	1	24	241	154	65	4	4	1	4	22	8	14	-.033	.003	.300	.386	.508	.307
Young D	91	65	93	681	485	186	38	0	13	263	127	26	2	3	0	7	10	3	23	-.008	.012	.288	.316	.408	.249
Harris B	71	72	59	576	392	149	35	3	12	226	96	42	1	4	8	1	4	1	19	-.013	.060	.286	.343	.434	.268
Iwamura A *	68	82	34	559	361	140	21	10	7	202	114	58	0	1	4	5	12	8	2	.008	-.043	.285	.359	.411	.270
Gomes J	51	48	49	394	268	85	20	2	17	160	126	35	1	7	0	4	12	4	1	-.019	.062	.244	.322	.460	.265
Wigginton T	44	47	49	417	286	104	21	0	16	173	73	28	0	5	0	6	1	4	8	.019	.050	.275	.329	.458	.268
Navarro D +	36	46	44	434	312	88	19	2	9	138	67	33	3	1	7	5	3	1	11	-.039	.023	.227	.286	.356	.222
Norton G +	28	25	23	240	155	49	9	0	4	70	55	37	3	0	0	1	1	1	1	-.025	-.069	.243	.358	.347	.253
Wilson J	24	25	24	285	204	66	15	3	2	93	51	12	0	4	3	3	6	2	5	-.016	.014	.251	.291	.354	.224
Dukes E	23	27	21	220	159	35	3	2	10	72	44	33	0	2	0	1	2	4	6	.073	.071	.190	.318	.391	.246
Baldelli R	15	16	12	150	111	28	6	0	5	49	35	9	1	3	1	0	4	1	1	.011	.025	.204	.268	.358	.215
Velandia J	12	7	11	60	34	16	4	0	2	26	17	8	0	1	1	0	0	0	0	-.243	-.218	.320	.424	.520	.327
Casanova R +	10	12	11	89	62	20	1	1	6	41	17	7	1	1	0	2	0	0	3	-.163	-.022	.253	.315	.519	.277
Paul J	7	8	9	115	86	20	3	0	1	26	30	6	0	0	4	0	1	0	1	.085	.062	.190	.234	.248	.171
Cantu J	3	4	4	65	49	12	1	0	0	13	16	5	0	1	0	1	0	0	3	-.037	.047	.207	.277	.224	.184
Guzman J	3	5	4	39	29	9	1	2	0	14	10	2	0	0	0	0	0	0	1	.091	-.170	.243	.282	.378	.226
Sonnanstine	1	1	1	5	3	2	0	0	0	2	2	0	0	0	0	0	0	0	0	-.280	--	.400	.400	.400	.286
Ruggiano J	1	2	3	15	11	3	0	0	0	3	5	1	0	0	0	0	0	0	0	.075	-.174	.214	.267	.214	.177
Kazmir S *	1	0	1	2	1	1	0	0	0	1	0	0	0	0	0	0	0	0	0	-.350	--	.500	.500	.500	.357
Hammel J	1	0	1	1	0	1	1	0	0	2	0	0	0	0	0	0	0	0	0	-.950	--	1.000	1.000	2.000	.969
Howell J *	1	1	1	6	4	2	0	0	0	2	2	0	0	0	0	0	0	0	0	-.233	.000	.333	.333	.333	.238
Jackson E	0	0	0	2	1	1	0	0	0	1	1	0	0	0	0	0	0	0	0	-.350	--	.500	.500	.500	.357
Zobrist B +	0	8	9	105	83	15	2	0	1	20	21	3	0	1	2	2	2	0	1	-.030	-.018	.155	.184	.206	.137
Riggans S	0	1	2	10	10	1	0	0	0	1	1	0	0	0	0	0	0	0	1	-.140	.700	.100	.100	.100	.071
Mohr D	0	1	2	16	15	2	0	0	1	5	6	0	0	0	0	0	0	1	0	-.179	.269	.125	.125	.313	.137
Shields J	-0	1	0	7	5	1	0	0	0	1	0	0	0	0	1	0	0	0	0	-.117	-.175	.167	.167	.167	.119

Italicized stats have been adjusted for home park.

Batted Ball Batting Stats

Player	% of PA		% of Batted Balls					Out %		Runs Per Event				Total Runs vs. Avg.				
	K%	BB%	GB%	LD%	FB%	IF/F	HR/OF	GB	OF	NIP	GB	LD	OF	NIP	GB	LD	FB	Tot
Pena C	23	18	37	18	45	.08	.32	78	85	.09	.02	.40	.47	16	-4	-3	46	54
Upton B	28	13	43	20	38	.07	.21	63	79	.03	.09	.48	.35	-0	5	3	17	26
Crawford C	18	6	48	20	32	.05	.08	69	73	.00	.07	.44	.23	-8	8	10	8	17
Wigginton T	18	8	44	19	37	.04	.14	72	89	.03	.06	.42	.18	-2	2	3	2	4
Iwamura A	20	11	46	20	34	.10	.06	65	88	.04	.11	.43	.10	0	12	3	-13	3
Gomes J	32	11	26	21	53	.09	.16	71	84	.00	.08	.43	.26	-5	-1	-1	10	3
Harris B	17	8	43	21	35	.11	.09	73	81	.04	.05	.41	.18	-3	-0	6	-1	2
Norton G	23	15	33	24	43	.16	.07	84	76	.07	-.01	.36	.17	3	-4	0	-2	-2
Dukes E	20	16	42	11	48	.18	.16	80	87	.09	.00	.33	.24	4	-3	-7	3	-3
Baldelli R	23	8	38	18	44	.22	.14	69	97	.00	.08	.35	.14	-2	1	-3	-3	-7
Paul J	26	5	39	15	46	.09	.03	59	90	-.04	.14	.28	.02	-3	1	-4	-5	-11
Young D	19	4	46	21	33	.09	.08	73	84	-.03	.04	.45	.13	-14	-0	13	-10	-11
Zobrist B	20	4	43	20	37	.11	.04	78	88	-.04	.02	.18	.03	-3	-1	-4	-5	-13
Wilson J	18	6	43	13	44	.11	.02	72	84	-.00	.07	.49	.06	-4	1	-2	-9	-14
Navarro D	15	8	42	17	41	.11	.08	82	85	.04	-.00	.35	.13	-2	-6	-6	-6	-20
MLB Average	17	9	43	19	38	.10	.10	74	83	.05	.05	.40	.18	--	--	--	--	--

Pitching Stats

Player	PRC	IP	BFP	G	GS	K	BB	IBB	HBP	H	HR	DP	DER	SB	CS	PO	W	L	Sv	Op	Hld	H-A	R^L	RA	ERA	FIP
Kazmir S *	107	206.7	887	34	34	239	89	1	7	196	18	22	.648	12	8	3	13	9	0	0	0	-.002	-.049	3.96	3.48	3.58
Shields J	101	215.0	874	31	31	184	36	0	10	202	28	15	.709	9	6	0	12	8	0	0	0	-.009	.013	4.10	3.85	4.00
Jackson E	46	161.0	755	32	31	128	88	3	4	195	19	15	.647	17	5	1	5	15	0	0	0	.020	-.039	6.48	5.76	4.98
Sonnanstine	40	130.7	554	22	22	97	26	2	5	151	18	20	.667	1	8	0	6	10	0	0	0	.034	-.039	5.99	5.85	4.35
Glover G	28	77.3	334	67	0	51	27	3	1	87	12	11	.691	6	2	0	6	5	2	4	11	-.016	-.013	5.12	4.89	5.05
Hammel J	26	85.0	384	24	14	64	40	1	2	100	12	6	.665	16	3	0	3	5	0	0	0	-.021	-.033	6.14	6.14	5.16
Reyes A	24	60.7	254	61	0	70	21	1	1	49	13	1	.743	2	0	0	2	4	26	30	0	-.053	-.057	5.19	4.90	4.95
Dohmann S	17	32.7	136	31	0	26	18	1	0	29	3	8	.697	3	2	1	3	0	0	0	4	-.072	.037	3.58	3.31	4.54
Fossum C *	15	76.0	364	40	10	53	27	1	6	109	15	9	.627	10	0	0	5	8	0	4	2	.031	.009	8.41	7.70	5.81
Stokes B	15	62.3	294	59	0	35	25	1	3	90	11	9	.641	3	1	0	2	7	0	2	8	-.017	-.014	7.07	7.07	5.85
Salas J	14	36.3	168	34	0	26	17	0	5	36	7	0	.726	2	1	1	1	1	0	1	2	-.062	.013	4.71	3.72	6.27
Howell J *	12	51.0	244	10	10	49	21	0	3	69	8	5	.607	2	1	1	1	6	0	0	0	-.107	-.010	7.94	7.59	4.91
Camp S	10	40.0	198	50	0	36	18	6	3	63	7	9	.560	2	0	0	0	3	0	2	11	-.120	-.024	7.43	7.20	4.98
Seo J	8	52.0	248	11	10	28	16	1	4	84	11	9	.598	3	2	0	3	4	0	0	0	.025	.011	9.17	8.13	6.15
Balfour G	7	22.0	103	22	0	27	16	0	0	26	1	2	.559	1	1	2	1	0	0	0	1	.027	-.091	6.14	6.14	3.70
Wheeler D	7	25.0	116	25	0	26	10	2	1	28	3	1	.645	1	0	0	0	5	0	3	12	-.055	-.046	7.20	5.76	3.94
Ryu J	5	23.3	110	17	0	14	11	0	4	31	2	4	.620	2	2	0	1	2	0	1	1	.053	-.059	7.33	7.33	5.22
Switzer J *	4	19.0	88	21	0	13	7	1	0	27	2	2	.621	0	1	0	0	2	0	0	3	-.078	-.138	8.05	8.05	4.33
Witasick J	4	16.3	81	20	0	8	18	1	0	17	1	3	.685	1	0	0	0	0	0	0	3	-.025	-.159	7.16	6.61	6.32
Corcoran T	4	17.3	79	9	0	6	12	3	1	17	2	3	.724	0	1	0	0	0	0	0	0	-.157	-.102	7.27	6.75	5.92
Lugo R	2	10.7	61	11	0	8	13	2	0	17	2	1	.605	0	0	0	2	0	0	2	0	-.173	-.036	9.28	9.28	7.41
Orvella C	0	8.0	56	10	0	6	10	1	1	18	3	0	.500	3	0	0	0	2	0	0	0	-.054	-.015	18.00	14.63	10.51
Wilson J	0	1.0	5	1	0	0	1	0	0	1	0	0	.750	0	0	0	0	0	0	0	0	--	.308	0.00	0.00	6.38
Ridgway J *	0	0.3	10	3	0	0	1	0	1	7	1	0	.143	0	0	0	0	0	0	0	0	-.223	.215	189.00	189.00	60.38

Italicized stats have been adjusted for home park.

Batted Ball Pitching Stats

Player	% of PA		% of Batted Balls			IF/F	HR/OF	Out %		Runs Per Event				Total Runs vs. Avg.				
	K%	BB%	GB%	LD%	FB%			GB	OF	NIP	GB	LD	OF	NIP	GB	LD	FB	Tot
Shields J	21	5	43	16	40	.09	.12	77	82	-.02	.03	.38	.21	-17	-1	-12	6	-24
Kazmir S	27	11	43	16	41	.10	.09	64	84	.02	.11	.46	.16	-6	12	-9	-7	-10
Reyes A	28	9	20	19	61	.10	.15	66	92	.00	.11	.34	.19	-4	-0	-4	4	-4
Dohmann S	19	13	39	24	38	.09	.10	76	93	.07	.01	.41	.12	1	-1	1	-2	-1
Wheeler D	22	9	38	24	38	.07	.07	72	72	.02	.05	.39	.21	-1	0	1	1	1
Salas J	15	14	31	16	53	.30	.16	70	84	.10	.09	.38	.24	3	1	-2	2	4
Glover G	15	8	38	14	48	.11	.11	70	77	.05	.07	.35	.23	-1	2	-6	10	5
Sonnanstine A	18	6	39	18	43	.08	.10	70	85	-.00	.06	.46	.17	-8	4	5	4	5
Howell J	20	10	46	23	31	.06	.16	73	78	.04	.05	.47	.30	-0	1	6	5	11
Hammel J	17	11	41	16	43	.08	.09	66	77	.07	.10	.42	.22	2	5	-2	7	13
Camp S	18	11	57	21	22	.07	.26	66	70	.06	.08	.51	.46	1	4	5	5	15
Stokes B	12	9	48	17	35	.09	.15	65	79	.09	.09	.40	.26	2	6	1	7	16
Fossum C	15	9	45	23	32	.09	.18	68	83	.06	.09	.43	.26	1	6	9	6	22
Seo J	11	8	37	21	41	.11	.15	61	81	.08	.13	.45	.25	1	7	8	8	24
Jackson E	17	12	45	19	36	.10	.11	68	80	.08	.09	.36	.22	8	12	-1	6	24
MLB Average	17	9	43	19	38	.10	.10	74	83	.05	.05	.40	.18	--	--	--	--	--

Fielding Stats

Name	INN	SBA/G	CS%	ERA	WP+PB/G	PO	A	TE	FE
Catcher									
Navarro D	956.3	0.89	25%	5.50	0.367	814	67	12	2
Paul J	277.7	0.71	41%	4.89	0.551	228	21	2	0
Casanova R	168.7	0.69	31%	6.99	0.587	138	9	3	0
Riggans S	27.0	1.00	0%	4.33	0.667	31	1	2	0

Name	Inn	PO	A	TE	FE	FPct	DPS	DPT	RZR	OOZ
First Base										
Pena C	1221.0	1054	130	0	8	.993	14	0	.769	38
Wigginton T	132.0	116	15	0	0	1.000	1	0	.548	1
Cantu J	51.0	49	3	0	0	1.000	0	0	.714	0
Guzman J	17.0	11	1	0	1	.923	0	0	.667	0
Norton G	8.7	5	1	0	0	1.000	0	0	0.000	1
Second Base										
Upton B	416.3	106	133	5	7	.952	11	13	.783	13
Harris B	404.0	75	96	0	1	.994	9	17	.826	2
Wigginton T	321.0	74	89	1	2	.982	9	15	.780	7
Wilson J	182.0	44	68	2	4	.949	10	9	.877	5
Velandia J	94.3	17	29	0	0	1.000	4	2	.893	2
Iwamura A	9.0	2	2	0	0	1.000	0	1	1.000	0
Cantu J	3.0	2	2	0	0	1.000	1	1	1.000	0
Shortstop										
Harris B	751.7	111	221	4	7	.968	26	25	.777	37
Wilson J	417.3	67	118	2	6	.959	15	14	.736	18
Zobrist B	224.7	37	63	2	4	.943	8	9	.700	10
Velandia J	27.0	7	12	0	0	1.000	4	0	1.000	2
Guzman J	9.0	0	0	0	0	0.000	0	0	0.000	0

Name	Inn	PO	A	TE	FE	FPct	DPS	DPT	RZR	OOZ
Third Base										
Iwamura A	1042.0	79	197	2	5	.975	15	0	.626	40
Wigginton T	254.7	23	52	0	4	.938	2	1	.643	11
Wilson J	64.0	3	19	0	3	.880	4	0	.704	0
Guzman J	44.0	3	7	0	0	1.000	1	0	.500	2
Harris B	24.7	2	1	1	0	.750	0	0	.667	0
Left Field										
Crawford C	1186.0	286	3	2	2	.986	2	0	.872	40
Gomes J	186.3	42	2	0	0	1.000	2	0	.740	5
Norton G	20.0	1	0	0	0	1.000	0	0	1.000	0
Mohr D	18.0	3	0	0	0	1.000	0	0	.500	0
Dukes E	12.0	5	0	0	0	1.000	0	0	1.000	0
Ruggiano J	7.0	2	0	0	0	1.000	0	0	1.000	1
Center Field										
Upton B	664.7	204	11	2	0	.991	4	0	.870	37
Dukes E	332.3	82	4	0	0	1.000	2	0	.830	4
Young D	242.7	62	0	1	2	.954	0	0	.841	4
Baldelli R	162.0	62	3	0	0	1.000	2	0	.903	6
Ruggiano J	20.0	3	0	0	0	1.000	0	0	.400	1
Mohr D	8.0	6	0	0	0	1.000	0	0	.833	1
Right Field										
Young D	1134.0	252	16	3	1	.985	14	0	.868	35
Gomes J	252.7	53	3	0	0	1.000	2	0	.750	11
Norton G	31.7	3	1	0	0	1.000	0	0	.600	0
Mohr D	9.0	0	0	0	0	0.000	0	0	--	--
Dukes E	1.3	0	0	0	0	0.000	0	0	--	--
Ruggiano J	1.0	1	0	0	0	1.000	0	0	1.000	0

Texas Rangers

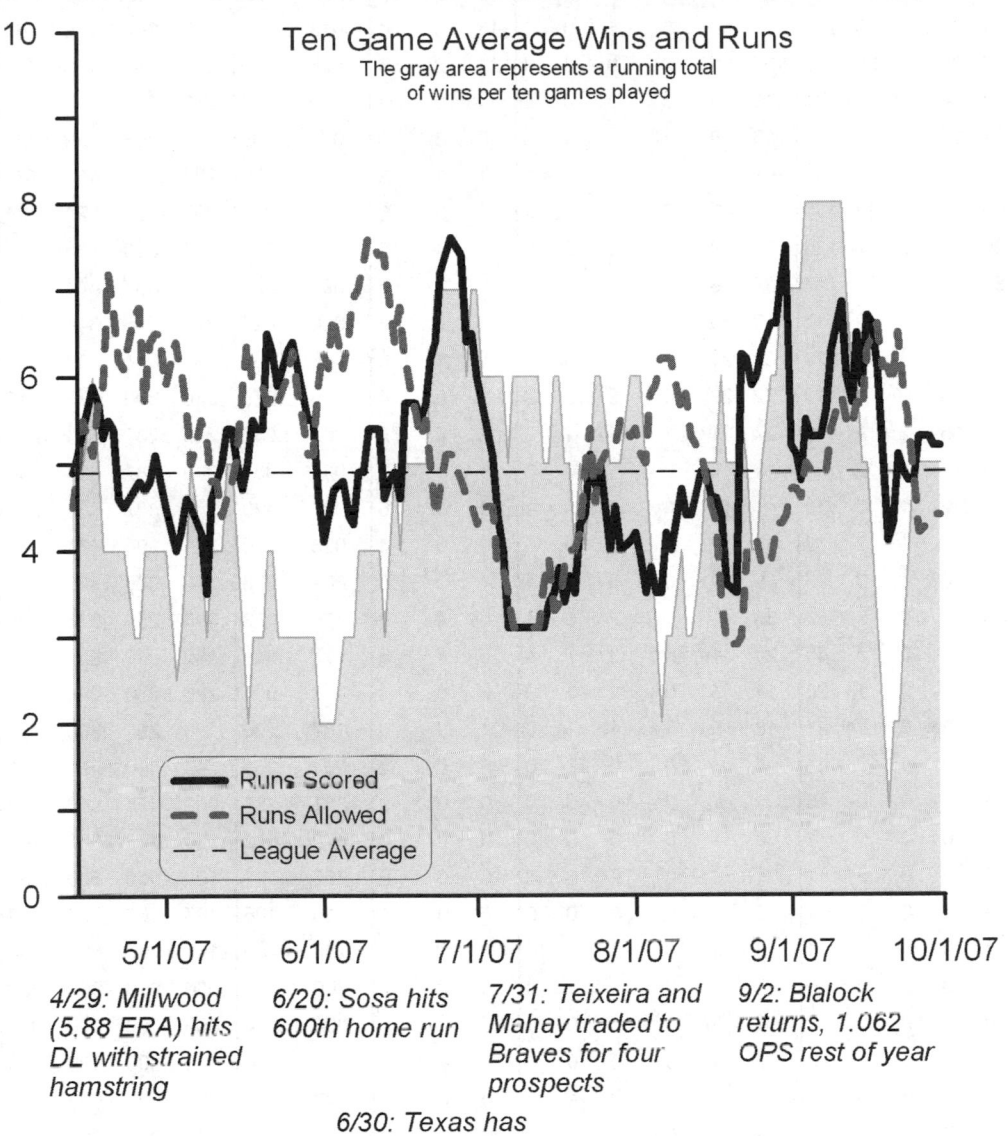

Ten Game Average Wins and Runs
The gray area represents a running total
of wins per ten games played

Legend:
- Runs Scored
- - Runs Allowed
- - League Average

4/29: Millwood (5.88 ERA) hits DL with strained hamstring

6/20: Sosa hits 600th home run

6/30: Texas has worst record in AL (33-47)

7/31: Teixeira and Mahay traded to Braves for four prospects

9/2: Blalock returns, 1.062 OPS rest of year

Stat Facts:
- Gerald Laird threw out 40% of base stealers
- Jarrod Saltalamacchia threw out 6% of base stealers
- Vicente Padilla allowed just three stolen bases in six attempts
- Victor Diaz walked once, struck out 33 times, and hit 9 HRs in 108 Pas
- 38% of Diaz's outfield flies were home runs
- Jamey Wright induced 17 double plays in 77 innings
- Michael Young's LD% of 27% was highest in the league
- Just 2% of Young's fly balls were infield pop-ups
- The DER of .643 behind Kevin Millwood was lowest in the league
- The LD% of 21% off Millwood was second-highest in the league
- 56% of the batted balls off Kameron Loe were grounders, and just 26% were fly balls

Team Batting and Pitching/Fielding Stats by Month						
	April	May	June	July	Aug	Sept/Oct
Wins	10	9	14	14	14	14
Losses	15	20	12	12	14	14
RS/G	4.7	5.0	5.8	3.8	5.3	5.5
RA/G	5.8	5.5	5.8	4.4	4.4	5.4
OBP	.303	.324	.353	.303	.328	.352
SLG	.401	.440	.452	.384	.421	.452
FIP	5.44	4.65	4.98	3.92	4.23	5.12
DER	.690	.684	.658	.684	.690	.688

Batting Stats

Player	BR	Runs	RBI	PA	Outs	H	2B	3B	HR	TB	K	BB	IBB	HBP	SH	SF	SB	CS	GDP	H-A	L^R	BA	OBP	SLG	GPA
Young M	97	80	94	692	462	201	37	1	9	267	107	47	5	5	0	1	13	3	21	.013	.005	.315	.366	.418	.256
Kinsler I	76	96	61	566	372	127	22	2	20	213	83	62	2	9	8	4	23	2	14	.078	.085	.263	.355	.441	.257
Sosa S	67	53	92	454	319	104	24	1	21	193	112	34	3	3	0	5	0	0	11	-.020	.116	.252	.311	.468	.245
Byrd M	61	60	70	454	299	127	17	8	10	190	88	29	3	5	0	6	5	3	9	.071	.009	.307	.355	.459	.261
Wilkerson B	57	54	62	389	262	79	17	1	20	158	107	43	0	1	3	4	4	1	2	.068	-.030	.234	.319	.467	.248
Teixeira M +	54	48	49	335	206	85	24	1	13	150	66	45	10	3	0	1	0	0	5	.010	.059	.297	.397	.524	.295
Lofton K *	49	62	23	363	230	96	16	3	7	139	28	39	1	2	2	3	21	4	5	.031	.099	.303	.380	.438	.267
Catalanotto	48	52	44	377	252	86	20	4	11	147	37	28	0	11	6	1	2	1	6	.093	.038	.260	.337	.444	.250
Laird G	43	48	47	448	321	91	18	3	9	142	103	30	1	2	5	4	6	2	3	.020	.027	.224	.278	.349	.202
Blalock H *	37	32	33	232	156	61	16	3	10	113	38	21	1	1	0	2	4	1	8	.066	.031	.293	.358	.543	.283
Vazquez R *	34	42	28	345	235	69	13	3	8	112	72	29	0	2	12	2	1	0	4	-.039	.075	.230	.300	.373	.218
Cruz N	32	35	34	333	244	72	15	2	9	118	87	21	1	2	1	1	2	4	5	.063	-.039	.235	.287	.384	.215
Murphy D *	20	16	14	110	69	35	12	1	2	55	19	7	0	0	0	0	0	0	1	-.091	-.031	.340	.382	.534	.291
Metcalf T	20	25	21	181	127	41	12	1	5	70	41	13	0	0	5	2	0	1	6	-.020	-.025	.255	.307	.435	.235
Saltalamacch	18	28	21	176	129	42	7	1	7	72	47	9	0	0	0	0	0	0	4	-.026	-.170	.251	.290	.431	.227
Botts J +	17	19	14	190	135	40	8	1	2	56	59	19	0	3	0	1	1	0	8	.001	.078	.240	.326	.335	.220
Diaz V	13	13	25	108	83	25	4	0	9	56	33	1	0	2	0	1	0	0	4	-.176	-.033	.240	.259	.538	.239
Hairston J	12	22	16	184	135	30	7	0	3	46	24	11	0	3	7	4	5	1	5	-.027	.019	.189	.249	.289	.175
Melhuse A +	6	6	7	73	57	14	3	0	1	20	18	3	0	1	1	0	0	0	3	-.073	.051	.206	.250	.294	.177
Kata M +	5	12	6	77	57	13	2	0	2	21	18	5	0	1	1	0	1	0	0	.107	-.126	.186	.250	.300	.179
Stewart C	3	4	3	43	30	9	2	0	0	11	6	3	0	0	3	0	0	0	2	-.004	.251	.243	.300	.297	.199
Quiroz G	3	1	2	11	6	4	1	0	0	5	2	1	0	0	0	0	0	0	0	-.364	.288	.400	.455	.500	.314
Loe K	1	1	0	3	1	1	0	0	0	1	0	1	0	0	0	0	0	0	0	-.425	-.475	.500	.667	.500	.405
Padilla V	0	1	0	2	1	1	0	0	0	1	1	0	0	0	0	0	0	0	0	-.350	--	.500	.500	.500	.333
Mahar K	0	2	1	18	16	3	1	0	0	4	7	0	0	0	0	0	0	0	1	-.168	.106	.167	.167	.222	.124
Guzman F +	0	2	1	6	6	1	0	0	1	4	2	0	0	0	0	0	0	1	0	-.290	1.450	.167	.167	.667	.230
Wright J	-0	0	0	2	1	0	0	0	0	0	1	0	0	0	1	0	0	0	0	.000	--	.000	.000	.000	.000
Littleton W	-0	0	0	1	1	0	0	0	0	0	1	0	0	0	0	0	0	0	0	.000	--	.000	.000	.000	.000
Koronka J *	-0	0	0	2	2	0	0	0	0	0	2	0	0	0	0	0	0	0	0	--	--	.000	.000	.000	.000
McCarthy B	-0	0	0	3	2	0	0	0	0	0	2	0	0	0	1	0	0	0	0	.000	--	.000	.000	.000	.000
Tejeda R	-0	0	0	4	3	0	0	0	0	0	3	0	0	0	1	0	0	0	0	.000	--	.000	.000	.000	.000
Millwood K	-0	0	0	4	4	0	0	0	0	0	4	0	0	0	0	0	0	0	0	.000	.000	.000	.000	.000	.000
Relaford D +	-1	2	0	28	26	3	0	0	0	3	6	2	0	0	0	0	0	1	2	.086	-.004	.115	.179	.115	.104

Italicized stats have been adjusted for home park.
Batted Ball Batting Stats are listed after Fielding Stats.

Pitching Stats

Player	PRC	IP	BFP	G	GS	K	BB	IBB	HBP	H	HR	DP	DER	SB	CS	PO	W	L	Sv	Op	Hld	H-A	R^L	RA	ERA	FIP
Millwood K	59	172.7	788	31	31	123	67	2	8	213	19	23	.643	14	5	0	10	14	0	0	0	-.034	-.017	5.79	5.16	4.65
Benoit J	55	82.0	337	70	0	87	28	2	2	68	6	9	.696	2	2	0	7	4	6	13	19	-.042	.093	3.07	2.85	3.23
Wilson C *	42	68.3	285	66	0	63	33	1	6	50	4	13	.715	2	0	0	2	1	12	14	15	.031	-.126	3.29	3.03	3.97
Loe K	40	136.0	615	28	23	78	56	6	4	162	13	17	.659	11	5	1	6	11	0	0	0	-.001	-.053	6.35	5.36	4.67
McCarthy B	35	101.7	459	23	22	59	48	0	3	111	9	8	.685	17	5	0	5	10	0	0	0	-.029	-.029	5.49	4.87	4.88
Wright J	34	77.0	330	20	9	39	41	2	5	72	6	17	.715	4	4	1	4	5	0	0	1	-.057	-.066	4.09	3.62	5.09
Padilla V	34	120.3	553	23	23	71	50	1	9	146	16	13	.668	3	3	1	6	10	0	0	0	-.086	-.046	6.58	5.76	5.37
Gagne E	28	33.3	132	34	0	29	12	0	1	23	2	4	.761	0	0	0	2	0	16	17	1	.088	.101	2.16	2.16	3.59
Mahay R *	27	39.0	164	28	0	32	21	0	1	33	3	7	.720	0	3	0	2	0	1	1	1	-.010	-.013	2.77	2.77	4.43
Tejeda R	25	95.3	454	19	19	69	60	1	6	110	17	9	.679	12	5	0	5	9	0	0	0	-.012	-.078	7.36	6.61	6.26
Francisco F	24	59.3	268	59	0	49	38	4	2	57	3	6	.676	4	4	0	1	1	0	0	21	.001	.026	5.01	4.55	4.21
Eyre W	24	68.0	307	33	2	42	32	4	1	78	8	8	.674	2	2	0	4	6	1	1	1	-.013	.042	5.56	5.16	4.95
Otsuka A	21	32.3	132	34	0	23	9	1	0	26	0	1	.710	3	2	0	2	1	4	7	11	-.072	.064	2.78	2.51	2.70
Littleton W	20	48.0	205	35	0	24	16	1	3	48	6	6	.718	3	1	0	3	2	2	3	2	.097	.033	4.31	4.31	5.13
Volquez E	15	34.0	149	6	6	29	15	0	2	34	4	4	.697	2	0	0	2	1	0	0	0	-.052	.080	4.76	4.50	4.70
Rheinecker J	15	50.3	239	23	7	40	28	2	2	61	9	7	.650	0	0	0	4	3	0	0	2	-.028	-.100	6.79	5.36	5.78
Wood M	14	50.7	234	21	4	25	15	1	4	68	9	5	.652	1	1	0	3	2	0	0	3	-.089	-.055	6.39	5.33	5.77
Gabbard K *	14	40.3	179	8	8	26	23	1	3	40	5	7	.713	5	1	1	2	1	0	0	0	-.021	.044	5.58	5.58	5.56
Feldman S	12	39.0	192	29	0	19	32	5	3	44	3	4	.681	6	2	0	1	2	0	0	0	-.142	-.061	6.00	5.77	5.71
Murray A *	11	28.0	123	14	2	18	15	1	0	25	6	2	.774	4	0	0	1	2	0	0	0	-.005	.104	4.82	4.50	6.38
Mendoza L	11	16.0	64	6	3	7	4	0	2	13	1	2	.760	0	1	1	1	0	0	0	0	.097	-.014	2.25	2.25	4.44
White B *	4	9.3	42	9	0	9	7	1	2	8	1	3	.696	1	0	0	2	0	0	0	3	-.021	.053	4.82	4.82	5.42
Galarraga A	3	8.7	40	3	1	6	7	0	0	8	2	1	.760	2	1	0	0	0	0	0	0	.021	-.068	6.23	6.23	7.42
Koronka J *	2	10.3	52	2	2	2	5	0	1	16	0	1	.636	0	0	0	0	2	0	0	0	--	-.116	7.84	7.84	4.74
Chen B *	2	10.0	46	5	0	7	6	1	0	11	3	2	.700	0	0	0	0	0	0	0	0	-.033	.084	9.90	7.20	7.38

Italicized stats have been adjusted for home park.
Batted Ball Pitching Stats are listed after Fielding Stats.

Fielding Stats

Name	INN	SBA/G	CS%	ERA	WP+PB/G	PO	A	TE	FE
Catcher									
Laird G	987.3	0.89	40%	4.78	0.383	675	75	9	3
Saltalamacchia	185.7	0.82	6%	4.80	0.533	127	5	2	0
Melhuse A	123.0	0.80	9%	4.02	1.024	80	5	0	0
Stewart C	105.3	1.03	33%	4.96	1.025	99	5	2	0
Quiroz G	28.7	1.57	0%	6.28	0.314	25	0	1	1

Name	Inn	PO	A	TE	FE	FPct	DPS	DPT	RZR	OOZ
First Base										
Teixeira M	624.0	614	47	0	1	.998	8	1	.755	19
Wilkerson B	456.0	497	19	0	3	.994	6	1	.703	10
Saltalamacchia	199.0	204	12	4	5	.960	0	0	.719	10
Catalanotto F	96.0	94	6	0	0	1.000	0	0	.750	3
Vazquez R	35.0	31	0	0	0	1.000	0	0	1.000	0
Kata M	20.0	25	0	0	0	1.000	0	0	.500	0
Second Base										
Kinsler I	1136.0	283	436	4	13	.977	32	66	.845	53
Hairston J	107.0	25	41	0	0	1.000	7	5	.784	6
Vazquez R	103.0	18	32	0	0	1.000	4	5	.706	3
Relaford D	70.3	11	27	0	0	1.000	2	3	.833	4
Kata M	13.0	3	1	1	0	.800	0	1	--	--
Shortstop										
Young M	1291.0	211	446	9	10	.972	50	48	.809	45
Vazquez R	110.7	16	42	0	0	1.000	7	1	.919	7
Kata M	25.0	7	6	0	0	1.000	0	2	1.000	1
Hairston J	3.0	1	0	0	0	1.000	0	0	--	--
Third Base										
Vazquez R	540.3	46	123	3	4	.960	15	1	.702	25
Metcalf T	430.3	35	89	3	4	.947	12	0	.699	12
Blalock H	339.3	18	69	2	4	.935	9	0	.600	15
Hairston J	44.7	3	13	1	0	.941	1	0	.643	3
Kata M	44.3	3	7	1	1	.833	0	0	.176	4
Melhuse A	31.0	0	12	0	0	1.000	1	0	.917	0

Name	Inn	PO	A	TE	FE	FPct	DPS	DPT	RZR	OOZ
Left Field										
Catalanotto F	483.3	98	2	0	0	1.000	0	0	.837	16
Wilkerson B	275.3	73	2	0	2	.974	0	0	.866	15
Botts J	212.0	62	1	0	0	1.000	0	0	.980	14
Cruz N	118.0	19	1	0	0	1.000	0	0	.846	8
Byrd M	116.7	31	0	0	0	1.000	0	0	1.000	6
Murphy D	94.3	25	0	1	0	.962	0	0	.786	3
Hairston J	62.0	15	1	0	1	.941	0	0	1.000	3
Kata M	54.0	12	2	0	0	1.000	2	0	1.000	3
Diaz V	10.3	2	0	0	0	1.000	0	0	1.000	1
Relaford D	2.0	0	0	0	0	0.000	0	0	--	--
Laird G	1.0	0	0	0	0	0.000	0	0	--	--
Guzman F	1.0	0	0	0	0	0.000	0	0	--	--
Center Field										
Lofton K	669.3	186	5	1	2	.985	6	0	.849	34
Byrd M	496.3	114	4	1	1	.983	2	0	.887	12
Hairston J	134.3	50	2	0	1	.981	0	0	.891	9
Murphy D	78.7	23	0	0	0	1.000	0	0	.840	2
Mahar K	37.3	9	0	0	0	1.000	0	0	.857	3
Guzman F	12.0	5	0	0	0	1.000	0	0	.750	2
Wilkerson B	2.0	1	0	0	0	1.000	0	0	1.000	0
Right Field										
Cruz N	604.3	148	5	2	3	.968	2	0	.869	22
Byrd M	304.3	78	5	1	0	.988	8	0	.870	18
Diaz V	161.3	33	0	0	1	.971	0	0	.828	9
Sosa S	131.0	32	1	0	0	1.000	0	0	.929	7
Wilkerson B	111.0	27	0	0	0	1.000	0	0	1.000	1
Murphy D	76.0	13	4	0	0	1.000	2	0	.786	2
Hairston J	39.0	8	0	0	0	1.000	0	0	1.000	2
Mahar K	3.0	1	0	0	0	1.000	0	0	1.000	0

Batted Ball Batting Stats

Player	% of PA		% of Batted Balls					Out %		Runs Per Event				Total Runs vs. Avg.				
	K%	BB%	GB%	LD%	FB%	IF/F	HR/OF	GB	OF	NIP	GB	LD	OF	NIP	GB	LD	FB	Tot
Teixeira M	20	14	40	22	38	.10	.17	80	70	.08	.01	.42	.37	5	-4	4	14	20
Lofton K	8	11	39	19	42	.12	.07	69	85	.16	.08	.38	.11	6	6	3	-3	12
Young M	15	8	48	27	24	.02	.07	71	78	.04	.06	.34	.17	-3	5	15	-6	11
Byrd M	19	7	47	20	33	.06	.09	69	77	.02	.07	.47	.20	-4	5	7	2	10
Blalock H	16	9	33	21	46	.13	.10	79	79	.06	-.00	.55	.22	0	-3	8	4	9
Kinsler I	15	13	35	20	46	.13	.12	78	89	.10	.02	.43	.16	8	-4	4	-1	7
Catalanotto F	10	10	51	19	30	.06	.12	77	91	.12	.03	.43	.16	4	-1	4	-3	4
Wilkerson B	28	11	39	17	45	.07	.21	76	84	.02	.04	.37	.31	-2	-1	-7	13	2
Sosa S	25	8	39	15	46	.08	.16	77	78	.00	.02	.40	.30	-6	-4	-6	18	1
Diaz V	31	3	61	6	33	.00	.38	77	73	-.07	.01	.19	.62	-4	-1	-6	10	-1
Metcalf T	23	7	39	19	42	.06	.11	64	83	-.00	.09	.34	.20	-3	1	-2	1	-3
Saltalamacchia J	27	5	52	14	34	.05	.18	77	72	-.04	.02	.37	.37	-5	-2	-4	6	-4
Botts J	31	12	40	22	38	.07	.05	70	83	.01	.03	.44	.11	-2	-1	0	-4	-7
Vazquez R	21	9	43	21	36	.08	.11	78	85	.03	.03	.35	.17	-2	-2	-3	-3	-11
Cruz N	26	7	38	16	46	.14	.10	70	87	-.02	.08	.47	.15	-7	1	-2	-3	-11
Hairston J	13	8	35	14	52	.22	.06	76	92	.06	.02	.28	.05	-1	-1	-6	-8	-15
Laird G	23	7	33	12	55	.13	.07	68	84	-.00	.09	.40	.13	-7	5	-12	-5	-19
MLB Average	*17*	*9*	*43*	*19*	*38*	*.10*	*.10*	*74*	*83*	*.05*	*.05*	*.40*	*.18*	--	--	--	--	--

Batted Ball Pitching Stats

Player	% of PA		% of Batted Balls					Out %		Runs Per Event				Total Runs vs. Avg.				
	K%	BB%	GB%	LD%	FB%	IF/F	HR/OF	GB	OF	NIP	GB	LD	OF	NIP	GB	LD	FB	Tot
Benoit J	26	9	37	24	39	.11	.08	79	80	.00	.02	.35	.16	-4	-4	-1	-4	-13
Wilson C	22	14	49	24	27	.08	.09	75	93	.06	.03	.28	.08	2	-2	-3	-9	-12
Gagne E	22	9	42	21	37	.06	.06	82	87	.02	-.01	.23	.10	-1	-2	-4	-3	-10
Otsuka A	17	8	55	20	25	.17	.00	75	95	.03	.05	.43	-.05	-1	0	1	-7	-7
Mahay R	20	13	52	12	36	.10	.09	77	72	.07	.03	.33	.25	2	-1	-4	1	-2
Littleton W	12	9	55	19	27	.02	.12	80	92	.09	.01	.46	.13	1	-2	3	-3	-1
Wright J	12	14	55	17	28	.12	.10	76	85	.14	.03	.35	.15	7	-1	-2	-5	-1
Volquez E	19	11	38	22	40	.12	.11	69	91	.06	.06	.32	.15	1	1	-1	-1	-1
Gabbard K	15	15	56	15	29	.00	.14	84	77	.12	-.03	.43	.27	4	-4	-1	3	2
Murray A	15	12	38	11	51	.09	.15	79	83	.10	.04	.38	.24	1	-1	-3	4	2
Francisco F	18	15	35	22	43	.09	.04	72	81	.09	.07	.37	.12	5	0	0	-3	2
McCarthy B	13	11	36	17	47	.09	.06	68	85	.10	.09	.42	.11	5	5	2	-5	7
Eyre W	14	11	45	19	36	.11	.11	71	78	.09	.06	.33	.24	3	3	-2	4	7
Feldman S	10	18	59	15	26	.09	.09	73	83	.18	.05	.41	.18	8	2	-0	-1	8
Rheinecker J	17	13	56	17	27	.00	.20	76	72	.08	.03	.40	.38	3	-0	-0	8	10
Padilla V	13	11	46	21	34	.11	.12	69	86	.10	.07	.37	.17	5	5	4	-1	13
Wood M	11	8	51	19	31	.10	.17	72	88	.09	.06	.53	.24	1	3	7	3	13
Loe K	13	10	56	18	26	.02	.11	74	81	.09	.05	.42	.21	4	7	4	1	16
Millwood K	16	10	46	21	32	.08	.10	72	83	.06	.05	.45	.18	2	4	16	-1	21
Tejeda R	15	15	35	14	51	.14	.09	60	86	.11	.14	.61	.14	9	8	5	-1	22
MLB Average	*17*	*9*	*43*	*19*	*38*	*.10*	*.10*	*74*	*83*	*.05*	*.05*	*.40*	*.18*	--	--	--	--	--

Toronto Blue Jays

Stat Facts:

- Troy Glaus's L^R was .155
- Just 30% of Frank Thomas's batted balls were grounders, and 53% were fly balls
- Roy Halladay induced 30 double plays
- A.J. Burnett allowed 31 stolen bases in 31 attempts
- Dustin McGowan allowed 29 steals in 30 attempts
- Gregg Zaun threw out 14% of base stealers
- Jason Phillips threw out just 4% of base stealers
- Just 7% of the outfield flies off Halladay were home runs
- 20% of the outfield flies against Burnett were home runs
- The DER of .739 behind Burnett tied for highest in the league
- McGowan's lefty/righty split of -.074 was second-lowest in the league

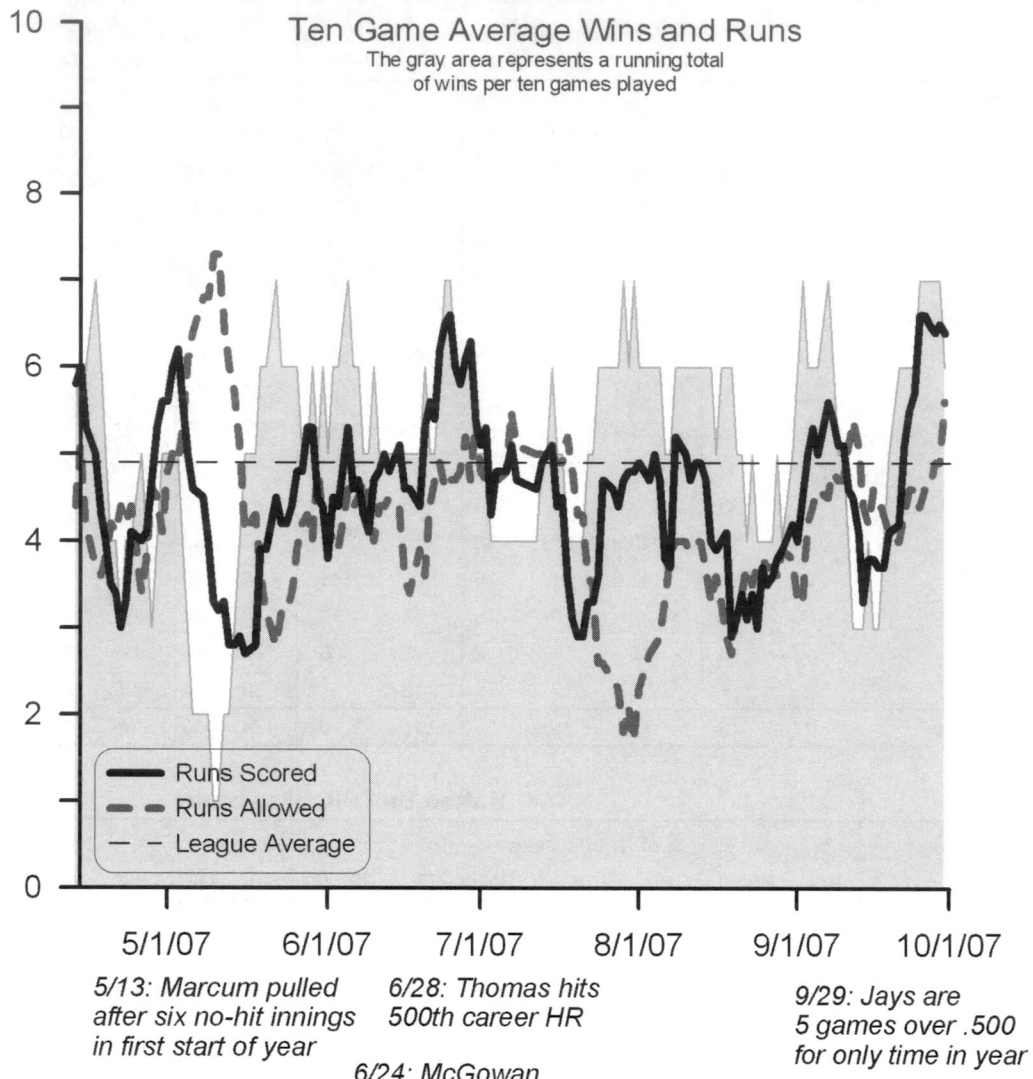

Ten Game Average Wins and Runs
The gray area represents a running total of wins per ten games played

Legend:
— Runs Scored
– – Runs Allowed
– · – League Average

5/13: Marcum pulled after six no-hit innings in first start of year

6/28: Thomas hits 500th career HR

6/24: McGowan loses no-hitter in ninth vs. COL

9/29: Jays are 5 games over .500 for only time in year

9/16: Hill hits 42nd double, breaking Alomar's club record for 2B

Team Batting and Pitching/Fielding Stats by Month						
	April	May	June	July	Aug	Sept/Oct
Wins	13	12	14	14	15	15
Losses	12	16	13	12	13	13
RS/G	5.2	3.9	5.2	4.3	4.2	5.2
RA/G	4.2	5.0	4.6	3.5	3.8	4.8
OBP	.347	.306	.329	.321	.323	.335
SLG	.450	.411	.420	.419	.409	.409
FIP	4.47	4.80	3.75	4.19	3.97	3.89
DER	.730	.705	.688	.710	.717	.686

Batting Stats

Player	BR	Runs	RBI	PA	Outs	H	2B	3B	HR	TB	K	BB	IBB	HBP	SH	SF	SB	CS	GDP	H-A	L^R	BA	OBP	SLG	GPA
Rios A	105	114	85	711	465	191	43	7	24	320	103	55	3	6	0	7	17	4	9	-.009	.073	.297	.354	.498	.278
Thomas F	97	63	95	624	398	147	30	0	26	255	94	81	3	7	0	5	0	0	14	.053	.081	.277	.377	.480	.284
Hill A	88	87	78	657	455	177	47	2	17	279	102	41	1	0	3	5	4	3	21	.026	.045	.291	.333	.459	.260
Wells V	75	85	80	642	454	143	36	4	16	235	89	49	4	3	0	6	10	4	9	-.003	.062	.245	.304	.402	.233
Stairs M *	67	58	64	405	262	103	28	1	21	196	66	44	5	2	0	2	2	1	7	.006	.022	.289	.368	.549	.297
Glaus T	66	60	62	456	292	101	19	1	20	182	102	61	2	5	0	5	0	1	7	.031	.155	.262	.366	.473	.277
Zaun G +	48	43	52	391	260	80	24	1	10	136	55	51	8	2	1	6	0	0	9	.066	.027	.242	.341	.411	.251
Overbay L *	46	49	44	476	335	102	30	2	10	166	78	47	4	1	0	3	2	0	12	-.031	-.031	.240	.315	.391	.235
Lind A *	40	34	46	311	230	69	14	0	11	116	65	16	0	1	2	2	1	2	7	.046	.054	.238	.278	.400	.221
McDonald J	34	32	31	353	251	82	20	2	1	109	48	11	0	2	12	1	7	2	4	.003	.092	.251	.279	.333	.205
Johnson R	24	31	14	307	219	65	13	2	2	88	56	16	0	11	5	0	4	2	7	-.000	.121	.236	.305	.320	.213
Clayton R	19	23	12	210	150	48	14	0	1	65	50	14	0	1	3	3	2	1	8	-.019	-.002	.254	.304	.344	.219
Thigpen C	13	13	11	110	81	24	5	0	0	29	17	8	0	0	1	0	2	0	4	-.075	.017	.238	.294	.287	.200
Phillips J	11	11	12	158	120	30	7	0	1	40	21	10	0	2	2	0	0	1	5	-.065	-.020	.208	.269	.278	.187
Adams R *	9	14	12	69	48	14	3	0	2	23	14	7	1	0	2	0	2	1	1	.280	.192	.233	.313	.383	.232
Griffin J *	4	4	3	14	7	3	1	0	1	7	5	1	0	0	0	1	0	0	0	-.214	--	.300	.429	.700	.361
Smith J *	3	7	4	56	41	11	1	1	0	14	22	3	0	1	0	0	0	0	0	.024	.132	.212	.268	.269	.184
Clark H *	3	6	2	57	40	10	2	0	0	12	5	7	1	0	0	1	1	0	1	-.007	.203	.204	.298	.245	.192
Fasano S	3	5	4	49	37	8	3	0	1	14	19	2	0	1	1	0	0	0	0	-.142	-.060	.178	.229	.311	.177
Inglett J *	2	0	2	5	2	3	0	1	0	5	0	0	0	0	0	0	1	0	0	-.225	.650	.600	.600	1.000	.510
Olmedo R +	2	6	1	54	41	11	4	0	0	15	9	2	0	0	1	0	0	0	1	.029	-.208	.216	.245	.294	.180
Luna H	1	5	4	46	35	7	0	0	1	10	10	2	0	1	0	1	2	0	0	-.044	.156	.167	.217	.238	.154
Halladay R	1	0	1	4	2	2	0	0	0	2	2	0	0	0	0	0	0	0	0	-.350	-.700	.500	.500	.500	.343
Roberts R	0	2	0	16	12	1	0	0	0	1	7	2	0	1	0	0	0	0	0	-.195	.073	.077	.250	.077	.129
McGowan D	-0	1	0	7	6	2	0	0	0	2	3	0	0	0	0	0	0	0	1	-.200	.583	.286	.286	.286	.088
Towers J	-0	0	0	1	1	0	0	0	0	0	0	0	0	0	0	0	0	0	0	.000	--	.000	.000	.000	.196
Litsch J	-0	0	0	1	1	0	0	0	0	0	0	0	0	0	0	0	0	0	0	.000	--	.000	.000	.000	.000
Burnett A	-0	0	0	2	2	0	0	0	0	0	0	0	0	0	0	0	0	0	0	.000	--	.000	.000	.000	.000

Italicized stats have been adjusted for home park.

Batted Ball Batting Stats

Player	% of PA		% of Batted Balls					Out %		Runs Per Event				Total Runs vs. Avg.				
	K%	BB%	GB%	LD%	FB%	IF/F	HR/OF	GB	OF	NIP	GB	LD	OF	NIP	GB	LD	FB	Tot
Rios A	14	9	36	20	44	.07	.11	70	84	.06	.08	.39	.19	0	5	6	12	23
Stairs M	16	11	40	18	42	.08	.18	77	81	.08	.03	.46	.31	3	-2	4	18	23
Thomas F	15	14	30	17	53	.09	.12	70	86	.11	.06	.39	.18	12	-0	-2	12	21
Glaus T	22	14	34	21	45	.10	.16	78	87	.07	.02	.44	.24	5	-4	4	8	13
Hill A	16	6	40	21	39	.08	.08	70	85	.02	.06	.43	.14	-6	3	11	-3	4
Zaun G	14	14	42	17	41	.18	.11	82	87	.11	-.00	.46	.16	7	-6	1	-4	-1
Thigpen C	15	7	43	24	33	.19	.00	75	77	.03	.03	.30	.05	-1	-0	-0	-4	-5
Overbay L	16	10	49	21	31	.03	.09	78	89	.06	.03	.36	.12	1	-2	0	-9	-9
Lind A	21	5	45	19	37	.11	.15	85	75	-.02	-.03	.36	.30	-6	-8	-3	7	-10
Clayton R	24	7	50	21	29	.10	.03	76	81	-.01	.02	.41	.10	-3	-2	0	-6	-11
Phillips J	13	8	46	20	34	.14	.03	88	83	.05	-.05	.36	.09	-1	-5	-0	-5	-11
Wells V	14	8	39	17	44	.19	.08	75	85	.06	.04	.41	.14	-1	-1	-2	-8	-12
Johnson R	18	9	47	19	34	.13	.03	78	72	.04	.02	.31	.15	-1	-3	-5	-5	-13
McDonald J	14	4	40	23	37	.08	.01	76	85	-.02	.04	.34	.04	-6	0	1	-13	-18
MLB Average	*17*	*9*	*43*	*19*	*38*	*.10*	*.10*	*74*	*83*	*.05*	*.05*	*.40*	*.18*	--	--	--	--	--

Pitching Stats

Player	PRC	IP	BFP	G	GS	K	BB	IBB	HBP	H	HR	DP	DER	SB	CS	PO	W	L	Sv	Op	Hld	H-A	R^L	RA	ERA	FIP
Halladay R	104	225.3	927	31	31	139	48	3	3	232	15	30	.691	20	7	1	16	7	0	0	0	-.020	-.002	4.03	3.71	3.65
Burnett A	86	165.7	691	25	25	176	66	2	12	131	23	19	.727	31	0	0	10	8	0	0	0	-.033	.019	4.02	3.75	4.44
McGowan D	80	169.7	705	27	27	144	61	3	2	146	14	14	.715	29	1	0	12	10	0	0	0	-.029	-.074	4.24	4.08	3.82
Marcum S	72	159.0	660	38	25	122	49	1	5	149	27	19	.724	6	2	1	12	6	1	2	1	.066	-.045	4.30	4.13	5.05
Accardo J	48	67.3	275	64	0	57	24	2	2	51	4	4	.739	10	1	0	4	4	30	35	2	-.040	.088	2.54	2.14	3.53
Downs S *	46	58.0	239	81	0	57	24	3	1	47	3	6	.708	0	1	1	4	2	1	4	24	-.063	-.027	2.33	2.17	3.23
Janssen C	45	72.7	297	70	0	39	20	2	3	67	4	12	.710	1	1	2	2	3	6	11	24	-.014	.001	2.72	2.35	3.89
Litsch J	43	111.0	478	20	20	50	36	2	7	116	14	17	.704	6	3	0	7	9	0	0	0	-.006	-.076	4.54	3.81	5.23
Towers J	33	107.0	469	25	15	76	22	2	6	129	18	11	.663	13	2	0	5	10	0	0	0	-.064	-.043	6.14	5.38	4.88
Tallet B *	33	62.3	267	48	0	54	28	7	6	49	1	5	.713	9	1	1	2	4	0	3	1	-.085	.047	3.75	3.47	3.16
Frasor J	26	57.0	242	51	0	59	23	1	2	47	3	1	.697	5	2	0	1	5	3	6	4	-.006	-.060	4.58	4.58	3.26
Wolfe B	23	45.3	174	38	0	22	9	2	2	36	5	6	.772	0	0	0	3	1	0	2	6	.002	-.212	3.38	2.98	4.44
Ohka T	15	56.0	251	10	10	21	22	1	0	68	10	7	.697	0	1	0	2	5	0	0	0	-.006	-.040	6.27	5.79	6.08
Chacin G *	8	27.3	118	5	5	11	7	1	2	29	6	2	.750	0	0	0	2	1	0	0	0	-.020	.050	5.60	5.60	6.31
League B	3	11.7	58	14	0	7	7	0	0	19	1	1	.581	0	1	0	0	0	0	1	0	.046	-.119	6.17	6.17	5.09
Gronkiewicz	3	4.0	15	1	0	2	2	0	0	2	1	1	.900	0	0	0	0	0	0	0	0	--	.056	2.25	2.25	7.13
Kennedy J *	2	7.0	32	9	0	8	5	0	0	6	0	0	.632	1	1	0	1	0	0	0	2	.002	-.067	7.71	5.14	3.24
De Jong J	2	9.0	42	6	0	7	5	0	0	11	0	2	.600	3	0	0	0	0	0	0	0	-.118	-.182	9.00	8.00	3.49
Banks J	1	7.3	35	3	1	2	2	0	0	11	1	0	.667	0	0	0	0	0	0	0	0	-.329	.189	7.36	7.36	5.43
Zambrano V	1	10.7	62	8	2	5	11	2	1	20	5	2	.600	0	0	0	0	2	0	0	0	-.050	.044	10.97	10.97	11.35
Taubenheim T	1	5.0	24	1	1	4	4	0	1	5	1	0	.714	0	0	0	0	0	0	0	0	--	.032	9.00	9.00	7.38
Ryan B *	0	4.3	25	5	0	3	4	0	0	7	1	0	.588	0	0	0	0	2	3	5	0	-.119	-.110	14.54	12.46	7.76
Vermilyea J	0	6.0	22	2	0	2	0	0	0	5	0	1	.750	0	0	0	0	0	0	0	0	-.041	.081	0.00	0.00	2.71

Italicized stats have been adjusted for home park.

Batted Ball Pitching Stats

Player	% of PA		% of Batted Balls					Out %		Runs Per Event				Total Runs vs. Avg.				
	K%	BB%	GB%	LD%	FB%	IF/F	HR/OF	GB	OF	NIP	GB	LD	OF	NIP	GB	LD	FB	Tot
Halladay R	15	6	53	18	29	.09	.07	78	80	.01	.02	.43	.14	-11	-6	4	-16	-29
McGowan D	20	9	53	16	31	.07	.10	79	81	.03	.02	.38	.19	-5	-7	-10	-5	-26
Burnett A	25	11	55	15	30	.12	.20	78	85	.03	.01	.35	.30	-3	-7	-15	3	-22
Accardo J	21	9	49	20	30	.07	.04	78	92	.03	.03	.37	.01	-1	-2	-1	-12	-17
Downs S	24	10	60	18	22	.12	.10	81	74	.03	-.00	.36	.22	-1	-4	-4	-4	-13
Tallet B	20	13	40	19	40	.11	.02	77	87	.06	.02	.43	.02	2	-2	-0	-11	-10
Janssen R	13	8	49	18	33	.07	.06	75	90	.06	.03	.41	.06	-1	-1	1	-9	-10
Wolfe B	13	6	56	12	32	.20	.14	81	90	.04	.01	.39	.19	-1	-2	-4	-2	-9
Frasor J	24	10	45	19	36	.09	.04	77	77	.02	.04	.40	.15	-1	-2	-2	-3	-8
Marcum S	18	8	40	18	42	.11	.15	77	85	.03	.02	.39	.23	-4	-6	-4	9	-5
Chacin G	9	8	40	19	41	.08	.16	82	87	.09	.00	.32	.24	0	-2	-0	4	2
Litsch J	10	9	48	18	34	.09	.12	76	83	.10	.03	.34	.21	3	-1	-2	3	3
Ohka T	8	9	44	20	36	.10	.15	78	86	.12	.02	.40	.22	2	-2	4	4	7
Towers J	16	6	44	20	36	.05	.15	76	79	.01	.04	.41	.26	-5	-0	5	12	11
MLB Average	17	9	43	19	38	.10	.10	74	83	.05	.05	.40	.18	--	--	--	--	--

Fielding Stats

Name	INN	SBA/G	CS%	ERA	WP+PB/G	PO	A	TE	FE
Catcher									
Zaun G	838.3	0.91	14%	3.55	0.268	590	41	7	1
Phillips J	363.7	1.11	4%	4.01	0.272	308	14	3	0
Thigpen C	126.3	0.78	36%	5.13	0.427	103	11	0	0
Fasano S	120.3	1.05	21%	5.91	0.449	93	5	3	0

Name	Inn	PO	A	TE	FE	FPct	DPS	DPT	RZR	OOZ
First Base										
Overbay L	972.3	1060	101	0	5	.996	18	0	.809	26
Stairs M	334.3	377	31	3	3	.986	2	2	.828	10
Thigpen C	96.0	99	10	0	1	.991	1	1	.733	5
Phillips J	23.0	22	2	0	0	1.000	0	0	.333	1
Clark H	13.0	17	1	0	0	1.000	0	0	1.000	0
Luna H	10.0	7	1	0	0	1.000	0	0	.333	0
Second Base										
Hill A	1410.0	244	560	6	8	.983	52	64	.865	57
Clark H	19.0	2	4	0	0	1.000	0	0	1.000	0
Adams R	17.0	4	3	0	0	1.000	0	0	1.000	0
Roberts R	2.7	0	1	0	0	1.000	0	0	1.000	0
Shortstop										
McDonald J	799.3	148	294	4	4	.982	26	30	.845	51
Clayton R	500.0	73	176	2	5	.973	13	17	.806	27
Olmedo R	134.3	24	60	0	1	.988	4	10	.896	4
Smith J	12.0	1	6	0	1	.875	1	1	.500	4
Clark H	3.0	0	0	0	0	.000	0	0	0.000	0

Name	Inn	PO	A	TE	FE	FPct	DPS	DPT	RZR	OOZ
Third Base										
Glaus T	928.0	63	197	5	3	.967	21	2	.706	48
Adams R	123.0	6	11	1	2	.850	0	0	.474	2
Smith J	101.3	12	28	0	0	1.000	5	1	.760	6
Luna H	100.3	6	23	0	2	.935	3	0	.679	5
McDonald J	93.0	10	29	0	1	.975	5	0	.758	4
Clark H	65.0	4	17	0	0	1.000	2	0	.800	5
Roberts R	22.0	0	2	1	0	.667	0	0	--	--
Inglett J	9.0	0	0	0	0	.000	0	0	--	--
Olmedo R	7.0	2	2	0	0	1.000	0	0	1.000	1
Left Field										
Lind A	651.7	137	5	0	0	1.000	0	0	.898	22
Johnson R	503.0	108	2	0	0	1.000	0	0	.841	18
Stairs M	288.0	46	3	0	0	1.000	0	0	.830	7
Roberts R	6.0	3	0	0	0	1.000	0	0	1.000	0
Center Field										
Wells V	1279.0	321	5	0	3	.991	0	0	.878	32
Rios A	161.7	44	1	1	1	.957	0	0	.909	4
Johnson R	8.0	1	0	0	0	1.000	0	0	1.000	0
Right Field										
Rios A	1250.0	243	10	1	4	.981	2	0	.905	43
Stairs M	102.0	20	0	0	0	1.000	0	0	.769	0
Johnson R	71.7	13	1	0	0	1.000	0	0	.929	0
Griffin J	24.0	5	0	0	0	1.000	0	0	1.000	0
Luna H	1.0	0	0	0	0	.000	0	0	--	--

Washington Nationals

Stat Facts:

- Mike Bacsik allowed 26 home runs (including #756) in 118 innings
- Bacsik's 118 innings were the second-most on the staff
- Jon Rauch and Saul Rivera were #1 and #2 in the league in appearances
- Austin Kearns had a .906 RZR, and made 68 OOZ plays
- 32% of Willy Mo Pena's fly balls were home runs
- 60% of Christian Guzman's batted balls were grounders
- Ryan Langerhans struck out in 34% of his plate appearances
- Matt Chico allowed 33% ground balls, second lowest in the league
- Shawn Hill allowed 55% ground balls
- Jay Bergmann allowed 50% fly balls
- Jason Simontacchi picked off five runners in 71 innings, and allowed zero steals in three attempts

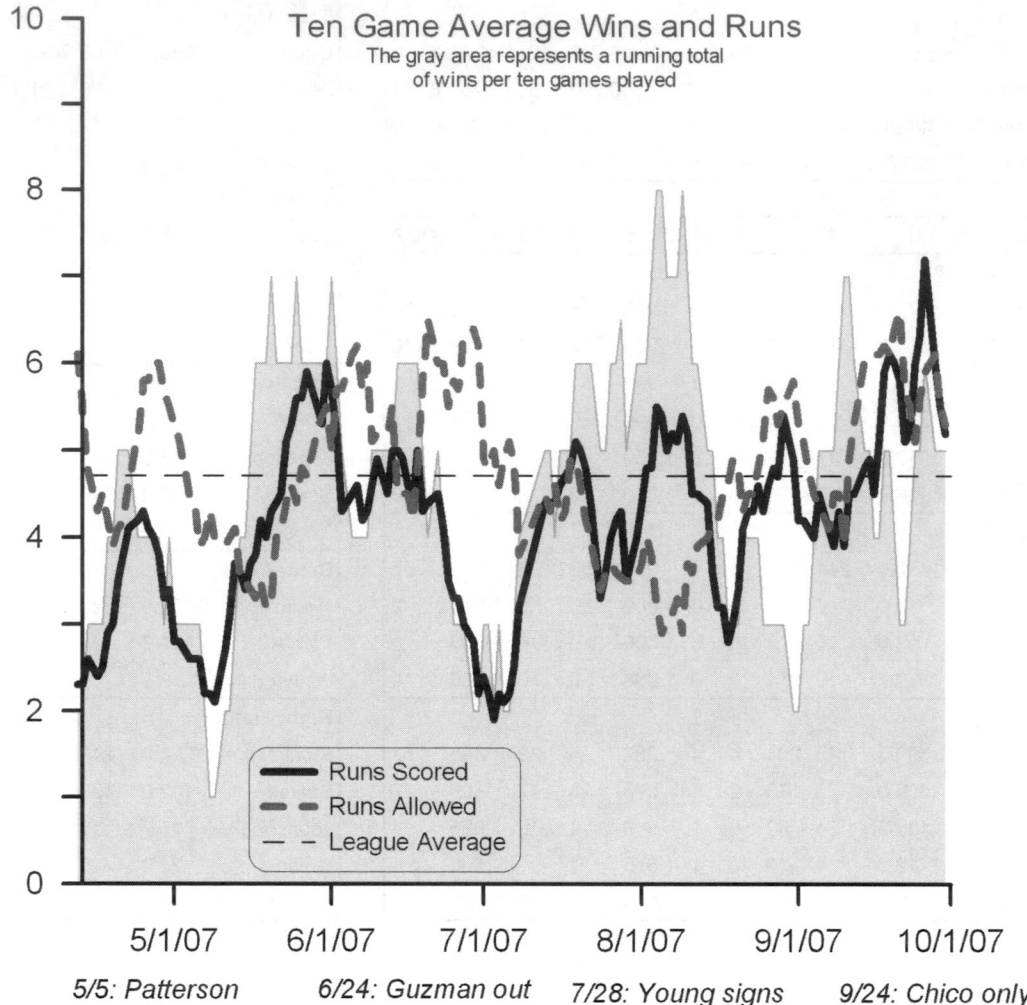

Ten Game Average Wins and Runs
The gray area represents a running total of wins per ten games played

Legend:
— Runs Scored
- - Runs Allowed
– – League Average

5/5: Patterson makes last start due to elbow injury

5/10: Nats at 9-25 but go 64-64 rest of way

6/24: Guzman out for year after hitting .328/.380/.466

7/28: Young signs 2-yr/$10M extension

8/18: Acquire Wily Mo Pena who goes .293/.352/.504

9/24: Chico only Nats pitcher to make 30 starts

Team Batting and Pitching/Fielding Stats by Month						
	April	May	June	July	Aug	Sept/Oct
Wins	9	13	10	14	12	15
Losses	17	15	16	12	17	12
RS/G	3.1	4.3	3.7	4.1	4.5	5.1
RA/G	5.2	4.4	5.6	4.0	4.6	5.3
OBP	.315	.310	.308	.328	.333	.351
SLG	.332	.376	.382	.376	.441	.427
FIP	5.11	4.29	4.78	4.74	4.94	4.89
DER	.708	.700	.685	.720	.700	.685

Batting Stats

Player	BR	Runs	RBI	PA	Outs	H	2B	3B	HR	TB	K	BB	IBB	HBP	SH	SF	SB	CS	GDP	H-A	L^R	BA	OBP	SLG	GPA
Kearns A	93	84	74	674	446	156	35	1	16	241	106	71	5	12	0	4	2	2	13	-.044	.051	.266	.355	.411	.273
Zimmerman R	92	99	91	722	506	174	43	5	24	299	125	61	3	3	0	5	4	1	26	.015	.132	.266	.330	.458	.274
Church R *	77	57	70	530	356	128	43	1	15	218	107	49	4	8	0	3	3	2	12	-.015	.062	.272	.349	.464	.284
Young D +	77	57	74	508	326	147	38	1	13	226	74	44	6	1	0	3	0	0	13	.065	-.042	.320	.378	.491	.305
Belliard R	67	57	58	557	375	148	35	1	11	218	72	34	1	1	6	5	3	0	12	.012	.056	.290	.332	.427	.267
Lopez F +	67	70	50	671	475	148	25	6	9	212	109	53	1	4	5	6	24	9	11	-.016	.029	.245	.308	.352	.236
Schneider B	44	33	54	477	327	96	21	1	6	137	56	56	7	2	4	7	0	0	15	-.014	.009	.235	.326	.336	.240
Logan N	36	39	21	350	253	86	18	4	0	112	86	19	1	0	5	1	23	5	9	-.003	.071	.265	.304	.345	.232
Guzman C +	30	31	14	192	118	57	6	6	2	81	21	15	1	1	0	2	2	0	1	.069	-.018	.328	.380	.466	.299
Langerhans R	25	24	22	187	131	32	6	2	6	60	63	22	1	1	1	1	3	0	1	-.101	-.062	.198	.296	.370	.235
Pena W	22	24	22	145	96	39	4	0	8	67	36	8	2	4	0	0	2	0	2	-.002	.122	.293	.352	.504	.296
Flores J	21	21	25	197	142	44	9	0	4	65	48	14	0	3	0	0	0	1	5	-.055	.063	.244	.310	.361	.239
Jimenez D +	18	14	10	128	81	25	7	0	2	38	22	21	0	1	4	0	2	1	3	.121	-.010	.245	.379	.373	.275
Fick R *	18	24	16	221	161	46	6	1	2	60	42	19	1	3	1	1	0	1	9	-.029	.081	.234	.309	.305	.224
Batista T	14	10	16	118	79	26	3	0	2	35	14	12	3	3	0	2	0	0	4	-.050	-.040	.257	.347	.347	.253
Snelling C *	7	6	7	61	41	10	1	1	1	16	11	9	1	3	0	0	0	1	1	-.079	.177	.204	.361	.327	.254
Maxwell J	4	5	5	27	19	7	0	0	2	13	8	1	0	0	0	0	0	0	0	-.156	.249	.269	.296	.500	.269
Hanrahan J	3	3	3	17	10	4	2	1	0	8	5	0	0	0	3	0	0	0	0	-.048	-.271	.286	.286	.571	.283
Watson B *	2	2	2	19	13	5	1	0	0	6	1	1	1	0	0	0	1	0	0	.287	.253	.278	.316	.333	.235
Chico M *	1	1	3	57	40	8	0	0	0	8	11	0	0	0	9	0	0	0	0	.089	.000	.167	.167	.167	.122
Wilson J	1	3	0	25	18	1	0	0	0	1	6	5	0	1	0	0	0	0	0	.126	.023	.053	.280	.053	.145
Lannan J *	0	1	1	13	12	2	1	0	0	3	5	0	0	0	0	0	0	0	1	.069	-.138	.154	.154	.231	.132
Restovich M	0	0	1	29	24	4	1	0	0	5	8	1	0	0	0	0	0	0	0	.027	-.341	.143	.172	.179	.127
Rivera S	0	0	0	2	1	0	0	0	0	0	0	1	0	0	0	0	0	0	0	.450	--	.000	.500	.000	.234
Casto K *	0	1	3	57	50	7	2	0	0	9	17	2	0	0	0	1	0	0	3	.052	.047	.130	.158	.167	.117
Bowie M *	-0	0	1	13	10	1	0	0	0	1	4	0	0	0	2	0	0	0	0	-.233	.088	.091	.091	.091	.066
Bacsik M *	-0	1	1	34	26	3	1	0	0	4	6	1	0	0	4	0	0	0	0	.073	-.034	.103	.133	.138	.098
Williams J	-0	0	0	9	6	1	0	0	0	1	4	0	0	1	1	0	0	0	0	.308	.063	.143	.250	.143	.154
Speigner L	-0	0	0	8	4	0	0	0	0	0	2	1	0	0	3	0	0	0	0	-.225	-.113	.000	.200	.000	.094
Colome J	-0	0	0	1	1	0	0	0	0	0	1	0	0	0	0	0	0	0	0	.000	--	.000	.000	.000	.000
Cordero C	-0	0	0	1	1	0	0	0	0	0	1	0	0	0	0	0	0	0	0	.000	--	.000	.000	.000	.000
Abreu W	-0	0	0	2	2	0	0	0	0	0	1	0	0	0	0	0	0	0	0	.000	.000	.000	.000	.000	.000
Schroder C	-0	0	0	2	2	0	0	0	0	0	1	0	0	0	0	0	0	0	0	.000	--	.000	.000	.000	.000
Rauch J	-0	0	0	3	3	0	0	0	0	0	2	0	0	0	0	0	0	0	0	.000	.000	.000	.000	.000	.000
Traber B *	-0	0	0	4	4	0	0	0	0	0	3	0	0	0	0	0	0	0	0	.000	.000	.000	.000	.000	.000
Hill S	-1	2	0	37	24	2	0	0	0	2	10	3	0	1	7	0	0	0	0	-.042	.051	.077	.200	.077	.114
Patterson J	-1	0	0	10	10	0	0	0	0	0	7	0	0	0	0	0	0	0	0	.000	.000	.000	.000	.000	.000
Redding T	-1	1	2	29	27	2	1	0	0	3	11	0	0	0	1	0	0	0	1	.103	.135	.071	.071	.107	.061
Simontacchi	-2	1	0	20	18	1	0	0	0	1	5	0	0	0	1	0	0	0	0	-.100	.350	.053	.053	.053	.038
Bergmann J	-2	2	0	44	33	5	0	0	0	5	17	1	0	0	6	0	0	0	1	-.041	.003	.135	.158	.135	.109

Italicized stats have been adjusted for home park.
Batted Ball Batting Stats are listed after Fielding Stats.

Pitching Stats

Player	PRC	IP	BFP	G	GS	K	BB	IBB	HBP	H	HR	DP	DER	SB	CS	PO	W	L	Sv	Op	Hld	H-A	R^L	RA	ERA	FIP
Chico M *	53	167.0	747	31	31	94	74	3	5	183	26	15	.695	9	6	2	7	9	0	0	0	.011	-.016	5.17	4.63	5.53
Bergmann J	44	115.3	480	21	21	86	42	1	2	99	18	8	.747	8	3	2	6	6	0	0	0	-.047	-.095	4.60	4.45	4.93
Hill S	43	97.3	399	16	16	65	25	2	5	86	9	11	.725	6	3	0	4	5	0	0	0	.016	-.083	3.88	3.42	4.00
Rivera S	42	93.0	398	85	0	64	42	4	2	88	1	13	.689	2	2	0	4	6	3	5	19	-.050	-.012	3.77	3.68	3.32
Rauch J	41	87.3	354	88	0	71	21	4	0	75	7	6	.718	5	1	1	8	4	4	10	33	-.031	.004	3.81	3.61	3.27
Redding T	36	84.0	366	15	15	47	38	4	4	84	10	10	.719	5	3	0	3	6	0	0	0	-.023	.026	3.75	3.64	5.05
Cordero C	36	75.0	321	76	0	62	29	3	0	75	8	8	.689	2	2	0	3	3	37	46	1	-.016	.074	3.72	3.36	4.04
Bacsik M *	32	118.0	520	29	20	45	29	3	6	141	26	17	.703	2	2	0	5	8	0	0	0	-.088	.009	5.57	5.11	6.18
Colome J	27	66.0	286	61	0	43	27	3	1	64	6	5	.722	3	0	0	5	1	1	4	12	-.053	-.081	4.09	3.82	4.28
Schroder C	22	45.3	192	37	0	43	15	1	2	36	2	2	.708	3	1	0	2	3	0	0	1	-.001	-.080	3.77	3.18	3.00
Bowie M *	21	57.3	248	30	8	42	27	0	2	55	7	8	.700	3	2	0	4	3	0	1	1	-.067	-.068	4.71	4.55	4.91
Ayala L	21	42.3	181	44	0	28	12	0	1	43	5	3	.704	1	1	0	2	2	1	2	6	-.070	.045	3.40	3.19	4.40
Simontacchi	17	70.7	322	13	13	42	23	4	3	95	13	8	.647	0	3	5	6	7	0	0	0	.014	.026	6.75	6.37	5.41
Hanrahan J	14	51.0	247	12	11	43	38	0	0	59	9	2	.675	4	2	0	5	3	0	0	0	-.076	.012	6.18	6.00	6.11
Traber B *	14	39.7	182	28	2	27	13	3	2	50	4	4	.640	5	1	0	2	2	0	1	2	-.110	-.141	4.99	4.76	4.13
King R *	12	33.7	149	55	0	18	18	1	2	31	5	3	.745	3	1	0	1	1	0	0	10	-.050	-.151	4.54	4.54	5.82
Albaladejo J	12	14.3	51	14	0	12	2	0	1	7	1	2	.800	1	0	0	1	1	0	1	2	-.031	-.090	1.88	1.88	3.13
Lannan J *	11	34.7	153	6	6	10	17	1	2	36	3	7	.702	4	2	1	2	2	0	0	0	-.015	.042	4.41	4.15	5.37
Abreu W	9	30.3	133	26	0	26	9	1	0	37	7	6	.659	4	0	0	0	1	0	1	3	.052	.120	6.23	5.93	5.35
Speigner L	6	40.0	198	19	6	19	23	2	0	58	4	5	.638	0	1	0	2	3	0	0	0	-.028	.007	8.78	8.78	5.19
Patterson J	6	31.3	152	7	7	15	22	1	0	39	5	3	.682	7	1	0	1	5	0	0	0	.065	-.035	7.47	7.47	6.40
Williams J	6	30.0	140	6	6	15	18	0	0	34	6	4	.703	2	0	0	0	5	0	0	0	-.058	.030	7.80	7.20	6.67
Wagner R	4	15.7	73	14	0	9	8	2	0	20	2	3	.630	1	0	0	0	2	0	0	1	-.108	.108	6.32	5.74	4.93
Munoz A *	1	5.3	32	13	0	3	7	1	2	6	2	0	.778	0	0	0	0	0	0	1	4	.032	.118	6.75	6.75	11.52
Booker C	0	1.0	5	3	0	1	1	0	0	1	1	0	1.000	0	0	0	0	1	0	1	0	-.725	-.800	18.00	18.00	17.27
Detwiler R *	0	1.0	4	1	0	1	0	0	0	0	0	0	.667	0	0	0	0	0	0	0	0	--	.000	0.00	0.00	1.27

Italicized stats have been adjusted for home park.
Batted Ball Pitching Stats are listed after Fielding Stats.

Fielding Stats

Name	INN	SBA/G	CS%	ERA	WP+PB/G	PO	A	TE	FE
Catcher									
Schneider B	1051.3	0.63	28%	4.79	0.368	702	53	6	0
Flores J	395.3	0.87	29%	4.01	0.410	262	30	2	0

Name	Inn	PO	A	TE	FE	FPct	DPS	DPT	RZR	OOZ
First Base										
Young D	884.7	788	61	1	8	.990	7	1	.639	19
Fick R	383.3	344	22	1	2	.989	2	2	.712	6
Batista T	127.0	121	3	0	1	.992	0	0	.733	1
Belliard R	42.0	39	0	0	1	.975	0	0	.750	0
Casto K	9.0	13	0	0	0	1.000	0	0	--	--
Schneider B	0.7	0	0	0	0	0.000	0	0	--	--
Second Base										
Belliard R	1004.0	277	286	2	4	.989	25	52	.800	31
Lopez F	373.3	90	113	0	1	.995	16	20	.817	11
Jimenez D	68.7	13	22	0	0	1.000	3	1	1.000	0
Shortstop										
Lopez F	927.0	154	289	15	5	.957	36	19	.784	30
Guzman C	376.0	67	105	1	7	.956	19	15	.786	11
Jimenez D	77.3	17	19	1	2	.923	3	1	.818	1
Wilson J	36.3	5	15	3	2	.000	4	0	.714	0
Belliard R	30.0	6	9	0	0	1.000	0	1	.750	4
Third Base										
Zimmerman R	1431.0	140	348	15	8	.955	32	7	.716	71
Belliard R	11.0	1	3	0	0	1.000	0	0	.333	2
Batista T	3.0	0	1	0	0	1.000	0	0	--	--
Jimenez D	1.0	0	0	0	0	0.000	0	0	--	--

Name	Inn	PO	A	TE	FE	FPct	DPS	DPT	RZR	OOZ
Left Field										
Church R	719.3	196	3	1	2	.985	2	0	.891	33
Pena W	274.3	55	0	0	0	1.000	0	0	.873	7
Snelling C	129.0	28	1	0	0	1.000	0	0	.774	4
Langerhans R	119.3	29	0	0	0	1.000	0	0	.958	6
Casto K	91.7	18	0	0	0	1.000	0	0	.947	0
Fick R	67.0	14	1	0	1	.938	0	0	.722	2
Restovich M	39.0	10	0	0	0	1.000	0	0	.700	3
Maxwell J	6.0	1	0	0	0	1.000	0	0	1.000	0
Watson B	1.0	0	0	0	0	0.000	0	0	--	--
Center Field										
Logan N	755.3	248	2	0	2	.992	0	0	.912	42
Church R	326.0	118	1	0	0	1.000	0	0	.912	14
Langerhans R	260.7	89	0	1	0	.989	0	0	.908	10
Watson D	42.0	9	0	0	0	1.000	0	0	1.000	3
Maxwell J	41.0	16	0	0	0	1.000	0	0	1.000	1
Kearns A	21.7	6	0	0	0	1.000	0	0	.800	2
Right Field										
Kearns A	1376.0	374	9	1	1	.995	8	0	.906	68
Fick R	30.7	4	0	0	0	1.000	0	0	1.000	0
Langerhans R	27.0	10	0	0	0	1.000	0	0	.833	0
Pena W	9.0	2	0	0	0	1.000	0	0	1.000	1
Restovich M	3.7	1	0	0	0	1.000	0	0	1.000	0

Batted Ball Batting Stats

	% of PA		% of Batted Balls					Out %		Runs Per Event				Total Runs vs. Avg.				
Player	K%	BB%	GB%	LD%	FB%	IF/F	HR/OF	GB	OF	NIP	GB	LD	OF	NIP	GB	LD	FB	Tot
Young D	15	9	43	22	35	.06	.10	75	75	.06	.04	.41	.23	1	-0	9	9	18
Church R	20	11	43	22	35	.09	.12	79	77	.05	.01	.47	.24	1	-6	11	5	11
Guzman C	11	8	60	17	23	.03	.06	65	74	.09	.12	.37	.20	1	8	0	-1	8
Kearns A	16	12	45	20	35	.08	.10	74	83	.09	.05	.35	.18	8	2	-1	-2	8
Zimmerman R	17	9	44	17	40	.12	.12	71	86	.04	.05	.46	.19	-2	1	3	3	5
Pena W	25	8	48	23	29	.21	.32	66	87	.00	.09	.34	.47	-2	2	-0	4	4
Jimenez D	17	17	41	19	40	.25	.08	67	91	.12	.10	.35	.09	3	1	-1	-4	-0
Batista T	12	13	35	16	49	.23	.06	71	84	.12	.04	.32	.10	2	-0	-2	-2	-2
Belliard R	13	6	44	17	39	.13	.07	72	78	.04	.06	.39	.17	-4	3	-1	-0	-2
Flores J	24	9	50	17	34	.11	.10	75	80	.01	.04	.41	.20	-2	-1	-2	-1	-6
Langerhans R	34	12	38	15	48	.11	.15	75	83	.01	.05	.36	.26	-2	-1	-6	2	-7
Fick R	19	10	35	29	36	.11	.04	77	85	.04	.01	.26	.06	-0	-3	-1	-7	-11
Schneider B	12	12	48	15	36	.08	.05	83	82	.12	-.02	.42	.11	7	-11	-3	-9	-15
Logan E	25	5	56	19	26	.04	.00	67	74	-.03	.09	.33	.13	-8	8	-7	-8	-15
Lopez F	16	8	50	20	30	.03	.06	78	84	.04	.03	.38	.11	-2	-4	0	-14	-20
MLB Average	*17*	*9*	*43*	*19*	*38*	*.10*	*.10*	*74*	*83*	*.05*	*.05*	*.40*	*.18*	*--*	*--*	*--*	*--*	*--*

Batted Ball Pitching Stats

	% of PA		% of Batted Balls					Out %		Runs Per Event				Total Runs vs. Avg.				
Player	K%	BB%	GB%	LD%	FB%	IF/F	HR/OF	GB	OF	NIP	GB	LD	OF	NIP	GB	LD	FB	Tot
Rauch J	20	6	33	13	53	.13	.05	68	86	-.01	.07	.51	.09	-6	-0	-3	-8	-18
Hill S	16	8	55	17	28	.07	.11	79	86	.03	.02	.38	.18	-3	-3	-3	-4	-13
Schroder C	22	9	34	15	52	.14	.04	58	91	.02	.15	.35	.02	-2	4	-4	-8	-10
Rivera S	16	11	49	18	32	.07	.01	74	77	.07	.05	.32	.11	3	1	-5	-8	-10
Bergmann J	18	9	33	16	50	.10	.11	71	89	.04	.06	.40	.15	-1	-1	-5	0	-7
Colome J	15	10	36	19	45	.14	.07	77	88	.07	.03	.42	.10	1	-3	1	-5	-6
Cordero C	19	9	38	19	43	.07	.09	67	88	.03	.08	.40	.12	-1	2	-1	-3	-3
Ayala L	15	7	39	21	40	.16	.11	72	85	.03	.06	.33	.16	-1	0	-1	-2	-3
Bowie M	17	12	43	18	40	.07	.11	73	79	.07	.04	.28	.21	2	-1	-5	2	-2
Redding T	13	11	38	22	39	.07	.10	80	92	.10	-.00	.42	.11	4	-6	6	-5	-1
Lannan J	7	12	51	14	35	.05	.05	72	87	.19	.04	.47	.08	4	0	0	-3	1
King R	12	13	39	25	36	.10	.11	88	84	.12	-.04	.40	.19	3	-4	3	0	2
Abreu W	20	7	33	11	55	.19	.16	50	83	.00	.19	.44	.25	-2	4	-2	4	5
Traber B	15	8	48	20	32	.07	.10	68	89	.05	.08	.48	.13	-0	4	4	-2	5
Williams J	11	13	48	15	37	.18	.16	73	85	.14	.05	.49	.24	3	1	1	2	6
Patterson J	10	14	36	19	46	.10	.11	73	80	.15	.07	.39	.22	4	0	1	4	9
Hanrahan J	17	15	31	25	44	.13	.13	67	93	.10	.10	.41	.15	5	2	4	-2	10
Speigner L	10	13	45	20	35	.00	.08	71	80	.15	.07	.43	.17	4	2	4	2	12
Bacsik M	9	7	41	18	41	.08	.16	74	89	.09	.04	.37	.22	0	1	2	13	17
Simontacchi J	13	8	34	22	44	.08	.13	72	82	.06	.05	.47	.22	0	0	9	8	18
Chico M	13	11	33	20	47	.11	.11	71	85	.10	.07	.37	.18	7	2	3	8	20
MLB Average	*17*	*9*	*43*	*19*	*38*	*.10*	*.10*	*74*	*83*	*.05*	*.05*	*.40*	*.18*	*--*	*--*	*--*	*--*	*--*

Win Statistics

You'll find an assortment of statistics related to wins in this appendix. Win-based stats assign responsibility for a team's wins and losses to specific players. In the *Annual*, we have referred to two win-based stats, Win Shares and Win Probability Added. Key stats associated with both systems are listed here.

In the Win Shares columns, you'll find each player's total Win Shares (WS), Win Shares Percentage (similar to a team's winning percentage, labeled WS%), Win Shares Above Bench (Win Shares contributed above a bench player's level, labeled WSAB) and Net Win Shares Value (WS$, expressed in thousands). All of these stats are defined in our Glossary, and you can read more about them on our website.

Win Probability Added (WPA) stats are also discussed in "The Story Stat," an article in this *Annual*. Here we've listed each player's batting and pitching WPA, as well as the Leverage Index of all pitchers.

The WPA stats are contributed by David Appelman of FanGraphs (www.fangraphs.com), based on tables supplied by Tom M. Tango.

We have listed win-based stats for all players with at least three expected Win Shares in 2007. You can download a complete list of win stats for all players who appeared in major league games last year at http://www.hardballtimes.com/THT2008Annual/. The user name is "tht08" and the password is "utley." This is a service to book purchasers only.

Player	WS	WS%	WSAB	WS$	bWPA	pWPA	pLI
Arizona Diamondbacks							
Byrnes E	26	0.669	12.9	$6,993	1.5		
Callaspo A +	0	0.000	-3.5	-$3,080	-1.3		
Clark T +	5	0.373	0.0	-$294	0.2		
Cruz J	6	0.783	3.9	$2,299	-0.0	0.5	0.7
Davis D	10	0.599	6.4	$308	-1.3	0.5	1.0
Drew S *	16	0.460	4.0	$3,558	-0.5		
Gonzalez E	4	0.431	2.3	$2,007	-0.3	0.4	0.7
Hairston S	3	0.273	-0.7	-$580	-0.0		
Hernandez L	10	0.573	5.6	$1,615	-0.8	-0.1	1.1
Hudson O +	20	0.599	8.9	$4,135	1.5		
Jackson C	14	0.537	5.0	$4,404	1.9		
Lyon B	11	0.905	6.8	$4,773		2.8	1.7
Montero M *	3	0.218	-1.3	-$1,161	-0.4		
Ojeda A +	4	0.539	1.5	$1,298	-0.2	0.0	0.0
Owings M	14	1.089	10.9	$9,551	0.6	-0.5	1.0
Pena T	10	0.764	5.9	$5,200	-0.0	2.6	1.3
Quentin C	6	0.398	0.4	$319	-0.4		
Reynolds M	14	0.603	6.4	$5,610	1.2		
Snyder C	17	0.769	9.8	$8,618	0.2		
Tracy C *	7	0.490	2.0	-$850	0.1		
Upton J	2	0.234	-1.2	-$1,028	-0.3		
Valverde J	12	0.799	6.7	$4,202		2.2	2.1
Webb B	22	1.071	16.7	$10,409	-1.2	3.3	1.1
Young C	16	0.459	4.3	$3,778	-0.6		
Atlanta Braves							
Carlyle B *	3	0.330	0.7	$600	-0.6	-1.0	0.9
Davies K	1	0.134	-0.9	-$807	-0.5	-1.7	1.0
Diaz M	11	0.529	3.9	$3,398	1.5		

Player	WS	WS%	WSAB	WS$	bWPA	pWPA	pLI
Escobar Y	11	0.564	4.6	$4,078	2.4		
Francoeur J	22	0.565	8.3	$7,215	-0.1		
Harris W *	9	0.421	2.1	$1,759	-0.5		
Hudson T	19	0.984	14.3	$8,489	-0.3	1.9	0.9
James C *	8	0.581	4.9	$4,267	-0.8	0.9	1.0
Johnson K *	19	0.571	7.7	$6,754	1.1		
Jones A	16	0.436	3.7	-$3,272	-2.5		
Jones C +	26	0.801	14.9	$7,130	4.2		
McCann B *	15	0.486	4.7	$3,800	-0.1		
Moylan P	10	0.853	6.0	$5,273	-0.0	2.4	0.8
Renteria E	18	0.608	7.8	$2,102	1.9		
Saltalamacch	2	0.239	-1.3	-$1,163	-0.7		
Smoltz J	16	0.889	11.3	$6,179	-0.9	2.2	1.0
Soriano R	8	0.655	4.1	$2,744		2.3	1.2
Teixeira M +	14	1.056	9.5	$4,404	1.5		
Thorman S *	2	0.118	-3.5	-$3,092	-0.9		
Villarreal O	4	0.413	0.3	-$330	-0.1	-0.4	0.8
Wickman B	3	0.295	0.0	-$2,761		-0.5	2.0
Woodward C	0	0.000	-2.7	-$2,642	-1.0		
Yates T	2	0.212	-1.6	-$1,432	-0.0	0.4	1.1
Baltimore Orioles							
Baez D	0	0.000	-2.4	-$4,765		-0.8	1.3
Bako P *	0	0.000	-4.1	-$3,859	-1.9		
Bedard E *	19	0.964	13.9	$9,095	0.0	3.9	1.1
Bell R	1	0.163	-0.6	-$637		-0.0	0.6
Bradford C	6	0.618	3.1	$1,389		-0.3	1.6
Burres B *	3	0.230	-0.3	-$229	0.0	-0.3	0.8
Cabrera D	6	0.273	0.4	-$1,115	-0.1	-2.0	1.0
Gibbons J *	1	0.076	-3.2	-$7,612	-2.2		

Player	WS	WS%	WSAB	WS$	bWPA	pWPA	pLI
Gomez C	3	0.308	-0.0	-$188	-0.3		
Guthrie J	13	0.677	8.7	$7,656	-0.1	1.4	1.0
Hernandez R	11	0.519	4.2	$601	-0.1		
Huff A *	13	0.497	4.5	$2,121	-0.0		
Markakis N *	22	0.608	9.3	$8,212	2.3		
Millar K	13	0.480	3.7	$2,056	-0.6		
Mora M	11	0.408	2.1	-$1,937	-1.1		
Patterson C	8	0.307	-0.6	-$4,605	-0.4		
Payton J	8	0.324	-0.8	-$2,747	-0.4		
Ray C	5	0.600	2.2	$1,902		-1.1	1.9
Redman T *	5	0.695	2.9	$2,510	0.5		
Roberts B +	24	0.668	11.7	$6,275	1.6		
Tejada M	15	0.525	4.9	-$2,462	-0.6		
Trachsel S	8	0.525	4.1	$2,447	-0.1	0.5	1.1
Walker J *	7	0.668	4.2	$2,376		1.0	1.4

Boston Red Sox

Player	WS	WS%	WSAB	WS$	bWPA	pWPA	pLI
Beckett J	19	0.867	13.1	$4,969	-0.1	3.0	0.9
Cora A *	4	0.317	-0.8	-$1,547	-1.3		
Crisp C +	16	0.504	5.0	$831	-0.7		
Delcarmen M	5	0.831	3.1	$2,738		1.1	1.0
Drew J *	12	0.409	1.7	-$5,308	0.9		
Ellsbury J *	6	0.884	4.1	$3,577	0.5		
Hinske E *	3	0.255	-0.8	-$6,197	-1.2		
Lester J *	4	0.593	1.9	$1,689		0.0	1.0
Lowell M	24	0.687	11.8	$6,113	1.3		
Lugo J	12	0.360	0.2	-$3,731	-1.3		
Matsuzaka D	12	0.544	6.8	$3,213	-0.1	1.7	1.1
Mirabelli D	2	0.284	-0.8	-$904	-0.7		
Okajima H *	10	0.938	5.9	$4,740		2.9	1.5
Ortiz D *	29	1.095	19.6	$10,989	4.8		
Papelbon J	12	0.944	7.5	$6,585		3.7	1.7
Pedroia D	19	0.617	8.0	$6,997	0.7		
Pena W	1	0.106	-2.7	-$3,223	-0.1		
Ramirez M	15	0.512	4.4	-$4,908	0.2		
Schilling C	10	0.616	6.3	-$785	-0.0	1.4	1.0
Snyder K +	3	0.477	0.8	$740		-0.2	0.6
Tavarez J *	4	0.273	0.3	-$1,051	0.1	-2.3	0.9
Timlin M	4	0.573	2.1	$635		1.2	0.8
Varitek J +	15	0.540	4.9	-$992	-0.1		
Wakefield T	10	0.492	5.0	$2,556	-0.1	0.3	0.9
Youkilis K	20	0.607	8.9	$7,772	0.8		

Chicago White Sox

Player	WS	WS%	WSAB	WS$	bWPA	pWPA	pLI
Buehrle M *	17	0.782	11.8	$5,802	-0.2	2.2	1.0
Cintron A +	3	0.301	0.1	-$1,489	-1.2		
Contreras J	5	0.247	0.3	-$4,040	-0.0	-2.9	1.0

Player	WS	WS%	WSAB	WS$	bWPA	pWPA	pLI
Crede J	3	0.317	0.3	-$4,543	0.1		
Danks J *	4	0.267	0.7	$598	-0.1	-1.9	0.9
Dye J	12	0.409	2.0	-$1,030	-0.8		
Erstad D *	5	0.282	-0.6	-$755	-0.4		
Fields J	12	0.547	4.6	$4,078	0.1		
Floyd G	2	0.267	0.4	$351		-0.2	0.8
Garland J	13	0.581	7.9	$2,150	-0.0	1.0	1.0
Gonzalez A	0	0.000	-4.5	-$3,993	-1.2		
Hall T	-1	-0.152	-4.2	-$4,375	-1.3		
Iguchi T	10	0.507	3.2	$1,824	-0.5		
Jenks B	14	0.989	9.5	$8,252		1.1	1.9
Konerko P	18	0.551	6.3	-$245	1.7		
Logan B	3	0.442	0.5	$438		0.0	0.9
MacDougal M	0	0.000	-2.7	-$3,562		-0.7	1.5
Mackowiak R	7	0.503	2.5	$224	-0.9		
Owens J *	6	0.301	-1.0	-$851	-1.4		
Pierzynski A	10	0.375	0.7	-$1,949	-1.4		
Podsednik S	0	0.000	-3.7	-$5,870	-0.4		
Richar D *	3	0.267	-0.4	-$331	-1.2		
Terrero L	4	0.531	1.1	$956	-0.1		
Thome J *	24	1.181	17.2	$7,809	2.9		
Thornton M *	4	0.461	1.4	$1,054	-0.1	-0.7	1.2
Uribe J	13	0.427	2.5	-$1,745	-0.2		
Vazquez J	19	0.810	13.2	$5,552	-0.2	2.0	1.0

Chicago Cubs

Player	WS	WS%	WSAB	WS$	bWPA	pWPA	pLI
Barrett M	4	0.307	-0.7	-$1,928	-0.9		
Dempster R	5	0.361	0.5	-$2,047	-0.0	1.0	1.6
DeRosa M	17	0.523	5.3	$3,477	0.6		
Eyre S *	3	0.403	0.8	-$1,144	-0.0	-0.9	0.8
Floyd C *	8	0.462	2.4	$773	-0.0		
Fontenot M *	5	0.349	-0.3	-$305	-0.4		
Hill K +	0	0.000	-2.6	-$2,318	-1.0		
Hill R *	13	0.766	8.4	$7,367	-1.0	1.4	1.0
Howry B *	9	0.664	4.7	$2,102		1.7	1.4
Izturis C +	1	0.085	-3.1	-$3,922	-0.7		
Jones J *	15	0.539	5.4	$2,017	-1.8		
Kendall J	4	0.348	0.4	-$2,334	0.3		
Lee D	24	0.663	11.1	$3,444	3.4		
Lilly T *	14	0.787	10.0	$6,527	-1.4	1.6	0.9
Marmol C	11	1.145	7.4	$6,483	-0.1	2.8	1.2
Marquis J *	8	0.492	3.9	$1,239	-0.8	-0.9	1.1
Marshall S *	6	0.663	4.2	$3,661	-0.6	0.2	1.0
Murton M	5	0.351	0.5	$407	-0.1		
Pagan A +	5	0.551	1.9	$1,668	0.3		
Pie F *	5	0.449	1.1	$928	-0.8		

Player	WS	WS%	WSAB	WS$	bWPA	pWPA	pLI
Ramirez A	23	0.741	12.3	$6,395	4.5		
Soriano A	22	0.646	9.8	$4,293	1.0		
Theriot R	11	0.331	-0.2	-$188	-0.6		
Ward D *	5	0.742	2.3	$1,692	1.1		
Wuertz M	6	0.645	2.5	$2,162	-0.0	0.1	0.9
Zambrano C +	16	0.870	11.4	-$2,542	-1.0	2.1	1.0
Cincinnati Reds							
Arroyo B	11	0.608	6.9	$1,486	-0.9	0.4	1.0
Belisle M	4	0.259	0.8	$668	-1.0	-1.9	1.0
Burton J	6	0.922	3.7	$3,222		0.7	1.0
Coffey T	1	0.138	-1.5	-$1,359		-0.9	0.9
Conine J	5	0.386	0.1	$100	0.0		
Coutlangus J	3	0.488	1.1	$1,002		-0.3	1.1
Dunn A *	21	0.615	9.2	-$2,508	2.7		
Encarnacion	17	0.551	6.5	$5,716	0.8		
Freel R	4	0.243	-1.2	-$2,420	-1.4		
Gonzalez A	10	0.423	2.1	$288	-0.8		
Griffey Jr.	16	0.476	4.4	-$2,202	1.1		
Hamilton J *	13	0.706	6.4	$5,603	0.7		
Harang A	17	0.856	12.3	$6,769	-1.6	2.4	1.0
Hatteberg S	11	0.490	3.2	$2,243	2.8		
Hopper N	8	0.446	1.6	$1,437	0.6		
Keppinger J	9	0.606	4.3	$3,789	0.8		
Lohse K	6	0.518	2.8	-$248	-0.4	-0.2	0.9
Phillips B	18	0.470	5.0	$4,330	1.1		
Ross D	6	0.299	-0.9	-$2,083	-2.1		
Santos V	2	0.334	-0.2	-$349	-0.1	-1.7	0.8
Stanton M *	1	0.122	-1.7	-$2,261	-0.0	0.1	1.0
Valentin J +	5	0.354	0.6	$92	-0.4		
Weathers D	11	0.658	4.9	$3,383		1.1	2.0
Cleveland Indians							
Barfield J	8	0.329	-0.4	-$387	-2.6		
Betancourt R	15	1.256	10.4	$8,657	-0.0	5.4	1.6
Blake C	12	0.347	-0.3	-$3,766	-0.2		
Borowski J	5	0.349	-0.2	-$2,022		1.4	2.3
Byrd P	11	0.532	6.3	$2,235	-0.0	-0.5	0.9
Cabrera A +	7	0.722	3.3	$2,875	1.1		
Carmona F	22	0.948	16.7	$14,645	-0.1	4.4	1.0
Dellucci D *	3	0.291	-1.0	-$2,570	-0.4		
Garko R	13	0.460	3.3	$2,940	1.0		
Gutierrez F	7	0.431	1.3	$1,138	-1.5		
Hafner T *	17	0.656	7.9	$3,423	1.8		
Lee C *	0	0.000	-2.6	-$4,732	-0.1	-1.8	0.9
Lofton K *	4	0.385	0.6	-$448	0.4		
Martinez V +	31	0.922	19.0	$13,781	2.6		

Player	WS	WS%	WSAB	WS$	bWPA	pWPA	pLI
Mastny T	4	0.570	1.9	$1,636		0.1	0.9
Michaels J	7	0.447	1.4	-$502	0.4		
Nixon T *	4	0.218	-1.9	-$2,995	-2.0		
Peralta J	22	0.641	10.0	$8,188	-0.4		
Perez R *	8	1.001	5.4	$4,747		2.4	1.1
Sabathia C *	24	0.926	17.5	$11,232	0.1	3.7	1.1
Shoppach K	7	0.718	4.1	$3,596	-0.0		
Sizemore G *	31	0.803	17.3	$14,642	2.3		
Sowers J *	0	0.000	-1.7	-$1,462	0.1	-1.3	1.0
Westbrook J	9	0.550	4.7	-$3,965	-0.1	0.7	1.0
Colorado Rockies							
Affeldt J *	5	0.586	2.5	$1,324		-1.4	1.1
Atkins G	20	0.529	6.4	$5,648	0.2		
Baker J	0	0.000	-3.3	-$2,871	-1.0		
Buchholz T	5	0.472	1.9	$1,641	-0.4	-0.2	0.9
Carroll J	4	0.266	-1.0	-$852	-1.1		
Cook A	10	0.697	6.3	$2,703	-0.3	-0.9	1.1
Corpas M	12	0.821	7.4	$6,520		2.7	1.4
Fogg J	6	0.423	2.3	-$1,401	-1.1	-0.5	1.0
Francis J *	14	0.754	9.6	$8,050	-0.6	2.0	0.9
Fuentes B *	8	0.615	3.7	$17		-1.0	1.9
Hawkins L	5	0.569	2.4	$639	-0.0	-0.5	1.1
Hawpe B *	22	0.651	10.2	$8,950	4.1		
Helton T *	24	0.637	10.6	$1,271	4.8		
Herges M *	5	0.793	3.0	$2,498	-0.1	1.8	1.0
Hirsh J	4	0.402	1.8	$1,539	-0.7	-1.3	0.9
Holliday M	30	0.764	16.4	$10,195	5.1		
Iannetta C	5	0.379	0.4	$323	0.4		
Jimenez U	3	0.427	1.8	$1,597	-0.6	0.3	0.9
Julio J	4	0.480	1.0	-$1,988	0.0	-0.2	1.1
Lopez R	3	0.427	1.7	-$2,606	-0.7	0.3	0.9
Matsui K +	14	0.564	5.4	$4,231	2.7		
Spilborghs R	9	0.560	3.9	$3,406	1.0		
Sullivan C *	4	0.490	1.0	$314	0.0		
Taveras W	12	0.547	4.3	$3,771	-0.5		
Torrealba Y	6	0.241	-2.7	-$3,839	-1.5		
Tulowitzki T	25	0.659	12.0	$10,578	2.9		
Detroit Tigers							
Bonderman J	7	0.371	2.3	-$2,249	-0.0	-0.4	0.9
Byrdak T *	4	0.671	1.7	$1,510		0.3	0.9
Casey S *	9	0.352	0.1	-$1,718	-0.5		
Durbin C	6	0.418	2.6	$2,324	-0.0	0.1	0.9
Granderson C	26	0.755	14.4	$12,629	0.6		
Grilli J	4	0.396	0.6	$570		-0.1	0.7
Guillen C +	19	0.586	8.2	$1,392	1.9		
Infante O	4	0.435	1.0	-$62	-0.9		

Player	WS	WS%	WSAB	WS$	bWPA	pWPA	pLI
Inge B	13	0.421	1.8	-$3,160	-1.8		
Jones T +	6	0.449	1.5	-$961		1.6	2.2
Maroth M *	3	0.351	1.1	-$917	0.0	0.1	1.0
Miller A *	1	0.142	-0.4	-$344	-0.1	-0.9	1.1
Miner Z	5	0.713	2.2	$1,968		-0.3	1.0
Monroe C	3	0.153	-3.5	-$7,034	-1.3		
Ordonez M	36	1.058	23.7	$14,475	6.3		
Polanco P	23	0.707	12.2	$8,602	2.9		
Rabelo M +	2	0.206	-0.9	-$826	-0.7		
Raburn R	5	0.653	1.9	$1,668	0.4		
Robertson N	8	0.421	3.3	-$112		0.4	1.0
Rodney F	3	0.428	0.5	-$200		-0.4	1.4
Rodriguez I	13	0.486	3.7	-$2,008	-1.9		
Rogers K *	3	0.440	1.2	-$2,735	-0.1	-0.2	0.9
Seay B *	6	0.957	3.6	$3,121	-0.0	1.7	0.9
Sheffield G	16	0.696	8.5	$1,156	0.8		
Thames M	7	0.492	2.3	$2,009	-0.0		
Verlander J	16	0.735	10.7	$8,730	-0.2	1.9	1.0
Florida Marlins							
Amezaga A +	5	0.209	-3.2	-$2,776	-2.5		
Boone A	7	0.572	2.5	$1,931	1.2		
Borchard J +	1	0.096	-2.2	-$1,920	-1.2		
Cabrera M	30	0.830	17.8	$8,331	4.6		
De Aza A *	1	0.119	-2.2	-$1,961	-0.6		
Gardner L	8	0.808	4.5	$3,970	-0.1	1.3	1.0
Gregg K	8	0.464	2.6	$2,276	-0.0	1.9	1.7
Hermida J *	15	0.575	5.6	$4,956	1.9		
Jacobs M *	8	0.326	-0.5	-$444	-0.9		
Kim B	2	0.211	-0.4	-$1,286	-0.4	-0.7	1.0
Linden T +	3	0.428	0.5	$415	-0.1		
Lindstrom M	6	0.617	2.3	$2,060	-0.0	0.7	1.1
Miller J	5	0.550	2.3	$2,059	-0.0	0.4	0.9
Mitre S	3	0.229	0.4	$320	-0.9	-0.7	1.0
Olivo M	8	0.313	-1.0	-$2,570	-1.9		
Olsen S *	0	0.000	-3.5	-$3,098	-0.6	-3.8	0.9
Pinto R *	4	0.436	1.2	$1,091	-0.0	0.3	1.1
Ramirez H	29	0.782	16.3	$14,310	2.4		
Ross C	11	1.042	8.0	$6,987	2.8		
Tankersley T	4	0.544	1.5	$1,346		0.9	1.2
Treanor M	6	0.549	2.8	$2,470	0.2		
Uggla D	17	0.441	3.7	$3,274	-0.4		
Vanden Hurk	-1	-0.140	-3.4	-$3,012	-0.5	-1.9	1.0
Willingham J	21	0.653	9.4	$8,291	1.0		
Willis D *	7	0.400	3.0	-$3,683	-0.1	-2.4	1.0
Wood J	3	0.473	0.6	$507	-0.0	0.0	0.0

Player	WS	WS%	WSAB	WS$	bWPA	pWPA	pLI
Houston Astros							
Albers M *	0	0.000	-3.0	-$2,636	-0.7	-0.4	0.9
Ausmus B	8	0.356	-0.0	-$1,810	-2.2		
Berkman L +	24	0.665	11.7	$3,269	3.5		
Biggio C	6	0.207	-3.7	-$5,628	-2.2		
Borkowski D	3	0.301	-0.6	-$695	-0.0	0.3	0.8
Bruntlett E	4	0.429	1.0	$685	-1.3		
Burke C	5	0.257	-1.9	-$1,664	-2.4		
Ensberg M	5	0.359	-0.2	-$3,539	-1.5		
Everett A	4	0.301	-0.7	-$3,183	-1.1		
Jennings J *	-1	-0.114	-3.6	-$8,549	-0.1	-1.7	0.9
Lamb M *	10	0.533	3.8	$871	1.0		
Lane J	3	0.285	-1.0	-$1,589	-0.7		
Lee C	23	0.609	10.3	$3,499	1.9		
Lidge B	9	0.660	3.8	-$1,836		1.2	1.7
Loretta M	11	0.400	1.8	$546	0.9		
Miller T	2	0.286	-0.3	-$744		-0.3	1.0
Moehler B	3	0.406	0.7	$572	-0.1	-0.4	0.7
Munson E *	1	0.120	-2.0	-$1,747	-0.7		
Oswalt R	18	0.985	13.8	-$1,051	-1.1	3.1	1.1
Pence H	20	0.761	11.0	$9,674	2.5		
Qualls C	9	0.677	4.8	$4,179		2.0	1.6
Rodriguez W	7	0.441	2.8	$2,460	-1.1	-0.4	0.9
Sampson C	6	0.552	3.0	$2,658	-0.8	-0.4	1.0
Scott L *	12	0.519	4.3	$3,819	0.2		
Wheeler D	3	0.325	-0.1	-$1,370		0.3	1.6
Wigginton T	5	0.484	1.0	$56	0.4		
Williams W	3	0.183	-0.7	-$3,393	-1.1	-1.7	1.0
Kansas City Royals							
Bannister B	13	0.730	8.1	$7,132	0.0	0.6	0.9
Brown E	8	0.391	1.1	-$2,248	0.3		
Buck J	8	0.369	0.6	$443	-1.1		
Butler B	8	0.548	3.0	$2,620	0.5		
de la Rosa J	3	0.213	-0.9	-$836	-0.1	-1.6	0.9
DeJesus D *	16	0.441	3.5	$2,889	0.1		
Gathright J	5	0.358	0.4	$331	-0.2		
German E	7	0.339	0.3	$221	-1.1		
Gload R *	7	0.382	1.0	$635	-0.7		
Gobble J *	5	0.659	2.7	$2,027		1.0	1.0
Gordon A *	13	0.407	1.4	$1,245	-2.0		
Greinke Z	10	0.672	4.6	$4,006	-0.1	2.9	1.0
Grudzielanek	12	0.476	3.5	$1,244	-0.4		
LaRue J	0	0.000	-3.6	-$5,606	-1.5		
Meche G	15	0.644	9.4	$4,947	-0.1	1.3	1.0
Pena T	10	0.340	0.3	$222	-2.9		

Player	WS	WS%	WSAB	WS$	bWPA	pWPA	pLI
Peralta J	7	0.617	2.7	$2,344	0.1	0.2	0.8
Perez O *	4	0.269	0.1	-$4,306	-0.1	-1.4	1.0
Riske D	8	0.778	4.6	$3,195		0.2	1.1
Shealy R	1	0.098	-2.5	-$2,183	-0.6		
Soria J	11	0.914	6.6	$5,796		3.8	1.8
Sweeney M	5	0.443	1.6	-$3,886	-0.2		
Teahen M *	16	0.503	4.8	$4,153	-0.3		

Los Angeles Angels of Anaheim

Player	WS	WS%	WSAB	WS$	bWPA	pWPA	pLI
Anderson G *	14	0.623	6.1	-$331	-0.2		
Aybar E +	2	0.178	-2.2	-$1,970	-0.7		
Bootcheck C	4	0.432	0.5	$446		-0.1	0.5
Cabrera O	25	0.686	12.6	$7,049	0.9		
Colon B	0	0.000	-2.5	-$9,950	-0.2	-1.9	1.0
Escobar K	18	0.848	13.1	$7,501	-0.1	3.1	1.0
Figgins C +	22	0.835	12.6	$7,848	2.9		
Guerrero V	31	0.967	20.4	$10,863	5.9		
Hillenbrand	0	0.000	-2.7	-$4,240	-1.3		
Izturis M +	16	0.805	9.5	$8,280	0.9		
Kendrick H	9	0.476	2.6	$2,264	-0.1		
Kotchman C *	16	0.595	7.0	$6,124	1.1		
Lackey J	22	0.914	15.9	$8,266	-0.1	3.1	1.0
Mathis J	2	0.105	-2.1	$1,872	0.7		
Matthews Jr.	15	0.493	4.5	$959	-0.5		
Molina J	2	0.273	-0.8	-$1,439	-0.1		
Moseley D	5	0.464	1.9	$1,644		0.0	0.8
Napoli M	8	0.557	3.1	$2,757	0.5		
Oliver D	5	0.638	2.1	$1,290		0.7	0.7
Quinlan R	1	0.098	-2.3	-$2,420	-1.0		
Rodriguez F	12	0.818	6.9	-$855		3.0	2.1
Santana E	3	0.185	-1.3	-$1,218	0.0	-1.9	1.0
Saunders J *	7	0.609	3.8	$3,327		-0.2	1.0
Shields S	7	0.584	2.9	-$565		1.2	1.6
Speier J	6	0.824	3.3	$1,243		1.3	1.1
Weaver J	12	0.690	7.7	$6,755	-0.1	1.0	1.0
Willits R +	15	0.562	5.5	$4,828	-0.3		

Los Angeles Dodgers

Player	WS	WS%	WSAB	WS$	bWPA	pWPA	pLI
Abreu T +	4	0.402	0.2	$200	-0.2		
Beimel J *	6	0.638	2.4	$1,535	-0.0	1.4	1.0
Betemit W +	5	0.471	1.6	$1,355	1.1		
Billingsley	12	0.892	9.2	$8,073	-0.6	1.9	1.0
Broxton J	10	0.740	5.1	$4,484		1.2	1.5
Ethier A *	14	0.487	3.8	$3,307	0.3		
Furcal R +	15	0.424	2.7	-$4,417	-1.3		
Garciaparra	11	0.423	1.9	-$1,905	-1.1		
Gonzalez L *	13	0.448	2.6	-$1,176	-0.3		
Hendrickson	2	0.176	-0.6	-$3,180	-0.5	-1.2	0.8
Kemp M	11	0.629	4.7	$4,131	0.8		
Kent J	18	0.578	6.9	$1,305	-0.3		
Laroche A	2	0.309	-0.1	-$45	0.2		
Loney J *	16	0.757	9.1	$8,002	2.8		
Lowe D	11	0.636	6.3	$957	-1.2	1.1	0.9
Martin R	24	0.691	11.5	$10,126	2.1		
Martinez R	1	0.117	-1.5	-$1,489	-0.1		
Penny B	21	1.168	16.5	$10,720	-0.3	2.7	1.0
Pierre J *	13	0.321	-0.8	-$4,280	-1.6		
Saenz O	0	0.000	-2.0	-$2,098	-0.9		
Saito T	16	1.066	10.3	$8,457		4.3	1.9
Seanez R	6	0.594	2.8	$2,280	-0.0	0.2	0.7
Tomko B	-1	-0.108	-3.5	-$4,530	-0.5	-2.3	0.8
Wolf R *	5	0.564	3.2	-$775	-0.3	-0.4	1.0

Milwaukee Brewers

Player	WS	WS%	WSAB	WS$	bWPA	pWPA	pLI
Braun R	22	0.817	12.5	$11,015	2.1		
Bush D	6	0.368	1.7	$1,386	-0.8	-0.9	1.0
Capuano C *	4	0.303	1.2	-$1,924	-0.3	-1.4	1.0
Cordero F	10	0.677	4.6	$1,509		1.5	2.0
Counsell C *	5	0.271	-1.6	-$2,641	-1.7		
Estrada J +	7	0.271	-1.7	-$4,619	-1.8		
Fielder P *	28	0.747	15.1	$13,231	5.2		
Gallardo Y	9	0.952	6.8	$6,007	0.0	1.7	0.9
Graffanino T	4	0.277	-0.9	-$2,184	-1.6		
Gross G *	4	0.365	0.1	$91	0.4		
Gwynn T *	3	0.421	0.3	$292	0.3		
Hall B	12	0.430	1.9	-$1,339	-0.3		
Hardy J	19	0.539	7.2	$6,275	0.8		
Hart C	23	0.741	12.0	$10,562	2.8		
Jenkins G *	12	0.462	3.1	-$763	0.3		
Mench K	8	0.474	2.5	-$973	-0.2		
Miller D	3	0.257	-0.8	-$1,592	-0.9		
Sheets B	9	0.737	6.2	$113	-0.9	1.7	0.9
Shouse B *	5	0.634	2.4	$1,446		0.9	1.0
Spurling C	2	0.319	-0.2	-$511		0.2	0.6
Suppan J	8	0.448	3.7	$488	-1.0	-0.9	1.0
Turnbow D	5	0.450	1.2	-$1,157		0.8	1.5
Vargas C	5	0.413	2.0	-$448	-0.4	-1.2	1.0
Villanueva C	8	0.535	2.9	$2,517	-0.2	1.7	1.0
Weeks R	15	0.540	5.2	$3,001	0.2		
Wise M	4	0.518	0.9	$139	0.0	0.6	0.8

Minnesota Twins

Player	WS	WS%	WSAB	WS$	bWPA	pWPA	pLI
Baker S	8	0.511	4.2	$3,680	-0.2	1.1	1.0
Bartlett J	16	0.524	5.1	$4,465	-0.3		

Player	WS	WS%	WSAB	WS$	bWPA	pWPA	pLI
Bonser B	5	0.267	0.3	$230	-0.1	-0.9	1.0
Casilla A +	0	0.000	-3.6	-$3,163	-2.1		
Castillo L +	8	0.400	1.4	-$395	0.1		
Cirillo J	4	0.501	1.3	$699	-0.6		
Cuddyer M	17	0.514	5.2	$1,194	0.4		
Ford L	2	0.281	-0.6	-$1,131	-0.4		
Garza M	5	0.555	2.6	$2,313	-0.0	0.2	1.0
Guerrier M	10	0.863	5.9	$5,148		1.6	1.0
Hunter T	24	0.696	12.5	$5,171	0.6		
Kubel J *	13	0.565	5.0	$4,422	-0.4		
Mauer J *	22	0.926	13.6	$8,414	0.5		
Morneau J *	19	0.546	6.8	$1,650	0.3		
Nathan J	14	0.917	9.1	$2,917		3.6	2.0
Neshek P +	8	0.847	5.0	$4,379		2.8	1.1
Ortiz R	3	0.304	0.5	-$718	-0.1	-0.6	0.6
Punto N +	4	0.136	-5.9	-$6,676	-2.6		
Redmond M	11	0.735	5.5	$4,572	-0.3		
Rincon J	2	0.250	-0.9	-$2,479		-0.5	0.9
Rodriguez L	0	0.000	-3.0	-$2,626	-1.6		
Santana J *	18	0.758	12.3	$4,562	0.3	1.8	0.9
Silva C	11	0.503	6.2	$1,638	-0.1	1.8	0.9
Slowey K	3	0.420	1.3	$1,115		0.3	0.9
Tyner J *	4	0.242	-1.4	-$1,291	-1.0		

New York Yankees

Player	WS	WS%	WSAB	WS$	bWPA	pWPA	pLI
Abreu B *	19	0.531	7.0	-$1,161	0.0		
Bruney B	2	0.311	0.3	$284		-0.5	0.8
Cabrera M +	13	0.408	1.7	$1,408	-0.5		
Cairo M	2	0.306	-0.6	-$615	-0.6		
Cano R *	21	0.597	9.0	$7,810	-0.0		
Clemens R	5	0.468	2.9	-$5,968	0.0	0.7	1.0
Damon J *	15	0.546	5.6	-$1,340	-0.2		
Farnsworth K	3	0.363	-0.1	-$2,684		0.4	1.1
Giambi J *	6	0.489	2.2	-$8,545	1.0		
Hughes P	4	0.514	2.0	$1,790		0.1	0.9
Igawa K *	1	0.137	-1.2	-$2,849	0.0	-1.2	0.9
Jeter D	24	0.663	11.3	-$835	2.6		
Matsui H *	17	0.552	6.0	-$979	1.4		
Mientkiewicz	4	0.382	0.5	-$119	-0.5		
Mussina M *	6	0.366	2.0	-$3,747	-0.0	-0.9	0.9
Pettitte A *	14	0.602	7.8	-$896	-0.1	0.7	1.0
Phillips A	3	0.273	-1.1	-$971	-0.3		
Posada J +	26	0.864	15.1	$7,517	2.7		
Proctor S	3	0.392	0.6	$474	-0.1	-0.8	1.1
Rivera M	9	0.642	4.4	-$1,138		2.3	1.8
Rodriguez A	39	1.081	26.1	$9,143	7.5		

Player	WS	WS%	WSAB	WS$	bWPA	pWPA	pLI
Vizcaino L	6	0.598	2.3	-$746	-0.0	1.3	1.0
Wang C	16	0.746	10.6	$9,163	-0.1	2.3	1.0

New York Mets

Player	WS	WS%	WSAB	WS$	bWPA	pWPA	pLI
Alou M	12	0.607	5.2	$1,037	-0.3		
Beltran C +	27	0.774	14.9	$6,488	2.0		
Castillo L +	6	0.478	2.1	$783	1.1		
Castro R	6	0.683	2.9	$2,081	0.1		
Chavez E *	4	0.431	1.2	$350	-0.4		
Delgado C *	14	0.417	1.9	-$5,329	2.0		
Easley D	8	0.670	4.2	$3,458	1.0		
Feliciano P	6	0.630	2.5	$1,990		1.3	1.1
Glavine T *	11	0.639	6.5	$2,185	-0.4	1.1	1.0
Gomez C	2	0.250	-1.1	-$927	-1.0		
Gotay R +	6	0.546	2.1	$1,834	0.1		
Green S *	12	0.440	2.8	-$3,691	0.6		
Heilman A	9	0.691	4.1	$3,488		-0.6	1.3
Hernandez O	10	0.785	6.7	$3,846	-0.8	1.8	1.0
Lo Duca P	8	0.297	-1.2	-$4,182	-1.7		
Maine J	11	0.677	7.3	$6,412	-0.9	1.0	0.9
Milledge L	6	0.526	2.4	$2,084	-0.3		
Mota G	1	0.122	-1.8	-$2,301	-0.0	-0.9	0.8
Pelfrey M	0	0.000	-1.5	-$1,329	-0.4	-1.3	0.9
Perez O *	11	0.716	6.8	$5,946	-0.8	0.6	1.0
Reyes J +	24	0.578	9.6	$5,870	0.5		
Schoeneweis	1	0.118	-1.6	-$2,992		-0.0	0.8
Sele A	1	0.155	-1.0	-$1,186	-0.1	0.3	0.6
Smith J	3	0.498	1.4	$1,254	-0.0	-0.0	0.9
Sosa J	7	0.513	2.0	$1,367	-0.2	0.5	1.1
Valentin J +	3	0.294	-0.6	-$2,237	-0.2		
Wagner B *	11	0.706	5.2	-$498		1.7	1.7
Wright D	34	0.867	20.6	$17,252	4.1		

Oakland Athletics

Player	WS	WS%	WSAB	WS$	bWPA	pWPA	pLI
Blanton J	15	0.604	8.8	$7,692	-0.2	2.1	1.0
Braden D *	-1	-0.128	-3.4	-$2,982		-1.2	1.0
Buck T *	10	0.574	4.4	$3,894	0.6		
Casilla S	4	0.544	1.2	$1,071		0.5	1.1
Chavez E *	6	0.302	-0.5	-$4,950	-3.0		
Crosby B	3	0.150	-3.7	-$5,506	-2.4		
Cust J *	19	0.842	11.5	$10,146	3.0		
DiNardo L *	7	0.492	3.2	$2,768	-0.0	-0.2	0.9
Ellis M	20	0.592	7.8	$3,580	-0.8		
Embree A *	6	0.487	2.3	$992		2.3	1.5
Gaudin C	10	0.464	4.4	$3,874	-0.1	-0.1	1.0
Hannahan J *	5	0.557	1.7	$1,497	-0.3		
Haren D	19	0.792	12.8	$9,379	-0.1	2.8	1.0
Johnson D *	10	0.402	1.5	$1,334	-0.8		

Player	WS	WS%	WSAB	WS$	bWPA	pWPA	pLI
Kendall J	3	0.177	-3.2	-$6,785	-1.2		
Kennedy J	5	0.451	2.1	-$442	0.2	-0.4	1.0
Kotsay M *	3	0.251	-1.2	-$4,842	-1.1		
Murphy D	3	0.433	1.2	$1,014	-0.4		
Piazza M	5	0.399	0.4	-$3,665	0.2		
Scutaro M	8	0.399	0.8	-$517	-0.5		
Stewart S	13	0.402	1.8	$1,272	-2.4		
Street H	8	0.831	4.7	$4,134		1.3	1.6
Suzuki K	7	0.529	2.4	$2,137	0.4		
Swisher N +	19	0.561	7.5	$6,208	1.3		

Philadelphia Phillies

Player	WS	WS%	WSAB	WS$	bWPA	pWPA	pLI
Alfonseca A	2	0.213	-0.9	-$803	-0.0	-0.9	1.5
Barajas R	3	0.372	0.4	-$694	-0.4		
Bourn M *	4	0.531	1.3	$1,174	-0.4		
Burrell P	21	0.667	9.6	$2,045	3.0		
Condrey C	3	0.463	0.6	$526	-0.2	1.6	0.6
Coste C	4	0.547	1.4	$1,274	-0.7		
Dobbs G *	7	0.371	0.2	$138	0.5		
Eaton A	1	0.074	-1.8	-$5,020	-1.0	-2.4	1.0
Geary G	3	0.325	-0.1	-$54	-0.1	0.3	1.1
Gordon T	3	0.386	0.6	$2,771		0.5	1.7
Hamels C *	15	0.960	11.2	$9,812	-1.0	2.5	1.0
Helms W	2	0.122	-4.1	-$4,393	0.7		
Howard R *	26	0.743	14.1	$11,829	3.5		
Iguchi T	5	0.610	2.2	$1,520	0.1		
Kendrick K	9	0.881	6.8	$5,967	-0.4	1.2	0.9
Lieber J *	3	0.431	1.4	-$2,505	0.1	-0.6	1.0
Madson R *	6	0.797	3.0	$1,872	-0.1	0.6	1.2
Moyer J *	8	0.476	3.6	$330	-1.5	-1.0	1.0
Myers B	7	0.551	2.2	-$3,008	-0.1	-0.6	1.7
Nunez A +	2	0.124	-3.5	-$3,860	-1.8		
Rollins J +	28	0.671	13.2	$7,789	3.2		
Romero J +	6	1.006	4.1	$3,210	-0.0	1.7	1.3
Rowand A	23	0.615	9.7	$4,414	2.5		
Ruiz C	13	0.546	5.1	$4,483	-0.8		
Utley C *	28	0.845	16.5	$9,918	3.8		
Victorino S	12	0.440	2.7	$2,378	1.4		
Werth J	14	0.854	7.8	$6,661	1.3		

Pittsburgh Pirates

Player	WS	WS%	WSAB	WS$	bWPA	pWPA	pLI
Armas Jr. T	0	0.000	-1.6	-$2,729	-0.2	-1.5	0.7
Bautista J	13	0.386	1.8	$1,604	-0.5		
Bay J	13	0.386	1.8	-$1,714	-1.0		
Capps M	13	0.899	7.8	$6,858	0.0	2.2	1.7
Castillo J	2	0.160	-2.4	-$3,667	-1.8		
Chacon S	7	0.518	2.8	-$1,151	-0.1	0.8	1.3
Doumit R +	7	0.460	1.3	$1,175	-0.3		

Player	WS	WS%	WSAB	WS$	bWPA	pWPA	pLI
Duffy C *	5	0.339	0.3	$269	-0.3		
Duke Z *	2	0.213	-0.5	-$449	-0.3	-1.5	0.9
Gorzelanny T	12	0.688	8.1	$7,095	-1.1	1.8	1.0
Grabow J *	3	0.418	0.7	$165	-0.0	0.4	1.0
Izturis C +	3	0.424	0.3	-$500	-0.4		
LaRoche A *	17	0.488	5.0	$1,415	0.7		
Maholm P *	5	0.324	1.2	$1,008	-0.5	-1.1	1.0
Marte D *	6	0.935	3.4	$790	-0.0	0.9	0.9
McLouth N *	11	0.543	4.3	$3,788	1.4		
Morgan N *	4	0.629	1.9	$1,672	0.1		
Nady X	11	0.432	2.3	$135	1.1		
Paulino R	11	0.397	1.3	$1,158	-1.7		
Sanchez F	21	0.592	9.0	$5,452	-0.6		
Snell I	13	0.719	8.2	$7,194	-1.2	1.6	1.0
Torres S	2	0.198	-1.4	-$2,413		-1.2	1.5
Wilson J	19	0.638	8.5	$2,203	-1.8		

San Diego Padres

Player	WS	WS%	WSAB	WS$	bWPA	pWPA	pLI
Bard J +	16	0.641	6.9	$5,327	-1.1		
Barrett M	0	0.000	-2.9	-$3,302	-1.7		
Bell H	13	0.884	8.1	$7,141		4.1	1.6
Blum G +	8	0.394	1.4	$967	-0.5		
Bradley M +	9	0.959	5.6	$2,245	1.4		
Branyan R *	4	0.517	1.2	$686	-0.8		
Brocail D *	6	0.603	2.8	$2,392	-0.0	1.2	0.8
Cameron K	4	0.568	1.9	$1,702	-0.0	0.8	0.6
Cameron M	22	0.603	9.4	$4,969	-0.1		
Cruz J +	5	0.310	-0.1	-$204	-0.1		
Germano J	5	0.424	1.8	$1,623	-0.6	0.0	0.9
Giles B *	17	0.557	6.3	$897	0.1		
Giles M	11	0.415	2.2	$484	-0.9		
Gonzalez A *	27	0.670	12.6	$10,695	4.1		
Greene K	19	0.510	6.4	$5,617	-0.5		
Hampson J *	4	0.602	1.9	$1,707	-0.3	0.4	0.8
Hoffman T	9	0.673	4.2	$434		1.0	2.3
Kouzmanoff K	15	0.496	4.5	$3,969	0.1		
Linebrink S	3	0.388	0.8	-$242		1.1	1.5
Maddux G	9	0.527	4.6	-$725	-1.0	1.3	0.9
Meredith C	5	0.443	1.2	$1,051	-0.0	-0.8	1.1
Peavy J	23	1.200	18.2	$11,385	-0.7	4.8	0.9
Sledge T *	4	0.316	-0.8	-$664	-0.8		
Wells D *	0	0.000	-2.7	-$3,324	-0.8	-1.3	1.1
Young C	13	0.860	9.3	$7,571	-0.8	2.7	1.0

Seattle Mariners

Player	WS	WS%	WSAB	WS$	bWPA	pWPA	pLI
Baek C	3	0.378	0.9	$751	-0.0	-0.2	0.9
Batista M	12	0.574	6.8	$3,399	-0.1	1.4	1.0
Beltre A	18	0.544	6.3	-$740	1.5		

Player	WS	WS%	WSAB	WS$	bWPA	pWPA	pLI
Betancourt Y	19	0.628	8.3	$7,229	0.3		
Bloomquist W	2	0.191	-1.2	-$1,552	-0.4		
Broussard B	5	0.374	0.8	-$2,608	0.3		
Burke J	6	0.842	3.8	$3,359	0.0		
Green S	6	0.662	2.5	$2,172		0.6	1.1
Guillen J	20	0.592	7.8	$5,050	0.4		
Hernandez F	15	0.731	9.6	$8,384	-0.0	1.8	1.0
Ibanez R *	24	0.754	12.9	$8,812	1.6		
Johjima K	18	0.664	8.6	$4,951	-0.9		
Lopez J	9	0.301	-1.6	-$1,693	-1.7		
Morrow B	5	0.579	1.6	$1,416		1.3	1.3
O'Flaherty E	4	0.621	2.2	$1,899	-0.0	0.0	0.8
Putz J	18	1.166	12.8	$8,861		6.2	1.7
Ramirez H *	-1	-0.095	-3.8	-$5,725		-2.5	1.0
Sexson R	7	0.275	-1.5	-$8,840	-1.3		
Sherrill G *	7	0.909	4.7	$4,101		1.2	1.3
Suzuki I *	33	0.888	20.4	$11,890	1.7		
Vidro J +	16	0.654	7.1	$2,734	0.7		
Washburn J *	11	0.528	5.9	$479	0.1	0.1	1.0
Weaver J	1	0.063	-2.7	-$2,349	-0.0	-2.6	0.9

San Francisco Giants

Player	WS	WS%	WSAB	WS$	bWPA	pWPA	pLI
Aurilia R	5	0.253	-2.2	-$3,460	-1.2		
Bonds B *	21	0.822	11.8	$2,678	4.3		
Cain M	12	0.685	7.7	$6,492	-1.2	2.3	1.0
Chulk V	5	0.683	2.3	$1,998	0.0	0.2	0.8
Correia K	8	0.612	3.1	$2,716	-0.4	-0.3	1.1
Davis R	5	0.559	2.0	$1,791	-0.1		
Durham R +	6	0.207	-4.4	-$7,177	-1.3		
Feliz P	13	0.392	1.6	-$957	-1.1		
Frandsen K	4	0.245	-1.3	-$1,102	-2.1		
Hennessey B	7	0.516	2.8	$2,475	-0.0	0.4	1.7
Klesko R *	7	0.309	-0.7	-$1,306	-0.9		
Kline S +	2	0.290	-0.4	-$1,063	-0.0	0.7	0.9
Lewis F *	6	0.603	2.4	$2,130	0.5		
Lincecum T *	7	0.551	4.3	$3,785	-0.8	0.8	1.0
Lowry N	9	0.678	6.1	$4,375	-1.0	0.4	1.1
Messenger R	1	0.161	-1.1	-$933		-1.5	1.1
Molina B	14	0.482	4.2	$1,922	-1.0		
Morris M	6	0.501	2.7	-$1,011	-0.7	-0.7	1.0
Ortmeier D +	4	0.428	0.7	$656	-0.4		
Roberts D *	10	0.415	2.1	-$425	-0.2		
Sanchez J *	0	0.000	-2.0	-$1,769	-0.1	-0.4	1.0
Schierholtz	2	0.311	0.2	$159	0.0		
Taschner J *	2	0.276	-0.5	-$460	0.0	-0.2	1.0
Vizquel O +	11	0.342	-0.5	-$2,845	-3.1		

Player	WS	WS%	WSAB	WS$	bWPA	pWPA	pLI
Winn R +	18	0.501	5.4	$2,587	1.0		
Zito B *	8	0.468	3.6	-$1,643	-0.9	0.5	1.0

St. Louis Cardinals

Player	WS	WS%	WSAB	WS$	bWPA	pWPA	pLI
Ankiel R *	9	0.874	5.0	$4,416	0.2		
Bennett G	2	0.208	-0.9	-$1,017	-0.7		
Duncan C *	18	0.773	9.6	$8,425	1.4		
Eckstein D	11	0.414	2.2	-$202	-0.5		
Edmonds J *	9	0.395	1.1	-$4,351	-0.8		
Encarnacion	5	0.294	-0.4	-$2,689	1.1		
Flores R *	3	0.377	0.7	$598	-0.0	-0.7	0.9
Franklin R	9	0.726	5.1	$4,146	-0.0	1.6	1.3
Isringhausen	12	0.840	7.3	$2,283		2.7	1.6
Kennedy A *	1	0.059	-4.8	-$5,233	-2.1		
Looper B	8	0.529	4.3	$1,707	-0.3	0.1	0.9
Ludwick R	11	0.605	4.5	$3,953	0.7		
Miles A +	9	0.358	0.5	-$205	-1.2	0.0	0.0
Molina Y	11	0.491	3.8	$3,155	-0.3		
Pujols A	32	0.858	18.8	$9,196	4.7		
Reyes A	-1	-0.105	-3.9	-$3,415	-0.8	-2.3	0.8
Rolen S	11	0.444	2.3	-$4,239	-0.8		
Ryan B	5	0.443	0.9	$826	0.5		
Schumaker S	7	0.708	3.8	$3,320	0.5		
Spiezio S +	7	0.516	2.4	$1,210	-0.8	0.0	0.0
Springer R	10	1.097	6.6	$5,138	-0.0	1.5	0.8
Taguchi S	9	0.490	2.5	$1,650	-0.2		
Thompson B	5	0.425	2.0	$1,754	-0.5	-0.1	0.8
Wainwright A	16	0.919	12.0	$10,479	-0.2	1.3	1.1
Wells K	3	0.211	-0.8	-$2,470	-0.3	-2.7	1.0

Tampa Bay Devil Rays

Player	WS	WS%	WSAB	WS$	bWPA	pWPA	pLI
Baldelli R	2	0.298	-0.5	-$799	-1.2		
Crawford C *	21	0.666	9.9	$4,835	3.5		
Dukes E	2	0.189	-1.4	-$1,236	-0.4		
Fossum C *	-1	-0.105	-5.2	-$7,020		-2.9	0.9
Glover G	4	0.393	0.9	$705		-0.0	0.9
Gomes J	8	0.451	2.1	$1,782	-0.2		
Hammel J	2	0.219	-0.3	-$283	0.1	-1.2	0.8
Harris B	13	0.437	3.0	$2,595	-1.2		
Iwamura A *	13	0.461	3.2	$2,072	-0.5		
Jackson E	2	0.116	-1.7	-$1,526	0.0	-2.0	1.1
Kazmir S *	17	0.766	11.7	$10,262	0.1	1.8	1.1
Navarro D +	6	0.262	-1.8	-$1,596	-2.7		
Norton G +	4	0.428	1.0	$639	-0.3		
Paul J	1	0.161	-1.0	-$873	-0.7		
Pena C *	30	0.957	19.2	$16,662	3.8		
Reyes A	5	0.413	1.2	$865		1.0	1.7

Player	WS	WS%	WSAB	WS$	bWPA	pWPA	pLI
Shields J	16	0.687	10.2	$8,925	-0.1	2.8	1.0
Sonnanstine	3	0.212	-0.0	-$12	0.0	-1.6	0.9
Stokes B	0	0.000	-3.5	-$3,033		-2.1	0.9
Upton B	23	0.822	12.9	$11,329	1.8		
Wigginton T	6	0.293	-0.5	-$2,051	-0.2		
Wilson J	3	0.195	-2.5	-$2,228	-1.3	0.0	0.0
Young D	16	0.457	4.2	$3,716	-1.1		

Texas Rangers

Player	WS	WS%	WSAB	WS$	bWPA	pWPA	pLI
Benoit J	10	0.786	5.5	$4,118		2.5	1.5
Blalock H *	8	0.725	4.0	-$1,017	0.5		
Botts J +	2	0.233	-1.1	-$934	-1.5		
Byrd M	13	0.556	5.3	$4,539	1.2		
Catalanotto	9	0.497	2.5	$681	1.3		
Cruz N	4	0.229	-1.8	-$1,563	-0.5		
Eyre W	2	0.249	-0.3	-$248		-1.7	0.9
Francisco F	3	0.375	0.3	$266		1.0	1.0
Gagne E	6	0.882	3.5	$1,138		1.9	1.6
Hairston J	1	0.104	-2.4	-$2,280	-0.8		
Kinsler I	17	0.585	6.9	$6,063	0.8		
Laird G	10	0.423	1.3	$1,119	-1.2		
Littleton W	3	0.486	1.1	$925	0.0	-0.0	0.7
Loe K	3	0.204	-0.2	-$160	0.0	-1.5	1.0
Lofton K *	11	0.603	4.9	$2,552	0.1		
McCarthy B	4	0.364	1.0	$897	-0.0	-0.9	1.0
Metcalf T	3	0.307	-0.3	-$230	0.1		
Millwood K	6	0.322	1.2	-$4,383	-0.1	-1.7	1.0
Padilla V	2	0.154	-1.1	-$5,274	0.0	-2.7	0.9
Saltalamacch	3	0.324	-0.4	-$389	-0.8		
Sosa S	12	0.673	5.8	$5,002	0.5		
Teixeira M +	12	0.711	6.3	$456	0.9		
Tejeda R	0	0.000	-2.7	-$2,358	-0.1	-2.4	1.0
Vazquez R *	6	0.326	-0.4	-$560	-0.9		
Wilkerson B	11	0.538	4.1	-$530	0.2		
Wilson C *	8	0.721	3.7	$3,274		1.7	1.3
Wood M	1	0.167	-0.6	-$575		-0.9	0.8
Wright J	5	0.597	3.2	$2,526	-0.0	0.2	1.0
Young M	23	0.660	10.6	$6,077	2.3		

Toronto Blue Jays

Player	WS	WS%	WSAB	WS$	bWPA	pWPA	pLI
Accardo J	12	0.866	7.1	$6,198		1.9	2.0
Burnett A	12	0.674	7.6	$298	-0.0	2.1	1.0
Clayton R	3	0.256	-0.7	-$794	-1.0		
Downs S *	8	0.918	5.0	$3,727		1.4	1.4
Frasor J	3	0.385	0.6	$70		-0.0	1.2
Glaus T	14	0.576	5.4	-$294	1.0		
Halladay R	18	0.741	11.5	$3,949	0.1	3.4	0.9

Player	WS	WS%	WSAB	WS$	bWPA	pWPA	pLI
Hill A	20	0.563	8.0	$7,071	-0.8		
Janssen C	9	0.776	5.1	$4,503		1.4	1.6
Johnson R	3	0.187	-2.8	-$5,251	-1.8		
Lind A *	7	0.419	1.5	$1,354	0.3		
Litsch J	7	0.587	4.1	$3,630	-0.1	0.8	1.1
Marcum S	11	0.625	6.6	$5,842	-0.1	1.6	1.0
McDonald J	8	0.399	0.9	$375	-1.2		
McGowan D	11	0.597	6.7	$5,917	-0.1	0.5	1.0
Ohka T	1	0.167	-0.8	-$1,227		-0.7	0.9
Overbay L *	6	0.236	-3.4	-$6,735	-2.1		
Phillips J	1	0.113	-2.5	-$2,346	-1.2		
Rios A	23	0.611	9.5	$6,108	1.3		
Stairs M *	14	0.671	6.9	$5,829	2.0		
Tallet B *	5	0.648	2.2	$1,942		-0.7	0.8
Thomas F	17	0.699	8.5	$4,926	1.6		
Towers J	2	0.174	-0.6	-$3,147	-0.0	-1.7	0.9
Wells V	15	0.441	3.4	-$2,478	-1.1		
Zaun G +	9	0.426	1.9	$108	-0.0		

Washington Nationals

Player	WS	WS%	WSAB	WS$	bWPA	pWPA	pLI
Ayala L	4	0.674	1.5	$354		-0.0	0.9
Bacsik M *	2	0.190	-0.0	-$673	0.5	-1.3	0.9
Bolliard R	16	0.526	5.0	$4,168	-0.2		
Bergmann J	4	0.405	1.2	$1,014	-0.9	0.6	1.0
Bowie M *	2	0.294	0.1	$53	-0.2	0.5	1.0
Chico M *	5	0.344	1.2	$1,028	-0.7	-0.8	1.0
Church R *	19	0.655	8.4	$7,413	0.1		
Colome J	5	0.524	1.8	$1,375	-0.0	1.1	1.1
Cordero C	8	0.458	1.8	-$2,379	-0.0	1.8	1.9
Fick R *	1	0.081	-3.3	-$3,151	-1.8		
Flores J	5	0.461	1.8	$1,561	1.2		
Guzman C +	8	0.762	4.1	$1,682	0.4		
Hill S	5	0.600	3.2	$2,819	-0.6	1.3	1.0
Jimenez D +	4	0.637	1.6	$1,292	0.2		
Kearns A	21	0.562	8.4	$4,152	0.3		
Langerhans R	6	0.571	2.0	$1,745	-1.2		
Logan N	7	0.357	0.5	$464	-0.8		
Lopez F +	11	0.301	-1.5	-$5,040	-1.9		
Pena W	5	0.631	2.3	$1,292	0.4		
Rauch J	9	0.621	4.1	$3,514	-0.1	1.5	1.6
Redding T	4	0.548	2.3	$1,972	-0.5	0.5	1.0
Rivera S	7	0.521	2.3	$1,981	-0.1	1.4	1.2
Schneider B	11	0.409	1.7	-$1,758	-2.0		
Simontacchi	-1	-0.159	-2.9	-$2,777	-0.4	-1.0	0.9
Young D +	17	0.629	7.3	$6,331	0.9		
Zimmerman R	21	0.530	7.2	$6,313	0.5		

Playing Time Constellations

We are pleased to once again bring you John Burnson's Playing Time Constellations. John is the publisher of the *2008 Graphical Player*, a truly unique publication featuring player profiles unlike anything you'll find in another book or on the Internet. The constellations on the following pages are just a small sample of John's work.

Elsewhere in this *Annual*, you have seen how many games each player played at each position. But the constellations tell you more: not only who played where, but when, and in what order. Take a look at the Arizona Diamondbacks constellation below. You'll find positions listed in the vertical axis and players listed in the horizontal axis. Upward trajectory indicates increased playing time; downward trajectory indicates decreased playing time.

Each dot represents a month's worth of playing time for that player at that position. In each cell, the plot moves from left to right, from April to September. A dot is displayed only if the player appeared at that position that month. Cells are 150 PA tall, and each team is represented by players with at least 100 appearances last year. Players with asterisks finished the year with another team.

So, let's see what the Arizona constellation tells us about their year. We see that Eric Byrnes initially played all three outfield positions but settled in left. Chris Young solidified his job in center. Carlos Quentin got time early in right but was displaced in the final two months by Justin Upton. We also see that a try-out with Chad Tracy at third quickly gave way to Mark Reynolds. Augie Ojeda stepped in at second when Orlando Hudson went down in September.

On the following ten pages, you'll find similar graphs for every major league team. You'll see when the Cubs' Ryan Theriot took over at shortstop, and when the Padres' Geoff Blum took over second base. Follow Melky Cabrera replacing Johnny Damon in center for the Yankees. As Rod Stewart once said, every picture tells a story, don't it.

John Burnson is also the publisher of *Heater Magazine*. *Heater* is an electronic baseball magazine, published twice a week during the season, and providing the very best in fantasy baseball coverage and statistics. These graphs are only a small sample of what you can receive with a one-year subscription. To learn more (and subscribe), visit the *Heater Magazine* website (http://www.heatermagazine.com/).

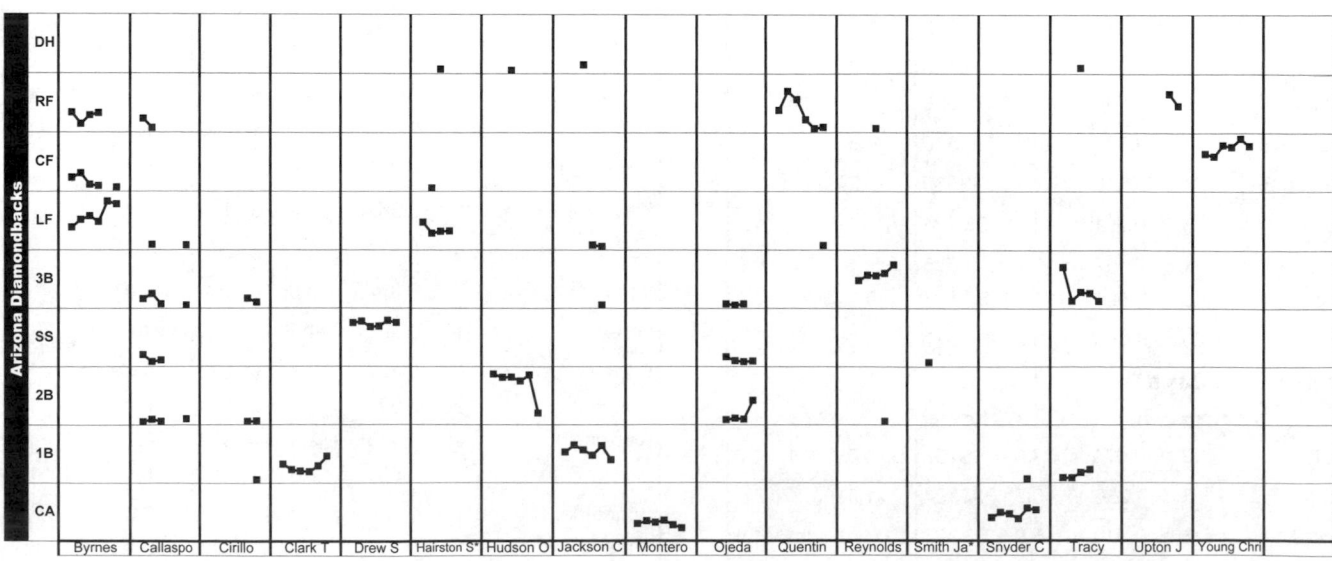

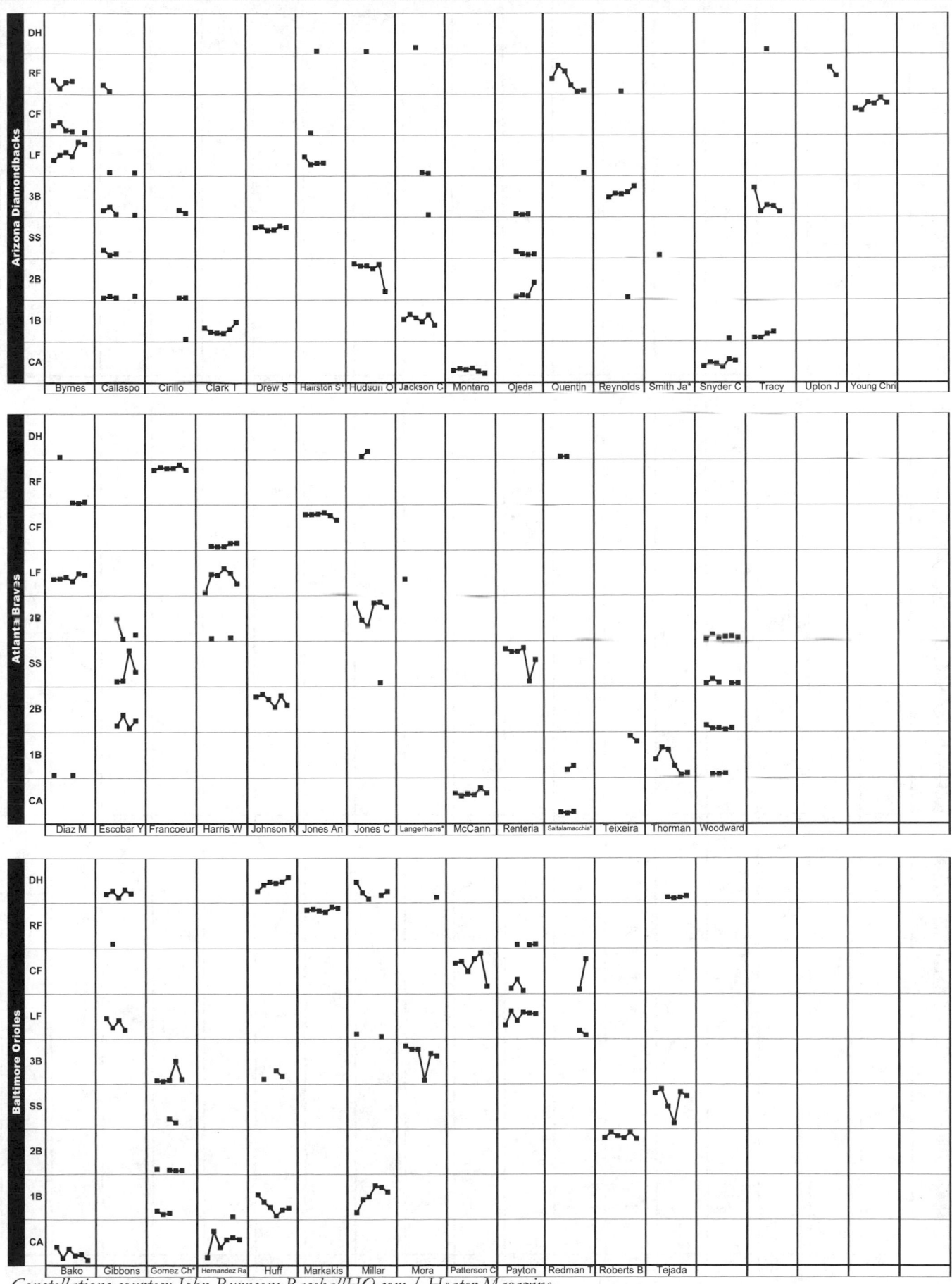

Constellations courtesy John Burnson; BaseballHQ.com / Heater Magazine

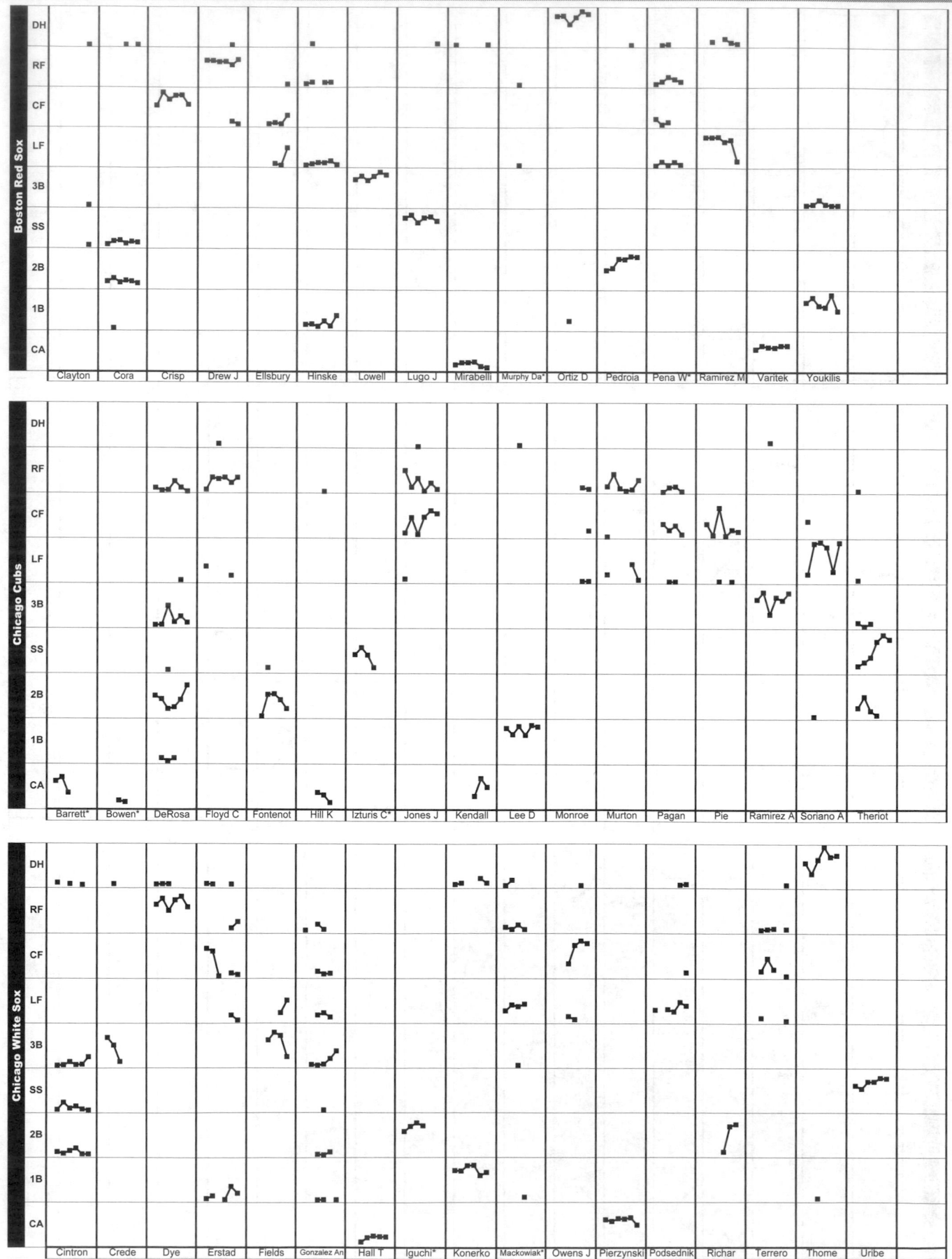

Constellations courtesy John Burnson; BaseballHQ.com / Heater Magazine

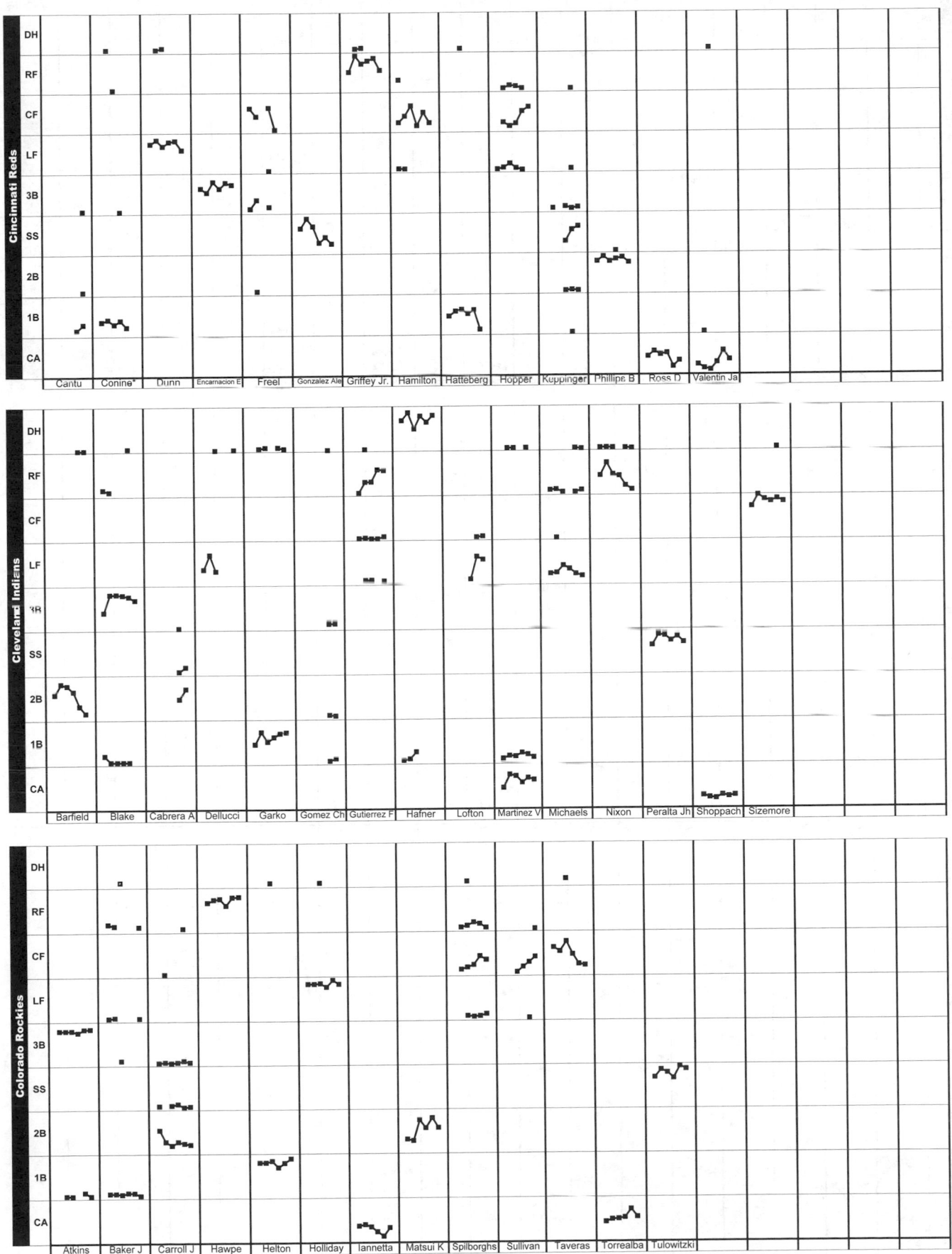

Constellations courtesy John Burnson; BaseballHQ.com / Heater Magazine

Playing Time Constellations

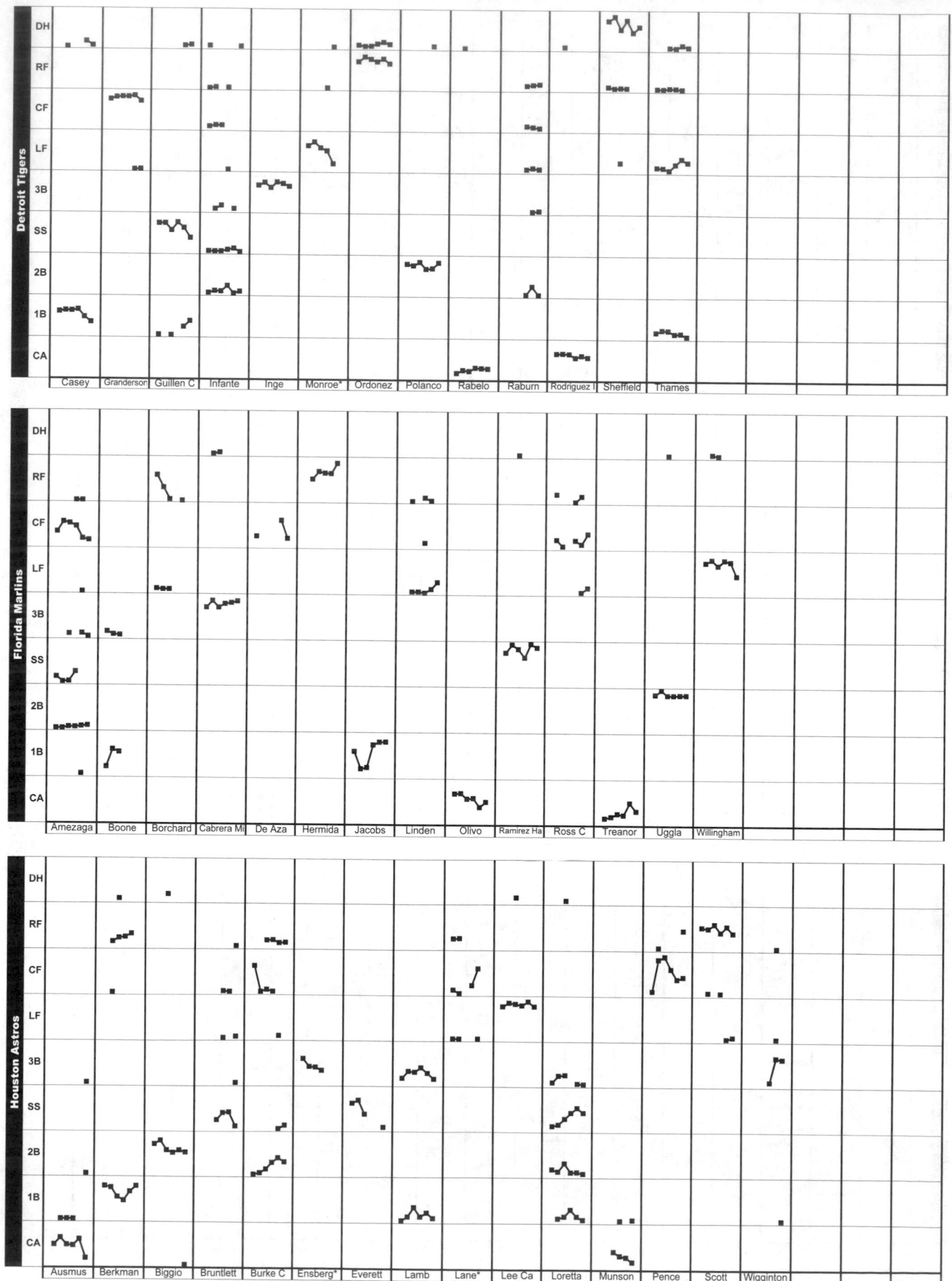

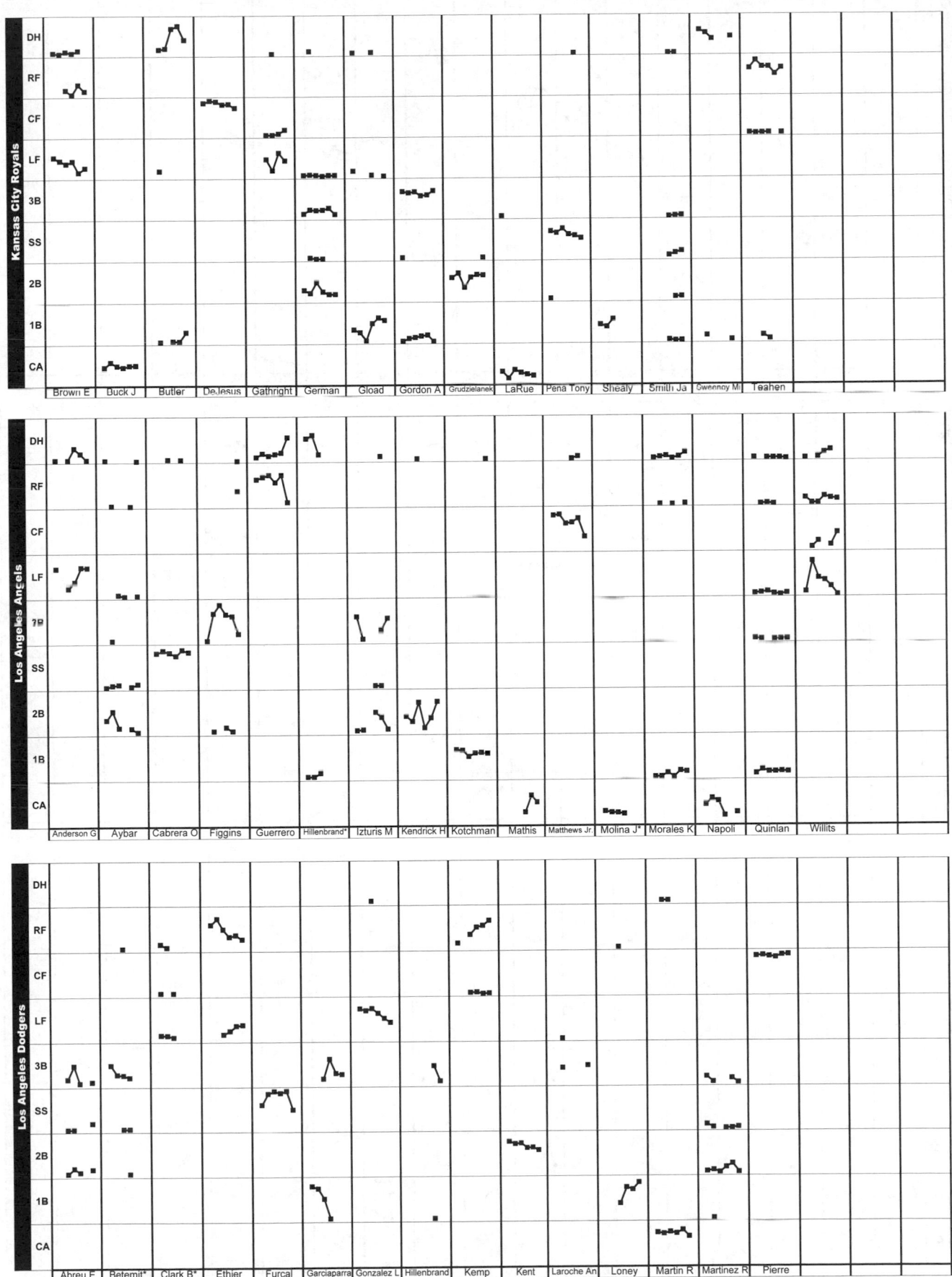

Constellations courtesy John Burnson; BaseballHQ.com / Heater Magazine

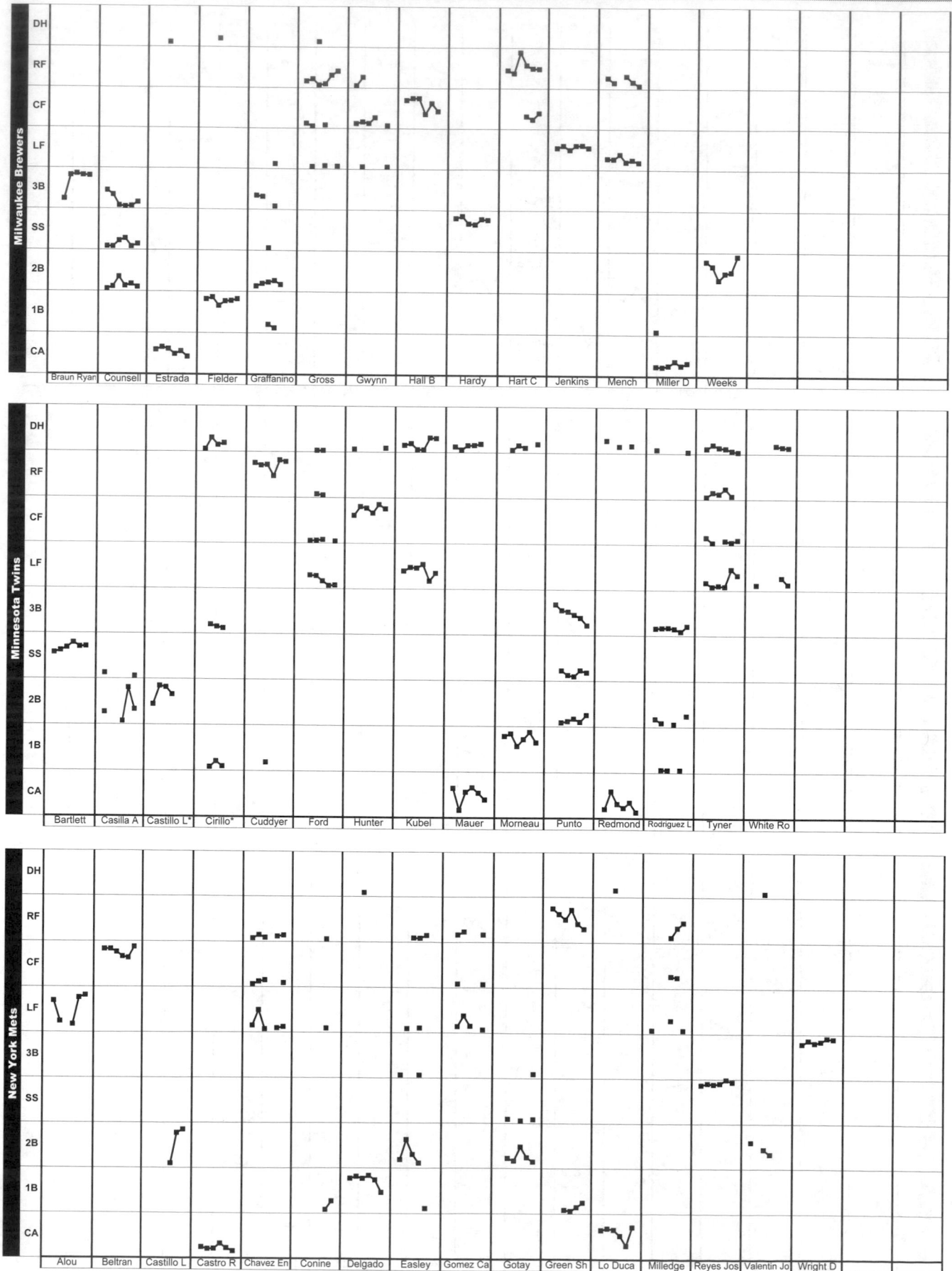

Constellations courtesy John Burnson; BaseballHQ.com / Heater Magazine

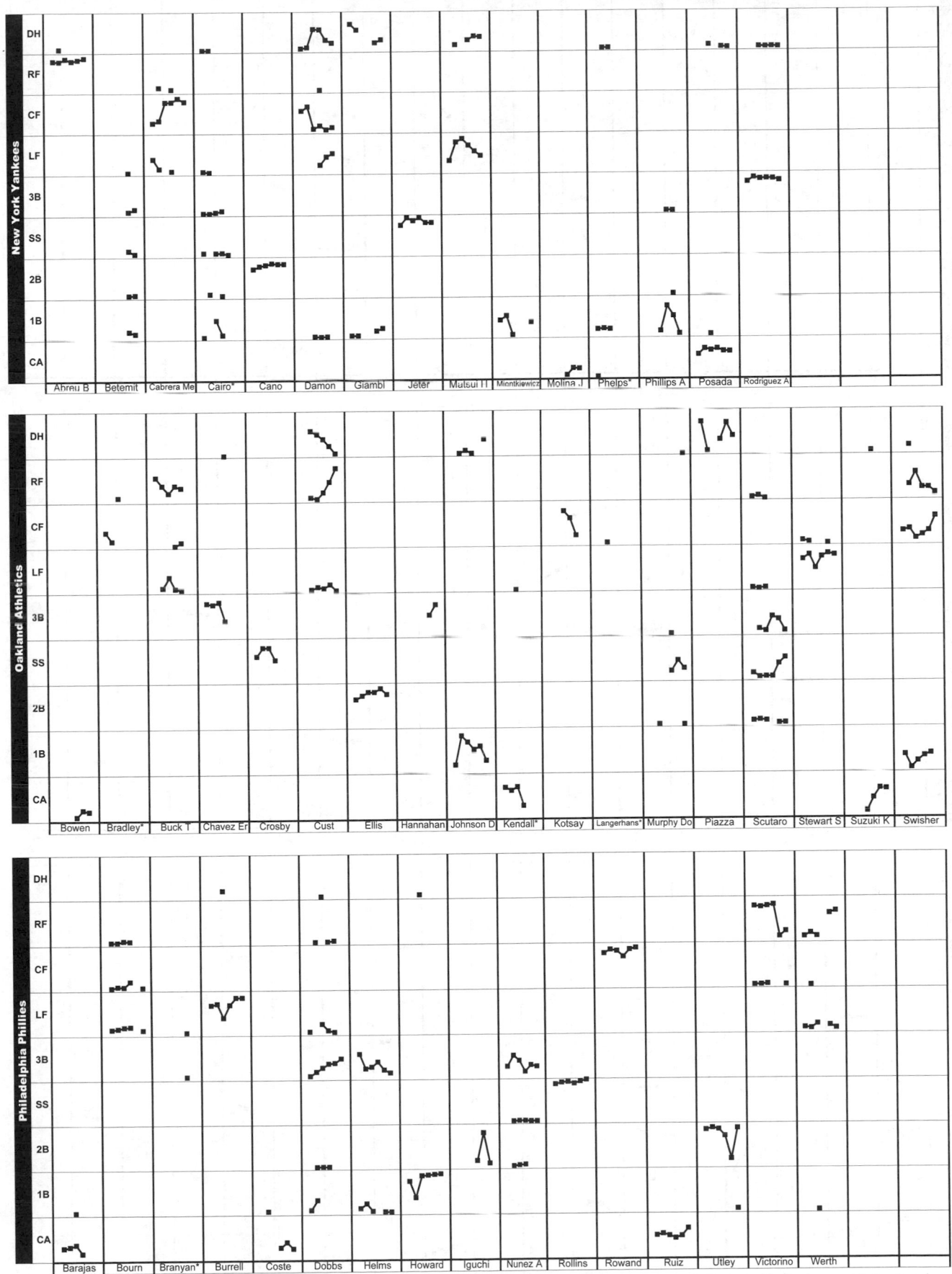

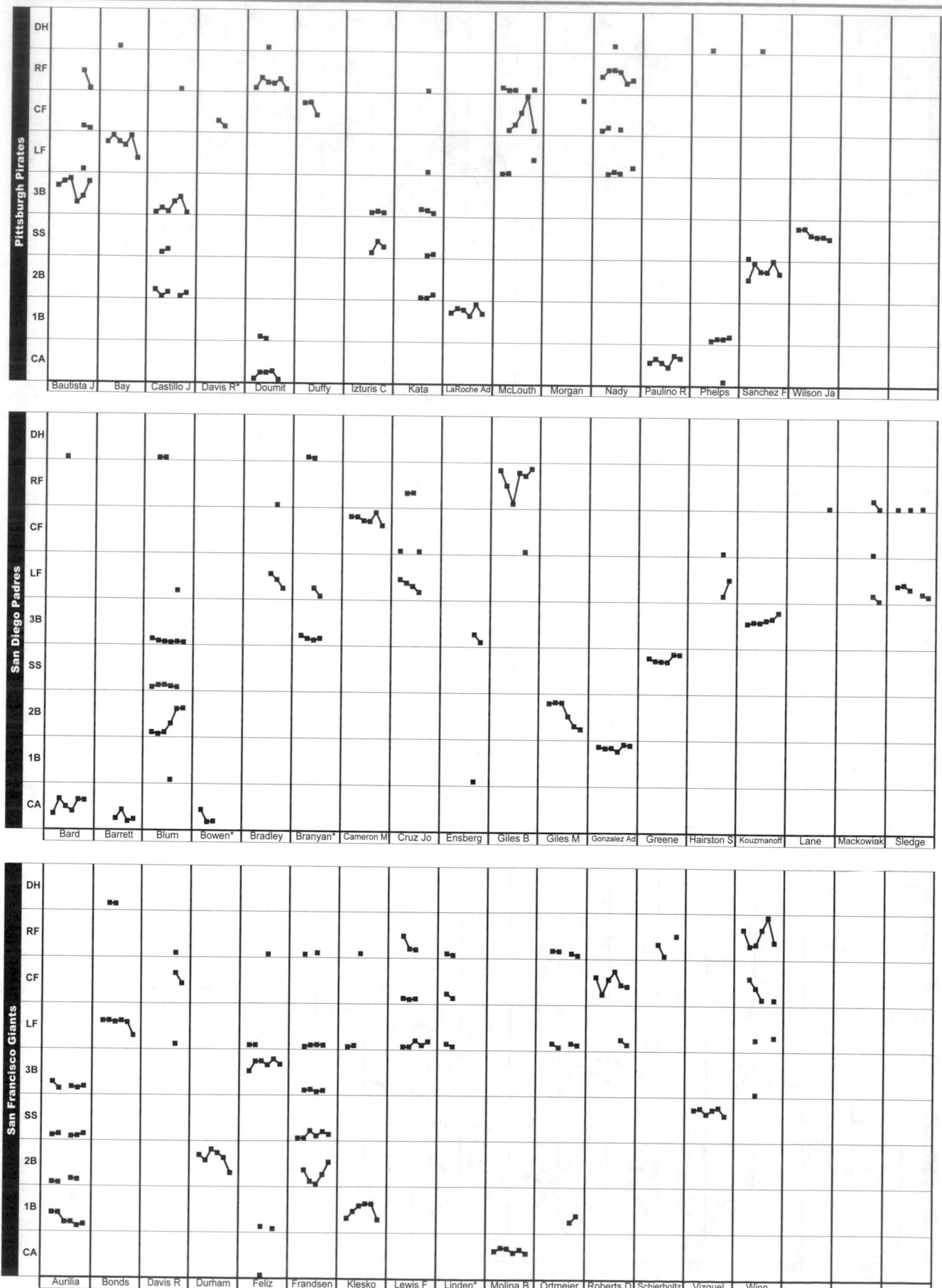

Constellations courtesy John Burnson; BaseballHQ.com / Heater Magazine

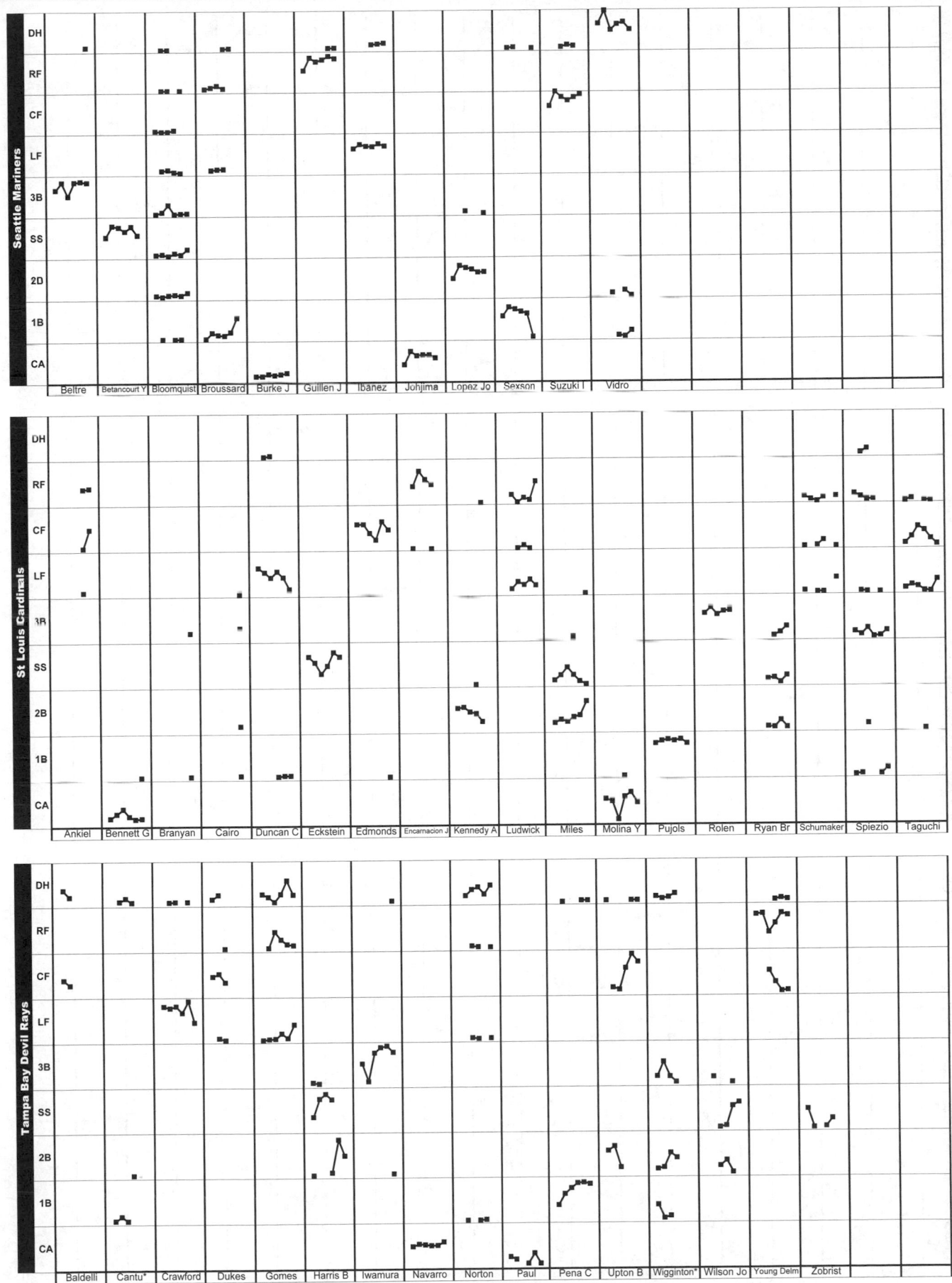

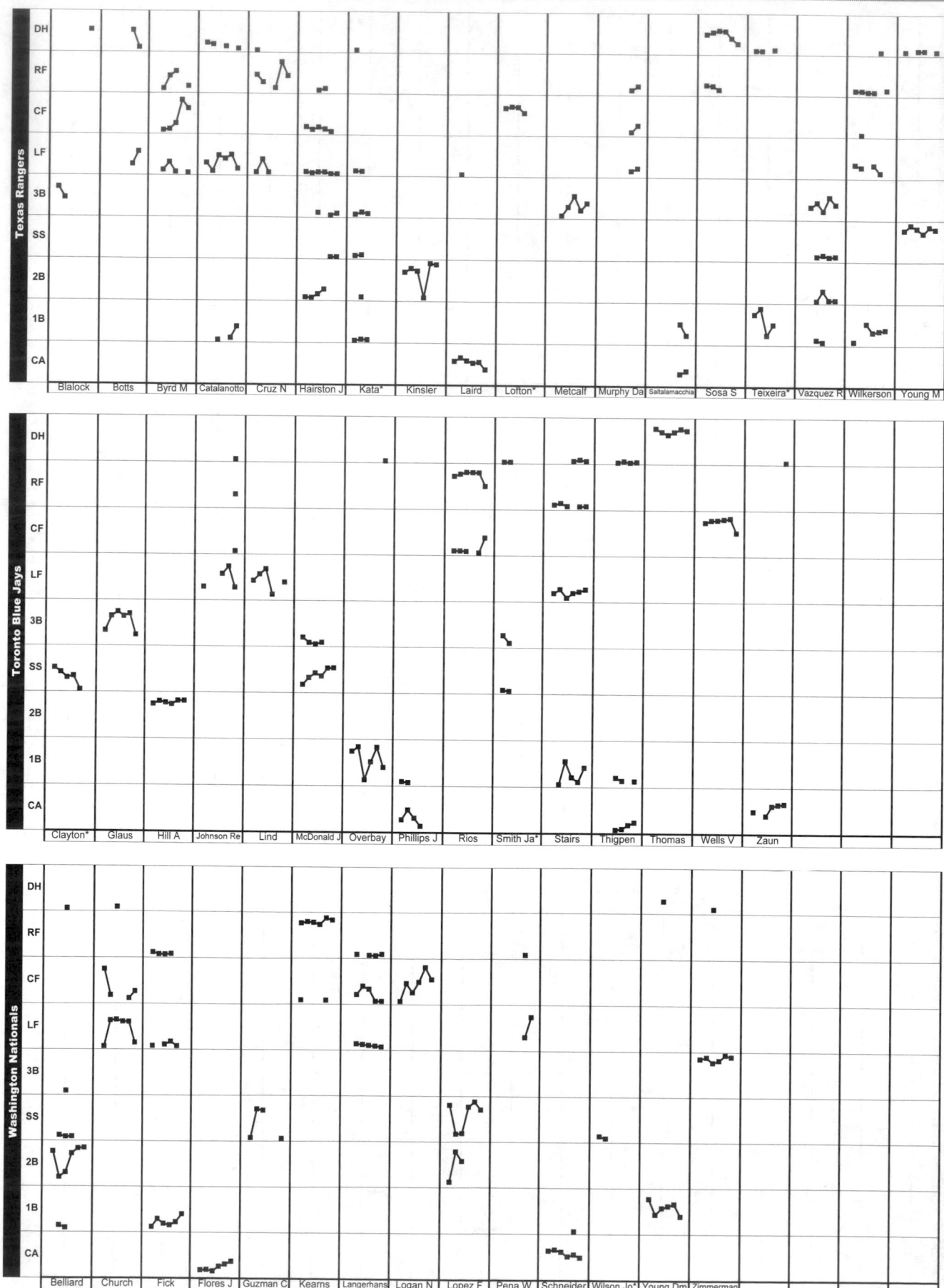

The THT Glossary

A: Assists. The number of times a fielder makes a throw that results in an out.

AB: At-Bats

AB/RSP: At-Bats with Runners in Scoring Position (second and/or third base)

BA: Batting Average; Hits divided by At-Bats

BA/RSP: Batting Average with Runners in Scoring Position (second and/or third base)

BABIP: Batting Average on Balls in Play. This is a measure of the number of batted balls that safely fall in for hits (not including home runs). The exact formula we use is (H-HR)/(AB-K-HR+SF). This is similar to DER, but from the batter's perspective.

BR: Base Runs, a run contribution formula created by David Smyth, which quantifies the number of runs contributed by a batter. The fundamental formula for Base Runs is (baserunners * scoring rate) + home runs. You can read more about Base Runs in the Stats Introduction to this *Annual*.

BB: Bases on Balls, otherwise known as walks

BB/G: Walks Allowed per Games pitched. This stat is based on the number of walks allowed divided by total number of batters faced, times the average number of batters per game in that specific league (generally around 38 batters a game).

BFP: Batters Faced by Pitcher; the pitching equivalent of Plate Appearances for batters

CS: Caught Stealing

CWS: Career Win Shares

DER: Defense Efficiency Ratio. The percent of times a batted ball is turned into an out by the team's fielders, not including home runs. The exact formula we use is (BFP-H-K-BB-HBP-0.6*E)/(BFP-HR-K-BB-HBP). This is similar to BABIP, but from the defensive team's perspective.

DP: Double Plays

DPS: Double Plays Started, in which the fielder typically gets only an assist

DPT: Double Plays Turned, in which the fielder records both an assist and a putout

ERA: Earned Run Average. Number of earned runs allowed divided by innings pitched multiplied by nine.

ERA+: ERA measured against the league average and adjusted for ballpark factors. An ERA+ over 100 is better than average, less than 100 is below average.

ExpWS: Expected Win Shares. See the Win Shares section for a fuller discussion.

FB: Fly ball, as categorized by BIS's scorekeepers. Includes both infield and outfield fly balls.

FE: Fielding Errors, as opposed to Throwing Errors (TE)

FIP: Fielding Independent Pitching, a measure of all those things for which a pitcher is specifically responsible. The formula is (HR*13+(BB+HBP)*3-K*2)/IP, plus a league-specific factor (usually around 3.2) to round out the number to an equivalent ERA number. FIP helps you understand how well a pitcher pitched, regardless of how well his fielders fielded. FIP was invented by Tom M. Tango.

FPct: Fielding Percentage, or the number of fielding chances handled without an error. The formula is (A+PO)/(A+PO+E).

G: Games played

GB%: The percent of batted balls that are grounders. GB% is a better way to measure ground ball tendencies than the more common Ground ball/Fly ball ratio (G/F), because ratios don't follow normal scales (a G/F ratio of 2 doesn't equal twice as many ground balls than 1) and definitions of fly balls can be inconsistent.

GIDP (or GDP): The number of times a batter Grounded Into Double Plays

GPA: Gross Production Average, a variation of OPS, but more accurate and easier to interpret. The exact formula is (OBP*1.8+SLG)/4, adjusted for ballpark. The scale of GPA is similar to BA: .200 is lousy, .265 is around average and .300 is a star.

GS: Games Started, a pitching stat.

H-A: Home minus Away, a stat for expressing the "home field advantage" enjoyed by each player. The exact formula is each player's GPA at home minus his GPA on the road. This is calculated for both batters and pitchers; since both tend to perform better at home, H-A is generally positive for batters and negative for pitchers.

Holds: A bullpen stat. According to MLB.com, *A relief pitcher is credited with a hold any time he enters a game in a save situation, records at least one out and leaves the game never having relinquished the lead. A pitcher cannot finish the game and receive credit for a hold, nor can he earn a hold and a save in the same game.*

HRA: Home Runs Allowed, also a pitching stat

HR/Fly or HR/F: Home Runs as a percent of outfield Fly balls. The home run totals are adjusted by the home ballpark's historic home run rates. Research has shown that about 11% of outfield flies are hit for home runs.

HR/G: Home Runs Allowed per Games pitched. This stat is based on the number of home runs allowed divided by total number of batters faced, times the average number of batters per game in that specific league (generally around 38 batters a game).

IBB: Intentional Base on Balls.

IF/Fly or IF/F: The percent of fly balls that are infield flies. Infield flies are those fly balls caught within the infield baselines.

ISO: Isolated Power, which measures the "true power" of a batter. The formula is SLG-BA.

K: Strikeouts

K/G: Strikeouts per games pitched. This stat is based on the number of strikeouts divided by total number of batters faced, times the average number of batters per game in that specific league (generally around 38 batters a game).

L: Losses

L^R: See R^L.

LD%: Line Drive Percentage. Baseball Info Solutions tracks the trajectory of each batted ball and categorizes it as a ground ball, fly ball or line drive. LD% is the percent of batted balls that are line drives. Line drives are not necessarily the hardest hit balls, but they do fall for a hit around 75% of the time.

LI: Leverage Index. Invented by Tom M. Tango, LI measures the criticality of a play. It is based on the range of potential WPA outcomes of a play, compared to all other plays. 1.0 is an average Index.

LOB and LOB%: LOB stands for Left On Base. It is the number of runners that are left on base at the end of an inning. LOB% is slightly different; it is the percentage of base runners allowed that didn't score a run. LOB% is used to track a pitcher's luck or effectiveness (depending on your point of view). The exact formula is (H+BB+HBP-R)/(H+BB+HBP-(1.4*HR)).

Net Stolen Bases: The effective impact of a player's stolen bases. For batters, the formula is SB-(2*CS) because being caught stealing hurts twice as much as a stolen base helps. For pitchers, the formula is (SB+balks)-2*(CS+pickoffs).

Net Win Shares Value: A dollar figure that represents the relative value of a player's contract, given how much the player contributed.

NIP: Stands for Not In Play, and represents plays in which the batter didn't put the ball in play: strikeouts, walks and hits by pitch.

OBP: On Base Percentage, the proportion of plate appearances in which a batter reached base successfully, including hits, walks and hit by pitches.

OF: Outfield Flies. BIS categorizes each fly ball as an infield fly or outfield fly, using the infield baselines as the boundary, depending on where the ball would have landed if not caught.

OOZ: Plays made out of zone. A zone is defined as all areas of the field in which that fielding position successfully converts 50% of chances into outs, on average.

Op: Save Opportunities

OPS: On Base plus Slugging Percentage, a crude but quick measure of a batter's true contribution to his team's offense. See GPA for a better approach.

OPS+: OPS measured against the league average, and adjusted for ballpark factors. An OPS+ over 100 is better than average, less than 100 is below average.

Outs: Outs. Not just outs at bat, by the way, but also outs when caught stealing. Two outs are included when hitting into a double play.

P/PA: Pitches per Plate Appearance.

PA: Plate Appearances, or AB+BB+HBP+SF+SH.

PO: Putouts, the number of times a fielder recorded an out in the field. First basemen and catchers get lots of these. From a pitching perspective, PO stands for pickoffs—the number of times a pitcher picks a base runner off a base.

POS: Position played in the field

PRC: Pitching Runs Created, a new stat developed by THT's David Gassko. PRC measures the impact of a pitcher by putting his production on the same scale as a batter's Runs Created. PRC is calculated by inserting the number of runs allowed by a pitcher into a league-average context, and then using the Pythagorean Formula to estimate how many wins that pitcher/team would achieve. That win total is then converted into the number of offensive runs it would take to achieve the same number of wins. The impact of fielders is separated in the process.

Pythagorean Formula: A formula for converting a team's Run Differential into a projected win-loss record. The formula is RS^2/(RS^2+RA^2). Teams' actual win-loss records tend to mirror their Pythagorean records, and variances can usually be attributed to luck.

You can improve the accuracy of the Pythagorean formula by using a different exponent (the 2 in the formula). In particular, a sabermetrician named US Patriot discovered that the best exponent can be calculated this way: $(RS/G+RA/G)^{.285}$, where RS/G is Runs Scored per Game and RA/G is Runs Allowed per Game. This is called the PythagoPat formula.

PWins: Pythagorean Wins. See the previous entry.

R: Runs Scored and/or Allowed.

R/G: Runs Scored Per Game. Literally, R divided by games played.

R^L (or L^R): The difference in GPA between a player's performance against left-handed and right-handed pitchers or batters. The order of subtraction depends on the player's natural platoon split—for right-handed batters, for instance, it's L-R. You can read more about R^L in the Stats Introduction of this *Annual*. Note that, for team stats, the formula is the more common L-R for batters and R-L for pitchers.

RA: Runs Allowed or Runs Allowed Per Nine Innings. Just like ERA, but with unearned runs, too.

RAA: Runs Above Average

RBI: Runs Batted In

RC: Runs Created. Invented by Bill James, RC is a very good measure of the number of runs a batter truly contributed to his team's offense. The basic formula for RC is OBP*TB, but it has evolved into over 14 different versions. We use the most complicated version, which includes the impact of hitting well with runners in scoring position, and we adjust for ballpark impact.

RCAA: Runs Created Above Average. A stat invented and tracked by Lee Sinins, the author of the *Sabermetric Baseball Encyclopedia*. Lee calculates each player's Runs Created and then compares it to the league average, given that player's number of plate appearances.

RF: Range Factor, a measure of the total chances fielded in a player's playing time. The formula we use is 9*(PO+A)/Innings in Field.

RISP: Runners In Scoring Position

RS: Runs Scored

RSAA: Runs Saved Above Average. This stat, which is also tracked and reported by Lee Sinins, is a measure of a pitcher's effectiveness and contribution.

Run Differential: Runs Scored minus Runs Allowed

RZR: Revised Zone Rating. RZR measures how often a fielder successfully fields a ball that is hit into his zone. A zone is defined as all areas of the field in which that fielding position successfully converts 50% of chances into outs, on average. RZR differs from the original Zone Rating by removing plays made out of zone and listing them separately.

SB: Stolen Bases

SB%: The percent of time a runner stole a base successfully. The formula is SB/SBA.

SBA: Stolen Bases Attempted.

SBA/G: Stolen Base Attempts per nine innings played.

ShO: Shutouts

Situational Hitting: The portion of Bill James's Runs Created formula that includes the impact of a batter's batting average with runners in scoring position and the number of home runs with runners on. It is an estimate of the number of runs a player created, compared to his overall Runs Created, by hitting with runners on base.

SLG and SLGA: Slugging Percentage. Total Bases divided by At-Bats. SLGA stands for Slugging Percentage Against. It represents SLG from the pitcher's perspective.

SO: Strikeouts

Superlwts: Super Linear Weights, an expansion of Pete Palmer's original Linear Weights formula, was created by Mitchel Lichtman. It quantifies the impact of a batter or pitcher, based on all aspects of play, including batting, pitching, fielding and baserunning. Superlwts is expressed as the number of runs better or worse than an average player.

Sv: Saves. According to MLB.com, *A pitcher is credited with a save when he finishes a game won by his club, is not the winning pitcher, and either (a) enters the game with a lead of no more than three runs and pitches for at least one inning, (b) enters the game with the potential tying run either on base, or at bat, or on deck, or (c) pitches effectively for at least three innings.*

Sv%: Saves divided by Save Opportunities

TB: Total Bases, calculated as 1B+2B*2+3B*3+HR*4

TBA: Total Bases Allowed. A pitching stat.

TE: Throwing Errors, as opposed to Fielding Errors (FE)

UER: Unearned Runs

UERA: Unearned Run Average, or the number of unearned runs allowed for each nine innings pitched.

UZR: A fielding system invented by Mitchel Lichtman, it is very similar to John Dewan's plus/minus system, except that it expresses fielding prowess in terms of runs above/below average instead of plays above/below average.

W: Wins

WHIP: Walks and Hits Per Inning Pitched, a variant of OBP for pitchers. This is a popular stat in rotisserie baseball circles.

wOBA: Introduced in *The Book*, this rate stat is similar to OPS and GPA, except that it is set to the scale of OBP. See David Gassko's article "Do Managers Matter?" for more information.

WPA: Win Probability Added. A system in which each player is given credit toward helping his team win, based on play-by-play data and the impact each specific play has on the team's probability of winning. See "The Story Stat" in this *Annual* for more information.

WPA/LI: Literally, the WPA of a play divided by its criticality (measured by LI). This stat takes WPA and effectively neutralizes the impact of the game situation. It's another approach for judging player impact on a game—removing the game context but leaving the player's impact on scoring.

WP+PB/G: Wild Pitches and Passed Balls per Nine Innings played. A fielding stat for catchers.

xFIP: Expected Fielding Independent Pitching. xFIP and "normalizes" the home run component. Research has shown that home runs allowed are pretty much a function of flyballs allowed and home park, so xFIP is based on the average number of home runs allowed per outfield fly. Theoretically, this should be a better predictor of a pitcher's future ERA.

Win Shares Definitions

WS: Win Shares. Invented by Bill James. Win Shares is a very complicated statistic that takes all the contributions a player made toward his team's wins and distills them into a single number that represents the number of wins he contributed to the team, times three.

There are three subcategories of Win Shares: batting, pitching and fielding.

We have tweaked James' original formula in two ways:

1) We allow players to accumulate negative Win Shares. Adding an artificial "floor" at zero (which the original formula does) has unfortunate repercussions for all players' totals.

2) We have somewhat de-emphasized the portion of Win Shares that credits relief pitchers. We feel this is appropriate in today's "save-happy" environment.

CWS: Career Win Shares. Each player's career Win Shares includes Bill James's totals through 2003 and our totals for the last three years.

WSAge: The average age of a team, weighted by each player's total Win Shares contribution.

NetWSValue: A dollar figure that represents the relative value of a player's contract, given how much the player contributed. You can read more about Net Wins Shares Value in previous *Annuals*, or online at http://www.hardballtimes.com/main/article/2007-net-win-shares-value/.

ExpWS: Expected Win Shares. This figure represents a player's average baseline, or the number of Win Shares he would have contributed if he were an average player, given his playing time. To calculate this, we include the number of each player's plate appearances, innings in the field, innings pitched and relief innings pitched.

WSAB: Win Shares Above Bench. WSAB is a refined approach to Win Shares, in which each player's total Win Shares are compared to the Win Shares an average bench player would have received.

Our research indicates that this is an important adjustment to Win Shares, because it gives greater context to the Win Shares totals. The impact is similar to adding "Loss Shares" for each player.

The bench player is defined as 70% of Expected Win Shares for all players except starting pitchers, for whom it is 50% of Expected Win Shares.

WSP: Win Shares Percentage is a rate stat, calculated as WS/(2*ExpWS). WSP is similar to winning percentage in that .500 is average, but WSP ranges above 1.000 and below .000.

Who's Who

Richard Barbieri graduated from college with a major in History, which he puts to use once a week writing his column for *The Hardball Times*. The rest of the time, he works in law enforcement.

Sal Baxamusa is a graduate student studying chemical engineering. A native of California, Sal currently resides in New England with his wife and son.

John Beamer earns his keep from Strategy Consulting, an endeavor that takes him to all corners of the globe. In his spare time he tries to follow the Atlanta Braves and he has mlbtv.com to thank for keeping him sane. Currently he lives among the rhinoceroses and leopards of South Africa with his wife and baby boy.

Carolina Bolado lives in Weehawken, New Jersey and is an online editor for a menu directory site in New York. In her spare time, she enjoys watching her beloved Marlins, swimming long distances in polluted bodies of water and experimenting with new foods in her kitchen.

A graduate of Michigan State University, **Brian Borawski** is a CPA who owns his private practice. A lifelong Tigers fan, Brian writes about his favorite team at Tiger Blog (www.tigerblog.net) and he's a member of SABR's Business of Baseball committee.

John Brattain's work can also be read regularly at MSN Canada and his blog "The Progenitor of Severe Glutial Discomfort." He wishes to thank the hard working support staff and editors at THT for making him look presentable as well as his wife Kelly and daughters Belinda and Kataryna for allowing him to monopolize the computer.

David Cameron resides in Winston-Salem, North Carolina. Along with Derek Zumsteg and Jason Barker, he blogs about the things that drive him crazy about the Seattle Mariners at ussmariner.com.

Matthew Carruth is a University of Pennsylvania graduate in computer science (among other things) who spends most of his time immersed in baseball, soccer, skiing, food and writing. He is heralding the return of Futurama to television with extreme gusto.

Derek Carty is currently a student in New Jersey. He is a huge fan of the Mets and loves fantasy baseball. When he isn't in school or doing something baseball related, he can usually be found visiting his friend Mickey Mouse in Walt Disney World.

Chris Constancio lives in the Midwest and crunches numbers for a living. He does more of the same in his spare time when writing about player development for the *Hardball Times* and maintaining a database of minor league statistics at *First Inning* (www.firstinning.com).

Jon Daly aspires to write the great American graphic novel, as soon as he can find a collaborator who can draw. In his free time, he works in the financial service industry.

John Dewan has consistently broken new ground in the area of sports statistical analysis, first as one of the founders and former CEO of STATS, Inc. and now as the owner of Baseball Info Solutions. He is also the co-publisher of ACTA Publications and the author of the ground-breaking book on defense in baseball, *The Fielding Bible*. As a noted sports expert, he is heard weekly on WSCR "The Score," an all-sports radio station in Chicago, where he lives with his wife and two children.

Joe Distelheim is the retired editor of *The Huntsville (Ala.) Times*. In previous incarnations, he was sports editor of *The Charlotte Oberver* and *Detroit Free Press*. He suffers from an incurable addiction to the Chicago Cubs.

Bill Ferris is a long time Tigers fan who started blogging about his favorite team at Detroit Tigers Weblog (www.DetroitTigersWeblog.com) in 2001. A graduate of the University of Michigan, he works as an industrial engineer in the health care industry.

David Gassko is a major league consultant, and wants to thank his uncle David for teaching him to love baseball and hate the Yankees.

Vince Gennaro is the author of *Diamond Dollars: The Economics of Winning in Baseball* (Maple Street Press), a consultant to several Major League teams, and adjunct professor in the Graduate Sports Business Management program at Manhattanville College. His innovative analysis has been featured in *The New York Times*, the *Wall Street Journal, CNNMoney.com* and on *CNBC*, he's also written for *Yahoo! Sports, Red Sox Annual*, and *The Hardball Times*.

Brian Gunn is a screenwriter living in Los Angeles.

A history instructor by trade, **Chris Jaffe** recently signed a contract with McFarland Publishers to write a book titled, "Evaluating Baseball's Managers." It is tentatively slated to be published in 2009.

Jonathan Helfgott graduated from Bard College in December of 2005 with a degree in history. He was rewarded for his life-long obsession with baseball by receiving a Thomas J. Watson fellowship in 2006 for his project Baseball's Globalization: Economics, Culture, and Sport. The fellowship sent him around the world for a year investigating the inner workings of the international baseball industry. Jonathan currently lives in the Pacific Northwest.

Bill James has been writing about baseball and compiling reference books about baseball since 1975. He is currently the Senior Baseball Operations Advisor for the Boston Red Sox.

Will Leitch is the editor of Deadspin and the author of *God Save The Fan*, in book stores now.

Mitchel Lichtman is a well-known sabermetrician and former consultant with the 2006 World Champion St. Louis Cardinals. He is also one of the co-authors of *The Book, Playing the Percentages in Baseball*. Mr. Lichtman is a graduate of The University of Nevada Boyd School of Law, and Cornell University in Ithaca, New York. He currently resides in the Finger Lakes region of central New York.

Greg Rybarczyk operates the Hit Tracker Online website, and watches way too much MLB video. A life-long Boston fan, he lives in the Portland, OR suburbs with his wife and two young children, who will hopefully live long, happy lives knowing the Red Sox only as "our team that always wins..."

Dave Studenmund is one of those "family men" you always hear about. He also likes baseball.

Tom Tango runs the *Tango on Baseball* website, where one will find a large number of research pieces devoted to sabermetrics. He is also one of the co-authors of *The Book, Playing the Percentages in Baseball*. His inspirations have been Pete Palmer and Bill James, and he is thankful for the generosity of Retrosheet and Baseball1 in providing data to the public. He works as a consultant for major league teams in hockey, and has worked as one in baseball. Born and raised in Canada, he now resides in New Jersey with his family.

Steve Treder's baseball writing has been presented in numerous forums and journals. He and his wife are enjoying their empty nest in the San Francisco Bay Area.

When he's not rooting for the A's serving or as THT's web editor, **Bryan Tsao** is a master's candidate at the School of Information at the University of California, Berkeley, where he studies the intersection of design, user research and strategy.

TUCK!'s award-winning cartoons, illustrations, and comics have appeared in outlets as diverse as hockeybuzz.com (where he was the house cartoonist for two seasons), as well as the Game Night Revue (program sold outside St. Louis Blues homegames). TUCK! also illustrated the recently published *Three Players Who Have Never Been in My Kitchen*, with other notable placements and contributions (including Pulitzer Newspapers, Gannett Newspapers, Marvel Comics, Image Comics), and many impressive near-misses that make for entertaining happy hour conversation.

SABR member **David Vincent**, called the "Sultan of Swat Stats" by ESPN, is the recognized authority on the history of the home run. He is the author of *Home Run: The Definitive History of Baseball's Ultimate Weapon*, published by Potomac Books, Inc.

John Walsh is a research physicist by day, baseball researcher by night. Despite living four thousand miles from Fenway Park, he remains an avid Red Sox fan.

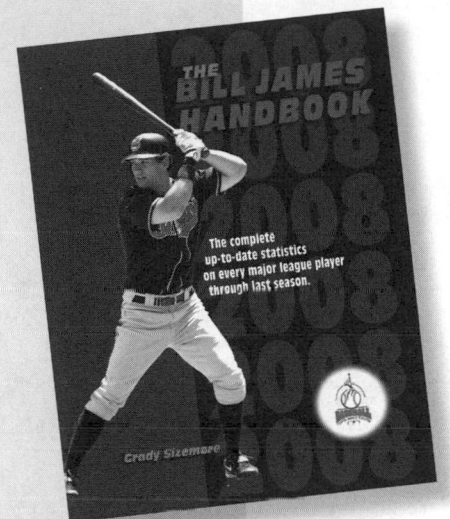
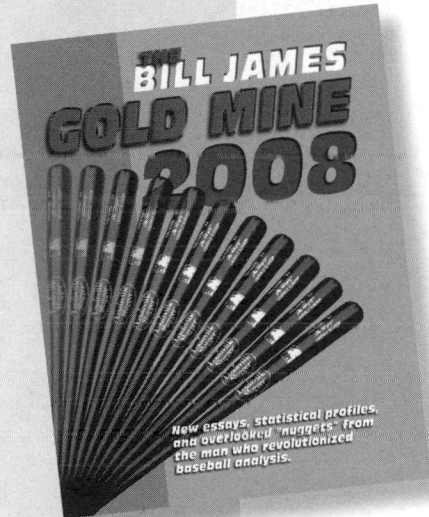